THE LIFE OF
SAMUEL JOHNSON, LL.D.

JAMES BOSWELL
by GEORGE WILLISON
in *The Scottish National Portrait Gallery*

THE LIFE OF

SAMUEL JOHNSON

LL.D.

BY JAMES BOSWELL, ESQ.

With marginal comments and markings
from two copies annotated by

HESTER LYNCH THRALE PIOZZI

Prepared for publication
with an Introduction by

EDWARD G. FLETCHER

IN THREE VOLUMES
II

THE HERITAGE PRESS
NEW YORK

THE LIFE OF
SAMUEL JOHNSON, LL.D.

THE LIFE OF
SAMUEL JOHNSON
LL.D.

ON the 21st of March, I was happy to find myself again in my friend's study, and was glad to see my old acquaintance, Mr. Francis Barber, who was now returned home. Dr. Johnson received me with a hearty welcome; saying, 'I am glad you are come, and glad you are come upon such an errand:' (alluding to the cause of the schoolmaster.) BOSWELL. 'I hope, Sir, he will be in no danger. It is a very delicate matter to interfere between a master and his scholars: nor do I see how you can fix the degree of severity that a master may use.' JOHNSON. 'Why, Sir, till you can fix the degree of obstinacy and negligence of the scholars, you cannot fix the degree of severity of the master. Severity must be continued until obstinacy be subdued, and negligence be cured.' He mentioned the severity of Hunter, his own master. 'Sir, (said I,) Hunter is a Scotch name: so it should seem this schoolmaster who beat you so severely, was a Scotchman. I can now account for your prejudice against the Scotch.' JOHNSON. 'Sir, he was not Scotch; and, abating his brutality, he was a very good master.'

We talked of his two political pamphlets, 'The False Alarm,' and 'Thoughts concerning Falkland's Islands.' JOHNSON. 'Well, Sir, which of them did you think the best?' BOSWELL. 'I liked the second best.' JOHNSON. 'Why, Sir, I liked the first best; and Beattie liked the first best. Sir, there is a subtlety of disquisition in the first, that is worth all the fire of the second.' BOSWELL. 'Pray, Sir, is it true that Lord North paid you a visit, and that you got two hundred a year in addition to your pension?' JOHNSON. 'No, Sir. Except what I had from the bookseller, I did not get a farthing by them. And between you

and me, I believe Lord North is no friend to me.'
BOSWELL. 'How so, Sir?' JOHNSON. 'Why, Sir, you
cannot account for the fancies of men.—Well, how does
Lord Elibank? and how does Lord Monboddo?' BOS-
WELL. 'Very well, Sir. Lord Monboddo still maintains
the superiority of the savage life.' JOHNSON. 'What
strange narrowness of mind now is that, to think the
things we have not known, are better than the things
which we have known.' BOSWELL. 'Why, Sir, that is a
common prejudice.' JOHNSON. 'Yes, Sir, but a common
prejudice should not be found in one whose trade it is to
rectify errour.'

A gentleman having come in who was to go as a Mate
in the ship along with Mr. Banks and Dr. Solander, Dr.
Johnson asked what were the names of the ships destined
for the expedition. The gentleman answered, they were
once to be called the Drake and the Ralegh, but now they
were to be called the Resolution and the Adventure.
JOHNSON. 'Much better; for had the Ralegh returned
without going round the world, it would have been
ridiculous. To give them the names of the Drake and the
Ralegh was laying a trap for satire.' BOSWELL. 'Had you
not some desire to go upon this expedition, Sir?' JOHNSON.
'Why yes, but I soon laid it aside. Sir, there is very little
of intellectual, in the course. Besides, I see but at a small
distance. So it was not worth my while to go to see birds
fly, which I should not have seen fly;[a] and fishes swim,
which I should not have seen swim.'

The gentleman being gone, and Dr. Johnson having
left the room for some time, a debate arose between
the Reverend Mr. Stockdale and Mrs. Desmoulins,
whether Mr. Banks and Dr. Solander were entitled to
any share of glory from their expedition. When Dr.
Johnson returned to us, I told him the subject of their
dispute. JOHNSON. 'Why, Sir, it was properly for botany
that they went out: I believe they thought only of culling
of simples.'

I thanked him for showing civilities to Beattie. 'Sir,
(said he,) I should thank *you*. We all love Beattie. Mrs.
Thrale says, if ever she has another husband, she'll have

marginal line:
but a . . . rectify errour
[H]

marginal line:
*ridiculous. To . . . for
satire* [H]

[a] *just so.* [1]

Beattie. He sunk upon us[1] that he was married; else we should have shown his lady more civilities. She is a very fine woman. But how can you show civilities to a nonentity? I did not think he had been married. Nay, I did not think about it one way or other; but he did not tell us of his lady till late.'

He then spoke of St. Kilda, the most remote of the Hebrides. I told him, I thought of buying it. JOHNSON. 'Pray do, Sir. We will go and pass a winter amid the blasts there. We shall have fine fish, and we will take some dried tongues with us, and some books. We will have a strong built vessel, and some Orkney men to navigate her. We must build a tolerable house: but we may carry with us a wooden house ready made, and requiring nothing but to be put up. Consider, Sir, by buying St. Kilda, you may keep the people from falling into worse hands. We must give them a clergyman, and he shall be one of Beattie's choosing. He shall be educated at Marischal College. I'll

[1] 'TO JAMES BOSWELL, ESQ.

'MY DEAR SIR,   'Edinburgh, May 3, 1792
     'As I suppose your great work will soon be reprinted, I beg leave to trouble you with a remark on a passage of it, in which I am a little misrepresented. Be not alarmed; the misrepresentation is not imputable to you. Not having the book at hand, I cannot specify the page, but I suppose you will easily find it. Dr. Johnson says, speaking of Mrs. Thrale's family, "Dr. Beattie *sunk upon us* that he was married, or words to that purpose." I am not sure that I understand *sunk upon us*, which is a very uncommon phrase: but it seems to me to imply, (and others, I find, have understood it in the same sense,) *studiously concealed from us his being married*. Now, Sir, this was by no means the case. I could have no motive to conceal a circumstance, of which I never was nor can be ashamed; and of which Dr. Johnson seemed to think, when he afterwards became acquainted with Mrs. Beattie, that I had, as was true, reason to be proud. So far was I from concealing her, that my wife had at that time almost as numerous an acquaintance in London as I had myself; and was, not very long after, kindly invited and elegantly entertained at Streatham by Mr. and Mrs. Thrale.
     'My request, therefore, is, that you would rectify this matter in your new edition. You are at liberty to make what use you please of this letter.
     'My best wishes ever attend you and your family. Believe me to be, with the utmost regard and esteem, dear Sir,

     'Your obliged and affectionate humble servant,

                                                  'J. BEATTIE'

I have, from my respect for my friend Dr. Beattie, and regard to his extreme sensibility, inserted the foregoing letter, though I cannot but wonder at his considering as any imputation a phrase commonly used among the best friends.

be your Lord Chancellor, or what you please.' BOSWELL. 'Are you serious, Sir, in advising me to buy St. Kilda? for if you should advise me to go to Japan, I believe I should do it.' JOHNSON. 'Why yes, Sir, I am serious.' BOSWELL. 'Why then, I'll see what can be done.'

I gave him an account of the two parties in the Church of Scotland, those for supporting the rights of patrons, independent of the people, and those against it. JOHNSON. 'It should be settled one way or other. I cannot wish well to a popular election of the clergy, when I consider that it occasions such animosities, such unworthy courting of the people, such slanders between the contending parties, and other disadvantages. It is enough to allow the people to remonstrate against the nomination of a minister for solid reasons.' (I suppose he meant heresy or immorality.)

He was engaged to dine abroad, and asked me to return to him in the evening, at nine, which I accordingly did.

We drank tea with Mrs. Williams, who told us a story of second sight, which happened in Wales where she was born. He listened to it very attentively, and said he should be glad to have some instances of that faculty well authenticated. His elevated wish for more and more evidence for spirit, in opposition to the grovelling belief of materialism, led him to a love of such mysterious disquisitions. He again justly observed, that we could have no certainty of the truth of supernatural appearances, unless something was told us which we could not know by ordinary means, or something done which could not be done but by supernatural power: that Pharaoh in reason and justice required such evidence from Moses; nay, that our Saviour said, 'If I had not done among them the works which none other man did, they had not had sin.' He had said in the morning, that 'Macaulay's History of St. Kilda' was very well written, except some foppery about liberty and slavery. I mentioned to him that Macaulay told me, he was advised to leave out of his book the wonderful story that upon the approach of a stranger all the inhabitants catch cold;[1] but that it had been so well authenticated, he determined to retain it. JOHNSON. 'Sir, to leave things out of a book, merely because people tell you they will

marginal line:
footnote 1 [H]

[1] See vol. i, p. 395.

not be believed, is meanness. Macaulay acted with more magnanimity.'

We talked of the Roman Catholick religion, and how little difference there was in essential matters between ours and it. JOHNSON. 'True, Sir; all denominations of Christians have really little difference in point of doctrine, though they may differ widely in external forms. There is a prodigious difference between the external form of one of your Presbyterian churches in Scotland, and a church in Italy; yet the doctrine taught is essentially the same.'

I mentioned the petition to Parliament for removing the subscription to the Thirty-nine Articles. JOHNSON. 'It was soon thrown out Sir, they talk of not making boys at the University subscribe to what they do not understand;[a] but they ought to consider, that our Universities were founded to bring up members for the Church of England, and we must not supply our enemies with arms from our arsenal. No, Sir, the meaning of subscribing is, not that they fully understand all the articles, but that they will adhere to the Church of England. Now take it in this way, and suppose that they should only subscribe their adherence to the Church of England, there would be still the same difficulty; for still the young men would be subscribing to what they do not understand. For if you should ask them, what do you mean by the Church of England? Do you know in what it differs from the Presbyterian Church? from the Romish Church? from the Greek Church? from the Coptick Church? they could not tell you. So, Sir, it comes to the same thing.' BOSWELL. 'But, would it not be sufficient to subscribe the Bible?' JOHNSON. 'Why no, Sir; for all sects will subscribe the Bible; nay, the Mahometans will subscribe the Bible; for the Mahometans acknowledge JESUS CHRIST, as well as Moses, but maintain that GOD sent Mahomet as a still greater prophet than either.'

I mentioned the motion which had been made in the House of Commons, to abolish the fast of the 30th of January. JOHNSON. 'Why, Sir, I could have wished that it had been a temporary act, perhaps, to have expired with the century. I am against abolishing it; because that would be declaring it wrong to establish it; but I should

[a] *Their Oath or Subscription will then be short indeed—for what do we understand? certainly not our own Existence.* [H]

have no objection to make an act, continuing it for another century, and then letting it expire.'

He disapproved of the Royal Marriage Bill; 'Because (said he) I would not have the people think that the validity of marriage depends on the will of man, or that the right of a King depends on the will of man. I should not have been against making the marriage of any of the royal family, without the approbation of King and Parliament, highly criminal.'[a]

In the morning we had talked of old families, and the respect due to them. JOHNSON. 'Sir, you have a right to that kind of respect, and are arguing for yourself. I am for supporting the principle, and am disinterested in doing it, as I have no such right.' BOSWELL. 'Why, Sir, it is one more incitement to a man to do well.' JOHNSON. 'Yes, Sir, and it is a matter of opinion very necessary to keep society together. What is it but opinion, by which we have a respect for authority, that prevents us, who are the rabble, from rising up and pulling down you who are gentlemen from your places, and saying, "We will be gentlemen in our turn?" Now, Sir, that respect for author-ity is much more easily granted to a man whose father has had it, than to an upstart, and so Society is more easily supported.' BOSWELL. 'Perhaps, Sir, it might be done by the respect belonging to office, as among the Romans, where the dress, the *toga*, inspired reverence.' JOHNSON. 'Why, we know very little about the Romans. But, surely, it is much easier to respect a man who has always had respect, than to respect a man who we know was last year no better than ourselves, and will be no better next year. In republicks there is no respect for authority, but a fear of power.' BOSWELL. 'At present, Sir, I think riches seem to gain most respect.' JOHNSON. 'No, Sir, riches do not gain hearty respect; they only procure external attention. A very rich man, from low beginnings, may buy his election in a borough; but, *cæteris paribus*, a man of family will be preferred. People will prefer a man for whose father their fathers have voted,[b] though they should get no more money, or even less. That shows that the respect for family is not merely fanciful, but has an actual operation. If gentlemen of family would

[a] *& now 1820 come out Books, saying how wrong it is not to permit the Royal Fam-ily to marry the first Girl they see   Any but German Princes's, is the Cry.* [H]

marginal line: *authority is . . . and so* [H]

marginal line: *next year . . . Bos-well. 'At* [H]
two marginal lines: *respect.' Johnson. . . . external attention* [H]

[b] *So they will.* [H]

allow the rich upstarts to spend their money profusely, which they are ready enough to do, and not vie with them in expence, the upstarts would soon be at an end, and the gentlemen would remain; but if the gentlemen will vie in expence with the upstarts, which is very foolish, they must be ruined.'

I gave him an account of the excellent mimickry of a friend of mine in Scotland; observing, at the same time, that some people thought it a very mean thing. JOHNSON. 'Why, Sir, it is making a very mean use of man's powers. But to be a good mimick, requires great powers; great acuteness of observation, great retention of what is observed, and great pliancy of organs to represent what is observed. I remember a lady of quality in this town, Lady ———— ————,[a] who was a wonderful mimick, and used to make me laugh immoderately. I have heard she is now gone mad.'[b] BOSWELL. 'It is amazing how a mimick can not only give you the gestures and voice of a person whom he represents; but even what a person would say on any particular subject.' JOHNSON. 'Why, Sir, you are to consider that the manner and some particular phrases of a person do much to impress you with an idea of him, and you are not sure that he would say what the mimick says in his character.' BOSWELL. 'I don't think Foote a good mimick, Sir.' JOHNSON. 'No, Sir; his imitations are not like. He gives you something different from himself, but not the character which he means to assume. He goes out of himself, without going into other people. He cannot take off any person unless he is strongly marked, such as George Faulkner. He is like a painter who can draw the portrait of a man who has a wen upon his face, and who therefore is easily known. If a man hops upon one leg, Foote can hop upon one leg. But he has not that nice discrimination which your friend seems to possess. Foote is, however, very entertaining with a kind of conversation between wit and buffoonery.'

On Monday, March 23, I found him busy, preparing a fourth edition of his folio Dictionary. Mr. Peyton, one of his original amanuenses, was writing for him. I put him in mind of a meaning of the word *side*, which he had omitted, viz. relationship; as father's side, mother's side.

[a] *Emily Hervey* [H & I]

[b] *She was never mad as I know of: Seven Years after this Date— or more; we met in a Library at Brighton: Don't you remember Your old Acquaintance Dr. Johnson? said she. Ah Lady Emily!— have you left off Your old Tricks? was the Reply. All the bad ones I hope, answer'd Lady Emily coldly;— & turned away.* [H]

He inserted it. I asked him if *humiliating* was a good word. He said, he had seen it frequently used, but he did not know it to be legitimate English. He would not admit *civilization*, but only *civility*. With great deference to him I thought *civilization*, from *to civilize*, better in the sense opposed to *barbarity* than *civility*; as it is better to have a distinct word for each sense, than one word with two senses, which *civility* is, in his way of using it.

He seemed also to be intent on some sort of chymical operation. I was entertained by observing how he contrived to send Mr. Peyton on an errand, without seeming to degrade him. 'Mr. Peyton,—Mr. Peyton, will you be so good as to take a walk to Temple-Bar? You will there see a chymist's shop, at which you will be pleased to buy for me an ounce of oil of vitriol; not spirit of vitriol, but oil of vitriol. It will cost three half-pence.' Peyton immediately went, and returned with it, and told him it cost but a penny.

I then reminded him of the schoolmaster's cause, and proposed to read to him the printed papers concerning it. 'No, Sir, (said he,) I can read quicker than I can hear.' So he read them to himself.

After he had read for some time, we were interrupted by the entrance of Mr. Kristrom, a Swede, who was tutor to some young gentlemen in the city. He told me that there was a very good History of Sweden, by Daline. Having at that time an intention of writing the history of that country, I asked Dr. Johnson whether one might write a history of Sweden without going thither. 'Yes, Sir, (said he,) one for common use.'

ᵃ *a wise Man* [H]

We talked of languages. Johnson observed that Leibnitzᵃ had made some progress in a work, tracing all languages up to the Hebrew. 'Why, Sir, (said he,) you would not imagine that the French *jour*, day, is derived from the Latin *dies*, and yet nothing is more certain; and the intermediate steps are very clear. From *dies*, comes *diurnus*. *Diu* is, by inaccurate ears, or inaccurate pronunciation, easily confounded with *giu?* then the Italians form a substantive of the ablative of an adjective, and thence *giurno*, or, as they make it, *giorno:* which is readily contracted into *giour*, or *jour*.' He observed, that the Bohemian language

marginal line: *contracted into . . . Sclavonick. The* [H]

was true Sclavonick. The Swede said, it had some similarity with the German. JOHNSON. 'Why, Sir, to be sure,
such parts of Sclavonia as confine with Germany will
borrow German words; and such parts as confine with
Tartary will borrow Tartar words.'

He said, he never had it properly ascertained that the
Scotch Highlanders and the Irish understood each other.
I told him that my Cousin Colonel Graham, of the Royal
Highlanders, whom I met at Drogheda, told me they did.
JOHNSON. 'Sir, if the Highlanders understood Irish, why
translate the New Testament into Erse, as was lately done
at Edinburgh, when there is an Irish translation?' BOS-
WELL. 'Although the Erse and Irish are both dialects of
the same language, there may be a good deal of diversity
between them, as between the different dialects in Italy.'—
The Swede went away, and Mr. Johnson continued his
reading of the papers. I said, 'I am afraid, Sir, it is troublesome.' 'Why, Sir, (said he,) I do not take much delight
in it; but I'll go through it.'

We went to the Mitre, and dined in the room where he
and I first supped together. He gave me great hopes of my
cause. 'Sir, (said he,) the government of a schoolmaster is
somewhat of the nature of military government; that is to
say, it must be arbitrary, it must be exercised by the will
of one man, according to particular circumstances. You
must shew some learning upon this occasion. You must
shew, that a schoolmaster has a prescriptive right to beat;
and that an action of assault and battery cannot be admitted against him unless there is some great excess, some
barbarity. This man has maimed none of his boys. They
are all left with the full exercise of their corporeal faculties.
In our schools in England, many boys have been maimed;
yet I never heard of an action against a schoolmaster on
that account. Puffendorf, I think, maintains the right of a
schoolmaster to beat his scholars.'

On Saturday, March 27, I introduced to him Sir
Alexander Macdonald, with whom he had expressed a
wish to be acquainted. He received him very courteously.

Sir Alexander observed, that the Chancellors in England
are chosen from views much inferiour to the office, being
chosen from temporary political views. JOHNSON. 'Why,

marginal line:
views. JOHNSON . . .
other government [H]

Sir, in such a government as ours, no man is appointed to an office because he is the fittest for it, nor hardly in any other government; because there are so many connections and dependencies to be studied. A despotick prince may choose a man to an office, merely because he is the fittest for it. The King of Prussia may do it.' SIR A. 'I think, Sir, almost all great lawyers, such at least as have written upon law, have known only law, and nothing else.' JOHNSON. 'Why, no, Sir; Judge Hale was a great lawyer, and wrote upon law; and yet he knew a great many other things, and has written upon other things. Selden too.' SIR A. 'Very true, Sir; and Lord Bacon. But was not Lord Coke a mere lawyer?' JOHNSON. 'Why, I am afraid he was; but he would have taken it very ill if you had told him so. He would have prosecuted you for scandal.' BOSWELL. 'Lord Mansfield is not a mere lawyer.' JOHNSON. 'No, Sir, I never was in Lord Mansfield's company; but Lord Mansfield was distinguished at the University. Lord Mansfield, when he first came to town, "drank champagne with the wits," as Prior says. He was the friend of Pope.' SIR A. 'Barristers, I believe, are not so abusive now as they were formerly. I fancy they had less law long ago, and so were obliged to take to abuse, to fill up the time. Now they have such a number of precedents, they have no occasion for abuse.' JOHNSON. 'Nay, Sir, they had more law long ago than they have now. As to precedents, to be sure they will increase in course of time; but the more precedents there are, the less occasion is there for law; that is to say, the less occasion is there for investigating principles.' SIR A. 'I have been correcting several Scotch accents in my friend Boswell. I doubt, Sir, if any Scotchman ever attains to a perfect English pronunciation.' JOHNSON. 'Why, Sir, few of them do,ᵃ because they do not persevere after acquiring a certain degree of it. But, Sir, there can be no doubt that they may attain to a perfect English pronunciation, if they will. We find how near they come to it; and certainly, a man who conquers nineteen parts of the Scottish accent, may conquer the twentieth. But, Sir, when a man has got the better of nine tenths he grows weary, he relaxes his diligence,ᵇ he finds he has corrected his accent so far as not to be disagreeable,

marginal line:
and dependencies . . . do it [H]

ᵃ *because they are proud of their Extraction.* [H]

ᵇ *He wishes to retain the Distinction.* [H]

and he no longer desires his friends to tell him when he is
wrong; nor does he choose to be told. Sir, when people
watch me narrowly, and I do not watch myself, they will
find me out to be of a particular county. In the same
manner, Dunning may be found out to be a Devonshire
man. So most Scotchmen may be found out. But, Sir, little
aberrations are of no disadvantage. I never catched
Mallet in a Scotch accent;[a] and yet Mallet, I suppose, was
past five-and-twenty before he came to London.'

    Upon another occasion I talked to him on this subject,
having myself taken some pains to improve my pronunciation, by the aid of the late Mr. Love, of Drury-lane
theatre, when he was a player at Edinburgh, and also of
old Mr. Sheridan. Johnson said to me, 'Sir, your pronunciation is not offensive.' With this concession I was pretty
well satisfied; and let me give my countrymen of North-
Britain an advice not to aim at absolute perfection in this
respect; not to speak *High English*, as we are apt to call
what is far removed from the *Scotch*, but which is by no
means *good English*, and makes 'the fools who use it,' truly
ridiculous. Good English is plain, easy, and smooth in the
mouth of an unaffected English Gentleman. A studied and
factitious pronunciation, which requires perpetual attention, and imposes perpetual constraint, is exceedingly
disgusting. A small intermixture of provincial peculiarities
may, perhaps, have an agreeable effect, as the notes of
different birds concur in the harmony of the grove, and
please more than if they were all exactly alike. I could
name some gentlemen of Ireland, to whom a slight
proportion of the accent and recitative of that country is
an advantage. The same observation will apply to the
gentlemen of Scotland. I do not mean that we should
speak as broad as a certain prosperous member of Parliament from that country; though it has been well observed,
that 'it has been of no small use to him; as it rouses the
attention of the House by its uncommonness: and is equal
to tropes and figures in a good English speaker.' I would
give as an instance of what I mean to recommend to my
countrymen, the pronunciation of the late Sir Gilbert
Elliot; and may I presume to add that of the present Earl
of Marchmont, who told me, with great good humour,

[a] *because he was not
proud of his Extraction.*
[H]

that the master of a shop in London, where he was not known, said to him, 'I suppose, Sir, you are an American.' 'Why so, Sir?' (said his Lordship.) 'Because, Sir, (replied the shopkeeper,) you speak neither English nor Scotch, but something different from both, which I conclude is the language of America.'

BOSWELL. 'It may be of use, Sir, to have a Dictionary to ascertain the pronunciation.' JOHNSON. 'Why, Sir, my Dictionary shows you the accent of words, if you can but remember them.' BOSWELL. 'But, Sir, we want marks to ascertain the pronunciation of the vowels. Sheridan, I believe, has finished such a work.' JOHNSON. 'Why, Sir, consider how much easier it is to learn a language by the ear, than by any marks. Sheridan's Dictionary may do very well; but you cannot always carry it about with you: and, when you want the word, you have not the Dictionary. It is like a man who has a sword that will not draw. It is an admirable sword, to be sure: but while your enemy is cutting your throat, you are unable to use it. Besides, Sir, what entitles Sheridan to fix the pronunciation of English? He has, in the first place, the disadvantage of being an Irishman: and if he says he will fix it after the example of the best company, why they differ among themselves. I remember an instance; when I published the Plan for my Dictionary, Lord Chesterfield told me that the word *great* should be pronounced so as to rhyme to *state;* and Sir William Yonge sent me word that it should be pronounced so as to rhyme to *seat,*[a] and that none but an Irishman would pronounce it *grait.*[b] Now here were two men of the highest rank, the one, the best speaker in the House of Lords, the other, the best speaker in the House of Commons, differing entirely.'

I again visited him at night. Finding him in a very good humour, I ventured to lead him to the subject of our situation in a future state, having much curiosity to know his notions on that point. JOHNSON. 'Why, Sir, the happiness of an unembodied spirit will consist in a consciousness of the favour of GOD, in the contemplation of truth, and in the possession of felicitating ideas.' BOSWELL. 'But, Sir, is there any harm in our forming to ourselves conjectures as to the particulars of our happiness, though the

marginal notes:

marginal line:
Sir, consider . . .
Sheridan's Dictionary
[H]

queried:
to rhyme etc. [H]

[a] *Sir.   Willm.   was*
right [H]

[b] *& that last was* true.
Chesterfield had kept
company with Swift
and Parnell till he had
learned his own Lan-
guage of them—who
were Irish [I]

scripture has said but very little on the subject? "We know not what we shall be." ' JOHNSON. 'Sir there is no harm. What philosophy suggests to us on this topick is probable: what scripture tells us is certain. Dr. Henry More has carried it as far as philosophy can. You may buy both his theological and philosophical works in two volumes folio, for about eight shillings.' BOSWELL. 'One of the most pleasing thoughts is, that we shall see our friends again.'[1] JOHNSON. 'Yes, Sir; but you must consider, that when we are become purely rational, many of our friendships will be cut off. Many friendships are formed by a community of sensual pleasures: all these will be cut off. We form many friendships with bad men, because they have agreeable qualities, and they can be useful to us; but, after death, they can no longer be of use to us. We form many friendships by mistake, imagining people to be different from what they really are. After death, we shall see every one in a true light. Then, Sir, they talk of our meeting our relations: but then all relationship is dissolved; and we shall have no regard for one person more than another, but for their real value. However, we shall either have the satisfaction of meeting our friends, or be satisfied without meeting them.'[a] BOSWELL. 'Yet, Sir, we see in scripture, that Dives still retained an anxious concern about his brethren.' JOHNSON. 'Why, Sir, we must either suppose that passage to be metaphorical, or hold with many divines, and all the Purgatorians, that departed souls do not all at once arrive at the utmost perfection of which they are capable.' BOSWELL. 'I think, Sir, that is a very rational supposition.' JOHNSON. 'Why yes, Sir; but we do not know it is a true one. There is no harm in believing it: but you must not compel others to make it an article of faith; for it is not revealed.' BOSWELL. 'Do you think, Sir, it is wrong in a man who holds the doctrine of Purgatory, to pray for the souls of his deceased friends?' JOHNSON. 'Why no, Sir.' BOSWELL. 'I have been told, that in the Liturgy of the Episcopal Church of Scotland, there was a form of prayer for the dead.' JOHNSON. 'Sir, it is not in

[a] *I should think many of one's Friends would be far above—some below our own Situation.* [H]

---

[1] [Bishop Hall, in his Epistle, 'discoursing of the different degrees of heavenly glory, and of our mutual knowledge of each other above,' (Dec. iii. c. 6,) holds the affirmative on both these questions.[b] MALONE.]

[b] *So sayd Watson when he was asked.* [H]

the Liturgy which Laud framed for the Episcopal Church of Scotland: if there is a liturgy older than that, I should be glad to see it.' BOSWELL. 'As to our employment in a future state, the sacred writings say little. The Revelation, however, of St. John gives us many ideas, and particularly mentions musick.' JOHNSON. 'Why, Sir, ideas must be given you by means of something which you know: and as to musick there are some philosophers and divines who have maintained that we shall not be spiritualized to such a degree, but that something of matter, very much refined, will remain. In that case, musick may make a part of our future felicity.'

BOSWELL. 'I do not know whether there are any well-attested stories of the appearance of ghosts. You know there is a famous story of the appearance of Mrs. Veal, prefixed to "Drelincourt on Death."' JOHNSON. 'I believe, Sir, that is given up. I believe the woman declared upon her death-bed that it was a lie.'[1] BOSWELL. 'This objection is made against the truth of ghosts appearing: that if they are in a state of happiness, it would be a punishment to them to return to this world; and if they are in a state of misery, it would be giving them a respite.' JOHNSON. 'Why, Sir, as the happiness or misery of embodied spirits does not depend upon place, but is intellectual, we cannot say that they are less happy or less miserable by appearing upon earth.'[a]

We went down between twelve and one to Mrs. Williams's room, and drank tea. I mentioned that we were to have the remains of Mr. Gray, in prose and verse, published by Mr. Mason. JOHNSON. 'I think we have had enough of Gray. I see they have published a splendid edition of Akenside's works. One bad ode may be suffered; but a number of them together makes one sick.' BOSWELL. 'Akenside's distinguished poem is his "Pleasures of Imagination:" but for my part, I never could admire it so much as most people do.' JOHNSON. 'Sir, I could not read it through.' BOSWELL. 'I have read it through; but I did not find any great power in it.'

[a] *Samuel said however 'Why hast thou disquieted me to call me up.'* [H]
& for so short a Time too!! [I]

---

[1] [This fiction is known to have been invented by Daniel Defoe, and was added to the second edition of the English translation of Drelincourt's work, (which was originally written in French,) to make it sell. The first edition had it not. MALONE.]

I mentioned Elwal, the heretick, whose trial Sir John Pringle had given me to read. JOHNSON. 'Sir, Mr. Elwal was, I think, an ironmonger at Wolverhampton; and he had a mind to make himself famous, by being the founder of a new sect, which he wished much should be called *Elwallians*. He held, that every thing in the Old Testament that was not typical, was to be of perpetual observance: and so he wore a ribband in the plaits of his coat, and he also wore a beard. I remember I had the honour of dining in company with Mr. Elwal. There was one Barter, a miller, who wrote against him; and you had the controversy between Mr. ELWAL and Mr. BARTER. To try to make himself distinguished he wrote a letter to King George the Second, challenging him to dispute with him, in which he said, "George, if you be afraid to come by yourself, to dispute with a poor old man, you may bring a thousand of your *black*-guards with you; and if you should still be afraid, you may bring a thousand of your *red*-guards." The letter had something of the impudence of Junius to our present King. But the men of Wolverhampton were not so inflammable as the Common-Council of London; so Mr. Elwal failed in his scheme of making himself a man of great consequence.'

On Tuesday, March 31, he and I dined at General Paoli's. A question was started whether the state of marriage was natural to man. JOHNSON. 'Sir, it is so far from being natural for a man and woman to live in a state of marriage, that we find all the motives which they have for remaining in that connection, and the restraints which civilized society imposes to prevent separation, are hardly sufficient to keep them together.' The General said, that in a state of nature a man and woman uniting together, would form a strong and constant affection, by the mutual pleasure each would receive; and that the same causes of dissention would not arise between them, as occur between husband and wife in a civilized state. JOHNSON. 'Sir, they would have dissentions enough, though of another kind. One would choose to go a hunting in this wood, the other in that; one would choose to go a fishing in this lake, the other in that; or, perhaps, one would choose to go a hunting, when the other would choose to go a fishing; and so

two marginal lines: *is so . . . state of* [H]

they would part. Besides, Sir, a savage man and a savage woman meet by chance: and when the man sees another woman that pleases him better, he will leave the first.'

We then fell into a disquisition whether there is any beauty independent of utility. The General maintained there was not. Dr. Johnson maintained that there was; and he instanced a coffee cup which he held in his hand, the painting of which was of no real use, as the cup could hold the coffee equally well if plain; yet the painting was beautiful.

We talked of the strange custom of swearing in conversation. The General said, that all barbarous nations swore from a certain violence of temper, that could not be confined to earth, but was always reaching at the powers above. He said, too, that there was greater variety of swearing, in proportion as there was a greater variety of *He said true.* [H] religious ceremonies.[a]

Dr. Johnson went home with me to my lodgings in Conduit-street and drank tea, previous to our going to the Pantheon, which neither of us had seen before.

He said, 'Goldsmith's Life of Parnell is poor; not that it is poorly written, but that he had poor materials; for nobody can write the life of a man, but those who have eat and drunk and lived in social intercourse with him.'

I said, that if it was not troublesome and presuming too much, I would request him to tell me all the little circumstances of his life; what schools he attended, when he came to Oxford, when he came to London, &c. &c. He did not disapprove of my curiosity as to these particulars; but said, 'They'll come out by degrees, as we talk together.'

He censured Ruffhead's Life of Pope; and said, 'he knew nothing of Pope, and nothing of poetry.' He praised Dr. Joseph Warton's Essay on Pope; but said, 'he supposed we should have no more of it, as the authour had not been able to persuade the world to think of Pope as he did.' BOSWELL. 'Why, Sir, should that prevent him from continuing his work? He is an ingenious Counsel, who has made the most of his cause: he is not obliged to gain it.' JOHNSON. 'But, Sir, there is a difference when the cause is of a man's own making.'

We talked of the proper use of riches. JOHNSON. 'If I were a man of great estate, I would drive all the rascals whom I did not like out of the country, at an election.'

I asked him, how far he thought wealth should be employed in hospitality. JOHNSON. 'You are to consider that ancient hospitality, of which we hear so much, was in an uncommercial country, when men being idle, were glad to be entertained at rich men's tables. But in a commercial country, a busy country, time becomes precious, and therefore hospitality is not so much valued. No doubt there is still room for a certain degree of it; and a man has a satisfaction in seeing his friends eating and drinking around him. But promiscuous hospitality is not the way to gain real influence. You must help some people at table before others; you must ask some people how they like their wine oftener than others. You therefore offend more people than you please. You are like the French statesman, who said, when he granted a favour, "*Jai fait dix mécontents et un ingrat.*" Besides, Sir, being entertained ever so well at a man's table, impresses no lasting regard or esteem. No, Sir, the way to make sure of power and influence is, by lending money confidentially to your neighbours at a small interest, or perhaps at no interest at all, and having their bonds in your possession.' BOSWELL. 'May not a man, Sir, employ his riches to advantage, in educating young men of merit?' JOHNSON. 'Yes, Sir, if they fall in your way; but if it be understood that you patronize young men of merit, you will be harassed with solicitations. You will have numbers forced upon you, who have no merit; some will force them upon you from mistaken partiality; and some from downright interested motives, without scruple; and you will be disgraced.'

'Were I a rich man, I would propagate all kinds of trees that will grow in the open air. A greenhouse is childish. I would introduce foreign animals into the country; for instance, the rein-deer.'[1]

The conversation now turned on critical subjects. JOHNSON. 'Bayes, in "The Rehearsal," is a mighty silly

marginal line:
You therefore . . . you please [H]
marginal line:
he granted . . . et un [H]

---

[1] This project has since been realized. Sir Henry Liddel, who made a spirited tour into Lapland, brought two rein-deer to his estate in Northumberland, where they bred: but the race has unfortunately perished.

character. If it was intended to be like a particular man, it could only be diverting while that man was remembered. But I question whether it was meant for Dryden, as has been reported; for we know some of the passages said to be ridiculed, were written since the Rehearsal; at least a passage mentioned in the Preface[1] is of a later date.' I maintained that it had merit as a general satire on the self-importance of dramatick authours. But even in this light he held it very cheap.

We then walked to the Pantheon. The first view of it did not strike us so much as Ranelagh, of which he said, the 'coup d'œil was the finest thing he had ever seen.' The truth is, Ranelagh is of a more beautiful form; more of it, or rather indeed the whole rotunda, appears at once, and it is better lighted. However, as Johnson observed, we saw the Pantheon in time of mourning, when there was a dull uniformity; whereas we had seen Ranelagh, when the view was enlivened with a gay profusion of colours. Mrs. Bosville, of Gunthwait, in Yorkshire, joined us, and entered into conversation with us. Johnson said to me afterwards, 'Sir, this is a mighty intelligent lady.'

marginal line:
is half ... I doubt [H]

I said there was not half a guinea's worth of pleasure in seeing this place. JOHNSON. 'But, Sir, there is half a guinea's worth of inferiority to other people in not having seen it.' BOSWELL. 'I doubt, Sir, whether there are many happy people here.' JOHNSON. 'Yes, Sir, there are many happy people here. There are many people here who are watching hundreds, and who think hundreds are watching them.'

marginal line:
encourage luxury ...
not been [H]

Happening to meet Sir Adam Ferguson, I presented him to Dr. Johnson. Sir Adam expressed some apprehension that the Pantheon would encourage luxury. 'Sir, (said Johnson,) I am a great friend to publick amusements; for they keep people from vice. You now (addressing

[1] [There is no preface to 'The Rehearsal,' as originally published. Dr. Johnson seems to have meant the Address to the Reader with a KEY subjoined to it; which have been prefixed to the modern editions of that play. He did not know, it appears, that several *additions* were made to 'The Rehearsal' after the first edition. The ridicule on the passages here alluded to is found among those *additions*. They therefore furnish no ground for the doubts here suggested. Unquestionably Bayes was meant to be the representative of Dryden, whose familiar phrases in his ordinary conversation are frequently introduced in this piece. MALONE.]

himself to me,) would have been with a wench, had you not been here.—O! I forgot you were married.'

Sir Adam suggested, that luxury corrupts a people, and destroys the spirit of liberty. JOHNSON. 'Sir, that is all visionary. I would not give half a guinea to live under one form of Government rather than another. It is of no moment to the happiness of an individual. Sir, the danger of the abuse of power is nothing to a private man. What Frenchman is prevented from passing his life as he pleases?' SIR ADAM. 'But, Sir, in the British constitution it is surely of importance to keep up a spirit in the people, so as to preserve a balance against the crown.' JOHNSON. 'Sir, I perceive you are a vile Whig.—Why all this childish jealousy of the power of the crown? The crown has not power enough. When I say that all governments are alike, I consider that in no government power can be abused long. Mankind will not bear it. If a sovereign oppresses his people to a great degree, they will rise and cut off his head. There is a remedy in human nature against tyranny, that will keep us safe under every form of government. Had not the people of France thought themselves honoured in sharing in the brilliant actions of Louis XIV. they would not have endured him; and we may say the same of the King of Prussia's people.' Sir Adam introduced the ancient Greeks and Romans. JOHNSON. 'Sir, the mass of both of them were barbarians. The mass of every people must be barbarous where there is no printing, and consequently knowledge is not generally diffused. Knowledge is diffused among our people by the news-papers.' Sir Adam mentioned the orators, poets, and artists of Greece. JOHNSON. 'Sir, I am talking of the mass of the people. We see even what the boasted Athenians were. The little effect which Demosthenes's orations had upon them, shews that they were barbarians.'

Sir Adam was unlucky in his topicks; for he suggested a doubt of the propriety of Bishops having seats in the House of Lords. JOHNSON. 'How so, Sir? Who is more proper for having the dignity of a peer, than a Bishop, provided a Bishop be what he ought to be; and if improper Bishops be made, that is not the fault of the Bishops, but of those who make them.'

On Sunday, April 5, after attending divine service at St. Paul's church, I found him alone. Of a schoolmaster of his acquaintance, a native of Scotland, he said, 'He has a great deal of good about him; but he is also very defective in some respects. His inner part is good, but his outer part is mighty awkward. You in Scotland do not attain that nice critical skill in languages, which we get in our schools in England. I would not put a boy to him, whom I intended for a man of learning. But for the sons of citizens, who are to learn a little, get good morals, and then go to trade, he may do very well.'

I mentioned a cause in which I had appeared as counsel at the bar of the General Assembly of the Church of Scotland, where a *Probationer*, (as one licensed to preach, but not yet ordained, is called,) was opposed in his application to be inducted, because it was alledged that he had been guilty of fornication five years before. JOHNSON. 'Why, Sir, if he has repented, it is not a sufficient objection. A man who is good enough to go to heaven, is good enough to be a clergyman.' This was a humane and liberal sentiment. But the character of a clergyman is more sacred than that of an ordinary christian. As he is to instruct with authority, he should be regarded with reverence, as one upon whom divine truth has had the effect to set him above such transgressions, as men, less exalted by spiritual habits and yet upon the whole not to be excluded from heaven, have been betrayed into by the predominance of passion. That clergymen may be considered as sinners in general, as all men are, cannot be denied; but this reflection will not counteract their good precepts so much, as the absolute knowledge of their having been guilty of certain specific immoral acts. I told him, that by the rules of the Church of Scotland, in their 'Book of Discipline,' if a *scandal*, as it is called, is not prosecuted for five years, it cannot afterwards be proceeded upon, 'unless it be *of a heinous nature*, or again become flagrant;' and that hence a question arose, whether fornication was a sin of a heinous nature; and that I had maintained, that it did not deserve that epithet, in as much as it was not one of those sins which argue very great depravity of heart: in short, was not, in the general acceptation of mankind, a heinous sin.

JOHNSON. 'No, Sir, it is not a heinous sin. A heinous sin is that for which a man is punished with death or banishment.' BOSWELL. 'But, Sir, after I had argued that it was not a heinous sin, an old clergyman rose up, and repeating the text of scripture denouncing judgment against whoremongers, asked, whether, considering this, there could be any doubt of fornication being a heinous sin.' JOHNSON. 'Why, Sir, observe the word *whoremonger*. Every sin, if persisted in, will become heinous. Whoremonger is a dealer in whores, as ironmonger is a dealer in iron. But as you don't call a man an ironmonger for buying and selling a pen-knife; so you don't call a man a whoremonger for getting one wench with child.'[1]

marginal line: *persisted in . . . in iron* [H]

I spoke of the inequality of the livings of the clergy in England, and the scanty provisions of some of the Curates. JOHNSON. 'Why yes, Sir; but it cannot be helped. You must consider, that the revenues of the clergy are not at the disposal of the state, like the pay of the army. Different men have founded different churches; and some are better endowed, some worse. The state cannot interfere and make an equal division of what has been particularly appropriated. Now when a clergyman has but a small living, or even two small livings, he can afford very little to the Curate.'

marginal line: *some worse . . . a small* [H]

He said, he went more frequently to church when there were prayers only, than when there was also a sermon, as the people required more an example for the one than the other; it being much easier for them to hear a sermon, than to fix their minds on prayer.

marginal line: *He said . . . an example* [H]

On Monday, April 6, I dined with him at Sir Alexander Macdonald's, where was a young officer in the regimentals of the Scots Royal, who talked with a vivacity, fluency, and precision so uncommon, that he attracted particular attention. He proved to be the Honourable Thomas Erskine, youngest brother to the Earl of Buchan, who has since risen into such brilliant reputation at the bar in Westminster-hall.

marginal line: *that he . . . Westminster-hall* [H]

Fielding being mentioned, Johnson exclaimed, 'he was a blockhead;' and upon my expressing my astonishment

---

[1] It must not be presumed that Dr. Johnson meant to give any countenance to licentiousness, though in the character of an Advocate he made a just and subtle distinction between occasional and habitual transgression.

at so strange an assertion, he said, 'What I mean by his being a blockhead is, that he was a barren rascal.' Bos-well. 'Will you not allow, Sir, that he draws very natural pictures of human life?' Johnson. 'Why, Sir, it is of very low life. Richardson used to say, that had he not known who Fielding was, he should have believed he was an ostler. Sir, there is more knowledge of the heart in one letter of Richardson's, than in all "Tom Jones."[1] I, indeed, never read "Joseph Andrews."' Erskine. 'Surely, Sir, Richardson is very tedious.' Johnson. 'Why, Sir, if you were to read Richardson for the story, your impatience would be so much fretted that you would hang yourself. But you must read him for the sentiment, and consider the story as only giving occasion to the sentiment.'—I have already given my opinion of Fielding; but I cannot refrain from repeating here my wonder at Johnson's excessive and unaccountable depreciation of one of the best writers that England has produced. 'Tom Jones' has stood the test of publick opinion with such success, as to have established its great merit, both for the story, the sentiments, and the manners, and also the varieties of diction, so as to leave no doubt of its having an animated truth of execution throughout.

A book of travels, lately published under the title of *Coriat Junior*, and written by Mr. Paterson,[2] was mentioned. Johnson said, this book was in imitation of Sterne,[3] and not of Coriat, whose name Paterson had chosen as a whimsical one. 'Tom Coriat (said he) was a humourist about the court of James the First. He had a mixture of learning, of wit, and of buffoonery. He first travelled through Europe, and published his travels. He afterwards travelled on foot through Asia, and had made many remarks; but he died at Mandoa and his remarks were lost.'

[1] [Johnson's severity against Fielding did not arise from any viciousness in his style, but from his loose life, and the profligacy of almost all his male characters. Who would venture to read one of his novels aloud to modest women? His novels are *male* amusements, and very amusing they certainly are. —Fielding's conversation was coarse, and so tinctured with the rank weeds of *the Garden*, that it would now be thought only fit for a brothel. Burney.]

[2] Mr. Samuel Paterson, eminent for his knowledge of books.

[3] Mr. Paterson, in a pamphlet, produced some evidence to shew that his work was written before Sterne's 'Sentimental Journey' appeared.

We talked of gaming, and animadverted on it with severity. JOHNSON. 'Nay, gentlemen, let us not aggravate the matter. It is not roguery to play with a man who is ignorant of the game, while you are master of it, and so win his money; for he thinks he can play better than you, as you think you can play better than he; and the superior skill carries it.' ERSKINE. 'He is a fool, but you are not a rogue.' JOHNSON. 'That's much about the truth, Sir. It must be considered, that a man who only does what every one of the society to which he belongs would do, is not a dishonest man. In the republic of Sparta it was agreed, that stealing was not dishonourable, if not discovered. I do not commend a society where there is an agreement that what would not otherwise be fair, shall be fair; but I maintain, that an individual of any society, who practises what is allowed, is not a dishonest man.' BOSWELL. 'So then, Sir, you do not think ill of a man who wins perhaps forty thousand pounds in a winter?' JOHNSON. 'Sir, I do not call a gamester a dishonest man; but I call him an unsocial man, an unprofitable man. Gaming is a mode of transferring property without producing any intermediate good. Trade gives employment to numbers, and so produces intermediate good.'

queried: It is not etc. [H]

queried: a man etc. [H]

queried: I maintain etc. [H]

Mr. Erskine told us, that when he was in the island of Minorca, he not only read prayers, but preached two sermons to the regiment. He seemed to object to the passage in scripture, where we are told that the angel of the Lord smote in one night forty thousand Assyrians.[1a] 'Sir, (said Johnson,) you should recollect that there was a supernatural interposition; they were destroyed by pestilence. You are not to suppose that the angel of the LORD went about and stabbed each of them with a dagger, or knocked them on the head, man by man.'

[a] They fell I fancy by the hot Samiel Wind . . . The Word Blast corroborates this Conjecture, & the Effects of the hot Wind are now well known. [H]

After Mr. Erskine was gone, a discussion took place, whether the present Earl of Buchan, when Lord Cardross, did right to refuse to go Secretary of the Embassy to Spain, when Sir James Gray, a man of inferior rank, went Ambassadour. Dr. Johnson said, that perhaps in point of interest he did wrong; but in point of dignity he did well.

[1] [One hundred and eighty-five thousand. See Isaiah xxxvii. 36, and 2 Kings xix. 35. MALONE.]

Sir Alexander insisted that he was wrong; and said that Mr. Pitt intended it as an advantageous thing for him. 'Why, Sir, (said Johnson,) Mr. Pitt might think it an advantageous thing for him to make him a vintner, and get him all the Portugal trade: but he would have demeaned himself strangely had he accepted of such a situation. Sir, had he gone Secretary while his inferiour was Ambassadour, he would have been a traitor to his rank and family.'

I talked of the little attachment which subsisted between near relations in London. 'Sir, (said Johnson,) in a country so commercial as ours, where every man can do for himself, there is not so much occasion for that attachment. No man is thought the worse of here, whose brother was hanged. In uncommercial countries, many of the branches of a family must depend on the stock; so, in order to make the head of the family take care of them, they are represented as connected with his reputation, that, self-love being interested, he may exert himself to promote their interest. You have first large circles, or clans; as commerce increases, the connection is confined to families; by degrees, that too goes off, as having become unnecessary, and there being few opportunities of intercourse. One brother is a merchant in the city, and another is an officer in the guards; how little intercourse can these two have!'

I argued warmly for the old feudal system. Sir Alexander opposed it, and talked of the pleasure of seeing all men free and independent. JOHNSON. 'I agree with Mr. Boswell, that there must be a high satisfaction in being a feudal Lord; but we are to consider that we ought not to wish to have a number of men unhappy for the satisfaction of one.'—I maintained that numbers, namely, the vassals or followers, were not unhappy; for that there was a reciprocal satisfaction between the Lord and them; he being kind in his authority over them; they being respectful and faithful to him.

On Thursday, April 9, I called on him to beg he would go and dine with me at the Mitre Tavern. He had resolved not to dine at all this day, I know not for what reason;[a] and I was so unwilling to be deprived of his company, that I was content to submit to suffer a want, which was at

[a] *It was probably in Passion Week by the Date.* [H]

first somewhat painful, but he soon made me forget it; and a man is always pleased with himself, when he finds his intellectual inclinations predominate.

He observed, that to reason philosophically on the nature of prayer, was very unprofitable.

Talking of ghosts, he said, he knew one friend, who was an honest man and a sensible man, who told him he had seen a ghost; old Mr. Edward Cave, the printer at St. John's Gate. He said, Mr. Cave did not like to talk of it, and seemed to be in great horrour whenever it was mentioned. BOSWELL. 'Pray, Sir, what did he say was the appearance?' JOHNSON. 'Why, Sir, something of a shadowy being.'

I mentioned witches, and asked him what they properly meant. JOHNSON. 'Why, Sir, they properly mean those who make use of the aid of evil spirits.' BOSWELL. 'There is no doubt, Sir, a general report and belief of their having existed.' JOHNSON. 'You have not only the general report and belief, but you have many voluntary solemn confessions.' He did not affirm any thing positively upon a subject which it is the fashion of the times to laugh at as a matter of absurd credulity. He only seemed willing, as a candid inquirer after truth, however strange and inexplicable, to show that he understood what might be urged for it.[1]

On Friday, April 10, I dined with him at General Oglethorpe's, where we found Dr. Goldsmith.

Armorial bearings having been mentioned, Johnson said they were as ancient as the siege of Thebes, which he proved by a passage in one of the tragedies of Euripides.[2][a]

I started the question, whether duelling was consistent with moral duty. The brave old General fired at this, and said, with a lofty air, 'Undoubtedly a man has a right to defend his honour.' GOLDSMITH, (turning to me,) 'I ask

[1] See this curious question treated by him with most acute ability, 'Journal of a Tour to the Hebrides,' 3d edit. p. 33.

[2] [The passage to which Johnson alluded is to be found (as I conjecture) in the PHŒNISSÆ, l. 1120.

Καὶ πρῶτα μὲν προσῆγε, κ. τ. λ.
Ὁ τῆς κυναγοῦ Παρθενοπαῖος ἔκγονος,
ΕΠΙΣΗΜ, ἔχων ΟΙΚΕΙΟΝ ἐν μέσῳ σάκει.

J. BOSWELL.]

[a] *They were older still. The Hebrew Standards were as Armorial Bearings — Joseph had the Branch Naphthali the Hind &c* [H]

They were as old as the 12 Tribes of Israel who carried their Standards with a Hind on one, a Bough on another, & so forth: he might have quoted Hebrew if Greek was not enough [I]

you first, Sir, what would you do if you were affronted?'
I answered, I should think it necessary to fight. 'Why then,
(replied Goldsmith,) that solves the question.' JOHNSON.
'No, Sir, it does not solve the question. It does not follow,
that what a man would do is therefore right.' I said, I
wished to have it settled, whether duelling was contrary
to the laws of Christianity. Johnson immediately entered
on the subject, and treated it in a masterly manner; and
so far as I have been able to recollect, his thoughts were
these: 'Sir, as men become in a high degree refined,
various causes of offence arise; which are considered to
be of such importance, that life must be staked to atone
for them, though in reality they are not so. A body that
has received a very fine polish may be easily hurt.[a] Before
men arrive at this artificial refinement, if one tells his
neighbour—he lies, his neighbour tells him—he lies; if one
gives his neighbour a blow, his neighbour gives him a blow:
but in a state of highly polished society, an affront is held
to be a serious injury. It must, therefore, be resented, or
rather a duel must be fought upon it; as men have agreed
to banish from their society one who puts up with an
affront without fighting a duel. Now, Sir, it is never unlawful to fight in self-defence. He, then, who fights a duel, does
not fight from passion against his antagonist, but out of
self-defence; to avert the stigma of the world, and to prevent himself from being driven out of society. I could wish
there was not that superfluity of refinement; but while such
notions prevail, no doubt a man may lawfully fight a duel.'

Let it be remembered, that this justification is applicable
only to the person who *receives* an affront. All mankind
must condemn the aggressor.

The General told us, that when he was a very young
man, I think only fifteen, serving under Prince Eugene
of Savoy, he was sitting in a company at table with a
Prince of Wirtemberg. The Prince took up a glass of wine,
and, by a fillip, made some of it fly in Oglethorpe's face.
Here was a nice dilemma. To have challenged him instantly, might have fixed a quarrelsome character upon the
young soldier: to have taken no notice of it, might have
been considered as cowardice. Oglethorpe, therefore,
keeping his eye upon the Prince, and smiling all the time,

[a] *very pretty.* [H]

as if he took what his Highness had done in jest, said, '*Mon Prince,*—' (I forget the French words he used, the purport however was,) 'That's a good joke: but we do it much better in England;' and threw a whole glass of wine in the Prince's face. An old General who sat by, said, '*Il a bien fait, mon Prince, vous l'avez commencé:*' and thus all ended in good humour.

marginal line: *Prince's face . . . good humour* [H]

Dr. Johnson said, 'Pray, General, give us an account of the siege of Belgrade.' Upon which the General, pouring a little wine upon the table, described every thing with a wet finger: 'Here we were, here were the Turks,' &c. &c. Johnson listened with the closest attention.

A question was started, how far people who disagree in a capital point can live in friendship together. Johnson said they might. Goldsmith said they could not, as they had not the *idem velle atque idem nolle*—the same likings and the same aversions. JOHNSON. 'Why, Sir, you must shun the subject as to which you disagree. For instance, I can live very well with Burke: I love his knowledge, his genius, his diffusion, and affluence of conversation; but I would not talk to him of the Rockingham party.' GOLDSMITH. 'But, Sir, when people live together who have something as to which they disagree, and which they want to shun, they will be in the situation mentioned in the story of Bluebeard: "You may look into all the chambers but one." But we should have the greatest inclination to look into that chamber, to talk of that subject.' JOHNSON, (with a loud voice.) 'Sir, I am not saying that *you* could live in friendship with a man from whom you differ as to some point: I am only saying that *I* could do it. You put me in mind of Sappho in Ovid.'[1]

[1] [Mr. Boswell's note here being rather short, as taken at the time, (with a view perhaps to future revision,) Johnson's remark is obscure, and requires to be a little opened. What he said, probably was, 'You seem to think that two friends, to live well together, must be in a perfect harmony with each other; that each should be to the other, what Sappho boasts she was to her lover, and uniformly agree in every particular; but this is by no means necessary,' &c. The words of Sappho alluded to, are:—'*om nique à parte placebam.*' Ovid. Epist. Sapp. ad Phaonem. l. 51. MALONE.]

[I should rather conjecture that the passage which Johnson had in view was the following, l. 45:

'Si, nisi quæ facie poterit te digna videri
    Nulla futura tua est; nulla futura tua est.'

Goldsmith told us, that he was now busy in writing a
Natural History; and, that he might have full leisure for it,
he had taken lodgings, at a farmer's house, near to the six
mile-stone, on the Edgeware-road, and had carried down
his books in two returned post-chaises. He said, he believed
the farmer's family thought him an odd character, similar
to that in which the *Spectator* appeared to his landlady and
her children: he was *The Gentleman*. Mr. Mickle, the translator of 'The Lusiad,' and I, went to visit him at this place
a few days afterwards. He was not at home; but having a
curiosity to see his apartment, we went in, and found
curious scraps of descriptions of animals, scrawled upon
the wall with a black lead pencil.

The subject of ghosts being introduced, Johnson repeated what he had told me of a friend of his, an honest
man, and a man of sense, having asserted to him, that he
had seen an apparition. Goldsmith told us, he was assured
by his brother, the Reverend Mr. Goldsmith, that he also
had seen one.[a] General Oglethorpe told us, that Prendergast, an officer in the Duke of Marlborough's army, had
mentioned to many of his friends, that he should die on a
particular day; that upon that day a battle took place
with the French; that after it was over, and Prendergast
was still alive, his brother officers, while they were yet in
the field, jestingly asked him, where was his prophecy
now. Prendergast gravely answered, 'I shall die, notwithstanding what you see.' Soon afterwards, there came a
shot from a French battery, to which the orders for a
cessation of arms had not reached, and he was killed upon

[a] *Who would believe
Goldy when he told of a
Ghost? a Man whom
One could not believe
when he told of a
Brother. It is ques-
tionable now whether
he had a Brother or not.*
[H]

His reasoning and its illustration I take to be this. If you are determined to
associate with no one whose sentiments do not universally coincide with your
own, you will by such a resolution exclude yourself from all society, for no
two men can be found who, on all points, invariably think alike. So Sappho
in Ovid tells Phaon, that if he will not unite himself to any one who is not a
complete resemblance of himself, it will be impossible for him to form any
union at all.

The lines which I have quoted are thus expanded in Pope's Paraphrase,
which, to say the truth, I suspect was at this moment more in Johnson's
recollection than the original:

'If to no charms thou wilt thy heart resign
But such as merit, such as equal thine,
By none, alas, by none, thou canst be mov'd,
Phaon alone by Phaon must be lov'd.'   J. BOSWELL.]

seventh act of correction, her daughter, says he, would have been ruined. The degrees of obstinacy in young minds are very different: as different must be the degrees of persevering severity. A stubborn scholar must be corrected till he is subdued. The discipline of a school is military. There must be either unbounded licence or absolute authority. The master, who punishes, not only consults the future happiness of him who is the immediate subject of correction, but he propagates obedience through the whole school; and establishes regularity by exemplary justice. The victorious obstinacy of a single boy would make his future endeavours of reformation or instruction totally ineffectual. Obstinacy, therefore, must never be victorious. Yet, it is well known, that there sometimes occurs a sullen and hardy resolution, that laughs at all common punishment, and bids defiance to all common degrees of pain. Correction must be proportionate to occasions. The flexible will be reformed by gentle discipline, and the refractory must be subdued by harsher methods. The degrees of scholastick, as of military punishment, no stated rules can ascertain. It must be enforced till it overpowers temptation; till stubbornness becomes flexible, and perverseness regular. Custom and reason have, indeed, set some bounds to scholastick penalties. The schoolmaster inflicts no capital punishments; nor enforces his edicts by either death or mutilation. The civil law has wisely determined, that a master who strikes at a scholar's eye shall be considered as criminal. But punishments, however severe, that produce no lasting evil, may be just and reasonable, because they may be necessary. Such have been the punishments used by the respondent. No scholar has gone from him either blind or lame, or with any of his limbs or powers injured or impaired. They were irregular, and he punished them: they were obstinate, and he enforced his punishment. But however provoked, he never exceeded the limits of moderation, for he inflicted nothing beyond present pain: and how much of that was required, no man is so little able to determine as those who have determined against him:—the parents of the offenders.—It has been said, that he used unprecedented and improper instruments of correction. Of this accusation the meaning

is not very easy to be found. No instrument of correction
is more proper than another, but as it is better adapted to
produce present pain without lasting mischief. Whatever
were his instruments, no lasting mischief has ensued; and
therefore, however unusual, in hands so cautious they were
proper.—It has been objected, that the respondent admits
the charge of cruelty by producing no evidence to confute
it. Let it be considered, that his scholars are either dispersed
at large in the world, or continue to inhabit the place in
which they were bred. Those who are dispersed cannot be
found; those who remain are the sons of his prosecutors,
and are not likely to support a man to whom their fathers
are enemies. If it be supposed that the enmity of their
fathers proves the justness of the charge, it must be considered how often experience shews us, that men who are
angry on one ground will accuse on another; with how
little kindness, in a town of low trade, a man who lives by
learning is regarded; and how implicitly, where the inhabitants are not very rich, a rich man is hearkened to
and followed. In a place like Campbelltown, it is easy for
one of the principal inhabitants to make a party. It is easy
for that party to heat themselves with imaginary griev-
ances. It is easy for them to oppress a man poorer than
themselves; and natural to assert the dignity of riches, by
persisting in oppression. The argument which attempts to
prove the impropriety of restoring him to the school, by
alledging that he has lost the confidence of the people, is
not the subject of juridical consideration; for he is to suffer,
if he must suffer, not for their judgment, but for his own
actions. It may be convenient for them to have another
master; but it is a convenience of their own making. It
would be likewise convenient for him to find another
school; but this convenience he cannot obtain.—The
question is not what is now convenient, but what is generally right. If the people of Campbelltown be distressed by
the restoration of the respondent, they are distressed only
by their own fault; by turbulent passions and unreasonable
desires; by tyranny, which law has defeated, and by malice,
which virtue has surmounted.'

'This, Sir, (said he,) you are to turn in your mind, and
make the best use of it you can in your speech.'

Of our friend Goldsmith he said, 'Sir, he is so much afraid of being unnoticed, that he often talks merely lest you should forget that he is in the company.' BOSWELL. 'Yes, he stands forward.' JOHNSON. 'True, Sir, but if a man is to stand forward, he should wish to do it not in an aukward posture, not in rags, not so as that he shall only be exposed to ridicule.' BOSWELL. 'For my part, I like very well to hear honest Goldsmith talk away carelessly.' JOHNSON. 'Why yes, Sir; but he should not like to hear himself.'

On Tuesday, April 14, the decree of the Court of Session in the schoolmaster's cause was reversed in the House of Lords, after a very eloquent speech by Lord Mansfield, who shewed himself an adept in school discipline, but I thought was too rigorous towards my client. On the evening of the next day I supped with Dr. Johnson, at the Crown and Anchor tavern, in the Strand, in company with Mr. Langton and his brother-in-law, Lord Binning. I repeated a sentence of Lord Mansfield's speech, of which by the aid of Mr. Longlands, the solicitor on the other side, who obligingly allowed me to compare his note with my own, I have a full copy: 'My Lords, severity is not the way to govern either boys or men.' 'Nay (said Johnson,) it is the way to *govern* them. I know not whether it be the way to *mend* them.'[a]

I talked of the recent expulsion of six students from the University of Oxford, who were methodists, and would not desist from publickly praying and exhorting. JOHNSON. 'Sir, that expulsion was extremely just and proper. What have they to do at an University, who are not willing to be taught, but will presume to teach? Where is religion to be learnt, but at an University? Sir, they were examined, and found to be mighty ignorant fellows.' BOSWELL. 'But, was it not hard, Sir, to expel them, for I am told they were good beings?' JOHNSON. 'I believe they might be good beings; but they were not fit to be in the University of Oxford. A cow is a very good animal in the field; but we turn her out of a garden.' Lord Elibank used to repeat this as an illustration uncommonly happy.

Desirous of calling Johnson forth to talk, and exercise his wit, though I should myself be the object of it, I resolutely ventured to undertake the defence of convivial indulgence in wine, though he was not to-night in the most genial humour. After urging the common plausible topicks, I at last had recourse to the maxim, *in vino veritas;* a man who is well warmed with wine will speak truth. JOHNSON. 'Why, Sir, that may be an argument for drinking, if you suppose men in general to be liars. But, Sir, I would not keep company with a fellow, who lyes as long as he is sober, and whom you must make drunk before you can get a word of truth out of him.'[1]

queried:
the maxim etc. [H]

Mr. Langton told us, he was about to establish a school upon his estate, but it had been suggested to him, that it might have a tendency to make the people less industrious. JOHNSON. 'No, Sir. While learning to read and write is a distinction, the few who have that distinction may be the less inclined to work; but when every body learns to read and write, it is no longer a distinction. A man who has a laced waistcoat is too fine a man to work; but if every body had laced waistcoats, we should have people working in laced waistcoats. There are no people whatever more industrious, none who work more, than our manufacturers; yet they have all learnt to read and write. Sir, you must not neglect doing a thing immediately good, from fear of remote evil;—from fear of its being abused. A man who has candles may sit up too late, which he would not do if he had not candles; but nobody will deny that the art of making candles, by which light is continued to us beyond the time that the sun gives us light, is a valuable art, and ought to be preserved.' BOSWELL. 'But, Sir, would it not be better to follow Nature; and go to bed and rise just as Nature gives us light or withholds it?' JOHNSON. 'No, Sir; for then we should have no kind of equality in the partition of our time between sleeping and waking. It would be very different in different seasons and in different places. In some of the northern parts of Scotland how little light is there in the depth of winter!'

We talked of Tacitus, and I hazarded an opinion, that

---

[1] Mrs. Piozzi, in her 'Anecdotes,' p. 261, has given an erroneous account of this incident, as of many others. She pretends to relate it from recollection, as if she herself had been present: when the fact is that it was communicated to her by me. She has represented it as a personality, and the true point has escaped her.

with all his merit for penetration, shrewdness of judgement, and terseness of expression, he was too compact, too much broken into hints, as it were, and therefore too difficult to be understood. To my great satisfaction Dr. Johnson sanctioned this opinion. 'Tacitus, Sir, seems to me rather to have made notes for an historical work, than to have written a history.'[1]

marginal line:
*Tacitus, Sir . . . a
history* [H]

At this time it appears from his 'Prayers and Meditations,' that he had been more than commonly diligent in religious duties, particularly in reading the holy scriptures. It was Passion Week, that solemn season which the Christian world has appropriated to the commemoration of the mysteries of our redemption, and during which, whatever embers of religion are in our breasts, will be kindled into pious warmth.

I paid him short visits both on Friday and Saturday, and seeing his large folio Greek Testament before him, beheld him with a reverential awe, and would not intrude upon his time. While he was thus employed to such good purpose, and while his friends in their intercourse with him constantly found a vigorous intellect and a lively imagination, it is melancholy to read in his private register, 'My mind is unsettled and my memory confused. I have of late turned my thoughts with a very useless earnestness upon past incidents. I have yet got no command over my thoughts; an unpleasing incident is almost certain to hinder my rest.'[2] What philosophick heroism was it in him to appear with such manly fortitude to the world, while he was inwardly so distressed! We may surely believe that the mysterious principle of being 'made perfect through suffering,' was to be strongly exemplified in him.

marginal line:
*over my . . . What
philosophick* [H]

On Sunday, April 19, being Easter-day, General Paoli and I paid him a visit before dinner. We talked of the notion that blind persons can distinguish colours by the touch. Johnson said, that Professor Sanderson mentions his having attempted to do it, but that he found he was

---

[1] It is remarkable that Lord Monboddo, whom, on account of his resembling Dr. Johnson in some particulars, Foote called an Elzevir edition of him, has, by coincidence, made the very same remark. *Origin and Progress of Language*, vol. iii. 2d edit. p. 219.

[2] Prayers and Meditations, p. 111.

aiming at an impossibility; that to be sure a difference in the surface makes the difference of colours; but that difference is so fine, that it is not sensible to the touch. The General mentioned jugglers and fraudulent gamesters, who could know cards by the touch. Dr. Johnson said, 'the cards used by such persons must be less polished than ours commonly are.'

We talked of sounds. The General said, there was no beauty in a simple sound, but only in an harmonious composition of sounds. I presumed to differ from this opinion, and mentioned the soft and sweet sound of a fine woman's voice. JOHNSON. 'No, Sir, if a serpent or a toad uttered it, you would think it ugly.' BOSWELL. 'So you would think, Sir, were a beautiful tune to be uttered by one of those animals.' JOHNSON. 'No, Sir, it would be admired. We have seen fine fiddlers whom we liked as little as toads.' (laughing.)

Talking on the subject of taste in the arts, he said, that difference of taste was, in truth, difference of skill. BOSWELL. 'But, Sir, is there not a quality called taste, which consists merely in perception or in liking; for instance, we find people differ much as to what is the best style of English composition. Some think Swift's the best; others prefer a fuller and grander way of writing.' JOHNSON. 'Sir, you must first define what you mean by style, before you can judge who has a good taste in style, and who has a bad. The two classes of persons whom you have mentioned don't differ as to good and bad. They both agree that Swift has a good neat style; but one loves a neat style, another loves a style of more splendour. In like manner, one loves a plain coat, another loves a laced coat; but neither will deny that each is good in its kind.'

While I remained in London this spring, I was with him at several other times, both by himself and in company. I dined with him one day at the Crown and Anchor tavern, in the Strand, with Lord Elibank, Mr. Langton, and Dr. Vansittart of Oxford. Without specifying each particular day, I have preserved the following memorable things.

I regretted the reflection in his preface to Shakspeare against Garrick, to whom we cannot but apply the following passage: 'I collated such copies as I could procure, and wished for more, but have not found the collectors of these rarities very communicative.' I told him, that Garrick had complained to me of it, and had vindicated himself by assuring me, that Johnson was made welcome to the full use of his collection, and that he left the key of it with a servant, with orders to have a fire and every convenience for him. I found Johnson's notion was, that Garrick wanted to be courted for them, and that, on the contrary, Garrick should have courted him, and sent him the plays of his own accord. But, indeed, considering the slovenly and careless manner in which books were treated by Johnson, it could not be expected that scarce and valuable editions should have been lent to him.

marginal line:
in which . . . to him [H]

A gentleman having to some of the usual arguments for drinking added this: 'You know, Sir, drinking drives away care, and makes us forget whatever is disagreeable. Would not you allow a man to drink for that reason?' JOHNSON. 'Yes, Sir, if he sat next *you*.'[a]

two exclamation points:
Would not etc. [H & I]

[a] *It was Boswell himself   Dr. Johnson said—The Man* compels *me to treat him so.* [H & I]

I expressed a liking for Mr. Francis Osborne's works, and asked him what he thought of that writer. He answered, 'A conceited fellow. Were a man to write so now, the boys would throw stones at him.' He, however, did not alter my opinion of a favourite authour, to whom I was first directed by his being quoted in 'The Spectator,' and in whom I have found much shrewd and lively sense, expressed indeed in a style somewhat quaint, which, however, I do not dislike. His book has an air of originality. We figure to ourselves an ancient gentleman talking to us.

marginal line:
life very . . . have tedious [H]

When one of his friends endeavoured to maintain that a country gentleman might contrive to pass his life very agreeably, 'Sir, (said he,) you cannot give me an instance of any man who is permitted to lay out his own time, contriving not to have tedious hours.' This observation, however, is equally applicable to gentlemen who live in cities, and are of no profession.

He said, 'there is no permanent national character; it varies according to circumstances. Alexander the Great swept India: now the Turks sweep Greece.'

A learned gentleman, who in the course of conversation wished to inform us of this simple fact, that the Counsel upon the circuit at Shrewsbury were much bitten by fleas, took, I suppose, seven or eight minutes in relating it circumstantially.[a] He in a plenitude of phrase told us, that large bales of woollen cloth were lodged in the town-hall;—that by reason of this, fleas nestled there in prodigious numbers;—that the lodgings of the counsel were near the town-hall;—and that those little animals moved from place to place with wonderful agility. Johnson sat in great impatience[b] till the gentleman had finished his tedious narrative, and then burst out (playfully however,) 'It is a pity, Sir, that you have not seen a lion; for a flea has taken you such a time, that a lion must have served you a twelvemonth.'[1]

He would not allow Scotland to derive any credit from Lord Mansfield; for he was educated in England. 'Much (said he,) may be made of a Scotchman, if he be *caught young*.'

Talking of a modern historian and a modern moralist, he said, 'There is more thought in the moralist than in the historian. There is but a shallow stream of thought in history.' BOSWELL. 'But surely, Sir, an historian has reflection.' JOHNSON. 'Why yes, Sir; and so has a cat when she catches a mouse for her kitten. But she cannot write like *******; neither can *********.'

He said, 'I am very unwilling to read the manuscripts of authours, and give them my opinion. If the authours who apply to me have money, I bid them boldly print without a name; if they have written in order to get money, I tell them to go to the booksellers and make the best bargain they can.' BOSWELL. 'But, Sir, if a bookseller should bring you a manuscript to look at.' JOHNSON. 'Why, Sir, I would desire the bookseller to take it away.'

I mentioned a friend of mine who had resided long in Spain, and was unwilling to return to Britain. JOHNSON. 'Sir, he is attached to some woman.' BOSWELL. 'I rather believe, Sir, it is the fine climate which keeps him there.' JOHNSON. 'Nay, Sir, how can you talk so? What is *climate* to happiness? Place me in the heart of Asia, should I not be exiled? What proportion does climate bear to the complex system of human life? You may advise me to go to

[a] *Mr. Vansittart did flourish away about a Mouse:—I don't know this story at all.* [i]

[b] *I saw old Mitchell of Brighthelmston affront him terribly once about Fleas . . . Johnson being tired of the Subject express'd his Impatience of it with Coarseness . . . Why Sir says the old Man—why should not Flea bite o' me be treated as Phlebotomy? It empties the Capillary Vessells.* [H]

Dr. Johnson complain'd of Fleas to Mr. Mitchell of Brighthelmstone I remember; & the old Man with much affected Gravity—said 'Why Sir perhaps they are beneficial in emptying the Capillary Vessels; & Flea bite o' me may be as good as Phlebotomy in such Cases.' Johnson was very ill pleas'd & disliked Mitchell ever after. [i]

marginal line: *England. 'Much . . . caught young* [H]

queried: *What is* climate etc. [H]
queried: *What proportion* etc. [H]

---

[1] Mrs. Piozzi, to whom I told this anecdote, has related it, as if the gentleman had given 'the *natural history* of the *mouse*.' Anecdotes, p. 191.

live at Bologna to eat sausages. The sausages there are the best in the world; they lose much by being carried.'

On Saturday, May 9, Mr. Dempster and I had agreed to dine by ourselves at the British Coffee-house. Johnson, on whom I happened to call in the morning, said, he would join us, which he did, and we spent a very agreeable day, though I recollect but little of what passed.

He said, 'Walpole was a minister given by the King to the people: Pitt was a minister given by the people to the King,—as an adjunct.'

'The misfortune of Goldsmith in conversation is this: he goes on without knowing how he is to get off. His genius is great, but his knowledge is small. As they say of a generous man, it is a pity he is not rich, we may say of Goldsmith, it is a pity he is not knowing. He would not keep his knowledge to himself.'

Before leaving London this year, I consulted him upon a question purely of Scotch law. It was held of old, and continued for a long period, to be an established principle in that law, that whoever intermeddled with the effects of a person deceased, without the interposition of legal authority to guard against embezzlement, should be subjected to pay all the debts of the deceased, as having been guilty of what was technically called *vicious intromission*. The Court of Session had gradually relaxed the strictness of this principle, where the interference proved had been inconsiderable. In a case[1] which came before that Court the preceding winter, I had laboured to persuade the Judge to return to the ancient law. It was my own sincere opinion, that they ought to adhere to it; but I had exhausted all my powers of reasoning in vain. Johnson thought as I did; and in order to assist me in my application to the Court for a revision and alteration of the judgement, he dictated to me the following argument:

'THIS, we are told, is a law which has its force only from the long practice of the Court: and may, therefore, be suspended or modified as the Court shall think proper.

'Concerning the power of the Court to make or to suspend a law, we have no intention to enquire. It is sufficient for our purpose that every just law is dictated by

[1] Wilson against Smith and Armour.

marginal note: marginal line:
rich, we . . . to himself
[H]

index sign:
an established principle
etc. [I]

reason; and that the practice of every legal Court is regulated by equity. It is the quality of reason to be invariable and constant; and of equity, to give to one man what, in the same case, is given to another. The advantage which humanity derives from law is this; that the law gives every man a rule of action, and prescribes a mode of conduct which shall entitle him to the support and protection of society. That the law may be a rule of action, it is necessary that it be known; it is necessary that it be permanent and stable. The law is the measure of civil right: but if the measure be changeable, the extent of the thing measured never can be settled.

'To permit a law to be modified at discretion, is to leave the community without law. It is to withdraw the direction of that publick wisdom, by which the deficiencies of private understanding are to be supplied. It is to suffer the rash and ignorant to act at discretion, and then to depend for the legality of that action on the sentence of the Judge. He that is thus governed, lives not by law, but by opinion: not by a certain rule to which he can apply his intention before he acts, but by an uncertain and variable opinion, which he can never know but after he has committed the act on which that opinion shall be passed. He lives by a law, (if a law it be,) which he can never know before he has offended it. To this case may be justly applied that important principle, *misera est servitus ubi jus est aut incognitum aut vagum*. If Intromission be not criminal till it exceeds a certain point, and that point be unsettled, and consequently different in different minds, the right of Intromission, and the right of the Creditor arising from it, are all *jura vaga*, and, by consequence, are *jura incognita;* and the result can be no other than a *misera servitus*, an uncertainty concerning the event of action, a servile dependance on private opinion.

'It may be urged, and with great plausibility, that there may be Intromission without fraud; which, however true, will by no means justify an occasional and arbitrary relaxation of the law. The end of law is protection as well as vengeance. Indeed, vengeance is never used but to strengthen protection. That society only is well governed, where life is freed from danger, and from suspicion; where

possession is so sheltered by salutary prohibitions, that
violation is prevented more frequently than punished.
Such a prohibition was this, while it operated with its
original force. The creditor of the deceased was not only
without loss, but without fear. He was not to seek a remedy
for an injury suffered; for, injury was warded off.

'As the law has been sometimes administered, it lays
us open to wounds, because it is imagined to have the
power of healing. To punish fraud when it is detected is
the proper art of vindictive justice; but to prevent frauds,
and make punishment unnecessary, is the great employment of legislative wisdom. To permit Intromission, and
to punish fraud, is to make law no better than a pitfall.
To tread upon the brink is safe; but to come a step further
is destruction. But, surely, it is better to enclose the gulph,
and hinder all access, than by encouraging us to advance
a little, to entice us afterwards a little further, and let us
perceive our folly only by our destruction.

'As law supplies the weak with adventitious strength,
it likewise enlightens the ignorant with extrinsick understanding. Law teaches us to know when we commit injury
and when we suffer it. It fixes certain marks upon actions,
by which we are admonished to do or to forbear them.
Qui sibi bene temperat in licitis, says one of the fathers,
nunquam cadet in illicita. He who never intromits at all, will
never intromit with fraudulent intentions.

'The relaxation of the law against vicious intromission
has been very favourably represented by a great master
of jurisprudence,[1] whose words have been exhibited with
unnecessary pomp, and seem to be considered as irresistibly decisive. The great moment of his authority makes it
necessary to examine his position. "Some ages ago, (says
he,) before the ferocity of the inhabitants of this part of
the island was subdued, the utmost severity of the civil law
was necessary, to restrain individuals from plundering each
other. Thus, the man who intermeddled irregularly with
the moveables of a person deceased, was subjected to all
the debts of the deceased without limitation. This makes
a branch of the law of Scotland, known by the name of
vicious intromission; and so rigidly was this regulation

marginal line:
temperat in . . . *all,*
will [H]

[1] Lord Kames, in his 'Historical Law Tracts.'

applied in our Courts of Law, that the most trifling move-
able abstracted *malâ fide*, subjected the intermeddler to the
foregoing consequences, which proved in many instances
a most rigorous punishment. But this severity was necessary, in order to subdue the undisciplined nature of our
people. It is extremely remarkable, that in proportion to
our improvement in manners, this regulation has been
gradually softened and applied by our sovereign Court
with a sparing hand."

'I find myself under a necessity of observing, that this
learned and judicious writer has not accurately distinguished the deficiencies and demands of the different
conditions of human life, which, from a degree of savageness and independence, in which all laws are vain, passes
or may pass, by innumerable gradations, to a state of
reciprocal benignity, in which laws shall be no longer
necessary. Men are first wild and unsocial, living each
man to himself, taking from the weak, and losing to the
strong. In their first coalitions of society, much of this
original savageness is retained. Of general happiness, the
product of general confidence, there is yet no thought.
Men continue to prosecute their own advantages by the
nearest way; and the utmost severity of the civil law is
necessary to restrain individuals from plundering each
other. The restraints then necessary, are restraints from
plunder, from acts of publick violence, and undisguised
oppression. The ferocity of our ancestors, as of all other
nations, produced not fraud, but rapine. They had not
yet learned to cheat, and attempted only to rob. As
manners grow more polished, with the knowledge of good,
men attain likewise dexterity in evil. Open rapine becomes
less frequent, and violence gives way to cunning. Those
who before invaded pastures and stormed houses, now
begin to enrich themselves by unequal contracts and
fraudulent intromissions. It is not against the violence of
ferocity, but the circumventions of deceit, that this law
was framed; and I am afraid the increase of commerce,
and the incessant struggle for riches which commerce
excites, give us no prospect of an end speedily to be expected of artifice and fraud. It therefore seems to be
no very conclusive reasoning, which connects those two

propositions:—"the nation is become less ferocious, and therefore the laws against fraud and *covin* shall be relaxed."

'Whatever reason may have influenced the Judges to a relaxation of the law, it was not that the nation was grown less fierce; and, I am afraid, it cannot be affirmed, that it is grown less fraudulent.

'Since this law has been represented as rigorously and unreasonably penal, it seems not improper to consider what are the conditions and qualities that make the justice or propriety of a penal law.

'To make a penal law reasonable and just, two conditions are necessary, and two proper. It is necessary that the law should be adequate to its end; that, if it be observed, it shall prevent the evil against which it is directed. It is, secondly, necessary that the end of the law be of such importance, as to deserve the security of a penal sanction. The other conditions of a penal law, which though not absolutely necessary, are to a very high degree fit, are, that to the moral violation of the law there are many temptations, and that of the physical observance there is great facility.

'All these conditions apparently concur to justify the law which we are now considering. Its end is the security of property; and property very often of great value. The method by which it effects the security is efficacious, because it admits, in its original rigour, no gradations of injury; but keeps guilt and innocence apart, by a distinct and definite limitation. He that intromits, is criminal; he that intromits not, is innocent. Of the two secondary considerations it cannot be denied that both are in our favour. The temptation to intromit is frequent and strong; so strong and so frequent, as to require the utmost activity of justice, and vigilance of caution, to withstand its prevalence; and the method by which a man may entitle himself to legal intromission is so open and so facile, that to neglect it is a proof of fraudulent intention; for why should a man omit to do (but for reasons which he will not confess,) that which he can do so easily, and that which he knows to be required by the law? If temptation were rare, a penal law might be deemed unnecessary. If the duty enjoined by the law were of difficult performance, omission, though it could not be justified, might be pitied. But in the present case, neither equity nor compassion operate against it. A useful, a necessary law is broken, not only without a reasonable motive, but with all the inducements to obedience that can be derived from safety and facility.

'I therefore return to my original position, that a law, to have its effect, must be permanent and stable. It may be said in the language of the schools, *Lex non recipit majus et minus*,—we may have a law, or we may have no law, but we cannot have half a law. We must either have a rule of action, or be permitted to act by discretion and by chance. Deviations from the law must be uniformly punished, or no man can be certain when he shall be safe.

'That from the rigour of the original institution this Court has sometimes departed, cannot be denied. But, as it is evident that such deviations, as they make law uncertain, make life unsafe, I hope, that of departing from it there will now be an end; that the wisdom of our ancestors will be treated with due reverence; and that consistent and steady decisions will furnish the people with a rule of action, and leave fraud and fraudulent intromission no future hope of impunity or escape.'

With such comprehension of mind, and such clearness of penetration, did he thus treat a subject altogether new to him, without any other preparation than my having stated to him the arguments which had been used on each side of the question. His intellectual powers appeared with peculiar lustre, when tried against those of a writer of such fame as Lord Kames, and that too in his Lordship's own department.

This masterly argument, after being prefaced and concluded with some sentences of my own, and garnished with the usual formularies, was actually printed and laid before the Lords of Session, but without success. My respected friend Lord Hailes, however, one of that honourable body, had critical sagacity enough to discover a more than ordinary hand in the *Petition*. I told him Dr. Johnson had favoured me with his pen. His Lordship, with wonderful *acumen*, pointed out exactly where his composition began, and where it ended. But that I may do impartial justice, and conform to the great rule of Courts, *Suum cuique tribuito*, I must add, that their Lordships in general, though they were pleased to call this 'a well-drawn paper,' preferred the former very inferiour petition, which I had written; thus confirming the truth of an observation made to me by one of their number, in a merry mood: 'My dear Sir, give yourself no trouble in the composition of the papers you present to us; for, indeed, it is casting pearls before swine.'

two marginal lines:
dear Sir . . . it is [H]

I renewed my solicitations that Dr. Johnson would this year accomplish his long-intended visit to Scotland.

'TO JAMES BOSWELL, ESQ.

'DEAR SIR,

'The regret has not been little with which I have missed a journey so pregnant with pleasing expectations, as that in which I could promise myself not only the gratification of curiosity, both rational and fanciful, but the delight of seeing those whom I love and esteem. * * * * * * * *. But such has been the course of things, that I could not come; and such has been, I am afraid, the state of my body, that it would not well have seconded my inclination. My body, I think grows better, and I refer my hopes to another year; for I am very sincere in my design to pay the visit, and take the ramble. In the mean time, do not omit any opportunity of keeping up a favourable opinion of me in the minds of any of my friends. Beattie's book is, I believe, every day more liked; at least, I like it more, as I look more upon it.

'I am glad if you got credit by your cause, and am yet of opinion, that our cause was good, and that the determination ought to have been in your favour. Poor Hastie, I think, had but his deserts.

'You promised to get me a little Pindar, you may add to it a little Anacreon.

'The leisure which I cannot enjoy, it will be a pleasure to hear that you employ upon the antiquities of the feudal establishment. The whole system of ancient tenures is gradually passing away; and I wish to have the knowledge of it preserved adequate and complete. For such an

institution makes a very important part of the history of
mankind. Do not forget a design so worthy of a scholar
who studies the laws of his country, and of a gentleman
who may naturally be curious to know the condition of his
own ancestors. I am, dear Sir,

'Your's with great affection,

'August 31, 1772.'   'SAM. JOHNSON'

'TO DR. JOHNSON

'MY DEAR SIR,   'Edinburgh, Dec. 25, 1772.

* * * * * *

'I WAS much disappointed that you did not come to
Scotland last autumn. However, I must own that your
letter prevents me from complaining; not only because I
am sensible that the state of your health was but too good
an excuse, but because you write in a strain which shews
that you have agreeable views of the scheme which we
have so long proposed.

* * * * * *

'I communicated to Beattie what you said of his book
in your last letter to me. He writes to me thus: "You judge
very rightly in supposing that Dr. Johnson's favourable
opinion of my book must give me great delight. Indeed it
is impossible for me to say how much I am gratified by it;
for there is not a man upon earth whose good opinion I
would be more ambitious to cultivate. His talents and his
virtues I reverence more than any words can express. The
extraordinary civilities (the paternal attentions I should
rather say,) and the many instructions I have had the
honour to receive from him, will to me be a perpetual
source of pleasure in the recollection,

'Dum memor ipse mei, dum spiritus hos reget artus.'

"I had still some thoughts, while the summer lasted, of
being obliged to go to London on some little business;
otherwise I should certainly have troubled him with a
letter several months ago, and given some vent to my
gratitude and admiration. This I intend to do, as soon as

I am left a little at leisure. Mean time, if you have occasion to write to him, I beg you will offer him my most respectful compliments, and assure him of the sincerity of my attachment and the warmth of my gratitude."

*   *   *   *   *   *

'I am, &c.

'JAMES BOSWELL'

In 1773, his only publication was an edition of his folio Dictionary, with additions and corrections; nor did he, so far as is known, furnish any productions of his fertile pen to any of his numerous friends or dependants, except the Preface*[1] to his old amanuensis Macbean's 'Dictionary of ancient Geography.' His Shakspeare, indeed, which had been received with high approbation by the publick, and gone through several editions, was this year re-published by George Steevens, Esq. a gentleman not only deeply skilled in ancient learning, and of very extensive reading in English literature, especially the early writers, but at the same time of acute discernment and elegant taste. It is almost unnecessary to say, that by his great and valuable additions to Dr. Johnson's work, he justly obtained considerable reputation:

'*Divisum imperium cum Jove Cæsar habet.*'

'TO JAMES BOSWELL, ESQ.

'DEAR SIR,

'I HAVE read your kind letter much more than the elegant Pindar which it accompanied. I am always glad to find myself not forgotten; and to be forgotten by you would give me great uneasiness. My northern friends have never been unkind to me; I have from you, dear Sir, testimonies of affection, which I have not often been able

---

^a *They would have it English, not Latin; which* vex'd *him.* [H]

[1] He, however, wrote, or partly wrote, an Epitaph on Mrs. Bell, wife of his friend John Bell, Esq. brother of the Rev. Dr. Bell, Prebendary of Westminster, which is printed in his Works. It is in English prose,^a and has so little of his manner, that I did not believe he had any hand in it, till I was satisfied of the fact by the authority of Mr. Bell.

to excite; and Dr. Beattie rates the testimony which I was
desirous of paying to his merit, much higher than I should
have thought it reasonable to expect.

'I have heard of your masquerade.[1] What says your
synod to such innovations? I am not studiously scrupulous,
nor do I think a masquerade either evil in itself, or very
likely to be the occasion of evil; yet as the world thinks it
a very licentious relaxation of manners, I would not have
been one of the *first* masquers in a country where no
masquerade had ever been before.[2]

'A new edition of my great Dictionary is printed, from
a copy which I was persuaded to revise; but having made
no preparation, I was able to do very little. Some super-
fluities I have expunged, and some faults I have corrected,
and here and there have scattered a remark; but the main
fabrick of the work remains as it was. I have looked very
little into it since I wrote it, and, I think, I found it full as
often better, as worse, than I expected.

'Baretti and Davies have had a furious quarrel; a quarrel,
I think, irreconcileable. Dr. Goldsmith has a new comedy,
which is expected in the spring. No name is yet given it.
The chief diversion arises from a stratagem by which a
lover is made to mistake his future father-in-law's house
for an inn. This, you see, borders upon farce. The dialogue
is quick and gay, and the incidents are so prepared as not
to seem improbable.[a]

underlined:
not, improbable [1]
[a] *impossible.* [1]

'I am sorry that you lost your cause of Intromission,
because I yet think the arguments on your side unanswer-
able. But you seem, I think, to say that you gained reputation even by your defeat; and reputation you will daily
gain, if you keep Lord Auchinleck's precept in your mind,
and endeavour to consolidate in your mind a firm and
regular system of law, instead of picking up occasional
fragments.

marginal line:
consolidate in . .
occasional fragments
[H]

'My health seems in general to improve; but I have been
troubled for many weeks with a vexatious catarrh, which
is sometimes sufficiently distressful. I have not found any
great effects from bleeding and physick; and am afraid,
that I must expect help from brighter days and softer air.

[1] Given by a lady at Edinburgh.
[2] There had been masquerades in Scotland; but not for a very long time.

'Write to me now and then; and whenever any good befalls you, make haste to let me know it, for no one will rejoice at it more than, dear Sir,

'Your most humble servant,

'London, Feb. 22, 1773.'   'SAM. JOHNSON'

'You continue to stand very high in the favour of Mrs. Thrale.'[a]

[a] *Poor Mrs. Thrale was forced to say so in order to keep well with Johnson.* [H]

While a former edition of my work was passing through the press, I was unexpectedly favoured with a packet from Philadelphia, from Mr. James Abercrombie, a gentleman of that country, who is pleased to honour me with very high praise of my 'Life of Dr. Johnson.' To have the fame of my illustrious friend, and his faithful biographer, echoed from the New World is extremely flattering; and my grateful acknowledgements shall be wafted across the Atlantick. Mr. Abercrombie has politely conferred on me a considerable additional obligation, by transmitting to me copies of two letters from Dr. Johnson to American gentlemen. 'Gladly, Sir, (says he,) would I have sent you the originals: but being the only relicks of the kind in America, they are considered by the possessors of such inestimable value, that no possible consideration would induce them to part with them. In some future publication of yours relative to that great and good man, they may perhaps be thought worthy of insertion.'

'TO MR. B———D[1]

'SIR,

'THAT in the hurry of a sudden departure you should yet find leisure to consult my convenience, is a degree of kindness, and an instance of regard, not only beyond my claims, but above my expectation. You are not mistaken in supposing that I set a high value on my American friends, and that you should confer a very valuable favour upon me by giving me an opportunity of keeping myself in their memory.

[1] This gentleman, who now resides in America in a publick character of considerable dignity, desired that his name might not be transcribed at full length.

'I have taken the liberty of troubling you with a packet, to which I wish a safe and speedy conveyance, because I wish a safe and speedy voyage to him that conveys it. I am, Sir,

'Your most humble servant,

'London, Johnson's-Court,   'SAM. JOHNSON'
Fleet-street, March 4, 1773.'

'TO THE REVEREND MR. WHITE[1]

'DEAR SIR,

'YOUR kindness for your friends accompanies you across the Atlantick. It was long since observed by Horace, that no ship could leave care behind: you have been attended in your voyage by other powers,—by benevolence and constancy: and I hope care did not often shew her face in their company.

'I received the copy of Rasselas. The impression is not magnificent, but it flatters an authour, because the printer seems to have expected that it would be scattered among the people. The little book has been well received, and is translated into Italian, French, German, and Dutch. It has now one honour more by an American edition.

'I know not that much has happened since your departure that can engage your curiosity. Of all public transactions the whole world is now informed by the newspapers. Opposition seems to despond; and the dissenters, though they have taken advantage of unsettled times, and a government much enfeebled, seem not likely to gain any immunities.

'Dr. Goldsmith has a new comedy in rehearsal at Covent-Garden, to which the manager predicts ill success. I hope he will be mistaken. I think it deserves a very kind reception.

'I shall soon publish a new edition of my large Dictionary; I have been persuaded to revise it, and have mended some faults, but added little to its usefulness.

---

[1] Now Doctor White, and Bishop of the Episcopal Church in Pennsylvania. During his first visit to England in 1771, as a candidate for holy orders, he was several times in company with Dr. Johnson, who expressed a wish to see the edition of Rasselas, which Dr. White told him had been printed in America. Dr. White, on his return, immediately sent him a copy.

'No book has been published since your departure, of which much notice is taken. Faction only fills the town with pamphlets, and greater subjects are forgotten in the noise of discord.

'Thus have I written, only to tell you how little I have to tell. Of myself I can only add, that having been afflicted many weeks with a very troublesome cough, I am now recovered.

'I take the liberty which you give me of troubling you with a letter, of which you will please to fill up the direction. I am, Sir,

'Your most humble servant,

'Johnson's-Court, Fleet-street,   'SAM. JOHNSON'
London, March 4, 1773.'

On Saturday, April 3, the day after my arrival in London this year, I went to his house late in the evening, and sat with Mrs. Williams till he came home. I found in the London Chronicle, Dr. Goldsmith's apology to the publick for beating Evans, a bookseller, on account of a paragraph[1] in a news-paper published by him, which Goldsmith thought impertinent to him and to a lady of his acquaintance. The apology was written so much in Dr. Johnson's manner, that both Mrs. Williams and I supposed it to be his; but when he came home, he soon undeceived us. When he said to Mrs. Williams, 'Well, Dr. Goldsmith's *manifesto* has got into your paper;' I asked him if Dr. Goldsmith had written it, with an air that made him see I suspected it was his, though subscribed by Goldsmith. JOHNSON. 'Sir, Dr. Goldsmith would no more have asked me to write such a thing as that for him, than he would have asked me to feed him with a spoon, or to do any thing else that denoted his imbecility. I as much believe that he wrote it, as if I had seen him do it. Sir, had he shewn it to any one friend, he would not have been allowed to publish it. He has, indeed, done it very well; but it is a foolish thing well

index sign:
done it etc. [H]

[1] [The offence given, was a long abusive letter in the London Packet. A particular account of this transaction, and Goldsmith's Vindication, (for such it was, rather than an Apology,) may be found in the new Life of that Poet, prefixed to his Miscellaneous Works in 4 vols. 8vo. pp. 105–108.

MALONE.]

done. I suppose he has been so much elated with the
success of his new comedy, that he has thought every thing
that concerned him must be of importance to the publick.'
BOSWELL. 'I fancy, Sir, this is the first time that he has
been engaged in such an adventure.' JOHNSON. 'Why,
Sir, I believe it is the first time he has *beat;* he may have
been beaten before. This, Sir, is a new plume to him.'

index sign:
he may have etc. [1]

I mentioned Sir John Dalrymple's 'Memoirs of Great
Britain and Ireland,' and his discoveries to the prejudice
of Lord Russell and Algernon Sydney. JOHNSON. 'Why,
Sir, every body who had just notions of Government
thought them rascals before. It is well that all mankind
now see them to be rascals.' BOSWELL. 'But, Sir, may not
those discoveries be true without their being rascals.'
JOHNSON. 'Consider, Sir, would any of them have been
willing to have had it known that they intrigued with
France? Depend upon it, Sir, he who does what he is
afraid should be known, has something rotten about him.
This Dalrymple seems to be an honest fellow; for he tells
equally what makes against both sides. But nothing can
be poorer than his mode of writing, it is the mere bouncing
of a school-boy; Great He![1] but greater She! and such
stuff.'

I could not agree with him in this criticism; for though
Sir John Dalrymple's style is not regularly formed in any
respect, and one cannot help smiling sometimes at his
affected *grandiloquence,* there is in his writing a pointed
vivacity, and much of a gentlemanly spirit.

At Mr. Thrale's, in the evening, he repeated his usual
paradoxical declamation against action in publick speaking. 'Action can have no effect upon reasonable minds.
It may augment noise, but it never can enforce argument.
If you speak to a dog, you use action; you hold up your
hand thus, because he is a brute; and in proportion as
men are removed from brutes, action will have the less
influence upon them.' MRS. THRALE. 'What then, Sir,
becomes of Demosthenes's saying? "Action, action, action!"' JOHNSON. 'Demosthenes, Madam, spoke to an
assembly of brutes; to a barbarous people.'[a]

queried:
Action can etc. [H]

a *The polish'd
Athenians!* [H]

---

[1] [A bombastick ode of Oldham's on Ben Jonson begins thus: 'GREAT
THOU!' which perhaps his namesake remembered.   MALONE.]

I thought it extraordinary, that he should deny the power of rhetorical action upon human nature, when it is proved by innumerable facts in all stages of society. Reasonable beings are not solely reasonable. They have fancies which may be pleased, passions which may be roused.

Lord Chesterfield being mentioned, Johnson remarked, that almost all of that celebrated nobleman's witty sayings were puns. He, however, allowed the merit of good wit to his Lordship's saying of Lord Tyrawley and himself, when both very old and infirm: 'Tyrawley and I have been dead these two years; but we don't choose to have it known.'

He talked with approbation of an intended edition of 'The Spectator,' with notes; two volumes of which had been prepared by a gentleman eminent in the literary world,[a] and the materials which he had collected for the remainder had been transferred to another hand. He observed, that all works which describe manners, require notes in sixty or seventy years,[b] or less; and told us, he had communicated all he knew that could throw light upon 'The Spectator.' He said, 'Addison had made his Sir Andrew Freeport a true Whig, arguing against giving charity to beggars, and throwing out other such ungracious sentiments; but that he had thought better, and made amends by making him found an hospital for decayed farmers.' He called for the volume of 'The Spectator,' in which that account is contained, and read it aloud to us. He read so well, that every thing acquired additional weight and grace from his utterance.

The conversation having turned on modern imitations of ancient ballads, and some one having praised their simplicity, he treated them with that ridicule which he always displayed when that subject was mentioned.

He disapproved of introducing scripture phrases into secular discourse. This seemed to me a question of some difficulty. A scripture expression may be used, like a highly classical phrase, to produce an instantaneous strong impression; and it may be done without being at all improper. Yet I own there is danger, that applying the language of our sacred book to ordinary subjects may tend to lessen

[a] *did he mean our new Percy Edition?* [1]

[b] *So they do.* [1]

our reverence for it. If therefore it be introduced at all, it should be with very great caution.

On Thursday, April 8, I sat a good part of the evening with him, but he was very silent. He said, 'Burnet's "History of his own Times" is very entertaining. The style, indeed, is mere chit-chat. I do not believe that Burnet intentionally lyed; but he was so much prejudiced, that he took no pains to find out the truth. He was like a man who resolves to regulate his time by a certain watch; but will not enquire whether the watch is right or not.'

Though he was not disposed to talk, he was unwilling that I should leave him; and when I looked at my watch, and told him it was twelve o'clock, he cried, 'What's that to you and me?' and ordered Frank to tell Mrs. Williams that we were coming to drink tea with her, which we did. It was settled that we should go to church together next day.

On the 9th of April, being Good-Friday, I breakfasted with him on tea and cross-buns: *Doctor* Levet, as Frank called him, making the tea. He carried me with him to the church of St. Clement Danes, where he had his seat; and his behaviour was, as I had imagined to myself, solemnly devout. I never shall forget the tremulous earnestness with which he pronounced the aweful petition in the Litany: 'In the hour of death, and at the day of judgment, good LORD deliver us.'

We went to church both in the morning and evening.[a] In the interval between the two services we did not dine; but he read in the Greek New Testament, and I turned over several of his books.

[a] *& Boswell going thither on a Good Fryday—merely out of Curiosity to see how Johnson behaved!* [H]

In Archbishop Laud's Diary, I found the following passage, which I read to Dr. Johnson:

'1623. February 1, Sunday. I stood by the most illustrious Prince Charles,[1] at dinner. He was then very merry, and talked occasionally of many things with his attendants. Among other things, he said, that if he were necessitated to take any particular profession of life, he could not be a lawyer, adding his reasons: "I cannot (saith he) defend a bad, nor yield in a good cause."' JOHNSON. 'Sir, this is false reasoning; because every cause has a bad side: and a

---

[1] Afterwards Charles I.

lawyer is not overcome, though the cause which he has endeavoured to support be determined against him.'

I told him that Goldsmith had said to me a few days before, 'As I take my shoes from the shoemaker, and my coat from the taylor, so I take my religion from the priest.' I regretted this loose way of talking. JOHNSON. 'Sir, he knows nothing; he has made up his mind about nothing.'

To my great surprize he asked me to dine with him on Easter-Day. I never supposed that he had a dinner at his house; for I had not then heard of any one of his friends having been entertained at his table. He told me, 'I have generally a meat pye on Sunday: it is baked at a publick oven, which is very properly allowed, because one man can attend it; and thus the advantage is obtained of not keeping servants from church to dress dinners.'

April 11, being Easter-Sunday, after having attended Divine Service at St. Paul's, I repaired to Dr. Johnson's. I had gratified my curiosity much in dining with JEAN JACQUES ROUSSEAU, while he lived in the wilds of Neufchatel: I had as great a curiosity to dine with DR. SAMUEL JOHNSON, in the dusky recess of a court in Fleet-street.[a] I supposed we should scarcely have knives and forks, and only some strange uncouth, ill-drest dish: but I found every thing in very good order. We had no other company but Mrs. Williams and a young woman whom I did not know.[b] As a dinner here was considered as a singular phenomenon, and as I was frequently interrogated on the subject, my readers may perhaps be desirous to know our bill of fare. Foote, I remember, in allusion to Francis, the *negro*, was willing to suppose that our repast was *black broth*. But the fact was, that we had a very good soup, a boiled leg of lamb and spinach, a veal pye, and a rice pudding.

Of Dr. John Campbell, the authour, he said, 'He is a very inquisitive and a very able man, and a man of good religious principles, though I am afraid he has been deficient in practice. Campbell is radically right; and we may hope, that in time there will be good practice.'

He owned that he thought Hawkesworth was one of his imitators, but he did not think Goldsmith was. Goldsmith, he said, had great merit. BOSWELL. 'But, Sir, he is much

[a] *Just the same* [H]

[b] *That was Poll.* [H]

indebted to you for his getting so high in the publick estimation.' JOHNSON. 'Why, Sir, he has, perhaps, got *sooner*
to it by his intimacy with me.'

Goldsmith, though his vanity often excited him to
occasional competition, had a very high regard for Johnson,
which he had at this time expressed in the strongest manner in the Dedication of his Comedy, entitled, 'She Stoops
to Conquer.'[1]

Johnson observed, that there were very few books
printed in Scotland before the Union. He had seen a
complete collection of them in the possession of the Hon.
Archibald Campbell, a non-juring Bishop.[2] I wish this
collection had been kept entire. Many of them are in the
library of the Faculty of Advocates at Edinburgh. I told
Dr. Johnson that I had some intention to write the life of
the learned and worthy Thomas Ruddiman. He said, 'I
should take pleasure in helping you to do honour to him.
But his farewell letter to the Faculty of Advocates, when
he resigned the office of their Librarian, should have been
in Latin.'

I put a question to him upon a fact in common life,
which he could not answer, nor have I found any one else
who could. What is the reason that women servants, though
obliged to be at the expence of purchasing their own
clothes, have much lower wages than men servants, to
whom a great proportion of that article is furnished, and
when in fact our female house servants work much harder
than the male?[3]

He told me that he had twelve or fourteen times
attempted to keep a journal of his life, but never could
persevere. He advised me to do it. 'The great thing to be
recorded, (said he,) is the state of your own mind; and you
should write down every thing that you remember, for

[1] 'By inscribing this slight performance to you, I do not mean so much to
compliment you as myself. It may do me some honour to inform the publick,
that I have lived many years in intimacy with you. It may serve the interests
of mankind also to inform them, that the greatest wit may be found in a
character, without impairing the most unaffected piety.'

[2] See an account of this learned and respectable gentleman, and of his
curious work on the *Middle State*, 'Journal of a Tour to the Hebrides,' 3d edit.
p. 371.

[3] [There is a greater variety of employments for men, than for women;
therefore the demand raises the price. KEARNEY.]

you cannot judge at first what is good or bad; and write immediately while the impression is fresh, for it will not be the same a week afterwards.'

I again solicited him to communicate to me the particulars of his early life. He said, 'You shall have them all for two pence. I hope you shall know a great deal more of me before you write my Life.' He mentioned to me this day many circumstances, which I wrote down when I went home, and have interwoven in the former part of this narrative.

On Tuesday, April 13, he and Dr. Goldsmith and I dined at General Oglethorpe's. Goldsmith expatiated on the common topick, that the race of our people was degenerated, and that this was owing to luxury. JOHNSON. 'Sir, in the first place, I doubt the fact. I believe there are as many tall men in England now, as ever there were. But, secondly, supposing the stature of our people to be diminished, that is not owing to luxury; for, Sir, consider to how very small a proportion of our people luxury can reach. Our soldiery, surely, are not luxurious, who live on six-pence a day; and the same remark will apply to almost all the other classes. Luxury, so far as it reaches the poor, will do good to the race of people; it will strengthen and multiply them. Sir, no nation was ever hurt by luxury; for, as I said before, it can reach but to a very few. I admit that the great increase of commerce and manufactures hurts the military spirit of a people; because it produces a competition for something else than martial honours,—a competition for riches. It also hurts the bodies of the people; for you will observe, there is no man who works at any particular trade, but you may know him from his appearance to do so. One part or the other of his body being more used than the rest, he is in some degree deformed: but, Sir, that is not luxury. A tailor sits cross-legged; but that is not luxury.' GOLDSMITH. 'Come, you're just going to the same place by another road.' JOHNSON. 'Nay, Sir, I say that is not *luxury*. Let us take a walk from Charing-cross to White-chapel, through, I suppose, the greatest series of shops in the world, what is there in any of these shops, (if you except gin-shops,) that can do any human being any harm?' GOLDSMITH. 'Well, Sir, I'll accept

your challenge. The very next shop to Northumberland-
house is a pickle-shop.' JOHNSON. 'Well, Sir: do we not
know that a maid can in one afternoon make pickles
sufficient to serve a whole family for a year? nay, that five
pickle-shops can serve all the kingdom?[a] Besides, Sir, there
is no harm done to any body by the making of pickles, or
the eating of pickles.'

[a] *I question the Fact
—& if 5 Pickle Shops
could serve all the
Kingdom, Why have
we 500?* [H]

We drank tea with the ladies; and Goldsmith sung Tony
Lumpkin's song in his comedy, 'She Stoops to Conquer,'
and a very pretty one, to an Irish tune,[1] which he had
designed for Miss Hardcastle; but as Mrs. Bulkeley, who
played the part, could not sing, it was left out. He afterwards wrote it down for me, by which means it was
preserved, and now appears amongst his poems. Dr.
Johnson, in his way home, stopped at my lodgings in
Piccadilly, and sat with me, drinking tea a second time,
till a late hour.

I told him that Mrs. Macaulay said, she wondered how
he could reconcile his political principles with his moral:
his notions of inequality and subordination with wishing
well to the happiness of all mankind, who might live so
agreeably, had they all their portions of land, and none
to domineer over another. JOHNSON. 'Why, Sir, I reconcile my principles very well, because mankind are happier
in a state of inequality and subordination. Were they to
be in this pretty state of equality, they would soon degenerate into brutes;—they would become Monboddo's
nation;—their tails would grow. Sir, all would be losers,
were all to work for all:—they would have no intellectual
improvement. All intellectual improvement arises from
leisure; all leisure arises from one working for another.'

marginal line:
principles very . . . in a
[H]

Talking of the family of Stuart, he said, 'It should seem
that the family at present on the throne has now established
as good a right as the former family, by the long consent
of the people; and that to disturb this right might be
considered as culpable. At the same time I own, that it
is a very difficult question, when considered with respect
to the house of Stuart. To oblige people to take oaths as
to the disputed right is wrong. I know not whether I
could take them: but I do not blame those who do.' So

[1] The humours of Ballamagairy.

conscientious and so delicate was he upon this subject, which has occasioned so much clamour against him.

three marginal lines:
Talking of . . . in writing [H]

Talking of law cases, he said, 'The English reports, in general, are very poor: only the half of what has been said is taken down; and of that half, much is mistaken. Whereas, in Scotland, the arguments on each side are deliberately put in writing, to be considered by the court. I think a collection of your cases upon subjects of importance, with the opinions of the Judges upon them, would be valuable.'

On Thursday, April 15, I dined with him and Dr. Goldsmith at General Paoli's. We found here Signor Martinelli, of Florence, authour of a History of England in Italian, printed at London.

I spoke of Allan Ramsay's 'Gentle Shepherd,' in the Scottish dialect, as the best pastoral that had ever been written; not only abounding with beautiful rural imagery, and just and pleasing sentiments, but being a real picture of manners; and I offered to teach Dr. Johnson to understand it. 'No, Sir, (said he,) I won't learn it. You shall retain your superiority by my not knowing it.'

This brought on a question whether one man is lessened by another's acquiring an equal degree of knowledge with him. Johnson asserted the affirmative. I maintained that the position might be true in those kinds of knowledge which produce wisdom, power, and force, so as to enable one man to have the government of others; but that a man is not in any degree lessened by others knowing as well as he what ends in mere pleasure:—eating fine fruits, drinking delicious wines, reading exquisite poetry.

The General observed, that Martinelli was a Whig. JOHNSON. 'I am sorry for it. It shews the spirit of the times: he is obliged to temporise.' BOSWELL. 'I rather think, Sir, that Toryism prevails in this reign.' JOHNSON. 'I know not why you should think so, Sir. You see your friend Lord Lyttelton, a nobleman, is obliged in his History to write the most vulgar Whiggism.'

An animated debate took place whether Martinelli should continue his History of England to the present day. GOLDSMITH. 'To be sure he should.' JOHNSON. 'No, Sir; he would give great offence. He would have to tell of almost all the living great what they do not wish told.'

GOLDSMITH. 'It may, perhaps, be necessary for a native to be more cautious; but a foreigner who comes among us without prejudice, may be considered as holding the place of a Judge, and may speak his mind freely.' JOHNSON. 'Sir, a foreigner, when he sends a work from the press, ought to be on his guard against catching the errour and mistaken enthusiasm of the people among whom he happens to be.' GOLDSMITH. 'Sir, he wants only to sell his history, and to tell truth; one an honest, the other a laudable motive.' JOHNSON. 'Sir, they are both laudable motives. It is laudable in a man to wish to live by his labours; but he should write so as he may *live* by them, not so as he may be knocked on the head. I would advise him to be at Calais before he publishes his history of the present age. A foreigner who attaches himself to a political party in this country, is in the worst state that can be imagined: he is looked upon as a mere intermeddler. A native may do it from interest.' BOSWELL. 'Or principle.' GOLDSMITH. 'There are people who tell a hundred political lies every day, and are not hurt by it. Surely, then, one may tell truth with safety.' JOHNSON. 'Why, Sir, in the first place, he who tells a hundred lies has disarmed the force of his lies. But besides; a man had rather have a hundred lies told of him, than one truth which he does not wish should be told.' GOLDSMITH. 'For my part, I'd tell truth, and shame the devil.' JOHNSON. 'Yes, Sir; but the devil will be angry. I wish to shame the devil as much as you do, but I should choose to be out of the reach of his claws.' GOLDSMITH. 'His claws can do you no harm, when you have the shield of truth.'

It having been observed that there was little hospitality in London; JOHNSON. 'Nay, Sir, any man who has a name, or who has the power of pleasing, will be very generally invited in London. The man, Sterne, I have been told, has had engagements for three months.' GOLDSMITH. 'And a very dull fellow.' JOHNSON. 'Why, no, Sir.'

Martinelli told us, that for several years he lived much with Charles Townshend, and that he ventured to tell him he was a bad joker. JOHNSON. 'Why, Sir, thus much I can say upon the subject. One day he and a few more agreed to go and dine in the country, and each of them

was to bring a friend in his carriage with him. Charles
Townshend asked Fitzherbert to go with him, but told
him, "You must find somebody to bring you back; I can
only carry you there." Fitzherbert did not much like this
arrangement. He however consented, observing sarcastically, "It will do very well; for then the same jokes will
serve you in returning as in going."'

An eminent publick character being mentioned;—
JOHNSON. 'I remember being present when he shewed
himself to be so corrupted, or at least something so different
from what I think right, as to maintain that a member of
parliament should go along with his party right or wrong.
Now, Sir, this is so remote from native virtue, from scholastick virtue, that a good man must have undergone a great
change before he can reconcile himself to such a doctrine.
It is maintaining that you may lie to the publick; for you
lie when you call that right which you think wrong, or the
reverse. A friend of ours who is too much an echo of that
gentleman observed, that a man who does not stick uniformly to a party, is only waiting to be bought. Why then,
said I, he is only waiting to be what that gentleman is
already.'

We talked of the King's coming to see Goldsmith's new
play.—'I wish he would,' said Goldsmith; adding, however, with an affected indifference, 'Not that it would do
me the least good.' JOHNSON. 'Well then, Sir, let us say
it would do *him* good, (laughing.) No, Sir, this affectation
will not pass;—it is mighty idle. In such a state as ours,
who would not wish to please the Chief Magistrate?'
GOLDSMITH. 'I *do* wish to please him. I remember a line
in Dryden,

> "And every poet is the monarch's friend."

It ought to be reversed.' JOHNSON. 'Nay, there are finer
lines in Dryden on this subject:

> "For colleges on bounteous Kings depend,
>   And never rebel was to arts a friend."'

General Paoli observed, that successful rebels might.
MARTINELLI. 'Happy rebellions.' GOLDSMITH. 'We
have no such phrase.' GENERAL PAOLI. 'But have you

not the *thing?*' GOLDSMITH. 'Yes; all our *happy* revolutions.
They have hurt our constitution, and will hurt it, till we
mend it by another HAPPY REVOLUTION.'—I never
before discovered that my friend Goldsmith had so much
of the old prejudice in him.

General Paoli, talking of Goldsmith's new play, said,
'*Il a fait un compliment très gracieux à une certaine grande dame;*'
meaning a Duchess of the first rank.

I expressed a doubt whether Goldsmith intended it, in
order that I might hear the truth from himself.[a] It, perhaps, was not quite fair to endeavour to bring him to a
confession, as he might not wish to avow positively his
taking part against the Court. He smiled and hesitated.
The General at once relieved him, by this beautiful
image: '*Monsieur Goldsmith est comme la mer, qui jette des
perles et beaucoup d'autres belles choses, sans s'en appercevoir.*'
GOLDSMITH, '*Très bien dit, et très élégamment.*'

A person was mentioned, who it was said could take
down in short hand the speeches in parliament with perfect
exactness. JOHNSON. 'Sir, it is impossible. I remember one
Angel, who came to me to write for him a Preface or
Dedication to a book upon short hand, and he professed
to write as fast as a man could speak. In order to try him,
I took down a book, and read while he wrote; and I
favoured him, for I read more deliberately than usual.
I had proceeded but a very little way, when he begged
I would desist, for he could not follow me.' Hearing now
for the first time of this Preface or Dedication, I said,
'What an expence, Sir, do you put us to in buying books,
to which you have written Prefaces or Dedications.'
JOHNSON. 'Why I have dedicated to the Royal Family
all round; that is to say, to the last generation of the Royal
Family.' GOLDSMITH. 'And perhaps, Sir, not one sentence of wit in a whole Dedication.' JOHNSON. 'Perhaps
not, Sir.' BOSWELL. 'What then is the reason for applying
to a particular person to do that which any one may do as
well?' JOHNSON. 'Why, Sir, one man has greater readiness
at doing it than another.'

I spoke of Mr. Harris, of Salisbury, as being a very
learned man, and in particular an eminent Grecian.
JOHNSON. 'I am not sure of that. His friends give him

[a] Trap, *always*
Trap. [H]

out as such, but I know not who of his friends are able to judge of it.' GOLDSMITH. 'He is what is much better: he is a worthy humane man.' JOHNSON. 'Nay, Sir, that is not to the purpose of our argument: that will as much prove that he can play upon the fiddle as well as Giardini, as that he is an eminent Grecian.' GOLDSMITH. 'The greatest musical performers have but small emoluments. Giardini, I am told, does not get above seven hundred a year.' JOHNSON. 'That is indeed but little for a man to get, who does best that which so many endeavour to do. There is nothing, I think, in which the power of art is shown so much as in playing on the fiddle. In all other things we can do something at first. Any man will forge a bar of iron, if you give him a hammer; not so well as a smith, but tolerably. A man will saw a piece of wood, and make a box, though a clumsy one; but give him a fiddle and a fiddle-stick,and he can do nothing.'

On Monday, April 19, he called on me with Mrs. Williams, in Mr. Strahan's coach, and carried me out to dine with Mr. Elphinston, at his Academy at Kensington. A printer having acquired a fortune sufficient to keep his coach, was a good topick for the credit of literature. Mrs. Williams said, that another printer, Mr. Hamilton, had not waited so long as Mr. Strahan, but had kept his coach several years sooner. JOHNSON. 'He was in the right. Life is short. The sooner that a man begins to enjoy his wealth, the better.'

Mr. Elphinston talked of a new book that was much admired, and asked Dr. Johnson if he had read it. JOHN-SON. 'I have looked into it.' 'What (said Elphinston,) have you not read it through?' Johnson, offended at being thus pressed, and so obliged to own his cursory mode of reading, answered tartly, 'No, Sir; do *you* read books *through?*'

He this day again defended duelling, and put his argument upon what I have ever thought the most solid basis; that if publick war be allowed to be consistent with morality, private war must be equally so. Indeed we may observe what strained arguments are used to reconcile war with the Christian religion. But, in my opinion, it is exceedingly clear that duelling having better reasons for its barbarous violence,is more justifiable than war in which considerable office in the law expatiated on the happiness of a savage life, and mentioned an instance of an officer who had actually lived for some time in the wilds of America, of whom, when in that state, he quoted this reflection with an air of admiration, as if it had been deeply philosophical: 'Here am I, free and unrestrained, amidst the rude magnificence of Nature, with this Indian woman by my side, and this gun, with which I can procure food when I want it: what more can be desired for human happiness?' It did not require much sagacity to foresee that such a sentiment would not be permitted to pass without due animadversion. JOHNSON. 'Do not allow yourself, Sir, to be imposed upon by such gross absurdity. It is sad stuff; it is brutish. If a bull could speak, he might as well exclaim,—Here am I with this cow and this grass; what being can enjoy greater felicity?'

We talked of the melancholy end of a gentleman who had destroyed himself.[a] JOHNSON. 'It was owing to imaginary difficulties in his affairs, which, had he talked of with any friend, would soon have vanished.' BOSWELL. 'Do you think, Sir, that all who commit suicide are mad?' JOHNSON. 'Sir, they are often not universally disordered in their intellects, but one passion presses so upon them, that they yield to it, and commit suicide, as a passionate man will stab another.' He added, 'I have often thought, that after a man has taken the resolution to kill himself, it is not courage in him to do any thing, however desperate, because he has nothing to fear.' GOLDSMITH. 'I don't see that.' JOHNSON. 'Nay, but my dear Sir, why should not you see what every one else sees?' GOLDSMITH. 'It is for fear of something that he has resolved to kill himself: and will not that timid disposition restrain him?' JOHNSON. 'It does not signify that the fear of something made him resolve; it is upon the state of his mind, after the resolution is taken, that I argue. Suppose a man either from fear, or pride, or conscience, or whatever motive, has resolved to kill himself; when once the resolution is taken, he has nothing to fear. He may then go and take the King of Prussia by the nose, at the head of his army. He cannot fear the rack, who is resolved to kill himself. When Eustace Budgel was walking down to the Thames, determined to drown

[a] Mr. Fitzherbert—Father to Lord St. Helen's [1]

queried: *when once* etc. [H]

queried: *He cannot fear* etc. [H]

himself, he might, if he pleased, without any apprehension of danger, have turned aside, and first set fire to St. James's palace.'

On Tuesday, April 27, Mr. Beauclerk and I called on him in the morning. As we walked up Johnson's-court, I said, 'I have a veneration for this court;' and was glad to find that Beauclerk had the same reverential enthusiasm. We found him alone. We talked of Sir Andrew Stuart's elegant and plausible Letters to Lord Mansfield: a copy of which had been sent by the authour to Dr. Johnson. JOHNSON. 'They have not answered the end. They have not been talked of; I have never heard of them. This is owing to their not being sold. People seldom read a book which is given to them; and few are given. The way to spread a work is to sell it at a low price. No man will send to buy a thing that costs even sixpence, without an intention to read it.' BOSWELL. 'May it not be doubted, Sir, whether it be proper to publish letters, arraigning the ultimate decision of an important cause by the supreme judicature of the nation?' JOHNSON. 'No, Sir, I do not think it was wrong to publish these letters. If they are thought to do harm, why not answer them? But they will do no harm, if Mr. Douglas be indeed the son of Lady Jane, he cannot be hurt: if he be not her son, and yet has the great estate of the family of Douglas, he may well submit to have a pamphlet against him by Andrew Stuart. Sir, I think such a publication does good, as it does good to shew us the possibilities of human life. And, Sir, you will not say that the Douglas cause was a cause of easy decision, when it divided your Court as much as it could do, to be determined at all. When your Judges are seven and seven, the casting vote of the President must be given on one side or other; no matter, for my argument, on which; one or the other *must* be taken; as when I am to move, there is no matter which leg I move first. And then, Sir, it was otherwise determined here. No, Sir, a more dubious determination of any question cannot be imagined.'[1]

index sign:
People seldom etc. [H]

[1] I regretted that Dr. Johnson never took the trouble to study a question which interested nations. He would not even read a pamphlet which I wrote upon it, entitled 'The Essence of the Douglas Cause;' which I have reason to flatter myself, had considerable effect in favour of Mr. Douglas; of whose legitimate filiation I was then, and am still, firmly convinced. Let me add

He said, 'Goldsmith should not be for ever attempting to shine in conversation: he has not temper for it, he is so much mortified when he fails. Sir, a game of jokes is composed partly of skill, partly of chance. A man may be beat at times by one who has not the tenth part of his wit. Now Goldsmith's putting himself against another, is like a man laying a hundred to one who cannot spare the hundred. It is not worth a man's while. A man should not lay a hundred to one, unless he can easily spare it, though he has a hundred chances for him: he can get but a guinea, and he may lose a hundred. Goldsmith is in this state. When he contends, if he gets the better, it is a very little addition to a man of his literary reputation: if he does not get the better, he is miserably vexed.'

Johnson's own superlative powers of wit set him above any risk of such uneasiness. Garrick had remarked to me of him, a few days before, 'Rabelais and all other wits are nothing compared with him. You may be diverted by them; but Johnson gives you a forcible hug, and shakes laughter out of you, whether you will or no.'

Goldsmith, however, was often very fortunate in his witty contests, even when he entered the lists with Johnson himself. Sir Joshua Reynolds was in company with them one day, when Goldsmith said, that he thought he could write a good fable, mentioned the simplicity which that kind of composition requires, and observed, that in most fables the animals introduced seldom talk in character. 'For instance, (said he,) the fable of the little fishes, who saw birds fly over their heads, and envying them, petitioned Jupiter to be changed into birds. The skill (continued he,) consists in making them talk like little fishes.' While he indulged himself in this fanciful reverie, he observed Johnson shaking his sides, and laughing. Upon which he smartly proceeded, 'Why, Dr. Johnson, this is not so easy as you seem to think; for if you were to make little fishes talk, they would talk like WHALES.'

Johnson, though remarkable for his great variety of

marginal line: that no fact can be more respectably ascertained, than by the judgement of
in which . . . a protest the most august tribunal in the world; a judgement in which Lord Mansfield
[H] and Lord Camden united in 1769, and from which only five of a numerous body entered a protest.

composition, never exercised his talents in fable, except
we allow his beautiful tale published in Mrs. Williams's
Miscellanies to be of that species. I have however found
among his manuscript collections the following sketch
of one:

'Glow-worm[1] lying in the garden saw a candle in a
neighbouring palace,—and complained of the littleness
of his own light;—another observed—wait a little;—soon
dark,—have outlasted πολλ [*many*] of these glaring lights
which are only brighter as they haste to nothing.'

On Thursday, April 29, I dined with him at General
Oglethorpe's, where were Sir Joshua Reynolds, Mr.
Langton, Dr. Goldsmith, and Mr. Thrale. I was very
desirous to get Dr. Johnson absolutely fixed in his resolution to go with me to the Hebrides this year; and I told
him that I had received a letter from Dr. Robertson the
historian, upon the subject, with which he was much
pleased, and now talked in such a manner of his long
intended tour, that I was satisfied he meant to fulfil his
engagement.

The custom of eating dogs at Otaheite being mentioned,
Goldsmith observed, that this was also a custom in China:
that a dog-butcher is as common there as any other
butcher; and that when he walks abroad all the dogs fall
on him. JOHNSON. 'That is not owing to his killing dogs,
Sir. I remember a butcher at Lichfield, whom a dog that
was in the house where I lived, always attacked. It is the
smell of carnage which provokes this, let the animals he
has killed be what they may.' GOLDSMITH. 'Yes, there is
a general abhorrence in animals[a] at the signs of massacre.
If you put a tub full of blood into a stable, the horses are
like to go mad.'[b] JOHNSON. 'I doubt that.' GOLDSMITH.
'Nay, Sir, it is a fact well authenticated.' THRALE. 'You
had better prove it before you put it into your book on
natural history. You may do it in my stable if you will.'
JOHNSON. 'Nay, Sir, I would not have him prove it. If he
is content to take his information from others, he may get
through his book with little trouble, and without much

[a] *in Carnivorous Ani-*
mals but The Horses
would not go mad
about it. Oxen however,
have a natural Horror
of Blood, & they as
Graminivorous as the
Horses. [H]

underlined:
animals at the signs [H]

underlined:
horses are . . . go mad
[I]

[b] *Mr.   Thrale   and*
every body conversant
with a Stable knows it
is not strictly true:
Careless Grooms bleed
their Horses & leave the
Pail uncleaned but too
often. Yet Horses &
Oxen dislike the Smell
of Blood & shew their
dislike plainly. [I]

[1] [It has already been observed, that one of his first Essays was a Latin
Poem on a glow-worm; but whether it be any where extant has not been
ascertained. MALONE.]

endangering his reputation. But if he makes experiments for so comprehensive a book as his, there would be no end to them; his erroneous assertions would then fall upon himself; and he might be blamed for not having made experiments as to every particular.'

The character of Mallet having been introduced, and spoken of slightingly by Goldsmith; JOHNSON. 'Why, Sir, Mallet had talents enough to keep his literary reputation alive as long as he himself lived; and that, let me tell you, is a good deal.' GOLDSMITH. 'But I cannot agree that it was so. His literary reputation was dead long before his natural death. I consider an authour's literary reputation to be alive only while his name will insure a good price for his copy from the booksellers. I will get you (to Johnson,) a hundred guineas for any thing whatever that you shall write, if you put your name to it.'

Dr. Goldsmith's new play, 'She stoops to Conquer,' being mentioned; JOHNSON. 'I know of no comedy for many years that has so much exhilarated an audience, that has answered so much the great end of comedy— making an audience merry.'

Goldsmith having said, that Garrick's compliment to the Queen, which he introduced into the play of 'The Chances,' which he had altered and revised this year, was mean and gross flattery;—JOHNSON. 'Why, Sir, I would not *write*, I would not give solemnly under my hand, a character beyond what I thought really true; but a speech on the stage, let it flatter ever so extravagantly, is formular. It has always been formular to flatter Kings and Queens; so much so, that even in our church-service we have "our most religious King," used indiscriminately, whoever is King. Nay, they even flatter themselves;—"we have been graciously pleased to grant."—No modern flattery, how-ever, is so gross as that of the Augustan age, where the Emperour was deified. "*Præsens Divus habebitur Augustus.*" And as to meanness, (rising into warmth) how is it mean in a player,—a showman,—a fellow who exhibits himself for a shilling, to flatter his Queen? The attempt, indeed, was dangerous; for if it had missed, what became of Garrick, and what became of the Queen? As Sir William Temple says of a great General, it is necessary not only that his designs be formed in a masterly manner, but that they should be attended with success. Sir, it is right, at a time when the Royal Family is not generally liked, to let it be seen that the people like at least one of them.' SIR JOSHUA REYNOLDS. 'I do not perceive why the profession of a player should be despised; for the great and ultimate end of all the employments of mankind is to produce amusement. Garrick produces more amusement than any body.' BOSWELL. 'You say, Dr. Johnson, that Garrick exhibits himself for a shilling. In this respect he is only on a footing with a lawyer who exhibits himself for his fee, and even will maintain any nonsense or absurdity, if the case require it. Garrick refuses a play or a part which he does not like: a lawyer never refuses.' JOHNSON. 'Why, Sir, what does this prove? only that a lawyer is worse. Boswell is now like Jack in "The Tale of a Tub," who, when he is puzzled by an argument, hangs himself. He thinks I shall cut him down, but I'll let him hang.' (laughing vociferously.) SIR JOSHUA REYNOLDS. 'Mr. Boswell thinks that the profession of a lawyer being unquestionably honourable, if he can show the profession of a player to be more honourable, he proves his argument.'

On Friday, April 30, I dined with him at Mr. Beauclerk's, where were Lord Charlemont, Sir Joshua Reynolds, and some more members of the LITERARY CLUB, whom he had obligingly invited to meet me, as I was this evening to be balloted for as candidate for admission into that distinguished society. Johnson had done me the honour to propose me, and Beauclerk was very zealous for me.

Goldsmith being mentioned: JOHNSON. 'It is amazing how little Goldsmith knows. He seldom comes where he is not more ignorant than any one else.' SIR JOSHUA REYNOLDS. 'Yet there is no man whose company is more liked.' JOHNSON. 'To be sure, Sir. When people find a man of the most distinguished abilities as a writer, their inferiour while he is with them, it must be highly gratifying to them. What Goldsmith comically says of himself is very true,—he always gets the better when he argues alone; meaning, that he is master of a subject in his study, and can write well upon it; but when he comes into company, grows confused, and unable to talk. Take him as a poet, his "Traveller" is a very fine performance; ay, and so is his "Deserted Village," were it not sometimes too much the echo of his "Traveller." Whether, indeed, we take him as a poet,—as a comick writer,—or as an historian, he stands in the first class.' BOSWELL. 'An historian! My dear Sir, you surely will not rank his compilation of the Roman History with the works of other historians of this age?' JOHNSON. 'Why, who are before him?' BOSWELL. 'Hume,—Robertson,—Lord Lyttelton.' JOHNSON. (His antipathy to the Scotch beginning to rise.) 'I have not read Hume; but, doubtless, Goldsmith's History is better than the *verbiage* of Robertson, or the foppery of Dalrymple.' BOSWELL. 'Will you not admit the superiority of Robertson, in whose History we find such penetration—such painting?' JOHNSON. 'Sir, you must

queried:
He who etc. [H]

consider how that penetration and that painting are employed. It is not history, it is imagination. He who describes what he never saw, draws from fancy. Robertson paints minds as Sir Joshua paints faces in a history-piece: he imagines an heroick countenance. You must look upon

marginal line:
great excellence . . . has
done [H]

Robertson's work as romance, and try it by that standard. History it is not. Besides, Sir, it is the great excellence of a writer to put into his book as much as his book will hold. Goldsmith has done this in his History. Now Robertson might have put twice as much into his book. Robertson is like a man who has packed gold in wool; the wool takes

^a *Very good* [I]

up more room than the gold.^a No, Sir; I always thought Robertson would be crushed by his own weight,—would be buried under his own ornaments. Goldsmith tells you shortly all you want to know: Robertson detains you a great deal too long. No man will read Robertson's cumbrous detail a second time; but Goldsmith's plain narrative will please again and again. I would say to Robertson what an old tutor of a college said to one of his pupils: "Read over your compositions, and wherever you meet with a passage which you think is particularly fine, strike it out." Goldsmith's abridgement is better than that of Lucius Florus or Eutropius; and I will venture to say, that if you compare him with Vertot, in the same places of the Roman History, you will find that he excels Vertot. Sir, he has the art of compiling, and of saying every thing he has to say in a pleasing manner. He is now writing a Natural History, and will make it as entertaining as a Persian Tale.'

I cannot dismiss the present topick without observing, that it is probable that Dr. Johnson, who owned that he often 'talked for victory,' rather urged plausible objections to Dr. Robertson's excellent historical works, in the ardour of contest, than expressed his real and decided opinion; for it is not easy to suppose, that he should so widely differ from the rest of the literary world.

JOHNSON. 'I remember once being with Goldsmith in Westminster-abbey. While we surveyed the Poets' Corner, I said to him,

"Forsitan et nostrum nomen miscebitur istis." [1]

> queried and
> underlined:
> istis [H]

When we got to Temple-bar, he stopped me, pointed to the heads upon it, and slily whispered me,

"Forsitan et nostrum nomen miscebitur ISTIS." ' [2]

Johnson praised John Bunyan highly. 'His "Pilgrim's Progress" has great merit, both for invention, imagination, and the conduct of the story; and it has had the best evidence of its merit, the general and continued approbation of mankind. Few books, I believe, have had a more extensive sale. It is remarkable, that it begins very much like the poem of Dante; yet there was no translation of Dante when Bunyan wrote. There is reason to think that he had read Spenser.'

> marginal line:
> *Dante when . . . to*
> *think* [H]

A proposition which had been agitated, that monuments to eminent persons should, for the time to come, be erected in St. Paul's church as well as in Westminster-abbey, was mentioned; and it was asked, who should be honoured by having his monument first erected there. Somebody suggested Pope. JOHNSON. 'Why, Sir, as Pope was a Roman Catholick, I would not have his to be first. I think Milton's rather should have the precedence. [3] I think

[1] Ovid de Art. Amand. i. iii. v. 13.

[2] In allusion to Dr. Johnson's supposed political principles, and perhaps his own.

[3] Here is another instance of his high admiration of Milton as a Poet, notwithstanding his just abhorrence of that sour Republican's political principles. His candour and discrimination are equally conspicuous. Let us hear no more of his 'injustice to Milton.'

more highly of him now than I did at twenty. There is more thinking in him and in Butler, than in any of our poets.'

Some of the company expressed a wonder why the authour of so excellent a book as 'The Whole Duty of Man,' should conceal himself.[1] JOHNSON. 'There may be different reasons assigned for this, any one of which would be very sufficient. He may have been a clergyman, and may have thought that his religious counsels would have less weight when known to come from a man whose profession was Theology. He may have been a man whose practice was not suitable to his principles, so that his character might injure the effect of his book, which he had written in a season of penitence. Or he may have been a man of rigid self-denial, so that he would have no reward for his pious labours while in this world, but refer it all to a future state.'

The gentlemen went away to their club, and I was left at Beauclerk's till the fate of my election should be announced to me. I sat in a state of anxiety which even the

charming conversation of Lady Di Beauclerkᵃ could not entirely dissipate. In a short time I received the agreeable intelligence that I was chosen. I hastened to the place of meeting, and was introduced to such a society as can seldom be found. Mr. Edmund Burke, whom I then saw for the first time, and whose splendid talents had long made me ardently wish for his acquaintance; Dr. Nugent, Mr. Garrick, Dr. Goldsmith, Mr. (afterwards Sir William)

Jones,ᵇ and the company with whom I had dined. Upon my entrance, Johnson placed himself behind a chair, on which he leaned as on a desk or pulpit, and with humourous formality gave me a *Charge*, pointing out the conduct expected from me as a good member of this club.

Goldsmith produced some very absurd verses which had been publickly recited to an audience for money. JOHNSON. 'I can match this nonsense. There was a poem called "Eugenio," which came out some years ago, and concludes thus:

[1] [In a manuscript in the Bodleian Library several circumstances are stated, which strongly incline me to believe that Dr. Accepted Frewen, Archbishop of York, was the authour of this work. MALONE.]

> "And now, ye trifling, self-assuming elves,
>   Brimful of pride, of nothing, of yourselves,
>   Survey Eugenio, view him o'er and o'er,
>   Then sink into yourselves, and be no more." [1]

Nay, Dryden, in his poem on the Royal Society, has these lines:

> "Then we upon our globe's last verge shall go,
>   And see the ocean leaning on the sky;
> From thence our rolling neighbours we shall know,
>   And on the lunar world securely pry." '

Talking of puns, Johnson, who had a great contempt for that species of wit, deigned to allow that there was one good pun in 'Menagiana,' I think on the word *corps*. [2]

Much pleasant conversation passed, which Johnson relished with great good humour. But his conversation

---

[1] Dr. Johnson's memory here was not perfectly accurate: 'Eugenio' does not conclude thus. There are eight more lines after the last of those quoted by him; and the passage which he meant to recite is as follows:

> 'Say now ye fluttering, poor assuming elves,
>   Stark full of pride, of folly, of—yourselves;
>   Say where's the wretch of all your impious crew
>   Who dares confront his character to view?
>   Behold Eugenio, view him o'er and o'er,
>   Then sink into yourselves, and be no more.'

Mr. Reed informs me that the Authour of Eugenio, Thomas Beech, a Wine Merchant at Wrexham[a] in Denbighshire, soon after its publication, viz. 17th May, 1737, cut his throat; and that it appears by Swift's Works, that the poem had been shewn to him, and received some of his corrections. Johnson had read 'Eugenio' on his first coming to town, for we see it mentioned in one of his letters to Mr. Cave, which has been inserted in this work.

[a] *I never heard of him but here, & yet he was a strange Fellow sure; & worthy to be remembered at* Wrexham *where Poets & Suicides are no common Things.* [1]

[2] I formerly thought that I had, perhaps, mistaken the word and imagined it to be *Corps*, from its similarity of sound to the real one. For an accurate and shrewd unknown gentleman, to whom I am indebted for some remarks on my work, observes on this passage—'Q. if not on the word, *Fort?* A vociferous French preacher said of Bourdaloue, "Il preche *fort bien*, et moi *bien fort*."—Menagiana. See also Anecdotes Littéraires, Article, Bourdaloue.' But my ingenious and obliging correspondent, Mr. Abercrombie of Philadelphia, has pointed out to me the following passage in 'Menagiana;' which renders the preceding conjecture unnecessary, and confirms my original statement:

'Mad^me de Bourdonne, Chanoinesse de Remiremont, venoit d'entendre un discours plein de feu et d'esprit, mais fort peu solide, et très irrégulier. Une de ses amies, qui y prenoit intérêt pour l'orateur, lui dit en sortant, "Eh bien, Mad^me que vous semble-t-il de ce que vous venez d'entendre? Qu'il y a d'esprit?—Il y a tant, répondit Mad^me de Bourdonne, que je n'y ai pas vû de *corps*." ' Menagiana, tome ii. p. 64. Amsterd. 1713.

alone, or what led to it, or was interwoven with it, is the business of this work.

On Saturday, May 1, we dined by ourselves at our old rendezvous, the Mitre tavern. He was placid, but not much disposed to talk. He observed, that 'The Irish mix better with the English than the Scotch do; their language is nearer to English; as a proof of which, they succeed very well as players, which Scotchmen do not. Then, Sir, they have not that extreme nationality which we find in the Scotch. I will do you, Boswell, the justice to say, that you are the most *unscottified* of your countrymen. You are almost the only instance of a Scotchman that I have known, who did not at every other sentence bring in some other Scotchman.'

We drank tea with Mrs. Williams. I introduced a question which has been much agitated in the Church of Scotland, whether the claim of lay-patrons to present ministers to parishes be well founded; and supposing it to be well founded, whether it ought to be exercised without the concurrence of the people? That Church is composed of a series of judicatures: a Presbytery, a Synod, and finally, a General Assembly; before all of which, this matter may be contended: and in some cases the Presbytery having refused to induct or *settle*, as they call it, the person presented by the patron, it has been found necessary to appeal to the General Assembly. He said, I might see the subject well treated in the 'Defence of Pluralities;' and although he thought that a patron should exercise his right with tenderness to the inclinations of the people of a parish, he was very clear as to his right. Then supposing the question to be pleaded before the General Assembly, he dictated to me what follows:

'AGAINST the right of patrons is commonly opposed, by the inferior judicatures, the plea of conscience. Their conscience tells them, that the people ought to choose their pastor; their conscience tells them, that they ought not to impose upon a congregation a minister ungrateful and unacceptable to his auditors. Conscience is nothing more than a conviction felt by ourselves of something to be done, or something to be avoided; and in questions of simple unperplexed morality, conscience is very often a guide that may be trusted. But before conscience can determine, the state of the question is supposed to be completely known. In questions of law, or of fact, conscience is very often confounded with opinion. No man's conscience can tell him the right of another man; they must be known by rational investigation or historical enquiry. Opinion, which he that holds it may call his conscience, may teach some men that religion would be promoted, and quiet preserved, by granting to the people universally the choice of their ministers. But it is a conscience very ill informed that violates the rights of one man, for the convenience of another. Religion cannot be promoted by injustice; and it was never yet found that a popular election was very quietly transacted.

'That justice would be violated by transferring to the people the right of patronage, is apparent to all who know whence that right had its original. The right of patronage was not at first a privilege torn by power from unresisting poverty. It is not an authority at first usurped in times of ignorance, and established only by succession and by precedents. It is not a grant capriciously made from a higher tyrant to a lower. It is a right dearly purchased by the first possessors, and justly inherited by those that succeeded them. When Christianity was established in this island, a regular mode of publick worship was prescribed. Publick worship requires a publick place; and the proprietors of lands, as they were converted, built churches for their families and their vassals. For the maintenance of ministers, they settled a certain portion of their lands; and a district, through which each minister was required to extend his care, was, by that circumscription, constituted a parish. This is a position so generally received in England, that the extent of a manor and of a parish are regularly received for each other. The churches which the proprietors of lands had thus built and thus endowed, they justly thought themselves entitled to provide with ministers; and where the episcopal government prevails, the Bishop has no power to reject a man nominated by the patron, but for some crime that might exclude him from the priesthood. For the endowment of the church being the gift of the landlord, he was consequently at liberty to give

marginal line:
who know . . . torn by
[H]

it according to his choice, to any man capable of performing the holy offices. The people did not choose him,
because the people did not pay him.

'We hear it sometimes urged, that this original right is
passed out of memory, and is obliterated and obscured by
many translations of property and changes of government;
that scarce any church is now in the hands of the heirs of
the builders; and that the present persons have entered
subsequently upon the pretended rights by a thousand
accidental and unknown causes. Much of this, perhaps, is
true. But how is the right of patronage extinguished? If the
right followed the lands, it is possessed by the same equity
by which the lands are possessed. It is, in effect, part of the
manor, and protected by the same laws with every other
privilege. Let us suppose an estate forfeited by treason,
and granted by the Crown to a new family. With the lands
were forfeited all the rights appendant to those lands; by
the same power that grants the lands, the rights also are
granted. The right lost to the patron falls not to the
people, but is either retained by the Crown, or, what to
the people is the same thing, is by the Crown given away.
Let it change hands ever so often, it is possessed by him
that receives it with the same right as it was conveyed.
It may, indeed, like all our possessions, be forcibly seized
or fraudulently obtained. But no injury is still done to the
people; for what they never had, they have never lost.
Caius may usurp the right of Titius, but neither Caius nor
Titius injure the people; and no man's conscience, however tender or however active, can prompt him to restore
what may be proved to have been never taken away.
Supposing, what I think cannot be proved, that a popular
election of ministers were to be desired, our desires are
not the measure of equity. It were to be desired that power
should be only in the hands of the merciful, and riches in
the possession of the generous; but the law must leave both
riches and power where it finds them: and must often
leave riches with the covetous, and power with the cruel.
Convenience may be a rule in little things, where no other
rule has been established. But as the great end of government is to give every man his own, no inconvenience is
greater than that of making right uncertain. Nor is any

marginal line:
effect, part . . . suppose
an [H]

man more an enemy to publick peace, than he who fills
weak heads with imaginary claims, and breaks the series
of civil subordination, by inciting the lower classes of
mankind to encroach upon the higher.

'Having thus shown that the right of patronage, being
originally purchased, may be legally transferred, and that
it is now in the hands of lawful possessors, at least as
certainly as any other right;—we have left to the advocates
of the people no other plea than that of convenience. Let
us, therefore, now consider what the people would really
gain by a general abolition of the right of patronage. What
is most to be desired by such a change is, that the country
should be supplied with better ministers. But why should
we suppose that the parish will make a wiser choice than
the patron? If we suppose mankind actuated by interest,
the patron is more likely to choose with caution, because
he will suffer more by choosing wrong. By the deficiencies
of his minister, or by his vices, he is equally offended with
the rest of the congregation; but he will have this reason
more to lament them, that they will be imputed to his
absurdity or corruption. The qualifications of a minister
are well known to be learning and piety. Of his learning
the patron is probably the only judge in the parish; and
of his piety not less a judge than others; and is more likely
to enquire minutely and diligently before he gives a
presentation, than one of the parochial rabble, who can
give nothing but a vote. It may be urged, that though the
parish might not choose better ministers, they would at
least choose ministers whom they like better, and who
would therefore officiate with greater efficacy. That
ignorance and perverseness should always obtain what
they like, was never considered as the end of government;
of which it is the great and standing benefit, that the wise
see for the simple, and the regular act for the capricious.
But that this argument supposes the people capable of
judging, and resolute to act according to their best
judgements, though this be sufficiently absurd, it is not all
its absurdity. It supposes not only wisdom, but unanimity
in those, who upon no other occasions are unanimous or
wise. If by some strange concurrence all the voices of a
parish should unite in the choice of any single man, though

marginal line:
diligently before . . . a
vote [H]

two marginal lines:
that the . . . argument
supposes [H]

I could not charge the patron with injustice for presenting a minister, I should censure him as unkind and injudicious. But, it is evident, that as in all other popular elections there will be contrariety of judgement and acrimony of passion, a parish upon every vacancy would break into factions, and the contest for the choice of a minister would set neighbours at variance, and bring discord into families. The minister would be taught all the arts of a candidate, would flatter some, and bribe others; and the electors, as in all other cases, would call for holidays and ale, and break the heads of each other during the jollity of the canvass. The time must, however, come at last, when one of the factions must prevail, and one of the ministers get possession of the church. On what terms does he enter upon his ministry but those of enmity with half his parish? By what prudence or what diligence can he hope to con-ciliate the affections of that party by whose defeat he has obtained his living? Every man who voted against him will enter the church with hanging head and downcast eyes, afraid to encounter that neighbour by whose vote and influence he has been overpowered. He will hate his neighbour for opposing him, and his minister for having prospered by the opposition; and as he will never see him but with pain, he will never see him but with hatred. Of a minister presented by the patron, the parish has seldom any thing worse to say than that they do not know him. Of a minister chosen by a popular contest, all those who do not favour him, have nursed up in their bosoms principles of hatred and reasons of rejection. Anger is excited principally by pride. The pride of a common man is very little exasperated by the supposed usurpation of an acknowledged superiour. He bears only his little share of a general evil, and suffers in common with the whole parish: but when the contest is between equals, the defeat has many aggravations; and he that is defeated by his next neighbour, is seldom satisfied without some revenge: and it is hard to say what bitterness of malignity would prevail in a parish where these elections should happen to be frequent, and the enmity of opposition should be re-kindled before it had cooled.'

Though I present to my readers Dr. Johnson's masterly

thoughts on the subject, I think it proper to declare, that notwithstanding I am myself a lay-patron, I do not entirely subscribe to his opinion.

On Friday, May 7, I breakfasted with him at Mr. Thrale's in the Borough. While we were alone, I endeavoured as well as I could to apologise for a lady who had been divorced from her husband by act of Parliament.[a] I said, that he had used her very ill, had behaved brutally to her, and that she could not continue to live with him without having her delicacy contaminated; that all affection for him was thus destroyed; that the essence of conjugal union being gone, there remained only a cold form, a mere civil obligation; that she was in the prime of life, with qualities to produce happiness; that these ought not to be lost; and, that the gentleman on whose account she was divorced had gained her heart while thus unhappily situated. Seduced, perhaps, by the charms of the lady in question, I thus attempted to palliate what I was sensible could not be justified; for when I had finished my harangue, my venerable friend gave me a proper check: 'My dear Sir, never accustom your mind to mingle virtue and vice. The woman's a whore, and there's an end on't.'

He described the father of one of his friends thus: 'Sir, he was so exuberant a talker at publick meetings, that the gentlemen of his county were afraid of him. No business could be done for his declamation.'[b]

He did not give me full credit when I mentioned that I had carried on a short conversation by signs with some Esquimaux, who were then in London, particularly with one of them who was a priest. He thought I could not make them understand me. No man was more incredulous as to particular facts, which were at all extraordinary; and therefore no man was more scrupulously inquisitive, in order to discover the truth.

I dined with him this day at the house of my friends, Messieurs Edward and Charles Dilly, booksellers in the Poultry: there were present, their elder brother Mr. Dilly of Bedfordshire, Dr. Goldsmith, Mr. Langton, Mr. Claxton, Reverend Dr. Mayo, a dissenting minister, the Reverend Mr. Toplady, and my friend the Reverend Mr. Temple.

[a] *Lady Diana Beauclerc* [H]
Lady Di. [I]

[b] *comical enough; I do not know who it was.* [H]

Hawkesworth's compilation of the voyages to the South Sea being mentioned;—JOHNSON. 'Sir, if you talk of it as a subject of commerce, it will be gainful; if as a book that is to increase human knowledge, I believe there will not be much of that. Hawkesworth can tell only what the voyagers have told him; and they have found very little, only one new animal, I think.' BOSWELL. 'But many insects, Sir.' JOHNSON. 'Why, Sir, as to insects, Ray reckons of British insects twenty thousand species. They might have staid at home and discovered enough in that way.'

Talking of birds, I mentioned Mr. Daines Barrington's ingenious Essay against the received notion of their migration. JOHNSON. 'I think we have as good evidence for the migration of woodcocks as can be desired. We find they disappear at a certain time of the year, and appear again at a certain time of the year; and some of them, when weary in their flight, have been known to alight on the rigging of ships far out at sea.' One of the company observed, that there had been instances of some of them found in summer in Essex. JOHNSON. 'Sir, that strengthens our argument. *Exceptio probat regulam.* Some being found shews, that, if all remained, many would be found. A few sick or lame ones may be found.' GOLDSMITH. 'There is a partial migration of the swallows; the stronger ones migrate, the others do not.'

BOSWELL. 'I am well assured that the people of Otaheite who have the bread tree, the fruit of which serves them for bread, laughed heartily when they were informed of the tedious process necessary with us to have bread;— plowing, sowing, harrowing, reaping, threshing, grinding, baking.' JOHNSON. 'Why, Sir, all ignorant savages will laugh when they are told of the advantages of civilized life. Were you to tell men who live without houses, how we pile brick upon brick, and rafter upon rafter, and that after a house is raised to a certain height, a man tumbles off a scaffold, and breaks his neck; he would laugh heartily at our folly in building; but it does not follow that men are better without houses. No, Sir, (holding up a slice of a good loaf,) this is better than the bread tree.'

He repeated an argument, which is to be found in his

'Rambler,' against the notion that the brute creation is
endowed with the faculty of reason: 'birds build by instinct;
they never improve; they build their first nest as well as
any one they ever build.' GOLDSMITH. 'Yet we see if you
take away a bird's nest with the eggs in it, she will make
a slighter nest and lay again.' JOHNSON. 'Sir, that is
because at first she has full time and makes her nest
deliberately. In the case you mention she is pressed to
lay,[a] and must therefore make her nest quickly, and consequently it will be slight.' GOLDSMITH. 'The nidification
of birds is what is least known in natural history, though
one of the most curious things in it.'[b]

I introduced the subject of toleration. JOHNSON.
'Every society has a right to preserve publick peace and
order, and therefore has a good right to prohibit the
propagation of opinions which have a dangerous tendency.
To say the *magistrate* has this right, is using an inadequate
word: it is the *society* for which the magistrate is agent. He
may be morally or theologically wrong in restraining the
propagation of opinions which he thinks dangerous, but
he is politically right.' MAYO. 'I am of opinion, Sir, that
every man is entitled to liberty of conscience in religion;
and that the magistrate cannot restrain that right.'
JOHNSON. 'Sir, I agree with you. Every man has a right
to liberty of conscience, and with that the magistrate cannot interfere. People confound liberty of thinking with
liberty of talking; nay, with liberty of preaching. Every
man has a physical right to think as he pleases; for it
cannot be discovered how he thinks. He has not a moral
right, for he ought to inform himself, and think justly.
But, Sir, no member of a society has a right to *teach* any
doctrine contrary to what the society holds to be true.
The magistrate, I say, may be wrong in what he thinks;
but while he thinks himself right, he may and ought to
enforce what he thinks.' MAYO. 'Then, Sir, we are to
remain always in errour, and truth never can prevail; and
the magistrate was right in persecuting the first Christians.'
JOHNSON. 'Sir, the only method by which religious truth
can be established is by martyrdom. The magistrate has
a right to enforce what he thinks; and he who is conscious
of the truth has a right to suffer. I am afraid there is no

underlined:
pressed to lay [I]

[a] *on the contrary I
wonder whence the 2d.
Set of Eggs come?
because had She been
let alone no more Eggs
would have appeared
till her young ones had
flown.* [I]

[b] *So it certainly is.* [H]

queried:
the only method etc.
[H]

queried:
no other way etc. [H]

other way of ascertaining the truth, but by persecution on the one hand and enduring it on the other.' GOLDSMITH. 'But how is a man to act, Sir? Though firmly convinced of the truth of his doctrine, may he not think it wrong to expose himself to persecution? Has he a right to do so? Is it not, as it were, committing voluntary suicide?' JOHNSON. 'Sir, as to voluntary suicide, as you call it, there are twenty thousand men in an army who will go without scruple to be shot at, and mount a breach for five-pence a day.' GOLDSMITH. 'But have they a moral right to do this?' JOHNSON. 'Nay, Sir, if you will not take the universal opinion of mankind, I have nothing to say. If mankind cannot defend their own way of thinking, I cannot defend it. Sir, if a man is in doubt whether it would be better for him to expose himself to martyrdom or not, he should not do it. He must be convinced that he has a delegation from heaven.' GOLDSMITH. 'I would consider whether there is the greater chance of good or evil upon the whole. If I see a man who has fallen into a well, I would wish to help him out; but if there is a greater probability that he shall pull me in, than that I shall pull him out, I would not attempt it. So were I to go to Turkey, I might wish to convert the Grand Signor to the Christian faith; but when I considered that I should probably be put to death without effectuating my purpose in any degree, I should keep myself quiet.' JOHNSON. 'Sir, you must consider that we have perfect and imperfect obligations. Perfect obligations, which are generally not to do something, are clear and positive; as, "thou shalt not kill." But charity, for instance, is not definable by limits. It is a duty to give to the poor; but no man can say how much another should give to the poor, or when a man has given too little to save his soul. In the same manner it is a duty to instruct the ignorant, and of consequence to convert infidels to Christianity; but no man in the common course of things is obliged to carry this to such a degree as to incur the danger of martyrdom, as no man is obliged to strip himself to the shirt, in order to give charity. I have said, that a man must be persuaded that he has a particular delegation from heaven.' GOLDSMITH. 'How is this to be known? Our first reformers, who were burnt for not

queried:
if you will not etc. [H]

believing bread and wine to be CHRIST.'—JOHNSON. queried twice: not burnt etc. [H] (interrupting him,) 'Sir, they were not burnt for not believing bread and wine to be CHRIST, but for insulting those who did believe it. And, Sir, when the first reformers began, they did not intend to be martyred: as many of them ran away as could.' BOSWELL. 'But, Sir, there was your countryman Elwal, who you told me challenged King George with his black-guards, and his red-guards.' JOHNSON. 'My countryman, Elwal, Sir, should have been put in the stocks: a proper pulpit for him; and he'd have had a numerous audience. A man who preaches in the stocks will always have hearers enough.' BOSWELL. 'But Elwal thought himself in the right.' JOHNSON. 'We are not providing for mad people; there are places for them in the neighbourhood.' (meaning Moorfields.) MAYO. 'But, Sir, is it not very hard that I should not be allowed to teach my children what I really believe to be the truth?' JOHNSON. 'Why, Sir, you might contrive to teach your children *extrà scandalum;* but, Sir, the magistrate, if he knows it, has a right to restrain you. Suppose you teach your children to be thieves?' MAYO. 'This is making a joke of the subject.' JOHNSON. 'Nay, Sir, take it thus:— that you teach them the community of goods: for which there are as many plausible arguments as for most erroneous doctrines. You teach them that all things at first were in common, and that no man had a right to any thing but as he laid his hands upon it; and that this still is, or ought to be, the rule amongst mankind. Here, Sir, you sap a great principle in society,—property. And don't you think the magistrate would have a right to prevent you? Or, suppose you should teach your children the notion of the Adamites, and they should run naked into the streets, would not the magistrate have a right to flog 'em into their doublets?' MAYO. 'I think the magistrate has no right to interfere till there is some overt act.' BOSWELL. 'So, Sir, though he sees an enemy to the state charging a blunderbuss, he is not to interfere till it is fired off !' MAYO. 'He must be sure of its direction against the state.' JOHNSON. 'The magistrate is to judge of that.—He has no right to restrain your thinking, because the evil centers in yourself. If a man were sitting at this table, and chopping off his

time with it in his hand, like a gamester, who, at the close
of a long night, lingers for a little while, to see if he can
have a favourable opening to finish with success. Once
when he was beginning to speak, he found himself overpowered by the loud voice of Johnson, who was at the
opposite end of the table, and did not perceive Goldsmith's
attempt. Thus disappointed of his wish to obtain the
attention of the company, Goldsmith in a passion threw
down his hat, looking angrily at Johnson, and exclaimed
in a bitter tone, '*Take it.*' When Toplady was going to
speak, Johnson uttered some sound, which led Goldsmith
to think that he was beginning again, and taking the
words from Toplady. Upon which, he seized this opportunity of venting his own envy and spleen, under the
pretext of supporting another person: 'Sir, (said he to
Johnson,) the gentleman has heard you patiently for an
hour: pray allow us now to hear him.' JOHNSON. (sternly,)
'Sir, I was not interrupting the gentleman. I was only
giving him a signal of my attention. Sir, you are impertinent.' Goldsmith made no reply, but continued in the
company for some time.

A gentleman present[a] ventured to ask Dr. Johnson if
there was not a material difference as to toleration of
opinions which lead to action, and opinions merely
speculative; for instance, would it be wrong in the magistrate to tolerate those who preach against the doctrine of
the TRINITY? Johnson was highly offended, and said, 'I
wonder, Sir,[b] how a gentleman of your piety can introduce
this subject in a mixed company.' He told me afterwards,
that the impropriety was, that perhaps some of the company might have talked on the subject in such terms as
might have shocked him; or he might have been forced
to appear in their eyes a narrow-minded man. The gentleman, with submissive deference, said, he had only hinted
at the question from a desire to hear Dr. Johnson's opinion
upon it. JOHNSON. 'Why, then, Sir, I think that permitting men to preach any opinion contrary to the doctrine
of the established church, tends, in a certain degree, to
lessen the authority of the church, and consequently, to
lessen the influence of religion.' 'It may be considered,
(said the gentleman,) whether it would not be politick to

[a] *Langton* [H]

[b] *Langton I think it
was—oh yes it was
Langton—& he's gone
too.* [I]

index sign:
permitting men etc. [H]

tolerate in such a case.' JOHNSON. 'Sir, we have been talking of *right:* this is another question. I think it is *not* politick to tolerate in such a case.'

Though he did not think it fit that so awful a subject should be introduced in a mixed company, and therefore at this time waved the theological question; yet his own orthodox belief in the sacred mystery of the TRINITY is evinced beyond doubt, by the following passage in his private devotions: 'O LORD, hear my prayer, for JESUS CHRIST'S sake; to whom, with thee and the HOLY GHOST, *three persons and one* GOD, be all honour and glory, world without end, Amen.'[1]

BOSWELL. 'Pray, Mr. Dilly, how does Dr. Leland's History of Ireland sell?' JOHNSON. (bursting forth with a generous indignation,) 'The Irish are in a most unnatural state; for we see there the minority prevailing over the majority. There is no instance, even in the ten persecutions, of such severity as that which the protestants of Ireland have exercised against the Catholicks. Did we tell them we have conquered them, it would be above board: to punish them by confiscation and other penalties, as rebels, was monstrous injustice. King William was not their lawful sovereign: he had not been acknowledged by the Parliament of Ireland, when they appeared in arms against him.'

I here suggested something favourable of the Roman Catholicks. TOPLADY. 'Does not their invocation[a] of saints suppose omnipresence in the saints?' JOHNSON. 'No, Sir; it supposes only pluri-presence; and when spirits are divested of matter, it seems probable that they should see with more extent than when in an embodied state. There is, therefore, no approach to an invasion of any of the divine attributes, in the invocation of saints. But I think it is will-worship, and presumption. I see no command for it, and therefore think it is safer not to practise it.'[b]

He and Mr. Langton and I went together to THE CLUB, where we found Mr. Burke, Mr. Garrick, and some other members, and amongst them our friend Goldsmith, who sat silently brooding over Johnson's

[a] *Their Invocation of one Set of Dead men, and their Prayers for ye. Salvation of another Set; are presumptuous, for they know not who is holy in God's eye—& it is useless, & it is contradictory.—Let the Dead bury their Dead—follow thou* me *says our Saviour.* [1]

[b] *Yes truly   So do I.* [1]

[1] Prayers and Meditations, p. 40.

reprimand to him after dinner. Johnson perceived this, and said aside to some of us, 'I'll make Goldsmith forgive me;' and then called to him in a loud voice, 'Dr. Goldsmith,—something passed to-day where you and I dined; I ask your pardon.' Goldsmith answered placidly, 'It must be much from you, Sir, that I take ill.' And so at once the difference was over, and they were on as easy terms as ever, and Goldsmith rattled away as usual.

In our way to the club to-night, when I regretted that Goldsmith would, upon every occasion, endeavour to shine, by which he often exposed himself, Mr. Langton observed, that he was not like Addison, who was content with the fame of his writings, and did not aim also at excellency in conversation, for which he found himself unfit; and that he said to a lady who complained of his having talked little in company, 'Madam, I have but nine-pence in ready money, but I can draw for a thousand pounds.' I observed that Goldsmith had a great deal of gold in his cabinet, but, not content with that, was always taking out his purse. JOHNSON. 'Yes, Sir, and that so often an empty purse!'

Goldsmith's incessant desire of being conspicuous in company, was the occasion of his sometimes appearing to such disadvantage as one should hardly have supposed possible in a man of his genius. When his literary reputation had risen deservedly high, and his society was much courted, he became very jealous of the extraordinary attention which was every where paid to Johnson. One evening, in a circle of wits, he found fault with me for talking of Johnson as entitled to the honour of unquestionable superiority. 'Sir, (said he,) you are for making a monarchy of what should be a republick.'

He was still more mortified, when talking in a company with fluent vivacity, and, as he flattered himself, to the admiration of all who were present; a German who sat next him, and perceived Johnson rolling himself as if about to speak, suddenly stopped him, saying, 'Stay, stay, —Toctor Shonson is going to say something.' This was, no doubt, very provoking, especially to one so irritable as Goldsmith, who frequently mentioned it[a] with strong expressions of indignation.

It may also be observed, that Goldsmith was sometimes
content to be treated with an easy familiarity, but upon
a just like himself [H] occasions, would be consequential and important.[a] An
instance of this occurred in a small particular. Johnson
had a way of contracting the names of his friends: as Beauclerk, Beau; Boswell, Bozzy; Langton, Lanky; Murphy,
Mur; Sheridan, Sherry. I remember one day, when Tom
Davies was telling that Dr. Johnson said, 'We are all in
labour for a name to *Goldy's* play,' Goldsmith seemed
displeased that such a liberty should be taken with his
name, and said, 'I have often desired him not to call me
Goldy.' Tom was remarkably attentive to the most minute
circumstance about Johnson. I recollect his telling me
once, on my arrival in London, 'Sir, our great friend has
made an improvement on his appellation of old Mr.
Sheridan. He calls him now *Sherry derry*.'

'TO THE REVEREND MR. BAGSHAW, AT BROMLEY[1]

'SIR,

'I RETURN you my sincere thanks for your additions
to my Dictionary; but the new edition has been published
some time, and therefore I cannot now make use of them.
Whether I shall ever revise it more, I know not. If many
readers had been as judicious, as diligent, and as communicative as yourself, my work had been better. The
world must at present take it as it is. I am, Sir,

'Your most obliged
'And most humble servant,

'May, 8, 1773.'   'SAM. JOHNSON'

[1] The Reverend Thomas Bagshaw, M.A. who died on November 20, 1787,
in the seventy-seventh year of his age, Chaplain of Bromley College, in Kent,
and Rector of Southfleet. He had resigned the cure of Bromley Parish some
time before his death. For this, and another letter from Dr. Johnson in 1784,
to the same truly respectable man, I am indebted to Dr. John Loveday, of
the Commons, a son of the late learned and pious John Loveday, Esq. of
Caversham in Berkshire, who obligingly transcribed them for me from the
originals in his possession. This worthy gentleman, having retired from
business, now lives in Warwickshire. The world has been lately obliged to
him as the Editor of the late Rev. Dr. Townson's excellent work, modestly
entitled 'A Discourse on the Evangelical History, from the Interment to
the Ascension of our Lord and Saviour Jesus Christ:' to which is prefixed,
a truly interesting and pleasing account of the authour, by the Reverend
Mr. Ralph Churton.

On Sunday, May 8, I dined with Johnson at Mr. Langton's with Dr. Beattie and some other company. He descanted on the subject of Literary Property. 'There seems (said he,) to be in authours a stronger right of property than that by occupancy; a metaphysical right, a right, as it were, of creation, which should from its nature be perpetual; but the consent of nations is against it; and indeed reason and the interest of learning are against it; for were it to be perpetual, no book, however useful, could be universally diffused amongst mankind, should the proprietor take it into his head to restrain its circulation. No book could have the advantage of being edited with notes, however necessary to its elucidation, should the proprietor perversely oppose it. For the general good of the world, therefore, whatever valuable work has once been created by an authour, and issued out by him, should be understood as no longer in his power, but as belonging to the publick; at the same time the authour is entitled to an adequate reward. This he should have by an exclusive right to his work for a considerable number of years.'

He attacked Lord Monboddo's strange speculation on the primitive state of human nature; observing, 'Sir, it is all conjecture about a thing useless, even were it known to be true. Knowledge of all kinds is good. Conjecture, as to things useful, is good; but conjecture as to what it would be useless to know, such as whether men went upon all four, is very idle.'

On Monday, May 9, as I was to set out on my return to Scotland next morning, I was desirous to see as much of Dr. Johnson as I could. But I first called on Goldsmith to take leave of him. The jealousy and envy which, though possessed of many most amiable qualities, he frankly avowed, broke out violently at this interview. Upon another occasion, when Goldsmith confessed himself to be of an envious disposition, I contended with Johnson that we ought not to be angry with him, he was so candid in owning it. 'Nay, Sir, (said Johnson,) we must be angry that a man has such a superabundance of an odious quality, that he cannot keep it within his own breast, but it boils over.' In my opinion, however, Goldsmith had not more of it than other people have, but only talked of it freely.

exclamation point: *In my opinion* etc. [H]

He now seemed very angry that Johnson was going to be a traveller; said 'he would be a dead weight for me to carry, and that I should never be able to lug him along through the Highlands and Hebrides.' Nor would he patiently allow me to enlarge upon Johnson's wonderful abilities: but exclaimed, 'Is he like Burke, who winds into a subject like a serpent?' 'But, (said I,) Johnson is the Hercules who strangled serpents in his cradle.'

I dined with Dr. Johnson at General Paoli's. He was obliged, by indisposition, to leave the company early; he appointed me, however, to meet him in the evening at Mr. (now Sir Robert) Chambers's in the Temple, where he accordingly came, though he continued to be very ill. Chambers, as is common on such occasions, prescribed various remedies to him. JOHNSON. (fretted by pain,) 'Pr'ythee don't tease me. Stay till I am well, and then you shall tell me how to cure myself.' He grew better, and talked with a noble enthusiasm of keeping up the representation of respectable families. His zeal on this subject was a circumstance in his character exceedingly remarkable, when it is considered that he himself had no pretensions to blood. I heard him once say, 'I have great merit in being zealous for subordination and the honours of birth; for I can hardly tell who was my grandfather.' He maintained the dignity and propriety of male succession, in opposition to the opinion of one of our friends, who had that day employed Mr. Chambers to draw his will, devising his estate to his three sisters, in preference to a remote heir male. Johnson called them 'three *dowdies*,' and said, with as high a spirit as the boldest Baron in the most perfect days of the feudal system, 'An ancient estate should always go to males. It is mighty foolish to let a stranger have it because he marries your daughter, and takes your name. As for an estate newly acquired by trade, you may give it, if you will, to the dog *Towser*, and let him keep his *own* name.'

I have known him at times exceedingly diverted at what seemed to others a very small sport. He now laughed immoderately, without any reason that we could perceive, at our friend's making his will: called him the *testator*, and added, 'I dare say he thinks he has done a mighty thing.ᵃ

ᵃ & this was Lang-ton, a Man of very high . . . meaning very old Family: if it was ridiculous in him to be careful about Succession —it was so in every body. [H]

The Testator was Langton who I suppose had but little to leave; his Will was so good a Joke to them all. [I]

He won't stay till he gets home to his seat in the country, to produce this wonderful deed: he'll call up the landlord of the first inn on the road; and, after a suitable preface upon mortality and the uncertainty of life, will tell him that he should not delay making his will; and here, Sir, will he say, is my will, which I have just made, with the assistance of one of the ablest lawyers in the kingdom; and he will read it to him, (laughing all the time.) He believes he has made this will; but he did not make it: you, Chambers, made it for him. I trust you have had more conscience than to make him say, "being of sound under-standing;" ha, ha, ha! I hope he has left me a legacy. I'd have his will turned into verse, like a ballad.'

In this playful manner did he run on, exulting in his own pleasantry, which certainly was not such as might be expected from the authour of 'The Rambler,' but which is here preserved, that my readers may be acquainted even with the slightest occasional characteristicks of so eminent a man.

Mr. Chambers did not by any means relish this jocularity upon a matter of which *pars magna fuit*, and seemed im-patient till he got rid of us. Johnson could not stop his merriment, but continued it all the way till he got without the Temple-gate. He then burst into such a fit of laughter, that he appeared to be almost in a convulsion; and, in order to support himself, laid hold of one of the posts at the side of the foot pavement, and sent forth peals so loud, that in the silence of the night his voice seemed to resound from Temple-bar to Fleet-ditch.

This most ludicrous exhibition[a] of the awful, melan-choly, and venerable Johnson, happened well to counteract the feelings of sadness which I used to experience when parting with him for a considerable time. I accompanied him to his door, where he gave me his blessing.

He records of himself this year, 'Between Easter and Whitsuntide, having always considered that time as propi-tious to study, I attempted to learn the Low Dutch lan-guage.'[1] It is to be observed, that he here admits an opinion of the human mind being influenced by seasons, which he ridicules in his writings. His progress, he says,

[a] *& concerning a Will of all Things* [H]

---

[1] Prayers and Meditations, p. 129.

was interrupted by a fever, 'which, by the imprudent use
of a small print, left an inflammation in his useful eye.' We
cannot but admire his spirit when we know, that amidst
a complication of bodily and mental distress, he was still
animated with the desire of intellectual improvement.[1]
Various notes of his studies appear on different days, in his
manuscript diary of this year; such as, '*Inchoavi lectionem
Pentateuchi—Finivi lectionem Conf. Fab. Burdonum.—Legi
primum actum Troadum.—Legi Dissertationem Clerici postremam
de Pent.—2 of Clark's Sermons.—L. Apollonii pugnam Betriciam.
—L. centum versus Homeri.*' Let this serve as a specimen of
what accessions of literature he was perpetually infusing
into his mind, while he charged himself with idleness.

This year died Mrs. Salusbury, (mother of Mrs. Thrale,)
a lady whom he appears to have esteemed much, and whose
memory he honoured with an Epitaph.[2]

In a letter from Edinburgh, dated the 29th of May, I
pressed him to persevere in his resolution to make this
year the projected visit to the Hebrides, of which he and
I had talked for many years, and which I was confident
would afford us much entertainment.

'TO JAMES BOSWELL, ESQ.

'DEAR SIR,

'WHEN your letter came to me, I was so darkened by
an inflammation in my eye that I could not for some time
read it. I can now write without trouble, and can read
large prints. My eye is gradually growing stronger; and
I hope will be able to take some delight in the survey of a
Caledonian loch.

'Chambers is going a Judge, with six thousand a year,
to Bengal. He and I shall come down together as far as
Newcastle, and thence I shall easily get to Edinburgh.
Let me know the exact time when your Courts intermit.
I must conform a little to Chambers's occasions, and he

---

[1] [Not six months before his death, he wished me to teach him the Scale
of Musick:—'Dr. Burney, teach me at least the alphabet of your language.'
BURNEY.]

[2] Mrs. Piozzi's Anecdotes of Johnson, p. 131.

must conform a little to mine. The time which you shall fix, must be the common point to which we will come as near as we can. Except this eye, I am very well.

'Beattie is so caressed, and invited, and treated, and liked, and flattered, by the great, that I can see nothing of him. I am in great hope that he will be well provided for, and then we will live upon him at the Marischal College, without pity or modesty.

'————[a] left the town without taking leave of me, and is gone in deep dudgeon to ————.[b] Is not this very childish? Where is now my legacy?

[a] *Langton* [H & I]

[b] *Lincolnshire* [H & I]

'I hope your dear lady and her dear baby are both well. I shall see them too when I come; and I have that opinion of your choice, as to suspect that when I have seen Mrs. Boswell, I shall be less willing to go away.

I am, dear Sir,

'Your affectionate humble servant,

'Johnson's-court, Fleet-
street, July 5, 1773.'

'SAM. JOHNSON'

'Write to me as soon as you can. Chambers is now at Oxford.'

I again wrote to him, informing him that the Court of Session rose on the twelfth of August, hoping to see him before that time, and expressing, perhaps in too extravagant terms, my admiration of him, and my expectation of pleasure from our intended tour.

'TO JAMES BOSWELL, ESQ.

'DEAR SIR,

'I SHALL set out from London on Friday the sixth of this month, and purpose not to loiter much by the way. Which day I shall be at Edinburgh, I cannot exactly tell. I suppose I must drive to an inn, and send a porter to find you.

'I am afraid Beattie will not be at his College soon enough for us, and I shall be sorry to miss him; but there is no staying for the concurrence of all conveniences. We will do as well as we can. I am, Sir,

'Your most humble servant,

'August 3, 1773.'   'SAM. JOHNSON'

TO THE SAME

'DEAR SIR,

'NOT being at Mr. Thrale's when your letter came, I had written the inclosed paper and sealed it; bringing it hither for a frank, I found your's. If any thing could repress my ardour, it would be such a letter as your's. To disappoint a friend is unpleasing: and he that forms expectations like your's, must be disappointed. Think only when you see me, that you see a man who loves you, and is proud and glad that you love him. I am, Sir,

underlined:
must [H]

'Your most affectionate,

'August 3, 1773.'   'SAM. JOHNSON'

TO THE SAME

'DEAR SIR,   'Newcastle, Aug. 11, 1773

'I CAME hither last night, and hope, but do not absolutely promise, to be in Edinburgh on Saturday. Beattie will not come so soon. I am, Sir,

'Your most humble servant,

'SAM. JOHNSON'

'My compliments to your lady.'

TO THE SAME

'Mr. JOHNSON sends his compliments to Mr. Boswell, being just arrived at Boyd's.'

'Saturday night.'

His stay in Scotland was from the 18th of August, on which day he arrived, till the 22d of November, when he set out on his return to London; and I believe ninety-four days were never passed by any man in a more vigorous exertion.

He came by the way of Berwick upon Tweed to Edinburgh, where he remained a few days, and then went by St. Andrew's, Aberdeen, Inverness, and Fort Augustus, to the Hebrides, to visit which was the principal object he had in view. He visited the isles of Sky, Rasay, Col, Mull, Inchkenneth, and Icolmkill. He travelled through Argyleshire by Inverary, and from thence by Lochlomond and Dunbarton to Glasgow, then by Loudon to Auckinleck in Ayrshire, the seat of my family, and then by Hamilton, back to Edinburgh, where he again spent some time. He thus saw the four Universities of Scotland, its three principal cities, and as much of the Highland and insular life as was sufficient for his philosophical contemplation. I had the pleasure of accompanying him during the whole of his journey. He was respectfully entertained by the great, the learned, and the elegant, wherever he went; nor was he less delighted with the hospitality which he experienced in humbler life.

His various adventures, and the force and vivacity of his mind, as exercised during this peregrination, upon innumerable topicks, have been faithfully, and to the best of my abilities, displayed in my 'Journal of a Tour to the Hebrides,' to which, as the publick has been pleased to honour it by a very extensive circulation, I beg leave to refer, as to a separate and remarkable portion of his life,[1] which may be there seen in detail, and which exhibits as striking a view of his powers in conversation, as his works do of his excellence in writing. Nor can I deny to myself the very flattering gratification of inserting here the character which my friend Mr. Courtenay has been pleased to give of that work:

'With Reynolds' pencil, vivid, bold, and true,
So fervent Boswell gives him to our view:
In every trait we see his mind expand;
The master rises by the pupil's hand;

---

[1] [The authour was not a small gainer by this extraordinary Journey; for Dr. Johnson thus writes to Mrs. Thrale, Nov. 3, 1773: 'Boswell will praise my resolution and perseverance, and I shall in return celebrate his good humour and perpetual cheerfulness. He has better faculties than I had imagined; more justness of discernment, and more fecundity of images. It is very convenient to travel with him; for there is no house where he is not received with kindness and respect.' Let. 90, to Mrs. Thrale. MALONE.]

We love the writer, praise his happy vein,
Grac'd with the naiveté of the sage Montaigne.
Hence not alone are brighter parts display'd,
But e'en the specks of character pourtray'd:
We *see* the Rambler with fastidious smile
Mark the lone tree, and note the heath-clad isle;
But when th' heroic tale of Flora[1] charms,
Deck'd in a kilt, he wields a chieftain's arms:
The tuneful piper sounds a martial strain,
And Samuel sings, "The King shall have his *ain*." '

During his stay at Edinburgh, after his return from the Hebrides, he was at great pains to obtain information concerning Scotland; and it will appear from his subsequent letters, that he was not less solicitous for intelligence on this subject after his return to London.

'TO JAMES BOSWELL, ESQ.

'DEAR SIR,

'I CAME home last night, without any incommodity, danger, or weariness, and am ready to begin a new journey. I shall go to Oxford on Monday. I know Mrs. Boswell wished me well to go;[2] her wishes have not been disappointed. Mrs. Williams has received Sir A.'s[3] letter.

'Make my compliments to all those to whom my compliments may be welcome.

'Let the box[4] be sent as soon as it can, and let me know when to expect it.

[1] [The celebrated Flora Macdonald. See Boswell's *Tour*. COURTENAY.]

[2] In this he shewed a very acute penetration. My wife paid him the most assiduous and respectful attention, while he was our guest; so that I wonder how he discovered her wishing for his departure. The truth is, that his irregular hours and uncouth habits, such as turning the candles with their heads downwards, when they did not burn bright enough, and letting the wax drop upon the carpet, could not but be disagreeable to a lady. Besides, she had not that high admiration of him which was felt by most of those who knew him; and what was very natural to a female mind, she thought he had too much influence over her husband. She once, in a little warmth, made, with more point than justice, this remark upon that subject: 'I have seen many a bear led by a man; but I never before saw a man led by a bear.'

[3] Sir Alexander Gordon, one of the Professors at Aberdeen.

[4] This was a box containing a number of curious things which he had picked up in Scotland, particularly some horn spoons.

marginal line:
was felt . . . *made,*
with [H]

marginal line:
seen many . . . *a bear*
[H]

'Enquire, if you can, the order of the Clans: Macdonald is first, Maclean second; further I cannot go. Quicken Dr. Webster.[1] I am, Sir,

'Your's affectionately,

'Nov. 27, 1773.'   'SAM. JOHNSON'

'MR. BOSWELL TO DR. JOHNSON

'Edinburgh, Dec. 2, 1773

*   *   *   *   *   *

'YOU shall have what information I can procure as to the order of the Clans. A gentleman of the name of Grant tells me, that there is no settled order among them; and he says, that the Macdonalds were not placed upon the right of the army at Culloden; the Stuarts were. I shall, however, examine witnesses of every name that I can find here. Dr. Webster shall be quickened too. I like your little memorandums; they are symptoms of your being in earnest with your book of northern travels.

'Your box shall be sent next week by sea. You will find in it some pieces of the broom bush, which you saw growing on the old castle of Auchinleck. The wood has a curious appearance when sawn across. You may either have a little writing-standish made of it, or get it formed into boards for a treatise on witchcraft, by way of a suitable binding.'   *   *   *   *   *   *

'MR. BOSWELL TO DR. JOHNSON

'Edinburgh, Dec. 18, 1773

*   *   *   *   *   *

'YOU promised me an inscription for a print to be taken from an historical picture of Mary, Queen of Scots, being forced to resign her crown, which Mr. Hamilton at Rome has painted for me. The two following have been sent to me:

"*Maria Scotorum Regina meliori seculo digna, jus regium civibus seditiosis invita resignat.*"

"*Cives seditiosi Mariam Scotorum Reginam sese muneri abdicare invitam cogunt.*"

[1] The Reverend Dr. Alexander Webster, one of the ministers of Edinburgh, a man of distinguished abilities, who had promised him information concerning the Highlands and Islands of Scotland.

'Be so good as to read the passage in Robertson, and see if you cannot give me a better inscription. I must have it both in Latin and English; so if you should not give me another Latin one, you will at least choose the best of these two, and send a translation of it.'

* * * * * *

His humane forgiving disposition was put to a pretty strong test on his return to London by a liberty which Mr. Thomas Davies had taken with him in his absence, which was, to publish two volumes entitled, 'Miscellaneous and Fugitive Pieces,' which he advertised in the newspapers, 'By the Authour of the Rambler.' In this collection, several of Dr. Johnson's acknowledged writings, several of his anonymous performances, and some which he had written for others, were inserted; but there were also some in which he had no concern whatever. He was at first very angry, as he had good reason to be. But, upon consideration of his poor friend's narrow circumstances, and that he had only a little profit in view, and meant no harm, he soon relented, and continued his kindness to him as formerly.

In the course of his self-examination with retrospect to this year, he seems to have been much dejected; for he says, January 1, 1774, 'This year has passed with so little improvement, that I doubt whether I have not rather impaired than increased my learning;'[1] and yet we have seen how he *read*, and we know how he *talked* during that period.

He was now seriously engaged in writing an account of our travels in the Hebrides, in consequence of which I had the pleasure of a more frequent correspondence with him.

'TO JAMES BOSWELL, ESQ.

'DEAR SIR,

'MY operations have been hindered by a cough; at least I flatter myself, that if my cough had not come, I should have been further advanced. But I have had no intelligence from Dr. W——, [Webster,] nor from the Excise-office, nor from you. No account of the little

[1] Prayers and Meditations, p. 129.

borough.[1] Nothing of the Erse language. I have yet heard
nothing of my box.

'You must make haste and gather me all you can, and
do it quickly, or I will and shall do without it.

'Make my compliments to Mrs. Boswell, and tell her
that I do not love her the less for wishing me away. I gave
her trouble enough, and shall be glad in recompence, to
give her any pleasure.

'I would send some porter into the Hebrides, if I knew
which way it could be got to my kind friends there.
Enquire, and let me know.

'Make my compliments to all the Doctors of Edinburgh,
and to all my friends, from one end of Scotland to the
other.

'Write to me, and send me what intelligence you can:
and if any thing is too bulky for the post, let me have it by
the carrier. I do not like trusting winds and waves. I am,
dear Sir,

'Your most, &c.

'Jan. 29, 1774.'   'SAM. JOHNSON'

TO THE SAME

'DEAR SIR,

'IN a day or two after I had written the last discontented letter, I received my box, which was very welcome.
But still I must entreat you to hasten Dr. Webster, and
continue to pick up what you can that may be useful.

'Mr. Oglethorpe was with me this morning. You know
his errand. He was not unwelcome.

'Tell Mrs. Boswell that my good intentions towards her
still continue. I should be glad to do any thing that would
either benefit or please her.

'Chambers is not yet gone, but so hurried, or so negligent, or so proud, that I rarely see him. I have indeed, for
some weeks past, been very ill of a cold and cough, and
have been at Mrs. Thrale's, that I might be taken care of.
I am much better: *novæ redeunt in prælia vires;* but I am yet
tender, and easily disordered. How happy it was that
neither of us were ill in the Hebrides.

marginal line: *easily disordered . . . the Hebrides* [H]

[1] The ancient Burgh of Prestick, in Ayrshire.

'The question of Literary Property is this day before the Lords. Murphy drew up the Appellants' case, that is, the plea against the perpetual right. I have not seen it, nor heard the decision. I would not have the right perpetual.

'I will write to you as any thing occurs, and do you send me something about my Scottish friends. I have very great kindness for them. Let me know likewise how fees come in, and when we are to see you. I am, Sir,

'Your's affectionately,

'London, Feb. 7, 1774.'   'SAM. JOHNSON'

He at this time wrote the following letters to Mr. Steevens, his able associate in editing Shakspeare:

'TO GEORGE STEEVENS, ESQ. IN HAMPSTEAD

'SIR,

'IF I am asked when I have seen Mr. Steevens, you know what answer I must give; if I am asked when I shall see him, I wish you would tell me what to say.

'If you have "Lesley's History of Scotland," or any other book about Scotland, except Boetius and Buchanan, it will be a kindness if you send them to, Sir,

'Your humble servant,

'Feb. 7, 1774.'   'SAM. JOHNSON'

'SIR,   TO THE SAME

'WE are thinking to augment our club, and I am desirous of nominating you, if you care to stand the ballot, and can attend on Friday nights at least twice in five weeks: less than this is too little, and rather more will be expected. Be pleased to let me know before Friday.

I am, Sir,

'Your most, &c.

Feb. 21, 1774.'   'SAM. JOHNSON'

'SIR,   TO THE SAME

'LAST night you became a member of the club; if you call on me on Friday, I will introduce you. A gentleman, proposed after you, was rejected.

'I thank you for Neander,[1] but wish he were not so fine.
I will take care of him. I am, Sir,

'Your humble servant,

'March 5, 1774.'   'SAM. JOHNSON'

'TO JAMES BOSWELL, ESQ.

'DEAR SIR,

'DR. WEBSTER's informations were much less exact,
and much less determinate than I expected: they are,
indeed, much less positive than, if he can trust his own
book[2] which he laid before me, he is able to give. But I
believe it will always be found, that he who calls much for
information will advance his work but slowly.

'I am, however, obliged to you, dear Sir, for your
endeavours to help me, and hope, that between us something
will sometime be done, if not on this on some occasion.

'Chambers is either married, or almost married, to Miss
Wilton, a girl of[a] sixteen, exquisitely beautiful,[b] whom he
has with his lawyer's tongue, persuaded[c] to take her chance
with him in the East.

'We have added to the club, Charles Fox, Sir Charles
Bunbury, Dr. Fordyce, and Mr. Steevens.

'Return my thanks to Dr. Webster. Tell Dr. Robertson
I have not much to reply to his censure of my negligence:
and tell Dr. Blair, that since he has written hither what I
said to him, we must now consider ourselves as even,
forgive one another, and begin again. I care not how soon,
for he is a very pleasing man. Pay my compliments to all
my friends, and remind Lord Elibank of his promise to
give me all his works.

'I hope Mrs. Boswell and little Miss are well.—When
shall I see them again? She is a sweet lady, only she was

exclamation point:
to Miss Wilton etc. [H]

[a] not inserted before
sixteen [1: text omits
of]

[b] a Pupil of Baretti [H]

[c] a Girl without a Groat
is easily persuaded to
marry a man with
6000 L a year. [1]

---

[1] [See the Catalogue of Mr. Steevens's Library, No. 265:—
'Neandri (Mich.) Opus aureum, Gr. et Lat. 2 tom. 4to. corio turciso, foliis
deauratis. Lipsiæ, 1577.'—This was doubtless the book which appears to have
been lent by Mr. Steevens to Dr. Johnson. MALONE.]

[2] A manuscript account drawn by Dr. Webster of all the parishes in Scotland, ascertaining their length, breadth, number of inhabitants, and
distinguishing Protestants and Roman Catholicks. This book had been
transmitted to government, and Dr. Johnson saw a copy of it in Dr. Webster's
possession.

so glad to see me go, that I have almost a mind to come again, that she may again have the same pleasure.

'Enquire if it be practicable to send a small present of a cask of porter to Dunvegan, Rasay, and Col. I would not wish to be thought forgetful of civilities. I am, Sir,

'Your humble servant,

'March 5, 1774.'   'SAM. JOHNSON'

On the 5th of March I wrote to him, requesting his counsel whether I should this spring come to London. I stated to him on the one hand some pecuniary embarrassments, which, together with my wife's situation at that time, made me hesitate: and, on the other, the pleasure and improvement which my annual visit to the metropolis always afforded me; and particularly mentioned a peculiar satisfaction which I experienced in celebrating the festival of Easter in St. Paul's cathedral; that to my fancy it appeared like going up to Jerusalem at the feast of the Passover; and that the strong devotion which I felt on that occasion diffused its influence on my mind through the rest of the year.

exclamation point: to my fancy etc. [H]

'TO JAMES BOSWELL, ESQ.

'DEAR SIR,   [*Not dated, but written about
                                        the* 15th *of March*]

'I AM ashamed to think that since I received your letter I have passed so many days without answering it.

'I think there is no great difficulty in resolving your doubts. The reasons for which you are inclined to visit London, are, I think, not of sufficient strength to answer the objections. That you should delight to come once a year to the fountain of intelligence and pleasure, is very natural; but both information and pleasure must be regulated by propriety. Pleasure, which cannot be obtained but by unseasonable or unsuitable expence, must always end in pain; and pleasure, which must be enjoyed at the expence of another's pain, can never be such as a worthy mind can fully delight in.

marginal line: to come . . . both information [H]

'What improvement you might gain by coming to London, you may easily supply or easily compensate, by enjoining yourself some particular study at home, or opening some new avenue to information. Edinburgh is not yet exhausted: and I am sure you will find no pleasure here which can deserve either that you should anticipate any part of your future fortune, or that you should condemn yourself and your lady to penurious frugality for the rest of the year.

'I need not tell you what regard you owe to Mrs. Boswell's entreaties; or how much you ought to study the happiness of her who studies yours with so much diligence, and of whose kindness you enjoy such good effects. Life cannot subsist in society but by reciprocal concessions. She permitted you to ramble last year, you must permit her now to keep you at home.

'Your last reason is so serious, that I am unwilling to oppose it. Yet you must remember, that your image of worshipping once a year in a certain place, in imitation of the Jews, is but a comparison; and *simile non est idem;* if the annual resort to Jerusalem was a duty to the Jews, it was a duty because it was commanded; and you have no such command, therefore no such duty. It may be dangerous to receive too readily, and indulge too fondly, opinions, from which, perhaps, no pious mind is wholly disengaged, of local sanctity and local devotion. You know what strange effects they have produced over a great part of the Christian world. I am now writing, and you, when you read this, are reading under the Eye of Omnipresence.

'To what degree fancy is to be admitted into religious offices, it would require much deliberation to determine. I am far from intending totally to exclude it. Fancy is a faculty bestowed by our Creator, and it is reasonable that all our faculties should co-operate in his worship; but they are to co-operate according to the will of him that gave them, according to the order which his wisdom has established. As ceremonies prudential or convenient are less obligatory than positive ordinances, as bodily worship is only the token to others or ourselves of mental adoration, so Fancy is always to act in subordination to Reason. We may take Fancy for a companion, but must follow Reason as our guide. We may allow Fancy to suggest certain ideas

index sign: *We may take* etc. [H]

in certain places; but Reason must always be heard, when she tells us, that those ideas and those places have no natural or necessary relation. When we enter a church we habitually recall to mind the duty of adoration, but we must not omit adoration for want of a temple: because we know, and ought to remember, that the Universal Lord is every where present; and that, therefore, to come to Jona, or to Jerusalem, though it may be useful, cannot be necessary.

'Thus I have answered your letter, and have not answered it negligently. I love you too well to be careless when you are serious.

'I think I shall be very diligent next week about our travels, which I have too long neglected. I am, dear Sir,

'Your most, &c.

'SAM. JOHNSON'

'Compliments to Madam and Miss.'

TO THE SAME

'DEAR SIR,

'THE lady who delivers this has a lawsuit, in which she desires to make use of your skill and eloquence, and she seems to think that she shall have something more of both for a recommendation from me; which, though I know how little you want any external incitement to your duty, I could not refuse her, because I know that at least it will not hurt her, to tell you that I wish her well. I am, Sir,

'Your most humble servant,

'May 10, 1774.'   'SAM. JOHNSON'

'MR. BOSWELL TO DR. JOHNSON

'Edinburgh, May 12, 1774

'LORD HAILES has begged of me to offer you his best respects, and to transmit to you specimens of "Annals of Scotland, from the Accession of Malcolm Kenmore to the Death of James V." in drawing up which, his Lordship has been engaged for some time. His Lordship writes to me thus: "If I could procure Dr. Johnson's criticisms, they would be of great use to me in the prosecution of my work, as they would be judicious and true. I have no right to ask that favour of him. If you could, it would highly oblige me."

'Dr. Blair requests you may be assured that he did not write to London what you said to him, and that neither by word nor letter has he made the least complaint of you; but on the contrary has a high respect for you, and loves you much more since he saw you in Scotland. It would both divert and please you to see his eagerness about this matter.'

'TO JAMES BOSWELL, ESQ.

'DEAR SIR,   'Streatham, June 12, 1774

'YESTERDAY I put the first sheets of the "Journey to the Hebrides" to the press. I have endeavoured to do you some justice in the first paragraph. It will be one volume in octavo, not thick.

'It will be proper to make some presents in Scotland. You shall tell me to whom I shall give; and I have stipulated twenty-five for you to give in your own name. Some will take the present better from me, others better from you. In this, you who are to live in the place ought to direct. Consider it. Whatever you can get for my purpose send me; and make my compliments to your lady and both the young ones.

'I am, Sir, your, &c.

'SAM. JOHNSON'

'MR. BOSWELL TO DR. JOHNSON

'Edinburgh, June 24, 1774

'YOU do not acknowledge the receipt of the various packets which I have sent to you. Neither can I prevail with you to *answer* my letters,[a] though you honour me with *returns*. You have said nothing to me about poor Goldsmith,[1] nothing about Langton.

'I have received for you, from the Society for propagating Christian Knowledge in Scotland, the following Erse books:—"The New Testament;"—"Baxter's Call;"

¹ Dr. Goldsmith died April 4, this year.[b]

[a] *Johnson was careful of his own Dignity* [H]
Johnson dared not answer him but in general Terms; he knew Mr. Boswell wanted his Letters chiefly for the Pleasure of shewing them. [I]

[b] *Alas! Alas! & now Johnson & Boswell & Blair & Robertson & Garrick & Reynolds— & almost all the People named in these Books add to the dead cold list—Alas Alas! cries the Survivor in 1808.* [I]

—"The Confession of Faith of the Assembly of Divines at Westminster;"—"The Mother's Catechism;"—"A Gaelick and English Vocabulary."'[1]

'TO JAMES BOSWELL, ESQ.

'DEAR SIR,

'I WISH you could have looked over my book before the printer, but it could not easily be. I suspect some mistakes; but as I deal, perhaps, more in notions than in facts, the matter is not great, and the second edition will be mended, if any such there be. The press will go on slowly for a time, because I am going into Wales to-morrow.[a]

[a] *to Wales!* [I]

'I should be very sorry if I appeared to treat such a character as Lord Hailes otherwise than with high respect. I return the sheets,[2] to which I have done what mischief I could; and finding it so little, thought not much of sending them. The narrative is clear, lively, and short.

'I have done worse to Lord Hailes than by neglecting his sheets: I have run him in debt. Dr. Horne, the President of Magdalen College in Oxford, wrote to me about three months ago, that he purposed to reprint Walton's Lives, and desired me to contribute to the work: my answer was, that Lord Hailes intended the same publication; and Dr. Horne has resigned it to him. His Lordship must now think seriously about it.

'Of poor dear Dr. Goldsmith there is little to be told, more than the papers have made publick. He died of a fever, made, I am afraid, more violent by uneasiness of mind. His debts began to be heavy, and all his resources were exhausted. Sir Joshua is of opinion that he owed not less than two thousand pounds. Was ever poet so trusted before?

two exclamation
points:
Was ever etc. [H]

'You may, if you please, put the inscription thus: "*Maria Scotorum Regina nata* 15—, *a suis in exilium acta* 15—, *ab hospitâ neci data* 15—." You must find the years.

---

[1] These books Dr. Johnson presented to the Bodleian Library.

[2] On the cover enclosing them Dr. Johnson wrote: 'If my delay has given any reason for supposing that I have not a very deep sense of the honour done me by asking my judgement, I am very sorry.'

'Of your second daughter you certainly gave the account yourself, though you have forgotten it. While Mrs. Boswell is well, never doubt of a boy. Mrs. Thrale brought, I think, five girls running, but while I was with you she had a boy.[a]

'I am obliged to you for all your pamphlets, and of the last I hope to make some use. I made some of the former.

'I am, dear Sir,

'Your most affectionate servant,

'SAM. JOHNSON'

'July 4, 1774.'

'My compliments to all the three ladies.'

[a] *Ay! poor Ralph: who lived but 26 Months; and died at Brighthelmstone* [H]

'TO BENNET LANGTON, ESQ. AT LANGTON, NEAR SPILSBY, LINCOLNSHIRE

'DEAR SIR,

'YOU have reason to reproach me that I have left your last letter so long unanswered, but I had nothing particular to say. Chambers, you find, is gone far,[b] and poor Goldsmith is gone much further. He died of a fever, exasperated, as I believe, by the fear of distress. He had raised money and squandered it, by every artifice of acquisition and folly of expence. But let not his frailties be remembered; he was a very great man.

'I have just begun to print my Journey to the Hebrides, and am leaving the press to take another journey into Wales, whither Mr. Thrale is going, to take possession of, at least, five hundred a year, fallen to his lady.[c] All at Streatham, that are alive, are well.

'I have never recovered from the last dreadful illness, but flatter myself that I grow gradually better; much, however, yet remains to mend. Κύριε ἐλέησον.

'If you have the Latin version of *Busy, curious, thirsty fly*, be so kind as to transcribe and send it; but you need not be in haste, for I shall be I know not where, for at least five weeks. I wrote the following tetrastick on poor Goldsmith:

[b] *Chambers has taken the long Journey too!!* [1]

underlined: *five hundred* [H]

[c] *I hope 1500 £: but they all lov'd to depreciate poor H. L. P.* [H]

Τὸν τάφον εἰσοράᾳς τὸν Ὀλιβάροιο, κονίην
Ἄφροσι μὴ σεμνήν, Ξεῖνε, πόδεσσι πάτει·
Οἷσι μέμηλε φύσις, μέτρων χάρις, ἔργα παλαιῶν,
Κλαίετε ποιητὴν, ἱστόρικὸν, φυσικόν.

'Please to make my most respectful compliments to all the ladies, and remember me to young George and his sisters. I reckon George begins to shew a pair of heels.

'Do not be sullen now, but let me find a letter when I come back. I am, dear Sir,

'Your affectionate, humble servant,

'July 5, 1774.'　　　　　　　　　　　'SAM. JOHNSON'

exclamation point and underlined:
Llewenny [H]
ª Poor dear Llewenny! no longer in Existence 1819. [H]

exclamation point:
Wales . . . is etc. [H]
ᵇ yet to please Mr. Thrale he feign'd Ab-horrence of it. [H]
two exclamation points:
Denbigh is etc. [H]
ᶜ It is less mean now 1808. [I]

'TO MR. ROBERT LEVET

'DEAR SIR,　　　　　'Llewenny,ª in Denbighshire, August 16, 1774

'MR. THRALE'S affairs have kept him here a great while, nor do I know exactly when we shall come hence. I have sent you a bill upon Mr. Strahan.

'I have made nothing of the Ipecacuanha, but have taken abundance of pills, and hope that they have done me good.

'Wales, so far as I have yet seen of it, is a very beautiful and rich country, all enclosed, and planted.ᵇ Denbigh is not a mean town.ᶜ Make my compliments to all my friends, and tell Frank I hope he remembers my advice. When his money is out, let him have more. I am, Sir,

'Your humble servant,

'SAM. JOHNSON'

'MR. BOSWELL TO DR. JOHNSON

'Edinburgh, Aug. 30, 1774

'YOU have given me an inscription for a portrait of Mary Queen of Scots, in which you, in a short and striking manner, point out her hard fate. But you will be pleased to keep in mind, that my picture is a representation of a particular scene in her history; her being forced to resign her crown, while she was imprisoned in the castle of Lochlevin. I must, therefore, beg that you will be kind enough to give me an inscription suited to that particular scene; or determine which of the two formerly transmitted to you is the best; and at any rate, favour me with an

English translation. It will be doubly kind if you comply with my request speedily.

'Your critical notes on the specimen of Lord Hailes's "Annals of Scotland," are excellent. I agreed with you on every one of them. He himself objected only to the alteration of *free* to *brave*, in the passage where he says that Edward "departed with the glory due to the conqueror of a free people." He says, to call the Scots brave would only add to the glory of their conquerour. You will make allowance for the national zeal of our annalist. I now send a few more leaves of the Annals, which I hope you will peruse, and return with observations, as you did upon the former occasion. Lord Hailes writes to me thus: "Mr. Boswell will be pleased to express the grateful sense which Sir David Dalrymple has of Dr. Johnson's attention to his little specimen. The further specimen will show, that

"Even in an *Edward* he can see desert."

'It gives me much pleasure to hear that a republication of Isaac Walton's Lives is intended. You have been in a mistake in thinking that Lord Hailes had it in view. I remember one morning, while he sat with you in my house, he said, that there should be a new edition of Walton's Lives; and you said that 'they should be benoted a little'. This was all that passed on that subject. You must, therefore, inform Dr. Horne, that he may resume his plan. I enclose a note concerning it; and if Dr. Horne will write to me, all the attention that I can give shall be cheerfully bestowed, upon what I think a pious work, the preservation and elucidation of Walton, by whose writings I have been most pleasingly edified.'

* * * * * *

'MR. BOSWELL TO DR. JOHNSON

'Edinburgh, Sept. 16, 1774

'WALES has probably detained you longer than I supposed. You will have become quite a mountaineer, by visiting Scotland one year and Wales another. You must

next go to Switzerland. Cambria will complain, if you do
not honour her also with some remarks. And I find *con-
cessere columnæ*, the booksellers expect another book. I am
impatient to see your "Tour to Scotland and the Hebrides."
Might you not send me a copy by the post as soon as it is
printed off?'

* * * * * *

'TO JAMES BOSWELL, ESQ.

'DEAR SIR,

'YESTERDAY I returned from my Welsh journey.
I was sorry to leave my book suspended so long; but having
an opportunity of seeing, with so much convenience, a
new part of the island, I could not reject it. I have been
in five of the six counties of North Wales; and have seen
St. Asaph and Bangor, the two seats of their Bishops;
have been upon Penmanmaur and Snowden, and passed
over into Anglesea. But Wales is so little different from
England, that it offers nothing to the speculation of the
traveller.

'When I came home, I found several of your papers,
with some pages of Lord Hailes's Annals, which I will
consider. I am in haste to give you some account
of myself, lest you should suspect me of negligence in
the pressing business which I find recommended to my
care, and which I knew nothing of till now, when
all care is vain.[1]

'In the distribution of my books I purpose to follow
your advice, adding such as shall occur to me. I am not
pleased with your notes of remembrance added to your
names, for I hope I shall not easily forget them.

'I have received four Erse books, without any direction,
and suspect that they are intended for the Oxford library.
If that is the intention, I think it will be proper to add the
metrical psalms, and whatever else is printed in Erse, that
the present may be complete. The donor's name should
be told.

[1] I had written to him, to request his interposition in behalf of a convict,
who I thought was very unjustly condemned.

'I wish you could have read the book before it was printed, but our distance does not easily permit it.

'I am sorry Lord Hailes does not intend to publish Walton; I am afraid it will not be done so well, if it be done at all.

'I purpose now to drive the book forward. Make my compliments to Mrs. Boswell, and let me hear often from you. I am, dear Sir,

'Your affectionate humble servant,

'London, Octob. 1, 1774.'   'SAM. JOHNSON'

This tour to Wales, which was made in company with Mr. and Mrs. Thrale, though it no doubt contributed to his health and amusement, did not give an occasion to such a discursive exercise of his mind as our tour to the Hebrides. I do not find that he kept any journal or notes of what he saw there.[a] All that I heard him say of it was, that 'instead of bleak and barren mountains, there were green and fertile ones; and that one of the castles in Wales would contain all the castles that he had seen in Scotland.'

Parliament having been dissolved, and his friend Mr. Thrale, who was a steady supporter of government, having again to encounter the storm of a contested election, he wrote a short political pamphlet, entitled, 'The Patriot,'* addressed to the electors of Great Britain; a title which, to factious men who consider a patriot only as an opposer of the measures of government, will appear strangely misapplied. It was, however, written with energetick vivacity; and, except those passages in which it endeavours to vindicate the glaring outrage of the House of Commons in the case of the Middlesex election, and to justify the attempt to reduce our fellow-subjects in America to unconditional submission, it contained an admirable display of the properties of a real patriot, in the original and genuine sense;—a sincere, steady, rational, and unbiassed friend to the interests and prosperity of his King and country. It must be acknowledged, however, that both in this and his two former pamphlets, there was, amidst many powerful arguments, not only a considerable portion of

index sign: *any journal* etc. [H]

[a] *I found out in the Year 1816 or 17 that he had kept a Journal, & since then Mr. Duppa printed it. 1820* [H]

two marginal lines: *was, amidst . . . a contemptuous* [H]

sophistry, but a contemptuous ridicule of his opponents, which was very provoking.

'TO MR. PERKINS[1]

'SIR,

'You may do me a very great favour. Mrs. Williams, a gentlewoman whom you may have seen at Mr. Thrale's, is a petitioner for Mr. Hetherington's charity; petitions are this day issued at Christ's Hospital.

'I am a bad manager of business in a crowd; and if I should send a mean man, he may be put away without his errand. I must therefore entreat that you will go, and ask for a petition for Anna Williams, whose paper of enquiries was delivered with answers at the counting-house of the hospital on Thursday the 20th. My servant will attend you thither, and bring the petition home when you have it.

'The petition, which they are to give us, is a form which they deliver to every petitioner, and which the petitioner is afterwards to fill up, and return to them again. This we must have, or we cannot proceed according to their directions. You need, I believe, only ask for a petition; if they enquire for whom you ask, you can tell them.

'I beg pardon for giving you this trouble; but it is a matter of great importance. I am, Sir,

'Your most humble servant,

'October 25, 1774.'   'SAM. JOHNSON'

'TO JAMES BOSWELL, ESQ.

'DEAR SIR,

'There has appeared lately in the papers an account of a boat overset between Mull and Ulva, in which many

[1] Mr. Perkins was for a number of years the worthy superintendent of Mr. Thrale's great brewery, and after his death became one of the Proprietors of it; and now resides in Mr. Thrale's house in Southwark, which was the scene of so many literary meetings, and in which he continues the liberal hospitality for which it was eminent. Dr. Johnson esteemed him much. He hung up in the counting-house a fine proof of the admirable mezzotinto of Dr. Johnson, by Doughty; and when Mrs. Thrale asked him somewhat flippantly, 'Why do you put him up in the counting-house?' he answered, 'Because, Madam, I wish to have one wise man there.' 'Sir, (said Johnson,) I thank you. It is a very handsome compliment, and I believe you speak sincerely.'

passengers were lost, and among them Maclean of Col. We, you know, were once drowned;[1] I hope, therefore, that the story is either wantonly or erroneously told. Pray satisfy me by the next post.

'I have printed two hundred and forty pages. I am able to do nothing much worth doing to dear Lord Hailes's book. I will, however, send back the sheets; and hope, by degrees, to answer all your reasonable expectations.

'Mr. Thrale has happily surmounted a very violent and acrimonious opposition; but all joys have their abatement: Mrs. Thrale has fallen from her horse and hurt herself very much.[a] The rest of our friends, I believe, are well. My compliments to Mrs. Boswell. I am, Sir,

[a] *Mrs. Thrale's Horse fell under her, & put his Foot upon her face   I trust—in rising.* [H]

'Your most affectionate servant,

'London, Octob. 27, 1774.'   'SAM. JOHNSON'

This letter, which shews his tender concern for an amiable young gentleman to whom he had been very much obliged in the Hebrides,[b] I have inserted according to its date, though before receiving it I had informed him of the melancholy event that the young Laird of Col was unfortunately drowned.

[b] *Yes; & it shows Johnson's Heady Resolution to believe no ill News.* [H]

'TO JAMES BOSWELL, ESQ.

'DEAR SIR,

'LAST night I corrected the last page of our "Journey to the Hebrides." The printer has detained it all this time, for I had, before I went into Wales, written all except two sheets. "The Patriot" was called for by my political friends on Friday, was written on Saturday, and I have heard little of it. So vague are conjectures at a distance.[2] As soon as I can, I will take care that copies be sent to you, for I would wish that they might be given before they are bought; but I am afraid that Mr. Strahan will send to you and to the booksellers at the same time.

---

[1] In the news-papers.

[2] Alluding to a passage in a letter of mine, where speaking of his 'Journey to the Hebrides,' I say, 'But has not "The Patriot" been an interruption, by the time taken to write it, and the time luxuriously spent in listening to its applauses?'

Trade is as diligent as courtesy. I have mentioned all that
you recommended. Pray make my compliments to Mrs.
Boswell and the younglings. The club has, I think, not
yet met.

'Tell me, and tell me honestly, what you think and what
others say of our travels. Shall we touch the continent?[1]

I am, dear Sir,

'Your most humble servant,

'Nov. 26, 1774.'   'SAM. JOHNSON'

IN his manuscript diary of this year, there is the following
entry:

'Nov. 27. Advent Sunday. I considered that this day,
being the beginning of the ecclesiastical year, was a proper
time for a new course of life. I began to read the Greek
Testament regularly at 160 verses every Sunday. This day
I began the Acts.

'In this week I read Virgil's Pastorals. I learned to
repeat the Pollio and Gallus. I read carelessly the first
Georgick.'

Such evidences of his unceasing ardour, both for 'divine
and human lore,' when advanced into his sixty-fifth year,
and notwithstanding his many disturbances from disease,
must make us at once honour his spirit, and lament that it
should be so grievously clogged by its material tegument.
It is remarkable, that he was very fond of the precision
which calculation produces. Thus we find in one of his
manuscript diaries, '12 pages in 4to Gr. Test. and 30
pages in Beza's folio, comprize the whole in 40 days.'

'DR. JOHNSON TO JOHN HOOLE, ESQ.

'DEAR SIR,

'I HAVE returned your play,[2] which you will find
underscored with red, where there was a word which
I did not like. The red will be washed off with a little
water.

---

[1] We had projected a voyage together up the Baltick, and talked of visiting
some of the more northern regions.

[2] 'Cleonice.'

'The plot is so well framed, the intricacy so artful, and the disentanglement so easy, the suspense so affecting, and the passionate parts so properly interposed,[a] that I have no doubt of its success.[b] I am, Sir,

[a] *all that was Metas-tasio's, not Hoole's.* [H]

[b] *it did not succeed.* [H]

'Your most humble servant,

'December 19, 1774.'   'SAM. JOHNSON'

THE first effort of his pen in 1775, was, 'Proposals for publishing the Works of Mrs. Charlotte Lennox,'✝ in three volumes quarto. In his diary, January 2, I find this entry: 'Wrote Charlotte's Proposals.' But, indeed, the internal evidence would have been quite sufficient. Her claim to the favour of the publick was thus enforced:

'Most of the pieces, as they appeared singly have been read with approbation, perhaps above their merits, but of no great advantage to the writer. She hopes, therefore, that she shall not be considered as too indulgent to vanity, or too studious of interest, if from that labour which has hitherto been chiefly gainful to others, she endeavours to obtain at last some profit to herself and her children. She cannot decently enforce her claim by the praise of her own performances: nor can she suppose, that, by the most artful and laboured address, any additional notice could be procured to a publication, of which Her MAJESTY has condescended to be the PATRONESS.'

He this year also wrote the Preface to Baretti's 'Easy Lessons in Italian and English.'✝

marginal line: *He this . . . and English* [H]

'TO JAMES BOSWELL, ESQ.

'DEAR SIR,

'You never did ask for a book by the post till now, and I did not think on it. You see now it is done. I sent one to the King, and I hear he likes it.

'I shall send a parcel into Scotland for presents, and intend to give to many of my friends. In your catalogue you left out Lord Auchinleck.

'Let me know, as fast as you read it, how you like it; and let me know if any mistake is committed, or any thing important left out. I wish you could have seen the sheets.

My compliments to Mrs. Boswell, and to Veronica, and to all my friends. I am, Sir,

'Your most humble servant,

'January 14, 1775.'   'SAM. JOHNSON'

'MR. BOSWELL TO DR. JOHNSON

'Edinburgh, Jan. 19, 1775

'BE pleased to accept of my best thanks for your "Journey to the Hebrides," which came to me by last night's post. I did really ask the favour twice; but you have been even with me by granting it so speedily. BIS *dat qui cito dat.* Though ill of a bad cold, you kept me up the greatest part of last night: for I did not stop till I had read every word of your book. I looked back to our first talking of a visit to the Hebrides, which was many years ago, when sitting by ourselves in the Mitre tavern in London, I think about *witching time o'night:* and then exulted in contemplating our scheme fulfilled, and a *monumentum perenne* of it erected by your superiour abilities. I shall only say, that your book has afforded me a high gratification. I shall afterwards give you my thoughts on particular passages. In the mean time, I hasten to tell you of your having mistaken two names, which you will correct in London, as I shall do here, that the gentlemen who deserve the valuable compliments which you have paid them, may enjoy their honours. In page 106, for *Gordon* read *Murchison;* and in page 357, for *Maclean* read *Macleod.*

*   *   *   *   *   *

'But I am now to apply to you for immediate aid in my profession, which you have never refused to grant when I requested it. I enclose you a petition for Dr. Memis, a physician at Aberdeen, in which Sir John Dalrymple has exerted his talents, and which I am to answer as Counsel for the managers of the Royal Infirmary in that city. Mr. Jopp, the Provost, who delivered to you your freedom, is one of my clients, and, *as a citizen of Aberdeen,* you will support him.

'The fact is shortly this. In a translation of the charter of the Infirmary from Latin into English, made under the authority of the managers, the same phrase in the original is in one place rendered *Physician,* but when applied to Dr. Memis is rendered *Doctor of Medicine.* Dr. Memis complained of this before the translation was printed, but was not indulged with having it altered; and he has brought an action for damages, on account of a supposed injury, as if the designation given to him was an inferiour one, tending to make it be supposed he is *not* a *Physician,* and consequently to hurt his practice. My father has dismissed the action as groundless, and now he has appealed to the whole Court.'[1]

'TO JAMES BOSWELL, ESQ.

'DEAR SIR,

'I LONG to hear how you like the book; it is, I think, much liked here. But Macpherson is very furious; can you give me any more intelligence about him, or his Fingal? Do what you can, and do it quickly. Is Lord Hailes on our side?

'Pray let me know what I owed you when I left you, that I may send it to you.

'I am going to write about the Americans. If you have picked up any hints among your lawyers, who are great masters of the law of nations, or if your own mind suggest any thing, let me know. But mum, it is a secret.

'I will send your parcel of books as soon as I can; but I cannot do as I wish. However, you find every thing mentioned in the book which you recommended.

'Langton is here; we are all that ever we were. He is a worthy fellow, without malice, though not without resentment.

'Poor Beauclerk is so ill, that his life is thought to be in danger. Lady Di nurses him with very great assiduity.

'Reynolds has taken too much to strong liquour,[2a] and seems to delight in his new character.

[a] *Johnson always fancied all the Men were drunk who drank any thing but Water.* [H]

[1] In the Court of Session of Scotland an action is first tried by one of the Judges, who is called the Lord Ordinary: and if either party is dissatisfied, he may appeal to the whole Court, consisting of fifteen, the Lord President and fourteen other Judges, who have both in and out of Court the title of Lords from the name of their estates; as, Lord Auchinleck, Lord Monboddo, &c.

[2] It should be recollected, that this fanciful description of his friend was given by Johnson after he himself had become a water-drinker.

'This is all the news that I have; but as you love verses, I will send you a few which I made upon Inchkenneth;[1] but remember the condition, you shall not shew them, except to Lord Hailes, whom I love better than any man whom I know so little. If he asks you to transcribe them for him, you may do it, but I think he must promise not to let them be copied again, nor to shew them as mine.

'I have at last sent back Lord Hailes's sheets. I never think about returning them, because I alter nothing. You will see that I might as well have kept them. However I am ashamed of my delay; and if I have the honour of receiving any more, promise punctually to return them by the next post. Make my compliments to dear Mrs. Boswell, and to Miss Veronica. I am, dear Sir,

'Yours most faithfully,

'Jan. 1, 1775.'   'SAM. JOHNSON'[2]

'MR. BOSWELL TO DR. JOHNSON

'Edinburgh, Jan. 27, 1775

*   *   *   *   *   *

'You rate our lawyers here too high, when you call them great masters of the law of nations.

*   *   *   *   *   *

[1] See them in 'Journal of a Tour to the Hebrides,' 3d edit. p. 337.

[2] He now sent me a Latin inscription for my historical picture Mary Queen of Scots, and afterwards favoured me with an English translation. Mr. Alderman Boydell, that eminent Patron of the Arts, has subjoined them to the engraving from my picture.

'*Maria Scotorum Regina,*
Hominum seditiosorum
Contumeliis lassata,
Minis territa, clamoribus victa,
Libello, per quem
Regno cedit,
Lacrimans trepidansque
Nomen apponit.'

'Mary Queen of Scots,
Harassed, terrified, and overpowered
By the insults, menaces,
And clamours
Of her rebellious subjects,
Sets her hand,
With tears and confusion,
To a resignation of the kingdom.'

'As for myself, I am ashamed to say I have read little and thought little on the subject of America. I will be much obliged to you, if you will direct me where I shall find the best information of what is to be said on both sides. It is a subject vast in its present extent and future consequences. The imperfect hints which now float in my mind, tend rather to the formation of an opinion that our government has been precipitant and severe in the resolutions taken against the Bostonians. Well do you know that I have no kindness for that race. But nations or bodies of men, should, as well as individuals, have a fair trial, and not be condemned on character alone. Have we not express contracts with our colonies, which afford a more certain foundation of judgment, than general political speculations on the mutual rights of States and their provinces or colonies? Pray let me know immediately what to read, and I shall diligently endeavour to gather for you any thing that I can find. Is Burke's speech on American taxation published by himself? Is it authentick? I remember to have heard you say, that you had never considered East-Indian affairs: though, surely, they are of much importance to Great-Britain. Under the recollection of this, I shelter myself from the reproach of ignorance about the Americans. If you write upon the subject, I shall certainly understand it. But, since you seem to expect that I should know something of it, without your instruction, and that my own mind should suggest something, I trust you will put me in the way.

* * * * * *

'What does Becket mean by the *Originals* of Fingal and other poems of Ossian, which he advertises to have lain in his shop.' * * * * * *

'TO JAMES BOSWELL, ESQ.

'DEAR SIR,

'You sent me a case to consider, in which I have no facts but what are against us, nor any principles on which to reason. It is vain to try to write thus without materials. The fact seems to be against you; at least I cannot know nor say any thing to the contrary. I am glad that you like the book so well. I hear no more of Macpherson. I shall long to know what Lord Hailes says of it. Lend it him privately. I shall send the parcel as soon as I can. Make my compliments to Mrs. Boswell. I am, Sir, &c.

'Jan. 28, 1775.'   'SAM. JOHNSON'

'MR. BOSWELL TO DR. JOHNSON

'Edinburgh, Feb. 2, 1775

*   *   *   *   *   *

'As to Macpherson, I am anxious to have from yourself a full and pointed account of what has passed between you and him. It is confidently told here, that before your book came out he sent to you, to let you know that he understood you meant to deny the authenticity of Ossian's poems; that the originals were in his possession; that you might have inspection of them, and might take the evidence of people skilled in the Erse language; and that he hoped after this fair offer, you would not be so uncandid as to assert that he had refused reasonable proof. That you paid no regard to his message but published your strong attack upon him; and then he wrote a letter to you, in such terms as he thought suited to one who had not acted as a man of veracity. You may believe it gives me pain to hear your conduct represented as unfavourable, while I can only deny what is said, on the ground that your character refutes it, without having any information to oppose. Let me, I beg it of you, be furnished with a sufficient answer to any calumny upon this occasion.

'Lord Hailes writes to me, (for we correspond more than we talk together,) "As to Fingal, I see a controversy arising, and purpose to keep out of its way. There is no doubt that I might mention some circumstances; but I do not chuse to commit them to paper."[1] What his opinion is, I do not know. He says, "I am singularly obliged to Dr. Johnson for his accurate and useful criticisms. Had he given some strictures on the general plan of the work, it would

[1] [His Lordship, notwithstanding his resolution, did commit his sentiments to paper, and in one of his notes affixed to his Collection of Old Scottish Poetry, he says, that 'to doubt the authenticity of those poems, is a refinement in Scepticism indeed.' J. BOSWELL.]

have added much to his favours." He is charmed with your verses on Inchkenneth, says they are very elegant, but bids me tell you he doubts whether

"*Legitimas faciunt pectora pura preces,*"

be according to the rubrick: but that is your concern; for, you know, he is a Presbyterian.'

*   *   *   *   *   *

'TO DR. LAWRENCE[1]

'SIR,   'Feb. 7, 1775

'ONE of the Scotch physicians is now prosecuting a corporation that in some publick instrument have stiled him *Doctor of Medicine* instead of *Physician*. Boswell desires, being advocate for the corporation, to know whether *Doctor of Medicine* is not a legitimate title, and whether it may be considered as a disadvantageous distinction. I am to write to-night; be pleased to tell me. I am, Sir, your most, &c.   'SAM. JOHNSON'

'TO JAMES BOSWELL, ESQ.

'MY DEAR BOSWELL,

'I AM surprised that, knowing as you do the disposition of your countrymen to tell lies in favour of each other,[2] you can be at all affected by any reports that circulate among them. Macpherson never in his life offered me a sight of any original or of any evidence of any kind; but thought only of intimidating me by noise and threats, till my last answer,—that I would not be deterred from detecting what I thought a cheat, by the menaces of a ruffian,—put an end to our correspondence.

'The state of the question is this. He, and Dr. Blair, whom I consider as deceived, say, that he copied the poem from old manuscripts. His copies, if he had them, and I believe him to have none, are nothing. Where are the

---

[1] The learned and worthy Dr. Lawrence, whom Dr. Johnson respected and loved as his physician and friend.

[2] My friend has, in his letter, relied upon my testimony, with a confidence, of which the ground has escaped my recollection.

manuscripts? They can be shown if they exist, but they were never shown. *De non existentibus et non apparentibus,* says our law, *eadem est ratio.* No man has a claim to credit upon his own word, when better evidence, if he had it, may be easily produced. But so far as we can find, the Erse language was never written till very lately for the purposes of religion. A nation that cannot write, or a language that was never written, has no manuscripts.

'But whatever he had he never offered to show. If old manuscripts should now be mentioned, I should, unless there were more evidence than can be easily had, suppose them another proof of Scotch conspiracy in national falsehood.

queried:
suppose them etc. [H]
queried:
Do not etc. [H]

'Do not censure the expression; you know it to be true.

'Dr. Memis's question is so narrow as to allow no speculation; and I have no facts before me but those which his advocate has produced against you.

'I consulted this morning the President of the London College of Physicians, who says, that with us, *Doctor of Physick* (we do not say *Doctor of Medicine*) is the highest title that a practicer of physick can have; that *Doctor* implies not only *Physician,* but teacher of physick; that every *Doctor* is legally a *Physician;* but no man, not a *Doctor,* can *practise physick* but by *licence* particularly granted. The Doctorate is a licence of itself. It seems to us a very slender cause of prosecution.

*   *   *   *   *   *

'I am now engaged, but in a little time I hope to do all you would have. My compliments to Madam and Veronica. I am, Sir,

'Your most humble servant,

'February 7, 1775.'   'SAM. JOHNSON'

What words were used by Mr. Macpherson in his letter to the venerable Sage, I have never heard; but they are generally said to have been of a nature very different from the language of literary contest. Dr. Johnson's answer appeared in the news-papers of the day, and has since been frequently re-published; but not with perfect accuracy. I give it as dictated to me by himself, written down in his presence, and authenticated by a note in his own handwriting, ' *This, I think, is a true copy.*'[1]

'MR. JAMES MACPHERSON,

'I RECEIVED your foolish and impudent letter. Any violence offered me I shall do my best to repel; and what I cannot do for myself, the law shall do for me. I hope I shall never be deterred from detecting what I think a cheat, by the menaces of a ruffian.

'What would you have me retract? I thought your book an imposture; I think it an imposture still. For this opinion I have given my reasons to the publick, which I here dare you to refute. Your rage I defy. Your abilities, since your Homer, are not so formidable; and what I hear of your morals inclines me to pay regard not to what you shall say, but to what you shall prove. You may print this if you will.

'SAM. JOHNSON'

Mr. Macpherson little knew the character of Dr. Johnson, if he supposed that he could be easily intimidated; for no man was ever more remarkable for personal courage. He had, indeed, an awful dread of death, or rather, 'of something after death;' and what rational man, who seriously thinks of quitting all that he has ever known, and going into a new and unknown state of being, can be without that dread? But his fear was from reflection; his courage natural.[a] His fear, in that one instance, was the result of philosophical and religious consideration. He feared death, but he feared nothing else, not even what might occasion death. Many instances of his resolution may be mentioned. One day, at Mr. Beauclerk's house in the country, when two large dogs were fighting, he went up to them, and beat them till they separated; and at another time, when told of the danger there was that a gun might burst if charged with many balls, he put in six or seven and fired it off against a wall. Mr. Langton told me, that when they were swimming together near Oxford, he cautioned Dr. Johnson against a pool,[b] which was

[a] *That is neatly said.* [H]

exclamation point: *he put in* etc. [H]
underlined: *and fired . . . a wall* [I]

[b] *There he was in real Danger.* [I]

[1] I have deposited it in the British Museum.

reckoned particularly dangerous; upon which Johnson directly swam into it. He told me himself that one night he was attacked in the street by four men, to whom he would not yield, but kept them all at bay, till the watch came up, and carried both him and them to the round-house. In the play-house at Lichfield, as Mr. Garrick informed me, Johnson having for a moment quitted a chair which was placed for him between the side-scenes, a gentleman took possession of it, and when Johnson on his return civilly demanded his seat, rudely refused to give it up; upon which Johnson laid hold of it, and tossed him and the chair into the pit. Foote, who so successfully revived the old comedy, by exhibiting living characters, had resolved to imitate Johnson on the stage, expecting great profits from his ridicule of so celebrated a man. Johnson being informed of his intention, and being at dinner at Mr. Thomas Davies's the bookseller, from whom I had the story, he asked Mr. Davies 'what was the common price of an oak stick;' and being answered six-pence, 'Why then, Sir, (said he,) give me leave to send your servant to purchase me a shilling one. I'll have a double quantity; for I am told Foote means to *take me off*, as he calls it, and I am determined the fellow shall not do it with impunity.' Davies took care to acquaint Foote of this, which effectually checked the wantonness of the mimick. Mr. Macpherson's menaces made Johnson pro-vide himself with the same implement of defence: and had he been attacked, I have no doubt that, old as he was, he would have made his corporal prowess be felt as much as his intellectual.

His 'Journey to the Western Islands of Scotland,'* is a most valuable performance. It abounds in extensive philosophical views of society, and in ingenious sentiment and lively description. A considerable part of it, indeed, consists of speculations, which many years before he saw the wild regions which we visited together, probably had employed his attention, though the actual sight of those scenes undoubtedly quickened and augmented them. Mr. Orme, the very able historian, agreed with me in this opinion, which he thus strongly expressed:—'There are in that book thoughts, which, by long revolution in the great mind of Johnson, have been formed and polished like pebbles rolled in the ocean!'

That he was to some degree of excess a *true born Englishman*, so as to have entertained an undue prejudice against both the country and the people of Scotland, must be allowed. But it was a prejudice of the head, and not of the heart. He had no ill will to the Scotch; for, if he had been conscious of that, he never would have thrown himself into the bosom of their country, and trusted to the protection of its remote inhabitants with a fearless confidence. His remark upon the nakedness of the country, from its being denuded of trees, was made after having travelled two hundred miles along the Eastern coast, where certainly trees are not to be found near the road; and he said it was 'a map of the road' which he gave. His disbelief of the authenticity of the poems ascribed to Ossian, a Highland bard, was confirmed in the course of his journey, by a very strict examination of the evidence offered for it; and although their authenticity was made too much a national point by the Scotch, there were many respectable persons in that country, who did not concur in this: so that his judgement upon the question ought not to be decried, even by those who differ from him. As to myself, I can only say, upon a subject now become very uninteresting, that when the fragments of Highland poetry first came out, I was much pleased with their wild peculiarity, and was one of those who subscribed to enable their editor, Mr. Macpherson, then a young man, to make a search in the Highlands and Hebrides for a long poem in the Erse language, which was reported to be preserved somewhere in those regions. But when there came forth an Epick Poem in six books, with all the common circumstances of former compositions of that nature; and when, upon an attentive examination of it, there was found a perpetual recurrence of the same images which appear in the fragments: and when no ancient manuscript, to authenticate the work, was deposited in any publick library, though that was insisted on as a reasonable proof, *who* could forbear to doubt?

Johnson's grateful acknowledgements of kindness received in the course of this tour, completely refute the brutal reflections which have been thrown out against him, as if he had made an ungrateful return; and his delicacy in sparing in his book those who we find, from his letters to Mrs. Thrale, were just objects of censure, is much to be admired. His candour and amiable disposition is conspicuous from his conduct, when informed by Mr. Macleod, of Rasay, that he had committed a mistake, which gave that gentleman some uneasiness. He wrote him a courteous and kind letter, and inserted in the news-papers an advertisement, correcting the mistake.[1]

The observations of my friend Mr. Dempster in a letter written to me, soon after he had read Dr. Johnson's book, are so just and liberal, that they cannot be too often repeated.

* * * * * *

'There is nothing in the book, from beginning to end, that a Scotchman need to take amiss. What he says of the country is true; and his observations on the people are what must naturally occur to a sensible, observing, and reflecting inhabitant of a convenient metropolis, where a man on thirty pounds a year may be better accommodated with all the little wants of life, than Col or Sir Allan.

marginal line:
convenient metropolis
... Sir Allan [H]
underlined:
convenient [H]

'I am charmed with his researches concerning the Erse language, and the antiquity of their manuscripts. I am quite convinced; and I shall rank Ossian and his Fingals and Oscars, amongst the nursery tales, not the true history of our country, in all time to come.

'Upon the whole, the book cannot displease, for it has no pretensions. The authour neither says he is a geographer, nor an antiquarian, nor very learned in the history of Scotland, nor a naturalist, nor a fossilist. The manners of the people, and the face of the country, are all he attempts to describe, or seems to have thought of. Much were it to be wished, that they who have travelled into more remote, and of course more curious regions, had all possessed his good sense. Of the state of learning, his observations on Glasgow University show he has formed a very sound judgment. He understands our climate too; and he has accurately observed the changes, however slow

[1] See 'Journal of a Tour to the Hebrides,' 3d edit. p. 520.

and imperceptible to us, which Scotland has undergone, in consequence of the blessings of liberty and internal peace.'

* * * * * *

marginal line:
Mr. Knox . . . an
account [H]

Mr. Knox, another native of Scotland, who has since made the same tour, and published an account of it, is equally liberal. 'I have read (says he,) his book again and again, travelled with him from Berwick to Glenelg, through countries with which I am well acquainted; sailed with him from Glenelg to Rasay, Sky, Rum, Col, Mull, and Icolmkill, but have not been able to correct him in any matter of consequence. I have often admired the accuracy, the precision, and the justness of what he advances, respecting both the country and the people.

'The Doctor has every where delivered his sentiments with freedom, and in many instances with a seeming regard for the benefit of the inhabitants, and the ornament of the country. His remarks on the want of trees and hedges for shade, as well as for shelter to the cattle, are well founded, and merit the thanks, not the illiberal censure of the natives. He also felt for the distresses of the High-landers, and explodes with great propriety the bad management of the grounds, and the neglect of timber in the Hebrides.'

Having quoted Johnson's just compliments on the Rasay family, he says, 'On the other hand, I found this family equally lavish in their encomiums upon the Doctor's conversation, and his subsequent civilities to a young gentleman of that country, who, upon waiting upon him at London, was well received, and experienced all the attention and regard that a warm friend could bestow. Mr. Macleod having also been in London, waited upon the Doctor, who provided a magnificent and ex-pensive entertainment in honour of his old Hebridean acquaintance.'

And, talking of the military road by Fort Augustus, he says, 'By this road, though one of the most rugged in Great Britain, the celebrated Dr. Johnson passed from Inverness to the Hebride Isles. His observations on the country and people are extremely correct, judicious, and instructive.'[1]

[1] Page 103.

Mr. Tytler, the acute and able vindicator of Mary Queen of Scots, in one of his letters to Mr. James Elphinstone, published in that gentleman's 'Forty Years' Correspondence,' says, 'I read Dr. Johnson's Tour with very great pleasure. Some few errours he has fallen into, but of no great importance, and those are lost in the numberless beauties of his work.

'If I had leisure, I could perhaps point out the most exceptionable places; but at present I am in the country, and have not his book at hand. It is plain he meant to speak well of Scotland: and he has in my apprehension done us great honour in the most capital article, the character of the inhabitants.'

His private letters to Mrs. Thrale, written during the course of his journey, which therefore may be supposed to convey his genuine feelings at the time, abound in such benignant sentiment towards the people who showed him civilities, that no man whose temper is not very harsh and sour, can retain a doubt of the goodness of his heart.

It is painful to recollect with what rancour he was assailed by numbers of shallow irritable North Britons, on account of his supposed injurious treatment of their country and countrymen, in his 'Journey.' Had there been any just ground for such a charge, would the virtuous and candid Dempster have given his opinion of the book, in the terms in which I have quoted? Would the patriotick Knox[1] have spoken of it as he has done? Would Mr. Tytler, surely

'—— a *Scot*, if ever *Scot* there were,'

have expressed himself thus? And let me add, that, citizen of the world as I hold myself to be, I have that degree of predilection for my *natale solum*, nay, I have that just sense of the merit of an ancient nation, which has been ever renowned for its valour, which in former times maintained its independence against a powerful neighbour, and in modern times has been equally distinguished for its ingenuity and industry in civilized life, that I should have

[1] I observed with much regret, while the first edition of this work was passing through the press, (August 1790,) that this ingenious gentleman was dead.

felt a generous indignation at any injustice done to it. Johnson treated Scotland no worse than he did even his best friends, whose characters he used to give as they appeared to him, both in light and shade. Some people, who had not exercised their minds sufficiently, condemned him for censuring his friends. But Sir Joshua Reynolds, whose philosophical penetration and justness of thinking were not less known to those who lived with him, than his genius in his art admired by the world, explained his conduct thus: 'He was fond of discrimination, which he could not show without pointing out the bad as well as the good in every character; and as his friends were those whose characters he knew best, they afforded him the best opportunity for showing the acuteness of his judgment.'

He expressed to his friend Mr. Windham of Norfolk, his wonder at the extreme jealousy of the Scotch, and their resentment at having their country described by him as it really was; when to say that it was a country as good as England, would have been a gross falsehood. 'None of us, (said he,) would be offended if a foreigner who has travelled here should say, that vines and olives don't grow in England.' And as to his prejudice against the Scotch, which I always ascribed to that nationality which he observed in *them*, he said to the same gentleman, 'When I find a Scotchman, to whom an Englishman is as a Scotchman, that Scotchman shall be as an Englishman to me.' His intimacy with many gentlemen of Scotland, and his employing so many natives of that country as his amanuenses, prove that his prejudice was not virulent; and I have deposited in the British Museum, amongst other pieces of his writing, the following note in answer to one from me, asking if he would meet me at dinner at the Mitre, though a friend of mine, a Scotchman, was to be there:—'Mr. Johnson does not see why Mr. Boswell should suppose a Scotchman less acceptable than any other man. He will be at the Mitre.'

marginal line: he would . . . though a [H]

My much-valued friend Dr. Barnard, now Bishop of Killaloe, having once expressed to him an apprehension, that if he should visit Ireland he might treat the people of that country more unfavourably than he had done the

Scotch, he answered, with strong pointed double-edged wit, 'Sir, you have no reason to be afraid of me. The Irish two marginal lines: are not in a conspiracy to cheat the world by false represen- *merits of . . . one* tations of the merits of their countrymen. No, Sir; the *another* [H] Irish are a FAIR PEOPLE;—they never speak well of one another.'

Johnson told me of an instance of Scottish nationality, which made a very unfavourable impression upon his mind. A Scotchman of some consideration in London, solicited him to recommend by the weight of his learned authority, to be master of an English school, a person of whom he who recommended him confessed he knew no more but that he was his countryman. Johnson was shocked at this unconscientious conduct.

All the miserable cavillings against his 'Journey,' in news-papers, magazines, and other fugitive publications, I can speak from certain knowledge, only furnished him with sport. At last there came out a scurrilous volume, larger than Johnson's own, filled with malignant abuse, under a name, real or fictitious, of some low man in an obscure corner of Scotland, though supposed to be the work of another Scotchman, who has found means to make himself well known both in Scotland and England. The effect which it had upon Johnson was, to produce this pleasant observation to Mr. Seward, to whom he lent the book: 'This fellow must be a blockhead. They don't know how to go about their abuse. Who will read a five shilling book against me? No, Sir, if they had wit, they should have kept pelting me with pamphlets.'

'MR. BOSWELL TO DR. JOHNSON

'Edinburgh, Feb. 18, 1775

'YOU would have been very well pleased if you had dined with me to-day. I had for my guests, Macquharrie, young Maclean of Col, the successor of our friend, a very amiable man, though not marked with such active qualities as his brother; Mr. Maclean of Torloisk in Mull, a gentle-man of Sir Allan's family; and two of the clan Grant; so that the Highland and Hebridean genius reigned. We had a great deal of conversation about you, and drank your health in a bumper. The toast was not proposed by me, which is a circumstance to be remarked, for I am now so connected with you, that any thing that I can say or do to your honour has not the value of an additional compliment. It is only giving you a guinea out of that treasure of admiration which already belongs to you, and which is no hidden treasure; for I suppose my admiration of you is co-existent with the knowledge of my character.

'I find that the Highlanders and Hebrideans in general are much fonder of your "Journey," than the low-country or *hither* Scots. One of the Grants said to-day, that he was sure you were a man of a good heart, and a candid man, and seemed to hope he should be able to convince you of the antiquity of a good proportion of the poems of Ossian. After all that has passed, I think the matter is capable of being proved to a certain degree. I am told that Macpherson got one old Erse MS. from Clanranald, for the restitution of which he executed a formal obligation; and it is affirmed, that the Gaelick (call it Erse or call it Irish,) has been written in the Highlands and Hebrides for many centuries. It is reasonable to suppose, that such of the inhabitants as acquired any learning, possessed the art of writing as well as their Irish neighbours, and Celtick cousins; and the question is, can sufficient evidence be shewn of this?

'Those who are skilled in ancient writings can determine the age of MSS. or at least can ascertain the century in which they were written; and if men of veracity, who are so skilled, shall tell us that MSS. in the possession of families in the Highlands and isles, are the works of a remote age, I think we should be convinced by their testimony.

'There is now come to this city, Ranald Macdonald from the Isle of Egg, who has several MSS. of Erse poetry, which he wishes to publish by subscription. I have engaged to take three copies of the book, the price of which is to be six shillings, as I would subscribe for all the Erse that can be printed be it old or new, that the language may be preserved. This man says, that some of his manuscripts are ancient; and, to be sure, one of them which was shewn to me does appear to have the duskyness of antiquity.

*   *   *   *   *   *

'The enquiry is not yet quite hopeless, and I should think that the exact truth may be discovered, if proper means be used. I am, &c.

'JAMES BOSWELL'

'TO JAMES BOSWELL, ESQ.

'DEAR SIR,

'I AM sorry that I could get no books for my friends in Scotland. Mr. Strahan has at last promised to send two dozen to you. If they come put the name of my friends into them; you may cut them out,[1] and paste them with a little starch in the book.

'You then are going wild about Ossian. Why do you think any part can be proved? The dusky manuscript of Egg is probably not fifty years old; if it be an hundred, it proves nothing. The tale of Clanranald is no proof. Has Clanranald told it? Can he prove it? There are, I believe, no Erse manuscripts. None of the old families had a single letter in Erse that we heard of. You say it is likely that they could write. The learned, if any learned there were, could; but knowing by that learning, some written language, in that language they wrote, as letters had never been applied to their own. If there are manuscripts, let them be shewn, with some proof that they are not forged for the occasion. You say many can remember parts of Ossian. I believe all those parts are versions of the English; at least there is no proof of their antiquity.

'Macpherson is said to have made some translations himself; and having taught a boy to write it, ordered him to say that he had learnt it of his grandmother. The boy, when he grew up, told the story. This Mrs. Williams heard at Mr. Strahan's table. Don't be credulous; you know how little a Highlander can be trusted. Macpherson is, so far as I know, very quiet. Is not that proof enough? Every thing is against him. No visible manuscript: no inscription in the language: no correspondence among friends: no transaction of business, of which a single scrap remains in the ancient families. Macpherson's pretence is, that the character was Saxon. If he had not talked unskilfully of

---

[1] From a list in his hand-writing.

manuscripts, he might have fought with oral tradition much longer. As to Mr. Grant's information, I suppose he knows much less of the matter than ourselves.

'In the mean time, the bookseller says that the sale[1] is sufficiently quick. They printed four thousand. Correct your copy wherever it is wrong, and bring it up. Your friends will all be glad to see you. I think of going myself into the country about May.

'I am sorry that I have not managed to send the book sooner. I have left four for you, and do not restrict you absolutely to follow my directions in the distribution. You must use your own discretion.

'Make my compliments to Mrs. Boswell: I suppose she is now beginning to forgive me. I am, dear Sir, your humble servant,   'SAM. JOHNSON'
'Feb. 25, 1775.'

On Tuesday, March 21, I arrived in London; and on repairing to Dr. Johnson's before dinner, found him in his study, sitting with Mr. Peter Garrick, the elder brother of David, strongly resembling him in countenance and voice,[a] but of more sedate and placid manners. Johnson informed me, that 'though Mr. Beauclerk was in great pain, it was hoped he was not in danger, and that he now wished to consult Dr. Heberden, to try the effect of a *new understanding.*[b] Both at this interview, and in the evening at Mr. Thrale's, where he and Mr. Peter Garrick and I met again, he was vehement on the subject of the Ossian controversy; observing, 'We do not know that there are any ancient Erse manuscripts; and we have no other reason to disbelieve that there are men with three heads, but that we do not know that there are any such men.' He also was outrageous, upon his supposition that my countrymen 'loved Scotland better than truth,' saying, 'All of them,— nay not all,—but *droves* of them, would come up, and attest any thing for the honour of Scotland.' He also persevered in his wild allegation, that he questioned if there was a tree between Edinburgh and the English border older than himself. I assured him he was mistaken, and suggested that the proper punishment would be that he should

[a] *very true* [1]

[b] *what can be meant by the Words in Italick?* [1]

---

[1] Of his 'Journey to the Western Islands of Scotland.'

receive a stripe at every tree above a hundred years old, that was found within that space. He laughed, and said, 'I believe I might submit to it for a *baubee!*'

The doubts which, in my correspondence with him, I had ventured to state as to the justice and wisdom of the conduct of Great Britain towards the American colonies, while I at the same time requested that he would enable me to inform myself upon that momentous subject, he had altogether disregarded; and had recently published a pamphlet, entitled 'Taxation no Tyranny; an Answer to the Resolutions and Address of the American Congress.'*

He had long before indulged most unfavourable sentiments of our fellow-subjects in America. For, as early as 1769, I was told by Dr. John Campbell, that he had said of them, 'Sir, they are a race of convicts, and ought to be thankful for any thing we allow them short of hanging.'

Of this performance I avoided to talk with him; for I had now formed a clear and settled opinion, that the people of America were well warranted to resist a claim that their fellow-subjects in the mother-country should have the entire command of their fortunes, by taxing them without their own consent; and the extreme violence which it breathed, appeared to me so unsuitable to the mildness of a Christian philosopher, and so directly opposite to the principles of peace which he had so beautifully recommended in his pamphlet respecting Falkland's Islands, that I was sorry to see him appear in so unfavourable a light. Besides, I could not perceive in it that ability of argument, or that felicity of expression, for which he was, upon other occasions, so eminent. Positive assertion, sarcastical severity, and extravagant ridicule, which he himself reprobated as a test of truth, were united in this rhapsody.

That this pamphlet was written at the desire of those who were then in power, I have no doubt; and, indeed, he owned to me, that it had been revised and curtailed by some of them. He told me, that they had struck out one passage, which was to this effect: 'That the Colonists could with no solidity argue from their not having been taxed while in their infancy, that they should not now be taxed. We do not put a calf into the plow; we wait till he is an ox.' He said, 'They struck it out either critically as too ludicrous, or politically as too exasperating. I care not which. It was their business. If an architect says, I will build five stories, and the man who employs him says, I will have only three, the employer is to decide.' 'Yes, Sir, (said I,) in ordinary cases. But should it be so when the architect gives his skill and labour *gratis?*'

Unfavourable as I am constrained to say my opinion of this pamphlet was, yet, since it was congenial with the sentiments of numbers at that time, and as every thing relating to the writings of Dr. Johnson is of importance in literary history, I shall therefore insert some passages which were struck out, it does not appear why, either by himself or those who revised it. They appear printed in a few proof leaves of it in my possession, marked with corrections in his own hand-writing. I shall distinguish them by *Italicks*.

In the paragraph where he says, the Americans were incited to resistance by European intelligence from 'men whom they thought their friends, but who were friends only to themselves,' there followed,—'*and made by their selfishness, the enemies of their country.*'

And the next paragraph ran thus: 'On the original contrivers of mischief, *rather than on those whom they have deluded*, let an insulted nation pour out its vengeance.'

The paragraph which came next was in these words: '*Unhappy is that country in which men can hope for advancement by favouring its enemies.*[a] *The tranquillity of stable government is not always easily preserved against the machinations of single innovators; but what can be the hope of quiet, when factions hostile to the legislature can be openly formed and openly avowed?*'

After the paragraph which now concludes the pamphlet, there followed this, in which he certainly means the great Earl of Chatham, and glances at a certain popular Lord Chancellor.

'*If, by the fortune of war, they drive us utterly away, what they will do next can only be conjectured. If a new monarchy is erected, they will want a* KING. *He who first takes into his hand the sceptre of America, should have a name of good omen.* WILLIAM *has been known both a conqueror and deliverer; and perhaps England, however contemned, might yet supply them with* ANOTHER WILLIAM. *Whigs, indeed, are not willing to be governed; and it is possible that* KING WILLIAM *may be strongly inclined to guide their measures: but Whigs have been cheated like other mortals, and suffered their leader to become their tyrant, under the name of their* PROTECTOR. *What more they will receive from England, no man can tell. In their rudiments of empire they may want a* CHANCELLOR.'

Then came this paragraph:

'*Their numbers are, at present, not quite sufficient for the greatness which, in some form of government or other, is to rival the ancient monarchies; but by Dr. Franklin's rule of progression, they will, in a century and a quarter, be more than equal to the inhabitants of Europe. When the Whigs of America are thus multiplied, let the Princes of the earth tremble in their palaces. If they should continue to double and to double, their own hemisphere would not contain them. But let not our boldest oppugners of authority look forward with delight to this futurity of Whiggism.*'

How it ended I know not, as it is cut off abruptly at the foot of the last of these proof pages.

His pamphlets in support of the measures of administration were published on his own account, and he afterwards collected them into a volume, with the title of 'Political Tracts, by the Authour of the Rambler,' with this motto:

> '*Fallitur egregio quisquis sub Principe credit*
> *Servitium; nunquam libertas gratior extat*
> *Quam sub Rege pio.*'   CLAUDIANUS

These pamphlets drew upon him numerous attacks. Against the common weapons of literary warfare he was hardened; but there were two instances of animadversion which I communicated to him, and from what I could judge, both from his silence and his looks, appeared to me to impress him much.

One was, 'A Letter to Dr. Samuel Johnson, occasioned by his late political Publications.' It appeared previous to his 'Taxation no Tyranny,' and was written by Dr. Joseph Towers. In that performance, Dr. Johnson was treated with the respect due to so eminent a man, while his conduct as a political writer was boldly and pointedly arraigned, as inconsistent with the character of one, who, if he did employ his pen upon politicks, 'it might reasonably be expected should distinguish himself, not by party violence and rancour, but by moderation and by wisdom.'

It concluded thus: 'I would, however, wish you to remember, should you again address the publick under the character of a political writer, that luxuriance of imagination or energy of language, will ill compensate for the want of candour, of justice, and of truth. And I shall only add, that should I hereafter be disposed to read, as I heretofore have done, the most excellent of all your performances, "THE RAMBLER," the pleasure which I have been accustomed to find in it will be much diminished by the reflection that the writer of so moral, so elegant, and so valuable a work, was capable of prostituting his talents in such productions as "The False Alarm," the "Thoughts on the Transactions respecting Falkland's Islands," and "The Patriot." '

I am willing to do justice to the merit of Dr. Towers, of whom I will say, that although I abhor his Whiggish democratical notions and propensities, (for I will not call them principles,) I esteem him as an ingenious, knowing, and very convivial man.

The other instance was a paragraph of a letter to me, from my old and most intimate friend, the Reverend Mr. Temple, who wrote the character of Gray, which has had the honour to be adopted both by Mr. Mason and Dr. Johnson in their accounts of that poet. The words were, 'How can your great, I will not say your *pious*, but your *moral* friend, support the barbarous measures of administration, which they have not the face to ask even their infidel pensioner Hume to defend.'

However confident of the rectitude of his own mind, Johnson may have felt sincere uneasiness that his conduct should be erroneously imputed to unworthy motives, by good men; and that the influence of his valuable writings should on that account be in any degree obstructed or lessened.

He complained to a Right Honourable friend of distinguished talents and very elegant manners, with whom he maintained a long intimacy, and whose generosity towards him will afterwards appear, that his pension having been given to him as a literary character, he had been exclamation point: so much irritated [H] applied to by administration to write political pamphlets; and he was even so much irritated, that he declared his resolution to resign his pension. His friend showed him the impropriety of such a measure, and he afterwards expressed his gratitude, and said he had received good advice. To that friend he once signified a wish to have his pension secured to him for his life; but he neither asked nor received from government any reward whatsoever for his political labours.

On Friday, March 24, I met him at the LITERARY CLUB, where were Mr. Beauclerk, Mr. Langton, Mr. Colman, Dr. Percy, Mr. Vesey, Sir Charles Bunbury, Dr. George Fordyce, Mr. Steevens, and Mr. Charles Fox. Before he came in, we talked of his 'Journey to the Western Islands,' and of his coming away, 'willing to believe the second sight,'[1] which seemed to excite some ridicule. I was then so impressed with the truth of many of the stories of which I had been told, that I avowed my conviction, saying, 'He is only *willing* to believe: I *do* believe. The evidence is enough for me, though not for his great mind. What will not fill a quart bottle will fill a pint bottle. I am filled with belief.' 'Are you? (said Colman,) then cork it up.'[a]

I found his 'Journey' the common topick of conversation in London at this time, wherever I happened to be. At one of Lord Mansfield's formal Sunday evening conversations, strangely called *Levées*, his Lordship addressed me, 'We have all been reading your travels, Mr. Boswell.' I answered, 'I was but the humble attendant of Dr. Johnson.' The Chief Justice replied, with that air and manner which none, who ever saw and heard him, can forget, 'He speaks ill of nobody but Ossian.'

Johnson was in high spirits this evening at the club, and talked with great animation and success. He attacked Swift, as he used to do upon all occasions. 'The "Tale of a Tub" is so much superiour to his other writings, that one

marginal line:
with belief . . . then
cork [H]
[a] *very good.* [H]

[1] Johnson's 'Journey to the Western Islands of Scotland,' edit. 1785, p. 256.

can hardly believe he was the authour of it:[1] there is in it such a vigour of mind, such a swarm of thoughts, so much of nature, and art, and life.' I wondered to hear him say of 'Gulliver's Travels,' 'When once you have thought of big men and little men, it is very easy to do all the rest.' I endeavoured to make a stand for Swift, and tried to rouse those who were much more able to defend him; but in vain. Johnson at last, of his own accord, allowed very great merit to the inventory of articles found in the pocket of 'the Man Mountain,' particularly the description of his watch, which it was conjectured was his G O D, as he consulted it upon all occasions. He observed, that 'Swift put his name to but two things, (after he had a name to put,) "The Plan for the Improvement of the English Language," and the last "Drapier's Letter."'

From Swift, there was an easy transition to Mr. Thomas Sheridan.—J O H N S O N. 'Sheridan is a wonderful admirer of the tragedy of Douglas, and presented its authour with a gold medal. Some years ago, at a coffee-house in Oxford, I called to him, "Mr. Sheridan, Mr. Sheridan, how came you to give a gold medal to Home, for writing that foolish play?" This, you see, was wanton and insolent; but I *meant* to be wanton and insolent. A medal has no value but as a stamp of merit. And was Sheridan to assume to himself the right of giving that stamp? If Sheridan was magnificent enough to bestow a gold metal as an honorary reward of dramatick excellence, he should have requested one of the Universities to choose the person on whom it

[1] This doubt has been much agitated on both sides, I think without good reason. See Addison's 'Freeholder,' May 4, 1714; An Apology for the Tale of a Tub:—Dr. Hawkesworth's Preface to Swift's Works, and Swift's Letter to Tooke the Printer, and Tooke's Answer in that collection:—Sheridan's Life of Swift;—Mr. Courtenay's note on p. 3 of his 'Poetical Review of the Literary and Moral Character of Dr. Johnson;' and Mr. Cooksey's 'Essay on the Life and Character of John Lord Somers, Baron of Evesham.'

Dr. Johnson here speaks only to the *internal evidence*. I take leave to differ from him, having a very high estimation of the powers of Dr. Swift. His 'Sentiments of a Church-of-Englandman;' his 'Sermon on the Trinity,' and other serious pieces, prove his learning as well as his acuteness in logick and metaphysicks; and his various compositions of a different cast exhibit not only wit, humour, and ridicule; but a knowledge 'of nature, and art, and life;' a combination, therefore, of those powers, when (as the 'Apology' says,) 'the authour was young, his invention at the height, and his reading fresh in his head,' might surely produce '*The Tale of a Tub.*'

should be conferred. Sheridan had no right to give a stamp
of merit: it was counterfeiting Apollo's coin.'ª

On Monday, March 27, I breakfasted with him at Mr.
Strahan's. He told us, that he was engaged to go that
evening to Mrs. Abington's benefit. 'She was visiting some
ladies whom I was visiting, and begged that I would come
to her benefit. I told her I could not hear: but she insisted
so much on my coming, that it would have been brutal to
have refused her.' This was a speech quite characteristical.
He loved to bring forward his having been in the gay circles
of life; and he was, perhaps, a little vain of the solicitations
of this elegant and fashionable actress. He told us, the
play was to be 'The Hypocrite,' altered from Cibber's
'Nonjuror,' so as to satirize the Methodists. 'I do not think
(said he,) the character of the Hypocrite justly applicable
to the Methodists, but it was very applicable to the Non-
jurors. I once said to Dr. Madan, a clergyman of Ireland,
who was a great Whig, that perhaps a Nonjuror would
have been less criminal in taking the oaths imposed by the
ruling power, than refusing them; because refusing them,
necessarily laid him under almost an irresistible temptation
to be more criminal; for, a man *must* live, and if he pre-
cludes himself from the support furnished by the establishment, will probably be reduced to very wicked shifts to
maintain himself.'[1] BOSWELL. 'I should think, Sir, that

[1] This was not merely a cursory remark; for in his Life of Fenton he
observes, 'With many other wise and virtuous men, who at that time of
discord and debate [about the beginning of this century,] consulted conscience well or ill formed, more than interest, he doubted the legality of the
government; and refusing to qualify himself for publick employment, by
taking the oaths required, left the University without a degree.' This
conduct Johnson calls 'perverseness of integrity.'

The question concerning the morality of taking oaths, of whatever kind,
imposed by the prevailing power at the time, rather than to be excluded
from all consequence, or even any considerable usefulness in society, has
been agitated with all the acuteness of casuistry. It is related, that he who
devised the oath of abjuration, profligately boasted, that he had framed a
test which should 'damn one half of the nation, and starve the other.'

Upon minds not exalted to inflexible rectitude, or minds in which zeal for
a party is predominant to excess, taking that oath against conviction, may
have been palliated under the plea of necessity, or ventured upon in heat, as
upon the whole producing more good than evil.

At a county election in Scotland, many years ago, when there was a
warm contest between the friends of the Hanoverian succession, and those
against it, the oath of abjuration having been demanded, the freeholders

a man who took the oaths contrary to his principles, was a determined wicked man, because he was sure he was committing perjury, whereas a Nonjuror might be insensibly led to do what was wrong, without being so directly conscious of it.' JOHNSON. 'Why, Sir, a man who goes to bed to his patron's wife is pretty sure that he is committing wickedness.' BOSWELL. 'Did the nonjuring clergymen do so, Sir?' JOHNSON. 'I am afraid many of them did.'

I was startled at this argument, and could by no means think it convincing. Had not his own father complied with the requisition of government, (as to which he once observed to me, when I pressed him upon it, ' *That*, Sir, he was to settle with himself,') he would probably have thought more unfavourably of a Jacobite who took the oaths:

> '———— had he not resembled
> My father as he *swore*.——'

Mr. Strahan talked of launching into the great ocean of London, in order to have a chance for rising into eminence; and, observing that many men were kept back from trying their fortunes there, because they were born to a competency, said, 'Small certainties are the bane[a] of men of talents;' which Johnson confirmed. Mr. Strahan put Johnson in mind of a remark which he had made to him; 'There are few ways in which a man can be more innocently employed than in getting money.' 'The more one thinks of this, (said Strahan,) the juster it will appear.'[b]

Mr. Strahan had taken a poor boy from the country as an apprentice, upon Johnson's recommendation. Johnson having enquired after him, said, 'Mr. Strahan, let me have five guineas on account, and I'll give this boy one. Nay, if a man recommends a boy, and does nothing for him, it is sad work. Call him down.'

I followed him into the court yard, behind Mr. Strahan's house; and there I had a proof of what I had heard him profess, that he talked alike to all. 'Some people tell you

[a] *Content! The bane of Industry says Mandevil* [1]

[b] very natural for Strahan to think so. [H]

upon one side rose to go away. Upon which a very sanguine gentleman, one of their number, ran to the door to stop them, calling out with much earnestness, 'Stay, stay, my friends, and let us swear the rogues out of it!'

that they let themselves down to the capacity of their hearers. I never do that. I speak uniformly, in as intelligible a manner as I can.'

'Well, my boy, how do you go on?'—'Pretty well, Sir; but they are afraid I an't strong enough for some parts of the business.' JOHNSON. 'Why, I shall be sorry for it; for when you consider with how little mental power and corporeal labour a printer can get a guinea a week, it is a very desirable occupation for you. Do you hear,—take all the pains you can; and if this does not do, we must think of some other way of life for you. There's a guinea.'

Here was one of the many, many instances of his active benevolence. At the same time, the slow and sonorous solemnity with which, while he bent himself down, he addressed a little thick short-legged boy, contrasted with the boy's aukwardness and awe, could not but excite some ludicrous emotions.

I met him at Drury-lane play-house in the evening. Sir Joshua Reynolds, at Mrs. Abington's request, had promised to bring a body of wits to her benefit; and having secured forty places in the front boxes, had done me the honour to put me in the group. Johnson sat on the seat directly behind me; and as he could neither see nor hear at such a distance from the stage, he was wrapped up in grave abstraction, and seemed quite a cloud, amidst all the sunshine of glitter and gaiety. I wondered at his patience in sitting out a play of five acts, and a farce of two. He said very little; but after the prologue to 'Bon Ton' had been spoken, which he could hear pretty well from the more slow and distinct utterance, he talked on prologue-writing, and observed, 'Dryden has written pro-logues superiour to any that David Garrick has written; but David Garrick has written more good prologues than Dryden has done. It is wonderful that he has been able to write such variety of them.'

At Mr. Beauclerk's, where I supped, was Mr. Garrick, whom I made happy with Johnson's praise of his prologues; and I suppose, in gratitude to him, he took up one of his favourite topicks, the nationality of the Scotch, which he maintained in a pleasant manner, with the aid of a little poetical fiction. 'Come, come, don't deny it: they are really national. Why, now, the Adams are as liberal-minded men as any in the world: but, I don't know how it is, all their workmen are Scotch. You are, to be sure, wonderfully free from that nationality: but so it happens, that you employ the only Scotch shoeblack in London.' He imitated the manner of his old master with ludicrous exaggeration; repeating, with pauses and half-whistlings interjected,

> '*Os homini sublime dedit,—cælumque tueri*
> *Jussit,—et erectos ad sidera—tollere vultus;*'

looking downwards all the time, and, while pronouncing the four last words, absolutely touching the ground with a kind of contorted gesticulation.

Garrick, however, when he pleased, could imitate Johnson very exactly; for that great actor, with his distinguished powers of expression which were so universally admired, possessed also an admirable talent of mimickry. He was always jealous that Johnson spoke lightly of him. I recollect his exhibiting him to me one day, as if saying, 'Davy has some convivial pleasantry about him, but 'tis a futile[a] fellow;' which he uttered perfectly with the tone and air of Johnson.

a little inserted after futile [H]

I cannot too frequently request of my readers, while they peruse my account of Johnson's conversation, to endeavour to keep in mind his deliberate and strong utterance. His mode of speaking was indeed very impressive;[1] and I wish it could be preserved as musick is written, according to the very ingenious method of Mr. Steele,[2] who has shown how the recitation of Mr. Garrick,

[1] My noble friend Lord Pembroke said once to me at Wilton, with a happy pleasantry and some truth, that 'Dr. Johnson's sayings would not appear so extraordinary, were it not for his *bow-wow way*.' The sayings themselves are generally of sterling merit; but, doubtless, his *manner* was an addition to their effect; and therefore should be attended to as much as may be. It is necessary, however, to guard those who were not acquainted with him, against overcharged imitations or caricatures of his manner, which are frequently attempted, and many of which are second-hand copies from the late Mr. Henderson the actor, who, though a good mimick of some persons, did not represent Johnson correctly.

[2] See '*Prosodia Rationalis;* or, an Essay towards establishing the Melody and Measure of Speech, to be expressed and perpetuated by peculiar Symbols.' London, 1779.

and other eminent speakers, might be transmitted to posterity *in score*.[1]

Next day I dined with Johnson at Mr. Thrale's. He attacked Gray, calling him 'a dull fellow.' BOSWELL. 'I understand he was reserved, and might appear dull in company; but surely he was not dull in poetry.' JOHNSON. 'Sir, he was dull in company, dull in his closet, dull every where. He was dull in a new way, and that made many people think him GREAT. He was a mechanical poet.' He then repeated some ludicrous lines, which have escaped my memory, and said, 'Is not that GREAT, like his Odes?' Mrs. Thrale maintained that his Odes were melodious; upon which he exclaimed,

'Weave the warp, and weave the woof;'—

I added, in a solemn tone,

'The winding-sheet of Edward's race.'

'*There* is a good line.'—'Ay, (said he,) and the next line is a good one,' (pronouncing it contemptuously;)

'Give ample verge and room enough.'—

'No, Sir, there are but two good stanzas in Gray's poetry, which are in his "Elegy in a Country Churchyard."' He then repeated the stanza,

'For who to dumb forgetfulness a prey,' &c.

mistaking one word; for instead of *precincts* he said *confines*. He added, 'The other Stanza I forget.'

A young lady who had married a man much her inferiour in rank being mentioned, a question arose how a woman's relations should behave to her in such a situation; and, while I recapitulate the debate, and recollect what has since happened, I cannot but be struck in a manner

---

[1] I use the phrase *in score*, as Dr. Johnson has explained it in his Dictionary. '*A song in* SCORE, the words with the musical notes of a song annexed.' But I understand that in scientifick propriety it means all the parts of a musical composition noted down in the characters by which it is exhibited to the eye of the skilful.

[It was *declamation* that Steele pretended to reduce to notation by new characters. This he called the *melody* of speech, not the *harmony*, which the term in *score* implies. BURNEY.][a]

[a] *Burney I suppose* [1: text reads *B.*]

that delicacy forbids me to express. While I contended that she ought to be treated with an inflexible steadiness of displeasure, Mrs. Thrale was all for mildness and forgiveness, and, according to the vulgar phrase, 'making the best of a bad bargain.' JOHNSON. 'Madam, we must distinguish. Were I a man of rank, I would not let a daughter starve who had made a mean marriage; but having voluntarily degraded herself from the station which she was originally entitled to hold, I would support her only in that which she herself had chosen; and would not put her on a level with my other daughters. You are to consider, Madam, that it is our duty to maintain the subordination of civilized society; and when there is a gross and shameful deviation from rank, it should be punished so as to deter others from the same perversion.'

marginal line: *station which . . . herself had* [H]

After frequently considering this subject, I am more and more confirmed in what I then meant to express, and which was sanctioned by the authority, and illustrated by the wisdom of Johnson; and I think it of the utmost consequence to the happiness of Society, to which subordination is absolutely necessary. It is weak and contemptible, and unworthy, in a parent to relax in such a case. It is sacrificing general advantage to private feelings. And let it be considered, that the claim of a daughter who has acted thus, to be restored to her former situation, is either fantastical or unjust. If there be no value in the distinction of rank, what does she suffer by being kept in the situation to which she has descended? If there be a value in that distinction, it ought to be steadily maintained. If indulgence be shown to such conduct, and the offenders know that in a longer or shorter time they shall be received as well as if they had not contaminated their blood by a base alliance, the great check upon that inordinate caprice which generally occasions low marriages, will be removed, and the fair and comfortable order of improved life will be miserably disturbed.

Lord Chesterfield's letters being mentioned, Johnson said, 'It was not to be wondered at that they had so great a sale, considering that they were the letters of a statesman, a wit, one who had been so much in the mouths of mankind, one long accustomed *virûm volitare per ora.*'

On Friday, March 31, I supped with him and some friends at a tavern. One of the company attempted,

with two ᵃ much forwardness, to rally him on his late appearance at the theatre; but had reason to repent of his temerity. 'Why, Sir, did you go to Mrs. Abington's benefit? Did you see?' JOHNSON. 'No, Sir.' 'Did you hear?' JOHNSON. 'No, Sir.' 'Why then, Sir, did you go?'

JOHNSON. 'Because, Sir, she is a favourite of the publick; and when the publick cares the thousandth part for you

that it does for her, I will go to your benefit too.' ᵇ

Next morning I won a small bet from Lady Diana Beauclerk, by asking him as to one of his particularities, which her Ladyship laid I durst not do. It seems he had been frequently observed at the Club to put into his pocket the Seville oranges, after he had squeezed the juice of them into the drink which he made for himself. Beauclerk and Garrick talked of it to me, and seemed to think that he had a strange unwillingness to be discovered. We could not divine what he did with them; and this was the bold question to be put. I saw on his table the spoils of the preceding night, some fresh peels nicely scraped and cut into pieces. 'O, Sir, (said I,) I now partly see what you do with the squeezed oranges which you put into your pocket at the Club.' JOHNSON. 'I have a great love for them.' BOSWELL. 'And pray, Sir, what do you do with them? You scrape them it seems, very neatly, and what next?' JOHNSON. 'Let them dry, Sir.' BOSWELL. 'And what next?' JOHNSON. 'Nay, Sir, you shall know their fate no further.' BOSWELL. 'Then the world must be left in the dark. It must be said (assuming a mock solemnity,) he scraped them and let them dry, but what he did with them next, he never could be prevailed upon to tell.' JOHNSON. 'Nay, Sir, you should say it more emphatically: —he could not be prevailed upon, even by his dearest friends, to tell.'

He had this morning received his Diploma as Doctor of Laws from the University of Oxford. He did not vaunt of his new dignity, but I understood he was highly pleased with it. I shall here insert the progress and completion of that high academical honour, in the same manner as I have traced his obtaining that of Master of Arts.

To the Reverend Dr. FOTHERGILL, *Vice-Chancellor of the University of* Oxford, *to be communicated to the Heads of Houses, and proposed in Convocation.*

'MR. VICE-CHANCELLOR AND GENTLEMEN,

'The honour of the degree of M. A. by diploma, formerly conferred upon Mr. SAMUEL JOHNSON, in consequence of his having eminently distinguished himself by the publication of a series of Essays, excellently calculated to form the manners of the people, and in which the cause of religion and morality has been maintained and recommended by the strongest powers of argument and elegance of language, reflected an equal degree of lustre upon the University itself.

'The many learned labours which have since that time employed the attention and displayed the abilities of that great man, so much to the advancement of literature and the benefit of the community, render him worthy of more distinguished honours in the Republick of letters: and I persuade myself, that I shall act agreeably to the sentiments of the whole University, in desiring that it may be proposed in Convocation to confer on him the degree of Doctor in Civil Law by diploma, to which I readily give my consent; and am,

'Mr. Vice-Chancellor and Gentlemen,

'Your affectionate friend and servant,

'Downing-street,   'NORTH'[1]
March 23, 1775.'

DIPLOMA

'*CANCELLARIUS, Magistri, et Scholares Universitatis Oxoniensis omnibus ad quos presentes Literæ pervenerint, Salutem in Domino Sempiternam.*

'SCIATIS, *virum illustrem,* SAMUELEM JOHNSON, *in omni humaniorum literarum genere eruditum, omniumque scientiarum comprehensione felicissimum, scriptis suis, ad popularium mores formandos summâ verborum elegantiâ ac sententiarum gravitate compositis, ita olim inclaruisse, ut dignus videretur cui ab Academiâ suâ eximia quædam laudis præmia deferentur, quique venerabilem Magistrorum Ordinem summâ cum dignitate cooptaretur:*

[1] Extracted from the Convocation Register, Oxford.

'*Cùm verò eundem clarissimum virum tot posteà tantique labores, in patriâ præsertim linguâ ornandâ et stabiliendâ feliciter impensi, ita insigniverint, ut in Literarum Republicâ* PRINCEPS *jam et* PRIMARIUS *jure habeatur;* Nos, CANCELLARIUS, *Magistri, et Scholares Universitatis Oxoniensis, quò talis viri merita pari honoris remuneratione exæquentur, et perpetuum suæ simul laudis, nostræque ergà literas propensissimæ voluntatis extet monumentum, in solenni Convocatione Doctorum et Magistrorum Regentium, et non Regentium, prædictum* SAMUELEM JOHNSON *Doctorem in Jure Civili renunciavimus et constituimus, eumque virtute præsentis Diplomatis singulis juribus, privilegiis et honoribus, ad istum gradum quàquà pertinentibus, frui et gaudere jussimus. In cujus rei testimonium commune Universitatis Oxoniensis sigillum præsentibus apponi fecimus.*

'*Datum in Domo nostræ Convocationis die tricesimo Mensis Martii, Anno Domini Millesimo septingentesimo, septuagesimo quinto.*'[1]

'*Viro Reverendo* THOMÆ FOTHERGILL, *S.T.P.*
Universitatis Oxoniensis Vice-Cancellario
'*S.P.D.*

'SAM. JOHNSON

'*MULTIS non est opus, ut testimonium quo, te præside, Oxonienses nomen meum posteris commendârunt, quali animo acceperim compertum faciam. Nemo sibi placens non lætatur; nemo sibi non placet, qui vobis, literarum arbitris, placere potuit. Hoc*

[1] The original is in my possession. He shewed me the Diploma, and allowed me to read it, but would not consent to my taking a copy of it, fearing perhaps that I should blaze it abroad in his life-time. His objection to this appears from his 99th letter to Mrs. Thrale, whom in that letter he thus scolds for the grossness of her flattery of him.—'The other Oxford news is, that they have sent me a degree of Doctor of Laws, with such praises in the Diploma as perhaps ought to make me ashamed; they are very like your praises. I wonder whether I shall ever show it to you.'

It is remarkable that he never, so far as I know, assumed his title of *Doctor*, but called himself *Mr.* Johnson, as appears from many of his cards or notes to myself, and I have seen many from him to other persons, in which he uniformly takes that designation.—I once observed on his table a letter directed to him with the addition of *Esquire*, and objected to it as being a designation inferiour to that of Doctor; but he checked me, and seemed pleased with it, because, as I conjectured, he liked to be sometimes taken out of the class of literary men, and to be merely *genteel,—un gentilhomme comme un autre.*

tamen habet incommodi tantum beneficium, quod mihi nunquam posthâc sine vestræ famæ detrimento vel labi liceat vel cessare; semperque sit timendum ne quod mihi tam eximiæ laudi est, vobis aliquando fiat opprobrio. Vale.'[1]

'*7. Id. Apr. 1775.*'

He revised some sheets of Lord Hailes's 'Annals of Scotland,' and wrote a few notes on the margin with red ink, which he bade me tell his Lordship did not sink into the paper, and might be wiped off with a wet sponge, so that he did not spoil his manuscript.—I observed to him that there were very few of his friends so accurate as that I could venture to put down in writing what they told me as his sayings. JOHNSON. 'Why should you write down *my* sayings?' BOSWELL. 'I write them when they are good.' JOHNSON. 'Nay, you may as well write down the sayings of any one else that are good.' But *where*, I might with great propriety have added, can I find such?

I visited him by appointment in the evening, and we drank tea with Mrs. Williams. He told me that he had been in the company of a gentleman whose extraordinary travels had been much the subject of conversation. But I found he had not listened to him with that full confidence, without which there is little satisfaction in the society of travellers. I was curious to hear what opinion so able a judge as Johnson had formed of his abilities, and I asked if he was not a man of sense. JOHNSON. 'Why, Sir, he is not a distinct relater; and I should say, he is neither abounding nor deficient in sense. I did not perceive any superiority of understanding.' BOSWELL. 'But will you not allow him a nobleness of resolution, in penetrating into distant regions?' JOHNSON. 'That, Sir, is not to the present purpose: we are talking of sense. A fighting cock has a nobleness of resolution.'

Next day, Sunday, April 2, I dined with him at Mr. Hoole's. We talked of Pope. JOHNSON. 'He wrote his "Dunciad" for fame. That was his primary motive. Had it not been for that, the dunces might have railed against him till they were weary, without his troubling himself

---

[1] ['The original is in the hands of Dr. Fothergill, then Vice-Chancellor, who made this transcript.' T. WARTON.]

about them. He delighted to vex them, no doubt; but he had more delight in seeing how well he could vex them.'

The 'Odes to Obscurity and Oblivion,' in ridicule of 'cool Mason and warm Gray,' being mentioned, Johnson said, 'They are Colman's best things.' Upon its being observed that it was believed these Odes were made by Colman and Lloyd jointly;—JOHNSON. 'Nay, Sir, how can two people make an Ode? Perhaps one made one of them, and one the other.' I observed that two people had made a play, and quoted the anecdote of Beaumont and Fletcher, who were brought under suspicion of treason, because while concerting the plan of a tragedy when sitting together at a tavern, one of them was overheard saying to the other, 'I'll kill the King.'[a] JOHNSON. 'The first of these Odes is the best; but they are both good. They exposed a very bad kind of writing.' BOSWELL. 'Surely, Sir, Mr. Mason's "Elfrida" is a fine Poem: at least you will allow there are some good passages in it.' JOHNSON. 'There are now and then some good imitations of Milton's bad manner.'

I often wondered at his low estimation of the writings of Gray and Mason. Of Gray's poetry I have in a former part of this work expressed my high opinion; and for that of Mr. Mason I have ever entertained a warm admiration. His 'Elfrida' is exquisite, both in poetical description and moral sentiment; and his 'Caractacus' is a noble drama. Nor can I omit paying my tribute of praise to some of his smaller poems, which I have read with pleasure, and which no criticism shall persuade me not to like. If I wondered at Johnson's not tasting the works of Mason and Gray, still more have I wondered at their not tasting his works: that they should be insensible to his energy of diction, to his splendour of images, and comprehension of thought. Tastes may differ as to the violin, the flute, the hautboy; in short, all the lesser instruments: but who can be insensible to the powerful impressions of the majestic organ?

His 'Taxation no Tyranny' being mentioned, he said, 'I think I have not been attacked enough for it. Attack is the re-action; I never think I have hit hard, unless it re-bounds.' BOSWELL. 'I don't know, Sir, what you would

underlined:
I'll kill the King [1]

[a] *The same is related in French of Scuderi & his Sister* [1]

be at. Five or six shots of small arms in every newspaper,
and repeated cannonading in pamphlets, might, I think,
satisfy you. But, Sir, you'll never make out this match, of
which we have talked, with a certain political lady,[a] since
you are so severe against her principles.' JOHNSON. 'Nay,
Sir, I have the better chance for that. She is like the Ama-
zons of old; she must be courted by the sword. But I have
not been severe upon her.' BOSWELL. 'Yes, Sir, you have
made her ridiculous.' JOHNSON. 'That was already done,
Sir. To endeavour to make *her* ridiculous, is like blacking
the chimney.'

I put him in mind that the landlord at Ellon in Scotland
said, that he heard he was the greatest man in England,—
next to Lord Mansfield. 'Ay, Sir, (said he,) the exception
defined the idea. A Scotchman could go no farther:

"The force of Nature could no farther go."'

Lady Miller's collection of verses by fashionable people,
which were put into her Vase at Batheaston villa, near
Bath, in competition for honorary prizes, being mentioned,
he held them very cheap: '*Bouts rimés* (said he) is a mere
conceit, and an *old* conceit *now;* I wonder how people were
persuaded to write in that manner for this lady.' I named
a gentleman of his acquaintance who wrote for the Vase.
JOHNSON. 'He was a blockhead for his pains.' BOSWELL.
'The Duchess of Northumberland wrote.' JOHNSON. 'Sir,
the Duchess of Northumberland may do what she pleases:
nobody will say any thing to a lady of her high rank. But
I should be apt to throw ******'s verses in his face.'

I talked of the cheerfulness of Fleet-street, owing to the
constant quick succession of people which we perceive
passing through it. JOHNSON. 'Why, Sir, Fleet-street has
a very animated appearance; but I think the full tide of
human existence is at Charing-cross.'

He made the common remark on the unhappiness which
men who have led a busy life experience, when they retire
in expectation of enjoying themselves at ease, and that
they generally languish for want of their habitual occupation, and wish to return to it. He mentioned as strong
an instance of this as can well be imagined.[b] 'An eminent

[a] *Mrs. Macaulay.* [H]

[b] *It was Murphy's
Story originally, who
always told it of dip-
ping Night instead of
melting day.* [H]
*It was originally a
Story of Murphy's, &
The Melting : day was
Dipping Night; I re-
member.* [I]

tallow-chandler in London, who had acquired a considerable fortune, gave up the trade in favour of his foreman, and went to live at a country-house near town. He soon grew weary, and paid frequent visits to his old shop, where he desired they might let him know their *melting-days*, and he would come and assist them; which he accordingly did. Here, Sir, was a man to whom the most disgusting circumstances in the business to which he had been used, was a relief from idleness.'

On Wednesday, April 5, I dined with him at Messieurs Dillys, with Mr. John Scott of Amwell, the Quaker, Mr. Langton, Mr. Miller, (now Sir John,) and Dr. Thomas Campbell, an Irish Clergyman, whom I took the liberty of inviting to Mr. Dilly's table, having seen him at Mr. Thrale's, and been told that he had come to England chiefly with a view to see Dr. Johnson, for whom he entertained the highest veneration. He[a] has since published 'A Philosophical Survey of the South of Ireland,' a very entertaining book, which has, however, one fault:—that it assumes the fictitious character of an Englishman.

We talked of public speaking. JOHNSON. 'We must not estimate a man's powers by his being able or not able to deliver his sentiments in publick. Isaac Hawkins Browne, one of the first wits of this country, got into Parliament, and never opened his mouth. For my own part, I think it is more disgraceful never to try to speak, than to try it, and fail; as it is more disgraceful not to fight, than to fight and be beaten.' This argument appeared to me fallacious; for if a man has not spoken, it may be said that he would have done very well if he had tried; whereas, if he has tried and failed, there is nothing to be said for him. 'Why then, (I asked,) is it thought disgraceful for a man not to fight, and not disgraceful not to speak in publick?' JOHNSON. 'Because there may be other reasons for a man's not speaking in publick than want of resolution: he may have nothing to say, (laughing.) Whereas, Sir, you know courage is reckoned the greatest of all virtues; because, unless a man has that virtue, he has no security for preserving any other.'

He observed, that 'the statutes against bribery were intended to prevent upstarts with money from getting into Parliament:' adding, that 'if he were a gentleman of

[a] *Dr. Campbell was a very tall handsome Man, & speaking of some other* Highbernian, *used this Expression—indeed now, & upon my Honour Sir; I am but a* Twitter *to him.* [1: *speaking of other* Highbernians . . . *a* twitter *to you.*] [H & 1]

landed property, he would turn out all his tenants who did not vote for the candidate whom he supported.' LANGTON. 'Would not that, Sir, be checking the freedom of election?' JOHNSON. 'Sir, the law does not mean that the privilege of voting should be independent of old family interest; of the permanent property of the country.'

On Thursday, April 6, I dined with him at Mr. Thomas Davies's, with Mr. Hicky the painter, and my old acquaintance Mr. Moody, the player.

Dr. Johnson, as usual, spoke contemptuously of Colley Cibber. 'It is wonderful that a man, who for forty years had lived with the great and the witty, should have acquired so ill the talents of conversation: and he had but half to furnish; for one half of what he said was oaths.' He, however, allowed considerable merit to some of his comedies, and said there was no reason to believe that the 'Careless Husband' was not written by himself. Davies said, he was the first dramatick writer who introduced genteel ladies upon the stage. Johnson refuted his observation by instancing several such characters in comedies before his time. DAVIES. (trying to defend himself from a charge of ignorance,) 'I mean genteel moral characters.' 'I think, (said Hicky,) gentility and morality are inseparable.' BOSWELL. 'By no means, Sir. The genteelest characters are often the most immoral. Does not Lord Chesterfield give precepts for uniting wickedness and the graces? A man, indeed, is not genteel when he gets drunk; but most vices may be committed very genteely: a man may debauch his friend's wife genteely: he may cheat at cards genteely.' HICKY. 'I do not think that is genteel.' BOSWELL. 'Sir, it may not be like a gentleman, but it may be genteel.' JOHNSON. 'You are meaning two different things. One means exteriour grace; the other honour. It is certain that a man may be very immoral with exteriour grace. Lovelace, in "Clarissa," is a very genteel and a very wicked character. Tom Hervey, who died t'other day, though a vicious man, was one of the genteelest men that ever lived.' Tom Davies instanced Charles the Second. JOHNSON, (taking fire at any attack upon that Prince, for whom he had an extraordinary partiality,) 'Charles the Second was licentious in his practice; but he always had a reverence for what was good. Charles the Second knew his people, and rewarded merit. The Church was at no time better filled than in his reign. He was the best King we have had from his time till the reign of his present Majesty, except James the Second, who was a very good King, but unhappily believed that it was necessary for the salvation of his subjects that they should be Roman Catholicks. *He* had the merit of endeavouring to do what he thought was for the salvation of the souls of his subjects, till he lost a great Empire. *We*, who thought that we should *not* be saved if we were Roman Catholicks, had the merit of maintaining our religion, at the expence of submitting ourselves to the government of King William, (for it could not be done otherwise,)—to the government of one of the most worthless scoundrels that ever existed. No, Charles the Second was not such a man as ———, (naming another King.) He did not destroy his father's will.

'He took money, indeed, from France: but he did not betray those over whom he ruled: he did not let the French fleet pass ours. George the First knew nothing, and desired to know nothing; did nothing, and desired to do nothing; and the only good thing that is told of him is, that he wished to restore the crown to its hereditary successor.' He roared with prodigious violence against George the Second. When he ceased, Moody interjected, in an Irish tone, and with a comick look, 'Ah! poor George the Second.'

I mentioned that Dr. Thomas Campbell had come from Ireland to London, principally to see Dr. Johnson. He seemed angry at this observation. DAVIES. 'Why, you know, Sir, there came a man from Spain to see Livy;[1] and Corelli came to England to see Purcell,[2] and when he heard he was dead, went directly back again to Italy.' JOHNSON. 'I should not have wished to be dead to disappoint Campbell, had he been so foolish as you represent him; but I should have wished to have been a hundred miles off.' This was apparently perverse; and I do believe it was not his real way of thinking: he could not but like a man who came so far to see him. He laughed with some

a no truly; nor wd. he have come on any such Errand; Purcell did certainly go to hear Corelli & did return without caring for ought else in Italy. They shd. tell their Stories right.
[1]

[1] Plin. Epist. Lib. ii. Ep. 3.
[2] [Mr. Davies was here mistaken. Corelli never was in England.[a]
BURNEY.]

complacency, when I told him Campbell's odd expression to me concerning him: 'That having seen such a man, was a thing to talk of a century hence,'—as if he could live so long.[a]

We got into an argument whether the Judges who went to India might with propriety engage in trade. Johnson warmly maintained that they might, 'For why (he urged) should not Judges get riches, as well as those who deserve them less?' I said, they should have sufficient salaries, and have nothing to take off their attention from the affairs of the publick. JOHNSON. 'No Judge, Sir, can give his whole attention to his office; and it is very proper that he should employ what time he has to himself, to his own advantage, in the most profitable manner.' 'Then, Sir, (said Davies, who enlivened the dispute by making it somewhat dramatick,) he may become an insurer; and when he is going to the bench, he may be stopped,—"Your Lordship cannot go yet; here is a bunch of invoices: several ships are about to sail."' JOHNSON. 'Sir, you may as well say a Judge should not have a house; for they may come and tell him, "Your Lordship's house is on fire;" and so, instead of minding the business of his Court, he is to be occupied in getting the engine with the greatest speed. There is no end of this. Every Judge who has land, trades to a certain extent in corn or in cattle; and in the land itself, undoubtedly. His steward acts for him, and so do clerks for a great merchant. A Judge may be a farmer; but he is not to geld his own pigs. A Judge may play a little at cards for his amusement; but he is not to play at marbles, or chuckfarthing in the Piazza. No, Sir, there is no profession to which a man gives a very great proportion of his time. It is wonderful when a calculation is made, how little the mind is actually employed in the discharge of any profession. No man would be a Judge, upon the condition of being totally a Judge.[b] The best employed lawyer has his mind at work but for a small proportion of his time: a great deal of his occupation is merely mechanical. —I once wrote for a magazine: I made a calculation, that if I should write but a page a day, at the same rate, I should, in ten years, write nine volumes in folio, of an ordinary size and print.' BOSWELL. 'Such as Carte's History?' JOHNSON.

[a] *I dare say he did say so; he was a fine Showy talking Man—Johnson liked him of all Things in a Year or Two.* [H & I]

[b] *A* brazen Face, *an* Iron Constitution, *&* a Leaden Bottom, *are by Sir John Popham said to be necessary for every* Judge: *The lastnamed Requisite is for* [the] *Purpose of holding him in his Seat to hear Senseless Arguments.* [H]

'Yes, Sir, when a man writes from his own mind, he writes very rapidly.[1] The greatest part of a writer's time is spent in reading, in order to write; a man will turn over half a library, to make one book.'

I argued warmly against the Judges trading, and mentioned Hale as an instance of a perfect Judge, who devoted himself entirely to his office. JOHNSON. 'Hale, Sir, attended to other things besides law: he left a great estate.' BOSWELL. 'That was because what he got, accumulated without any exertion and anxiety on his part.'

While the dispute went on, Moody once tried to say something on our side. Tom Davies clapped him on the back, to encourage him. Beauclerk, to whom I mentioned this circumstance, said, 'that he could not conceive a more humiliating situation than to be clapped on the back by Tom Davies.'[a]

a *how severe!* [1]

We spoke of Rolt, to whose Dictionary of Commerce, Dr. Johnson wrote the Preface. JOHNSON. 'Old Gardner, the bookseller, employed Rolt and Smart to write a monthly miscellany, called, "The Universal Visitor." There was a formal written contract, which Allen the printer saw. Gardner thought as you do of the Judge. They were bound to write nothing else; they were to have, I think, a third of the profits of his sixpenny pamphlet; and the contract was for ninety-nine years. I wish I had thought of giving this to Thurlow, in the cause about Literary Property. What an excellent instance would it have been of the oppression of booksellers towards poor authours!'[2] (smiling). Davies, zealous for the honour of *the Trade*, said, Gardner was not properly a bookseller. JOHNSON. 'Nay, Sir; he certainly was a bookseller. He had served his time regularly, was a member of the Stationers' company, kept a shop in the face of mankind, purchased copyright, and was a *bibliopole*, Sir, in every sense. I wrote for some months

[1] Johnson certainly did, who had a mind stored with knowledge, and teeming with imagery: but the observation is not applicable to writers in general.

[2] There has probably been some mistake as to the terms of this supposed extraordinary contract, the recital of which from hearsay afforded Johnson so much play for his sportive acuteness. Or if it was worded as he supposed, it is so strange that I should conclude it was a joke. Mr. Gardner, I am assured, was a worthy and liberal man.

in "The Universal Visitor," for poor Smart, while he was mad, not then knowing the terms on which he was engaged to write, and thinking I was doing him good. I hoped his wits would soon return to him. Mine returned to me, and I wrote in "The Universal Visitor" no longer.'

Friday, April 7, I dined with him at a tavern, with a numerous company. JOHNSON. 'I have been reading "Twiss's Travels in Spain," which are just come out. They are as good as the first book of travels that you will take up. They are as good as those of Keysler or Blainville: nay, as Addison's,[1] if you except the learning. They are not so good as Brydone's, but they are better than Pococke's. I have not, indeed, cut the leaves yet; but I have read in them where the pages are open, and I do not suppose that what is in the pages which are closed is worse than what is in the open pages.—It would seem (he added,) that Addison had not acquired much Italian learning, for we do not find it introduced into his writings. The only instance that I recollect, is his quoting "*Stavo bene; per star meglio, sto qui.*"[2][a]

I mentioned Addison's having borrowed many of his classical remarks from Leandro Alberti. Mr. Beauclerk said, 'It was alledged that he had borrowed also from another Italian authour.' JOHNSON. 'Why, Sir, all who go to look for what the Classicks have said of Italy, must find the same passages;[3] and I should think it would be one of the first things the Italians would do on the revival of learning, to collect all that the Roman authours have said of their country.'

Ossian being mentioned;—JOHNSON. 'Supposing the Irish and Erse languages to be the same, which I do not believe, yet as there is no reason to suppose that the

[a] *a small Specimen indeed.* [H]

[b] *Addison suffer'd some strange ill spelt Italian to be printed in his Spectator* [1]

[c] *It is to be found—or was to be found at Milan.* [H]

he need not. I read it in Church at Milan—by mere Chance I did not think of looking for it. [1]

[1] [Speaking of Addison's *Remarks on Italy* in 'The Journal of a Tour to the Hebrides,' (p. 320, 3d edit.) he says, 'it is a tedious book, and if it were not attached to Addison's previous reputation, one would not think much of it. Had he written nothing else, his name would not have lived. Addison does not seem to have gone deep into Italian literature: he shews nothing of it in his subsequent writings.[b]—He shews a great deal of French learning.' MALONE.]

[2] [Addison, however, does not mention where this celebrated Epitaph, which has eluded a very diligent enquiry, is found.[c] MALONE.]

[3] ['But if you find the same *applications* in another book, then Addison's learning falls to the ground.' 'Journal of a Tour to the Hebrides,' *ut supra.* MALONE.]

inhabitants of the Highlands and Hebrides ever wrote their native language, it is not to be credited that a long poem was preserved among them. If we had no evidence of the art of writing being practised in one of the counties of England, we should not believe that a long poem was preserved *there*, though in the neighbouring counties, where the same language was spoken, the inhabitants could write.' BEAUCLERK. 'The ballad of Lilliburlero was once in the mouths of all the people of this country, and is said to have had a great effect in bringing about the Revolution. Yet I question whether any body can repeat it now; which shews how improbable it is that much poetry should be preserved by tradition.'

One of the company suggested an internal objection to the antiquity of the poetry said to be Ossian's, that we do not find the wolf in it, which must have been the case had it been of that age.

The mention of the wolf had led Johnson to think of other wild beasts; and while Sir Joshua Reynolds and Mr. Langton were carrying on a dialogue about something which engaged them earnestly, he, in the midst of it, broke out, 'Pennant tells of Bears—' [what he added, I have forgotten.] They went on, which he being dull of hearing, did not perceive, or, if he did, was not willing to break off his talk; so he continued to vociferate his remarks, and *Bear* ('like a word in a catch' as Beauclerk said,) was repeatedly heard at intervals, which coming from him who, by those who did not know him, had been so often assimilated to that ferocious animal, while we who were sitting round could hardly stifle laughter, produced a very ludicrous effect. Silence having ensued, he proceeded: 'We are told, that the black bear is innocent; but I should not like to trust myself with him.' Mr. Gibbon muttered, in a low tone of voice, 'I should not like to trust myself with *you*.' This piece of sarcastick pleasantry was a prudent resolution, if applied to a competition of abilities.

Patriotism having become one of our topicks, Johnson suddenly uttered, in a strong determined tone, an apophthegm, at which many will start: 'Patriotism is the last refuge of a scoundrel.' But let it be considered, that he did not mean a real and generous love of our country, but that pretended patriotism which so many, in all ages and countries, have made a cloak for self-interest. I maintained, that certainly all patriots were not scoundrels. Being urged, (not by Johnson) to name one exception, I mentioned an eminent person, whom we all greatly admired. JOHNSON. 'Sir, I do not say that he is *not* honest; but we have no reason to conclude from his political conduct that he *is* honest. Were he to accept a place from this ministry, he would lose that character of firmness which he has, and might be turned out of his place in a year. This ministry is neither stable, nor grateful to their friends, as Sir Robert Walpole was: so that he may think it more for his interest to take his chance of his party coming in.'

Mrs. Pritchard being mentioned, he said, 'Her playing was quite mechanical. It is wonderful how little mind she had. Sir, she had never read the tragedy of Macbeth all through. She no more thought of the play out of which her part was taken, than a shoemaker thinks of the skin, out of which the piece of leather of which he is making a pair of shoes, is cut.'

On Saturday, May 8, I dined with him at Mr. Thrale's, where we met the Irish Dr. Campbell. Johnson had supped the night before at Mrs. Abington's with some fasionable people whom he named; and he seemed much pleased with having made one in so elegant a circle. Nor did he omit to pique his *mistress* a little with jealousy of her house-wifery; for he said, (with a smile,) 'Mrs. Abington's jelly, my dear lady, was better than yours.'

Mrs. Thrale, who frequently practised a coarse mode of flattery, by repeating his *bon-mots* in his hearing, told us that he had said, a certain celebrated actor[a] was just fit to stand at the door of an auction-room with a long pole, and cry, 'Pray, gentlemen, walk in;' and that a certain authour,[b] upon hearing this, had said, that another still more cele- brated actor was fit for nothing better than that, and would pick your pocket after you came out. JOHNSON. 'Nay, my dear lady, there is no wit in what our friend added; there is only abuse. You may as well say of any man that he will pick a pocket. Besides, the man who is stationed at the door does not pick people's pockets; that is done within by the auctioneer.'

[a] *Barry.* [H]

underlined: *certain authour* [I]

underlined: *authour* [H]

[b] *Murphy.* [H & I]

Mrs. Thrale told us, that Tom Davies repeated, in a very bald manner, the story of Dr. Johnson's first repartee to me, which I have related exactly.[1] He made me say, 'I *was born* in Scotland,' instead of 'I *come from* Scotland;' so that Johnson's saying, 'That, Sir, is what a great many of your countrymen cannot help,' had no point, or even meaning: and that upon this being mentioned to Mr. Fitzherbert, he observed, 'It is not every man that can *carry a bon mot.*'

On Monday, April 10, I dined with him at General Oglethorpe's, with Mr. Langton and the Irish Dr. Campbell, whom the General had obligingly given me leave to bring with me. This learned gentleman was thus gratified with a very high intellectual feast, by not only being in company with Dr. Johnson, but with General Oglethorpe, who had been so long a celebrated name both at home and abroad.[2]

I must, again and again, intreat of my readers not to suppose that my imperfect record of conversation contains the whole of what was said by Johnson, or other eminent persons who lived with him. What I have preserved, however, has the value of the most perfect authenticity.

He this day enlarged upon Pope's melancholy remark,

'Man never *is*, but always *to be* blest.'

He asserted, that *the present* was never a happy state to any human being; but that, as every part of life, of which we are

[1] P. 278. vol. i.

[2] Let me here be allowed to pay my tribute of most sincere gratitude to the memory of that excellent person, my intimacy with whom was the more valuable to me, because my first acquaintance with him was unexpected and unsolicited. Soon after the publication of my 'Account of Corsica,' he did me the honour to call on me, and approaching me with a frank courteous air, said, 'My name, Sir, is Oglethorpe, and I wish to be acquainted with you.' I was not a little flattered to be thus addressed by an eminent man, of whom I had read in Pope, from my early years,

'Or driven by strong benevolence of soul,
Will fly, like Oglethorpe, from pole to pole.'

I was fortunate enough to be found worthy of his good opinion, insomuch, that I not only was invited to make one in the many respectable companies whom he entertained at his table, but had a cover at his hospitable board every day when I happened to be disengaged; and in his society I never failed to enjoy learned and animated conversation, seasoned with genuine sentiments of virtue and religion.

conscious, was at some point of time a period yet to come, in which felicity was expected, there was some happiness produced by hope. Being pressed upon this subject, and asked if he really was of opinion, that though, in general, happiness was very rare in human life, a man was not sometimes happy in the moment that was present, he answered, 'Never, but when he is drunk.'[a]

He urged General Oglethorpe to give the world his Life. He said, 'I know no man whose Life would be more interesting. If I were furnished with materials, I should be very glad to write it.'[1]

Mr. Scott of Amwell's Elegies were lying in the room. Dr. Johnson observed, 'They are very well; but such as twenty people might write.' Upon this I took occasion to controvert Horace's maxim,

'—— —— *mediocribus esse poetis*
Non Di, non homines, non concessêre columnæ:'

for here, (I observed,) was a very middle-rate poet, who pleased many readers, and therefore poetry of a middle sort was entitled to some esteem; nor could I see why poetry should not, like every thing else, have different gradations of excellence, and consequently of value. Johnson repeated the common remark, that 'as there is no necessity for our having poetry at all, it being merely a luxury, an instrument of pleasure, it can have no value, unless when exquisite in its kind.' I declared myself not satisfied. 'Why, then, Sir, (said he,) Horace and you must settle it.' He was not much in the humour of talking.

No more of his conversation for some days appears in my journal, except that when a gentleman told him he had bought a suit of lace for his lady, he said, 'Well, Sir, you have done a good thing and a wise thing.'[b] 'I have done a good thing, (said the gentleman,) but I do not know that I have done a wise thing.' JOHNSON. 'Yes, Sir; no money is better spent than what is laid out for domestic satisfaction.

[a] *That was the Reply of a true* Englishman. [I]

[b] *That was not Mr. Thrale; I know not who it was.* [H]

I wonder who the Man & his Wife were; I never heard the Story but in this Book:—it bears every Mark of Truth tho'. [I]

[1] The General seemed unwilling to enter upon it at this time; but upon a subsequent occasion he communicated to me a number of particulars, which I have committed to writing; but I was not sufficiently diligent in obtaining more from him, not apprehending that his friends were so soon to lose him; for notwithstanding his great age, he was very healthy and vigorous, and was at last carried off by a violent fever, which is often fatal at any period of life.

A man is pleased that his wife is drest as well as other people; and a wife is pleased that she is drest.'

On Friday, April 14, being Good-Friday, I repaired to him in the morning, according to my usual custom on that day, and breakfasted with him. I observed that he fasted so very strictly, that he did not even taste bread, and took no milk with his tea; I suppose because it is a kind of animal food.

He entered upon the state of the nation, and thus discoursed: 'Sir, the great misfortune now is, that government has too little power. All that it has to bestow must of necessity be given to support itself; so that it cannot reward merit. No man, for instance, can now be made a Bishop for his learning and piety;[1] his only chance for promotion is his being connected with somebody who has parliamentary interest. Our several ministers in this reign have out-bid each other in concessions to the people. Lord Bute, though a very honourable man,—a man who meant well,—a man who had his blood full of prerogative,—was a theoretical statesman,—a book-minister,—and thought this country could be governed by the influence of the Crown alone. Then, Sir, he gave up a great deal. He advised the King to agree that the Judges should hold their places for life, instead of losing them at the accession of a new King. Lord Bute, I suppose, thought to make the King popular by this concession; but the people never minded it; and it was a most impolitick measure. There is no reason why a Judge should hold his office for life, more than any other person in publick trust. A Judge may be partial otherwise than to the Crown: we have seen Judges partial to the populace. A Judge may become corrupt, and yet there may not be legal evidence against him. A Judge may become froward from age. A Judge may grow unfit for his office in many ways. It was desirable that there should be a possibility of being delivered from him by a new King. That is now gone by an act of Parliament *ex gratiâ* of the Crown. Lord Bute advised the King to give up a very large sum of money,[2]

---

[1] From this too just observation there are some eminent exceptions.

[2] The money arising from the property of the prizes taken before the declaration of war, which were given to his Majesty by the peace of Paris, and amounted to upwards of 700,000l. and from the lands in the ceded

for which nobody thanked him. It was of consequence to the King, but nothing to the publick, among whom it was divided. When I say Lord Bute advised, I mean, that such acts were done when he was minister, and we are to suppose that he advised them. —Lord Bute shewed an undue partiality to Scotchmen. He turned out Dr. Nichols, a very eminent man, from being physician to the King, to make room for one of his countrymen, a man very low in his profession. He had ********** and **** to go on errands for him. He had occasion for people to go on errands for him; but he should not have had Scotchmen; and, certainly, he should not have suffered them to have access to him before the first people in England.'

I told him, that the admission of one of them before the first people in England, which had given the greatest offence, was no more than what happens at every minister's levee, where those who attend are admitted in the order that they have come, which is better than admitting them according to their rank; for if that were to be the rule, a man who has waited all the morning might have the mortification to see a peer, newly come, go in before him, and keep him waiting still. JOHNSON. 'True, Sir; but **** should not have come to the levee, to be in the way of people of consequence. He saw Lord Bute at all times; and could have said what he had to say at any time, as well as at the levee. There is now no Prime Minister: there is only an agent for government in the House of Commons. We are governed by the Cabinet; but there is no one head there since Sir Robert Walpole's time.' BOSWELL. 'What then, Sir, is the use of Parliament?' JOHNSON. 'Why, Sir, Parliament is a large council to the King; and the advantage of such a council is, having a great number of men of property concerned in the legislature, who, for their own

islands, which were estimated at 200,000l. more. Surely, there was a noble munificence in this gift from a Monarch to his people. And let it be remembered, that during the Earl of Bute's administration, the King was graciously pleased to give up the hereditary revenues of the Crown, and to accept, instead of them, of the limited sum of 800,000l. a year; upon which Blackstone observes, that 'The hereditary revenues, being put under the same management as the other branches of the public patrimony, will produce more, and be better collected than heretofore; and the publick is a gainer of upwards of 100,000l. *per annum*, by this disinterested bounty of his Majesty.'[a] Book I. Chap. viii. p. 330.

a *which nobody thinks of as Johnson says— or thanks him for.* [1]

interest, will not consent to bad laws. And you must have observed, Sir, the administration is feeble and timid, and cannot act with that authority and resolution which is necessary. Were I in power, I would turn out every man who dared to oppose me. Government has the distribution of offices, that it may be enabled to maintain its authority.'

'Lord Bute (he added,) took down too fast, without building up something new.' BOSWELL. 'Because, Sir, he found a rotten building. The political coach was drawn by a set of bad horses; it was necessary to change them.' JOHNSON. 'But he should have changed them one by one.'

I told him that I had been informed by Mr. Orme, that many parts of the East Indies were better mapped than the Highlands of Scotland. JOHNSON. 'That a country may be mapped, it must be travelled over.' 'Nay, (said I, meaning to laugh with him at one of his prejudices,) can't you say, it is not *worth* mapping?'

As we walked to St. Clement's church, and saw several shops open upon this most solemn fast-day of the Christian world, I remarked, that one disadvantage arising from the immensity of London, was, that nobody was heeded by his neighbour; there was no fear of censure for not observing Good-Friday, as it ought to be kept, and as it is kept in country-towns. He said, it was, upon the whole, very well observed even in London. He however owned that London was too large; but added, 'It is nonsense to say the head is too big for the body. It would be as much too big, though the body were ever so large; that is to say, though the country were ever so extensive. It has no similarity to a head connected with a body.'

Dr. Wetherell, Master of University College, Oxford, accompanied us home from church; and after he was gone, there came two other gentlemen, one of whom uttered the common-place complaints, that by the increase of taxes, labour would be dear, other nations would undersell us, and our commerce would be ruined. JOHNSON, (smiling). 'Never fear, Sir. Our commerce is in a very good state; and suppose we had no commerce at all, we could live very well on the produce of our own country.' I cannot omit to mention, that I never knew any man who was less disposed to be querulous than Johnson.[a] Whether the subject was

exclamation point: *I cannot omit* etc. [H]

[a] *Bravo* [H]

his own situation, or the state of the publick, or the state of human nature in general, though he saw the evils, his mind was turned to resolution, and never to whining or complaint.

We went again to St. Clement's in the afternoon. He had found fault with the preacher in the morning for not choosing a text adapted to the day. The preacher in the afternoon had chosen one extremely proper: 'It is finished.'

After the evening service, he said, 'Come, you shall go home with me, and sit just an hour.' But he was better than his word; for after we had drunk tea with Mrs. Williams, he asked me to go up to his study with him, where we sat a long while together in a serene undisturbed frame of mind, sometimes in silence, and sometimes conversing, as we felt ourselves inclined, or more properly speaking, as *he* was inclined; for during all the course of my long intimacy with him, my respectful attention never abated, and my wish to hear him was such, that I constantly watched every dawning of communication from that great and illuminated mind.

He observed, 'All knowledge is of itself of some value. There is nothing so minute or inconsiderable, that I would not rather know it than not. In the same manner, all power, of whatever sort, is of itself desirable. A man would not submit to learn to hem a ruffle, of his wife, or his wife's maid: but if a mere wish could attain it, he would rather wish to be able to hem a ruffle.'

He again advised me to keep a journal fully and minutely, but not to mention such trifles as, that meat was too much or too little done, or that the weather was fair or rainy. He had till very near his death, a contempt for the notion that the weather affects the human frame.

queried:
He had etc. [H]

I told him that our friend Goldsmith had said to me that he had come too late into the world, for that Pope and other poets had taken up the places in the Temple of Fame; so that as but a few at any period can possess poetical reputation, a man of genius can now hardly acquire it. JOHNSON. 'That is one of the most sensible things I have ever heard of Goldsmith. It is difficult to get literary fame, and it is every day growing more difficult. Ah, Sir, that should make a man think of securing happiness in another world, which all who try sincerely for it may attain. In comparison of that, how little are all other things! The belief of immortality is impressed upon all men, and all men act under an impression of it, however they may talk, and though, perhaps, they may be scarcely sensible of it.' I said, it appeared to me that some people had not the least notion of immortality; and I mentioned a distinguished gentleman of our acquaintance. JOHNSON. 'Sir, if it were not for the notion of immortality, he would cut a throat to fill his pockets.' When I quoted this to Beauclerk, who knew much more of the gentleman than we did, he said in his acid manner, 'He would cut a throat to fill his pockets, if it were not for fear of being hanged.'[a]

queried:
Sir, if it etc. [H]

[a] *Who was this I wonder!* [H]

Dr. Johnson proceeded: 'Sir, there is a great cry about infidelity: but there are, in reality, very few infidels. I have heard a person, originally a Quaker, but now, I am afraid, a Deist, say, that he did not believe there were, in all England, above two hundred infidels.'[b]

[b] *The Number is much increased 1807.* [I]

He was pleased to say, 'If you come to settle here, we will have one day in the week on which we will meet by ourselves. That is the happiest conversation where there is no competition, no vanity, but a calm quiet interchange of sentiments.' In his private register this evening is thus marked, 'Boswell sat with me till night; we had some serious talk.'[1] It also appears from the same record, that after I left him he was occupied in religious duties, in 'giving Francis, his servant, some directions for preparation to communicate; in reviewing his life, and resolving on better conduct.' The humility and piety which he discovers on such occasions, is truly edifying. No saint, however, in the course of his religious warfare, was more sensible of the unhappy failure of pious resolves, than Johnson. He said one day, talking to an acquaintance on this subject, 'Sir, Hell is paved with good intentions.'[2][c]

[c] *'Tis a Quotation.* [H]
That The Road to Hell is paved with good Resolutions is in Some Devotional Work. [I]

On Sunday, April 16, being Easter-day, after having attended the solemn service at St. Paul's, I dined with Dr. Johnson and Mrs. Williams. I maintained that Horace was wrong in placing happiness in *Nil admirari*, for that I

[1] Prayers and Meditations, p. 138.

[2] [This is a proverbial sentence. 'Hell (says Herbert) is full of good meanings and wishings.' JACULA PRUDENTUM, p. 11. edit. 1651. MALONE.]

thought admiration one of the most agreeable of all our
feelings; and I regretted that I had lost much of my disposition to admire, which people generally do as they advance
in life. JOHNSON. 'Sir, as a man advances in life, he gets
what is better than admiration,—judgement, to estimate
things at their true value.' I still insisted that admiration
was more pleasing than judgement, as love is more pleasing
than friendship. The feeling of friendship is like that of
being comfortably filled with roast beef; love, like being
enlivened with champagne. JOHNSON. 'No, Sir; admiration and love are like being intoxicated with champagne;
judgement and friendship like being enlivened. Waller has
hit upon the same thought with you:[1] but I don't believe
you have borrowed from Waller. I wish you would enable
yourself to borrow more.'

    He then took occasion to enlarge on the advantages of
reading, and combated the idle superficial notion, that
knowledge enough may be acquired in conversation. 'The
foundation (said he) must be laid by reading. General
principles must be had from books, which, however, must
be brought to the test of real life. In conversation you
never get a system. What is said upon a subject is to be
gathered from a hundred people. The parts of a truth
which a man gets thus, are at such a distance from each
other that he never attains to a full view.'

        'TO BENNET LANGTON, ESQ.

'DEAR SIR,

    'I HAVE enquired more minutely about the medicine
for the rheumatism, which I am sorry to hear that you still
want. The receipt is this:
    'Take equal quantities of flour of sulphur, and *flour* of
mustard-seed, make them an electuary with honey or

queried:
he gets etc. [H]

marginal line:
Take equal . . . *it:*
drinking [H]

----

[1] 'Amoret's as sweet and good
    As the most delicious food;
    Which but tasted does impart
    Life and gladness to the heart.

    Sacharissa's beauty's wine,
    Which to madness does incline;
    Such a liquor as no brain
    That is mortal can sustain.'

treacle; and take a bolus as big as a nutmeg several times a day, as you can bear it: drinking after it a quarter of a pint of the infusion of the root of Lovage.

'Lovage, in Ray's "Nomenclature," is Levisticum: perhaps the Botanists may know the Latin name.

'Of this medicine I pretend not to judge. There is all the appearance of its efficacy, which a single instance can afford: the patient was very old, the pain very violent, and the relief, I think, speedy and lasting.

'My opinion of alterative medicine is not high, but *quid tentasse nocebit?* if it does harm, or does no good, it may be omitted; but that it may do good, you have, I hope, reason to think is desired by, Sir, your most affectionate,

'Humble servant,

'April 17, 1775.'   'SAM. JOHNSON'

On Tuesday, April 11, he and I were engaged to go with Sir Joshua Reynolds to dine with Mr. Cambridge, at his beautiful villa on the banks of the Thames, near Twickenham. Dr. Johnson's tardiness was such, that Sir Joshua, who had an appointment at Richmond, early in the day, was obliged to go by himself on horseback, leaving his coach to Johnson and me. Johnson was in such good spirits, that every thing seemed to please him as we drove along.

Our conversation turned on a variety of subjects. He thought portrait-painting an improper employment for a woman. 'Publick practice of any art, (he observed,) and staring in men's faces, is very indelicate in a female.' I happened to start a question, whether when a man knows that some of his intimate friends are invited to the house of another friend, with whom they are all equally inti-
^a *a strange Question* mate, he may join them without an invitation.^a JOHNSON.
sure. [1]   'No, Sir; he is not to go when he is not invited. They may be invited on purpose to abuse him.' (smiling).

As a curious instance how little man knows, or wishes to know his own character in the world, or, rather as a convincing proof that Johnson's roughness was only external, and did not proceed from his heart, I insert the following dialogue. JOHNSON. 'It is wonderful, Sir, how

rare a quality good humour is in life. We meet with very
few good humoured men.' I mentioned four of our friends,
none of whom he would allow to be good humoured. One
was *acid*, another was *muddy*, and to the others he had
objections which have escaped me. Then, shaking his head
and stretching himself at ease in the coach, and smiling
with much complacency, he turned to me and said, 'I look
upon *myself* as a good humoured fellow.' The epithet
fellow, applied to the great Lexicographer, the stately
Moralist, the masterly Critick, as if he had been *Sam
Johnson*, a mere pleasant companion, was highly diverting;
and this light notion of himself struck me with wonder.
I answered, also smiling, 'No, no, Sir; that will *not* do. You
are good natured, but not good humoured: you are
irascible. You have not patience with folly and absurdity.
I believe you would pardon them, if there were time to
deprecate your vengeance; but punishment follows so
quick after sentence, that they cannot escape.'

I had brought with me a great bundle of Scotch magazines and news-papers, in which his 'Journey to the
Western Islands' was attacked in every mode; and I read
a great part of them to him, knowing they would afford
him entertainment. I wish the writers of them had been
present: they would have been sufficiently vexed. One
ludicrous imitation of his style, by Mr. Maclaurin, now
one of the Scotch Judges, with the title of Lord Dreghorn,
was distinguished by him from the rude mass. 'This (said
he,) is the best. But I could caricature my own style much
better myself.' He defended his remark upon the general
insufficiency of education in Scotland; and confirmed to
me the authenticity of his witty saying on the learning of
the Scotch;—'Their learning is like bread in a besieged
town: every man gets a little, but no man gets a full meal.'
'There is (said he,) in Scotland a diffusion of learning, a
certain portion of it widely and thinly spread. A merchant
has as much learning as one of their clergy.'

He talked of Isaac Walton's Lives, which was one of his
most favourite books. Dr. Donne's Life, he said, was the
most perfect of them. He observed, that 'it was wonderful
that Walton, who was in a very low situation of life, should
have been familiarly received by so many great men, and

that at a time when the ranks of society were kept more separate than they are now.' He supposed that Walton had then given up his business as a linen-draper and sempster, and was only an author;[1] and added, 'that he was a great panegyrist.' BOSWELL. 'No quality will get a man more friends than a disposition to admire the qualities of others. I do not mean flattery, but a sincere admiration.' JOHNSON. 'Nay, Sir, flattery pleases very generally. In the first place, the flatterer may think what he says to be true: but, in the second place, whether he thinks so or not, he certainly thinks those whom he flatters of consequence enough to be flattered.'

marginal line:
certainly thinks . . . be
flattered [H]

No sooner had we made our bow to Mr. Cambridge, in his library, than Johnson ran eagerly to one side of the room intent on poring over the backs of the books.[2] Sir Joshua observed, (aside,) 'He runs to the books as I do to the pictures: but I have the advantage. I can see much more of the pictures than he can of the books.' Mr. Cambridge, upon this, politely said, 'Dr. Johnson, I am going with your pardon, to accuse myself, for I have the same custom which I perceive you have. But it seems odd that one should have such a desire to look at the backs of books.' Johnson, ever ready for contest, instantly started from his reverie, wheeled about and answered, 'Sir, the reason is very plain. Knowledge is of two kinds. We know a subject ourselves, or we know where we can find information upon it. When we enquire into any subject, the first thing we have to do is to know what books have treated of it. This leads us to look at catalogues, and the backs of books in libraries.' Sir Joshua observed to me the extraordinary promptitude with which Johnson flew upon an argument. 'Yes, (said I,) he has no formal preparation, no

marginal line:
Yes, (said . . . your
body [H]

[1] [Johnson's conjecture was erroneous. Walton did not retire from business till 1643. But in 1664, Dr. King, Bishop of Chichester, in a letter prefixed to his LIVES, mentions his having been familiarly acquainted with him for forty years: and in 1631 he was so intimate with Dr. Donne, that he was one of the friends who attended him on his death bed. J. BOSWELL.]

[2] [The first time he dined with me, he was shewn into my book room, and instantly pored over the lettering of each volume within his reach. My collection of books is very miscellaneous, and I feared there might be some among them that he would not like. But seeing the number of volumes very considerable, he said, 'You are an honest man to have formed so great an accumulation of knowledge.' BURNEY.]

flourishing with his sword; he is through your body in an instant.'

Johnson was here solaced with an elegant entertainment, a very accomplished family, and much good company; among whom was Mr. Harris of Salisbury,[a] who paid him many compliments on his 'Journey to the Western Islands.'

[a] *a Man of the quietest Manners possible* [I]

The common remark as to the utility of reading history being made;—JOHNSON. 'We must consider how very little history there is; I mean real authentick history. That certain Kings reigned, and certain battles were fought, we can depend upon as true; but all the colouring, all the philosophy of history is conjecture.' BOSWELL. 'Then, Sir, you would reduce all history to no better than an almanack, a mere chronological series of remarkable events.' Mr. Gibbon, who must at that time have been employed upon his history, of which he published the first volume in the following year, was present; but did not step forth in defence of that species of writing. He probably did not like to *trust* himself with JOHNSON![1]

two marginal lines: *species of . . . like to* [H]

Johnson observed, that the force of our early habits was so great, that though reason approved, nay, though our senses relished a different course, almost every man returned to them. I do not believe there is any observation upon human nature better founded than this; and in many cases, it is a very painful truth; for where early habits have been mean and wretched, the joy and elevation resulting from better modes of life, must be damped by the gloomy consciousness of being under an almost inevitable doom to sink back into a situation which we recollect with disgust. It surely may be prevented, by constant attention and unremitting exertion to establish contrary habits of superiour efficacy.

'The Beggar's Opera,' and the common question, whether it was pernicious in its effects, having been introduced;—JOHNSON. 'As to this matter, which has been very much contested, I myself am of opinion, that more influence has been ascribed to "The Beggar's Opera," than it in reality ever had; for I do not believe that any man was ever made a rogue by being present at its representation. At the same time I do not deny that it may have

[1] See p. 158.

some influence, by making the character of a rogue familiar, and in some degree pleasing.'[1] Then collecting himself, as it were, to give a heavy stroke: 'There is in it such a *labefactation* of all principles as may be injurious to morality.'

While he pronounced this response, we sat in a comical sort of restraint, smothering a laugh, which we were afraid might burst out. In his life of Gay, he has been still more decisive as to the inefficiency of 'The Beggar's Opera' in corrupting society. But I have ever thought somewhat differently; for, indeed, not only are the gaiety and heroism of a highwayman very captivating to a youthful imagination, but the arguments for adventurous depredation are so plausible, the allusions so lively, and the contrasts with the ordinary and more painful modes of acquiring property are so artfully displayed, that it requires a cool and strong judgement to resist so imposing an aggregate: yet, I own, I should be very sorry to have 'The Beggar's Opera' suppressed; for there is in it so much of real London life, so much brilliant wit, and such a variety of airs, which, from early association of ideas, engage, soothe, and enliven the mind, that no performance which the theatre exhibits, delights me more.

The late '*worthy*' Duke of Queensbury, as Thomson, in his 'Seasons,' justly characterizes him, told me, that when Gay shewed him 'The Beggar's Opera,' his Grace's observation was, 'This is a very odd thing, Gay; I am satisfied that it is either a very good thing, or a very bad thing.' It proved the former, beyond the warmest expectations of the authour or his friends. Mr. Cambridge, however, shewed us to-day, that there was good reason enough to doubt concerning its success. He was told by Quin, that

---

[1] A very eminent physician, whose discernment is as acute and penetrating in judging of the human character as it is in his own profession, remarked once at a club where I was, that a lively young man, fond of pleasure, and without money, would hardly resist a solicitation from his mistress to go upon the highway, immediately after being present at the representation of 'The Beggar's Opera.' I have been told of an ingenious observation by Mr. Gibbon, that 'The Beggar's Opera may, perhaps, have sometimes increased the number of highwaymen; but that it has had a beneficial effect in refining that class of men, making them less ferocious, more polite, in short, more like gentlemen.' Upon this Mr. Courtenay said, that 'Gay was the Orpheus of highwaymen.'

during the first night of its appearance it was long in a very
dubious state; that there was a disposition to damn it, and
that it was saved by the song,

'Oh ponder well! be not severe!'

the audience being much affected by the innocent looks
of Polly, when she came to those two lines, which exhibit
at once a painful and ridiculous image,

'For on the rope that hangs my Dear,
Depends poor Polly's life.'

Quin himself had so bad an opinion of it, that he refused
the part of Captain Macheath, and gave it to Walker,
who acquired great celebrity by his grave yet animated
performance of it.

We talked of a young gentleman's marriage with an
eminent singer,[a] and his determination that she should no
longer sing in publick, though his father was very earnest
she should, because her talents would be liberally rewarded,
so as to make her a good fortune. It was questioned
whether the young gentleman, who had not a shilling in
the world, but was blest with very uncommon talents, was
not foolishly delicate, or foolishly proud, and his father
truly rational without being mean. Johnson, with all the
high spirit of a Roman senator, exclaimed, 'He resolved
wisely and nobly to be sure. He is a brave man. Would not
a gentleman be disgraced by having his wife singing
publickly for hire?[b] No, Sir, there can be no doubt here.
I know not if I should not *prepare* myself for a publick
singer, as readily as let my wife be one.'

Johnson arraigned the modern politicks of this country,
as entirely devoid of all principle of whatever kind. 'Politicks (said he) are now nothing more than means of rising
in the world. With this sole view do men engage in politicks, and their whole conduct proceeds upon it. How
different in that respect is the state of the nation now from
what it was in the time of Charles the First, during the
Usurpation, and after the Restoration, in the time of
Charles the Second. Hudibras affords a strong proof how
much hold political principles had then upon the minds
of men. There is in Hudibras a great deal of bullion which

[a] *Sheridan & his 1st.
Wife* [H]
*Sheridan & Miss
Linley* [I]

[b] *but how was Sheri-
dan a Gentleman? any
more than Miss Linley
was a Lady—? They
were Gens à Talens—
both of them. Complete
Equals* [H]

will always last. But to be sure the brightest strokes of his wit owed their force to the impression of the characters, which was upon men's minds at the time; to their knowing them, at table and in the street; in short, being familiar with them; and above all, to his satire being directed against those whom a little while before they had hated and feared. The nation in general has ever been loyal, has been at all times attached to the monarch, though a few daring rebels have been wonderfully powerful for a time. The murder of Charles the First was undoubtedly not committed with the approbation or consent of the people. Had that been the case, Parliament would not have ventured to consign the regicides to their deserved punishment. And we know what exuberance of joy there was when Charles the Second was restored. If Charles the Second had bent all his mind to it, had made it his sole object, he might have been as absolute as Louis the Fourteenth.' A gentleman observed he would have done no harm if he had. JOHNSON. 'Why, Sir, absolute princes seldom do any harm. But they who are governed by them are governed by chance. There is no security for good government.' CAMBRIDGE. 'There have been many sad victims to absolute government.' JOHNSON. 'So, Sir, have there been to popular factions.' BOSWELL. 'The question is, which is worst, one wild beast or many?'

Johnson praised 'The SPECTATOR,' particularly the character of Sir Roger de Coverley. He said, 'Sir Roger did not die a violent death, as has been generally fancied. He was not killed; he died only because others were to die, and because his death afforded an opportunity to Addison for some very fine writing. We have the example of Cervantes making Don Quixote die.—I never could see why Sir Roger is represented as a little cracked. It appears to me that the story of the widow was intended to have something superinduced upon it; but the superstructure did not come.'

Somebody found fault with writing verses in a dead language, maintaining that they were merely arrangements of so many words, and laughed at the Universities of Oxford and Cambridge, for sending forth collections of them not only in Greek and Latin, but even in Syriack,

marginal line:
time. The . . . appro-
bation or [H]

marginal line:
There is . . . govern-
ment.' CAMBRIDGE
[H]

Arabick, and other more unknown tongues. JOHNSON.
'I would have as many of these as possible; I would have
verses in every language that there are the means of
acquiring. Nobody imagines that an University is to have
at once two hundred poets; but it should be able to shew
two hundred scholars. Pearce's death was lamented, I
think, in forty languages. And I would have had at every
coronation, and every death of a king, every *Gaudium*, and
every *Luctus*, University-verses, in as many languages as
can be acquired.[a] I would have the world to be thus told,
"Here is a school where every thing may be learnt."'

Having set out next day on a visit to the Earl of Pembroke, at Wilton, and to my friend, Mr. Temple,[1] at
Mamhead, in Devonshire, and not having returned to
town till the second of May, I did not see Dr. Johnson for
a considerable time, and during the remaining part of my
stay in London kept very imperfect notes of his conversation, which had I according to my usual custom written
out at large soon after the time, much might have been
preserved, which is now irretrievably lost. I can now only
record some particular scenes, and a few fragments of his
memorabilia. But to make some amends for my relaxation
of diligence in one respect, I have to present my readers
with arguments upon two law cases, with which he
favoured me.

On Saturday, the sixth of May, we dined by ourselves
at the Mitre, and he dictated to me what follows, to obviate
the complaint already mentioned,[2] which had been made
in the form of an action in the Court of Session, by Dr.
Memis, of Aberdeen, that in the same translation of a
charter in which *physicians* were mentioned, he was called
Doctor of Medicine.

'THERE are but two reasons for which a physician can
decline the title of *Doctor of Medicine*, because he supposes
himself disgraced by the doctorship, or supposes the
doctorship disgraced by himself. To be disgraced by a title
which he shares in common with every illustrious name of
his profession, with Boerhaave, with Arbuthnot, and with
Cullen, can surely diminish no man's reputation. It is, I
suppose, to the doctorate, from which he shrinks, that he

[a] *but he liked the Joke well enough when one who knew nothing of Oriental Languages saw various Copies of Unintelligible Charac-ters. Is not this said She the last Set turned Bottom upwards?* [I]

---

[1] Page 137.   [2] Page 117.

owes his right of practising physick. A doctor of Medicine is a physician under the protection of the laws, and by the stamp of authority. The physician who is not a Doctor, usurps a profession, and is authorized only by himself to decide upon health and sickness, and life and death. That this gentleman is a Doctor, his diploma makes evident; a diploma not obtruded upon him, but obtained by solicitation, and for which fees were paid. With what countenance any man can refuse the title which he has either begged or bought, is not easily discovered.

'All verbal injury must comprise in it either some false position, or some unnecessary declaration of defamatory truth. That in calling him Doctor, a false appellation was given him, he himself will not pretend, who at the same time that he complains of the title would be offended if we supposed him to be not a Doctor. If the title of Doctor be a defamatory truth, it is time to dissolve our colleges; for why should the publick give salaries to men whose approbation is reproach? It may likewise deserve the notice of the publick to consider what help can be given to the professors of physick, who all share with this unhappy gentleman the ignominious appellation, and of whom the very boys in the street are not afraid to say, *There goes the Doctor.*

'What is implied by the term Doctor is well known. It distinguishes him to whom it is granted, as a man who has attained such knowledge of his profession as qualifies him to instruct others. A Doctor of Laws is a man who can form lawyers by his precepts. A Doctor of Medicine is a man who can teach the art of curing diseases. This is an old axiom which no man has yet thought fit to deny, *Nil dat quod non habet.* Upon this principle to be Doctor implies skill, for *nemo docet quod non didicit.* In England, whoever practises physic, not being a Doctor, must practise by a licence: but the doctorate conveys a licence in itself.

'By what accident it happened that he and the other physicians were mentioned in different terms, where the terms themselves were equivalent, or where in effect that which was applied to him was the most honourable, perhaps they who wrote the paper cannot now remember. Had they expected a lawsuit to have been the consequence of such petty variation, I hope they would have avoided it.[1] But, probably, as they meant no ill, they suspected no danger, and, therefore, consulted only what appeared to them propriety or convenience.'

A few days afterwards, I consulted him upon a cause, *Paterson and others* against *Alexander and others*, which had been decided by a casting vote in the Court of Session, determining that the Corporation of Stirling was corrupt, and setting aside the election of some of their officers, because it was proved that three of the leading men who influenced the majority, had entered into an unjustifiable compact, of which, however, the majority were ignorant. He dictated to me, after a little consideration, the following sentences upon the subject:

'THERE is a difference between majority and superiority; majority is applied to number, and superiority to power; and power, like many other things, is to be estimated *non numero sed pondere*. Now though the greater *number* is not corrupt, the greater *weight* is corrupt, so that corruption predominates in the borough, taken *collectively*, though, perhaps, taken *numerically*, the greater part may be uncorrupt. That borough, which is so constituted as to act corruptly, is in the eye of reason corrupt, whether it be by the uncontrollable power of a few, or by an accidental pravity of the multitude. The objection, in which is urged the injustice of making the innocent suffer with the guilty, is an objection not only against society, but against the possibility of society. All societies, great and small, subsist upon this condition; that as the individuals derive advantages from union, they may likewise suffer inconveniences; that as those who do nothing, and sometimes those who do ill, will have the honours and emoluments of general virtue and general prosperity, so those likewise who do nothing, or perhaps do well, must be involved in the consequences of predominant corruption.'

This, in my opinion, was a very nice case; but the decision was affirmed in the House of Lords.

---

[1] In justice to Dr. Memis, though I was against him as an Advocate, I must mention, that he objected to the variation very earnestly, before the translation was printed off.

On Monday, May 8, we went together and visited the mansions of Bedlam. I had been informed that he had once been there before with Mr. Wedderburne, (now Lord Loughborough,) Mr. Murphy, and Mr. Foote; and I had heard Foote give a very entertaining account of Johnson's happening to have his attention arrested by a man who was very furious, and who, while beating his straw, supposed it was William Duke of Cumberland, whom he was punishing for his cruelties in Scotland, in 1746.[1] There was nothing peculiarly remarkable this day; but the general contemplation of insanity was very affecting. I accompanied him home, and dined and drank tea with him.

Talking of an acquaintance of ours, distinguished for knowing an uncommon variety of miscellaneous articles both in antiquities and polite literature, he observed, 'You know, Sir, he runs about with little weight upon his mind.' And talking of another very ingenious gentleman, who from the warmth of his temper was at variance with many of his acquaintance, and wished to avoid them, he said, 'Sir, he leads the life of an outlaw.'

On Friday, May 12, as he had been so good as to assign me a room in his house, where I might sleep occasionally, when I happened to sit with him to a late hour, I took possession of it this night, found every thing in excellent order, and was attended by honest Francis with a most civil assiduity. I asked Johnson whether I might go to a consultation with another lawyer upon Sunday, as that appeared to me to be doing work as much in my way, as if an artisan should work on the day appropriated for religious rest. JOHNSON. 'Why, Sir, when you are of consequence enough to oppose the practice of consulting upon Sunday, you should do it: but you may go now. It is not criminal, though it is not what one should do, who is anxious for the preservation and increase of piety, to which a peculiar observance of Sunday is a great help. The distinction is clear between what is of moral and what is of ritual obligation.'

[1] My very honourable friend General Sir George Howard, who served in the Duke of Cumberland's army, has assured me that the cruelties were not imputable to his Royal Highness.

On Saturday, May 13, I breakfasted with him by invitation, accompanied by Mr. Andrew Crosbie, a Scotch Advocate, whom he had seen at Edinburgh, and the Hon. Colonel (now General) Edward Stopford, brother to Lord Courtown, who was desirous of being introduced to him. His tea and rolls and butter, and whole breakfast apparatus were all in such decorum, and his behaviour was so courteous, that Colonel Stopford was quite surprized, and wondered at his having heard so much said of Johnson's slovenliness and roughness. I have preserved nothing of what passed, except that Crosbie pleased him much by talking learnedly of alchymy, as to which Johnson was not a positive unbeliever, but rather delighted in considering what progress had actually been made in the transmutation of metals, what near approaches there had been to the making of gold; and told us that it was affirmed, that a person in the Russian dominions had discovered the secret, but died without revealing it, as imagining it would be prejudicial to society. He added, that it was not impossible but it might in time be generally known.

It being asked whether it was reasonable for a man to be angry at another whom a woman had preferred to him;—JOHNSON. 'I do not see, Sir, that it is reasonable for a man to be angry at another, whom a woman has preferred to him: but angry he is, no doubt; and he is loath to be angry at himself.'

Before setting out for Scotland on the 23d, I was frequently in his company at different places, but during this period have recorded only two remarks; one concerning Garrick: 'He has not Latin enough. He finds out the Latin by the meaning rather than the meaning by the Latin.' And another concerning writers of travels, who, he observed, 'were more defective than any other writers.'

I passed many hours with him on the 17th, of which I find all my memorial is, 'much laughing.' It should seem he had that day been in a humour for jocularity and merriment, and upon such occasions I never knew a man laugh more heartily. We may suppose, that the high relish of a state so different from his habitual gloom, produced more than ordinary exertions of that distinguishing faculty of man, which has puzzled philosophers so much to explain.

marginal line:
humoured growl . . . it
drolly [H]

Johnson's laugh was as remarkable as any circumstance in his manner. It was a kind of good humoured growl. Tom Davies described it drolly enough: 'He laughs like a rhinoceros.'

'TO BENNET LANGTON, ESQ.

'DEAR SIR,

'I HAVE an old amanuensis in great distress. I have given what I think I can give, and begged till I cannot tell where to beg again. I put into his hands this morning four guineas. If you could collect three guineas more, it would clear him from his present difficulty. I am, Sir,

'Your most humble servant,

'May 21, 1775.'   'SAM. JOHNSON'

'TO JAMES BOSWELL, ESQ.

'DEAR SIR,

'I MAKE no doubt but you are now safely lodged in your own habitation, and have told all your adventures to Mrs. Boswell and Miss Veronica. Pray teach Veronica to love me. Bid her not mind mamma.

'Mrs. Thrale has taken cold, and been very much disordered, but I hope is grown well. Mr. Langton went yesterday to Lincolnshire, and has invited Nicolaida[1] to follow him. Beauclerk talks of going to Bath. I am to set out on Monday; so there is nothing but dispersion.

'I have returned Lord Hailes's entertaining sheets, but must stay till I come back for more, because it will be inconvenient to send them after me in my vagrant state.

'I promised Mrs. Macaulay[2] that I would try to serve her son at Oxford. I have not forgotten it, nor am unwilling to perform it. If they desire to give him an English education, it should be considered whether they cannot send him for a year or two to an English school. If he comes immediately from Scotland, he can make no figure in our Universities. The schools in the north, I believe, are cheap; and when I was a young man, were eminently good.

[1] A learned Greek.

[2] Wife of the Reverend Mr. Kenneth Macaulay, authour of 'The History of St. Kilda.'

'There are two little books published by the Foulis, Telemachus and Collins's Poems, each a shilling; I would be glad to have them.

'Make my compliments to Mrs. Boswell, though she does not love me. You see what perverse things ladies are, and how little fit to be trusted with feudal estates. When she mends and loves me, there may be more hope of her daughters.

'I will not send compliments to my friends by name, because I would be loath to leave any out in the enumeration. Tell them, as you see them, how well I speak of Scotch politeness, and Scotch hospitality, and Scotch beauty, and of every thing Scotch, but Scotch oat-cakes, and Scotch prejudices.

'Let me know the answer of Rasay, and the decision relating to Sir Allan.[1] I am, my dearest Sir, with great affection,
                              'Your most obliged, and
                                  'Most humble servant,

'May 27, 1775.'   'SAM. JOHNSON'

After my return to Scotland, I wrote three letters to him, from which I extract the following passages:

'I have seen Lord Hailes since I came down. He thinks it wonderful that you are pleased to take so much pains in revising his "Annals." I told him that you said you were well rewarded by the entertainment which you had in reading them.'

'There has been a numerous flight of Hebrideans in Edinburgh this summer, whom I have been happy to entertain at my house. Mr. Donald Macqueen[2] and Lord Monboddo supped with me one evening. They joined in controverting your proposition, that the Gaelick of the Highlands and Isles of Scotland was not written till of late.'

'My mind has been somewhat dark this summer. I have need of your warming and vivifying rays; and I hope I shall have them frequently. I am going to pass some time with my father at Auchinleck.'

[1] A law-suit carried on by Sir Allan Maclean, Chief of his Clan, to recover certain parts of his family estates from the Duke of Argyle.

[2] A very learned minister in the Isle of Sky, whom both Dr. Johnson and I have mentioned with regard.

'TO JAMES BOSWELL, ESQ.

'DEAR SIR,

'I AM returned from the annual ramble into the middle counties. Having seen nothing I had not seen before, I have nothing to relate. Time has left that part of the island few antiquities; and commerce has left the people no singularities. I was glad to go abroad, and, perhaps, glad to come home; which is in other words, I was, I am afraid, weary of being at home, and weary of being abroad. Is not this the state of life? But, if we confess this weariness let us not lament it; for all the wise and all the good say, that we may cure it.

'For the black fumes which rise in your mind, I can prescribe nothing but that you disperse them by honest business or innocent pleasure, and by reading, sometimes easy and sometimes serious. Change of place is useful; and I hope that your residence at Auchinleck will have many good effects.

*   *   *   *   *   *

'That I should have given pain to Rasay, I am sincerely sorry; and am therefore very much pleased that he is no longer uneasy. He still thinks that I have represented him as personally giving up the Chieftainship. I meant only that it was no longer contested between the two houses, and supposed it settled, perhaps, by the cession of some remote generation, in the house of Dunvegan. I am sorry the advertisement was not continued for three or four times in the paper.

'That Lord Monboddo and Mr. Macqueen should controvert a position contrary to the imaginary interest of literary or national prejudice, might be easily imagined; but of a standing fact there ought to be no controversy; if there are men with tails, catch an *homo caudatus;* if there was writing of old in the Highlands or Hebrides, in the Erse language, produce the manuscripts. Where men write they will write to one another, and some of their letters, in families studious of their ancestry, will be kept. In Wales there are many manuscripts.

'I have now three parcels of Lord Hailes's history,

which I purpose to return all the next week: that his respect for my little observations should keep his work in suspense, makes one of the evils of my journey. It is in our language, I think, a new mode of history which tells all that is wanted, and, I suppose, all that is known, without laboured splendour of language, or affected subtilty of conjecture. The exactness of his dates raises my wonder. He seems to have the closeness of Henault without his constraint.

'Mrs. Thrale was so entertained with your "Journal,"[1] that she almost read herself blind.[a] She has a great regard for you.[b]

'Of Mrs. Boswell, though she knows in her heart that she does not love me, I am always glad to hear any good, and hope that she and the little dear ladies will have neither sickness nor any other affliction. But she knows that she does not care what becomes of me, and for that she may be sure that I think her very much to blame.

'Never, my dear Sir, do you take it into your head to think that I do not love you; you may settle yourself in full confidence both of my love and my esteem; I love you as a kind man, I value you as a worthy man, and hope in time to reverence you as a man of exemplary piety. I hold you, as Hamlet has it "in my heart of hearts," and therefore, it is little to say, that I am, Sir,

'Your affectionate humble servant,

'London, August 27, 1775.'   'SAM. JOHNSON'

                    TO THE SAME
'SIR,
'IF in these papers,[2] there is little alteration attempted, do not suppose me negligent. I have read them perhaps more closely than the rest; but I find nothing worthy of an objection.

'Write to me soon, and write often, and tell me all your honest heart.   'I am, Sir,
                    'Your's affectionately,
'August 30, 1775.'   'SAM. JOHNSON'

[1] My 'Journal of a Tour to the Hebrides,' which that lady read in the original manuscript.

[2] Another parcel of Lord Hailes's 'Annals of Scotland.'

[a] That is true [H]

[b] *not I—never had: I thought him a clever & a comical Fellow.* [H]

TO THE SAME

'MY DEAR SIR,

'I NOW write to you, lest in some of your freaks and humours you should fancy yourself neglected. Such fancies I must entreat you never to admit, at least never to indulge; for my regard for you is so radicated and fixed, that it is become part of my mind and cannot be effaced but by some cause uncommonly violent; therefore whether I write or not, set your thoughts at rest. I now write to tell you that I shall not very soon write again, for I am to set out to-morrow on another journey.

*   *   *   *   *   *

'Your friends are all well at Streatham, and in Leicester-fields.[1] Make my compliments to Mrs. Boswell, if she is in good humour with me.

'I am, Sir, &c.

'September 14, 1775.'   'SAM. JOHNSON'

What he mentions in such light terms as, 'I am to set out to-morrow on another journey,' I soon afterwards discovered was no less than a tour to France with Mr. and Mrs. Thrale. This was the only time in his life that he went upon the Continent.

'TO MR. ROBERT LEVET

'DEAR SIR,   'Sept. 18, 1775, Calais

'WE are here in France, after a very pleasing passage of no more than six hours. I know not when I shall write again, and therefore I write now, though you cannot suppose that I have much to say. You have seen France yourself. From this place we are going to Rouen, and from Rouen to Paris, where Mr. Thrale designs to stay about five or six weeks. We have a regular recommendation to the English resident, so we shall not be taken for vagabonds. We think to go one way and return another, and for as much as we can, I will try to speak a little French; I tried hitherto but little, but I spoke sometimes. If I heard better, I suppose I should learn faster. I am, Sir,

'Your humble servant,

'SAM. JOHNSON'

[1] Where Sir Joshua Reynolds lived.

TO THE SAME

'DEAR SIR,   'Paris, Oct. 22, 1775

'WE are still here, commonly very busy in looking about us. We have been to-day at Versailles. You have seen it, and I shall not describe it. We came yesterday from Fontainbleau, where the Court is now. We went to see the King and Queen at dinner, and the Queen was so impressed by Miss,[1] that she sent one of the Gentlemen to enquire who she was. I find all true that you have ever told me of Paris. Mr. Thrale is very liberal, and keeps us two coaches, and a very fine table; but I think our cookery very bad. Mrs. Thrale got into a convent of English nuns, and I talked with her through the grate, and I am very kindly used by the English Benedictine friars. But upon the whole I cannot make much acquaintance here; and though the churches, palaces, and some private houses are very magnificent, there is no very great pleasure after having seen many, in seeing more; at least the pleasure, whatever it be, must some time have an end, and we are beginning to think when we shall come home. Mr. Thrale calculates that as we left Streatham on the fifteenth of September, we shall see it again about the fifteenth of November.

'I think I had not been on this side of the sea five days before I found a sensible improvement in my health. I ran a race in the rain this day, and beat Baretti. Baretti is a fine fellow, and speaks French, I think, quite as well as English.

'Make my compliments to Mrs. Williams; and give my love to Francis; and tell my friends that I am not lost.

I am, dear Sir,
'Your affectionate humble, &c.
'SAM. JOHNSON'

'TO DR. SAMUEL JOHNSON

'MY DEAR SIR,   'Edinburgh, Oct. 24, 1775

'IF I had not been informed that you were at Paris, you should have had a letter from me by the earliest

---

[1] Miss Thrale.

opportunity, announcing the birth of my son, on the 9th instant; I have named him Alexander, after my father. I now write, as I suppose your fellow-traveller, Mr. Thrale, will return to London this week, to attend his duty in Parliament, and that you will not stay behind him.

'I send another parcel of Lord Hailes's "Annals." I have undertaken to solicit you for a favour to him, which he thus requests in a letter to me: "I intend soon to give you 'The Life of Robert Bruce,' which you will be pleased to transmit to Dr. Johnson. I wish that you could assist me in a fancy which I have taken, of getting Dr. Johnson to draw a character of Robert Bruce, from the account that I give of that prince. If he finds materials for it in my work, it will be a proof that I have been fortunate in selecting the most striking incidents."

'I suppose by "*The Life of Robert Bruce*," his Lordship means that part of his "Annals" which relates the history of that prince, and not a separate work.

'Shall we have "*A Journey to Paris*" from you in the winter? You will, I hope, at any rate be kind enough to give me some account of your French travels very soon, for I am very impatient. What a different scene have you viewed this autumn, from that which you viewed in autumn 1773!

I ever am, my dear Sir,

'Your much obliged and

'Affectionate humble servant,

'JAMES BOSWELL'

'TO JAMES BOSWELL, ESQ.

'DEAR SIR,

'I AM glad that the young Laird is born, and an end, as I hope, put to the only difference that you can ever have with Mrs. Boswell.[1] I know that she does not love me; but I intend to persist in wishing her well till I get the better of her.

'Paris is, indeed, a place very different from the Hebrides, but it is to a hasty traveller not so fertile of novelty,

---

[1] This alludes to my old feudal principle of preferring male to female succession.

nor affords so many opportunities of remark. I cannot pretend to tell the publick any thing of a place better known to many of my readers than to myself. We can talk of it when we meet.

'I shall go next week to Streatham, from whence I purpose to send a parcel of the "History" every post. Concerning the character of Bruce, I can only say, that I do not see any great reason for writing it; but I shall not easily deny what Lord Hailes and you concur in desiring.

'I have been remarkably healthy all the journey, and hope you and your family have known only that trouble and danger which has so happily terminated. Among all the congratulations that you may receive, I hope you believe none more warm or sincere, than those of, dear Sir,

'Your most affectionate,

'November 16, 1775.'   'SAM. JOHNSON'

'TO MRS. LUCY PORTER, IN LICHFIELD[1]

'DEAR MADAM,

'THIS week I came home from Paris. I have brought you a little box, which I thought pretty; but I know not whether it is properly a snuff-box, or a box for some other use. I will send it, when I can find an opportunity. I have been through the whole journey remarkably well. My fellow-travellers were the same whom you saw at Lichfield, only we took Baretti with us. Paris is not so fine a place as you would expect. The palaces and churches, however, are very splendid and magnificent; and what would please you, there are many very fine pictures; but I do not think their way of life commodious or pleasant.

'Let me know how your health has been all this while. I hope the fine summer has given you strength sufficient to encounter the winter.

---

[1] There can be no doubt that many years previous to 1775, he corresponded with this lady, who was his step-daughter, but none of his earlier letters to her have been preserved.

[Since the death of the authour, several of Johnson's letters to Mrs. Lucy Porter, written before 1775, were obligingly communicated to me by the Rev. Dr. Vyse, and are printed in the present edition. MALONE.]

'Make my compliments to all my friends; and, if your fingers will let you, write to me, or let your maid write, if it be troublesome to you. I am, dear Madam,

'Your most affectionate humble servant,

'Nov. 16, 1775.'   'SAM. JOHNSON'

TO THE SAME

'DEAR MADAM,

'SOME weeks ago I wrote to you, to tell you that I was just come home from a ramble, and hoped that I should have heard from you. I am afraid winter has laid hold on your fingers, and hinders you from writing. However, let somebody write, if you cannot, and tell me how you do, and a little of what has happened at Lichfield among our friends. I hope you are all well.

'When I was in France, I thought myself growing young, but am afraid that cold weather will take part of my new vigour from me. Let us, however, take care of ourselves, and lose no part of our health by negligence.

'I never knew whether you received the Commentary on the New Testament, and the Travels, and the glasses.

'Do, my dear love, write to me; and do not let us forget each other. This is the season of good wishes, and I wish you all good. I have not lately seen Mr. Porter,[1] nor heard of him. Is he with you?

'Be pleased to make my compliments to Mrs. Adey, and Mrs. Cobb, and all my friends; and when I can do any good, let me know. I am, dear Madam,

'Yours most affectionately,

'December 1775.'   'SAM. JOHNSON'

It is to be regretted, that he did not write an account of his travels in France; for as he is reported to have once said, that 'he could write the Life of a Broomstick,'[2a] so, notwithstanding so many former travellers have exhausted almost every subject for remark in that great kingdom, his

a he did not say it—Miss Reynolds said it of Him. [1]

[1] Son of Mrs. Johnson, by her first husband.

[2] [It is probable that the authour's memory here deceived him, and that he was thinking of Stella's remark, that Swift could write finely upon a broomstick. See Johnson's Life of Swift. J. BOSWELL.]

very accurate observation, and peculiar vigour of thought
and illustration, would have produced a valuable work.
During his visit to it, which lasted but about two months,
he wrote notes or minutes of what he saw. He promised to
show me them, but I neglected to put him in mind of it;
and the greatest part of them has been lost, or perhaps,
destroyed in a precipitate burning of his papers a few days
before his death, which must ever be lamented. One small
paper-book, however, entitled 'FRANCE II,' has been
preserved, and is in my possession. It is a diurnal register
of his life and observations, from the 10th of October to
the 4th of November, inclusive, being twenty-six days, and
shows an extraordinary attention to various minute
particulars. Being the only memorial of this tour that
remains, my readers, I am confident, will peruse it with
pleasure, though his notes are very short, and evidently
written only to assist his own recollection.

'OCT. 10, Tuesday. We saw the *Ecole Militaire*,[a] in
which one hundred and fifty young boys are educated for
the army. They have arms of different sizes, according to
the age;—flints of wood. The building is very large, but
nothing fine except the council-room. The French have
large squares in the windows;—they make good iron
palisades. Their meals are gross.

*a Buonaparte was there
no doubt. — how little
did we think that in that
School resides ye. future
Tyrant of all Europe!
1807. [1]*

'We visited the Observatory, a large building of a great
height. The upper stones of the parapet very large, but
not cramped with iron. The flat on the top is very extensive;
but on the insulated part there is no parapet. Though it
was broad enough, I did not care to go upon it. Maps were
printing in one of the rooms.

'We walked to a small convent of the Fathers of the
Oratory. In the reading-desk of the refectory lay the lives
of the Saints.

'Oct. 11. Wednesday. We went to see *Hôtel de Chatlois*,
a house not very large, but very elegant. One of the rooms
was gilt to a degree that I never saw before. The upper
part for servants and their masters was pretty.

'Thence we went to Mr. Monville's, a house divided into
small apartments, furnished with effeminate and minute
elegance.—Porphyry.

'Thence we went to St. Roque's church, which is very large;—the lower part of the pillars incrusted with marble.—Three chapels behind the high altar;—the last a mass of low arches.—Altars, I believe all round.

'We passed through *Place de Vendôme*, a fine square, about as big as Hanover-square.—Inhabited by the high families.—Lewis XIV. on horse-back in the middle.

'Monville is the son of a farmer-general. In the house of Chatlois is a room furnished with japan, fitted up in Europe.

'We dined with Boccage, the Marquis Blanchetti, and his lady.—The sweetmeats taken by the Marchioness Blanchetti, after observing that they were dear. Mr. Le Roy, Count Manucci, the Abbé, the Prior, and Father Wilson, who staid with me, till I took him home in the coach.

'Bathiani is gone.

'The French have no laws for the maintenance of their poor.—Monk not necessarily a priest.—Benedictines rise at four;—are at church an hour and half; at church again half an hour before, half an hour after, dinner; and again from half an hour after seven to eight. They may sleep eight hours.—Bodily labour wanted in monasteries.

'The poor taken to hospitals, and miserably kept.— Monks in the convent fifteen:—accounted poor.

'Oct. 12. Thursday. We went to the Gobelins.—Tapestry makes a good picture:—imitates flesh exactly.—One piece with a gold ground;—the birds not exactly coloured.— Thence we went to the King's cabinet;—very neat, not, perhaps, perfect.—Gold ore.—Candles of the candle-tree. —Seeds.—Woods.—Thence to Gagnier's house, where I saw rooms nine, furnished with a profusion of wealth and elegance which I never had seen before.—Vases.—Pictures.—The dragon china.—The lustre said to be of crystal, and to have cost 3,500l.—The whole furniture said to have cost 125,000l.—Damask hangings covered with pictures.—Porphyry.—This house struck me.—Then we waited on the ladies to Monville's.—Captain Irwin with us.[1]—Spain. County towns all beggars.—At Dijon he

[1] The rest of this paragraph appears to be a minute of what was told by Captain Irwin.

could not find the way to Orleans.—Cross roads of France very bad.—Five soldiers.—Woman.—Soldiers escaped. ——The Colonel would not lose five men for the death of one woman.—The magistrate cannot seize a soldier but by the Colonel's permission.—Good inn at Nismes.— Moors of Barbary fond of Englishmen.—Gibraltar eminently healthy;—it has beef from Barbary.—There is a large garden.—Soldiers sometimes fall from the rock.

'Oct. 13. Friday. I staid at home all day, only went to find the prior, who was not at home.—I read something in Canus.[1]—*Nec admiror, nec multum laudo.*

'Oct. 14. Saturday. We went to the house of Mr. Argenson, which was almost wainscotted with looking-glasses, and covered with gold.—The ladies' closet wainscotted with large squares of glass over painted paper. They always place mirrours to reflect their rooms.

'Then we went to Julien's, the Treasurer of the Clergy:— 30,000l. a year.—The house has no very large room, but is set with mirrours, and covered with gold.—Books of wood here, and in another library.

'At D********'s I looked into the books in the lady's closet, and, in contempt, shewed them to Mr. T.—*Prince Titi; Bibl. des Fées,* and other books.—She was offended, and shut up, as we heard afterwards, her apartment.

'Then we went to Julien Le Roy, the King's watch-maker, a man of character in his business, who shewed a small clock made to find the longitude.—A decent man.

'Afterwards we saw the *Palais Marchand,* and the Courts of Justice, civil and criminal.—Queries on the *Sellette.*— This building has the old Gothick passages, and a great appearance of antiquity.—Three hundred prisoners sometimes in the gaol.

'Much disturbed; hope no ill will be.[2]

'In the afternoon I visited Mr. Freron the journalist. He spoke Latin very scantily, but seemed to understand me.—His house not splendid, but of commodious size.—

---

[1] Melchior Canus, a celebrated Spanish Dominican, who died at Toledo, in 1560. He wrote a treatise *De Locis Theologicis,* in twelve books.

[2] This passage, which so many think superstitious, reminds me of Archbishop Laud's Diary.

His family, wife, son, and daughter, not elevated but decent.—I was pleased with my reception.—He is to translate my books, which I am to send him with notes.

'Oct. 15. Sunday. At Choisi, a royal palace on the banks of the Seine, about 7 m. from Paris.—The terrace noble along the river.—The rooms numerous and grand, but not discriminated from other palaces.—The chapel beautiful, but small.—China globes.—Inlaid tables.—Labyrinth.—Sinking table.—Toilet tables.

'Oct. 16. Monday. The Palais Royal very grand, large, and lofty.—A very great collection of pictures.—Three of Raphael.—Two Holy Family.—One small piece of M. Angelo.—One room of Rubens.—I thought the pictures of Raphael fine.

'The Thuilleries.—Statues.—Venus.—Æn. and Anchises in his arms.—Nilus.—Many more. The walks not open to mean persons.—Chairs at night hired for two sous a piece. —Pont tournant.

'Austin Nuns.—Grate.—Mrs. Fermor, Abbess.—She knew Pope, and thought him disagreeable.—Mrs. ――― has many books;—has seen life.—Their frontlet disagreeable.—Their hood.—Their life easy.—Rise about five; hour and half in chapel.—Dine at ten.—Another hour and half at chapel; half an hour about three, and half an hour more at seven:—four hours in chapel.—A large garden.—Thirteen pensioners.—Teacher complained.

'At the Boulevards saw nothing, yet was glad to be there.—Rope-dancing and farce.—Egg dance.

'N. [Note.] Near Paris, whether on week-days or Sundays, the roads empty.

'Oct. 17. Tuesday. At the Palais Marchand I bought

A snuff-box,	24 L.
	6
Table book	15
Scissars 3 p [pair]	18
	63—2 12 6

'We heard the lawyers plead.—N. As many killed at Paris as there are days in the year.—*Chambre de question.*—

Tournelle at the Palais Marchand.—An old venerable building.

'The Palais Bourbon, belonging to the Prince of Condé. Only one small wing shewn;—lofty;—splendid;—gold and glass.—The battles of the great Condé are painted in one of the rooms. The present Prince a grandsire at thirty-nine.

'The sight of palaces, and other great buildings, leaves no very distinct images, unless to those who talk of them. As I entered, my wife was in my mind:[1] she would have been pleased. Having now nobody to please, I am little pleased.

'N. In France there is no middle rank.

'So many shops open, that Sunday is little distinguished at Paris.—The palaces of Louvre and Thuilleries granted out in lodgings.[a]

[a] *So were those of Hampton Court &c.*—[1]

'In the *Palais de Bourbon*, gilt globes of metal at the fire place.

'The French beds commended.—Much of the marble, only paste.

'The colosseum a mere wooden building, at least much of it.

'Oct. 18. Wednesday. We went to Fontainebleau, which we found a large mean town, crowded with people—The forest thick with woods, very extensive.—Manucci secured us lodgings.—The appearance of the country pleasant.—No hills, few streams, only one hedge.—I remember no chapels nor crosses on the road.—Pavement still, and rows of trees.

'N. Nobody but mean people walk in Paris.

'Oct. 19. Thursday. At Court, we saw the apartments;—the King's bed-chamber and council-chamber extremely splendid.—Persons of all ranks in the external rooms through which the family passes;—servants and masters.—Brunet with us the second time.

'The introductor came to us;—civil to me.—Presenting. —I had scruples.—Not necessary.—We went and saw the

---

[1] His tender affection for his departed wife, of which there are many evidences in his 'Prayers and Meditations,' appears very feelingly in this passage.

King and Queen at dinner.—We saw the other ladies at dinner—Madame Elizabeth, with the Princess of Guimené. —At night we went to a comedy. I neither saw nor heard. —Drunken women.—Mrs. Th. preferred one to the other.

'Oct. 20. Friday. We saw the Queen mount in the forest—Brown habit; rode aside: one lady rode aside.—The Queen's horse light grey;—martingale.—She galloped.— We then went to the apartments, and admired them.— Then wandered through the palace.—In the passages, stalls and shops.—Painting in Fresco by a great master, worn out.—We saw the King's horses and dogs.—The dogs almost all English.—Degenerate.

'The horses not much commended.—The stables cool; the kennel filthy.

'At night the ladies went to the opera. I refused but should have been welcome.

marginal line: *The King . . . as we* [H]

'The King fed himself with his left hand as we.[a]

[a] *This I do not understand* [I]

'Saturday, 21. In the night I got round.—We came home to Paris.—I think we did not see the chapel.—Tree broken by the wind.—The French chairs made all of boards painted.

marginal line: *N. Soldiers . . . Dijon woman* [H]

'N. Soldiers at the court of justice.—Soldiers not amenable to the magistrates.—Dijon woman.[1]

'Faggots in the palace.—Every thing slovenly, except in the chief rooms.—Trees in the roads, some tall, none old, many very young and small.

'Women's saddles seem ill made. Queen's bridle woven with silver.—Tags to strike the horse.

'Sunday, Oct. 22. To Versailles, a mean town. Carriages of business passing.—Mean shops against the wall.—Our way lay through Sêve, where the China manufacture.— Wooden bridge at Sêve, in the way to Versailles.—The palace of great extent.—The front long; I saw it not perfectly.—The Menagerie. Cygnets dark; their black feet; on the ground; tame.—Halcyons, or gulls.—Stag and hind, young.—Aviary, very large: the net, wire.—Black stag of China, small.—Rhinoceros, the horn broken and pared away, which, I suppose, will grow; the basis, I

[1] See p. 191.

think, four inches 'cross; the skin folds like loose cloth doubled over his body, and cross his hips; a vast animal, though young; as big, perhaps, as four oxen. —The young elephant, with his tusks just appearing. —The brown bear put out his paws; —all very tame. —The lion. —The tigers I did not well view. —The camel, or dromedary with two bunches call the Huguin,[1] taller than any horse. —Two camels with one bunch. —Among the birds was a pelican, who being let out, went to a fountain, and swam about to catch fish. His feet well webbed: he dipped his head, and turned his long bill sidewise. He caught two or three fish, but did not eat them.

'Trianon is a kind of retreat appendant to Versailles. It has an open portico; the pavement, and, I think, the pillars, of marble. —There are many rooms, which I do not distinctly remember. —A table of porphyry, about five feet long, and between two and three broad, given to Louis XIV. by the Venetian State. —In the council-room almost all that was not door or window, was, I think, looking-glass. —Little Trianon is a small palace like a gentleman's house. —The upper floor paved with brick. — Little Vienne. —The court is ill paved. —The rooms at the top are small, fit to sooth the imagination with privacy. In the front of Versailles are small basons of water on the terrace, and other basons, I think, below them. There are little courts. —The great gallery is wainscotted with mir-rours, not very large, but joined by frames. I suppose the large plates were not yet made. —The play-house was very large. —The chapel I do not remember if we saw— We saw one chapel, but I am not certain whether there or at Trianon. —The foreign office paved with bricks. —The dinner half a Louis each, and, I think, a Louis over. —Money given at Menagerie, three livres; at palace, six livres.

'Oct. 23. Monday. Last night I wrote to Levet.——We went to see the looking-glasses wrought. They come from Normandy in cast plates, perhaps the third of an inch thick. At Paris they are ground upon a marble table, by rubbing one plate upon another with grit between them.

---

[1] This epithet should be applied to this animal with one bunch.

The various sands, of which there are said to be five, I could not learn. The handle, by which the upper glass is moved, has the form of a wheel, which may be moved in all directions. The plates are sent up with their surfaces ground, but not polished, and so continue till they are bespoken, lest time should spoil the surface, as we were told. Those that are to be polished, are laid on a table covered with several thick cloths, hard strained, that the resistance may be equal: they are then rubbed with a hand rubber, held down hard by a contrivance which I did not well understand. The powder which is used last seemed to me to be iron dissolved in aqua fortis; they called it, as Baretti said, *marc de l'eau forte*, which he thought was dregs. They mentioned vitriol and saltpetre. The cannon ball swam in the quicksilver. To silver them, a leaf of beaten tin is laid, and rubbed with quicksilver, to which it unites. Then more quicksilver is poured upon it, which, by its mutual [attraction] rises very high. Then a paper is laid at the nearest end of the plate, over which the glass is slided till it lies upon the plate, having driven much of the quicksilver before it. It is then, I think, pressed upon cloth, and then set sloping to drop the superfluous mercury: the slope is daily heightened towards a perpendicular.

'In the way I saw the Grêve, the mayor's house, and the Bastile.

'We then went to Sans-terre, a brewer.[1] He brews with about as much malt as Mr. Thrale, and sells his beer at the same price, though he pays no duty for malt, and little more than half as much for beer. Beer is sold retail at 6d. a bottle. He brews 4,000 barrels a year. There are seventeen brewers in Paris, of whom none is supposed to brew more than he;—reckoning them at 3,000 each, they make 51,000 a year.—They make their malt, for malting is here no trade.

'The moat of the Bastile is dry.

'Oct. 24, Tuesday. We visited the King's library—I saw the *Speculum humanæ Salvationis*, rudely printed, with ink, sometimes pale, sometimes black; part supposed to be

marginal line:
cannon ball . . . silver them [H]

a *Ay—& when some Voices cried out Grace —he beat the Drum to drown them. he yet lives. 1807.* [I]

[1] [The detestable ruffian, who afterwards conducted Louis the Sixteenth to the scaffold, and commanded the troops that guarded it, during his murder.[a] MALONE.]

with wooden types, and part with pages cut in boards. The Bible, supposed to be older than that of Mentz, in 62; it has no date; it is supposed to have been printed with wooden types.—I am in doubt; the print is large and fair, in two folios.—Another book was shewn me, supposed to have been printed with wooden types;—I think, *Durandi Sanctuarium* in 58. This is inferred from the difference of form sometimes seen in the same letter, which might be struck with different puncheons.—The regular similitude of most letters proves better that they are metal.—I saw nothing but the *Speculum* which I had not seen, I think, before.

'Thence to the Sorbonne.—The library very large, not in lattices like the King's. *Marbone* and *Durandi*, q. collection 14 vol. *Scriptores de rebus Gallicis.* many folios.—*Histoire Généalogique of France*, 9 vol.—*Gallia Christiana*, the first edition, 4to. the last, f. 12 vol.—The Prior and Librarian dined [with us]:—I waited on them home.—Their garden pretty, with covered walks, but small; yet may hold many students.—The Doctors of the Sorbonne are all equal;—choose those who succeed to vacancies.—Profit little.

'Oct. 25. Wednesday. I went with the Prior to St. Cloud, to see Dr. Hooke.—We walked round the palace, and had some talk.—I dined with our whole company at the Monastery.—In the library, *Beroald*,—*Cymon*,—*Titus*, from Boccace.—*Oratio Proverbialis* to the Virgin, from Petrarch; Falkland to Sandys;—Dryden's Preface to the third vol. of Miscellanies.[1]

'Oct. 26. Thursday. We saw the china at Sêve, cut, glazed, painted. Bellevue, a pleasing house, not great: fine prospect.—Meudon, an old palace.—Alexander, in Porphyry: hollow between eyes and nose, thin cheeks.—Plato and Aristotle.—Noble terrace overlooks the town.—St. Cloud.—Gallery not very high, nor grand, but pleasing.— In the rooms, Michael Angelo, drawn by himself, Sir Thomas More, Des Cartes, Bochart, Naudæus, Mazarine. —Gilded wainscot, so common that it is not minded.— Gough and Keene.—Hooke came to us at the inn.—A message from Drumgold.

[1] He means, I suppose, that he read these different pieces, while he remained in the library.

'Oct. 27. Friday. I staid at home.—Gough and Keene,
ᵃ *Strickland's* [H & 1] and Mrs. S———'sᵃ friend dined with us.—This day we
began to have a fire.—The weather is grown very cold,
and, I fear, has a bad effect upon my breath, which has
grown much more free and easy in this country.

'Sat. Oct. 28. I visited the Grand Chartreux built by
St. Louis.—It is built for forty, but contains only twenty-
four, and will not maintain more.—The friar that spoke
to us had a pretty apartment.—Mr. Baretti says four rooms;
I remember but three.—His books seemed to be French.—
His garden was neat; he gave me grapes.—We saw the
Place de Victoire, with the statues of the King, and the
captive nations.

'We saw the palace and gardens of Luxembourg, but
the gallery was shut.—We climbed to the top stairs.—I
dined with Colbrooke, who had much company:—Foote,
Sir George Rodney, Motteaux, Udson, Taaf.—Called on
the Prior, and found him in bed.

'Hotel—a guinea a day.—Coach, three guineas a week.
—Valet de place, three l. a day.—*Avantcoureur*, a guinea a
week.—Ordinary dinner, six l. a head.—Our ordinary
seems to be about five guineas a day.—Our extraordinary
expences, as diversions, gratuities, clothes, I cannot reckon.
Our travelling is ten guineas a day.

'White stockings, 18l.[1] Wig.—Hat.

'Sunday, Oct. 29. We saw the boarding-school.—The
Enfans trouvés.—A room with about eighty-six children in
cradles, as sweet as a parlour.—They lose a third; take in
to perhaps more than seven [years old]; put them to
trades; pin to them the papers sent with them.—Want
nurses.—Saw their chapel.

'Went to St. Eustatia; saw an innumerable company of
girls catechised, in many bodies, perhaps 100 to a catechist.
—Boys taught at one time, girls at another.—The Sermon;
the preacher wears a cap, which he takes off at the name:—
his action uniform, not very violent.

'Oct. 30. Monday. We saw the library of St. Germain.—
A very noble collection.—*Codex Divinorum Officiorum*, 1459;

[1] [i.e. 18 *livres*. Two pair of white silk stockings were probably purchased.
MALONE.]

—a letter, square like that of the *Offices*, perhaps the same.
—The *Codex*, by Fust and Gernsheym.—*Meursius*, 12 v. fol.
—*Amadis*, in French, 3 v. fol.—CATHOLICON *sine colophone*,
but of 1460.—Two other editions,[1] one by
Augustin. de Civitate Dei, without name, date, or place, but
of Fust's square letter as it seems.

'I dined with Col. Drumgold; had a pleasing afternoon.
'Some of the books of St. Germain's stand in presses
from the wall, like those at Oxford.

'Oct. 31. Tuesday. I lived at the Benedictines; meagre
day; soup meagre, herrings, eels, both with sauce; fryed
fish; lentils, tasteless in themselves. In the library; where
I found *Maffeus's de Historiâ Indicâ: Promontorium flectere,
to double the Cape.* I parted very tenderly from the Prior and
Friar Wilkes.

'*Maitre des Arts*, 2 y.—*Bacc. Theol.* 3 y.—*Licentiate*, 2 y.—
Doctor Th. 2 y. in all 9 years.—For the Doctorate three
disputations, *Major, Minor, Sorbonica.*—Several colleges
suppressed, and transferred to that which was the Jesuit's
College.

'Nov. 1. Wednesday. We left Paris.—St. Denis, a large
town; the church not very large, but the middle isle is very
lofty and aweful.—On the left are chapels built beyond the
line of the wall, which destroy the symmetry of the sides.
The organ is higher above the pavement than any I have
ever seen.—The gates are of brass.—On the middle gate
is the history of our Lord.—The painted windows are
historical, and said to be eminently beautiful.—We were
at another church belonging to a convent, of which the
portal is a dome; we could not enter further, and it was
almost dark.

'Nov. 2. Thursday. We came this day to Chantilly, a
seat belonging to the Prince of Condé.—This place is
eminently beautified by all varieties of waters starting up

---

[1] I have looked in vain into De Bure, Meerman, Mattaire, and other typo-
graphical books, for the two editions of the '*Catholicon*,' which Dr. Johnson
mentions here, with *names* which I cannot make out. I read 'one by *Latinius*,
one by *Boedinus*.' I have deposited the original MS. in the British Museum,
where the curious may see it. My grateful acknowledgements are due to
Mr. Planta for the trouble he was pleased to take in aiding my researches.

in fountains, falling in cascades, running in streams, and spread in lakes.—The water seems to be too near the house. —All this water is brought from a source or river three leagues off, by an artificial canal, which for one league is carried under ground.—The house is magnificent.—The cabinet seems well stocked; what I remember was, the jaws of a hippopotamus, and a young hippopotamus preserved, which, however, is so small, that I doubt its reality.—It seems too hairy for an abortion, and too small for a mature birth.—Nothing was in spirits; all was dry.— The dog; the deer; the ant-bear with long snout.—The toucan, long broad beak.—The stables were of very great length.—The kennel had no scents.—There was a mockery of a village.—The Menagerie had few animals.[1]—Two faussans,[2] or Brasilian weasels, spotted, very wild.—There is a forest, and, I think, a park.—I walked till I was very weary, and next morning felt my feet battered, and with pains in the toes.

'Nov. 3. Friday. We came to Compeigne, a very large town, with a royal palace built round a pentagonal court. —The court is raised upon vaults, and has, I suppose, an entry on one side by a gentle rise.—Talk of painting.— The church is not very large, but very elegant and splendid.—I had at first great difficulty to walk, but motion grew continually easier.—At night we came to Noyon, an episcopal city.—The cathedral is very beautiful, the pillars alternately Gothick and Corinthian.—We entered a very noble parochial church.—Noyon is walled, and is said to be three miles round.

'Nov. 4. Saturday. We rose very early, and came through St. Quintin to Cambray, not long after three.—We went

underlined and index sign:
Talk of painting [1]

[1] The writing is so bad here, that the names of several of the animals could not be decyphered without much more acquaintance with natural history that I possess.—Dr. Blagden, with his usual politeness, most obligingly examined the MS. To that gentleman, and to Dr. Gray, of the British Museum, who also very readily assisted me, I beg leave to express my best thanks.

[2] It is thus written by Johnson, from the French pronunciation of *fossane*. It should be observed, that the person who shewed this Menagerie was mistaken in supposing the *fossane* and the Brasilian weasel to be the same, the *fossane* being a different animal, and a native of Madagascar. I find them, however, upon one plate in Pennant's ' Synopsis of Quadrupeds.'

to an English nunnery, to give a letter to Father Welch, the confessor, who came to visit us in the evening.

'Nov. 5, Sunday. We saw the Cathedral.—It is very beautiful, with chapels on each side.—The choir splendid. —The balustrade in one part brass.—The Neff very high and grand.—The altar silver as far as it is seen.—The vestments very splendid. ——At the Benedictines church———'

Here his Journal[1] ends abruptly. Whether he wrote any more after this time, I know not; but probably not much, as he arrived in England about the 12th of November. These short notes of his tour, though they may seem minute taken singly, make together a considerable mass of information, and exhibit such an ardour of enquiry and acuteness of examination, as, I believe, are found in but few travellers, especially at an advanced age. They completely refute the idle notion which has been propagated, *that he could not see;* and, if he had taken the trouble to revise and digest them, he undoubtedly could have expanded them into a very entertaining narrative.

When I met him in London the following year, the account which he gave me of his French tour, was, 'Sir, I have seen all the visibilities of Paris, and around it: but to have formed an acquaintance with the people there, would have required more time than I could stay. I was just beginning to creep into acquaintance by means of Colonel Drumgould, a very high man, Sir, head of *L'Ecole Militaire,* a most complete character, for he had first been a professor of rhetorick, and then became a soldier. And, Sir, I was very kindly treated by the English Benedictines, and have a cell appropriated to me in their convent.'

He observed, 'The great in France live very magnificently, but the rest very miserably. There is no happy middle state as in England. The shops of Paris are mean; the meat in the markets is such as would be sent to a gaol in England; and Mr. Thrale justly observed, that the cookery of the French was forced upon them by necessity; for they could not eat their meat, unless they added some

---

[1] My worthy and ingenious friend, Mr. Andrew Lumisden, by his accurate acquaintance with France, enabled me to make out many proper names which Dr. Johnson had written indistinctly, and sometimes spelt erroneously.

ª *Bocage's* [H & I]

taste to it. The French are an indelicate people; they will spit upon any place. At Madame ——————'s,ª a literary lady of rank, the footman took the sugar in his fingers, and threw it into my coffee. I was going to put it aside; but hearing it was made on purpose for me, I e'en tasted Tom's fingers. The same lady would needs make tea *à l'Angloise.* The spout of the tea-pot did not pour freely; she bade the footman blow into it. France is worse than Scotland in every thing but climate. Nature has done more for the French; but they have done less for themselves than the Scotch have done.'[1]

It happened that Foote was at Paris at the same time with Dr. Johnson, and his description of my friend while there, was abundantly ludicrous. He told me, that the French were quite astonished at his figure and manner, and at his dress, which he obstinately continued exactly as in London;[2]—his brown clothes, black stockings, and plain shirt. He mentioned, that an Irish gentleman said to Johnson, 'Sir, you have not seen the best French players.' JOHNSON. 'Players, Sir! I look on them as no better than creatures set upon tables, and joint stools to make faces and produce laughter, like dancing dogs.'—'But, Sir, you will allow that some players are better than others?' JOHNSON. 'Yes, Sir, as some dogs dance better than others.'

While Johnson was in France, he was generally very resolute in speaking Latin. It was a maxim with him that a man should not let himself down by speaking a language which he speaks imperfectly. Indeed, we must have often

[1] [In a letter to a friend, written a few days after his return from France, he says, 'The French have a clear air and a fruitful soil; but their mode of common life is gross and incommodious, and disgusting. I am come home convinced that no improvement of general use is to be found among them.' MALONE.]

[2] [Mr. Foote seems to have *embellished* a little in saying that Johnson did not alter his dress at Paris; as in his Journal is a memorandum about white stockings, wig, and hat. In another place we are told that 'during his travels in France he was furnished with a French-made wig of handsome construction.' That Johnson was not inattentive to his appearance is certain,[b] from a circumstance related by Mr. Steevens, and inserted by Mr. Boswell, in vol. iii. between June 15 and June 22, 1784. J. BLAKEWAY.]

ᵇ *Mr. Thrale was attentive for him.* [H]

[Mr. Blakeway's observation is further confirmed by a note in Johnson's diary (quoted by Sir John Hawkins, *Life of Johnson*, p. 517,) by which it appears, that he laid out thirty pounds in cloaths for his French journey.
MALONE.]

observed how inferiour, how much like a child a man appears, who speaks a broken tongue. When Sir Joshua Reynolds, at one of the dinners of the Royal Academy, presented him to a Frenchman of great distinction, he would not deign to speak French, but talked Latin, though his Excellency did not understand it, owing, perhaps, to Johnson's English pronunciation: yet upon another occasion he was observed to speak French to a Frenchman of high rank, who spoke English; and being asked the reason, with some expression of surprise,—he answered, 'because I think my French is as good as his English.' Though Johnson understood French perfectly, he could not speak it readily, as I have observed at his first interview with General Paoli, in 1769; yet he wrote it, I imagine, pretty well, as appears from some of his letters in Mrs. Piozzi's collection, of which I shall transcribe one:

A Madame La Comtesse de ———ᵃ   ᵃ *Bouflers.* [H]

'July 16, 1775

'OUI, *Madame, le moment est arrivé, et il faut que je parte. Mais pourquoi faut il partir? Est ce que je m'ennuye? Je m'ennuyerai ailleurs. Est ce que je cherche ou quelque plaisir, ou quelque soulagement? Je ne cherche rien, je n'espere rien. Aller voir ce que j'ai vû, etre un peu rejoué, un peu degouté, me resouvenir que la vie se passe, et qu'elle se passe en vain, me plaindre de moi, m'endurcir aux dehors; voici le tout de ce qu'on compte pour les delices de l'année. Que Dieu vous donne, Madame, tous les agrémens de la vie, avec un esprit qui peut en jouir sans s'y livrer trop.*'

Here let me not forget a curious anecdote, as related to me by Mr. Beauclerk, which I shall endeavour to exhibit as well as I can in that gentleman's lively manner; and in justice to him it is proper to add, that Dr. Johnson told me I might rely both on the correctness of his memory, and the fidelity of his narrative. 'When Madame de Boufflers was first in England, (said Beauclerk,) she was desirous to see Johnson. I accordingly went with her to his chambers in the Temple, where she was entertained with his conversation for some time. When our visit was over, she and I left him, and were got into Inner Temple-lane, when all at once I heard a noise like thunder. This was occasioned by

Johnson, who it seems, upon a little recollection, had taken it into his head that he ought to have done the honours of his literary residence to a foreign lady of quality, and eager to show himself a man of gallantry, was hurrying down the stair-case in violent agitation. He overtook us before we reached the Temple-gate, and brushing in between me and Madame de Boufflers, seized her hand, and conducted her to her coach. His dress was a rusty brown morning suit, a pair of old shoes by way of slippers, a little shrivelled wig sticking on the top of his head, and the sleeves of his shirt and the knees of his breeches hanging loose. A considerable crowd of people gathered round, and were not a little struck by this singular appearance.'

He spoke Latin with wonderful fluency and elegance. When Pere Boscovich was in England, Johnson dined in company with him at Sir Joshua Reynolds's, and at Dr. Douglas's, now Bishop of Salisbury. Upon both occasions that celebrated foreigner expressed his astonishment at Johnson's Latin conversation. When at Paris, Johnson thus characterised Voltaire to Freron the Journalist: '*Vir est acerrimi ingenii et paucarum literarum.*'

'TO DR. SAMUEL JOHNSON

'MY DEAR SIR,   'Edinburgh, Dec. 5, 1775

'MR. ALEXANDER MACLEAN, the young Laird of Col, being to set out to-morrow for London, I give him this letter to introduce him to your acquaintance. The kindness which you and I experienced from his brother, whose unfortunate death we sincerely lament, will make us always desirous to show attention to any branch of the family. Indeed, you have so much of the true Highland cordiality, that I am sure you would have thought me to blame if I had neglected to recommend to you this Hebridean prince, in whose island we were hospitably entertained. I ever am with respectful attachment, my dear Sir,

'Your most obliged
'And most humble servant,
'JAMES BOSWELL'

Mr. Maclean returned with the most agreeable accounts of the polite attention with which he was received by Dr. Johnson.

In the course of the year Dr. Burney informs me, that 'he very frequently met Dr. Johnson at Mr. Thrale's, at Streatham, where they had many long conversations, often sitting up as long as the fire and candles lasted, and much longer than the patience of the servants subsisted.'[a]

> [a] *Yes truly* [H]

A few of Johnson's sayings, which that gentleman recollects, shall here be inserted.

'I never take a nap after dinner but when I have had a bad night, and then the nap takes me.'

'The writer of an epitaph should not be considered as saying nothing but what is strictly true. Allowance must be made for some degree of exaggerated praise. In lapidary inscriptions a man is not upon oath.'

'There is now less flogging in our great schools than formerly, but then less is learned there; so that what the boys get at one end they lose at the other.'

'More is learned in publick than in private schools, from emulation; there is the collision of mind with mind, or the radiation of many minds pointing to one centre. Though few boys make their own exercises, yet if a good exercise is given up, out of a great number of boys, it is made by somebody.'

'I hate by-roads in education. Education is as well known, and has long been as well known, as ever it can be. Endeavouring to make children prematurely wise is useless labour. Suppose they have more knowledge at five or six years old than other children, what use can be made of it? It will be lost before it is wanted, and the waste of so much time and labour of the teacher can never be repaid. Too much is expected from precocity, and too little performed. Miss ————[b] was an instance of early cultivation, but in what did it terminate? In marrying a little Presbyterian parson,[c] who keeps an infant boarding-school, so that all her employment now is,

> [b] *Letitia Aikin* [H & I]
>
> [c] *Barbauld* [H]

"To suckle fools, and chronicle small-beer."

She tells the children, "This is a cat, and that is a dog, with four legs, and a tail; see there! you are much better than a cat or a dog, for you can speak." If I had bestowed such an education on a daughter, and had discovered that she thought of marrying such a fellow, I would have sent her to the *Congress.*'

'After having talked slightingly of musick, he was observed to listen very attentively while Miss Thrale played on the harpsichord, and with eagerness he called to her, "Why don't you dash away like Burney?" Dr. Burney upon this said to him, "I believe, Sir, we shall make a musician of you at last." Johnson with candid complacency replied, "Sir, I shall be glad to have a new sense given to me."'

marginal line:
last. '*Johnson* . . . *given to* [H]
underlined:
candid complacency [H]

'He had come down one morning to the breakfast-room, and been a considerable time by himself before any body appeared. When on a subsequent day he was twitted by Mrs. Thrale for being very late, which he generally was, he defended himself by alluding to the extraordinary morning when he had been too early. "Madam, I do not like to come down to *vacuity.*"'

'Dr. Burney having remarked that Mr. Garrick was beginning to look old, he said, "Why, Sir, you are not to wonder at that; no man's face has had more wear and tear."'

Not having heard from him for a longer time than I supposed he would be silent, I wrote to him December 18, not in good spirits. 'Sometimes I have been afraid that the cold which has gone over Europe this year like a sort of pestilence has seized you severely: sometimes my imagination, which is upon occasions prolifick of evil, hath figured that you may have somehow taken offence at some part of my conduct.'

'TO JAMES BOSWELL, ESQ.

'DEAR SIR,

'NEVER dream of any offence. How should you offend me? I consider your friendship as a possession, which I intend to hold till you take it from me, and to lament if ever by my fault I should lose it. However, when such suspicions find their way into your mind, always give them vent; I shall make haste to disperse them; but hinder their first ingress if you can. Consider such thoughts as morbid.

'Such illness as may excuse my omission to Lord Hailes, I cannot honestly plead. I have been hindered, I know not how, by a succession of petty obstructions. I hope to mend immediately, and to send next post to his Lordship. Mr. Thrale would have written to you if I had omitted; he sends his compliments and wishes to see you.

'You and your lady will now have no more wrangling about feudal inheritance. How does the young Laird of Auchinleck? I suppose Miss Veronica is grown a reader and discourser.

'I have just now got a cough, but it has never yet hindered me from sleeping; I have had quieter nights than are common with me.

'I cannot but rejoice that Joseph[1] has had the wit to find the way back. He is a fine fellow, and one of the best travellers in the world.

'Young Col brought me your letter. He is a very pleasing youth. I took him two days ago to the Mitre, and we dined together. I was as civil as I had the means of being.

'I have had a letter from Rasay, acknowledging, with great appearance of satisfaction, the insertion in the Edinburgh paper. I am very glad that it was done.

'My compliments to Mrs. Boswell, who does not love me; and of all the rest, I need only send them to those that do; and I am afraid it will give you very little trouble to distribute them. I am, my dear, dear Sir,

'Your affectionate humble servant,
'December 23, 1775.'   'SAM. JOHNSON'

IN 1776, Johnson wrote, so far as I can discover, nothing for the publick: but that his mind was still ardent, and fraught with generous wishes to attain to still higher degrees of literary excellence, is proved by his private notes of this year, which I shall insert in their proper place.

'TO JAMES BOSWELL, ESQ.
'DEAR SIR,
'I HAVE at last sent you all Lord Hailes's papers. While I was in France, I looked very often into Henault;

[1] Joseph Ritter a Bohemian, who was in my service many years, and attended Dr. Johnson and me in our Tour to the Hebrides. After having left me for some time, he had now returned to me.

but Lord Hailes, in my opinion, leaves him far and far behind. Why I did not dispatch so short a perusal sooner, when I look back, I am utterly unable to discover: but human moments are stolen away by a thousand petty impediments which leave no trace behind them. I have been afflicted, through the whole Christmas, with the general disorder, of which the worst effect was a cough, which is now much mitigated, though the country, on which I look from a window at Streatham, is now covered with a deep snow. Mrs. Williams is very ill: every body else is as usual.

'Among the papers, I found a letter to you which I think you had not opened; and a paper for "The Chronicle," which I suppose it not necessary now to insert. I return them both.

'I have within these few days, had the honour of receiving Lord Hailes's first volume, for which I return my most respectful thanks.

'I wish you, my dearest friend, and your haughty lady, (for I know she does not love me,) and the young ladies, and the young Laird, all happiness. Teach the young gentleman, in spite of his mamma, to think and speak well of, Sir,
                    'Your affectionate humble servant,
'Jan. 10, 1776.'   'SAM. JOHNSON'

At this time was in agitation a matter of great consequence to me and my family, which I should not obtrude upon the world, were it not that the part which Dr. Johnson's friendship for me made him take in it, was the occasion of an exertion of his abilities, which it would be injustice to conceal. That what he wrote upon the subject may be understood, it is necessary to give a state of the question, which I shall do as briefly as I can.

In the year 1504, the barony or manour of Auchinleck (pronounced *Affléck,*) in Ayrshire, which belonged to a family of the same name with the lands, having fallen to the Crown by forfeiture, James the Fourth, King of Scotland, granted it to Thomas Boswell, a branch of an ancient family in the county of Fife, stiling him in the charter, '*dilecto familiari nostro;*' and assigning as the cause of the grant, '*pro bono et fideli servitio nobis præstito.*' Thomas Boswell was slain in battle, fighting along with his Sovereign, at the fatal field of Floddon, in 1513.

From this very honourable founder of our family, the estate was transmitted, in a direct series of heirs male to David Boswell, my father's great grand uncle, who had no sons, but four daughters, who were all respectably married, the eldest to Lord Cathcart.

David Boswell, being resolute in the military feudal principle of continuing the male succession, passed by his daughters, and settled the estate on his nephew by his next brother, who approved of the deed, and renounced any pretensions which he might possibly have, in preference to his son. But the estate having been burthened with large portions to the daughters, and other debts, it was necessary for the nephew to sell a considerable part of it, and what remained was still much encumbered.

The frugality of the nephew preserved, and, in some degree, relieved the estate. His son, my grandfather, an eminent lawyer, not only re-purchased a great part of what had been sold, but acquired other lands; and my father, who was one of the Judges of Scotland, and had added considerably to the estate, now signified his inclination to take the privilege allowed by our law,[1] to secure it to his family in perpetuity by an entail, which, on account of his marriage articles, could not be done without my consent.

In the plan of entailing the estate, I heartily concurred with him, though I was the first to be restrained by it; but we unhappily differed as to the series of heirs which should be established, or in the language of our law, called to the succession. My father had declared a predilection for heirs general, that is, males and females indiscriminately. He was willing, however, that all males descending from his grandfather, should be preferred to females; but would not extend that privilege to males deriving their descent from a higher source. I, on the other hand, had a zealous partiality for heirs male, however remote, which I maintained by arguments which appeared to me to have considerable

[1] Acts of Parliament of Scotland, 1685, Cap. 22.

weight.[1] And in the particular case of our family, I appre-
hended that we were under an implied obligation, in
honour and good faith, to transmit the estate by the same
tenure which we held it, which was as heirs male, excluding
nearer females. I therefore, as I thought conscientiously,
objected to my father's scheme.

My opposition was very displeasing to my father, who
was entitled to great respect and deference; and I had
reason to apprehend disagreeable consequences from my
non-compliance with his wishes. After much perplexity
and uneasiness, I wrote to Dr. Johnson, stating the case,
with all its difficulties, at full length, and earnestly requesting that he would consider it at leisure, and favour me
with his friendly opinion and advice.

'TO JAMES BOSWELL, ESQ.

'DEAR SIR,

'I WAS much impressed by your letter, and if I can
form upon your case any resolution satisfactory to myself,
will very gladly impart it: but whether I am equal to it,
I do not know. It is a case compounded of law and justice,
and requires a mind versed in juridical disquisitions.
Could not you tell your whole mind to Lord Hailes? He is,
you know, both a Christian and a Lawyer. I suppose he is
above partiality, and above loquacity: and, I believe, he
will not think the time lost in which he may quiet a disturbed, or settle a wavering mind. Write to me, as any

[1] As first, the opinion of some distinguished naturalists, that our species is
transmitted through males only, the female being all along no more than a
nidus, or nurse, as Mother Earth is to plants of every sort; which notion
seems to be confirmed by that text of scripture, 'He was yet *in the loins of his*
FATHER when Melchisedeck met him;' (Heb. vii. 10.) and consequently,
that a man's grandson by a daughter, instead of being his *surest* descendant,
as is vulgarly said, has, in reality, no connection whatever with his blood.—
And secondly, independent of this theory, (which, if true, should completely
exclude heirs general,) that if the preference of a male to a female, without
regard to primogeniture, (as a son, though much younger, nay, even a
grandson by a son, to a daughter,) be once admitted, as it universally is, it
must be equally reasonable and proper in the most remote degree of descent
from an original proprietor of an estate, as in the nearest; because,—however distant from the representative at the time,—that remote heir male,
upon the failure of those nearer to the *original proprietor* than he is, becomes
in fact the nearest male to *him*, and is, therefore, preferable as *his* representative, to a female descendant.—A little extension of mind will enable us

thing occurs to you; and if I find myself stopped by want of facts necessary to be known, I will make enquiries of you as my doubts arise.

'If your former resolutions should be found only fanciful, you decide rightly in judging that your father's fancies may claim the preference; but whether they are are fanciful or rational, is the question. I really think Lord Hailes could help us.

'Make my compliments to dear Mrs. Boswell; and tell her, that I hope to be wanting in nothing that I can contribute to bring you all out of your troubles.

I am, dear Sir, most affectionately,
'Your humble servant,
'London, Jan. 15, 1776.'   'SAM. JOHNSON'

TO THE SAME

'DEAR SIR,

'I AM going to write upon a question which requires more knowledge of local law, and more acquaintance with the general rules of inheritance, than I can claim; but I write, because you request it.

'Land is, like any other possession, by natural right wholly in the power of its present owner; and may be sold, given or bequeathed, absolutely or conditionally, as judgement shall direct, or passion incite.

'But natural right would avail little without the protection of law; and the primary notion of law is restraint in the exercise of natural right. A man is therefore, in society, not fully master of what he calls his own, but he still retains all the power which law does not take from him.

easily to perceive that a son's son, in continuation to whatever length of time, is preferable to a son's daughter, in the succession to an ancient inheritance; in which regard should be had to the representation of the original proprietor, and not to that of one of his descendants.

I am aware of Blackstone's admirable demonstration of the reasonableness of the legal succession, upon the principle of there being the greatest probability that the nearest heir of the person who last dies proprietor of an estate, is of the blood of the first purchaser. But supposing a pedigree to be carefully authenticated through all its branches, instead of mere *probability* there will be a *certainty* that *the nearest heir male, at whatever period*, has the same right of blood with the first heir male, namely, *the original purchaser's eldest son.*

'In the exercise of the right which law either leaves or gives, regard is to be paid to moral obligations.

'Of the estate which we are now considering, your father still retains such possession, with such power over it, that he can sell it, and do with the money what he will without any legal impediment. But when he extends his power beyond his own life, by settling the order of succession, the law makes your consent necessary.

'Let us suppose that he sells the land to risk the money in some specious adventure, and in that adventure loses the whole; his posterity would be disappointed; but they could not think themselves injured or robbed. If he spent it upon vice or pleasure, his successors could only call him vicious and voluptuous; they could not say that he was injurious or unjust.

'He that may do more may do less. He that by selling, or squandering, may disinherit a whole family, may certainly disinherit part, by a partial settlement.

'Laws are formed by the manners and exigencies of particular times, and it is but accidental that they last longer than their causes: the limitation of feudal succession to the male arose from the obligation of the tenant to attend his chief in war.

'As times and opinions are always changing, I know not whether it be not usurpation to prescribe rules to posterity, by presuming to judge of what we cannot know; and I know not whether I fully approve either your design or your father's, to limit that succession which descended to you unlimited. If we are to leave *sartum tectum* to posterity, what we have without any merit of our own received from our ancestors, should not choice and free-will be kept unviolated?—Is land to be treated with more reverence than liberty?—If this consideration should restrain your father from disinheriting some of the males, does it leave you the power of disinheriting all the females?

'Can the possessor of a feudal estate make any will? Can he appoint, out of the inheritance, any portion to his daughters? There seems to be a very shadowy difference between the power of leaving land, and of leaving money to be raised from land; between leaving an estate to females, and leaving the male heir, in effect, only their steward.

'Suppose at one time a law that allowed only males to inherit, and during the continuance of this law many estates to have descended, passing by the females, to remoter heirs. Suppose afterwards the law repealed in correspondence with a change of manners, and women made capable of inheritance; would not then the tenure of estates be changed? Could the women have no benefit from a law made in their favour? Must they be passed by upon moral principles for ever, because they were once excluded by a legal prohibition? Or may that which passed only to males by one law, pass likewise to females by another?

'You mention your resolution to maintain the right of your brothers:[1] I do not see how any of their rights are invaded.

'As your whole difficulty arises from the act of your ancestor, who diverted the succession from the females, you enquire, very properly, what were his motives, and what was his intention; for you certainly are not bound by his act more than he intended to bind you, nor hold your land on harder or stricter terms than those on which it was granted.

'Intentions must be gathered from acts. When he left the estate to his nephew, by excluding his daughters, was it, or was it not, in his power to have perpetuated the succession to the males? If he could have done it, he seems to have shewn, by omitting it, that he did not desire it to be done, and, upon your own principles, you will not easily prove your right to destroy that capacity of succession which your ancestors have left.

'If your ancestor had not the power of making a perpetual settlement; and if, therefore, we cannot judge distinctly of his intentions, yet his act can only be considered as an example; it makes not an obligation. And, as you observe, he set no example of rigorous adherence to the line of succession. He that overlooked a brother, would not wonder that little regard is shewn to remote relations.

'As the rules of succession are, in a great part, purely legal, no man can be supposed to bequeath any thing, but upon legal terms; he can grant no power which the law

---

[1] Which term I applied to all the heirs male.

denies; and if he makes no special and definite limitation, he confers all the power which the law allows.

'Your ancestor, for some reason, disinherited his daughters; but it no more follows that he intended this act as a rule for posterity, than the disinheriting of his brother.

'If therefore, you ask by what right your father admits daughters to inheritance, ask yourself, first, by what right you require them to be excluded?

'It appears, upon reflection, that your father excludes nobody; he only admits nearer females to inherit before males more remote; and the exclusion is purely consequential.

'These, dear Sir, are my thoughts, immethodical and deliberative; but, perhaps, you may find in them some glimmering of evidence.

'I cannot, however, but again recommend to you a conference with Lord Hailes, whom you know to be both a Lawyer and a Christian.

'Make my compliments to Mrs. Boswell, though she does not love me.
                    'I am, Sir,
                        'Your affectionate servant,
'Feb. 3, 1776.'   'SAM. JOHNSON'

I had followed his recommendation and consulted Lord Hailes, who upon this subject had a firm opinion contrary to mine. His Lordship obligingly took the trouble to write me a letter, in which he discussed with legal and historical learning, the points in which I saw much difficulty, maintaining that 'the succession of heirs general was the succession, by the law of Scotland, from the throne to the cottage, as far as we can learn it by record;' observing that the estate of our family had not been limited to heirs male: and that though an heir male had in one instance been chosen in preference to nearer females, that had been an arbitrary act, which had seemed to be best in the embarrassed state of affairs at that time: and the fact was, that upon a fair computation of the value of land and money at the time, applied to the estate and the burthens upon it, there was nothing given the heirs male but the skeleton of an estate. 'The plea of conscience (said his Lordship,) which you put, is a most respectable one, especially when *conscience* and *self* are on different sides. But I think that conscience is not well informed, and that *self* and *she* ought on this occasion to be of a side.'

This letter, which had considerable influence upon my mind, I sent to Dr. Johnson, begging to hear from him again, upon this interesting question.

'TO JAMES BOSWELL, ESQ.

'DEAR SIR,

'HAVING not any acquaintance with the laws or customs of Scotland, I endeavoured to consider your question upon general principles, and found nothing of much validity that I could oppose to this position: "He who inherits a fief unlimited by his ancestors, inherits the power of limiting it according to his own judgement or opinion." If this be true, you may join with your father.

'Further consideration produces another conclusion: "He who receives a fief unlimited by his ancestors, gives his heirs some reason to complain if he does not transmit it unlimited to posterity. For why should he make the state of others worse than his own, without a reason?" If this be true, though neither you nor your father are about to do what is quite right, but as your father violates (I think) the legal succession least, he seems to be nearer the right than yourself.

'It cannot but occur that "Women have natural and equitable claims as well as men, and these claims are not to be capriciously or lightly superseded or infringed." When fiefs implied military service, it is easily discerned why females could not inherit them; but that reason is now at an end. As manners make laws, manners likewise repeal them.

'These are the general conclusions which I have attained. None of them are very favourable to your scheme of entail, nor perhaps to any scheme. My observation, that only he who acquires an estate may bequeath it capriciously,[1] if it contains any conviction, includes this position likewise, that only he who acquires an estate may entail it capriciously. But I think it may be safely presumed, that "he who inherits an estate, inherits all the power legally

---

[1] I had reminded him of his observation, mentioned p. 90.

concomitant;" and that "He who gives or leaves unlimited
an estate legally limitable, must be presumed to give that
power of limitation which he omitted to take away, and
to commit future contingencies to future prudence." In
these two positions I believe Lord Hailes will advise you
to rest; every other notion of possession seems to me full
of difficulties, and embarrassed with scruples.

'If these axioms be allowed, you have arrived now at
full liberty without the help of particular circumstances,
which, however, have in your case great weight. You very
rightly observe, that he who passing by his brother gave
the inheritance to his nephew, could limit no more than
he gave; and by Lord Hailes's estimate of fourteen years'
purchase, what he gave was no more than you may easily
entail according to your own opinion, if that opinion
should finally prevail.

'Lord Hailes's suspicion that entails are encroachments
on the dominion of Providence, may be extended to all
hereditary privileges and all permanent institutions; I do
not see why it may not be extended to any provision for
the present hour, since all care about futurity proceeds
upon a supposition, that we know at least in some degree
what will be future. Of the future we certainly know
nothing; but we may form conjectures from the past; and
the power of forming conjectures, includes, in my opinion,
the duty of acting in conformity to that probability which
we discover. Providence gives the power, of which reason
teaches the use. I am, dear Sir,

'Your most faithful servant,
'Feb. 9, 1776.'   'SAM. JOHNSON'

'I hope I shall get some ground now with Mrs. Boswell;
make my compliments to her, and to the little people.

'Don't burn papers; they may be safe enough in your
own box,—you will wish to see them hereafter.'

TO THE SAME
'DEAR SIR,

'To the letters which I have written about your great
question I have nothing to add. If your conscience is
satisfied, you have now only your prudence to consult. I

long for a letter, that I may know how this troublesome and vexatious question is at last decided.[1] I hope that it will at last end well. Lord Hailes's letter was very friendly, and very seasonable, but I think his aversion from entails has something in it like superstition. Providence is not counteracted by any means which Providence puts into our power. The continuance and propagation of families makes a great part of the Jewish law, and is by no means prohibited in the Christian institution, though the necessity of it continues no longer. Hereditary tenures are established in all civilized countries, and are accompanied in most with hereditary authority. Sir William Temple considers our constitution as defective, that there is not an unalienable estate in land connected with a peerage: and Lord Bacon mentions as a proof that the Turks are Barbarians, their want of *Stirpes*, as he calls them, or hereditary rank. Do not let your mind, when it is freed from the supposed necessity of a rigorous entail, be entangled with contrary objections, and think all entails unlawful, till you have cogent arguments, which I believe you will never find. I am afraid of scruples.

'I have now sent all Lord Hailes's papers; part I found hidden in a drawer in which I had laid them for security, and had forgotten them. Part of these are written twice; I have returned both the copies. Part I had read before.

'Be so kind as to return Lord Hailes my most respectful thanks for his first volume: his accuracy strikes me with wonder; his narrative is far superiour to that of Henault, as I have formerly mentioned.

'I am afraid that the trouble, which my irregularity and delay has cost him, is greater, far greater, than any good that I can do him will ever recompense; but if I have any more copy, I will try to do better.

---

[1] The entail framed by my father with various judicious clauses, was settled by him and me, settling the estate upon the heirs male of his grandfather, which I found had been already done by my grandfather, imperfectly, but so as to be defeated only by selling the lands. I was freed by Dr. Johnson from scruples of conscientious obligation, and could, therefore, gratify my father. But my opinion and partiality for male succession, in its full extent, remained unshaken. Yet let me not be thought harsh or unkind to daughters: for my notion is, that they should be treated with great affection and tenderness, and always participate of the prosperity of the family.

'Pray let me know if Mrs. Boswell is friends with me, and pay my respects to Veronica, and Euphemia, and Alexander. I am, Sir,

                    'Your most humble servant,
'February 15, 1776.'   'SAM. JOHNSON'

'MR. BOSWELL TO DR. JOHNSON

                              'Edinburgh, Feb. 20, 1776

        *   *   *   *   *

'You have illuminated my mind, and relieved me from imaginary shackles of conscientious obligation. Were it necessary, I could immediately join in an entail upon the series of heirs approved by my father; but it is better not to act too suddenly.'

'DR. JOHNSON TO MR. BOSWELL

'DEAR SIR,

'I AM glad that what I could think or say has at all contributed to quiet your thoughts. Your resolution not to act, till your opinion is confirmed by more deliberation, is very just. If you have been scrupulous, do not be rash. I hope that as you think more, and take opportunities of talking with men intelligent in questions of property, you will be able to free yourself from every difficulty.

'When I wrote last, I sent, I think, ten packets. Did you receive them all?

'You must tell Mrs. Boswell that I suspected her to have written without your knowledge,[1] and therefore did not return any answer, lest a clandestine correspondence should have been perniciously discovered. I will write to her soon. * * * * * *.

                    'I am, dear Sir,
                        'Most affectionately yours,
'Feb. 24, 1776.'   'SAM. JOHNSON'

Having communicated to Lord Hailes what Dr. Johnson wrote concerning the question which perplexed me so much, his Lordship wrote to me; 'Your scruples have

---

[1] A letter to him on the interesting subject of the family settlement, which I had read.

produced more fruit than I ever expected from them; an excellent dissertation on general principles of morals and law.'

I wrote to Dr. Johnson on the 20th of February, complaining of melancholy, and expressing a strong desire to be with him; informing him that the ten packets came all safe; that Lord Hailes was much obliged to him, and said he had almost wholly removed his scruples against entails.

'TO JAMES BOSWELL, ESQ.

'DEAR SIR,

'I HAVE not had your letter half an hour; as you lay so much weight upon my notions, I should think it not just to delay my answer.

'I am very sorry that your melancholy should return, and should be sorry likewise if it could have no relief but from my company. My counsel you may have when you are pleased to require it; but of my company you cannot in the next month have much, for Mr. Thrale will take me to Italy, he says on the first of April.

'Let me warn you very earnestly against scruples. I am glad that you are reconciled to your settlement, and think it a great honour to have shaken Lord Hailes's opinion of entails. Do not, however, hope wholly to reason away your troubles; do not feed them with attention, and they will die imperceptibly away. Fix your thoughts upon your business, fill your intervals with company, and sunshine will again break in upon your mind. If you will come to me, you must come very quickly; and even then I know not but we may scour the country together, for I have a mind to see Oxford and Lichfield, before I set out on this long journey. To this I can only add that I am, dear Sir,

'Your most affectionate humble servant,

'March 5, 1776.'   'SAM. JOHNSON'

TO THE SAME

'DEAR SIR,

'VERY early in April we leave England, and in the beginning of the next week I shall leave London for a short time; of this I think it necessary to inform you, that you may not be disappointed in any of your enterprises. I had not fully resolved to go into the country before this day.

'Please to make my compliments to Lord Hailes; and mention very particularly to Mrs. Boswell my hope that she is reconciled to, Sir,

'Your faithful servant,

'March 12, 1776.'   'SAM. JOHNSON'

Above thirty years ago, the heirs of Lord Chancellor Clarendon presented the University of Oxford with the continuation of his History, and such other of his Lordship's manuscripts as had not been published, on condition that the profits arising from their publication should be applied to the establishment of a *Manège* in the University. The gift was accepted in full convocation. A person being now recommended to Dr. Johnson, as fit to superintend this proposed riding school, he exerted himself with that zeal for which he was remarkable upon every similar occasion. But, on enquiry into the matter, he found that the scheme was not likely to be soon carried into execution; the profits arising from the Clarendon press being, from some mismanagement, very scanty. This having been explained to him by a respectable dignitary of the church, who had good means of knowing it, he wrote a letter upon the subject, which at once exhibits his extraordinary precision and acuteness, and his warm attachment to his ALMA MATER.

'TO THE REVEREND DR. WETHERELL, MASTER
OF UNIVERSITY-COLLEGE, OXFORD

'DEAR SIR,

'FEW things are more unpleasant than the transaction of business with men who are above knowing or caring what they have to do; such as the trustees for Lord Cornbury's institution will, perhaps, appear, when you have read Dr. *******'s letter.

'The last part of the Doctor's letter is of great importance.

The complaint[1] which he makes I have heard long ago, and did not know but it was redressed. It is unhappy that a practice so erroneous has not been altered; for altered it must be, or our press will be useless with all its privileges. The booksellers, who, like all other men, have strong prejudices in their own favour, are enough inclined to think the practice of printing and selling books by any but themselves, an encroachment on the rights of their fraternity; and have need of stronger inducements to circulate academical publications than those of another: for, of that mutual co-operation by which the general trade is carried on, the University can bear no part. Of those whom he neither loves nor fears, and from whom he expects no reciprocation of good offices, why should any man promote the interest but for profit? I suppose, with all our scholastick ignorance of mankind, we are still too knowing to expect that the booksellers will erect themselves into patrons, and buy and sell under the influence of a disinterested zeal for the promotion of learning.

'To the booksellers, if we look for either honour or profit from our press, not only their common profit, but something more must be allowed; and if books, printed at Oxford, are expected to be rated at a high price, that price must be levied on the publick, and paid by the ultimate purchaser, not by the intermediate agents. What price shall be set upon the book, is, to the booksellers, wholly indifferent, provided that they gain a proportionate profit by negociating the sale.

'Why books printed at Oxford should be particularly dear, I am, however, unable to find. We pay no rent; we inherit many of our instruments and materials; lodging and victuals are cheaper than at London; and, therefore, workmanship ought, at least, not to be dearer. Our expences are naturally less than those of booksellers; and in most cases, communities are content with less profit than individuals.

'It is, perhaps, not considered through how many hands a book often passes, before it comes into those of the

---

[1] I suppose the complaint was, that the trustees of the Oxford press did not allow the London booksellers a sufficient profit upon vending their publications.

reader; or what part of the profit each hand must retain, as a motive for transmitting it to the next.

'We will call our primary agent in London, Mr. Cadell, who receives our books from us, gives them room in his warehouse, and issues them on demand; by him they are sold to Mr. Dilly, a wholesale bookseller, who sends them into the country; and the last seller is the country book-seller. Here are three profits to be paid between the printer and the reader, or in the style of commerce, between the manufacturer and the consumer; and if any of these profits is too penuriously distributed, the process of commerce is interrupted.

'We are now come to the practical question, what is to be done? You will tell me, with reason, that I have said nothing, till I declare how much, according to my opinion, of the ultimate price ought to be distributed through the whole succession of sale.

'The deduction, I am afraid, will appear very great; but let it be considered before it is refused. We must allow, for profit, between thirty and thirty-five *per cent.* between six and seven shillings in the pound; that is, for every book which costs the last buyer twenty shillings, we must charge Mr. Cadell with something less than fourteen. We must set the copies at fourteen shillings each, and superadd what is called the quarterly-book, or for every hundred books so charged we must deliver an hundred and four.

'The profits will then stand thus:

'Mr. Cadell, who runs no hazard, and gives no credit, will be paid for warehouse room and attendance by a shilling profit on each book, and his chance of the quarterly-book.

'Mr. Dilly, who buys the book for fifteen shillings, and who will expect the quarterly-book if he takes five and twenty, will send it to his country-customer at sixteen and sixpence, by which, at the hazard of loss, and the certainty of long credit, he gains the regular profit of ten *per cent.* which is expected in the wholesale trade.

'The country bookseller, buying at sixteen and sixpence, and commonly trusting a considerable time, gains but three and sixpence, and if he trusts a year, not much more than two and sixpence; otherwise than as he may, perhaps, take as long credit as he gives.

'With less profit than this, and more you see he cannot have, the country bookseller cannot live; for his receipts are small, and his debts sometimes bad.

'Thus, dear Sir, I have been incited by Dr. *******'s letter to give you a detail of the circulation of books, which, perhaps, every man has not had opportunity of knowing; and which those who know it, do not, perhaps, always distinctly consider.

'I am, &c.

'March 12, 1776.'   'SAM. JOHNSON'[1]

Having arrived in London late on Friday, the 15th of March, I hastened next morning to wait on Dr. Johnson, at his house; but found he was removed from Johnson's-court, No. 7, to Bolt-court, No. 8, still keeping to his favourite Fleet-street. My reflection at the time upon this change as marked in my Journal, is as follows: 'I felt a foolish regret that he had left a court which bore his name;[2] but it was not foolish to be affected with some tenderness of regard for a place in which I had seen him a great deal, from whence I had often issued a better and a happier man than when I went in, and which had often appeared to my imagination while I trod its pavement, in the solemn darkness of the night, to be sacred to wisdom and piety.' Being informed that he was at Mr. Thrale's in the Borough, I hastened thither, and found Mrs. Thrale and him at breakfast. I was kindly welcomed. In a moment he was in a full flow of conversation, and I felt myself elevated as if brought into another state of being. Mrs. Thrale and I looked to each other while he talked, and our looks expressed our congenial admiration and affection for him. I shall ever recollect this scene with great pleasure. I exclaimed to her, 'I am now, intellectually, *Hermippus*

---

[1] I am happy in giving this full and clear statement to the publick, to vindicate, by the authority of the greatest authour of his age, that respectable body of men, the Booksellers of London, from vulgar reflections, as if their profits were exorbitant, when, in truth, Dr. Johnson has here allowed them more than they usually demand.

[2] He said, when in Scotland, that he was *Johnson of that Ilk*.

redivivus,[1] I am quite restored by him, by transfusion of *mind*.' 'There are many (she replied) who admire and respect Mr. Johnson; but you and I *love* him.'

He seemed very happy in the near prospect of going to Italy with Mr. and Mrs. Thrale. 'But, (said he,) before leaving England I am to take a jaunt to Oxford, Birmingham, my native city Lichfield, and my old friend, Dr. Taylor's, at Ashbourne, in Derbyshire. I shall go in a few days, and you, Boswell, shall go with me.' I was ready to accompany him; being willing even to leave London to have the pleasure of his conversation.

I mentioned with much regret the extravagance of the representative of a great family in Scotland, by which there was danger of its being ruined; and as Johnson respected it for its antiquity, he joined with me in thinking it would be happy if this person should die. Mrs. Thrale seemed shocked at this, as feudal barbarity; and said, 'I do not understand this preference of the estate to its owner; of the land to the man who walks upon that land.' JOHNSON. 'Nay, Madam, it is not a preference of the land to its owner; it is the preference of a family to an individual. Here is an establishment in a country, which is of importance for ages, not only to the chief but to his people; an establishment which extends upwards and downwards; that this should be destroyed by one idle fellow is a sad thing.'

He said, 'Entails are good, because it is good to preserve in a country serieses of men, to whom the people are accustomed to look up as to their leaders. But I am for leaving a quantity of land in commerce, to excite industry, and keep money in the country; for if no land were to be bought in the country, there would be no encouragement to acquire wealth, because a family could not be founded there; or if it were acquired, it must be carried away to another country where land may be bought. And although the land in every country will remain the same, and be as fertile where there is no money, as where there is, yet all that portion of the happiness of civil life, which is produced by money circulating in a country, would be lost.' BOSWELL. 'Then, Sir, would it be for the advantage of a

[1] See vol. i. p. 296.

country that all its lands were sold at once?' JOHNSON.
'So far, Sir, as money produces good, it would be an
advantage; for, then that country would have as much
money circulating in it as it is worth. But to be sure this
would be counterbalanced by disadvantages attending a
total change of proprietors.'

I expressed my opinion that the power of entailing should
be limited thus: 'That there should be one third, or perhaps one half of the land of a country kept free for commerce; that the proportion allowed to be entailed, should
be parcelled out so that no family could entail above a
certain quantity. Let a family, according to the abilities
of its representatives, be richer or poorer in different
generations, or always rich if its representatives be always
wise: but let its absolute permanency be moderate. In this
way we should be certain of there being always a number
of established roots; and as in the course of nature, there
is in every age an extinction of some families, there would
be continual openings for men ambitious of perpetuity,
to plant a stock in the entail ground.'[1] JOHNSON. 'Why,
Sir, mankind will be better able to regulate the system of
entails, when the evil of too much land being locked
up by them is felt, than we can do at present when it
is not felt.'

I mentioned Dr. Adam Smith's book on 'The Wealth
of Nations,' which was just published, and that Sir John
Pringle had observed to me, that Dr. Smith, who had never
been in trade, could not be expected to write well on that
subject any more than a lawyer upon physick. JOHNSON.
'He is mistaken, Sir; a man who has never been engaged
in trade himself may undoubtedly write well upon trade,
and there is nothing which requires more to be illustrated
by philosophy than trade does. As to mere wealth, that is
to say, money, it is clear that one nation or one individual

[1] The privilege of perpetuating in a family an estate and arms indefeasibly
from generation to generation, is enjoyed by none of his Majesty's subjects
except in Scotland, where the legal fiction of fine and recovery is unknown. It
is a privilege so proud, that I should think it would be proper to have the
exercise of it dependent on the royal prerogative. It seems absurd to permit
the power of perpetuating their representation to men, who having had no
eminent merit, have truly no name. The King, as the impartial father of
his people, would never refuse to grant the privilege to those who deserved it.

queried:
as the impartial father
etc. [H]

cannot increase its store but by making another poorer: but trade procures what is more valuable, the reciprocation of the peculiar advantages of different countries. A merchant seldom thinks but of his own particular trade. To write a good book upon it, a man must have extensive views. It is not necessary to have practised, to write well upon a subject.' I mentioned law as a subject on which no man could write well without practice. JOHNSON. 'Why, Sir, in England, where so much money is to be got by the practice of the law, most of our writers upon it have been in practice; though Blackstone had not been much in practice when he published his "Commentaries." But upon the Continent, the great writers on law have not all been in practice: Grotius, indeed, was; but Puffendorf was not, Burlamaqui was not.'

When we had talked of the great consequence which a man acquired by being employed in his profession, I suggested a doubt of the justice of the general opinion, that it is improper in a lawyer to solicit employment; for why, I urged, should it not be equally allowable to solicit that as the means of consequence, as it is to solicit votes to be elected a member of Parliament? Mr. Strahan had told me that a countryman of his and mine, who had risen to eminence in the law, had, when first making his way, solicited him to get him employed in city causes. JOHNSON. 'Sir, it is wrong to stir up law-suits; but when once it is certain that a law-suit is to go on, there is nothing wrong in a lawyer's endeavouring that he shall have the benefit, rather than another.' BOSWELL. 'You would not solicit employment, Sir, if you were a lawyer.' JOHNSON. 'No, Sir; but not because I should think it wrong, but because I should disdain it.' This was a good distinction, which will be felt by men of just pride. He proceeded: 'However, I would not have a lawyer to be wanting to himself in using fair means. I would have him to inject a little hint now and then, to prevent his being overlooked.'

Lord Mountstuart's bill for a Scotch Militia, in supporting which his Lordship had made an able speech in the House of Commons, was now a pretty general topick of conversation. JOHNSON. 'As Scotland contributes so little land-tax towards the general support of the nation, it ought not to have a militia paid out of the general fund, unless it should be thought for the general interest, that Scotland should be protected from an invasion, which no man can think will happen; for what enemy would invade Scotland, where there is nothing to be got? No, Sir; now that the Scotch have not the pay of English soldiers spent among them, as so many troops are sent abroad, they are trying to get money another way, by having a militia paid. If they are afraid, and seriously desire to have an armed force to defend them, they should pay for it. Your scheme is to retain a part of your land-tax, by making us pay and clothe your militia.' BOSWELL. 'You should not talk of *we* and *you*, Sir; there is now an *Union*.' JOHNSON. 'There must be a distinction of interest, while the proportions of land-tax are so unequal. If Yorkshire should say, "Instead of paying our land-tax, we will keep a greater number of militia," it would be unreasonable.' In this argument my friend was certainly in the wrong. The land-tax is as unequally proportioned between different parts of England, as between England and Scotland; nay, it is considerably unequal in Scotland itself. But the land-tax is but a small part of the numerous branches of publick revenue, all of which Scotland pays precisely as England does. A French invasion made in Scotland would soon penetrate into England.

He thus discoursed upon supposed obligation in settling estates:—'Where a man gets the unlimited property of an estate, there is no obligation upon him in *justice* to leave it to one person rather than to another. There is a motive of preference from *kindness*, and this kindness is generally entertained for the nearest relation. If I *owe* a particular man a sum of money, I am obliged to let that man have the next money I get, and cannot in justice let another have it; but if I owe money to no man, I may dispose of what I get as I please. There is not a *debitum justitiæ* to a man's next heir; there is only a *debitum caritatis*. It is plain, then, that I have morally a choice according to my liking. If I have a brother in want, he has a claim from affection to my assistance; but if I have also a brother in want, whom I like better, he has a preferable claim. The right of an heir at law is only this, that he is to have the succession to an estate, in case no other person is appointed to it by the owner. His right is merely preferable to that of the King.'

We got into a boat to cross over to Black-friars; and as we moved along the Thames, I talked to him of a little volume, which, altogether unknown to him, was advertised to be published in a few days, under the title of '*Johnsoniana, or Bon-Mots* of Dr. Johnson.' JOHNSON. 'Sir, it is a mighty impudent thing.' BOSWELL. 'Pray, Sir, could you have no redress if you were to prosecute a publisher for bringing out, under your name, what you never said, and ascribing to you dull stupid nonsense, or making you swear profanely, as many ignorant relaters of your *bon-mots* do?' JOHNSON. 'No, Sir; there will always be some truth mixed with the falsehood, and how can it be ascertained how much is true and how much is false? Besides, Sir, what damages would a jury give me for having been represented as swearing?' BOSWELL. 'I think, Sir, you should at least disavow such a publication, because the world and posterity might with much plausible foundation say, "Here is a volume which was publickly advertised and came out in Dr. Johnson's own time, and, by his silence, was admitted by him to be genuine."' JOHNSON. 'I shall give myself no trouble about the matter.'

marginal line:
I shall . . . the matter
[H]

He was, perhaps, above suffering from such spurious publications; but I could not help thinking, that many men would be much injured in their reputation, by having absurd and vicious sayings imputed to them; and that redress ought in such cases to be given.

He said, 'The value of every story depends on its being true. A story is a picture either of an individual or of human nature in general: if it be false, it is a picture of nothing. For instance: suppose a man should tell that Johnson, before setting out for Italy, as he had to cross the Alps, sat down to make himself wings. This many people would believe: but it would be a picture of nothing. ******* (naming a worthy friend of ours,) used to think a story, a story, till I shewed him that truth was essential to it.' I observed, that Foote entertained us with stories which were not true; but that, indeed, it was properly not as narratives that Foote's stories pleased us, but as collections of ludicrous images. JOHNSON. 'Foote is quite impartial, for he tells lies of every body.'

The importance of strict and scrupulous veracity cannot be too often inculcated. Johnson was known to be so rigidly attentive to it, that even in his common conversation the slightest circumstance was mentioned with exact precision. The knowledge of his having such a principle and habit made his friends have a perfect reliance on the truth of every thing that he told, however it might have been doubted if told by many others. As an instance of this, I may mention an odd incident which he related as having happened to him one night in Fleet-street. 'A gentlewoman (said he) begged I would give her my arm to assist her in crossing the street, which I accordingly did; upon which she offered me a shilling, supposing me to be the watchman. I perceived that she was somewhat in liquor.' This, if told by most people, would have been thought an invention; when told by Johnson, it was believed by his friends as much as if they had seen what passed.

We landed at the Temple-stairs, where we parted.

I found him in the evening in Mrs. Williams's room. We talked of religious orders. He said, 'It is as unreasonable for a man to go into a Carthusian convent for fear of being immoral, as for a man to cut off his hands for fear he should steal. There is, indeed, great resolution in the immediate act of dismembering himself; but when that is once done, he has no longer any merit: for though it is out of his power to steal, yet he may all his life be a thief in his heart.[a] So when a man has once become a Carthusian, he is obliged to continue so, whether he chooses it or not. Their silence, too, is absurd. We read in the Gospel of the apostles being sent to preach, but not to hold their tongues. All severity that does not tend to increase good, or prevent evil, is idle. I said to the Lady Abbess of a convent, "Madam, you are here, not for the love of virtue, but the fear of vice." She said, "She should remember this as long as she lived."'

I thought it hard to give her this view of her situation, when she could not help it; and, indeed, I wondered at the whole of what he now said: because, both in his 'Rambler' and 'Idler,' he treats religious austerities with much solemnity of respect.

Finding him still persevering in his abstinence from
wine, I ventured to speak to him of it.—JOHNSON. 'Sir, I
have no objection to a man's drinking wine, if he can do
it in moderation. I found myself apt to go to excess in it,
and therefore, after having been for some time without it,
on account of illness, I thought it better not to return to
it. Every man is to judge for himself, according to the
effects which he experiences. One of the fathers tells us,
he found fasting made him so peevish that he did not
practise it.'

Though he often enlarged upon the evil of intoxication,
he was by no means harsh and unforgiving to those who
indulged in occasional excess in wine. One of his friends, I
well remember, came to sup at a tavern with him and
some other gentlemen, and too plainly discovered that he
had drunk too much at dinner. When one who loved
mischief, thinking to produce a severe censure, asked
Johnson, a few days afterwards, 'Well, Sir, what did your
friend say to you, as an apology for being in such a situation?' Johnson answered, 'Sir, he said all that a man
should say: he said he was sorry for it.'

I heard him once give a very judicious practical advice
upon this subject: 'A man who has been drinking wine at
all freely, should never go into a new company. With those
who have partaken of wine with him, he may be pretty
well in unison; but he will probably be offensive, or appear
ridiculous, to other people.'

He allowed very great influence to education. 'I do not
deny, Sir, but there is some original difference in minds;
but it is nothing in comparison of what is formed by education. We may instance the science of *numbers*, which all
minds are equally capable of attaining:[a] yet we find a
prodigious difference in the powers of different men, in
that respect, after they are grown up, because their minds
have been more or less exercised in it: and I think the same
cause will explain the difference of excellence in other
things, gradations admitting always some difference in the
first principles.'

This is a difficult subject: but it is best to hope that diligence may do a great deal. We are *sure* of what it can do,
in increasing our mechanical force and dexterity.

[a] *Oh no, not equally*
[H]

I again visited him on Monday. He took occasion to
enlarge, as he often did, upon the wretchedness of a sea-
life. 'A ship is worse than a gaol. There is, in a gaol, better
air, better company, better conveniency of every kind;
and a ship has the additional disadvantage of being in
danger. When men come to like a sea-life, they are not fit
to live on land.'—'Then (said I) it would be cruel in a
father to breed his son to the sea.' JOHNSON. 'It would be
cruel in a father who thinks as I do. Men go to sea, before
they know the unhappiness of that way of life; and when
they have come to know it, they cannot escape from it,
because it is then too late to choose another profession; as
indeed is generally the case with men, when they have
once engaged in any particular way of life.'

On Tuesday, March 19, which was fixed for our proposed
jaunt, we met in the morning at the Somerset coffee-house
in the Strand, where we were taken up by the Oxford
coach. He was accompanied by Mr. Gwyn, the architect;
and a gentleman of Merton College, whom he did not
know, had the fourth seat. We soon got into conversation;
for it was very remarkable of Johnson, that the presence
of a stranger had no restraint upon his talk. I observed that
Garrick, who was about to quit the stage, would soon have
an easier life. JOHNSON. 'I doubt that, Sir.' BOSWELL.
'Why, Sir, he will be Atlas with the burthen off his back.'
JOHNSON. 'But I know not, Sir, if he will be so steady
without his load. However, he should never play any more,
but be entirely the gentleman, and not partly the player:
he should no longer subject himself to be hissed by a mob,
or to be insolently treated by performers, whom he used
to rule with a high hand, and who would gladly retaliate.'
BOSWELL. 'I think he should play once a year for the
benefit of decayed actors, as it has been said he means to
do.' JOHNSON. 'Alas, Sir! he will soon be a decayed actor
himself.'

Johnson expressed his disapprobation of ornamental
architecture, such as magnificent columns supporting a
portico, or expensive pilasters supporting merely their own
capitals, 'because it consumes labour disproportionate to
its utility.' For the same reason he satyrised statuary.
'Painting (said he) consumes labour not disproportionate

to its effect; but a fellow will hack half a year at a block of marble to make something in stone that hardly resembles a man. The value of statuary is owing to its difficulty. You would not value the finest head cut upon a carrot.' Here he seemed to me to be strangely deficient in taste; for surely statuary is a noble art of imitation, and preserves a wonderful expression of the varieties of the human frame; and although it must be allowed that the circumstances of difficulty enhance the value of a marble head, we should consider, that if it requires a long time in the performance, it has a proportionate value in durability.

Gwyn was a fine lively rattling fellow. Dr. Johnson kept him in subjection, but with a kindly authority. The spirit of the artist, however, rose against what he thought a Gothick attack, and he made a brisk defence. 'What, Sir, you will allow no value to beauty in architecture or in statuary? Why should we allow it then in writing? Why do you take the trouble to give us so many fine allusions, and bright images, and elegant phrases? You might convey all your instruction without these ornaments.' Johnson smiled with complacency; but said, 'Why, Sir, all these ornaments are useful, because they obtain an easier reception for truth; but a building is not at all more convenient for being decorated with superfluous carved work.'

Gwyn at last was lucky enough to make one reply to Dr. Johnson, which he allowed to be excellent. Johnson censured him for taking down a church which might have stood many years, and building a new one at a different place, for no other reason but that there might be a direct road to a new bridge; and his expression was, 'You are taking a church out of the way, that the people may go in a straight line to the bridge.'—'No, Sir, (said Gwyn,) I am putting the church *in* the way, that the people may not *go out of the way*.' JOHNSON. (with a hearty loud laugh of approbation,) 'Speak no more. Rest your colloquial fame upon this.'

Upon our arrival at Oxford, Dr. Johnson and I went directly to University College, but were disappointed on finding that one of the fellows, his friend Mr. Scott, who accompanied him from Newcastle to Edinburgh, was gone to the country. We put up at the Angel inn, and passed the evening by ourselves in easy and familiar conversation. Talking of constitutional melancholy, he observed, 'A man so afflicted, Sir, must divert distressing thoughts, and not combat with them.' BOSWELL. 'May not he think them down, Sir?' JOHNSON. 'No, Sir. To attempt to *think them down* is madness. He should have a lamp constantly burning in his bed chamber during the night, and if wakefully disturbed, take a book, and read, and compose himself to rest. To have the management of the mind is a great art, and it may be attained in a considerable degree by experience and habitual exercise.' BOSWELL. 'Should not he provide amusements for himself? Would it not, for instance, be right for him to take a course of chymistry?' JOHNSON. 'Let him take a course of chymistry, or a course of rope-dancing, or a course of any thing to which he is inclined at the time. Let him contrive to have as many retreats for his mind as he can, as many things to which it can fly from itself. Burton's "Anatomy of Melancholy" is a valuable work. It is, perhaps, overloaded with quotation. But there is a great spirit and great power in what Burton says, when he writes from his own mind.'

Next morning we visited Dr. Wetherell, Master of University College, with whom Dr. Johnson conferred on the most advantageous mode of disposing of the books printed at the Clarendon press, on which subject his letter has been inserted in a former page. I often had occasion to remark, Johnson loved business, loved to have his wisdom actually operate on real life. Dr. Wetherell and I talked of him without reserve in his own presence. WETHERELL. 'I would have given him a hundred guineas if he would have written a preface to his "Political Tracts," by way of a Discourse on the British Constitution.' BOSWELL. 'Dr. Johnson, though in his writings, and upon all occasions, a great friend to the constitution both in church and state, has never written expressly in support of either. There is really a claim upon him for both. I am sure he could give a volume of no great bulk upon each, which would comprise all the substance, and with his spirit would effectually maintain them. He should erect a fort on the confines of each.' I could perceive that he was displeased with this dialogue. He burst out, 'Why should I be always writing?' I hoped he was conscious that the debt was just, and meant to discharge it, though he disliked being dunned.

We then went to Pembroke College, and waited on his old friend Dr. Adams, the master of it, whom I found to be a most polite, pleasing, communicative man. Before his advancement to the headship of his college, I had intended to go and visit him at Shrewsbury, where he was rector of St. Chad's, in order to get from him what particulars he could recollect of Johnson's academical life. He now obligingly gave me part of that authentick information, which, with what I afterwards owed to his kindness, will be found incorporated in its proper place in this work.

Dr. Adams had distinguished himself by an able answer to David Hume's 'Essay on Miracles.' He told me he had once dined in company with Hume in London: that Hume shook hands with him, and said, 'You have treated me much better than I deserve;' and that they exchanged visits. I took the liberty to object to treating an infidel writer with smooth civility. Where there is a controversy concerning a passage in a classick authour, or concerning a question in antiquities, or any other subject in which human happiness is not deeply interested, a man may treat his antagonist with politeness and even respect. But where the controversy is concerning the truth of religion, it is of such vast importance to him who maintains it, to obtain the victory, that the person of an opponent ought not to be spared. If a man firmly believes that religion is an invaluable treasure, he will consider a writer who endeavours to deprive mankind of it as a *robber;* he will look upon him as *odious*, though the infidel might think himself in the right. A robber who reasons as the gang do in the 'Beggar's Opera,' who call themselves *practical* philosophers, and may have as much sincerity as pernicious *speculative* philosophers, is not the less an object of just indignation. An abandoned profligate may think that it is not wrong to debauch my wife? but shall I, therefore, not detest him? And if I catch him in making an attempt, shall I treat him with politeness? No, I will kick him down stairs, or run him through the body; that is, if I really love my wife, or

have a true rational notion of honour. An Infidel then
shall not be treated handsomely by a Christian, merely
because he endeavours to rob with ingenuity. I do declare,
however, that I am exceedingly unwilling to be provoked
to anger, and could I be persuaded that truth would not
suffer from a cool moderation in its defenders, I should wish
to preserve good humour, at least, in every controversy;
nor, indeed, do I see why a man should lose his temper
while he does all he can to refute an opponent. I think
ridicule may be fairly used against an infidel; for instance,
if he be an ugly fellow, and yet absurdly vain of his person,
we may contrast his appearance with Cicero's beautiful
image of Virtue, could she be seen. Johnson coincided with
me and said, 'when a man voluntarily engages in an important controversy, he is to do all he can to lessen his
antagonist, because authority from personal respect has
much weight with most people, and often more than
reasoning. If my antagonist writes bad language, though
that may not be essential to the question, I will attack him
for his bad language.' ADAMS. 'You would not jostle a
chimney-sweeper.' JOHNSON. 'Yes, Sir, if it were necessary
to jostle him *down*.'

   Dr. Adams told us, that in some of the Colleges at
Oxford, the fellows had excluded the students from social
intercourse with them in the common room. JOHNSON.
'They are in the right, Sir: there can be no real conversation, no fair exertion of mind amongst them, if the young
men are by; for a man who has a character does not
choose to stake it in their presence.' BOSWELL. 'But, Sir,
may there not be very good conversation without a contest
for superiority?' JOHNSON. 'No animated conversation,
Sir, for it cannot be but one or other will come off
superiour.[a] I do not mean that the victor must have the
better of the argument, for he may take the weak side;
but his superiority of parts and knowledge will necessarily
appear; and he to whom he thus shews himself superiour is
lessened in the eyes of the young men. You know it was said,
"*Mallem cum Scaligero errare quam cum Clavio rectè sapere.*"
In the same manner take Bentley's and Jason de Nores'
Comments upon Horace, you will admire Bentley more
when wrong, than Jason when right.'

[a] *& the Boys would
be on the Catch to
laugh at both.* [H]

We walked with Dr. Adams into the master's garden, and into the common room. JOHNSON. (after a reverie of meditation,) 'Ay! Here I used to play at draughts with Phil. Jones and Fluyder. Jones loved beer, and did not get very forward in the church. Fluyder turned out a scoundrel, a Whig, and said he was ashamed of having been bred at Oxford. He had a living at Putney, and got under the eye of some retainers to the court at that time, and so became a violent Whig: but he had been a scoundrel all along to be sure.' BOSWELL. 'Was he a scoundrel, Sir, in any other way than that of being a political scoundrel? Did he cheat at draughts?' JOHNSON. 'Sir, we never played for *money.*'

He then carried me to visit Dr. Bentham, Canon of Christ-Church, and Divinity Professor, with whose learned and lively conversation we were much pleased. He gave us an invitation to dinner, which Dr. Johnson told me was a high honour. 'Sir, it is a great thing to dine with the Canons of Christ-Church.' We could not accept his invitation, as we were engaged to dine at University College. We had an excellent dinner there, with the Masters and Fellows, it being St. Cuthbert's day, which is kept by them as a festival, as he was a saint of Durham, with which this college is much connected.

We drank tea with Dr. Horne, late President of Magdalen College, and Bishop of Norwich, of whose abilities in different respects, the publick has had eminent proofs, and the esteem annexed to whose character was increased by knowing him personally. He had talked of publishing an edition of Walton's Lives, but had laid aside that design, upon Dr. Johnson's telling him, from mistake, that Lord Hailes intended to do it. I had wished to negociate between Lord Hailes and him, that one or other should perform so good a work. JOHNSON. 'In order to do it well, it will be necessary to collect all the editions of Walton's Lives. By way of adapting the book to the taste of the present age, they have, in a late edition, left out a vision which he relates Dr. Donne had, but it should be restored;[1] and

[1] [The vision which Johnson speaks of, was not in the original publication of Walton's life of Dr. Donne, in 1640. It is not found in the three earliest editions; but was first introduced into the fourth, in 1675. I have not been able to discover what modern republication is alluded to in which it was omitted. It has very properly been restored by Dr. Zouch. JAMES BOSWELL.]

there should be a critical catalogue given of the works of the different persons whose lives were written by Walton, and therefore their works must be carefully read by the editor.'

We then went to Trinity College, where he introduced me to Mr. Thomas Warton, with whom we passed a part of the evening. We talked of biography.—JOHNSON. 'It is rarely well executed. They only who live with a man can write his life with any genuine exactness and discrimination; and few people who have lived with a man know what to remark about him. The chaplain of a late Bishop, whom I was to assist in writing some memoirs of his Lordship, could tell me scarcely any thing.'[1]

I said, Mr. Robert Dodsley's life should be written, as he had been so much connected with the wits of his time, and by his literary merit had raised himself from the station of a footman. Mr. Warton said, he had published a little volume under the title of 'The Muse in Livery.' JOHNSON. 'I doubt whether Dodsley's brother would thank a man who should write his life; yet Dodsley himself was not unwilling that his original low condition should be recollected.[a] When Lord Lyttelton's "Dialogues of the Dead" came out, one of which is between Apicius, an ancient epicure, and Dartineuf, a modern epicure, Dodsley said to me, "I knew Dartineuf well, for I was once his footman."'

Biography led us to speak of Dr. John Campbell, who had written a considerable part of the 'Biographia Britannica.' Johnson, though he valued him highly, was of opinion that there was not so much in his great work, 'A Political Survey of Great Britain,' as the world had been taught to expect;[2] and had said to me, that he believed Campbell's disappointment on account of the bad success of that work, had killed him. He this evening observed of it, 'That work was his death.' Mr. Warton, not adverting to his meaning,

[a] *There was a Man at Bath who walked the Pumproom, & had a pretty Daughter, who used to tell People he had carried Coals to Mrs. Piozzi's Fire; & She called him Wise George: but his Girl did not approve the Conversation I remember. Their Names were Gaskell.* [H]

---

[1] It has been mentioned to me by an accurate English friend, that Dr. Johnson could never have used the phrase *almost nothing*, as not being English; and therefore I have put another in its place. At the same time, I am not quite convinced it is not good English. For the best writers use this phrase '*little or nothing;*' i.e. almost so little as to be nothing.

[2] Yet surely it is a very useful work, and of wonderful research and labour for one man to have executed.

answered, 'I believe so; from the great attention he bestowed on it.' JOHNSON. 'Nay, Sir, he died of *want* of attention, if he died at all by that book.'

We talked of a work much in vogue at that time, written in a very mellifluous style, but which, under pretext of another subject, contained much artful infidelity. I said it was not fair to attack us unexpectedly; he should have warned us of our danger, before we entered his garden of flowery eloquence, by advertising, 'Spring-guns and man-traps set here.' The authour had been an Oxonian, and was remembered there for having 'turned Papist.' I observed, that as he had changed several times—from the Church of England to the Church of Rome,—from the Church of Rome to infidelity,—I did not despair yet of seeing him a methodist preacher. JOHNSON. (laughing.) 'It is said, that his range has been more extensive, and that he has once been Mahometan. However, now that he has published his infidelity, he will probably persist in it.' BOSWELL. 'I am not quite sure of that, Sir.'

I mentioned Sir Richard Steele having published his 'Christian Hero,' with the avowed purpose of obliging himself to lead a religious life; yet that his conduct was by no means strictly suitable. JOHNSON. 'Steele, I believe, practised the lighter vices.'

Mr. Warton, being engaged, could not sup with us at our inn; we had therefore another evening by ourselves. I asked Johnson, whether a man's being forward to make himself known to eminent people, and seeing as much of life, and getting as much information as he could in every way, was not yet lessening himself by his forwardness. JOHNSON. 'No, Sir; a man always makes himself greater as he increases his knowledge.'

I censured some ludicrous fantastick dialogues between two coach horses and other such stuff, which Baretti had lately published.[a] He joined with me, and said, 'Nothing odd will do long. "Tristram Shandy" did not last.' I expressed a desire to be acquainted with a lady, who had been much talked of, and universally celebrated for extraordinary address and insinuation. JOHNSON. 'Never believe extraordinary characters which you hear of people. Depend upon it, Sir, they are exaggerated. You do not see

[a] *Stuff indeed! yet there was some humour in it —mixed with incomprehensible Oddity* [H]

one man shoot a great deal higher than another.' I
mentioned Mr. Burke. JOHNSON. 'Yes; Burke *is* an extraordinary man. His stream of mind is perpetual.' It is very
pleasing to me to record, that Johnson's high estimation
of the talents of this gentleman was uniform from their
early acquaintance. Sir Joshua Reynolds informs me, that
when Mr. Burke was first elected a member of Parliament,
and Sir John Hawkins expressed a wonder at his attaining
a seat,[a] Johnson said, 'Now we who know Mr. Burke,
know, that he will be one of the first men in the country.'
And once, when Johnson was ill, and unable to exert himself as much as usual without fatigue, Mr. Burke having
been mentioned, he said, 'That fellow calls forth all my
powers. Were I to see Burke now it would kill me.' So
much was he accustomed to consider conversation as a
contest, and such was his notion of Burke as an opponent.

underlined:
Sir John . . . a wonder
[I]
[a] *what a Man was
that Sir John Hawkins!*
[I]

Next morning, Thursday, March 21, we set out in a
post-chaise to pursue our ramble. It was a delightful day,
and we rode through Blenheim Park. When I looked at the
magnificent bridge built by John Duke of Marlborough,
over a small rivulet, and recollected the Epigram made
upon it—

> 'The lofty arch his high ambition shows,
>   The stream an emblem of his bounty flows:'

and saw that now, by the genius of Brown, a magnificent
body of water was collected, I said, 'They have *drowned*
the Epigram.' I observed to him, while in the midst of the
noble scene around us, 'You and I, Sir, have, I think, seen
together the extremes of what can be seen in Britain—the
wild rough island of Mull, and Blenheim Park.'

three marginal lines:
*and saw . . . a magni-
ficent* [H]
underlined:
genius, Brown [H]
marginal line:
*extremes of . . . Blen-
heim Park* [H]

We dined at an excellent inn at Chapel-house, where he
expatiated on the felicity of England in its taverns and
inns, and triumphed over the French for not having, in
any perfection, the tavern life. 'There is no private house,
(said he,) in which people can enjoy themselves so well, as
at a capital tavern. Let there be ever so great plenty of
good things, ever so much grandeur, ever so much elegance, ever so much desire that every body should be
easy; in the nature of things it cannot be: there must
always be some degree of care and anxiety. The master of

the house is anxious to entertain his guests; the guests are
anxious to be agreeable to him; and no man, but a very
impudent dog indeed, can as freely command what is in
another man's house, as if it were his own. Whereas at a
tavern, there is a general freedom from anxiety. You are
sure you are welcome: and the more noise you make, the
more trouble you give, the more good things you call for,
the welcomer you are. No servants will attend you with the
alacrity which waiters do, who are incited by the prospect
of an immediate reward in proportion as they please. No,
Sir; there is nothing which has yet been contrived by man,
by which so much happiness is produced as by a good
tavern or inn.'[1] He then repeated, with great emotion,
Shenstone's lines:

> 'Whoe'er has travell'd life's dull round,
> Where'er his stages may have been,
> May sigh to think he still has found
> The warmest welcome at an inn.'[2]

My illustrious friend, I thought, did not sufficiently
admire Shenstone. That ingenious and elegant gentleman's opinion of Johnson appears in one of his letters to
Mr. Greaves, dated Feb. 9, 1760. 'I have lately been reading one or two volumes of the Rambler; who, excepting

[1] Sir John Hawkins has preserved very few *Memorabilia* of Johnson. There
is, however, to be found in his bulky tome, a very excellent one upon this
subject. 'In contradiction to those, who, having a wife and children, prefer
domestick enjoyments to those which a tavern affords, I have heard him
assert, *that a tavern chair was the throne of human felicity.*—"As soon (said he) as
I enter the door of a tavern, I experience an oblivion of care, and a freedom
from solicitude: when I am seated, I find the master courteous, and the
servants obsequious to my call; anxious to know and ready to supply my
wants: wine there exhilarates my spirits, and prompts me to free conversation
and an interchange of discourse with those whom I most love: I dogmatise
and am contradicted, and in this conflict of opinion and sentiments I find
delight."'

[2] We happened to lie this night at the inn at Henley, where Shenstone
wrote these lines.*

* I give them as they are found in the corrected edition of his Works,
published after his death. In Dodsley's collection the stanza ran thus:

> 'Whoe'er has travell'd life's dull round,
> Whate'er his *various tour has* been,
> May sigh to think *how oft* he found
> *His* warmest welcome at an Inn.'

against some few hardnesses[1] in his manner, and the want
of more examples to enliven, is one of the most nervous,
most perspicuous, most concise, most harmonious prose
writers I know. A learned diction improves by time.'

In the afternoon, as we were driven rapidly along in the
post-chaise, he said to me, 'Life has not many things better
than this.'[a]

We stopped at Stratford-upon-Avon, and drank tea and
coffee; and it pleased me to be with him upon the classick
ground of Shakspeare's native place.

He spoke slightingly of 'Dyer's Fleece.'—'The subject,
Sir, cannot be made poetical. How can a man write
poetically of serges and druggets! Yet you will hear many
people talk to you gravely of that *excellent* poem, "THE
FLEECE."' Having talked of Grainger's 'Sugar-Cane,' I
mentioned to him Mr. Langton's having told me, that this
poem, when read in manuscript at Sir Joshua Reynolds's,
had made all the assembled wits burst into a laugh,
when, after much blank verse pomp, the poet began a new
paragraph thus:

> 'Now, Muse, let's sing of *rats*.'[b]

And what increased the ridicule was, that one of the
company, who slyly overlooked the reader, perceived that
the word had been originally *mice*, and had been altered
to *rats*, as more dignified.'[2]

[a] *than   what?—oh;
than driving in a Post
Chaise!!* [i]

[b] *no, no, it begins
Where shall the Muse
her breathless Race
begin
Where breathless end?
Say: shall we sing
of Rats* [i]

---

[1] 'He too often makes use of the *abstract* for the *concrete*.'

[2] Such is this little laughable incident, which has been often related. Dr.
Percy, the Bishop of Dromore, who was an intimate friend of Dr. Grainger,
and has a particular regard for his memory, has communicated to me the
following explanation:

'The passage in question was originally not liable to such a perversion:
for the authour having occasion in that part of his work to mention the
havock made by rats and mice, had introduced the subject in a kind of mock
heroick, and a parody of Homer's battle of the frogs and mice, invoking the
Muse of the old Grecian bard in an elegant and well-turned manner. In
that state I had seen it; but afterwards unknown to me and other friends,
he had been persuaded, contrary to his own better judgement, to alter it, so
as to produce the unlucky effect above-mentioned.'

The above was written by the Bishop when he had not the Poem itself to
recur to: and though the account given was true of it at one period, yet as
Dr. Grainger afterwards altered the passage in question; the remarks in the
text do not now apply to the printed poem.

The Bishop gives this character of Dr. Grainger:—'He was not only a
man of genius and learning, but had many excellent virtues; being one of
the most generous, friendly, and benevolent men I ever knew.'

This passage does not appear in the printed work. Dr. Grainger, or some of his friends, it should seem, having become sensible that introducing even *rats*, in a grave poem, might be liable to banter. He, however, could not bring himself to relinquish the idea; for they are thus, in a still more ludicrous manner, periphrastically exhibited in his poem as it now stands:

> 'Nor with less waste the whisker'd vermin race
> A countless clan despoil the lowland cane.'

Johnson said, that Dr. Grainger was an agreeable man; a man who would do any good that was in his power. His translation of Tibullus, he thought, was very well done; but 'The Sugar-Cane, a poem,' did not please him;[1] for, he exclaimed, 'What could he make of a sugar-cane? One might as well write the "Parsley-bed, a poem;" or "The Cabbage-garden, a poem."' BOSWELL. 'You must then *pickle* your cabbage with the *sal atticum.*' JOHNSON. 'You know there is already "The Hop-Garden, a poem:" and, I think, one could say a great deal about cabbage. The poem might begin with the advantages of civilized society over a rude state, exemplified by the Scotch, who had no cabbages till Oliver Cromwell's soldiers introduced them; and one might thus shew how arts are propagated by conquest, as they were by the Roman arms.' He seemed to be much diverted with the fertility of his own fancy.

I told him, that I heard Dr. Percy was writing the history of the wolf in Great-Britain. JOHNSON. 'The wolf, Sir! why the wolf? Why does he not write of the bear, which we had formerly? Nay, it is said we had the beaver. Or why does he not write of the grey rat, the Hanover rat, as it is called, because it is said to have come into this country about the time that the family of Hanover came? I should like to see " *The History of the Grey Rat, by Thomas Percy, D.D. Chaplain in Ordinary to His Majesty,*"' (laughing immoderately). BOSWELL. 'I am afraid a court chaplain could not decently write of the grey rat.' JOHNSON. 'Sir, he need not give it the name of the Hanover rat.' Thus

a *It begins*

Where shall the Muse her arduous Course begin?
Where breathless end?
—Say, shall we sing of Mice Rats? [H]

[1] Dr. Johnson said to me, 'Percy, Sir, was angry with me for laughing at the Sugar-cane: for he had a mind to make a great thing of Grainger's rats.'a

could he indulge a luxuriant sportive imagination, when
talking of a friend whom he loved and esteemed.[a]

underlined:
loved, esteemed [H]

[a]*Qu! not Percy sure* [H]

He mentioned to me the singular history of an ingenious
acquaintance. 'He had practised physick in various situa-
tions with no great emolument. A West-India gentleman,
whom he delighted by his conversation, gave him a bond
for a handsome annuity during his life, on the condition
of his accompanying him to the West-Indies, and living
with him there for two years. He accordingly embarked
with the gentleman; but upon the voyage fell in love with
a young woman who happened to be one of the passengers,
and married the wench. From the imprudence of his disposition he quarrelled with the gentleman, and declared he
would have no connection with him. So he forfeited the
annuity. He settled as a physician in one of the Leeward
Islands. A man was sent out to him merely to compound
his medicines. This fellow set up as rival to him in his
practice of physick, and got so much the better of him in
the opinion of the people of the island, that he carried
away all the business, upon which he returned to England,
and soon after died.'

On Friday, March 22, having set out early from Henley,
where we had lain the preceding night, we arrived at
Birmingham about nine o'clock, and, after breakfast, went
to call on his old schoolfellow Mr. Hector. A very stupid
maid, who opened the door, told us, that 'her master was
gone out; he was gone to the country; she could not tell
when he would return.' In short, she gave us a miserable
reception; and Johnson observed, 'She would have behaved no better to people who wanted him in the way of
his profession.' He said to her, 'My name is Johnson; tell
him I called. Will you remember the name?' She answered
with rustick simplicity, in the Warwickshire pronunciation,
'I don't understand you, Sir.'—'Blockhead, (said he,) I'll
write.' I never heard the word *blockhead* applied to a
woman before, though I do not see why it should not,
when there is evident occasion for it.[1] He, however, made

[1] My worthy friend Mr. Langton, to whom I am under innumerable
obligations in the course of my Johnsonian History, has furnished me with a
droll illustration of this question. An honest carpenter, after giving some
anecdote, in his presence, of the ill treatment which he had received from a
clergyman's wife, who was a noted termagant, and whom he accused of

another attempt to make her understand him, and roared loud in her ear, '*Johnson*,' and then she catched the sound.

We next called on Mr. Lloyd, one of the people called Quakers. He too was not at home, but Mrs. Lloyd was, and received us courteously, and asked us to dinner. Johnson said to me, 'After the uncertainty of all human things at Hector's, this invitation came very well.' We walked about the town, and he was pleased to see it increasing.

I talked of legitimation by subsequent marriage, which obtained in the Roman law, and still obtains in the law of Scotland. JOHNSON. 'I think it a bad thing; because the chastity of women being of the utmost importance, as all property depends upon it, they who forfeit it should not have any possibility of being restored to good character; nor should the children, by an illicit connection, attain the full right of lawful children, by the posteriour consent of the offending parties.' His opinion upon this subject deserves consideration. Upon his principle there may, at times, be a hardship, and seemingly a strange one, upon individuals; but the general good of society is better secured. And, after all, it is unreasonable in an individual to repine that he has not the advantage of a state which is made different from his own, by the social institution under which he is born. A woman does not complain that her brother who is younger than her, gets their common father's estate. Why then should a natural son complain that a younger brother, by the same parents lawfully begotten, gets it? The operation of law is similar in both cases. Besides, an illegitimate son, who has a younger legitimate brother by the same father and mother, has no stronger claim to the father's estate, than if that legitimate brother had only the same father, from whom alone the estate descends.

Mr. Lloyd joined us in the street; and in a little while we met *Friend Hector*, as Mr. Lloyd called him. It gave me pleasure to observe the joy which Johnson and he expressed on seeing each other again. Mr. Lloyd and I left them

unjust dealing in some transaction with him, added, 'I took care to let her know what I thought of her.' And being asked, 'What did you say?' answered, 'I told her she was a *scoundrel*.'

together, while he obligingly shewed me some of the manufactures of this very curious assemblage of artificers. We all met at dinner at Mr. Lloyd's, where we were entertained with great hospitality. Mr. and Mrs. Lloyd had been married the same year with their Majesties, and like them, had been blessed with a numerous family of fine children, their numbers being exactly the same. Johnson said, 'Marriage is the best state for a man in general; and every man is a worse man, in proportion as he is unfit for the married state.'

I have always loved the simplicity of manners, and the spiritual-mindedness of the Quakers; and talking with Mr. Lloyd, I observed, that the essential part of religion was piety, a devout intercourse with the Divinity; and that many a man was a Quaker without knowing it.

As Dr. Johnson had said to me in the morning, while we walked together, that he liked individuals among the Quakers, but not the sect; when we were at Mr. Lloyd's, I kept clear of introducing any questions concerning the peculiarities of their faith. But I having asked to look at Baskerville's edition of 'Barclay's Apology,' Johnson laid hold of it; and the chapter on baptism happening to open, Johnson remarked, 'He says there is neither precept nor practice for baptism, in the scriptures; that is false.' Here he was the aggressor, by no means in a gentle manner; and the good Quakers had the advantage of him; for he had read negligently, and had not observed that Barclay speaks of *infant* baptism; which they calmly made him perceive. Mr. Lloyd, however, was in a great mistake; for when insisting that the rite of baptism by water was to cease, when the *spiritual* administration of CHRIST began, he maintained, that John the Baptist said, '*My baptism* shall decrease, but *his* shall increase.' Whereas the words are, '*He* must increase, but *I* must decrease.'[1]

One of them having objected to the 'observance of days, and months, and years,' Johnson answered, 'The Church does not superstitiously observe days, merely as days, but as memorials of important facts. Christmas might be kept as well upon one day of the year as another; but there should be a stated day for commemorating the birth

---

[1] John iii. 30.

of our Saviour, because there is danger that what may be done on any day, will be neglected.'

He said to me at another time, 'Sir, the holidays observed by our church are of great use in religion.'[a] There can be no doubt of this, in a limited sense, I mean if the number of such consecrated portions of time be not too extensive. The excellent Mr. Nelson's 'Festivals and Fasts,' which has, I understand, the greatest sale of any book ever printed in England, except the Bible, is a most valuable help to devotion; and in addition to it I would recommend two sermons on the same subject, by Mr. Pott, Archdeacon of St. Alban's, equally distinguished for piety and elegance. I am sorry to have it to say, that Scotland is the only Christian country, Catholic or Protestant, where the great events of our religion are not solemnly commemorated by its ecclesiastical establishment, on days set apart for the purpose.[b]

Mr. Hector was so good as to accompany me to see the great works of Mr. Bolton, at a place which he has called Soho, about two miles from Birmingham, which the very ingenious proprietor shewed me himself to the best advantage. I wished Johnson had been with us: for it was a scene which I should have been glad to contemplate by his light. The vastness and the contrivance of some of the machinery would have 'matched his mighty mind.' I shall never forget Mr. Bolton's expression to me, 'I sell here, Sir, what all the world desires to have—POWER.' He had about seven hundred people at work. I contemplated him as an *iron chieftain*, and he seemed to be a father to his tribe. One of them came to him, complaining grievously of his landlord for having distrained his goods. 'Your landlord is in the right, Smith (said Bolton.)[c] But I'll tell you what: find you a friend who will lay down one half of your rent, and I'll lay down the other half; and you shall have your goods again.'

From Mr. Hector I now learnt many particulars of Dr. Johnson's early life, which, with others that he gave me at different times since, have contributed to the formation of this work.

Dr. Johnson said to me in the morning, 'You will see, Sir, at Mr. Hector's, his sister, Mrs. Careless, a clergyman's

---

[a] *It is so true yt one Cause why Religion runs to decay is that Boys at private Schools now do not observe the old stated Festivals, but make a Summer and a Winter Vacation at Pleasure of ye. Master.* [I]

[b] *Is it so?—do they keep Saint's days at Geneva or Amsterdam? I thought not.* [H]

[c] *The Land Lord was in the right sure enough: and after such Encouragement would I suppose, do it again.* [H]

widow. She was the first woman with whom I was in love. It dropt out of my head imperceptibly; but she and I shall always have a kindness for each other.' He laughed at the notion that a man can never be really in love but once, and considered it as a mere romantick fancy.

On our return from Mr. Bolton's Mr. Hector took me to his house, where we found Johnson sitting placidly at tea, with his *first love;* who though now advanced in years, was a genteel woman, very agreeable and well bred.

Johnson lamented to Mr. Hector the state of one of their school fellows, Mr. Charles Congreve, a clergyman, which he thus described: 'He obtained, I believe, considerable preferment in Ireland, but now lives in London, quite as a valetudinarian, afraid to go into any house but his own. He takes a short airing in his post-chaise every day. He has an elderly woman, whom he calls cousin, who lives with him, and jogs his elbow, when his glass has stood too long empty, and encourages him in drinking, in which he is very willing to be encouraged; not that he gets drunk, for he is a very pious man, but he is always muddy. He confesses to one bottle of port every day, and he probably drinks more. He is quite unsocial; his conversation is quite monosyllabical; and when, at my last visit, I asked him what o'clock it was? that signal of my departure had so pleasing an effect on him, that he sprung up to look at his watch, like a greyhound bounding at a hare.' When Johnson took leave of Mr. Hector, he said, 'Don't grow like Congreve; nor let me grow like him, when you are near me.'

When he again talked of Mrs. Careless to-night, he seemed to have had his affection revived; for he said, 'If I had married her, it might have been as happy for me.' BOSWELL. 'Pray, Sir, do you not suppose that there are fifty women in the world, with any one of whom a man may be as happy, as with any one woman in particular?' JOHNSON. 'Ay, Sir, fifty thousand.' BOSWELL. 'Then, Sir, you are not of opinion with some who imagine that certain men and certain women are made for each other; and that they cannot be happy if they miss their counterparts.' JOHNSON. 'To be sure not, Sir. I believe marriages would in general be as happy, and often more so, if they

marginal line:
more so . . . the matter
[H]

were all made by the Lord Chancellor, upon a due consideration of the characters and circumstances, without the parties having any choice in the matter.'

I wished to have staid at Birmingham to-night, to have talked more with Mr. Hector; but my friend was impatient to reach his native city; so we drove on that stage in the dark, and were long pensive and silent. When we came within the focus of the Lichfield lamps, 'Now (said he,) we are getting out of a state of death.' We put up at the Three Crowns, not one of the great inns, but a good old fashioned one, which was kept by Mr. Wilkins, and was the very next house to that in which Johnson was born and brought up, and which was still his own property.[1] We had a comfortable supper, and got into high spirits. I felt all my Toryism glow in this old capital of Staffordshire. I could have offered incense *genio loci;* and I indulged in libations of that ale, which Boniface, in 'The Beaux Stratagem,' recommends with such an eloquent jollity.

Next morning he introduced me to Mrs. Lucy Porter, his step-daughter. She was now an old maid, with much simplicity of manner. She had never been in London. Her brother, a Captain in the navy, had left her a fortune of ten thousand pounds; about a third of which she had laid out in building a stately house, and making a handsome garden, in an elevated situation in Lichfield. Johnson, when here by himself, used to live at her house. She reverenced him, and he had a parental tenderness for her.

We then visited Mr. Peter Garrick, who had that morning received a letter from his brother David, announcing our coming to Lichfield. He was engaged to dinner, but asked us to tea, and to sleep at his house. Johnson, however, would not quit his old acquaintance Wilkins, of the Three Crowns. The family likeness of the Garricks was very striking; and Johnson thought that David's vivacity was not so peculiar to himself as was supposed. 'Sir, (said he,) I don't know but if Peter had cultivated all the arts of gaiety as much as David has done, he might have been as

---

[1] I went through the house where my illustrious friend was born, with a reverence with which it doubtless will long be visited. An engraved view of it, with the adjacent buildings, is in 'The Gentleman's Magazine' for February, 1785.

brisk and lively. Depend upon it, Sir, vivacity is much an
art, and depends greatly on habit.' I believe there is a
good deal of truth in this, notwithstanding a ludicrous
story told me by a lady abroad, of a heavy German baron,
who had lived much with the young English at Geneva,
and was ambitious to be as lively as they;[a] with which
view, he, with assiduous exertion, was jumping over the
tables and chairs in his lodgings; and when the people
of the house ran in and asked, with surprise, what was the
matter, he answered, '*Sh' apprens t'etre fif.*'

    We dined at our inn, and had with us a Mr. Jackson,
one of Johnson's schoolfellows, whom he treated with
much kindness, though he seemed to be a low man, dull
and untaught. He had a coarse grey coat, black waistcoat,
greasy leather breeches, and a yellow uncurled wig; and
his countenance had the ruddiness which betokens one
who is in no haste to 'leave his can.' He drank only ale. He
had tried to be a cutler at Birmingham, but had not succeeded; and now he lived poorly at home, and had some
scheme of dressing leather in a better manner than common; to his indistinct account of which, Dr. Johnson
listened with patient attention, that he might assist him
with his advice. Here was an instance of genuine humanity
and real kindness in this great man, who has been most
unjustly represented as altogether harsh and destitute of
tenderness. A thousand such instances might have been
recorded in the course of his long life; though that his
temper was warm and hasty, and his manner often rough,
cannot be denied.

    I saw here, for the first time, *oat ale;* and oat cakes, not
hard as in Scotland, but soft like a Yorkshire cake, were
served at breakfast. It was pleasant to me to find, that
'*Oats,*' the '*food of horses,*' were so much used as the *food
of the people* in Dr. Johnson's own town. He expatiated in
praise of Lichfield and its inhabitants, who, he said, were
'the most sober, decent people in England, the genteelest
in proportion to their wealth, and spoke the purest English.'
I doubted as to the last article of this eulogy: for they had
several provincial sounds: as *there,* pronounced like *fear,*
instead of like *fair; once* pronounced *woonse,* instead of
wunse, or *wonse.* Johnson himself never got entirely free of

[a] *lively as the English!!!* [1]

these provincial accents. Garrick sometimes used to take him off, squeezing a lemon into a punch-bowl, with uncouth gesticulations, looking round the company, and calling out, 'Who's for *poonsh?*' [1]

Very little business appeared to be going forward in Lichfield. I found, however, two strange manufactures for so inland a place, sail-cloth and streamers for ships; and I observed them making some saddle-cloths, and dressing sheepskins: but upon the whole, the busy hand of industry seemed to be quite slackened. 'Surely, Sir, (said I,) you are an idle set of people.' 'Sir, (said Johnson,) we are a city of philosophers, we work with our heads, and make the boobies of Birmingham work for us with their hands.'

There was at this time a company of players performing at Lichfield. The manager, Mr. Stanton, sent his compliments, and begged leave to wait on Dr. Johnson. Johnson received him very courteously, and he drank a glass of wine with us. He was a plain decent well-behaved man, and expressed his gratitude to Dr. Johnson for having once got him permission from Dr. Taylor at Ashbourne to play there upon moderate terms. Garrick's name was soon introduced. JOHNSON. 'Garrick's conversation is gay and grotesque. It is a dish of all sorts, but all good things.[a] There is no solid meat in it: there is a want of sentiment in it. Not but that he has sentiment sometimes, and sentiment too very powerful and very pleasing: but it has not its full proportion in his conversation.'

When we were by ourselves he told me, 'Forty years ago, Sir, I was in love with an actress here, Mrs. Emmet, who acted Flora, in "Hob in a Well."' What merit this lady had as an actress, or what was her figure, or her manner, I have not been informed; but if we may believe Mr. Garrick, his old master's taste in theatrical merit was by no means refined; he was not an *elegans formarum spectator.* Garrick used to tell, that Johnson said of an actor,

[a] *our Garrick's a Sallad says Goldsmith* [1]

[b] *I fear I say so too. & Johnson said He cured him of saying Feyther for Father. Herbert Lawrence a Man of the World, who had left Cheshire or Staffordshire very early for a gay London Life, always said The Pooblic Advertiser.* [H]

[1] [Garrick himself, like the Lichfieldians, always said—*shupreme, shuperior.*[b] BURNEY.]

[This is still the vulgar pronunciation of Ireland, where the pronunciation of the English language by those who have not expatriated, is doubtless that which generally prevailed in England in the time of Queen Elizabeth. MALONE.]

who played Sir Harry Wildair at Lichfield, 'There is a courtly vivacity[a] about the fellow;' when in fact, according to Garrick's account, 'he was the most vulgar ruffian that ever went upon *boards*.'

We had promised Mr. Stanton to be at his theatre on Monday. Dr. Johnson jocularly proposed to me to write a Prologue for the occasion: 'A Prologue, by James Boswell, Esq. from the Hebrides.' I was really inclined to take the hint. Methought, 'Prologue, spoken before Dr. Samuel Johnson, at Lichfield, 1776,' would have sounded as well as, 'Prologue, spoken before the Duke of York at Oxford,' in Charles the Second's time. Much might have been said of what Lichfield had done for Shakspeare, by producing Johnson and Garrick. But I found he was averse to it.

We went and viewed the museum of Mr. Richard Green, apothecary here, who told me he was proud of being a relation of Dr. Johnson's. It was, truely, a wonderful collection, both of antiquities and natural curiosities, and ingenious works of art. He had all the articles accurately arranged, with their names upon labels, printed at his own little press; and on the staircase leading to it was a board, with the names of contributors marked in gold letters. A printed catalogue of the collection was to be had at a bookseller's. Johnson expressed his admiration of the activity and diligence and good fortune of Mr. Green, in getting together, in his situation, so great a variety of things; and Mr. Green told me that Johnson once said to him, 'Sir, I should as soon have thought of building a man of war, as of collecting such a museum.' Mr. Green's obliging alacrity in showing it was very pleasing. His engraved portrait, with which he has favoured me, has a motto truely characteristical of his disposition, '*Nemo sibi vivat*.'

A physician being mentioned who had lost his practice, because his whimsically changing his religion had made people distrustful of him, I maintained that this was unreasonable, as religion is unconnected with medical skill. JOHNSON. 'Sir, it is not unreasonable; for when people see a man absurd in what they understand, they may conclude the same of him in what they do not understand. If a physician were to take to eating of horse-flesh,

underlined: *courtly vivacity* [1]

[a] *Johnson had not ever seen Courtliness at that Time or any Vivacity but of the coarsest Kind.* [1]

nobody would employ him; though one may eat horse-flesh, and be a very skilful physician. If a man were educated in an absurd religion, his continuing to profess it would not hurt him, though his changing to it would.'[1]

We drank tea and coffee at Mr. Peter Garrick's, where was Mrs. Aston, one of the maiden sisters of Mrs. Walmsley, wife of Johnson's first friend, and sister also of the lady of whom Johnson used to speak with the warmest admiration, by the name of Molly Aston, who was afterwards married to Captain Brodie of the navy.

On Sunday, March 24, we breakfasted with Mrs. Cobb, a widow lady, who lived in an agreeable sequestered place close by the town, called the Friary, it having been formerly a religious house. She and her niece, Miss Adey, were great admirers of Dr. Johnson; and he behaved to them with a kindness and easy pleasantry, such as we see between old and intimate acquaintance. He accompanied Mrs. Cobb to St. Mary's church, and I went to the cathedral, where I was very much delighted with the musick, finding it to be peculiarly solemn, and accordant with the words of the service.

We dined at Mr. Peter Garrick's, who was in a very lively humour, and verified Johnson's saying, that if he had cultivated gaiety as much as his brother David, he might have equally excelled in it. He was to-day quite a London narrator, telling us a variety of anecdotes with that earnestness and attempt at mimickry which we usually find in the wits of the metropolis. Dr. Johnson went with me to the cathedral in the afternoon. It was grand and pleasing to contemplate this illustrious writer, now full of fame, worshipping in 'the solemn temple' of his native city.

I returned to tea and coffee at Mr. Peter Garrick's, and then found Dr. Johnson at the Reverend Mr. Seward's, Canon Residentiary, who inhabited the Bishop's palace, in which Mr. Walmsley lived, and which had been the scene of many happy hours in Johnson's early life. Mr. Seward had, with ecclesiastical hospitality and politeness, asked me in the morning, merely as a stranger, to dine

[1] [Fothergill a Quaker, and Schomberg a Jew, had the greatest practice of any two physicians of their time. BURNEY.]

with him; and in the afternoon, when I was introduced to him, he asked Dr. Johnson and me to spend the evening and sup with him. He was a genteel well-bred dignified clergyman, had travelled with Lord Charles Fitzroy, uncle of the present Duke of Grafton, who died when abroad, and he had lived much in the great world. He was an ingenious and literary man, had published an edition of Beaumont and Fletcher, and written verses in Dodsley's collection. His lady was the daughter of Mr. Hunter, Johnson's first schoolmaster. And now, for the first time, I had the pleasure of seeing his celebrated daughter, Miss Anna Seward, to whom I have since been indebted for many civilities, as well as some obliging communications concerning Johnson.

Mr. Seward mentioned to us the observations which he had made upon the strata of earth in volcanos, from which it appeared, that they were so very different in depth at different periods, that no calculation whatever could be made as to the time required for their formation. This fully refuted an anti-mosaical remark introduced into Captain Brydone's entertaining Tour, I hope heedlessly, from a kind of vanity which is too common in those who have not sufficiently studied the most important of all subjects. Dr. Johnson, indeed, had said before, independent of this observation, 'Shall all the accumulated evidence of the history of the world;—shall the authority of what is unquestionably the most ancient writing, be overturned by an uncertain remark such as this?'

On Monday, March 25, we breakfasted at Mrs. Lucy Porter's. Johnson had sent an express to Dr. Taylor's, acquainting him of our being at Lichfield, and Taylor had returned an answer that his post-chaise should come for us this day. While we sat at breakfast, Dr. Johnson received a letter by the post, which seemed to agitate him very much. When he had read it, he exclaimed, 'One of the most dreadful things that has happened in my time.' The phrase *my time*, like the word *age*, is usually understood to refer to an event of a publick or general nature. I imagined something like an assassination of the King— like a gunpowder plot carried into execution—or like another fire of London. When asked, 'What is it, Sir?' he answered, 'Mr. Thrale has lost his only son!' This was, no doubt, a very great affliction to Mr. and Mrs. Thrale, which their friends would consider accordingly; but from the manner in which the intelligence of it was communicated by Johnson, it appeared for the moment to be comparatively small. I, however, soon felt a sincere concern, and was curious to observe how Dr. Johnson would be affected. He said, 'This is a total extinction to their family, as much as if they were sold into captivity.' Upon my mentioning that Mr. Thrale had daughters who might inherit his wealth;—'Daughters, (said Johnson, warmly,) he'll no more value his daughters than—' I was going to speak.—'Sir, (said he,) don't you know how you yourself think? Sir, he wishes to propagate his name.' In short, I saw male succession strong in his mind, even where there was no name, no family of any long standing. I said, it was lucky he was not present when this misfortune happened. JOHNSON. 'It is lucky for *me*. People in distress never think that you feel enough.' BOSWELL. 'And, Sir, they will have the hope of seeing you, which will be a relief in the mean time; and when you get to them, the pain will be so far abated, that they will be capable of being consoled by you, which, in the first violence of it, I believe, would not be the case.' JOHNSON. 'No, Sir; violent pain of mind, like violent pain of body, *must* be severely felt.' BOSWELL. 'I own, Sir, I have not so much feeling for the distress of others, as some people have, or pretend to have: but I know this, that I would do all in my power to relieve them.' JOHNSON. 'Sir, it is affectation to pretend to feel the distress of others, as much as they do themselves. It is equally so, as if one should pretend to feel as much pain while a friend's leg is cutting off, as he does. No, Sir; you have expressed the rational and just nature of sympathy. I would have gone to the extremity of the earth to have preserved this boy.'

He was soon quite calm. The letter was from Mr. Thrale's clerk, and concluded, 'I need not say how much they wish to see you in London.' He said, 'We shall hasten back from Taylor's.'

Mrs. Lucy Porter and some other ladies of the place talked a great deal of him when he was out of the room, not only with veneration but affection. It pleased me to find that he was so much *beloved* in his native city.

Mrs. Aston, whom I had seen the preceding night, and her sister, Mrs. Gastrel, a widow lady, had each a house and garden, and pleasure-ground, prettily situated upon Stowhill, a gentle eminence, adjoining to Lichfield. Johnson walked away to dinner there, leaving me by myself without any apology; I wondered at this want of that facility of manners, from which a man has no difficulty in carrying a friend to a house where he is intimate; I felt it very unpleasant to be thus left in solitude in a country town, where I was an entire stranger, and began to think myself unkindly deserted: but I was soon relieved, and convinced that my friend, instead of being deficient in delicacy, had conducted the matter with perfect propriety, for I received the following note in his handwriting: 'Mrs. Gastrel, at the lower house on Stowhill, desires Mr. Boswell's company to dinner at two.' I accepted of the invitation, and had here another proof how amiable his character was in the opinion of those who knew him best. I was not informed, till afterwards, that Mrs. Gastrel's husband was the clergyman who, while he lived at Stratford-upon-Avon, where he was proprietor of Shakspeare's garden, with Gothick barbarity cut down his mulberry-tree,[1] and, as Dr. Johnson told me, did it to vex his neighbours. His lady, I have reason to believe, on the same authority, participated in the guilt of what the enthusiasts of our immortal bard deem almost a species of sacrilege.

After dinner Dr. Johnson wrote a letter to Mrs. Thrale, on the death of her son. I said it would be very distressing to Thrale, but she would soon forget it, as she had so many things to think of. JOHNSON. 'No, Sir, Thrale will forget it first. *She* has many things that she *may* think of. *He* has many things that he *must* think of.' This was a very just remark upon the different effects of those light pursuits which occupy a vacant and easy mind, and those serious engagements which arrest attention, and keep us from brooding over grief.

marginal line:
JOHNSON. '*No* . . .
has many [H]

marginal line:
footnote 1 [H]

[1] See an accurate and animated statement of Mr. Gastrel's barbarity, by Mr. Malone, in a note on 'Some account of the Life of William Shakspeare,' prefixed to his admirable edition of that Poet's works, Vol. I. p. 118.

He observed of Lord Bute, 'It was said of Augustus, that it would have been better for Rome that he had never been born, or had never died. So it would have been better for this nation if Lord Bute had never been minister, or had never resigned.'

In the evening we went to the Town-hall, which was converted into a temporary theatre, and saw 'Theodosius,' with 'The Stratford Jubilee.' I was happy to see Dr. Johnson sitting in a conspicuous part of the pit, and receiving affectionate homage from all his acquaintance. We were quite gay and merry. I afterwards mentioned to him that I condemned myself for being so, when poor Mr. and Mrs. Thrale were in such distress. JOHNSON. 'You are wrong, Sir; twenty years hence Mr. and Mrs. Thrale will not suffer much pain from the death of their son. Now, Sir, you are to consider, that distance of place, as well as distance of time, operates upon the human feelings. I would not have you be gay in the presence of the distressed, because it would shock them; but you may be gay at a distance. Pain for the loss of a friend, or of a relation whom we love, is occasioned by the want which we feel. In time the vacuity is filled with something else; or sometimes the vacuity closes up of itself.'

Mr. Seward and Mr. Pearson, another clergyman here, supped with us at our inn, and after they left us, we sat up late as we used to do in London.

Here I shall record some fragments of my friend's conversation during this jaunt.

'Marriage, Sir, is much more necessary to a man than to a woman: for he is much less able to supply himself with domestick comforts. You will recollect my saying to some ladies the other day, that I had often wondered why young women should marry, as they have so much more freedom, and so much more attention paid to them while unmarried, than when married. I indeed did not mention the *strong* reason for their marrying—the *mechanical* reason.' BOSWELL. 'Why that *is* a strong one. But does not imagination make it much more important than it is in reality? Is it not, to a certain degree, a delusion in us as well as in women?' JOHNSON. 'Why yes, Sir; but it is a delusion that is always beginning again.' BOSWELL. 'I don't know but there is upon the whole more misery than happiness produced by that passion.' JOHNSON. 'I don't think so, Sir.'

'Never speak of a man in his own presence. It is always indelicate, and may be offensive.'

'Questioning is not the mode of conversation among gentlemen. It is assuming a superiority, and it is particularly wrong to question a man concerning himself. There may be parts of his former life which he may not wish to be made known to other persons, or even brought to his own recollection.'

'A man should be careful never to tell tales of himself to his own disadvantage. People may be amused and laugh at the time, but they will be remembered and brought out against him upon some subsequent occasion.'

'Much may be done if a man puts his whole mind to a particular object. By doing so, Norton[1] has made himself the great lawyer that he is allowed to be.'

I mentioned an acquaintance of mine, a sectary, who was a very religious man, who not only attended regularly on publick worship with those of his communion, but made a particular study of the Scriptures, and even wrote a commentary on some parts of them, yet was known to be very licentious in indulging himself with women; maintaining that men are to be saved by faith alone, and that the Christian religion had not prescribed any fixed rule for the intercourse between the sexes. JOHNSON. 'Sir, there is no trusting to that crazy piety.'

I observed that it was strange how well Scotchmen were known to one another in their own country, though born in very distant counties; for we do not find that the gentlemen of neighbouring counties in England are mutually known to each other. Johnson, with his usual acuteness, at once saw and explained the reason of this: 'Why, Sir, you have Edinburgh, where the gentlemen from all your counties meet, and which is not so large but they are all known. There is no such common place of collection in England, except London, where from its great size and diffusion, many of those who reside in contiguous counties of England, may long remain unknown to each other.'

[1] [Sir Fletcher Norton, afterwards Speaker of the House of Commons, and in 1782 created Baron Grantly. MALONE.]

On Tuesday, March 26, there came for us an equipage properly suited to a wealthy well-beneficed clergyman: Dr. Taylor's large, roomy post-chaise, drawn by four stout plump horses, and driven by two steady jolly postillions, which conveyed us to Ashbourne; where I found my friend's schoolfellow living upon an establishment perfectly corresponding with his substantial creditable equipage: his house, garden, pleasure-grounds, table, in short every thing good, and no scantiness appearing. Every man should form such a plan of living as he can execute completely. Let him not draw an outline wider than he can fill up. I have seen many skeletons of shew and magnificence which excite at once ridicule and pity. Dr. Taylor had a good estate of his own, and good preferment in the church, being a prebendary of Westminster, and rector of Bosworth. He was a diligent justice of the peace, and presided over the town of Ashbourne, to the inhabitants of which I was told he was very liberal; and as a proof of this it was mentioned to me, he had the preceding winter, distributed two hundred pounds among such of them as stood in need of his assistance. He had consequently a considerable political interest in the county of Derby, which he employed to support the Devonshire family; for though the schoolfellow and friend of Johnson, he was a Whig. I could not perceive in his character much congeniality of any sort with that of Johnson, who, however, said to me, 'Sir, he has a very strong understanding.' His size, and figure, and countenance, and manner, were that of a hearty English 'Squire, with the parson super-induced: and I took particular notice of his upper-servant, Mr. Peters, a decent grave man, in purple clothes, and a large white wig, like the butler or *major domo* of a bishop.

Dr. Johnson and Dr. Taylor met with great cordiality; and Johnson soon gave him the same sad account of their schoolfellow, Congreve, that he had given to Mr. Hector; adding a remark of such moment to the rational conduct of a man in the decline of life, that deserves to be imprinted upon every mind: 'There is nothing against which an old man should be so much upon his guard as putting himself to nurse.' Innumerable have been the melancholy instances of men once distinguished for firmness, resolution, and spirit, who in their latter days have been governed like children, by interested female artifice.

Dr. Taylor commended a physician who was known to him and Dr. Johnson, and said, 'I fight many battles for him, as many people in the country dislike him.' JOHNSON. 'But you should consider, Sir, that by every one of your victories he is a loser; for, every man of whom you get the better, will be very angry, and resolve not to employ him; whereas if people get the better of you in argument about him, they'll think, "We'll send for Dr. ***** nevertheless."' This was an observation deep and sure in human nature.

Next day we talked of a book in which an eminent judge was arraigned before the bar of the publick, as having pronounced an unjust decision in a great cause. Dr. Johnson maintained that this publication would not give any uneasiness to the judge. 'For (said he,) either he acted honestly, or he meant to do injustice. If he acted honestly, his own consciousness will protect him; if he meant to do injustice, he will be glad to see the man who attacks him, so much vexed.'

Next day, as Dr. Johnson had acquainted Dr. Taylor of the reason for his returning speedily to London, it was resolved that we should set out after dinner. A few of Dr. Taylor's neighbours were his guests that day.

Dr. Johnson talked with approbation of one who had attained to the state of the philosophical wise man, that is, to have no want of any thing. 'Then Sir, (said I,) the savage is a wise man.' 'Sir, (said he,) I do not mean simply being without,—but not having a want.' I maintained, against this proposition, that it was better to have fine clothes, for instance, than not to feel the want of them. JOHNSON. 'No, Sir; fine clothes are good only as they supply the want of other means of procuring respect. Was Charles the Twelfth, think you, less respected for his coarse blue coat and black stock? And you find the King of Prussia dresses plain, because the dignity of his character is sufficient.' I here brought myself into a scrape, for I heedlessly said, 'Would not *you*, Sir, be the better for velvet embroidery?' JOHNSON. 'Sir, you put an end to all argument when you introduce your opponent himself.

marginal line: *Was Charles . . . here brought* [H]

underlined:
is your want [H]
ᵃ So it was.—*Curiosity
carried Boswell further
than it ever carried any
Mortal breathing. he
cared not what he pro-
voked so as he saw what
such a one would say
or do.* [H]

Have you no better manners? There is *your want.*ᵃ I apologised by saying, I had mentioned him as an instance of one who wanted as little as any man in the world, and yet, perhaps, might receive some additional lustre from dress.

Having left Ashbourne in the evening, we stopped to change horses at Derby, and availed ourselves of a moment to enjoy the conversation of my countryman, Dr. Butter, then physician there. He was in great indignation because Lord Mountstuart's bill for a Scotch militia had been lost. Dr. Johnson was as violent against it. 'I am glad, (said he,) that Parliament has had the spirit to throw it out. You wanted to take advantage of the timidity of our scoundrels; (meaning, I suppose, the ministry.) It may be observed, that he used the epithet scoundrel, very commonly, not quite in the sense in which it is generally understood, but as a strong term of disapprobation; as when he abruptly answered Mrs. Thrale, who had asked him how he did, 'Ready to become a scoundrel, Madam; with a little more spoiling you will, I think, make me a complete rascal:'[1]— he meant, easy to become a capricious and self-indulgent valetudinarian; a character for which I have heard him express great disgust.

Johnson had with him upon this jaunt, '*Il Palmerino d' Inghilterra,*' a romance praised by Cervantes; but did not like it much. He said, he read it for the language, by way of preparation for his Italian expedition.—We lay this night at Loughborough.

On Thursday, March 28, we pursued our journey. I mentioned that old Mr. Sheridan complained of the ingratitude of Mr. Wedderburne and General Fraser, who had been much obliged to him when they were young Scotchmen entering upon life in England. JOHNSON. 'Why, Sir, a man is very apt to complain of the ingratitude of those who have risen far above him. A man when he gets into a higher sphere, into other habits of life, cannot keep up all his former connections. Then, Sir, those who knew him formerly upon a level with themselves, may think that they ought still to be treated as on a level, which cannot be; and an acquaintance in a former situation may bring out things which it would be very

[1]Anecdotes of Johnson, p. 176.

disagreeable to have mentioned before higher company, though, perhaps, every body knows of them.' He placed this subject in a new light to me, and showed, that a man who has risen in the world, must not be condemned too harshly, for being distant to former acquaintance, even though he may have been much obliged to them. It is, no doubt, to be wished, that a proper degree of attention should be shewn by great men to their early friends. But if either from obtuse insensibility to difference of situation, or presumptuous forwardness, which will not submit even to an exterior observance of it, the dignity of high place cannot be preserved, when they are admitted into the company of those raised above the state in which they once were, encroachment must be repelled, and the kinder feelings sacrificed. To one of the very fortunate persons whom I have mentioned, namely, Mr. Wedderburne, now Lord Loughborough, I must do the justice to relate, that I have been assured by another early acquaintance of his, old Mr. Macklin, who assisted in improving his pronunciation, that he found him very grateful. Macklin, I suppose, had not pressed upon his elevation with so much eagerness, as the gentleman who complained of him. Dr. Johnson's remark as to the jealousy entertained of our friends who rise far above us, is certainly very just. By this was withered the early friendship between Charles Townshend and Akenside; and many similar instances might be adduced.

He said, 'It is commonly a weak man, who marries for love.' We then talked of marrying women of fortune; and I mentioned a common remark, that a man may be, upon the whole, richer by marrying a woman with a very small portion, because a woman of fortune will be proportionably expensive; whereas a woman who brings none will be very moderate in expenses. JOHNSON. 'Depend upon it, Sir, this is not true. A woman of fortune being used to the handling of money, spends it judiciously; but a woman who gets the command of money for the first time upon her marriage, has such a gust in spending it, that she throws it away with great profusion.'

He praised the ladies of the present age, insisting that they were more faithful to their husbands, and more

marginal line:
Sir, this . . . great profusion [H]

virtuous in every respect, than in former times, because their understandings were better cultivated. It was an undoubted proof of his good sense and good disposition, that he was never querulous, never prone to inveigh against the present times, as is so common when superficial minds are on the fret. On the contrary, he was willing to speak favourably of his own age; and, indeed, maintained its superiority in every respect, except in its reverence for government; the relaxation of which he imputed, as its grand cause, to the shock which our monarchy received at the Revolution, though necessary; and secondly, to the timid concessions made to faction by successive administrations in the reign of his present Majesty. I am happy to think, that he lived to see the Crown at last recover its just influence.

At Leicester we read in the news-paper that Dr. James was dead. I thought that the death of an old school-fellow, and one with whom he had lived a good deal in London, would have affected my fellow-traveller much: but he only said, 'Ah! poor Jamy.' Afterwards, however, when we were in the chaise, he said, with more tenderness, 'Since I set out on this jaunt, I have lost an old friend and a young one;—Dr. James, and poor Harry,' (meaning Mr. Thrale's son.)

Having lain at St. Alban's, on Thursday, March 28, we breakfasted the next morning at Barnet. I expressed to him a weakness of mind which I could not help; an uneasy apprehension that my wife and children, who were at a great distance from me, might, perhaps, be ill. 'Sir, (said he,) consider how foolish you would think it in *them* to be apprehensive that *you* are ill.' This sudden turn relieved me for the moment; but I afterwards perceived it to be an ingenious fallacy.[1] I might, to be sure, be satisfied that they had no reason to be apprehensive about me, because I *knew* that I myself was well: but we might have a mutual anxiety, without the charge of folly; because each

<hr/>

[a] *He said it merely that he might have an Answer to record.* [H & I]

[1] [Surely it is no fallacy, but a sound and rational argument.[a] He who is perfectly well, and apprehensive concerning the state of another at a distance from him, *knows* to a certainty that the fears of that person concerning *his* health are imaginary and delusive; and hence has a rational ground for supposing that his own apprehensions concerning his absent wife or friend, are equally unfounded. MALONE.]

and Miss Thrale, and Signor Baretti, their Italian master, to Bath. This was not showing the attention which might have been expected to the 'Guide, Philosopher, and Friend;' the *Imlac* who had hastened from the country to console a distressed mother, who he understood was very anxious for his return. They had, I found, without ceremony, proceeded on their intended journey. I was glad to understand from him that it was still resolved that his tour to Italy with Mr. and Mrs. Thrale should take place, of which he had entertained some doubt,[a] on account of the loss which they had suffered; and his doubts afterwards appeared to be well founded. He observed, indeed very justly, that 'their loss was an additional reason for their going abroad; and if it had not been fixed that he should have been one of the party, he would force them out; but he would not advise them unless his advice was asked, lest they might suspect that he recommended what he wished on his own account.' I was not pleased that his intimacy with Mr. Thrale's family, though it no doubt contributed much to his comfort and enjoyment, was not without some degree of restraint.[b] Not, as has been grossly suggested,[c] that it was required of him as a task to talk for the entertainment of them and their company; but that he was not quite at his ease; which, however, might partly be owing to his own honest pride—that dignity of mind which is always jealous of appearing too compliant.

On Sunday, March 31, I called on him, and shewed him as a curiosity which I had discovered, his 'Translation of Lobo's Account of Abyssinia,' which Sir John Pringle had lent me, it being then little known as one of his works. He said, 'Take no notice of it,' or 'don't talk of it.' He seemed to think it beneath him, though done at six-and-twenty. I said to him, 'Your style, Sir, is much improved since you translated this.' He answered with a sort of triumphant smile, 'Sir, I hope it is.'

On Wednesday, April 3, in the morning, I found him very busy putting his books in order, and as they were generally very old ones, clouds of dust were flying around him. He had on a pair of large gloves such as hedgers use. His present appearance put me in mind of my uncle,

[a] *very rationally sure.* [H & I]

[b] *What Restraint can he mean? Johnson kept every body else under Restraint.* [H & I]

[c] *I do not believe it ever was suggested.* [H & I]

Dr. Boswell's, description of him, 'A robust genius, born to grapple with whole libraries.'

I gave him an account of a conversation which had passed between me and Captain Cook, the day before, at dinner at Sir John Pringle's; and he was much pleased with the conscientious accuracy of that celebrated circumnavigator, who set me right as to many of the exaggerated accounts given by Dr. Hawkesworth of his Voyages. I told him that while I was with the Captain, I catched the enthusiasm of curiosity and adventure, and felt a strong inclination to go with him on his next voyage. JOHNSON. 'Why, Sir, a man *does* feel so, till he considers how very little he can learn from such voyages.' BOSWELL. 'But one is carried away with the general grand and indistinct notion of A VOYAGE ROUND THE WORLD.' JOHNSON. 'Yes, Sir, but a man is to guard himself against taking a thing in general.' I said I was certain that a great part of what we are told by the travellers to the South Sea must be conjecture, because they had not enough of the language of those countries to understand so much as they have related. Objects falling under the observation of the senses might be clearly known; but every thing intellectual, every thing abstract—politicks, morals, and religion, must be darkly guessed. Dr. Johnson was of the same opinion. He upon another occasion, when a friend mentioned to him several extraordinary facts, as communicated to him by the circumnavigators, slily observed, 'Sir, I never before knew how much I was respected by these gentlemen; they told me none of these things.'

He had been in company with Omai, a native of one of the South Sea Islands, after he had been some time in this country. He was struck with the elegance of his behaviour, and accounted for it thus: 'Sir, he had passed his time, while in England, only in the best company; so that all that he had acquired of our manners was genteel. As a proof of this, Sir, Lord Mulgrave and he dined one day at Streatham; they sat with their backs to the light fronting me, so that I could not see distinctly; and there was so little of the savage in Omai, that I was afraid to speak to either, lest I should mistake one for the other.'[a]

a *When Omai played at Chess and Backgammon with Baretti, every body admired at the Savage's good Breeding, & at the European's Impatient Spirit.* [H]
comical enough [I]

We agreed to dine to-day at the Mitre-tavern, after the rising of the House of Lords, where a branch of the litigation concerning the Douglas Estate, in which I was one of the counsel, was to come on. I brought with me Mr. Murray, Solicitor-General of Scotland, now one of the Judges of the Court of Session, with the title of Lord Henderland. I mentioned Mr. Solicitor's relation, Lord Charles Hay, with whom I knew Dr. Johnson had been acquainted. JOHNSON. 'I wrote something for Lord Charles; and I thought he had nothing to fear from a court-martial. I suffered a great loss when he died; he was a mighty pleasing man in conversation, and a reading man. The character of a soldier is high. They who stand forth the foremost in danger, for the community, have the respect of mankind. An officer is much more respected than any other man who has as little money. In a commercial country, money will always purchase respect. But you find, an officer, who has, properly speaking, no money, is every where well received and treated with attention. The character of a soldier always stands him in stead.' BOSWELL. 'Yet, Sir, I think that common soldiers are worse thought of than other men in the same rank of life; such as labourers.' JOHNSON. 'Why, Sir, a common soldier is usually a very gross man, and any quality which procures respect may be overwhelmed by grossness. A man of learning may be so vicious or so ridiculous that you cannot respect him. A common soldier too, generally eats more than he can pay for. But when a common soldier is civil in his quarters, his red coat procures him a degree of respect.' The peculiar respect paid to the military character in France was mentioned. BOSWELL. 'I should think that where military men are so numerous, they would be less valuable as not being rare.' JOHNSON. 'Nay, Sir, wherever a particular character or profession is high in the estimation of a people, those who are of it will be valued above other men. We value an Englishman high in this country, and yet Englishmen are not rare in it.'

Mr. Murray praised the ancient philosophers for the candour and good humour with which those of different sects disputed with each other. JOHNSON. 'Sir, they disputed with good humour, because they were not in earnest as to religion. Had the ancients been serious in their belief, we should not have had their Gods exhibited in the manner we find them represented in the Poets. The people would not have suffered it. They disputed with good humour upon their fanciful theories, because they were not interested in the truth of them: when a man has nothing to lose, he may be in good humour with his opponent. Accordingly you see in Lucian, the Epicurean, who argues only negatively, keeps his temper; the Stoick, who has something positive to preserve, grows angry. Being angry with one who controverts an opinion which you value, is a necessary consequence of the uneasiness which you feel. Every man who attacks my belief, diminishes in some degree my confidence in it, and therefore makes me uneasy; and I am angry with him who makes me uneasy. Those only who believed in revelation have been angry at having their faith called in question; because they only had something upon which they could rest as matter of fact.' MURRAY. 'It seems to me that we are not angry at a man for controverting an opinion which we believe and value; we rather pity him.' JOHNSON. 'Why, Sir, to be sure when you wish a man to have that belief which you think is of infinite advantage, you wish well to him; but your primary consideration is your own quiet. If a madman were to come into this room with a stick in his hand, no doubt we should pity the state of his mind; but our primary consideration would be to take care of ourselves. We should knock him down first, and pity him afterwards. No, Sir, every man will dispute with great good humour upon a subject in which he is not interested. I will dispute very calmly upon the probability of another man's son being hanged; but if a man zealously enforces the probability that my own son will be hanged, I shall certainly not be in a very good humour with him.' I added this illustration, 'If a man endeavours to convince me that my wife, whom I love very much, and in whom I place great confidence, is a disagreeable woman, and is even unfaithful to me, I shall be very angry, for he is putting me in fear of being unhappy.' MURRAY. 'But, Sir, truth will always bear an examination.' JOHNSON. 'Yes, Sir, but it is painful to be forced to defend it. Consider, Sir, how

marginal line:
opponent. Accordingly ... positive to [H]

marginal line:
of his ... every man [H]

should you like, though conscious of your innocence, to be tried before a jury for a capital crime, once a week.'

We talked of education at great schools; the advantages and disadvantages of which Johnson displayed in a luminous manner; but his arguments preponderated so much in favour of the benefit which a boy of good parts might receive at one of them, that I have reason to believe Mr. Murray was very much influenced by what he had heard to-day in his determination to send his own son to Westminster school.—I have acted in the same manner with regard to my own two sons; having placed the eldest at Eton, and the second at Westminster. I cannot say which is best. But in justice to both those noble seminaries, I with high satisfaction declare, that my boys have derived from them a great deal of good, and no evil: and I trust they will, like Horace, be grateful to their father[a] for giving them so valuable an education.

[a] *Their Father was a fine Fellow—but a very strange one sure. Any Father but Thos. Fitzmaurice or James Boswell.* [H & I]

I introduced the topick, which is often ignorantly urged, that the Universities of England are too rich;[1] so that learning does not flourish in them as it would do, if those who teach had smaller salaries, and depended on their assiduity for a great part of their income. JOHNSON. 'Sir, the very reverse of this is the truth; the English Universities are not rich enough. Our fellowships are only sufficient to support a man during his studies to fit him for the world, and accordingly in general they are held no longer than till an opportunity offers of getting away. Now and then, perhaps, there is a fellow who grows old in his college; but this is against his will, unless he be a man very indolent indeed. A hundred a year is reckoned a good fellowship, and that is no more than is necessary to keep a man decently as a scholar. We do not allow our fellows to marry, because we consider academical institutions as preparatory to a settlement in the world. It is only by being employed as a tutor, that a fellow can obtain any thing more than a livelihood. To be sure a man, who has enough without teaching, will probably not teach; for we would all be idle if we could. In the same manner, a man who is

[1] Dr. Adam Smith, who was for some time a professor in the University of Glasgow, has uttered, in his 'Wealth of Nations', some reflections upon this subject which are certainly not well founded, and seem to be invidious.

to get nothing by teaching, will not exert himself. Gresham-College was intended as a place of instruction for London; able professors were to read lectures gratis, they contrived to have no scholars; whereas, if they had been allowed to receive but sixpence a lecture from each scholar, they would have been emulous to have had many scholars. Every body will agree that it should be the interest of those who teach to have scholars; and this is the case in our Universities. That they are too rich is certainly not true; for they have nothing good enough to keep a man of eminent learning with them for his life. In the foreign Universities a professorship is a high thing. It is as much almost as a man can make by his learning; and therefore we find the most learned men abroad are in the Universities. It is not so with us. Our Universities are impoverished of learning, by the penury of their provisions. I wish there were many places of a thousand a year at Oxford, to keep first-rate men of learning from quitting the University.' Undoubtedly if this were the case, Literature would have a still greater dignity and splendour at Oxford, and there would be grander living sources of instruction.

I mentioned Mr. Maclaurin's uneasiness on account of a degree of ridicule carelessly thrown on his deceased father, in Goldsmith's 'History of Animated Nature,' in which that celebrated mathematician is represented as being subject to fits of yawning so violent as to render him incapable of proceeding in his lecture; a story altogether unfounded, but for the publication of which the law would give no reparation.[1] This led us to agitate the question, whether legal redress could be obtained, even when a man's deceased relation was calumniated in a publication.[a] Mr. Murray maintained there should be reparation, unless the authour could justify himself by proving the fact. JOHNSON. 'Sir, it is of so much more consequence that truth should be told, than that individuals should not be made uneasy, that it is much better that the law does not restrain writing freely concerning the characters of the

index sign:
fits of yawning etc. [1]

underlined:
calumniated [H]

[a] & where was the Calumny? Saying a man was subject to Fits of Yawning! He should have said Oscitancy—& then nobody would have minded. [H]

[1] Dr. Goldsmith was dead before Mr. Maclaurin discovered the ludicrous errour. But Mr. Nourse, the bookseller, who was the proprietor of the work, upon being applied to by Sir John Pringle, agreed very handsomely to have the leaf on which it was contained, cancelled, and reprinted without it, at his own expence.

dead. Damages will be given to a man who is calumniated in his lifetime, because he may be hurt in his worldly interest, or at least hurt in his mind: but the law does not regard that uneasiness which a man feels on having his ancestor calumniated. That is too nice. Let him deny what is said, and let the matter have a fair chance by discussion. But if a man could say nothing against a character but what he can prove, history could not be written; for a great deal is known of men of which proof cannot be brought. A minister may be notoriously known to take bribes, and yet you may not be able to prove it.' Mr. Murray suggested, that the authour should be obliged to show some sort of evidence, though he would not require a strict legal proof: but Johnson firmly and resolutely opposed any restraint whatever, as adverse to a free investigation of the characters of mankind.[1]

marginal line:
books, that . . . the
peace [H]

[1] What Dr. Johnson has here said, is undoubtedly good sense; yet I am afraid that law, though defined by *Lord Coke* 'the perfection of reason,' is not altogether *with him;* for it is held in the books, that an attack on the reputation even of a dead man, may be punished as a libel, because tending to a breach of the peace. There is, however, I believe, no modern decided case to that effect. In the King's Bench, Trinity Term, 1790, the question occurred on occasion of an indictment, *The King* v. *Topham,* who as a *proprietor* of a newspaper entitled 'THE WORLD,' was found guilty of a libel against Earl Cowper, deceased, because certain injurious charges against his Lordship were published in that paper. An arrest of judgment having been moved for, the case was afterwards solemnly argued. My friend Mr. Const, whom I delight in having an opportunity to praise, not only for his abilities but his manners; a gentleman whose ancient German blood has been mellowed in England, and who may be truly said to unite the *Baron* and the *Barrister,* was one of the Counsel for Mr. Topham. He displayed much learning and ingenuity upon the general question; which, however, was not decided, as the Court granted an arrest chiefly on the informality of the indictment. No man has a higher reverence for the law of England than I have; but, with all deference I cannot help thinking, that prosecution by indictment, if a defendant is never to be allowed to justify, must often be very oppressive, unless Juries, whom I am more and more confirmed in holding to be judges of law as well as of fact, resolutely interpose. Of late an act of Parliament has passed declaratory of their full right to one as well as the other, in matter of libel; and the bill having been brought in by a popular gentleman, many of his party have in most extravagant terms declaimed on the wonderful acquisition to the liberty of the press. For my own part I ever was clearly of opinion that this right was inherent in the very constitution of a Jury, and indeed in sense and reason inseparable from their important function. To establish it, therefore, by statute, is, I think, narrowing its foundation, which is the broad and deep basis of Common Law. Would it not rather weaken the right of primo-geniture, or any other old and universally acknowledged right, should the legislature pass an act in favour of it. In my 'Letter to the People of Scotland, against diminishing

On Thursday, April 4, having called on Dr. Johnson, I said, it was a pity that truth was not so firm as to bid defiance to all attacks, so that it might be shot at as much as people chose to attempt, and yet remain unhurt. JOHNSON. 'Then, Sir, it would not be shot at. Nobody attempts to dispute that two and two make four: but with contests concerning moral truth, human passions are generally mixed, and therefore it must be ever liable to assault and misrepresentation.'

On Friday, April 5, being Good Friday, after having attended the morning service at St. Clement's church, I walked home with Johnson. We talked of the Roman Catholick religion. JOHNSON. 'In the barbarous ages, Sir, priests and people were equally deceived; but afterwards there were gross corruptions introduced by the clergy, such as indulgences to priests to have concubines, and the worship of images, not, indeed, inculcated, but knowingly permitted.' He strongly censured the licensed stews at Rome. BOSWELL. 'So then, Sir, you would allow of no irregular intercourse whatever between the sexes?' JOHNSON. 'To be sure I would not, Sir. I would punish it much more than it is done, and so restrain it. In all countries there has been fornication, as in all countries there has been theft; but there may be more or less of the one, as well as of the other, in proportion to the force of law. All men will naturally commit fornication, as all men will naturally steal. And, Sir, it is very absurd to argue, as has been often done, that prostitutes are necessary to prevent the violent effects of appetite from violating the decent order of life; nay, should be permitted in order to

the number of the Lords of Session,' published in 1785, there is the following passage, which, as a concise, and I hope a fair and rational state of the matter, I presume to quote: 'The Juries of England are Judges of *law* as well as of *fact* in *many civil* and in *all criminal* trials. That my principles of *resistance* may not be misapprehended any more than my principles of *submission*, I protest that I should be the last man in the world to encourage Juries to contradict rashly, wantonly, or perversely, the opinion of the Judges. On the contrary, I would have them listen respectfully to the advice they receive from the Bench, by which they may often be well directed in forming *their own opinion;* which, "and not another's," is the opinion they are to return *upon their oaths.* But where, after due attention to all that the Judge has said, they are decidedly of a different opinion from him, they have not only a *power* and a *right*, but they are *bound in conscience* to bring in a verdict accordingly.'

preserve the chastity of our wives and daughters. Depend upon it, Sir, severe laws, steadily enforced, would be sufficient against those evils, and would promote marriage.'

I stated to him this case:—'Suppose a man has a daughter, who he knows has been seduced, but her misfortune is concealed from the world? should he keep her in his house? Would he not, by doing so, be accessary to imposition? And, perhaps, a worthy, unsuspecting man might come and marry this woman, unless the father inform him of the truth.' JOHNSON. 'Sir, he is accessary to no imposition. His daughter is in his house; and if a man courts her, he takes his chance. If a friend, or, indeed, if any man asks his opinion whether he should marry her, he ought to advise him against it, without telling why, because his real opinion is then required. Or, if he has other daughters who know of her frailty, he ought not to keep her in his house. You are to consider the state of life is this; we are to judge of one another's characters as well as we can; and a man is not bound in honesty or honour, to tell us the faults of his daughter or of himself. A man who has debauched his friend's daughter is not obliged to say to every body—'Take care of me; don't let me into your house without suspicion. I once debauched a friend's daughter. I may debauch yours.'

Mr. Thrale called upon him, and appeared to bear the loss of his son with a manly composure. There was no affectation about him; and he talked, as usual, upon indifferent subjects. He seemed to me to hesitate as to the intended Italian tour, on which, I flattered myself, he and Mrs. Thrale and Dr. Johnson were soon to set out; and, therefore, I pressed it as much as I could. I mentioned that Mr. Beauclerk had said, that Baretti, whom they were to carry with them, would keep them so long in the little towns of his own district, that they would not have time to see Rome. I mentioned this to put them on their guard. JOHNSON. 'Sir, we do not thank Mr. Beauclerk for supposing that we are to be directed by Baretti. No, Sir; Mr. Thrale is to go by my advice, to Mr. Jackson,[1] (the

---

[1] A gentleman, who, from his extraordinary stores of knowledge, has been stiled *omniscient*. Johnson, I think very properly, altered it to all-knowing, as it is a *verbum solenne*, appropriated to the Supreme Being.

all-knowing) and get from him a plan for seeing the most that can be seen in the time that we have to travel. We must, to be sure, see Rome, Naples, Florence, and Venice, and as much more as we can.' (Speaking with a tone of animation.)

When I expressed an earnest wish for his remarks on Italy, he said, 'I do not see that I could make a book upon Italy; yet I should be glad to get two hundred pounds, or five hundred pounds, by such a work.' This shewed both that a journal of his Tour upon the Continent was not wholly out of his contemplation, and that he uniformly adhered to that strange opinion which his indolent disposition made him utter: 'No man but a blockhead ever wrote except for money.' Numerous instances to refute this will occur to all who are versed in the history of literature.

He gave us one of the many sketches of character which were treasured in his mind, and which he was wont to produce quite unexpectedly in a very entertaining manner. 'I lately, (said he,) received a letter from the East-Indies, from a gentleman whom I formerly knew very well; he had returned from that country with a handsome fortune, as it was reckoned, before means were found to acquire those immense sums which have been brought from thence of late; he was a scholar, and an agreeable man, and lived very prettily in London, till his wife died. After her death, he took to dissipation and gaming, and lost all he had. One evening he lost a thousand pounds to a gentleman whose name I am sorry I have forgotten. Next morning he sent the gentleman five hundred pounds, with an apology that it was all he had in the world. The gentleman sent the money back to him, declaring he would not accept of it; and adding, that if Mr. ⸺ had occasion for five hundred pounds more, he would lend it to him. He resolved to go out again to the East-Indies, and make his fortune anew. He got a considerable appointment, and I had some intention of accompanying him. Had I thought then as I do now, I should have gone: but at that time, I had objections to quitting England.'

It was a very remarkable circumstance about Johnson, whom shallow observers have supposed to have been ignorant of the world, that very few men had seen greater variety of characters; and none could observe them better, as was evident from the strong, yet nice portraits which he often drew. I have frequently thought that if he had made out what the French call *une catalogue raisonnée* of all the people who had passed under his observation, it would have afforded a very rich fund of instruction and entertainment. The suddenness with which his accounts of some of them started out in conversation, was not less pleasing than surprising. I remember he once observed to me, 'It is wonderful, Sir, what is to be found in London. The most literary conversation that I ever enjoyed, was at the table of Jack Ellis, a money-scrivener behind the Royal Exchange, with whom I at one period used to dine generally once a week.'[1]

Volumes would be required to contain a list of his numerous and various acquaintance, none of whom he ever forgot; and could describe and discriminate them all with precision and vivacity. He associated with persons the most widely different in manners, abilities, rank, and accomplishments. He was at once the companion of the brilliant Colonel Forrester of the Guards, who wrote 'The Polite Philosopher,' and of the aukward and uncouth Robert Levet; of Lord Thurlow, and Mr. Sastres, the Italian master; and has dined one day with the beautiful, gay, and fascinating Lady Craven,[2] and the next with good Mrs. Gardiner, the tallow-chandler, on Snow-hill.

index sign:
the authour of etc. [H]

[1] This Mr. Ellis was, I believe, the last of that profession called *Scriveners*, which is one of the London companies, but of which the business is no longer carried on separately, but is transacted by attornies and others. He was a man of literature and talents. He was the authour of a Hudibrastick version of Maphæus's Canto, in addition to the Æneid; of some poems in Dodsley's collections; and various other small pieces; but being a very modest man, never put his name to any thing. He shewed me a translation which he had made of Ovid's Epistles, very prettily done. There is a good engraved portrait of him by Pether, from a picture by Fry, which hangs in the hall of the Scriveners' company. I visited him October 4, 1790, in his ninety-third year, and found his judgement distinct and clear, and his memory, though faded so as to fail him occasionally, yet, as he assured me, and I indeed perceived, able to serve him very well, after a little recollection. It was agreeable to observe, that he was free from the discontent and fretfulness which too often molest old age. He in the summer of that year walked to Rotherhithe, where he dined, and walked home in the evening. He died on the 31st of December, 1791.

[2] Lord Macartney, who with his other distinguished qualities, is remarkable also for an elegant pleasantry, told me that he met Johnson at Lady Craven's, and that he seemed jealous of any interference: 'So, (said his Lordship, smiling,) *I kept back.*'

On my expressing my wonder at his discovering so much of the knowledge peculiar to different professions, he told me, 'I learnt what I know of law chiefly from Mr. Ballow,[1] a very able man. I learnt some too from Chambers; but was not so teachable then. One is not willing to be taught by a young man.' When I expressed a wish to know more about Mr. Ballow, Johnson said, 'Sir, I have seen him but once these twenty years. The tide of life has driven us different ways.' I was sorry at the time to hear this; but whoever quits the creeks of private connections, and fairly gets into the great ocean of London, will, by imperceptible degrees, unavoidably experience such cessations of acquaintance.

'My knowledge of physick, (he added,) I learnt from Dr. James, whom I helped in writing the proposals for his Dictionary, and also a little in the Dictionary itself.[2] I also learnt from Dr. Lawrence, but was then grown more stubborn.'

A curious incident happened to-day, while Mr. Thrale and I sat with him. Francis announced that a large packet was brought to him from the post-office, said to have come from Lisbon, and it was charged *seven pounds ten shillings.* He would not receive it, supposing it to be some trick, nor did he even look at it. But upon enquiry afterwards he found that it was a real packet for him, from that very friend in the East-Indies of whom he had been speaking; and the ship which carried it having come to Portugal, this packet with others had been put into the post-office at Lisbon.

I mentioned a new gaming club, of which Mr. Beauclerk had given me an account, where the members played to a desperate extent. JOHNSON. 'Depend upon it, Sir, this is mere talk. *Who* is ruined by gaming? You will not find six

[1] There is an account of him in Sir John Hawkins's Life of Johnson, p. 244.

[Mr. Thomas Ballow was authour of an excellent TREATISE OF EQUITY, printed anonymously in 1742, and lately republished with very valuable additions, by John Fonblanque, Esq.

Mr. Ballow died suddenly in London, July 26, 1782, aged seventy-five, and is mentioned in the Gentleman's Magazine for that year as 'a great Greek scholar, and famous for his knowledge of the old philosophy.' MALONE.]

[2] I have in vain endeavoured to find out what parts Johnson wrote for Dr. James. Perhaps medical men may.

instances in an age. There is a strange rout made about deep play; whereas you have many more people ruined by adventurous trade, and yet we do not hear such an outcry against it.' THRALE. 'There may be few people absolutely ruined by deep play; but very many are much hurt in their circumstances by it.' JOHNSON. 'Yes, Sir, and so are very many by other kinds of expence.' I had heard him talk once before in the same manner; and at Oxford he said, 'he wished he had learned to play at cards.' The truth, however, is, that he loved to display his ingenuity in argument; and therefore would sometimes in conversation maintain opinions which he was sensible were wrong, but in supporting which, his reasoning and wit would be most conspicuous. He would begin thus: 'Why, Sir, as to the good or evil of card playing—' 'Now, (said Garrick,) he is thinking which side he shall take.' He appeared to have a pleasure in contradiction, especially when any opinion whatever was delivered with an air of confidence; so that there was hardly any topick, if not one of the great truths of Religion and Morality, that he might not have been incited to argue, either for or against. Lord Elibank[1] had the highest admiration of his powers. He once observed to me, 'Whatever opinion Johnson maintains, I will not say that he convinces..ie; but he never fails to shew me, that he had good reasons for it.' I have heard Johnson pay his Lordship this high compliment:

'I never was in Lord Elibank's company without learning something.'

We sat together till it was too late for the afternoon service. Thrale said, he had come with intention to go to church with us. We went at seven to evening prayers at St. Clement's church, after having drank coffee; an indulgence, which I understood Johnson yielded to on this occasion, in compliment to Thrale.

On Sunday, April 7, Easter-day, after having been at St. Paul's cathedral, I came to Dr. Johnson, according to my usual custom. It seemed to me, that there was always something peculiarly mild and placid in his manner upon this holy festival, the commemoration of the most joyful event in the history of our world, the resurrection of our

two marginal lines: wished he . . . He would [H]

[1] Patrick, Lord Elibank, who died in 1778.

LORD and SAVIOUR, who, having triumphed over death and the grave, proclaimed immortality to mankind.

I repeated to him an argument of a lady of my acquaintance, who maintained, that her husband's having been guilty of numberless infidelities, released her from conjugal obligations, because they were reciprocal. JOHNSON. 'This is miserable stuff, Sir. To the contract of marriage, besides the man and wife, there is a third party—Society; and if it be considered as a vow—GOD: and, therefore, it cannot be dissolved by their consent alone. Laws are not made for particular cases, but for men in general. A woman may be unhappy with her husband; but she cannot be freed from him without the approbation of the civil and ecclesiastical power. A man may be unhappy, because he is not so rich as another; but he is not to seize upon another's property with his own hand.' BOSWELL. 'But, Sir, this lady does not want that the contract should be dissolved; she only argues that she may indulge herself in gallantries with equal freedom as her husband does, provided she takes care not to introduce a spurious issue into his family. You know, Sir, what Macrobius has told of Julia.'[1] JOHNSON. 'This lady of yours, Sir, I think, is very fit for a brothel.'

Mr. Macbean, authour of the 'Dictionary of Ancient Geography,' came in. He mentioned that he had been forty years absent from Scotland. 'Ah, Boswell! (said Johnson, smiling,) what would you give to be forty years from Scotland?' I said, 'I should not like to be so long absent from the seat of my ancestors.' This gentleman, Mrs. Williams, and Mr. Levett, dined with us.

Dr. Johnson made a remark, which both Mr. Macbean and I thought new. It was this: that 'the law against usury is for the protection of creditors as well as debtors; for if there were no such check, people would be apt, from the temptation of great interest, to lend to desperate persons, by whom they would lose their money. Accordingly there are instances of ladies being ruined, by having injudiciously sunk their fortunes for high annuities, which, after a few years, ceased to be paid, in consequence of the ruined circumstances of the borrower.'

[1] '*Nunquam enim nisi navi plenâ tollo vectorem.*' Lib. ii. c. vi.

Mrs. Williams was very peevish; and I wondered at Johnson's patience with her now, as I had often done on similar occasions. The truth is, that his humane consideration of the forlorn and indigent state in which this lady was left by her father, induced him to treat her with the utmost tenderness, and even to be desirous of procuring her amusement, so as sometimes to incommode many of his friends,[a] by carrying her with him to their houses, where, from her manner of eating, in consequence of her blindness, she could not but offend the delicacy of persons of nice sensations.[b]

[a] Yes truly. [I]

[b] & was Johnson one of them? [H]

After coffee, we went to afternoon service in St. Clement's church. Observing some beggars in the street as we walked along, I said to him, I supposed there was no civilized country in the world, where the misery of want in the lowest classes of the people was prevented. JOHNSON. 'I believe, Sir, there is not; but it is better that some should be unhappy, than that none should be happy, which would be the case in a general state of equality.'[c]

[c] very true. [H]

When the service was ended, I went home with him, and we sat quietly by ourselves. He recommended Dr. Cheyne's books. I said, I thought Cheyne had been reckoned whimsical. — 'So he was, (said he,) in some things; but there is no end of objections. There are few books to which some objection or other may not be made.' He added, 'I would not have you read any thing else of Cheyne, but his book on Health, and his "English Malady."'

Upon the question whether a man who had been guilty of vicious actions would do well to force himself into solitude and sadness; JOHNSON. 'No, Sir, unless it prevent him from being vicious again. With some people, gloomy penitence is only madness turned upside down. A man may be gloomy, till in order to be relieved from gloom, he has recourse again to criminal indulgencies.'

marginal line: *With some . . . be gloomy* [H]

On Wednesday, April 10, I dined with him at Mr. Thrale's, where were Mr. Murphy and some other company. Before dinner, Dr. Johnson and I passed some time by ourselves. I was sorry to find it was now resolved that the proposed journey to Italy should not take place this year. He said, 'I am disappointed to be sure; but it is not a great disappointment.' I wondered to see him bear, with a philosophical calmness, what would have made most people peevish and fretful. I perceived, however, that he had so warmly cherished the hope of enjoying classical scenes, that he could not easily part with the scheme; for he said, 'I shall probably contrive to get to Italy some other way. But I won't mention it to Mr. and Mrs. Thrale, as it might vex them.' I suggested that going to Italy might have done Mr. and Mrs. Thrale good. JOHNSON. 'I rather believe not, Sir. While grief is fresh, every attempt to divert only irritates. You must wait till grief be *digested*, and then amusement will dissipate the remains of it.'

marginal line: *attempt to . . . will dissipate* [H]

At dinner, Mr. Murphy entertained us with the history of Mr. Joseph Simpson, a schoolfellow of Dr. Johnson's, a barrister at law, of good parts, but who fell into a dissipated course of life, incompatible with that success in his profession which he once had, and would otherwise have deservedly maintained; yet he still preserved a dignity in his deportment. He wrote a tragedy on the story of Leonidas, entitled 'The Patriot.' He read it to a company of lawyers, who found so many faults that he wrote it over again: so then there were two tragedies on the same subject and with the same title. Dr. Johnson told us, that one of them was still in his possession. This very piece was, after his death, published by some person who had been about him, and, for the sake of a little hasty profit, was fallaciously advertised so as to make it be believed to have been written by Johnson himself.

I said, I disliked the custom which some people had of bringing their children into company, because it in a manner forced us to pay foolish compliments to please their parents. JOHNSON. 'You are right, Sir. We may be excused for not caring much about other people's children, for there are many who care very little about their own children. It may be observed, that men, who from being engaged in business, or from their course of life in whatever way, seldom see their children, do not care much about them. I myself should not have had much fondness for a child of my own.' MRS. THRALE. 'Nay, Sir, how can you talk so?' JOHNSON. 'At least, I never wished to have a child.'

Mr. Murphy mentioned Dr. Johnson's having a design
to publish an edition of Cowley. Johnson said, he did not
know but he should; and he expressed his disapprobation
of Dr. Hurd, for having published a mutilated edition
under the title of 'Select Works of Abraham Cowley.'
Mr. Murphy thought it a bad precedent; observing, that
any authour might be used in the same manner; and that
it was pleasing to see the variety of an authour's compositions, at different periods.

We talked of Flatman's Poems; and Mrs. Thrale observed, that Pope had partly borrowed from him, 'The
dying Christian to his Soul.' Johnson repeated Rochester's
verses upon Flatman, which, I think by much too severe:

> 'Nor that slow drudge in swift Pindarick strains,
> Flatman, who Cowley imitates with pains,
> And rides a jaded Muse, whipt with loose reins.'

I like to recollect all the passages that I heard Johnson
repeat: it stamps a value on them.

He told us that the book entitled 'The Lives of the Poets,
by Mr. Cibber,' was entirely compiled by Mr. Shiels,[1] a

[1] In the Monthly Review for May, 1792, there is such a correction of the
above passage, as I should think myself very culpable not to subjoin. 'This
account is very inaccurate. The following statement of facts we know to be
true, in every material circumstance:—Shiels was the principal collector and
digester of the materials for the work: but as he was very raw in authourship,
an indifferent writer in prose, and his language full of Scotticisms, Cibber,
who was a clever, lively fellow, and then soliciting employment among the
booksellers, was engaged to correct the style and diction of the whole work,
then intended to make only four volumes, with power to alter, expunge, or
add, as he liked. He was also to supply *notes*, occasionally, especially concerning those dramatick poets with whom he had been chiefly conversant.
He also engaged to write several of the Lives, which, (as we are told,) he,
accordingly, performed. He was farther useful in striking out the Jacobitical
and Tory sentiments, which Shiels had industriously interspersed wherever
he could bring them in:—and as the success of the work appeared, after all,
very doubtful, he was content with twenty-one pounds for his labour besides
a few sets of the books, to disperse among his friends.—Shiels had nearly
seventy pounds, beside the advantage of many of the best Lives in the work
being communicated by friends to the undertaking; and for which Mr.
Shiels had the same consideration as for the rest, being paid by the sheet for
the whole. He was, however, so angry with his Whiggish supervisor, (THE.,
like his father, being a violent stickler for the political principles which prevailed in the reign of George the Second,) for so unmercifully mutilating his
copy, and scouting his politicks, that he wrote Cibber a challenge: but was
prevented from sending it, by the publisher, who fairly laughed him out of
his fury. The proprietors, too, were discontented, in the end, on account of

Scotchman, one of his amanuenses. 'The booksellers, (said he,) gave Theophilus Cibber, who was then in prison, ten guineas, to allow *Mr. Cibber* to be put upon the title-page, as the authour; by this, a double imposition was intended: in the first place, that it was the work of a Cibber at all; and, in the second place, that it was the work of old Cibber.'

Mr. Murphy said, that 'The Memoirs of Gray's Life set him much higher in his estimation than his poems did: for you there saw a man constantly at work in literature.' Johnson acquiesced in this; but depreciated the book, I thought very unreasonably. For he said, 'I forced myself

Mr. Cibber's unexpected industry; for his corrections and alterations in the proof-sheets were so numerous and considerable, that the printer made for them a grievous addition to his bill; and, in fine, all parties were dissatisfied. On the whole, the work was productive of no profit to the undertakers, who had agreed, in case of success, to make Cibber a present of some addition to the twenty guineas which he had received, and for which his receipt is now in the booksellers' hands. We are farther assured, that he actually obtained an additional sum; when he, soon after, (in the year 1758,) unfortunately embarked for Dublin, on an engagement for one of the theatres there: but the ship was cast away, and every person on board perished. There were about sixty passengers, among whom was the Earl of Drogheda, with many other persons of consequence and property.

'As to the alledged design of making the compilement pass for the work of old Mr. Cibber, the charges seem to have been founded on a somewhat uncharitable construction. We are assured that the thought was not harboured by some of the proprietors, who are still living: and we hope that it did not occur to the first designer of the work, who was also the printer of it, and who bore a respectable character.

'We have been induced to enter circumstantially into the foregoing detail of facts relating to the Lives of the Poets, compiled by Messrs. Cibber and Shiels, from a sincere regard to that sacred principle of Truth, to which Dr. Johnson so rigidly adhered, according to the best of his knowledge; and which, we believe, *no consideration* would have prevailed on him to violate. In regard to the matter, which we now dismiss, he had, no doubt, been misled by partial and wrong information: Shiels was the Doctor's amanuensis; he had quarrelled with Cibber; it is natural to suppose that he told his story in his own way; and it is certain that *he* was not "a very sturdy moralist."'
This explanation appears to me very satisfactory. It is, however, to be observed, that the story told by Johnson does not rest solely upon my record of his conversation; for he himself has published it in his life of Hammond, where he says, 'the manuscript of Shiels is now in my possession.' Very probably he had trusted to Shiels's word, and never looked at it so as to compare it with 'The Lives of the Poets,' as published under Mr. Cibber's name. What became of that manuscript I know not. I should have liked much to examine it. I suppose it was thrown into the fire in that impetuous combustion of papers, which Johnson I think rashly executed when *moribundus*.

to read it, only because it was a common topic of conversation. I found it mighty dull; and, as to the style, it is fit for the second table.' Why he thought so I was at a loss to conceive. He now gave it as his opinion, that 'Akenside was a superiour poet both to Gray and Mason.'

queried three times
and underlined:
Gray [H]

Talking of the Reviews, Johnson said, ' I think them very impartial: I do not know an instance of partiality.' He mentioned what had passed upon the subject of the Monthly and Critical Reviews, in the conversation with which his Majesty had honoured him. He expatiated a little more on them this evening. 'The Monthly Reviewers (said he) are not Deists; but they are Christians with as little christianity as may be; and are for pulling down all establishments. The Critical Reviewers are for supporting the constitution both in Church and state.[1] The Critical Reviewers, I believe, often review without reading the books through; but lay hold of a topick, and write chiefly from their own minds. The Monthly Reviewers are duller men, and are glad to read the books through.'

He talked of Lord Lyttelton's extreme anxiety as an authour; observing, that 'he was thirty years in preparing his History, and that he employed a man to point it for him; as if (laughing) another man could point his sense better than himself.'[a] Mr. Murphy said, he understood his history was kept back several years for fear of Smollett. JOHNSON. 'This seems strange to Murphy and me, who never felt that anxiety, but sent what we wrote to the press, and let it take its chance.' MRS. THRALE. 'The time has been, Sir, when you felt it.' JOHNSON. 'Why really, Madam, I do not recollect a time when that was the case.'

underlined:
point, point [I]
[a] *Yes, a Cork-cutter.*
[H]
*a Cork-cutter as I re-
member* [I]

Talking of 'The Spectator,' he said, 'It is wonderful that there is such a proportion of bad papers, in the half of the work which was not written by Addison; for there was all the world to write that half, yet not a half of that half is good. One of the finest pieces in the English language is the paper on Novelty, yet we do not hear it talked of. It was written by Grove, a dissenting *teacher*.' He would not, I perceived, call him a *clergyman*, though he was

[1] [Johnson's opinions concerning the Monthly and Critical Reviews would not be accurate now [1803]. BLAKEWAY.]

candid enough to allow very great merit to his composition. Mr. Murphy said, he remembered when there were
several people alive in London, who enjoyed a considerable reputation merely from having written a paper in
'The Spectator.' He mentioned particularly Mr. Ince,
who used to frequent Tom's coffee-house. 'But (said
Johnson,) you must consider how highly Steele speaks of
Mr. Ince.' He would not allow that the paper on carrying
a boy to travel, signed *Philip Homebred*, which was reported
to be written by the Lord Chancellor Hardwicke, had
merit. He said, 'it was quite vulgar, and had nothing
luminous.'

index sign:
*He would not allow
etc.* [I]

Johnson mentioned Dr. Barry's[1] System of Physick. 'He
was a man (said he,) who had acquired a high reputation
in Dublin, came over to England, and brought his reputation with him, but had not great success. His notion was,
that pulsation occasions death by attrition; and that,
therefore, the way to preserve life is to retard pulsation.
But we know that pulsation is strongest in infants, and that
we increase in growth while it operates in its regular
course; so it cannot be the cause of destruction.' Soon after
this, he said something very flattering to Mrs. Thrale,
which I do not recollect; but it concluded with wishing
her long life. 'Sir, (said I,) if Dr. Barry's system be true,
you have now shortened Mrs. Thrale's life, perhaps, some
minutes, by accelerating her pulsation.'[a]

[a] *he checked it often
enough to be sure.* [H]

On Thursday, April 11, I dined with him at General
Paoli's, in whose house I now resided, and where I had
ever afterwards the honour of being entertained with the
kindest attention as his constant guest, while I was in
London, till I had a house of my own there. I mentioned
my having that morning introduced to Mr. Garrick, Count
Neni, a Flemish Nobleman of great rank and fortune, to
whom Garrick talked of Able[b] Drugger as *a small part;* and
related, with pleasant vanity, that a Frenchman, who had
seen him in one of his low characters, exclaimed, '*Comment!
je ne le crois pas. Ce n'est pas Monsieur Garrick, ce Grand
Homme!*' Garrick added, with an appearance of grave
recollection, 'If I were to begin life again, I think I should
not play those low characters.' Upon which I observed,

[b] *Able* corrected to
Abel [H]

[1] Sir Edward Barry, Baronet.

'Sir, you would be in the wrong, for your great excellence is your variety of playing, your representing so well, characters so very different.' JOHNSON. 'Garrick, Sir, was not in earnest in what he said; for, to be sure, his peculiar excellence is his variety; and, perhaps, there is not any one character which has not been as well acted by somebody else, as he could do it.' BOSWELL. 'Why then, Sir, did he talk so?' JOHNSON. 'Why, Sir, to make you answer as you did.' BOSWELL. 'I don't know, Sir; he seemed to dip deep into his mind for the reflection.' JOHNSON. 'He had not far to dip, Sir; he had said the same thing, probably, twenty times before.'[a]

queried:
as well acted etc. [H]

[a] *Bravo Johnson.*
[H & I]

Of a nobleman raised at a very early period to high office, he said, 'His parts, Sir, are pretty well for a Lord; but would not be distinguished in a man who had nothing else but his parts.'

A journey to Italy was still in his thoughts. He said, 'A man who has not been in Italy, is always conscious of an inferiority, from his not having seen what it is expected a man should see. The grand object of travelling is to see the shores of the Mediterranean. On those shores were the four great Empires of the world; the Assyrian, the Persian, the Grecian, and the Roman.—All our religion, almost all our law, almost all our arts, almost all that sets us above savages, has come to us from the shores of the Mediterranean.' The General observed, that 'THE MEDITERRANEAN would be a noble subject for a poem.'

marginal line:
THE MEDITERRA-
NEAN . . . *subject for*
[H]

We talked of translation. I said, I could not define it, nor could I think of a similitude to illustrate it; but that it appeared to me the translation of poetry could be only imitation. JOHNSON. 'You may translate books of science exactly. You may also translate history, in so far as it is not embellished with oratory, which is poetical. Poetry, indeed, cannot be translated; and, therefore, it is the poets that preserve languages; for we would not be at the trouble to learn a language, if we could have all that is written in it just as well in a translation. But as the beauties of poetry cannot be preserved in any language except that in which it was originally written, we learn the language.'

A gentleman maintained that the art of printing had hurt real learning, by disseminating idle writings.—

JOHNSON. 'Sir, if it had not been for the art of printing, we should now have no learning at all; for books would have perished faster than they could have been transcribed.' This observation seems not just, considering for how many ages books were preserved by writing alone.[1]

The same gentleman maintained, that a general diffusion of knowledge among a people was a disadvantage; for it made the vulgar rise above their humble sphere. JOHNSON. 'Sir, while knowledge is a distinction, those who are possessed of it will naturally rise above those who are not. Merely to read and write was a distinction at first; but we see when reading and writing have become general, the common people keep their stations. And so, were higher attainments to become general, the effect would be the same.'

'Goldsmith (he said), referred every thing to vanity; his virtues, and his vices too were from that motive. He was not a social man. He never exchanged mind with you.'

We spent the evening at Mr. Hoole's. Mr. Mickle, the excellent translator of 'The Lusiad,' was there. I have preserved little of the conversation of this evening. Dr. Johnson said, 'Thomson had a true poetical genius, the power of viewing every thing in a poetical light. His fault is such a cloud of words sometimes, that the sense can hardly peep through. Shiels, who compiled "Cibber's Lives of the Poets,"[2] was one day sitting with me. I took down Thomson, and read aloud a large portion of him, and then asked,—Is not this fine? Shiels having expressed the highest admiration. Well, Sir, (said I,) I have omitted every other line.'

I related a dispute between Goldsmith and Mr. Robert Dodsley, one day when they and I were dining at Tom Davies's, in 1762. Goldsmith asserted, that there was no poetry produced in this age. Dodsley appealed to his own Collection, and maintained, that though you could not find a palace like Dryden's 'Ode on St. Cecilia's Day,'

[1] [The authour did not recollect that of the books preserved (and an infinite number was lost) all were confined to two languages. In modern times and modern languages, France and Italy alone produce more books in a given time than Greece and Rome; put England, Spain, Germany, and the Northern kingdoms out of the question. BLAKEWAY.]

[2] See ante, Note, pp. 280, 281.

you had villages composed of very pretty houses; and he mentioned particularly 'The Spleen.' JOHNSON. 'I think Dodsley gave up the question. He and Goldsmith said the same thing; only he said it in a softer manner than Goldsmith did; for he acknowledged that there was no poetry, nothing that towered above the common mark. You may find wit and humour in verse, and yet no poetry. "Hudibras" has a profusion of these; yet it is not to be reckoned a poem. "The Spleen," in Dodsley's collection, on which you say he chiefly rested, is not poetry.' BOSWELL. 'Does not Gray's poetry, Sir, tower above the common mark?' JOHNSON. 'Yes, Sir; but we must attend to the difference between what men in general cannot do if they would, and what every man may do if he would. Sixteen-string Jack[1] towered above the common mark.' BOSWELL. 'Then, Sir, what is poetry?' JOHNSON. 'Why, Sir, it is much easier to say what it is not. We all *know* what light is; but it is not easy to *tell* what it is.'

On Friday, April 12, I dined with him at our friend Tom Davies's, where we met Mr. Cradock, of Leicestershire, authour of 'Zobeide,' a tragedy; a very pleasing gentleman, to whom my friend Dr. Farmer's very excellent Essay on the Learning of Shakspeare is addressed; and Dr. Harwood, who has written and published various works; particularly a fantastical translation of the New Testament, in modern phrase, and with a Socinian twist.

I introduced Aristotle's doctrine in his 'Art of Poetry,' of 'the κάθαρσις τῶν παθημάτων, the purging of the passions,' as the purpose of tragedy.[2] 'But how are the passions to be purged by terrour and pity?' (said I, with an assumed air of ignorance, to incite him to talk, for which it was often necessary to employ some address). JOHNSON. 'Why, Sir, you are to consider what is the

[a] *Footpad rather. The Remarkable was, his adding a String to his Knees every Time he was acquitted in honour of his Escape.* [H]

Jack added a String every Time he was acquitted—or perhaps I should say every Time he escaped Punishment; —& he managed his System of Escape so ably that at last he was 16 String Jack. he had been Coachman to a Sister of Mr. Thrale [I]

[1] A noted highwayman, who after having been several times tried and acquitted, was at last hanged. He was remarkable for foppery in his dress, and particularly for wearing a bunch of sixteen strings at the knees of his breeches.[a]

[2] See an ingenious Essay on this subject by the late Dr. Moor, Greek professor at Glasgow.

[See also a learned note on this passage of Aristotle, by Mr. Twining, in his admirable translation of the Poeticks, in which the various explanations of other criticks are considered, and in which Dr. Moor's Essay is particularly discussed. J. BOSWELL.]

meaning of purging in the original sense. It is to expel
impurities from the human body. The mind is subject to
the same imperfection. The passions are the great movers
of human actions; but they are mixed with such impurities,
that it is necessary they should be purged or refined by
means of terrour and pity. For instance, ambition is a
noble passion; but by seeing upon the stage, that a man
who is so excessively ambitious as to raise himself by
injustice, is punished, we are terrified at the fatal consequences of such a passion. In the same manner a certain
degree of resentment is necessary; but if we see that a man
carries it too far, we pity the object of it, and are taught
to moderate that passion.' My record upon this occasion
does great injustice to Johnson's expression, which was so
forcible and brilliant, that Mr. Cradock whispered me,
'O that his words were written in a book!'

I observed the great defect of the tragedy of 'Othello'
was, that it had not a moral; for that no man could resist
the circumstances of suspicion which were artfully suggested to Othello's mind. JOHNSON. 'In the first place,
Sir, we learn from Othello this very useful moral, not to
make an unequal match; in the second place, we learn
not to yield too readily to suspicion. The handkerchief is
merely a trick, though a very pretty trick; but there are
no other circumstances of reasonable suspicion, except
what is related by Iago of Cassio's warm expressions concerning Desdemona in his sleep; and that depended entirely
upon the assertion of one man. No, Sir, I think Othello
has more moral than almost any play.'

Talking of a penurious gentleman of our acquaintance,
Johnson said, 'Sir, he is narrow, not so much from avarice,
as from impotence to spend his money. He cannot find in
his heart to pour out a bottle of wine; but he would not
much care if it should sour.'

He said, he wished to see 'John Dennis's Critical Works'
collected. Davies said, they would not sell. Dr. Johnson
seemed to think otherwise.

Davies said of a well known dramatick authour, that 'he
lived upon *potted stories,* and that he made his way as
Hannibal did, by vinegar; having begun by attacking
people, particularly the players.'

index sign:
Davies said etc. [H]

He reminded Dr. Johnson of Mr. Murphy's having paid him the highest compliment that ever was paid to a layman, by asking his pardon for repeating some oaths in the course of telling a story.

Johnson and I supped this evening at the Crown and Anchor tavern, in company with Sir Joshua Reynolds, Mr. Langton, Mr. Nairne, now one of the Scotch Judges, with the title of Lord Dunsinan, and my very worthy friend, Sir William Forbes, of Pitsligo.

We discussed the question, whether drinking improved conversation and benevolence. Sir Joshua maintained, it did. JOHNSON. 'No, Sir: before dinner men meet with great inequality of understanding; and those who are conscious of their inferiority, have the modesty not to talk. When they have drunk wine, every man feels himself happy, and loses that modesty, and grows impudent and vociferous: but he is not improved: he is only not sensible of his defects.' Sir Joshua said the Doctor was talking of the effects of excess in wine; but that a moderate glass enlivened the mind, by giving a proper circulation to the blood. 'I am, (said he,) in very good spirits, when I get up in the morning. By dinner time I am exhausted; wine puts me in the same state as when I got up: and I am sure that moderate drinking makes people talk better.' JOHNSON. 'No, Sir; wine gives not light, gay, ideal hilarity; but tumultuous, noisy, clamorous merriment. I have heard none of those drunken, —nay, drunken is a coarse word,— none of those *vinous* flights.' SIR JOSHUA. 'Because you have sat by, quite sober, and felt an envy of the happiness of those who were drinking.' JOHNSON. 'Perhaps, contempt.—And, Sir, it is not necessary to be drunk one's self, to relish the wit of drunkenness. Do we not judge of the drunken wit of the dialogue between Iago and Cassio, the most excellent in its kind, when we are quite sober? Wit is wit, by whatever means it is produced; and, if good, will appear so at all times. I admit that the spirits are raised by drinking, as by the common participation of any pleasure: cock-fighting, or bear-baiting, will raise the spirits of a company, as drinking does, though surely they will not improve conversation. I also admit, that there are some sluggish men who are improved by drinking; as

there are fruits which are not good till they are rotten.
There are such men, but they are medlars. I indeed allow
that there have been a very few men of talents who were
improved by drinking; but I maintain that I am right as
to the effects of drinking in general: and let it be considered, that there is no position, however false in its
universality, which is not true of some particular man.' Sir
William Forbes said, 'Might not a man warmed with wine
be like a bottle of beer, which is made brisker by being
set before the fire!'—'Nay, (said Johnson, laughing,) I
cannot answer that: that is too much for me.'

I observed, that wine did some people harm, by inflaming, confusing, and irritating their minds; but that
the experience of mankind had declared in favour of
moderate drinking. JOHNSON. 'Sir, I do not say it is
wrong to produce self-complacency by drinking; I only
deny that it improves the mind. When I drank wine, I
scorned to drink it when in company. I have drunk many
a bottle by myself; in the first place, because I had need of
it to raise my spirits: in the second place, because I would
have nobody to witness its effects upon me.'

He told us, 'almost all his Ramblers were written just
as they were wanted for the press; that he sent a certain
portion of the copy of an essay, and wrote the remainder,
while the former part of it was printing. When it was
wanted, and he had fairly sat down to it, he was sure it
would be done.'

He said, that for general improvement, a man should
read whatever his immediate inclination prompts him to;
though to be sure, if a man has a science to learn, he must
regularly and resolutely advance. He added, 'what we
read with inclination makes a much stronger impression.
If we read without inclination, half the mind is employed
in fixing the attention; so there is but one half to be employed on what we read.' He told us, he read Fielding's
'Amelia' through without stopping.[1] He said, 'if a man

[1] We have here an involuntary testimony to the excellence of this admirable writer, to whom we have seen that Dr. Johnson *directly* allowed
so little merit.

[Johnson appears to have been particularly pleased with the character of
the heroine of this novel. 'His attention to veracity (says Mrs. Piozzi,) was
without equal or example, and when I mentioned Clarissa as a perfect

begins to read in the middle of a book, and feels an inclination to go on, let him not quit it, to go to the beginning.[a]
He may, perhaps, not feel again the inclination.'

[a] *I began the Rom-
ance of St. Leon so, and
never wanted the first
Vol. at all.* [H]
*I begun Godwin's
St. Leon the 2d. Vol:
& went on to the End;
& never miss'd the
first Volume at all—Is
that Praise or Censure?*
[I]

Sir Joshua mentioned Mr. Cumberland's Odes, which
were just published. JOHNSON. 'Why, Sir, they would
have been thought as good as Odes commonly are, if
Cumberland had not put his name to them; but a name
immediately draws censure, unless it be a name that bears
down every thing before it. Nay, Cumberland has made
his Odes subsidiary to the fame of another man.[1] They
might have run well enough by themselves; but he has
not only loaded them with a name, but has made them
carry double.'

We talked of the Reviews, and Dr. Johnson spoke of
them as he did at Thrale's.[2] Sir Joshua said, what I have
often thought, that he wondered to find so much good
writing employed in them, when the authours were to
remain unknown, and so could not have the motive of
fame. JOHNSON. 'Nay, Sir, those who write in them, write
well in order to be paid well.'

Soon after this day, he went to Bath with Mr. and Mrs.
Thrale. I had never seen that beautiful city, and wished to
take the opportunity of visiting it, while Johnson was there.
Having written to him, I received the following answer:

'TO JAMES BOSWELL, ESQ.

'DEAR SIR,

'WHY do you talk of neglect? When did I neglect
you? If you will come to Bath, we shall all be glad to see
you. Come, therefore, as soon as you can.

'But I have a little business for you at London. Bid
Francis look in the paper drawer of the chest of drawers in
my bed-chamber, for two cases; one for the Attorney-
General, and one for the Solicitor-General. They lie, I think,

character, "On the contrary, (said he), you may observe there is always
something which she prefers to truth. Fielding's Amelia was the most
pleasing heroine of all the romances, (he said,) but that vile broken nose,
never cured, ruined the sale of perhaps the only book, which being printed
off [published] betimes one morning, a new edition was called for before
night."' ANECDOTES, p. 221. MALONE.]

[1] Mr. Romney, the painter, who has now deservedly established a high
reputation.   [2] Page 282 of this volume.

at the top of my papers; otherwise they are somewhere else, and will give me more trouble.

'Please to write to me immediately, if they can be found. Make my compliments to all our friends round the world, and to Mrs. Williams at home.

'I am, Sir, your, &c.

'SAM. JOHNSON.'

'Search for the papers as soon as you can, that, if it is necessary, I may write to you again before you come down.'

On the 26th of April, I went to Bath; and on my arrival at the Pelican inn,[a] found lying for me an obliging invitation from Mr. and Mrs. Thrale, by whom I was agreeably entertained almost constantly during my stay. They were gone to the rooms: but there was a kind note from Dr. Johnson, that he should sit at home all the evening. I went to him directly, and before Mr. and Mrs. Thrale returned, we had by ourselves some hours of tea-drinking and talk.

underlined, with Qu. in margin: Pelican [H]

[a] I do think there never was a Pelican Inn at Bath. [I]

I shall group together such of his sayings as I preserved during the few days that I was at Bath.

Of a person who differed from him in politicks, he said, 'In private life he is a very honest gentleman; but I will not allow him to be so in publick life. People *may* be honest, though they are doing wrong: that is, between their Maker and them. But *we*, who are suffering by their pernicious conduct, are to destroy them. We are sure that ————[b] acts from interest. We know what his genuine principles were. They who allow their passions to confound the distinctions between right and wrong, are criminal. They may be convinced; but they have not come honestly by their conviction.'

[b] Burke I suppose [I]

It having been mentioned, I know not with what truth, that a certain female political writer,[c] whose doctrines he disliked, had of late become very fond of dress, sat hours together at her toilet, and even put on rouge:—JOHNSON. 'She is better employed at her toilet, than using her pen. It is better she should be reddening her own cheeks, than blackening other people's characters.'

[c] Mrs. Macaulay [H]

marginal line: her toilet . . . blackening other [H]

He told us that 'Addison wrote Budgell's papers in the Spectator, at least mended them so much, that he made them almost his own; and that Draper, Tonson's partner, assured Mrs. Johnson, that the much admired Epilogue to "The Distressed Mother," which came out in Budgell's name, was in reality written by Addison.'

'The mode of government by one may be ill adapted to a small society, but is best for a great nation. The characteristick of our own government at present is imbecility.[a] The magistrates dare not call the guards for fear of being hanged. The guards will not come for fear of being given up to the blind rage of popular juries.'

[a] *in 1820 the Same.* [H]

[b] *Old Langton.* [I]

Of the father of one of our friends,[b] he observed, 'He never clarified his notions, by filtrating them through other minds. He had a canal upon his estate, where at one place the bank was too low.—I dug the canal deeper,' said he.[c]

[c] *Langton* [H]

He told me that 'so long ago as 1748 he had read "The Grave, a Poem,"[1] but did not like it much.' I differed from him: for though it is not equal throughout, and is seldom elegantly correct, it abounds in solemn thought, and poetical imagery beyond the common reach.[d] The world has differed from him; for the poem has passed through many editions, and is still much read by people of a serious cast of mind.

[d] *oh it is very fine See how the Soul &* [I]

[e] *Mrs. Montagu I suppose* [I]

A literary lady of large fortune was mentioned,[e] as one who did good to many, but by no means 'by stealth,' and instead of 'blushing to find it fame,' acted evidently from vanity. JOHNSON. 'I have seen no beings who do as much good from benevolence, as she does from whatever motive. If there are such under the earth, or in the clouds, I wish they would come up, or come down. What Soame Jenyns says upon this subject is not to be minded; he is a wit. No, Sir; to act from pure benevolence is not possible for finite beings. Human benevolence is mingled with vanity, interest, or some other motive.'

queried: to act etc. [H]

[1] I am sorry that there are no memoirs of the Reverend Robert Blair, the authour of this poem. He was the representative of the ancient family of Blair, of Blair, in Ayrshire, but the estate had descended to a female, and afterwards passed to the son of her husband by another marriage. He was minister of the parish of Athelstaneford, where Mr. John Home was his successor; so that it may truly be called classick ground. His son, who is of the same name, and a man eminent for talents and learning, is now, with universal approbation, Solicitor-general of Scotland.

He would not allow me to praise a lady then at Bath;[a] observing, 'She does not gain upon me, Sir; I think her empty-headed.' He was, indeed, a stern critick upon characters and manners. Even Mrs. Thrale did not escape his friendly animadversion at times. When he and I were one day endeavouring to ascertain article by article, how one of our friends could possibly spend as much money in his family as he told us he did, she interrupted us by a lively extravagant sally, on the expence of clothing his children, describing it in a very ludicrous and fanciful manner. Johnson looked a little angry, and said, 'Nay, Madam, when you are declaiming, declaim; and when you are calculating, calculate.' At another time, when she said, perhaps affectedly, 'I don't like to fly.' JOHNSON. 'With *your* wings, Madam, you *must* fly: but have a care, there are *clippers* abroad.' How very well was this said, and how fully has experience proved the truth of it![b] But have they not *clipped* rather *rudely*, and gone a great deal *closer* than was necessary?

A gentleman expressed a wish to go and live three years at Otaheité, or New Zealand, in order to obtain a full acquaintance with people, so totally different from all that we have ever known, and be satisfied what pure nature can do for man. JOHNSON. 'What could you learn, Sir? What can savages tell, but what they themselves have seen? Of the past, or the invisible, they can tell nothing. The inhabitants of Otaheité and New Zealand are not in a state of pure nature; for it is plain they broke off from some other people. Had they grown out of the ground, you might have judged of a state of pure nature. Fanciful people may talk of a mythology being amongst them; but it must be invention. They have once had religion, which has been gradually debased. And what account of their religion can you suppose to be learnt from savages? Only consider, Sir, our own state: our religion is in a book; we have an order of men whose duty it is to teach it, we have one day in the week set apart for it, and this is in general pretty well observed: yet ask the first ten gross men you meet, and hear what they can tell of their religion.'

On Monday, April 29, he and I made an excursion to Bristol, where I was entertained with seeing him enquire

[a] *I can't guess who ys. was.* [1]

[b] *I flew* from *the Clippers.* [1]

upon the spot, into the authenticity of '*Rowley's* Poetry,'
as I had seen him enquire upon the spot into the authenticity of '*Ossian's* Poetry.' George Catcot, the pewterer,
who was as zealous for Rowley, as Dr. Hugh Blair was
for *Ossian*, (I trust my Reverend friend will excuse the
comparison,) attended us at our inn, and with a triumphant air of lively simplicity called out, 'I'll make Dr.
Johnson a convert.' Dr. Johnson, at his desire, read aloud
some of Chatterton's fabricated verses, while Catcot stood
at the back of his chair, moving himself like a pendulum,
and beating time with his feet, and now and then looking
into Dr. Johnson's face, wondering that he was not yet
convinced. We called on Mr. Barret, the surgeon, and saw
some of the *originals* as they were called, which were
executed very artificially; but from a careful inspection of
them, and a consideration of the circumstances with
which they were attended, we were quite satisfied of the
imposture, which, indeed, has been clearly demonstrated
from internal evidence, by several able criticks.[1]

Honest Catcot seemed to pay no attention whatever to
any objections, but insisted, as an end of all controversy,
that we should go with him to the tower of the church of
St. Mary, Redcliff, and *view with our own eyes* the ancient
chest in which the manuscripts were found. To this, Dr.
Johnson good-naturedly agreed; and though troubled with
a shortness of breathing, laboured up a long flight of steps,
till we came to the place where the wonderous chest stood.
'*There*, (said Catcot, with a bouncing confident credulity,)
there is the very chest itself.' After this *ocular demonstration*,
there was no more to be said. He brought to my recollection a Scotch Highlander, a man of learning too, and who
had seen the world, attesting, and at the same time giving
his reasons for the authenticity of Fingal:—'I have heard
all that poem when I was young.'—'Have you, Sir? Pray
what have you heard?'—'I have heard Ossian, Oscar,
and *every one of them*.'

Johnson said of Chatterton, 'This is the most extraordinary young man that has encountered my knowledge.
It is wonderful how the whelp has written such things.'

[1] Mr. Tyrwhitt, Mr. Warton, Mr. Malone.

We were by no means pleased with our inn at Bristol. 'Let us see now, (said I,) how we should describe it.' Johnson was ready with his raillery. 'Describe it, Sir? — Why, it was so bad, that Boswell wished to be in Scotland!'

After Dr. Johnson's return to London, I was several times with him at his house, where I occasionally slept, in the room that had been assigned to me. I dined with him at Dr. Taylor's, at General Oglethorpe's, and at General Paoli's. To avoid a tedious minuteness, I shall group together what I have preserved of his conversation during this period also, without specifying each scene where it passed, except one, which will be found so remarkable as certainly to deserve a very particular relation. Where the place or the persons do not contribute to the zest of the conversation, it is unnecessary to encumber my page with mentioning them. To know of what vintage our wine is, enables us to judge of its value, and to drink it with more relish: but to have the produce of each vine of one vine-yard, in the same year, kept separate, would serve no purpose. To know that our wine, (to use an advertising phrase,) is 'of the stock of an Ambassadour lately deceased,' heightens its flavour: but it signifies nothing to know the bin where each bottle was once deposited.

'Garrick (he observed) does not play the part of Archer in "The Beaux Stratagem" well.[a] The gentleman should break out through the footman, which is not the case as he does it.'[b]

'Where there is no education, as in savage countries, men will have the upper hand of women. Bodily strength, no doubt, contributes to this; but it would be so, exclusive of that; for it is mind that always governs. When it comes to dry understanding, man has the better.'

'The little volumes entitled "*Respublicæ*," which are very well done, were a bookseller's work.'

'There is much talk of the misery which we cause to the brute creation; but they are recompensed by existence. If they were not useful to man, and therefore protected by him, they would not be nearly so numerous.' This argument is to be found in the able and benignant Hutchinson's 'Moral Philosophy.' But the question is, whether the animals who endure such sufferings of various kinds, for

[a] *There was a Mr. Farren did it better in 1816 or 17 or 18* [H]

[b] *Oh but it did—in* the last Act [I]

the service and entertainment of man, would accept of existence upon the terms on which they have it. Madame Sévigné, who, though she had many enjoyments, felt with delicate sensibility the prevalence of misery, complains of the task of existence having been imposed upon her without her consent.

'That man is never happy for the present is so true, that all his relief from unhappiness is only forgetting himself for a little while. Life is a progress from want to want, not from enjoyment to enjoyment.'[a]

'Though many men are nominally entrusted with the administration of hospitals and other publick institutions, almost all the good is done by one man, by whom the rest are driven on; owing to confidence in him, and indolence in them.'

'Lord Chesterfield's Letters to his son, I think, might be made a very pretty book. Take out the immorality, and it should be put into the hands of every young gentleman. An elegant manner and easiness of behaviour are acquired gradually and imperceptibly. No man can say, "I'll be genteel." There are ten genteel women for one genteel man, because they are more restrained. A man without some degree of restraint is insufferable; but we are all less restrained than women. Were a woman sitting in company to put out her legs before her as most men do, we should be tempted to kick them in.' No man was a more attentive and nice observer of behaviour in those in whose company he happened to be, than Johnson; or however strange it may seem to many, had a higher estimation of its refinements. Lord Eliot informs me, that one day when Johnson and he were at dinner in a gentleman's house in London, upon Lord Chesterfield's Letters being mentioned, Johnson surprized the company by this sentence: 'Every man of any education would rather be called a rascal, than accused of deficiency in *the graces*.' Mr. Gibbon, who was present, turned to a lady who knew Johnson well, and lived much with him, and in his quaint manner, tapping his box, addressed her thus: 'Don't you think, Madam, (looking towards Johnson,) that among *all* your acquaintance you could find *one* exception?' The lady smiled, and seemed to acquiesce.

Marginal notes:

two marginal lines: *of misery . . . her consent* [H]

marginal line: *forgetting himself . . . a progress* [H]

[a] *Life is a School-Room, not a Play ground.* [H & J]

marginal line: *by whom . . . in them* [H]

'I read (said he,) Sharpe's Letters on Italy over again, when I was at Bath. There is a great deal of matter in them.'

'Mrs. Williams was angry that Thrale's family did not send regularly to her every time they heard from me while I was in the Hebrides. Little people are apt to be jealous: but they should not be jealous; for they ought to consider, that superiour attention will necessarily be paid to superiour fortune or rank. Two persons may have equal merit, and on that account may have an equal claim to attention; but one of them may have also fortune and rank, and so may have a double claim.'

Talking of his notes on Shakspeare, he said, 'I despise those who do not see that I am right in the passage where *as* is repeated, and "asses of great charge" introduced. That on "To be, or not to be," is disputable.'[1]

A gentleman, whom I found sitting with him one morning, said,[a] that in his opinion the character of an infidel was more detestable than that of a man notoriously guilty of an atrocious crime. I differed from him, because we are surer of the odiousness of the one, than of the errour of the other. JOHNSON. 'Sir, I agree with him; for the infidel would be guilty of any crime if he were inclined to it.'[b]

'Many things which are false are transmitted from book to book, and gain credit in the world. One of these is the cry against the evil of luxury. Now the truth is, that luxury produces much good. Take the luxury of buildings in London. Does it not produce real advantage in the conveniency and elegance of accommodation, and this all from the exertion of industry? People will tell you, with a melancholy face, how many builders are in gaol. It is plain they are in gaol, not for building; for rents are not fallen. — A man gives half a guinea for a dish of green peas. How much gardening does this occasion? how many labourers must the competition to have such things early in the market keep in employment? You will hear it said, very

[a] *no need to ask any Gentleman's opinion. Jesus Christ says it shall be more* tolerable *&c for the one than for the other; & says it himself expressly   10:th Chapr. of St Matthew 15:th Verse* [1]

[b] *no need of Johnson or his Parasite to teach us that; Our Saviour says expressly, it shall be more tolerable in the Day of Judgment for Sodom and Gomorrah than for them—meaning Infidels.* [H]

---

[1] It may be observed, that Mr. Malone, in his very valable edition of Shakspeare, has fully vindicated Dr. Johnson from the idle censures which the first of these notes has given rise to. The interpretation of the other passage, which Dr. Johnson allows to be *disputable*, he has clearly shewn to be erroneous.

gravely, "Why was not the half guinea, thus spent in luxury, given to the poor? To how many might it have afforded a good meal. Alas! has it not gone to the *industrious* poor, whom it is better to support than the *idle* poor? You are much surer that you are doing good when you *pay* money to those who work, as the recompence of their labour, than when you *give* money merely in charity. Suppose the ancient luxury of a dish of peacock's brains were to be revived, how many carcases would be left to the poor[a] at a cheap rate: and as to the rout that is made about people who are ruined by extravagance, it is no matter to the nation that some individuals suffer. When so much general productive exertion is the consequence of luxury, the nation does not care though there are debtors in gaol: nay, they would not care though their creditors were there too.'

The uncommon vivacity of General Oglethorpe's mind, and variety of knowledge, having sometimes made his conversation seem too desultory, Johnson observed, 'Oglethorpe, Sir, never *completes* what he has to say.'

He on the same account made a smiliar remark on Patrick Lord Elibank; 'Sir, there is nothing *conclusive* in his talk.'

When I complained of having dined at a splendid table without hearing one sentence of conversation worthy of being remembered, he said, 'Sir, there seldom is any such conversation.' BOSWELL. 'Why then meet at table?' JOHNSON. 'Why to eat and drink together, and to promote kindness: and, Sir, this is better done when there is no solid conversation: for when there is, people differ in opinion, and get into bad humour, or some of the company who are not capable of such conversation, are left out, and feel themselves uneasy. It was for this reason Sir Robert Walpole said, he always talked bawdy at his table, because in that all could join.'[b]

Being irritated by hearing a gentleman[c] ask Mr. Levett a variety of questions concerning him, when he was sitting by, he broke out, 'Sir, you have but two topicks, yourself and me. I am sick of both.' 'A man, (said he,) should not talk of himself, nor much of any particular person. He should take care not to be made a proverb; and, therefore,

marginal line:
the idle . . . *who work*
[H]

underlined:
carcases, poor [H]
[a] *as if none but the Poor would eat Peacocks!*
[H & I]

[b] *Comical enough* [I]
underlined:
gentleman [H]
[c] *Boswell himself* [H]
marginal line:
he was . . . of both [H]

should avoid having any one topick of which people can
say, "We shall hear him upon it." There was a Dr. Oldfield, who was always talking of the Duke of Marlborough.
He came into a coffee house one day, and told that his
Grace had spoken in the House of Lords for half an hour.
"Did he indeed speak for half an hour?" (said Belchier,
the surgeon.)—"Yes."—"And what did he say of Dr.
Oldfield?"—"Nothing."—"Why then, Sir, he was very
ungrateful; for Dr. Oldfield could not have spoken for a
quarter of an hour, without saying something of him."'

'Every man is to take existence on the terms on which
it is given to him. To some men it is given on condition of
not taking liberties, which other men may take without
much harm. One may drink wine, and be nothing the
worse for it; on another, wine may have effects so inflam-
matory as to injure him both in body and mind, and
perhaps, make him commit something for which he may
deserve to be hanged.'

'Lord Hailes's "Annals of Scotland" have not that
painted form which is the taste of this age; but it is a book
which will always sell, it has such a stability of dates, such
a certainty of facts, and such a punctuality of citation.
I never before read Scotch history with certainty.'

I asked him whether he would advise me to read the
Bible with a commentary, and what commentaries he
would recommend. JOHNSON. 'To be sure, Sir, I would
have you read the Bible with a commentary; and I would
recommend Lowth and Patrick on the Old Testament, and
Hammond on the New.'

During my stay in London this spring, I solicited his
attention to another law case, in which I was engaged. In
the course of a contested election for the Borough of Dumfermline, which I attended as one of my friend Colonel
(afterwards Sir Archibald) Campbell's counsel; one of his
political agents, who was charged with having been
unfaithful to his employer, and having deserted to the
opposite party for a pecuniary reward—attacked very
rudely in the newspapers the Reverend Mr. James Thomson, one of the ministers of that place, on account of a
supposed allusion to him in one of his sermons. Upon this
the minister, on a subsequent Sunday, arraigned him by

name from the pulpit with some severity; and the agent, after the sermon was over, rose up and asked the minister aloud, 'What bribe he had received for telling so many lies from the chair of verity.' I was present at this very extraordinary scene. The person arraigned, and his father and brother, who also had a share both of the reproof from the pulpit, and in the retaliation, brought an action against Mr. Thomson, in the Court of Session, for defamation and damages, and I was one of the counsel for the reverend defendant. The *Liberty of the Pulpit* was our great ground of defence; but we argued also on the provocation of the previous attack, and on the instant retaliation. The Court of Session, however—the fifteen Judges, who are at the same time the Jury, decided against the minister, contrary to my humble opinion; and several of them expressed themselves with indignation against him. He was an aged gentleman, formerly a military chaplain, and a man of high spirit and honour. Johnson was satisfied that the judgement was wrong, and dictated to me the following argument in confutation of it:

'Of the censure pronounced from the pulpit, our determination must be formed, as in other cases, by a consideration of the act itself, and the particular circumstances with which it is invested.

'The right of censure and rebuke seems necessarily appendant to the pastoral office. He, to whom the care of a congregation is entrusted, is considered as the shepherd of a flock, as the teacher of a school, as the father of a family. As a shepherd tending not his own sheep but those of his master, he is answerable for those that stray, and that lose themselves by straying. But no man can be answerable for losses which he has not power to prevent, or for vagrancy which he has not authority to restrain.

'As a teacher giving instruction for wages, and liable to reproach, if those whom he undertakes to inform make no proficiency, he must have the power of enforcing attendance, of awakening negligence, and repressing contradiction.

'As a father, he possesses the paternal authority of admonition, rebuke, and punishment. He cannot, without reducing his office to an empty name, be hindered from the exercise of any practice necessary to stimulate the idle, to reform the vicious, to check the petulant, and correct the stubborn.

'If we enquire into the practice of the primitive church, we shall, I believe, find the ministers of the word, exercising the whole authority of this complicated character. We shall find them not only encouraging the good by exhortation, but terrifying the wicked by reproof and denunciation. In the earliest ages of the Church, while religion was yet pure from secular advantages, the punishment of sinners was publick censure, and open penance; penalties inflicted merely by ecclesiastical authority, at a time while the Church had yet no help from the civil power; while the hand of the magistrate lifted only the rod of persecution; and when governours were ready to afford a refuge to all those who fled from clerical authority.

'That the Church, therefore, had once a power of publick censure is evident, because that power was frequently exercised. That it borrowed not its power from the civil authority is likewise certain, because civil authority was at that time its enemy.

'The hour came at length, when after three hundred years of struggle and distress, Truth took possession of imperial power, and the civil laws lent their aid to the ecclesiastical constitutions. The magistrate from that time co-operated with the priest, and clerical sentences were made efficacious by secular force. But the State, when it came to the assistance of the Church, had no intention to diminish its authority. Those rebukes and those censures which were lawful before, were lawful still. But they had hitherto operated only upon voluntary submission. The refractory and contemptuous were at first in no danger of temporal severities, except what they might suffer from the reproaches of conscience, or the detestation of their fellow Christians. When religion obtained the support of law, if admonitions and censures had no effect, they were seconded by the magistrates with coercion and punishment.

'It therefore appears from ecclesiastical history, that the right of inflicting shame by publick censure has been always considered as inherent in the Church; and that this right was not conferred by the civil power; for it was exercised when the civil power operated against it. By the civil power it was never taken away; for the Christian magistrate interposed his office, not to rescue sinners from censure, but to supply more powerful means of reformation; to add pain where shame was insufficient; and when men were proclaimed unworthy of the society of the faithful, to restrain them by imprisonment, from spreading abroad the contagion of wickedness.

'It is not improbable that from this acknowledged power of publick censure, grew in time the practice of auricular confession. Those who dreaded the blast of publick repre-hension, were willing to submit themselves to the priest, by a private accusation of themselves; and to obtain a reconciliation with the Church by a kind of clandestine absolution and invisible penance; conditions with which the priest would, in times of ignorance and corruption, easily comply, as they increased his influence, by adding the knowledge of secret sins to that of notorious offences, and enlarged his authority, by making him the sole arbiter of the terms of reconcilement.[a]

'From this bondage the Reformation set us free. The minister has no longer power to press into the retirements of conscience, to torture us by interrogatories, or put himself in possession of our secrets and our lives. But though we have thus controlled his usurpations, his just and original power remains unimpaired. He may still see, though he may not pry: he may yet hear, though he may not question. And that knowledge which his eyes and ears force upon him it is still his duty to use, for the benefit of his flock. A father who lives near a wicked neighbour, may forbid a son to frequent his company. A minister who has in his congregation a man of open and scandalous wicked-ness, may warn his parishioners to shun his conversation. To warn them is not only lawful, but not to warn them would be criminal. He may warn them one by one in friendly converse, or by a parochial visitation. But if he may warn each man singly, what shall forbid him to warn them all together? Of that which is to be made known to all, how is there any difference whether it be communicated to each singly, or to all together? What is known to all, must necessarily be publick. Whether it shall be publick at once, or publick by degrees, is the only question. And of a sudden and solemn publication the impression is deeper, and the warning more effectual.

'It may easily be urged, if a minister be thus left at liberty to delate sinners from the pulpit, and to publish at will the crimes of a parishioner, he may often blast the innocent, and distress the timorous. He may be suspicious, and condemn without evidence; he may be rash, and judge without examination; he may be severe, and treat slight offences with too much harshness; he may be malignant and partial, and gratify his private interest or resentment under the shelter of his pastoral character.

'Of all this there is possibility, and of all this there is danger. But if possibility of evil be to exclude good, no good ever can be done. If nothing is to be attempted in which there is danger, we must all sink into hopeless inactivity. The evils that may be feared from this practice arise not from any defect in the institution, but from the infirmities of human nature. Power, in whatever hands it is placed, will be sometimes improperly exerted; yet courts of law must judge, though they will sometimes judge amiss. A father must instruct his children, though he himself may often want instruction. A minister must censure sinners, though his censure may be sometimes erroneous by want of judgement, and sometimes unjust by want of honesty.

'If we examine the circumstances of the present case, we shall find the sentence neither erroneous nor unjust; we shall find no breach of private confidence, no intrusion into secret transactions. The fact was notorious and indubitable; so easy to be proved, that no proof was desired. The act was base and treacherous, the perpetration insolent and open, and the example naturally mischievous. The minister, however, being retired and recluse, had not yet heard what was publickly known throughout the parish; and on occasion of a publick election, warned his people, according to his duty, against the crimes which publick elections frequently produce. His warning was felt by one of his parishioners, as pointed particularly at himself. But instead of producing, as might be wished, private compunction and immediate reformation, it kindled only rage and resentment. He charged his minster, in a publick paper, with scandal, defamation, and falsehood. The minister, thus reproached, had his own character to vindicate, upon which his pastoral authority must necessarily depend. To be charged with a defamatory lie is an injury which no man patiently endures in common life. To be charged with polluting the pastoral office with scandal and falsehood, was a violation of character still more atrocious, as it affected not only his personal but his clerical veracity. His indignation naturally rose in proportion to his honesty, and with all the fortitude of injured honesty, he dared this calumniator in the church, and at once exonerated himself from censure, and rescued his flock from deception and from danger. The man whom he accuses pretends not to be innocent; or at least only pretends; for he declines a trial. The crime of which he is accused has frequent opportunities and strong temptations. It has already spread far, with much depravation of private morals, and much injury to publick happiness. To warn the people, therefore, against it was not wanton and officious, but necessary and pastoral.

'What then is the fault with which this worthy minister is charged? He has usurped no dominion over conscience. He has exerted no authority in support of doubtful and controverted opinions. He has not dragged into light a bashful and corrigible sinner. His censure was directed against a breach of morality, against an act which no man justifies. The man who appropriated this censure to himself, is evidently and notoriously guilty. His consciousness of his own wickedness incited him to attack his faithful reprover with open insolence and printed accusations. Such an attack made defence necessary; and we hope it will be at last decided that the means of defence were just and lawful.'

When I read this to Mr. Burke, he was highly pleased, and exclaimed, 'Well; he does his work in a workman-like manner.'[1]

---

[1] As a proof of Dr. Johnson's extraordinary powers of composition, it appears from the original manuscript of this excellent dissertation, of which he dictated the first eight paragraphs on the 10th of May, and the remainder on the 13th, that there are in the whole only seven corrections, or rather variations, and those not considerable. Such were at once the vigorous and accurate emanations of his mind.

Mr. Thomson wished to bring the cause by appeal before the House of Lords, but was dissuaded by the advice of the noble person who lately presided so ably in that Most Honourable House, and who was then Attorney-General. As my readers will no doubt be glad also to read the opinion of this eminent man upon the same subject, I shall here insert it.

CASE

'THERE is herewith laid before you,

'1. Petition for the Reverend Mr. James Thomson, minister of Dumfermline.

'2. Answers thereto.

'3. Copy of the judgement of the Court of Session upon both.

'4. Notes of the opinions of the Judges, being the reasons upon which their decree is grounded.

'These papers you will please to peruse, and give your opinion,

'Whether there is a probability of the above decree of the Court of Session's being reversed, if Mr. Thomson should appeal from the same?'

'I DON'T think the appeal adviseable; not only because the value of the judgment is in no degree adequate to the expence; but because there are many chances, that upon the general complexion of the case, the impression will be taken to the disadvantage of the appellant.

'It is impossible to approve the style of that sermon. But the *complaint* was not less ungracious from that man, who had behaved so ill by his original libel, and, at the time, when he received the reproach he complains of. In the last article, all the plaintiffs are equally concerned. It struck me also with some wonder, that the Judges should think so much fervour apposite to the occasion of reproving the defendant for a little excess.

'Upon the matter, however, I agree with them in condemning the behaviour of the minister; and in thinking it a subject fit for ecclesiastical censure; and even for an action, if any individual could qualify[1] a wrong, and a damage arising from it. But this I doubt. The circumstance of publishing the reproach in a pulpit, though extremely indecent, and culpable in another view, does not constitute a different sort of wrong, or any other rule of law, than would have obtained, if the same words had been pronounced elsewhere. I don't know, whether there be any difference in the law of Scotland, in the definition of slander, before the Commissaries, or the Court of Session. The common law of England does not give way to actions for every reproachful word. An action cannot be brought for general damages, upon any words which import less than an offence cognisable by law; consequently no action could have been brought here for the words in question. Both laws admit the truth to be a justification in action *for words;* and the law of England does the same in actions for libels. The judgement, therefore, seems to me to have been wrong, in that the Court repelled that defence.

'E. THURLOW'

I am now to record a very curious incident in Dr. Johnson's life, which fell under my own observation; of which *pars magna fui,* and which I am persuaded will, with the liberal-minded, be much to his credit.

My desire of being acquainted with celebrated men of every description, had made me, much about the same time, obtain an introduction to Dr. Samuel Johnson and to John Wilkes, Esq. Two men more different could perhaps not be selected out of all mankind. They had even attacked one another with some asperity in their writings; yet I lived in habits of friendship with both. I could fully relish the excellence of each; for I have ever delighted in that intellectual chymistry, which can separate good qualities from evil in the same person.

Sir John Pringle, 'mine own friend and my Father's friend,' between whom and Dr. Johnson I in vain wished to establish an acquaintance, as I respected and lived in intimacy with both of them, observed to me once, very

[1] It is curious to observe that Lord Thurlow has here, perhaps in compliment to North Britain, made use of a term of the Scotch Law, which to an English reader may require explanation. To *qualify* a wrong, is to point out and establish it.

ingeniously, 'It is not in friendship as in mathematicks, where two things, each equal to a third, are equal between themselves. You agree with Johnson as a middle quality, and you agree with me as a middle quality; but Johnson and I should not agree.' Sir John was not sufficiently flexible; so I desisted: knowing, indeed, that the repulsion was equally strong on the part of Johnson; who, I know not from what cause, unless his being a Scotchman, had formed a very erroneous opinion of Sir John. But I conceived an irresistible wish, if possible, to bring Dr. Johnson and Mr. Wilkes together. How to manage it, was a nice and difficult matter.

My worthy booksellers and friends, Messieurs Dilly in the Poultry, at whose hospitable and well-covered table I have seen a greater number of literary men, than at any other, except that of Sir Joshua Reynolds, had invited me to meet Mr. Wilkes and some more gentlemen, on Wednesday, May 15. 'Pray, (said I,) let us have Dr. Johnson.'— 'What, with Mr. Wilkes? not for the world, (said Mr. Edward Dilly;) Dr. Johnson would never forgive me.'— 'Come, (said I,) if you'll let me negociate for you, I will be answerable that all shall go well.' DILLY. 'Nay, if you will take it upon you, I am sure I shall be very happy to see them both here.'

Notwithstanding the high veneration which I entertained for Dr. Johnson, I was sensible that he was sometimes a little actuated by the spirit of contradiction, and by means of that I hoped I should gain my point. I was persuaded that if I had come upon him with a direct proposal, 'Sir, will you dine in company with Jack Wilkes?' he would have flown into a passion, and would probably have answered, 'Dine with Jack Wilkes, Sir! I'd as soon dine with Jack Ketch.'[1] I therefore, while we were sitting quietly by ourselves at his house in an evening, took occasion to open my plan thus:—'Mr. Dilly, Sir, sends his respectful compliments to you, and would be happy if you would do him the honour to dine with him on Wednesday next along with me, as I must soon go to Scotland.' JOHNSON. 'Sir, I am obliged to Mr. Dilly. I will wait upon him—'

[1] This has been circulated as if actually said by Johnson; when the truth is, it was only *supposed* by me.

Boswell. 'Provided, Sir, I suppose, that the company which he is to have, is agreeable to you.' Johnson. 'What do you mean, Sir? What do you take me for? Do you think I am so ignorant of the world, as to imagine that I am to prescribe to a gentleman what company he is to have at his table?' Boswell. 'I beg your pardon, Sir, for wishing to prevent you from meeting people whom you might not like. Perhaps he may have some of what he calls his patriotick friends with him.' Johnson. 'Well, Sir, and what then? What care *I* for his *patriotick friends?* Poh!' Boswell. 'I should not be surprized to find Jack Wilkes there.' Johnson. 'And if Jack Wilkes *should* be there, what is that to *me*, Sir? My dear friend, let us have no more of this. I am sorry to be angry with you; but really it is treating me strangely to talk to me as if I could not meet any company whatever, occasionally.' Boswell. 'Pray forgive me, Sir: I meant well. But you shall meet whoever comes, for me.' Thus I secured him, and told Dilly that he would find him very well pleased to be one of his guests on the day appointed.

Upon the much expected Wednesday, I called on him about half an hour before dinner, as I often did when we were to dine out together, to see that he was ready in time, and to accompany him. I found him buffeting his books, as upon a former occasion,[1] covered with dust, and making no preparation for going abroad. 'How is this, Sir? (said I.) Don't you recollect that you are to dine at Mr. Dilly's?' Johnson. 'Sir, I did not think of going to Dilly's: it went out of my head. I have ordered dinner at home with Mrs. Williams.' Boswell. 'But, my dear Sir, you know you were engaged to Mr. Dilly, and I told him so. He will expect you, and will be much disappointed if you don't come.' Johnson. 'You must talk to Mrs. Williams about this.'

Here was a sad dilemma. I feared that what I was so confident I had secured, would yet be frustrated. He had accustomed himself to shew Mrs. Williams such a degree of humane attention, as frequently imposed some restraint upon him; and I knew that if she should be obstinate, he would not stir. I hastened down stairs to the blind lady's

[1] See page 264 of this volume.

room, and told her I was in great uneasiness, for Dr. Johnson had engaged to me to dine this day at Mr. Dilly's, but that he had told me he had forgotten his engagement, and had ordered dinner at home. 'Yes, Sir, (said she, pretty peevishly,) Dr. Johnson is to dine at home.'—'Madam, (said I,) his respect for you is such, that I know he will not leave you, unless you absolutely desire it. But as you have so much of his company, I hope you will be good enough to forego it for a day: as Mr. Dilly is a very worthy man, has frequently had agreeable parties at his house for Dr. Johnson, and will be vexed if the Doctor neglects him to-day. And then, Madam, be pleased to consider my situation; I carried the message, and I assured Mr. Dilly that Dr. Johnson was to come; and no doubt he has made a dinner, and invited a company, and boasted of the honour he expected to have. I shall be quite disgraced if the Doctor is not there.' She gradually softened to my solicitations, which were certainly as earnest as most entreaties to ladies upon any occasion, and was graciously pleased to empower me to tell Dr. Johnson, 'That all things considered, she thought he should certainly go.' I flew back to him, still in dust, and careless of what should be the event, 'indifferent in his choice to go or stay;' but as soon as I had announced to him Mrs. Williams's consent, he roared, 'Frank, a clean shirt,' and was very soon drest. When I had him fairly seated in a hackney-coach with me, I exulted as much as a fortune-hunter who has got an heiress into a post-chaise with him to set out for Gretna-Green.

When we entered Mr. Dilly's drawing-room, he found himself in the midst of a company he did not know. I kept myself snug and silent, watching how he would conduct himself. I observed him whispering to Mr. Dilly, 'Who is that gentleman, Sir?'—'Mr. Arthur Lee.'—JOHNSON. 'Too, too, too,' (under his breath,) which was one of his habitual mutterings. Mr. Arthur Lee could not but be very obnoxious to Johnson, for he was not only a *patriot*, but an *American*. He was afterwards minister from the United States at the court of Madrid. 'And who is the gentleman in lace?'—'Mr. Wilkes, Sir.' This information confounded him still more; he had some difficulty to restrain himself, and taking up a book, sat down upon a window-seat and read, or at least kept his eye upon it intently for some time, till he composed himself. His feelings, I dare say, were aukward enough. But he no doubt recollected his having rated me for supposing that he could be at all disconcerted by any company, and he, therefore, resolutely set himself to behave quite as an easy man of the world, who could adapt himself at once to the disposition and manners of those whom he might chance to meet.

The cheering sound of 'Dinner is upon the table,' dissolved his reverie, and we *all* sat down without any symptom of ill humour. There were present, beside Mr. Wilkes, and Mr. Arthur Lee, who was an old companion of mine when he studied physick at Edinburgh, Mr. (now Sir John) Miller, Dr. Lettsom, and Mr. Slater, the druggist. Mr. Wilkes placed himself next to Dr. Johnson, and behaved to him with so much attention and politeness, that he gained upon him insensibly. No man eat more heartily than Johnson, or loved better what was nice and delicate.[a] Mr. Wilkes was very assiduous in helping him to some fine veal. 'Pray give me leave, Sir;—It is better here—A little of the brown—Some fat, Sir—A little of the stuffing— Some gravy—Let me have the pleasure of giving you some butter—Allow me to recommend a squeeze of this orange; —or the lemon, perhaps, may have more zest.'—'Sir, Sir, I am obliged to you, Sir,' cried Johnson, bowing, and turning his head to him with a look for some time of 'surly virtue,'[1] but, in a short while, of complacency.

Foote being mentioned, Johnson said, 'He is not a good mimick.' One of the company added, 'A merry Andrew, a buffoon.' JOHNSON. 'But he has wit too, and is not deficient in ideas, or in fertility and variety of imagery, and not empty of reading; he has knowledge enough to fill up his part. One species of wit he has in an eminent degree, that of escape. You drive him into a corner with both hands; but he's gone, Sir, when you think you have got him—like an animal that jumps over your head. Then he has a great range for wit; he never lets truth stand between him and a jest, and he is sometimes mighty coarse. Garrick is under many restraints from which Foote is free.' WILKES. 'Garrick's wit is more like Lord Chesterfield's.'

underlined:
nice, delicate [H]

[a] *what was gustful rather . . . what was strong that he could taste it; what was tender that he could chew it.* [H]

[1] Johnson's 'London, a Poem,' v. 145.

JOHNSON. 'The first time I was in company with Foote was at Fitzherbert's. Having no good opinion of the fellow, I was resolved not to be pleased; and it is very difficult to please a man against his will. I went on eating my dinner pretty sullenly, affecting not to mind him. But the dog was so very comical, that I was obliged to lay down my knife and fork, throw myself back upon my chair, and fairly laugh it out. No, Sir, he was irresistible.[1] He upon one occasion experienced, in an extraordinary degree, the efficacy of his powers of entertaining. Amongst the many and various modes which he tried of getting money, he became a partner with a small-beer brewer, and he was to have a share of the profits for procuring customers amongst his numerous acquaintance. Fitzherbert was one who took his small-beer; but it was so bad that the servants resolved not to drink it. They were at some loss how to notify their resolution, being afraid of offending their master, who they knew liked Foote much as a companion. At last they fixed upon a little black boy, who was rather a favourite, to be their deputy, and deliver their remonstrance; and having invested him with the whole authority of the kitchen, he was to inform Mr. Fitzherbert, in all their names, upon a certain day, that they would drink Foote's small-beer no longer. On that day Foote happened to dine at Fitzherbert's, and this boy served at table; he was so delighted with Foote's stories, and merriment, and grimace, that when he went down stairs, he told them, "This is the finest man I have ever seen. I will not deliver your message. I will drink his small-beer."'

Somebody observed that Garrick could not have done this. WILKES. 'Garrick would have made the small-beer still smaller. He is now leaving the stage; but he will play *Scrub* all his life.' I knew that Johnson would let nobody attack Garrick but himself, as Garrick said to me, and I had heard him praise his liberality; so to bring out his commendation of his celebrated pupil, I said, loudly, 'I have heard Garrick is liberal.' JOHNSON. 'Yes, Sir, I know that Garrick has given away more money than any man in England that I am acquainted with, and that not from

---

[1] Foote told me, that Johnson said of him, 'For loud obstreperous broad-faced mirth, I know not his equal.'

ostentatious views. Garrick was very poor when he began life; so when he came to have money, he probably was very unskilful in giving away, and saved when he should not. But Garrick began to be liberal as soon as he could; and I am of opinion, the reputation of avarice which he has had, has been very lucky for him, and prevented his having many enemies. You despise a man for avarice, but do not hate him. Garrick might have been much better attacked for living with more splendour than is suitable to a player: if they had had the wit to have assaulted him in that quarter, they might have galled him more. But they have kept clamouring about his avarice, which has rescued him from much obloquy and envy.'

Talking of the great difficulty of obtaining authentick information for biography, Johnson told us, 'When I was a young fellow I wanted to write the "Life of Dryden," and in order to get materials, I applied to the only two persons then alive who had seen him; these were old Swinney,[1] and old Cibber. Swinney's information was no more than this, "That at Will's coffee-house Dryden had a particular chair for himself, which was set by the fire in winter, and was then called his winter-chair; and that it was carried out for him to the balcony in summer, and was then called his summer-chair." Cibber could tell no more but "That he remembered him a decent old man, arbiter of critical disputes at Will's." You are to consider that Cibber was then at a great distance from Dryden, had perhaps one leg only in the room, and durst not draw in the other.' BOSWELL. 'Yet Cibber was a man of observation?' JOHNSON. 'I think not.' BOSWELL. 'You will allow his "Apology" to be well done.' JOHNSON. 'Very well done, to be sure, Sir. That book is a striking proof of the justice of Pope's remark:

"Each might his several province well command,
     Would all but stoop to what they understand."'

BOSWELL. 'And his plays are good.' JOHNSON. 'Yes;

[1] [Owen M'Swinney, who died in 1754, and bequeathed his fortune to Mrs. Woffington, the actress. He had been a Manager of Drury Lane Theatre, and afterwards of the Queen's Theatre in the Haymarket. He was also a dramatick writer, having produced a comedy entitled—'The Quacks, or Love's the Physician,' 1705, and two operas. MALONE.]

but that was his trade; *l'esprit du corps;* he had been all his life among players and play-writers. I wondered that he had so little to say in conversation, for he had kept the best company, and learnt all that can be got by the ear. He abused Pindar to me, and then shewed me an ode of his own, with an absurd couplet, making a linnet soar on an eagle's wing.[1] I told him that when the ancients made a simile, they always made it like something real.'

Mr. Wilkes remarked, that 'among all the bold flights of Shakspeare's imagination, the boldest was making Birnam-wood march to Dunsinane; creating a wood where there never was a shrub; a wood in Scotland! ha! ha! ha!' And he also observed, that 'the clannish slavery of the Highlands of Scotland was the single exception to Milton's remark of "The Mountain Nymph, sweet Liberty," being worshipped in all hilly countries.'—'When I was at Inverary (said he,) on a visit to my old friend Archibald, Duke of Argyle, his dependents congratulated me on being such a favourite of his Grace. I said "It is then, gentlemen, truly lucky for me; for if I had displeased the Duke, and he had wished it, there is not a Campbell among you but would have been ready to bring John Wilkes's head to him in a charger. It would have been only

"Off with his head! so much for *Aylesbury*."

I was then member for Aylesbury.'

Dr. Johnson and Mr. Wilkes talked of the contested passage in Horace's Art of Poetry, '*Difficile est propriè communia dicere.*' Mr. Wilkes, according to my note, gave the interpretation thus: 'It is difficult to speak with propriety of common things; as, if a poet had to speak of Queen Caroline drinking tea, he must endeavour to avoid the vulgarity of cups and saucers.' But upon reading my note, he tells me that he meant to say, that 'the word *communia*, being a Roman law-term, signifies here things *communis juris*, that is to say, what have never yet been treated by any body; and this appears clearly from what followed,

cross:
talked of etc. [H]

"——— Tuque
Rectiùs Iliacum carmen deducis in actus
Quàm si proferres ignota indictaque primus."

[1] See page 285 of vol. i.

You will easier make a tragedy out of the Iliad than on any subject not handled before.'¹ JOHNSON. 'He means that it is difficult to appropriate to particular persons qualities which are common to all mankind, as Homer has done.' WILKES. 'We have no City-Poet now: that is an office which has gone into disuse. The last was Elkanah Settle.

¹ My very pleasant friend himself, as well as others *who remember old stories*, will no doubt be surprized, when I observe that *John Wilkes* here shews himself to be of the WARBURTONIAN SCHOOL. It is nevertheless true, as appears from Dr. Hurd the Bishop of Worcester's very elegant commentary and notes on the '*Epistola ad Pisones.*'

It is necessary to a fair consideration of the question, that the whole passage in which the words occur should be kept in view:

> 'Si quid inexpertum scenæ committis, et audes
> Personam formare novam, servetur ad imum
> Qualis ab incepto processerit, et sibi constet.
> Difficile est propriè communia dicere: tuque
> Rectiùs Iliacum carmen deducis in actus,
> Quàm si proferres ignota indictaque primus.
> Publica materies privati juris erit, si
> Non circa vilem patulumque moraberis orbem,
> Nec verbum verbo curabis reddere fidus
> Interpres; nec desilies imitator in artum
> Unde pedem proferre pudor vetat aut operis lex.'

The 'Commentary' thus illustrates it: 'But the formation of quite *new characters* is a work of great difficulty and hazard. For here there is no generally received and fixed *archetype* to work after, but every one *judges* of common right, according to the extent and comprehension of his own idea; therefore he advises to labour and refit *old characters and subjects*, particularly those made known and authorized by the practice of Homer and the Epic writers.'

The 'Note' is

'*Difficile* EST PROPRIÈ COMMUNIA DICERE.' Lambin's Comment is 'Communia hoc loco appellat Horatius argumenta fabularum à nullo adhuc tractata: et ita, quæ cuivis exposita sunt et in medio quodammodo posita, quasi vacua et à nemine occupata.' And that this is the true meaning of *communia* is evidently fixed by the words *ignota indictaque*, which are explanatory of it; so that the sense given it in the commentary is unquestionably the right one. Yet notwithstanding the clearness of the case, a late critick has this strange passage: 'Difficile quidem esse propriè communia dicere, hoc est, materiam vulgarem, notam et è medio petitam, ita immutare atque exornare, ut nova et scriptori propria videatur, ultro concedimus; et maximi procul dubio ponderis ista est observatio. Sed omnibus utrinque collatis, et tum difficilis tum venusti, tam judicii quam ingenii ratione habitâ, major videtur esse gloria fabulam formare penitùs novam, quam veterem, utcunque mutatum de novo exhibere.' (Poet. Præl. v. ii. p. 164.) Where, having first put a wrong construction on the word *communia*, he employs it to introduce an impertinent criticism. For where does the poet prefer the glory of refitting *old* subjects to that of inventing new ones? The contrary is implied in what he urges about the superiour difficulty of the latter, from which he dissuades his countrymen, only in respect of their abilities and inexperience

There is something in *names* which one cannot help feeling. Now *Elkanah Settle* sounds so *queer*, who can expect much from that name? We should have no hesitation to give it for John Dryden, in preference to Elkanah Settle, from the names only, without knowing their different merits.' JOHNSON. 'I suppose, Sir, Settle did as well for Aldermen

in these matters; and in order to cultivate in them, which is the main view of the Epistle, a spirit of correctness, by sending them to the old subjects, treated by the Greek writers.'

For my own part (with all deference for Dr. Hurd, who thinks the *case clear*,) I consider the passage, '*Difficile est propriè communia dicere,*' to be a *crux* for the criticks on Horace.

The explication which my Lord of Worcester treats with so much contempt, is nevertheless countenanced by authority which I find quoted by the learned Baxter in his edition of Horace, '*Difficile est propriè communia dicere*, h. e. res vulgares disertis verbis enarrare, vel humile thema cum dignitate tractare. *Difficile est communes res propriis explicare verbis.* Vet. Schol.' I was much disappointed to find that the great critick, Dr. Bentley, has no note upon this very difficult passage, as from his vigorous and illuminated mind I should have expected to receive more satisfaction than I have yet had.

Sanadon thus treats of it. 'Propriè communia dicere; c'est à dire, qu'il n'est pas aisé de former à ces personnages d'imagination, des caractêres particuliers et cependant vraisemblables. Comme l'on a eté le maitre de les former tels qu'on a voulu, les fautes que l'on fait en cela sont moins pardonnables. C'est pourquoi Horace conseille de prendre toujours des sujets connus, tels que sont par exemple ceux que l'on peut tirer des poèmes d'Homere.'

And *Dacier* observes upon it, 'Apres avoir marqué les deux qualités qu'il faut donner aux personnages qu'on invente, il conseille aux Poêtes tragiques, de n'user pas trop facilement de cette liberté qu'ils ont d'en inventer, car il est três difficile de reussir dans ces nouveaux caractêres. Il est mal aisé, dit Horace, de traiter proprement, c'est à dire convenablement, des sujets communs; c'est à dire, des sujets inventés, et qui n'ont aucun fondement ni dans l'Histoire ni dans la Fable; et il les appelle communs, parce qu'ils sont en disposition à tout le monde, et que tout le monde a le droit de les inventer, et qu'ils sont, comme on dit, au premier occupant.' See his observations at large on this expression and the following.

After all, I cannot help entertaining some doubt whether the words, *Difficile est propriè communia dicere,* may not have been thrown in by Horace to form a *separate* article in a 'choice of difficulties' which a poet has to encounter, who chooses a new subject; in which case it must be uncertain which of the various explanations is the true one, and every reader has a right to decide as it may strike his own fancy. And even should the words be understood as they generally are, to be connected both with what goes before and what comes after, the exact sense cannot be absolutely ascertained; for instance, whether *propriè* is meant to signify *in an appropriated manner*, as Dr. Johnson here understands it, or, as it is often used by Cicero, *with propriety*, or *elegantly*. In short, it is a rare instance of a defect in perspicuity in an admirable writer, who with almost every species of excellence, is peculiarly remarkable for that quality. The length of this note perhaps requires an apology. Many of my readers, I doubt not, will admit that a critical discussion of a passage in a favourite classick is very engaging.

in his time, as John Home could do now. Where did Beckford and Trecothick learn English?'

Mr. Arthur Lee mentioned some Scotch who had taken possession of a barren part of America, and wondered why they should choose it. JOHNSON. 'Why, Sir, all barrenness, is comparative. The *Scotch* would not know it to be barren.' BOSWELL. 'Come, come, he is flattering the English. You have now been in Scotland, Sir, and say if you did not see meat and drink enough there.' JOHNSON. 'Why yes, Sir; meat and drink enough to give the inhabitants sufficient strength to run away from home.' All these quick and lively sallies were said sportively, quite in jest, and with a smile, which showed that he meant only wit. Upon this topick he and Mr. Wilkes could perfectly assimilate; here was a bond of union between them, and I was conscious that as both of them had visited Caledonia, both were fully satisfied of the strange narrow ignorance of those who imagine that it is a land of famine.[a] But they amused themselves with persevering in the old jokes. When I claimed a superiority for Scotland over England in one respect, that no man can be arrested there for a debt merely because another swears it against him; but there must first be the judgement of a court of law ascertaining its justice; and that a seizure of the person, before judgement is obtained, can take place only, if his creditor should swear that he is about to fly from the country, or, as it is technically expressed, is *in meditatione fugæ.* WILKES. 'That, I should think, may be safely sworn of all the Scotch nation.' JOHNSON. (To Mr. Wilkes) 'You must know, Sir, I lately took my friend Boswell, and shewed him genuine civilized life in an English provincial town. I turned him loose at Lichfield, my native city, that he might see for once real civility: for you know he lives among savages in Scotland, and among rakes in London.' WILKES. 'Except when he is with grave, sober, decent people, like you and me.' JOHNSON. (smiling) 'And we ashamed of him.'

They were quite frank and easy. Johnson told the story of his asking Mrs. Macaulay to allow her footman to sit down with them, to prove the ridiculousness of the argument for the equality of mankind; and he said to me afterwards, with a nod of satisfaction, 'You saw Mr. Wilkes

[a] *The English have a vulgar Prejudice of thinking—or Saying at least that all Foreigners are Starvelings no Roast Beef 300 Miles from Hyde Park Corner.* [H]

acquiesced.' Wilkes talked with all imaginable freedom of the ludicrous title given to the Attorney-General, *Diabolus Regis;* adding, 'I have reason to know something about that officer; for I was prosecuted for a libel.' Johnson, who many people would have supposed must have been furiously angry at hearing this talked of so lightly, said not a word. He was now, *indeed,* 'a good-humoured fellow.'

After dinner we had an accession of Mrs. Knowles, the Quaker lady, well known for her various talents, and of Mr. Alderman Lee. Amidst some patriotick groans, somebody (I think the Alderman) said, 'Poor old England is lost.' JOHNSON. 'Sir, it is not so much to be lamented that old England is lost, as that the Scotch have found it.'[1] WILKES. 'Had Lord Bute governed Scotland only, I should not have taken the trouble to write his eulogy, and dedicate "MORTIMER" to him.'

Mr. Wilkes held a candle to shew a fine print of a beautiful female figure which hung in the room, and pointed out the elegant contour of the bosom with the finger of an arch connoisseur. He afterwards in a conversation with me waggishly insisted, that all the time Johnson shewed visible signs of a fervent admiration of the corresponding charms of the fair Quaker.[a]

This record, though by no means so perfect as I could wish, will serve to give a notion of a very curious interview, which was not only pleasing at the time, but had the agreeable and benignant effect of reconciling any animosity, and sweetening any acidity, which, in the various bustle of political contest, had been produced in the minds of two men, who though widely different had so many things in common—classical learning, modern literature, wit and humour, and ready repartee—that it would have been much to be regretted if they had been for ever at a distance from each other.

Mr. Burke gave me much credit for this successful *negotiation;* and pleasantly said, 'that there was nothing equal to it in the whole history of the *Corps Diplomatique.'*

I attended Dr. Johnson home, and had the satisfaction to hear him tell Mrs. Williams how much he had been

---

[1] It would not become me to expatiate on this strong and pointed remark, in which a very great deal of meaning is condensed.

pleased with Mr. Wilkes's company, and what an agreeable day he had passed.

I talked a good deal to him of the celebrated Margaret Caroline Rudd, whom I had visited, induced by the fame of her talents, address, and irresistible power of fascination. To a lady who disapproved of my visiting her, he said on a former occasion, 'Nay, Madam, Boswell is in the right; I should have visited her myself, were it not that they have now a trick of putting every thing into the news-papers.' This evening he exclaimed, 'I envy him his acquaintance with Mrs. Rudd.'

I mentioned a scheme which I had of making a tour to the Isle of Man, and giving a full account of it; and that Mr. Burke had playfully suggested as a motto,

'The proper study of mankind is MAN.'

JOHNSON. 'Sir, you will get more by the book than the jaunt will cost you; so you will have your diversion for nothing, and add to your reputation.'

On the evening of the next day I took leave of him, being to set out for Scotland. I thanked him with great warmth for all his kindness. 'Sir, (said he,) you are very welcome. Nobody repays it with more.'

How very false is the notion that has gone round the world of the rough, and passionate, and harsh manners of this great and good man. That he had occasional sallies of heat of temper, and that he was sometimes, perhaps, too 'easily provoked' by absurdity and folly, and sometimes too desirous of triumph in colloquial contest, must be allowed. The quickness both of his perception and sensibility disposed him to sudden explosions of satire; to which his extraordinary readiness of wit was a strong and almost irresistible incitement. To adopt one of the finest images in Mr. Home's 'Douglas,'

'————— On each glance of thought
        Decision followed, as the thunderbolt
        Pursues the flash!'—————

I admit that the beadle within him was often so eager to apply the lash, that the Judge had not time to consider the case with sufficient deliberation.

That he was occasionally remarkable for violence of temper may be granted: but let us ascertain the degree, and not let it be supposed that he was in a perpetual rage, and never without a club in his hand to knock down every one who approached him. On the contrary, the truth is, that by much the greatest part of his time he was civil, obliging, nay, polite in the true sense of the word; so much so, that many gentlemen who were long acquainted with him never received, or even heard a strong expression from him.

The following letters concerning an Epitaph which he wrote for the monument of Dr. Goldsmith, in Westminster-Abbey, afford at once a proof of his unaffected modesty, his carelessness as to his own writings, and of the great respect which he entertained for the taste and judgement of the excellent and eminent person to whom they are addressed:

'TO SIR JOSHUA REYNOLDS

'DEAR SIR,

'I HAVE been kept away from you, I know not well how, and of these vexatious hindrances I know not when there will be an end. I therefore send you the poor dear Doctor's epitaph. Read it first yourself; and if you then think it right, show it to the Club. I am, you know, willing to be corrected. If you think any thing much amiss, keep it to yourself, till we come together. I have sent two copies, but prefer the card. The dates must be settled by Dr. Percy. I am, Sir,

'Your most humble servant,

'May 16, 1776.'   'SAM. JOHNSON'

TO THE SAME

'SIR,

'MISS REYNOLDS has a mind to send the Epitaph to Dr. Beattie; I am very willing, but having no copy, cannot immediately recollect it. She tells me you have lost it. Try to recollect, and put down as much as you retain; you perhaps may have kept what I have dropped. The lines for which I am at a loss are something of *rerum civilium sivè naturalium.*[1] It was a sorry trick to lose it; help me if you can. I am, Sir,

'Your most humble servant,

'June 22, 1776.'   'SAM. JOHNSON'

'The gout grows better but slowly.'

It was, I think, after I had left London in this year, that this Epitaph gave occasion to a *Remonstrance* to the MONARCH OF LITERATURE, for an account of which I am indebted to Sir William Forbes, of Pitsligo.

That my readers may have the subject more fully and clearly before them, I shall first insert the Epitaph.

'OLIVARII GOLDSMITH,
Poetæ, Physici, Historici,
Qui nullum ferè scribendi genus
Non tetigit,

marginal line:
Nullum ... ornavit [H]

Nullum quod tetigit non ornavit:
Sive risus essent movendi,
Sive lacrymæ,
Affectuum potens at lenis dominator:
Ingenio sublimis, vividus, versatilis,
Oratione grandis, nitidus, venustus:
Hoc monumento memoriam coluit
Sodalium amor,
Amicorum fides,
Lectorum veneratio.
Natus in Hiberniâ Forniæ Longfordiensis,
In loco cui nomen Pallas,
Nov. XXIX. MDCCXXXI;[2]

marginal line:
Obiit Londini [H]

Eblanæ literis institutus;
Obiit Londini,
April. IV, MDCCLXXIV.'

Sir William Forbes writes to me thus: 'I enclose the *Round Robin*. This *jeu d'esprit* took its rise one day at dinner at our friend Sir Joshua Reynolds's. All the company

---

[1] These words must have been in the other copy. They are not in that which was preferred.

[2] [This was a mistake, which was not discovered till after Goldsmith's monument was put up in Westminster Abbey. He was born Nov. 29, 1728; and therefore, when he died, he was in his forty-sixth year. MALONE.]

present, except myself, were friends and acquaintance of Dr. Goldsmith. The Epitaph, written for him by Dr. Johnson, became the subject of conversation, and various emendations were suggested, which it was agreed should be submitted to the Doctor's consideration.—But the question was, who should have the courage to propose them to him? At last it was hinted, that there could be no way so good as that of a *Round Robin*, as the sailors call it, which they make use of when they enter into a conspiracy, so as not to let it be known who puts his name first or last to the paper. This proposition was instantly assented to; and Dr. Barnard, Dean of Derry, now Bishop of Killaloe,[1] drew up an address to Dr. Johnson on the occasion, replete with wit and humour, but which it was feared the Doctor might think treated the subject with too much levity. Mr. Burke then proposed the address as it stands in the paper in writing, to which I had the honour to officiate as clerk.

'Sir Joshua agreed to carry it to Dr. Johnson, who received it with much good humour,[2] and desired Sir

---

[1] [This prelate, who was afterwards translated to the See of Limerick, died at Wimbledon in Surrey, June 7, 1806, in his eightieth year. The original *Round Robin* remained in his possession; the paper which Sir William Forbes transmitted to Mr. Boswell, being only a copy. MALONE.]

[2] He however, upon seeing Dr. Warton's name to the suggestion, that the Epitaph should be in English, observed to Sir Joshua, 'I wonder that Joe Warton, a scholar by profession, should be such a fool.' He said too, 'I should have thought Mund Burke would have had more sense.' Mr. Langton, who was one of the company at Sir Joshua's, like a sturdy scholar, resolutely refused to sign the *Round Robin*. This Epitaph is engraved upon Dr. Goldsmith's monument without any alteration. At another time, when somebody endeavoured to argue in favour of its being in English, Johnson said, 'The language of the country of which a learned man was a native, is not the language fit for his epitaph, which should be in ancient and permanent language. Consider, Sir, how you should feel, were you to find at Rotterdam an epitaph upon Erasmus *in Dutch!*'[a]—For my own part, I think it would be best to have epitaphs written both in a learned language, and in the language of the country; so that they might have the advantage of being more universally understood, and at the same time be secured of classical stability. I cannot, however, but be of opinion, that it is not sufficiently discriminative. Applying to Goldsmith equally the epithets of '*Poetæ, Historici, Physici*,' is surely not right;[b] for as to his claim to the last of those epithets, I have heard Johnson himself say, 'Goldsmith, Sir, will give us a very fine book upon the subject; but if he can distinguish a cow from a horse, that, I believe, may be the extent of his knowledge of natural history.' His book is indeed an excellent performance, though in some instances he appears to have trusted too much to Buffon, who, with all his theoretical ingenuity and extraordinary eloquence, I suspect had little actual information in the

marginal line:
engraved upon . . . any alteration [H]

underlined:
Erasmus in Dutch [I]
   [a] *That is very good.* [I]

underlined:
not right [I]
underlined:
knowledge [I]

   [b] *Why Johnson does not say in the Epitaph that he understood any thing—he says that he adorned everything &* *he says true.* [I]

Joshua to tell the gentlemen, that he would alter the Epitaph in any manner they pleased, as to the sense of it; but *he would never consent to disgrace the walls of Westminster Abbey with an English inscription.*

'I consider this *Round Robin* as a species of literary curiosity worth preserving, as it marks, in a certain degree, Dr. Johnson's character.'

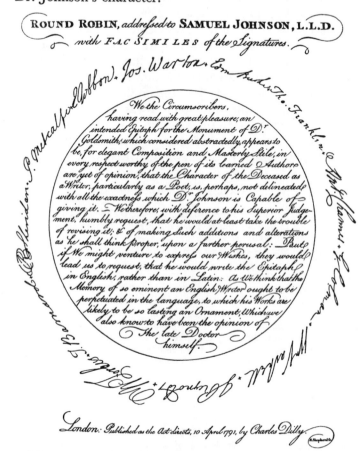

ROUND ROBIN, *addressed to* SAMUEL JOHNSON, L.L.D. *with* FAC SIMILES *of the Signatures.*

My readers are presented with a faithful transcript of a paper, which I doubt not of their being desirous to see.

marginal line:
years; a . . . who lived
[H]

science on which he wrote so admirably. For instance, he tells us that the cow sheds her horns every two years; a most palpable errour, which Goldsmith has faithfully transferred into his book. It is wonderful that Buffon, who lived so much in the country, at his noble seat, should have fallen into such a blunder. I suppose he has confounded the *cow* with the *deer*.

Sir William Forbes's observation is very just. The anecdote now related proves, in the strongest manner, the reverence and awe with which Johnson was regarded, by some of the most eminent men of his time, in various departments, and even by such of them as lived most with him; while it also confirms what I have again and again inculcated, that he was by no means of that ferocious and irascible character which has been ignorantly imagined.

This hasty composition is also to be remarked as one of the thousand instances which evince the extraordinary promptitude of Mr. Burke; who while he is equal to the greatest things, can adorn the least; can, with equal facility, embrace the vast and complicated speculations of politicks or the ingenious topicks of literary investigation.[1]

'DR. JOHNSON TO MRS. BOSWELL

'MADAM,

'You must not think me uncivil in omitting to answer the letter with which you favoured me some time ago. I imagined it to have been written without Mr. Boswell's knowledge, and therefore supposed the answer to require, what I could not find, a private conveyance.

'The difference with Lord Auchinleck is now over; and since young Alexander has appeared, I hope no more difficulties will arise among you; for I sincerely wish you all happy. Do not teach the young ones to dislike me, as you dislike me yourself; but let me at least have Veronica's kindness, because she is my acquaintance.

'You will now have Mr. Boswell home; it is well that you have him; he has led a wild life. I have taken him to Lichfield, and he has followed Mr. Thrale to Bath. Pray take care of him, and tame him. The only thing in which I have the honour to agree with you is, in loving him: and while we are so much of a mind in a matter of so much importance, our other quarrels will, I hope, produce no great bitterness. I am, Madam,

'Your most humble servant,

'May 16, 1776.'   'SAM. JOHNSON'

---

[1] Besides this Latin Epitaph, Johnson honoured the memory of his friend Goldsmith with a short one in Greek. See this volume, p. 107.

'MR. BOSWELL TO DR. JOHNSON

'Edinburgh, June 25, 1776

'You have formerly complained that my letters were too long. There is no danger of that complaint being made at present; for I find it difficult for me to write to you at all. [Here an account of having been afflicted with a return of melancholy or bad spirits.]

'The boxes of books[1] which you sent to me are arrived; but I have not yet examined the contents.

* * * * * *

'I send you Mr. Maclaurin's paper for the negro, who claims his freedom in the Court of Session.'

'DR. JOHNSON TO MR. BOSWELL

'DEAR SIR,

'These black fits, of which you complain, perhaps hurt your memory as well as your imagination. When did I complain that your letters were too long?[2] Your last letter, after a very long delay, brought very bad news. [Here a series of reflections upon melancholy, and—what I could not help thinking strangely unreasonable in him who had suffered so much from it himself,—a good deal of severity and reproof, as if it were owing to my own fault, or that I was, perhaps, affecting it from a desire of distinction.]

'Read Cheyne's "English Malady;" but do not let him teach you a foolish notion that melancholy is a proof of acuteness. * * * * *

'To hear that you have not opened your boxes of books is very offensive. The examination and arrangement of so many volumes might have afforded you an amusement very seasonable at present, and useful for the whole of life. I am, I confess, very angry that you manage yourself so ill. * * * * *

[a] not *certainly true, because Baretti said it; Baretti excelled in a malicious Lie: He beat Boswell himself in Courage of Coining Untruths; I know not whether his Skill was superior.* [H]

[1] Upon a settlement of our account of expences on a Tour to the Hebrides, there was a balance due to me, which Dr. Johnson chose to discharge by sending books.

[2] Baretti told me that Johnson complained of my writing very long letters to him when I was upon the Continent: which was most certainly true:[a] but it seems my friend did not remember it.

'I do not now say any more, than that I am, with great kindness and sincerity, dear Sir,

'Your humble servant,

'July 2, 1776.'   'SAM. JOHNSON'

'It was last year determined by Lord Mansfield in the Court of King's Bench, that a negro cannot be taken out of the kingdom without his own consent.'

'DR. JOHNSON TO MR. BOSWELL

'DEAR SIR,

'I MAKE haste to write again, lest my last letter should give you too much pain. If you are really oppressed with overpowering and involuntary melancholy, you are to be pitied rather than reproached. * * * *

'Now, my dear Bozzy, let us have done with quarrels and with censure. Let me know whether I have not sent you a pretty library. There are, perhaps, many books among them which you never need read through; but there are none which it is not proper for you to know, and sometimes to consult. Of these books, of which the use is only occasional, it is often sufficient to know the contents, that, when any question arises, you may know where to look for information.

'Since I wrote, I have looked over Mr. Maclaurin's plea, and think it excellent. How is the suit carried on? If by subscription, I commission you to contribute, in my name, what is proper. Let nothing be wanting in such a case. Dr. Drummond,[1] I see, is superseded. His father would have grieved; but he lived to obtain the pleasure of his son's election, and died before that pleasure was abated.

'Langton's lady has brought him a girl, and both are well; I dined with him the other day. * * * * *

'It vexes me to tell you, that on the evening of the 29th of May I was seized by the gout, and am not quite well. The pain has not been violent, but the weakness and tenderness were very troublesome, and what is said to be

[1] The son of Johnson's old friend, Mr. William Drummond. (See vol. i. p. 376.) He was a young man of such distinguished merit, that he was nominated to one of the medical professorships in the College of Edinburgh, without solicitation, while he was at Naples. Having other views, he did not accept of the honour, and soon afterwards died.

very uncommon, it has not alleviated my other disorders. Make use of youth and health while you have them; make my compliments to Mrs. Boswell. I am, my dear Sir,

'Your most affectionate

'July 6, 1776.'   'SAM. JOHNSON'

'MR. BOSWELL TO DR. JOHNSON

'MY DEAR SIR,   'Edinburgh, July 18, 1776

'YOUR letter of the second of this month was rather a harsh medicine; but I was delighted with that spontaneous tenderness, which, a few days afterwards, sent forth such balsam as your next brought me. I found myself for some time so ill that all I could do was to preserve a decent appearance, while all within was weakness and distress. Like a reduced garrison that has some spirit left, I hung out flags, and planted all the force I could muster, upon the walls. I am now much better, and I sincerely thank you for your kind attention and friendly counsel.

*   *   *   *   *   *

'Count Manucci[1] came here last week from travelling in Ireland. I have shown him what civilities I could on his own account, on your's, and on that of Mr. and Mrs. Thrale. He has had a fall from his horse, and been much hurt. I regret this unlucky accident, for he seems to be a very amiable man.'

As the evidence of what I have mentioned at the begining of this year, I select from his private register the following passage:

'July 25, 1776. O GOD, who hast ordained that whatever is to be desired should be sought by labour, and who, by thy blessing, bringest honest labour to good effect, look with mercy upon my studies and endeavours. Grant me, O LORD, to design only what is lawful and right; and afford me calmness of mind, and steadiness of purpose, that I may so do thy will in this short life, as to obtain

[1] A Florentine nobleman, mentioned by Johnson, in his 'Notes of his Tour in France.' I had the pleasure of becoming acquainted with him in London, in the spring of this year.

happiness in the world to come, for the sake of JESUS
CHRIST our Lord. Amen.'[1]

It appears from a note subjoined, that this was composed when he 'purposed to apply vigorously to study,
particularly of the Greek and Italian tongues.'

Such a purpose, so expressed, at the age of sixty-seven,
is admirable and encouraging; and it must impress all the
thinking part of my readers with a consolatory confidence
in habitual devotion, when they see a man of such enlarged intellectual powers as Johnson, thus in the genuine
earnestness of secrecy, imploring the aid of that Supreme
Being, 'from whom cometh down every good and every
perfect gift.'

'TO SIR JOSHUA REYNOLDS

'SIR,

'A YOUNG man, whose name is Paterson, offers himself this evening to the Academy. He is the son of a man[2]
for whom I have long had a kindness, and who is now
abroad in distress. I shall be glad that you will be pleased
to shew him any little countenance, or pay him any small
distinction. How much it is in your power to favour or to
forward a young man I do not know; nor do I know how
much this candidate deserves favour by his personal merit,
or what hopes his proficiency may now give of future
eminence. I recommend him as the son of my friend. Your
character and station enable you to give a young man great
encouragement by very easy means. You have heard of a
man who asked no other favour of Sir Robert Walpole,
than that he would bow to him at his levee. I am, Sir,

'Your most humble servant,

'August 3, 1776.'   'SAM. JOHNSON'

'MR. BOSWELL TO DR. JOHNSON

'Edinburgh, August 30, 1776

[After giving him an account of my having examined
the chests of books which he had sent to me,[a] and which

[a] *Boswell does not
seem pleased with this
Mode of payment—
Books from Stalls for
Monies expended on a
Journey.* [H & I]

[1] Prayers and Meditations, p. 151.

[2] [Samuel Paterson, formerly a bookseller, latterly an auctioneer, and well
known for his skill in forming catalogues of books. He died in London,
October 29, 1802. MALONE.]

contained what may be truly called a numerous and miscellaneous *Stall Library*, thrown together at random:—]

'Lord Hailes was against the decree in the case of my client, the minister; not that he justified the minister, but because the parishioner both provoked and retorted. I sent his Lordship your able argument upon the case for his perusal. His observation upon it in a letter to me was, "Dr. Johnson's *Suasorium* is pleasantly[1] and artfully composed. I suspect, however, that he has not convinced himself; for I believe that he is better read in ecclesiastical history, than to imagine that a Bishop or a Presbyter has a right to begin censure or discipline *è cathedrâ*."[2]

* * * * * *

'For the honour of Count Manucci, as well as to observe that exactness of truth which you have taught me, I must correct what I said in a former letter. He did not fall from his horse, which might have been an imputation on his skill as an officer of cavalry; his horse fell with him.

'I have, since I saw you, read every word of "Granger's Biographical History." It has entertained me exceedingly, and I do not think him the *Whig* that you supposed. Horace Walpole's being his patron is, indeed, no good sign of his political principles. But he denied to Lord Mountstuart that he was a Whig, and said he had been accused by both parties of partiality. It seems he was like Pope,

"While Tories call me Whig, and Whigs a Tory."

a It is sufficient to look at his Portrait;—he looks like a Whig. [1] I wish you would look more into his book;[a] and as Lord Mountstuart wishes much to find a proper person to continue the work upon Granger's plan, and has desired I would mention it to you; if such a man occurs, please to let me know. His Lordship will give him generous encouragement.'

[1] Why his Lordship uses the epithet *pleasantly*, when speaking of a grave piece of reasoning, I cannot conceive. But different men have different notions of pleasantry. I happened to sit by a gentleman one evening at the Opera-house in London, who at the moment when *Medea* appeared to be in great agony at the thought of killing her children, turned to me with a smile, and said, '*funny* enough.'

[2] Dr. Johnson afterwards told me, that he was of opinion that a clergyman had this right.

'TO MR. ROBERT LEVETT

'DEAR SIR,

'HAVING spent about six weeks at this place, we have at length resolved upon returning. I expect to see you all in Fleet-street on the 30th of this month.

'I did not go into the sea till last Friday, but think to go most of this week, though I know not that it does me any good. My nights are very restless and tiresome, but I am otherwise well.

'I have written word of my coming to Mrs. Williams. Remember me kindly to Francis and Betsy.[1] I am, Sir,

'Your humble servant,

'Brighthelmstone, Oct. 21, 1776.'   'SAM. JOHNSON'[2]

I again wrote to Dr. Johnson on the 21st of October, informing him, that my father had, in the most liberal manner, paid a large debt for me, and that I had now the happiness of being upon very good terms with him; to which he returned the following answer.

'TO JAMES BOSWELL, ESQ.

'DEAR SIR,

'I HAD great pleasure in hearing that you are at last on good terms with your father. Cultivate his kindness by all honest and manly means. Life is but short; no time can be afforded but for the indulgence of real sorrow, or contests upon questions seriously momentous. Let us not throw away any of our days upon useless resentment, or contend who shall hold out longest in stubborn malignity. It is best not to be angry; and best, in the next place, to be quickly reconciled. May you and your father pass the remainder of your time in reciprocal benevolence!

*   *   *   *   *   *

[1] [His female servant.[a] MALONE.]

[2] For this and Dr. Johnson's other letters to Mr. Levett, I am indebted to my old acquaintance Mr. Nathaniel Thomas, whose worth and ingenuity have been long known to a respectable though not a wide circle; and whose collection of medals would do credit to persons of greater opulence.

[Mr. Nathaniel Thomas, who was many years Editor of the St. James's Chronicle, died March 1, 1795. MALONE.]

[a] *I don't recollect Betsy —I knew Poll*. [1]

'Do you ever hear from Mr. Langton? I visit him some-times, but he does not talk. I do not like his scheme of life; but as I am not permitted to understand it, I cannot set any thing right that is wrong. His children are sweet babies.

'I hope my irreconcileable enemy, Mrs. Boswell, is well. Desire her not to transmit her malevolence to the young people. Let me have Alexander, and Veronica, and Euphemia, for my friends.

'Mrs. Williams, whom you may reckon as one of your well-wishers, is in a feeble and languishing state, with little hopes of growing better. She went for some part of the autumn into the country, but is little benefited; and Dr. Lawrence confesses that his art is at an end. Death is, however, at a distance: and what more than that can we say of ourselves? I am sorry for her pain, and more sorry for her decay. Mr. Levett is sound, wind and limb.

'I was some weeks this autumn at Brighthelmstone. The place was very dull, and I was not well; the expedition to the Hebrides was the most pleasant journey that I ever made. Such an effort annually would give the world a little diversification.

'Every year, however, we cannot wander, and must therefore endeavour to spend our time at home as well as we can. I believe it is best to throw life into a method, that every hour may bring its employment, and every employ-ment have its hour. Xenophon observes, in his "Treatise of Œconomy," that if every thing be kept in a certain place, when any thing is worn out or consumed, the vacuity which it leaves will shew what is wanting; so if every part of time has its duty, the hour will call into remembrance its proper engagement.

'I have not practised all this prudence myself, but I have suffered much for want of it; and I would have you, by timely recollection and steady resolution, escape from those evils which have lain heavy upon me. I am, my dearest Boswell,
                              'Your most humble servant,

'Bolt Court, Nov. 16, 1776.'   'SAM. JOHNSON'

On the 16th of November I informed him that Mr. Strahan had sent me *twelve* copies of the 'Journey to the

Western Islands,' handsomely bound, instead of the
twenty copies which were stipulated; but which, I supposed,
were to be only in sheets; requested to know how they
should be distributed: and mentioned that I had another
son born to me, who was named David, and was a
sickly infant.

'TO JAMES BOSWELL, ESQ.

'DEAR SIR,

   'I HAVE been for some time ill of a cold, which,
perhaps, I made an excuse to myself for not writing, when
in reality I knew not what to say.

   'The books you must at last distribute as you think best,
in my name, or your own, as you are inclined, or as you
judge most proper. Every body cannot be obliged; but I
wish that nobody may be offended. Do the best you can.

   'I congratulate you on the increase of your family, and
hope that little David is by this time well, and his mamma
perfectly recovered. I am much pleased to hear of the
re-establishment of kindness between you and your father.
Cultivate his paternal tenderness as much as you can. To
live at variance at all is uncomfortable; and variance with
a father is still more uncomfortable. Besides that, in the
whole dispute you have the wrong side; at least you gave
the first provocations, and some of them very offensive.
Let it now be all over. As you have no reason to think that
your new mother has shown you any foul play, treat her
with respect, and with some degree of confidence; this will
secure your father. When once a discordant family has felt
the pleasure of peace they will not willingly lose it. If Mrs.
Boswell would but be friends with me, we might now shut
the temple of Janus.

   'What came of Dr. Memis's cause? Is the question about
the negro determined? Has Sir Allan any reasonable
hopes? What is become of poor Macquarry? Let me know
the event of all these litigations. I wish particularly well to
the negro and Sir Allan.

   'Mrs. Williams has been much out of order; and though
she is something better, is likely, in her physician's opinion,
to endure her malady for life, though she may, perhaps, die
of some other. Mrs. Thrale is big, and fancies that she

carries a boy; if it were very reasonable to wish much about it, I should wish her not to be disappointed. The desire of male heirs is not appendant only to feudal tenures. A son is almost necessary to the continuance of Thrale's fortune; for what can misses do with a brewhouse? Lands are fitter for daughters than trades.

'Baretti went away from Thrale's in some whimsical fit of disgust, or ill-nature, without taking any leave. It is well if he finds in any other place as good an habitation, and as many conveniencies. He has got five-and-twenty guineas by translating Sir Joshua's Discourses into Italian, and Mr. Thrale gave him an hundred in the spring; so that he is yet in no difficulties.

'Colman has bought Foote's patent, and is to allow Foote for life sixteen hundred pounds a year, as Reynolds told me, and to allow him to play so often on such terms that he may gain four hundred pounds more. What Colman can get by this bargain,[1] but trouble and hazard, I do not see.

'I am, dear Sir,

'Your humble servant,

'Dec. 21, 1776.'   'SAM. JOHNSON'

The Reverend Dr. Hugh Blair, who had long been admired as a preacher at Edinburgh, thought now of diffusing his excellent sermons more extensively, and increasing his reputation, by publishing a collection of them. He transmitted the manuscript to Mr. Strahan, the printer, who after keeping it for some time, wrote a letter to him, discouraging the publication. Such at first was the unpropitious state of one of the most successful theological books that has ever appeared. Mr. Strahan, however, had sent one of the sermons to Dr. Johnson for his opinion; and after his unfavourable letter to Dr. Blair had been sent off, he received from Johnson on Christmas-eve, a note in which was the following paragraph:

'I have read over Dr. Blair's first sermon with more than approbation; to say it is good, is to say too little.'

marginal line:
though not . . . than a
[H]

[1] [It turned out, however, a very fortunate bargain; for Foote, though not then fifty-six, died at an inn in Dover, in less than a year, Oct. 21, 1777. MALONE.]

I believe Mr. Strahan had very soon after this time a conversation with Dr. Johnson concerning them; and then he very candidly wrote again to Dr. Blair, enclosing Johnson's note, and agreeing to purchase the volume, for which he and Mr. Cadell gave one hundred pounds. The sale was so rapid and extensive, and the approbation of the public so high, that to their honour be it recorded, the proprietors made Dr. Blair a present first of one sum, and afterwards of another, of fifty pounds, thus voluntarily doubling the stipulated price; and when he prepared another volume, they gave him at once three hundred pounds, being in all five hundred pounds, by an agreement to which I am a subscribing witness; and now for a third octavo volume he has received no less than six hundred pounds.

In 1777, it appears from his 'Prayers and Meditations,' that Johnson suffered much from a state of mind 'unsettled and perplexed,' and from that constitutional gloom, which, together with his extreme humility and anxiety with regard to his religious state, made him contemplate himself through too dark and unfavourable a medium. It may be said of him, that he 'saw GOD in clouds.' Certain we may be of his injustice to himself in the following lamentable paragraph, which it is painful to think came from the contrite heart of this great man, to whose labours the world is so much indebted: 'When I survey my past life, I discover nothing but a barren waste of time, with some disorders of body, and disturbances of the mind, very near to madness, which I hope He that made me will suffer to extenuate many faults, and excuse many deficiencies.'[1] But we find his devotions in this year eminently fervent; and we are comforted by observing intervals of quiet, composure, and gladness.

index sign:
near to madness etc.
[H]

On Easter-day we find the following emphatick prayer: 'Almighty and most merciful Father, who seest all our miseries, and knowest all our necessities, look down upon me, and pity me. Defend me from the violent incursion of evil thoughts, and enable me to form and keep such resolutions as may conduce to the discharge of the duties which thy providence shall appoint me; and so help me, by thy

[1] Prayers and Meditations, p. 155.

Holy Spirit, that my heart may surely there be fixed, where true joys are to be found, and that I may serve thee with pure affection and a cheerful mind. Have mercy upon me, O GOD, have mercy upon me; years and infirmities oppress me; terrour and anxiety beset me. Have mercy upon me, my Creator and my Judge. In all perplexities relieve and free me; and so help me by thy Holy Spirit, that I may now so commemorate the death of thy Son our Saviour JESUS CHRIST, as that when this short and painful life shall have an end, I may, for his sake, be received to everlasting happiness. Amen.'[1]

index sign: years and infirmities etc. [H]

While he was at church, the agreeable impressions upon his mind are thus commemorated: 'I was for some time distressed, but at last obtained, I hope from the GOD of Peace, more quiet than I have enjoyed for a long time. I had made no resolution, but as my heart grew lighter, my hopes revived, and my courage increased; and I wrote with my pencil, in my Common Prayer Book,

> "*Vita ordinanda.*
> *Biblia legenda.*
> *Theologiæ opera danda.*
> *Serviendum et lætandum.*"'

Mr. Steevens, whose generosity is well known, joined Dr. Johnson in kind assistance to a female relation of Dr. Goldsmith, and desired that on her return to Ireland she would procure authentick particulars of the life of her celebrated relation. Concerning her is the following letter:

'TO GEORGE STEEVENS, ESQ.

'DEAR SIR,

'YOU will be glad to hear that from Mrs. Goldsmith, whom we lamented as drowned, I have received a letter full of gratitude to us all, with promise to make the enquiries which we recommended to her.

'I would have had the honour of conveying this intelligence to Miss Caulfield, but that her letter is not at hand, and I know not the direction. You will tell the good news. I am, Sir,   'Your most, &c.

'February 25, 1777.'   'SAM. JOHNSON'

[1] Prayers and Meditations, p. 158.

'MR. BOSWELL TO DR. JOHNSON

'MY DEAR SIR,   'Edinburgh, February 14, 1777

'My state of epistolary accounts with you at present is extraordinary. The balance, as to number, is on your side. I am indebted to you for two letters; one dated the 16th of November, upon which very day I wrote to you, so that our letters were exactly exchanged; and one dated the 21st of December last.

'My heart was warmed with gratitude by the truly kind contents of both of them; and it is amazing and vexing that I have allowed so much time to elapse without writing to you. But delay is inherent in me, by nature or by bad habit. I waited till I should have an opportunity of paying you my compliments on a new year. I have procrastinated till the year is no longer new.

*   *   *   *   *

'Dr. Memis's cause was determined against him, with 40l. costs. The Lord President, and two other of the Judges, dissented from the majority, upon this ground; that although there may have been no intention to injure him by calling him *Doctor of Medicine*, instead of *Physician*, yet, as he remonstrated against the designation before the charter was printed off, and represented that it was disagreeable, and even hurtful to him, it was ill-natured to refuse to alter it, and let him have the designation to which he was certainly entitled. My own opinion is, that our court has judged wrong. The defendants were *in malâ fide*, to persist in naming him in a way that he disliked. You remember poor Goldsmith, when he grew important, and wished to appear *Doctor Major*, could not bear your calling him *Goldy*. Would it not have been wrong to have named him so in your "Preface to Shakspeare," or in any serious permanent writing of any sort? The difficulty is, whether an action should be allowed on such petty wrongs. *De minimis non curat lex.*

'The negro cause is not yet decided. A memorial is preparing on the side of slavery. I shall send you a copy as soon as it is printed. Maclaurin is made happy by your approbation of his memorial for the black.

'Macquarry was here in the winter, and we passed an evening together. The sale of his estate cannot be prevented.

'Sir Allan Maclean's suit against the Duke of Argyle, for recovering the ancient inheritance of his family, is now fairly before all our judges. I spoke for him yesterday, and Maclaurin to-day; Crosbie spoke to-day against him. Three more counsel are to be heard, and next week the cause will be determined. I send you the *Informations*, or *Cases*, on each side, which I hope you will read. You said to me when we were under Sir Allan's hospitable roof, "I will help you with my pen." You said it with a generous glow; and though his Grace of Argyle did afterwards mount you upon an excellent horse, upon which "you looked like a Bishop," you must not swerve from your purpose at Inchkenneth. I wish you may understand the points at issue, amidst our Scotch law principles and phrases.

[Here followed a full state of the case, in which I endeavoured to make it as clear as I could to an Englishman who had no knowledge of the formularies and technical language of the law of Scotland.]

'I shall inform you how the cause is decided here. But as it may be brought under the review of our Judges, and is certainly to be carried by appeal to the House of Lords, the assistance of such a mind as your's will be of consequence. Your paper on *Vicious Intromission* is a noble proof[a] of what you can do even in Scotch law.

[a] *So it is very good!* [1]

*   *   *   *   *   *

'I have not yet distributed all your books. Lord Hailes and Lord Monboddo have each received one, and return you thanks. Monboddo dined with me lately, and having drank tea, we were a good while by ourselves, and as I knew that he had read the "Journey" superficially, as he did not talk of it as I wished, I brought it to him, and read aloud several passages; and then he talked so, that I told him he was to have a copy *from the authour.* He begged *that* might be marked on it.

*   *   *   *   *   *

'I ever am, my dear Sir,
            'Your most faithful
      'And affectionate humble servant,
                  'JAMES BOSWELL'

'SIR ALEXANDER DICK TO DR. SAMUEL JOHNSON

'SIR,   'Prestonfield, Feb. 17, 1777

'I HAD yesterday the honour of receiving your book of your "*Journey to the Western Islands of Scotland*," which you was so good as to send me, by the hands of our mutual friend, Mr. Boswell, of Auchinleck; for which I return you my most hearty thanks; and after carefully reading it over again, shall deposit it in my little collection of choice books, next our worthy friend's "Journey to Corsica." As there are many things to admire in both performances, I have often wished that no Travels or Journey should be published but those undertaken by persons of integrity and capacity to judge well, and describe faithfully, and in good language, the situation, condition, and manners of the countries past through. Indeed our country of Scotland, in spite of the union of the crowns, is still in most places so devoid of clothing, or cover from hedges and plantations, that it was well you gave your readers a sound *Monitoire* with respect to that circumstance. The truths you have told, and the purity of the language in which they are expressed, as your "Journey" is universally read, may, and already appear to have a very good effect. For a man of my acquaintance, who has the largest nursery for trees and hedges in this country, tells me, that of late the demand upon him for these articles is doubled, and sometimes tripled. I have, therefore, listed Dr. Samuel Johnson in some of my memorandums of the principal planters and favourers of the enclosures, under a name which I took the liberty to invent from the Greek, *Papadendrion*. Lord Auchinleck and some few more are of the list. I am told that one gentleman in the shire of Aberdeen, *viz.* Sir Archibald Grant, has planted above fifty millions of trees on a piece of very wild ground at Monimusk: I must enquire if he has fenced them well, before he enters my list; for, that is the soul of enclosing. I began myself to plant a little, our ground being too valuable for much, and that is now fifty years ago; and the trees, now in my seventy-fourth year, I look up to with reverence, and shew them to my eldest son, now in his fifteenth year, and they are full the height of my country-house here, where I had the pleasure of receiving you, and hope again to have that satisfaction with our mutual friend, Mr. Boswell. I shall always continue, with the truest esteem, dear Doctor,

'Your much obliged,
'And obedient humble servant,
'ALEXANDER DICK'[1]

'TO JAMES BOSWELL, ESQ.

'DEAR SIR,

'IT is so long since I heard any thing from you,[2] that I am not easy about it; write something to me next post. When you sent your last letter, every thing seemed to be mending; I hope nothing has lately grown worse. I suppose young Alexander continues to thrive, and Veronica is now very pretty company. I do not suppose the lady is yet reconciled to me, yet let her know that I love her very well, and value her very much.

'Dr. Blair is printing some sermons. If they are all like the first, which I have read, they are *sermones aurei, ac auro magis aurei.* It is excellently written both as to doctrine and language. Mr. Watson's book[3] seems to be much esteemed.

* * * * * *

'Poor Beauclerk still continues very ill. Langton lives on as he used to do. His children are very pretty, and, I think, his lady loses her Scotch. Paoli I never see.

'I have been so distressed by difficulty of breathing, that I lost, as was computed, six-and-thirty ounces of blood in a few days. I am better, but not well.

'I wish you would be vigilant and get me Graham's "Telemachus," that was printed at Glasgow, a very little book; and "*Johnstoni Poemata,*" another little book, printed at Middleburgh.

'Mrs. Williams sends her compliments, and promises that when you come hither, she will accommodate you as

---

[1] For a character of this very amiable man, see 'Journal of a Tour to the Hebrides,' 3d edit. p. 36.

[2] By the then course of the post, my long letter of the 14th had not yet reached him.

[3] History of Philip the Second.

well as ever she can in the old room. She wishes to know whether you sent her book to Sir Alexander Gordon.

'My dear Boswell, do not neglect to write to me; for your kindness is one of the pleasures of my life, which I should be sorry to lose,   'I am, Sir,

'Your humble servant,

'February 18, 1777.'   'SAM. JOHNSON'

'TO DR. SAMUEL JOHNSON

'DEAR SIR,   'Edinburgh, Feb. 24, 1777

'Your letter dated the 18th instant, I had the pleasure to receive last post. Although my late long neglect, or rather delay, was truly culpable, I am tempted not to regret it, since it has produced me so valuable a proof of your regard. I did, indeed, during that inexcusable silence, sometimes divert the reproaches of my own mind, by fancying that I should hear again from you, enquiring with some anxiety about me, because, for aught you knew, I might have been ill.

'You are pleased to shew me, that my kindness is of some consequence to you. My heart is elated at the thought. Be assured, my dear Sir, that my affection and reverence for you are exalted and steady. I do not believe that a more perfect attachment ever existed in the history of mankind. And it is a noble attachment; for the attractions are Genius, Learning, and Piety.

'Your difficulty of breathing alarms me, and brings into my imagination an event, which although in the natural course of things, I must expect at some period, I cannot view with composure.

*   *   *   *   *   *

'My wife is much honoured by what you say of her. She begs you may accept of her best compliments. She is to send you some marmalade of oranges of her own making.[a]

*   *   *   *   *   *

'I ever am, my dear Sir,

'Your most obliged

'And faithful humble servant,

'JAMES BOSWELL'

underlined:
marmalade, oranges [1]

[a] *Orange* Marmalade *of her own making— would have been right; She could not make the Oranges. 1820* [H]

rather orange-Marmalade: She did not make the Oranges. *This is a Conserve which cannot be well made but by Scotch hands.* [1]

'TO JAMES BOSWELL, ESQ.

'DEAR SIR,

'I HAVE been much pleased with your late letter, and am glad that my old enemy, Mrs. Boswell, begins to feel some remorse. As to Miss Veronica's Scotch, I think it cannot be helped. An English maid you might easily have; but she would still imitate the greater number, as they would be likewise those whom she must most respect. Her dialect will not be gross. Her mamma has not much Scotch, and you have yourself very little. I hope she knows my name, and does not call me *Johnston*.[1]

two marginal lines: Johnston [H]

'The immediate cause of my writing is this:—One Shaw, who seems a modest and a decent man, has written an Erse Grammar, which a very learned Highlander, Macbean, has, at my request, examined and approved.

'The book is very little, but Mr. Shaw has been persuaded by his friends to set it at half a guinea, though I advised only a crown, and thought myself liberal. You, whom the authour considers as a great encourager of ingenious men, will receive a parcel of his proposals and receipts. I have undertaken to give you notice of them, and to solicit your countenance. You must ask no poor man, because the price is really too high. Yet such a work deserves patronage.

'It is proposed to augment our club from twenty to thirty, of which I am glad; for as we have several in it whom I do not much like to consort with,[2] I am for reducing it to a mere miscellaneous collection of conspicuous men, without any determinate character.   *   *   *   *

'I am, dear Sir,
'Most affectionately your's,

'March 14, 1777.'   'SAM. JOHNSON'

'My respects to Madam, to Veronica, to Alexander, to Euphemia, to David.'

[1] John*son* is the most common English formation of the sirname from *John;* John*ston* the Scotch.ᵃ My illustrious friend observed, that many North Britons pronounced his name in their own way.

[2] On account of their differing from him as to religion and politicks.

'MR. BOSWELL TO DR. JOHNSON

'Edinburgh, April 4, 1777

[After informing him of the death of my little son David, and that I could not come to London this spring:—]

'I think it hard that I should be a whole year without seeing you. May I presume to petition for a meeting with you in the autumn? You have, I believe, seen all the cathedrals in England, except that of Carlisle. If you are to be with Dr. Taylor, at Ashbourne, it would not be a great journey to come thither. We may pass a few most agreeable days there by ourselves, and I will accompany you a good part of the way to the southward again. Pray think of this.

'You forget that Mr. Shaw's Erse Grammar was put into your hands by myself last year. Lord Eglintoune put it into mine. I am glad that Mr. Macbean approves of it. I have received Mr. Shaw's Proposals for its publication, which I can perceive are written *by the hand of a* MASTER.

* * * * * *

'Pray get for me all the editions of "Walton's Lives." I have a notion that the republication of them with Notes will fall upon me, between Dr. Horne and Lord Hailes.'[1]

Mr. Shaw's Proposals† for 'An Analysis of the Scotch Celtick Language,' were thus illuminated by the pen of Johnson:

'THOUGH the Erse dialect of the Celtick language has, from the earliest times, been spoken in Britain, and still subsists in the northern parts and adjacent islands, yet, by the negligence of a people rather warlike than lettered, it has hitherto been left to the caprice and judgement of every speaker, and has floated in the living voice, without the steadiness of analogy, or direction of rules. An Erse Grammar is an addition to the stores of literature; and its authour hopes for the indulgence always shewn to those

---

[1] [None of the persons here mentioned executed the work which they had in contemplation. Walton's valuable book, however, has been correctly republished in quarto and octavo, with notes and illustrations, by the Rev. Mr. Zouch. MALONE.]

that attempt to do what was never done before. If his work shall be found defective, it is at least all his own: he is not like other grammarians, a compiler or transcriber; what he delivers, he has learned by attentive observation among his countrymen, who perhaps will be themselves surprized to see that speech reduced to principles, which they have used only by imitation.

'The use of this book will, however, not be confined to the mountains and islands: it will afford a pleasing and important subject of speculation, to those whose studies lead them to trace the affinity of languages, and the migrations of the ancient races of mankind.'

'TO DR. SAMUEL JOHNSON

'MY DEAR SIR,   'Glasgow, April 24, 1777

'OUR worthy friend Thrale's death having appeared in the news-papers,[a] and been afterwards contradicted, I have been placed in a state of very uneasy uncertainty, from which I hoped to be relieved by you: but my hopes have as yet been vain. How could you omit to write to me on such an occasion? I shall wait with anxiety.

'I am going to Auchinleck to stay a fortnight with my father. It is better not to be there very long at one time. But frequent renewals of attention are agreeable to him.

'Pray tell me about this edition of "The English Poets, with a Preface, biographical and critical, to each Authour, by Samuel Johnson, LL.D." which I see advertised. I am delighted with the prospect of it. Indeed I am happy to feel that I am capable of being so much delighted with literature. But is not the charm of this publication chiefly owing to the *magnum nomen* in the front of it?

'What do you say of Lord Chesterfield's Memoirs and last Letters?

'My wife has made marmalade of oranges for you. I left her and my daughters and Alexander all well yesterday. I have taught Veronica to speak of you thus;— Dr. John*son*, not John*ston*. I remain, my dear Sir,

'Your most affectionate,
'And obliged humble servant,
'JAMES BOSWELL'

[a] *some gay Fellow put it in to fright us—on me the Effect was miss'd, because I was going to join him & Tom Cotton (my Cousin) at Brighton & they were the first who told me. Mr. Thrale's Sisters were much terrified:—The more, as hearing I had left Streatham for Sussex.* [H]

It was a curious Trick to make some Man an April Fool, & so win a Wager: but it frighted many Friends, & hurt some. [I]

'TO JAMES BOSWELL, ESQ.

'DEAR SIR,

'THE story of Mr. Thrale's death, as he had neither been sick nor in any other danger, made so little impression upon me, that I never thought about obviating its effects on any body else. It is supposed to have been produced by the English custom of making April fools, that is, of sending one another on some foolish errand on the first of April.

'Tell Mrs. Boswell that I shall taste her marmalade cautiously at first. *Timeo Danaos et dona ferentes.* Beware, says the Italian proverb, of a reconciled enemy. But when I find it does me no harm, I shall then receive it and be thankful for it, as a pledge of firm, and, I hope, of unalterable kindness. She is, after all, a dear, dear lady.

'Please to return Dr. Blair thanks for his sermons. The Scotch write English wonderfully well.

*   *   *   *   *   *

'Your frequent visits to Auchinleck, and your short stay there, are very laudable and very judicious. Your present concord with your father gives me great pleasure; it was all that you seemed to want.

'My health is very bad, and my nights are very unquiet. What can I do to mend them? I have for this summer nothing better in prospect than a journey into Staffordshire and Derbyshire, perhaps with Oxford and Birmingham in my way.

'Make my compliments to Miss Veronica; I must leave it to *her* philosophy to comfort you for the loss of little David. You must remember, that to keep three out of four is more than your share. Mrs. Thrale[a] has but four out of eleven.   ᵃ *Poor Soul!—!!!!* [1]

'I am engaged to write little Lives, and little Prefaces, to a little edition of the English Poets. I think I have persuaded the booksellers to insert something of Thomson; and if you could give me some information about him, for the life which we have is very scanty, I should be glad. I am, dear Sir,

'Your most affectionate humble servant,

'May 3, 1777.'   'SAM. JOHNSON'

To those who delight in tracing the progress of works of literature, it will be an entertainment to compare the limited design with the ample execution of that admirable performance, 'The Lives of the English Poets,' which is the richest, most beautiful, and indeed most perfect, production of Johnson's pen. His notion of it at this time appears in the preceding letter. He has a memorandum in this year, '29 March, Easter-Eve, I treated with booksellers on a bargain, but the time was not long.'[1] The bargain was concerning that undertaking; but his tender conscience seems alarmed, lest it should have intruded too much on his devout preparation for the solemnity of the ensuing day. But, indeed, very little time was necessary for Johnson's concluding a treaty with the booksellers; as he had, I believe, less attention to profit from his labours, than any man to whom literature has been a profession. I shall here insert from a letter to me from my late worthy friend Mr. Edward Dilly, though of a later date, an account of this plan so happily conceived; since it was the occasion of procuring for us an elegant collection of the best biography and criticism of which our language can boast.

'TO JAMES BOSWELL, ESQ.

'DEAR SIR,   'Southill, Sept. 26, 1777

'You find by this letter, that I am still in the same calm retreat, from the noise and bustle of London, as when I wrote to you last. I am happy to find you had such an agreeable meeting with your old friend Dr. Johnson; I have no doubt your stock is much increased by the interview; few men, nay I may say, scarcely any man has got that fund of knowledge and entertainment as Dr. Johnson in conversation. When he opens freely, every one is attentive to what he says, and cannot fail of improvement as well as pleasure.

'The edition of the Poets, now printing, will do honour to the English press; and a concise account of the life of each authour, by Dr. Johnson, will be a very valuable addition, and stamp the reputation of this edition superiour to any thing that is gone before. The first cause that gave rise to this undertaking, I believe, was owing to the little trifling

[1] Prayers and Meditations, p. 155.

edition of the Poets, printing by the Martins at Edinburgh, and to be sold by Bell, in London. Upon examining the volumes which were printed, the type was found so extremely small, that many persons could not read them; not only this inconvenience attended it, but the inaccuracy of the press was very conspicuous. These reasons, as well as the idea of an invasion of what we call our Literary Property, induced the London Booksellers to print an elegant and accurate edition of all the English poets of reputation, from Chaucer to the present time.

'Accordingly a select number of the most respectable booksellers met on the occasion; and, on consulting together, agreed, that all the proprietors of copy-right in the various Poets should be summoned together; and when their opinions were given, to proceed immediately on the business. Accordingly a meeting was held, consisting of about forty of the most respectable booksellers of London, when it was agreed that an elegant and uniform edition of "The English Poets" should be immediately printed, with a concise account of the life of each authour, by Dr. Samuel Johnson; and that three persons should be deputed to wait upon Dr. Johnson, to solicit him to undertake the Lives, *viz*. T. Davies, Strahan, and Cadell. The Doctor very politely undertook it, and seemed exceedingly pleased with the proposal. As to the terms, it was left entirely to the Doctor to name his own; he mentioned two hundred guineas;[1] it was immediately agreed to; and a farther compliment, I believe, will be made him. A committee was likewise appointed to engage the best engravers, *viz*. Bartolozzi, Sherwin, Hall, &c. Likewise another committee for giving directions about the paper, printing, &c. so that the whole will be conducted with spirit, and in the best manner, with respect to authourship, editorship, engravings, &c. &c. My brother will give you a list of the Poets we mean to give, many of which are within the time of the Act of Queen Anne, which Martin and Bell cannot give, as they have no property in them; the

[1] [Johnson's moderation in demanding so small a sum is extraordinary. Had he asked one thousand, or even fifteen hundred guineas, the booksellers, who knew the value of his name, would doubtless have readily given it. They have probably got five thousand guineas by this work in the course of twenty-five years. MALONE.]

proprietors are almost all the booksellers in London, of consequence.   I am, dear Sir,

'Ever your's,

'EDWARD DILLY'

I shall afterwards have occasion to consider the extensive and varied range which Johnson took, when he was once led upon ground which he trod with a peculiar delight, having long been intimately acquainted with all the circumstances of it that could interest and please.

'DR. JOHNSON TO CHARLES O'CONNOR, ESQ.[1]

'SIR,

'HAVING had the pleasure of conversing with Dr. Campbell about your character and your literary undertaking, I am resolved to gratify myself by renewing a correspondence which began and ended a great while ago, and ended, I am afraid, by my fault; a fault which, if you have not forgotten it, you must now forgive.

'If I have ever disappointed you, give me leave to tell you, that you have likewise disappointed me. I expected great discoveries in Irish antiquity, and large publications in the Irish language; but the world still remains as it was, doubtful and ignorant. What the Irish language is in itself, and to what languages it has affinity, are very interesting questions, which every man wishes to see resolved that has any philological or historical curiosity. Dr. Leland begins his history too late: the ages which deserve an exact enquiry are those times (for such there were) when Ireland was the school of the west, the quiet habitation of sanctity and literature. If you could give a history, though imperfect, of the Irish nation, from its conversion to Christianity to the invasion from England, you would amplify

[1] Mr. Joseph Cooper Walker, of the Treasury, Dublin, who obligingly communicated to me this and a former letter from Dr. Johnson to the same gentleman, (for which see vol. i, page 222) writes to me as follows:—
'Perhaps it would gratify you to have some account of Mr. O'Connor. He is an amiable, learned, venerable old gentleman, of an independent fortune, who lives at Belanagar, in the county of Roscommon; he is an admired writer, and member of the Irish Academy.—The above Letter is alluded to in the Preface to the 2d edit. of his Dissert. p. 3.'—Mr. O'Connor afterwards died at the age of eighty-two, July 1, 1791. See a well-drawn character of him in the Gentleman's Magazine for August 1791.

knowledge with new views and new objects. Set about it
therefore, if you can: do what you can easily do without
anxious exactness. Lay the foundation, and leave the
superstructure to posterity. I am, Sir,

'Your humble servant,

'May 19, 1777.'   'SAM. JOHNSON'

Early in this year came out, in two volumes quarto, the
posthumous works of the learned Dr. Zachary Pearce,
Bishop of Rochester; being 'A Commentary, with Notes,
on the four Evangelists and the Acts of the Apostles,' with
other theological pieces. Johnson had now an opportunity
of making a grateful return to that excellent prelate, who,
we have seen, was the only person who gave him any
assistance in the compilation of his Dictionary. The Bishop
had left some account of his life and character, written by
himself. To this Johnson made some valuable additions,✝
and also furnished to the editor, the Reverend Mr. Derby,
a Dedication,✝ which I shall here insert, both because it
will appear at this time with peculiar propriety; and
because it will tend to propagate and increase that
'fervour of *Loyalty*,' which in me, who boast of the name
of TORY, is not only a principle, but a passion.

'TO THE KING

'SIR,

'I presume to lay before your Majesty the last labours
of a learned Bishop, who died in the toils and duties of his
calling. He is now beyond the reach of all earthly honours
and rewards; and only the hope of inciting others to
imitate him, makes it now fit to be remembered, that he
enjoyed in his life the favour of your Majesty.

'The tumultuary[a] life of Princes seldom permits them to
survey the wide extent of national interest, without losing
sight of private merit; to exhibit qualities which may be
imitated by the highest and the humblest of mankind: and
to be at once amiable and great.

'Such characters, if now and then they appear in
history, are contemplated with admiration. May it be the
ambition of all your subjects to make haste with their
tribute of reverence; and as posterity may learn from your

[a] underlined with *Qu:* in margin [1]

exclamation point: *and as posterity* etc. [H]

Majesty how Kings should live, may they learn likewise
from your people how they should be honoured.ᵃ I am,

> 'May it please your Majesty,
>> 'With the most profound respect,
>>> 'Your Majesty's
>>> 'Most dutiful and devoted
>>>> 'Subject and Servant.'

In the summer he wrote a Prologue* which was spoken
before 'A Word to the Wise,' a comedy by Mr. Hugh
Kelly, which had been brought upon the stage in 1770;
but he being a writer for ministry in one of the news-
papers, it fell a sacrifice to popular fury, and, in the play-
house phrase, was *damned*. By the generosity of Mr. Harris,
the proprietor of Covent-Garden theatre, it was now
exhibited for one night, for the benefit of the authour's
widow and children. To conciliate the favour of the
audience was the intention of Johnson's Prologue, which,
as it is not long, I shall here insert, as a proof that his
poetical talents were in no degree impaired.

> 'THIS night presents a play, with publick rage,
> Or right or wrong, once hooted from the stage:
> From zeal or malice, now no more we dread,
> For English vengeance *wars not with the dead*.
> A generous foe regards with pitying eye
> The man whom Fate has laid where all must lie.
> To wit, reviving from its authour's dust,
> Be kind, ye judges, or at least be just:
> Let no renewed hostilities invade
> Th' oblivious grave's inviolable shade.
> Let one great payment every claim appease,
> And him who cannot hurt, allow to please;
> To please by scenes, unconscious of offence,
> By harmless merriment, or useful sense.
> Where aught of bright or fair the piece displays,
> Approve it only;—'tis too late to praise.
> If want of skill or want of care appear,
> Forbear to hiss;—the poet cannot hear.
> Byᵃ all, like him, must praise and blame be found,
> At last, a fleeting gleam, or empty sound:

Yet then shall calm reflection bless the night,
When liberal pity dignified delight;
When pleasure fir'd her torch at virtue's flame,
And mirth was bounty with an humbler name.'

marginal line:
When liberal . . . dig-
nified delight [H]

A circumstance which could not fail to be very pleasing to Johnson, occurred this year. The Tragedy of 'Sir Thomas Overbury,' written by his early companion in London, Richard Savage, was brought out with alterations at Drury-lane theatre.[1] The Prologue to it was written by Mr. Richard Brinsley Sheridan; in which, after describing very pathetically the wretchedness of

'Ill-fated Savage, at whose birth was giv'n
No parent but the Muse, no friend but Heav'n:'

he introduced an elegant compliment to Johnson on his Dictionary, that wonderful performance which cannot be too often or too highly praised; of which Mr. Harris, in his 'Philological Inquiries,'[2] justly and liberally observes, 'Such is its merit, that our language does not possess a more copious, learned, and valuable work.' The concluding lines of this Prologue were these:

'So pleads the tale[3] that gives to future times
The son's misfortunes and the parent's crimes;
There shall his fame (if own'd to-night) survive,
Fix'd by THE HAND THAT BIDS OUR LANGUAGE
LIVE.'

marginal line:
Fix'd by . . . LAN-
GUAGE LIVE [H]

Mr. Sheridan here at once did honour to his taste and to his liberality of sentiment, by showing that he was not prejudiced from the unlucky difference which had taken place between his worthy father and Dr. Johnson. I have already mentioned, that Johnson was very desirous of reconciliation with old Mr. Sheridan. It will, therefore, not seem at all surprising that he was zealous in acknowledging the brilliant merit of his son. While it had as yet been displayed only in the drama, Johnson proposed him

[1] [Our authour has here fallen into a slight mistake: the prologue to this revived tragedy being written by Mr. Sheridan, Mr. Boswell very naturally supposed that it was performed at Drury-lane theatre. But in fact, as Mr. Kemble observes to me, it was acted at the theatre in Covent Garden. MALONE.]

[2] Part First, Chap. 4.   [3] 'Life of Richard Savage, by Dr. Johnson.'

as a member of THE LITERARY CLUB, observing, that
'He who has written the two best comedies of his age, is
surely a considerable man.' And he had, accordingly, the
honour to be elected; for an honour it undoubtedly must
be allowed to be, when it is considered of whom that society
consists, and that a single black ball excludes a candidate.

'MR. BOSWELL TO DR. JOHNSON

'MY DEAR SIR,   'June 9, 1777

'FOR the health of my wife and children, I have taken
the little country-house at which you visited my uncle,
Dr. Boswell, who, having lost his wife, is gone to live with
his son. We took possession of our villa about a week ago;
we have a garden of three quarters of an acre, well stocked
with fruit-trees and flowers, and gooseberries and currants,
and pease and beans, and cabbages, &c. &c. and my
children are quite happy. I now write to you in a little
study, from the window of which I see around me a
verdant grove, and beyond it the lofty mountain called
Arthur's Seat.

'Your last letter, in which you desire me to send you
some additional information concerning Thomson, reached
me very fortunately just as I was going to Lanark, to put
my wife's two nephews, the young Campbells, to school
there, under the care of Mr. Thomson, the master of it,
whose wife is sister to the author of "The Seasons." She is
an old woman; but her memory is very good; and she will
with pleasure give me for you every particular that you
wish to know, and she can tell. Pray then take the trouble
to send me such questions as may lead to biographical
materials. You say that the Life which we have of Thomson
is scanty. Since I received your letter, I have read his Life,
published under the name of Cibber, but as you told
me, really written by a Mr. Shiels;[1] that written by
Dr. Murdoch; one prefixed to an edition of the "Seasons,"
published at Edinburgh, which is compounded of both,
with the addition of an anecdote of Quin's relieving
Thomson from prison; the abridgement of Murdoch's
account of him, in the "Biographia Britannica," and

[1] See pp. 280, 281 of this volume.

another abridgement of it in the "Biographical Dictionary," enriched with Dr. Joseph Warton's critical
panegyrick on the "Seasons" in his "Essay on the Genius
and Writings of Pope:" from all these it appears to me
that we have a pretty full account of this poet. However,
you will, I doubt not, shew me many blanks, and I shall
do what can be done to have them filled up. As Thomson
never returned to Scotland, (which *you* will think very wise,)
his sister can speak from her own knowledge only as to the
early part of his life. She has some letters from him, which
may probably give light as to his more advanced progress,
if she will let us see them, which I suppose she will. I
believe George Lewis Scott[1] and Dr. Armstrong are now
his only surviving companions, while he lived in and about
London; and they, I dare say, can tell more of him than
is yet known. My own notion is, that Thomson was a
much coarser man than his friends are willing to acknowledge. His "Seasons" are indeed full of elegant and pious
sentiments: but a rank soil, nay a dunghill, will produce
beautiful flowers.

'Your edition[2] of the "English Poets" will be very valuable, on account of the "Prefaces and Lives." But I have
seen a specimen of an edition of the Poets at the Apollo
press, at Edinburgh, which, for excellence in printing and
engraving, highly deserves a liberal encouragement.

'Most sincerely do I regret the bad health and bad rest
with which you have been afflicted; and I hope you are
better. I cannot believe that the prologue which you
generously gave to Mr. Kelly's widow and children the
other day, is the effusion of one in sickness and in dis-
quietude: but external circumstances are never sure

[1] [George Lewis Scott, Esq. F.R.S. an amiable[a] and learned man, formerly
Sub-preceptor to his present Majesty, and afterwards appointed a Com-
missioner of Excise. He died in 1780. MALONE.]

[2] [Dr. Johnson was not the *editor* of this Collection of the English Poets; he
merely furnished the biographical prefaces with which it is enriched; as is
rightly stated in a subsequent page.

He indeed, from a virtuous motive recommended the works of four or five
poets (whom he has named) to be added to the collection; but he is no
otherwise answerable for any which are found there, or any which are
omitted.—The poems of Goldsmith (whose Life I know he intended to write,
for I collected some materials for it by his desire,) were omitted, in consequence of a petty exclusive interest in some of them, vested in Mr. Carnan,
a bookseller. MALONE.]

marginal lines:
*Biographical Diction-
ary . . . Pope:' from*
[H]

[a] *so he was an Agree-
able Man. he married
Mrs. Montagu's Sister
after a Courtship of
ten Years . . . & did
not live with her ten
Weeks.* [H & I]

marginal line:
*Dr. Johnson . . . of
the* [H]

indications of the state of man. I send you a letter which I wrote to you two years ago at Wilton; and did not send it at the time, for fear of being reproved as indulging too much tenderness; and one written to you at the tomb of Melancthon, which I kept back, lest I should appear at once too superstitious and too enthusiastick. I now imagine that perhaps they may please you.

'You do not take the least notice of my proposal for our meeting at Carlisle.[1] Though I have meritoriously refrained from visiting London this year, I ask you if it would not be wrong that I should be two years without having the benefit of your conversation, when, if you come down as far as Derbyshire, we may meet at the expence of a few days' journeying, and not many pounds. I wish you to see Carlisle, which made me mention that place. But if you have not a desire to complete your tour of the English cathedrals, I will take a larger share of the road between this place and Ashbourne. So tell me *where* you will fix for our passing a few days by ourselves. Now don't cry "foolish fellow," or "idle dog." Chain your humour, and let your kindness play.

'You will rejoice to hear that Miss Macleod, of Rasay, is married to Colonel Mure Campbell,[a] an excellent man, with a pretty good estate of his own, and the prospect of having the Earl of Loudoun's fortune and honours. Is not this a noble lot for our fair Hebridean? How happy am I that she is to be in Ayrshire. We shall have the Laird of Rasay, and old Malcolm, and I know not how many gallant Macleods, and bagpipes, &c. &c. at Auchinleck. Perhaps you may meet them all there.

'Without doubt you have read what is called "The *Life* of David Hume," written by himself, with the letter from

a & her Sister long afterwards married a McLeod of Coldback; I saw her at Cheltenham in 1811 with Two or Three beautiful Daughters—Flora very handsome indeed. [H]

underlined:
high [H]

b So She was poor Dear! [H]

---

[1] Dr. Johnson had himself talked of our seeing Carlisle together. *High* was a favourite word of his to denote a person of rank. He said to me, 'Sir, I believe we may meet at the house of a Roman Catholick lady in Cumberland; a high[b] lady, Sir.' I afterwards discovered that he meant Mrs. Strickland, sister of Charles Townley, Esq. whose very noble collection of statues and pictures is not more to be admired, than his extraordinary and polite readiness in shewing it, which I and several of my friends have agreeably experienced. They who are possessed of valuable stores of gratification to persons of taste, should exercise their benevolence in imparting the pleasure. Grateful acknowledgements are due to Welbore Ellis Agar, Esq. for the liberal access which he is pleased to allow to his exquisite collection of pictures.

Dr. Adam Smith subjoined to it. Is not this an age of daring effrontery? My friend Mr. Anderson, Professor of Natural Philosophy at Glasgow, at whose house you and I supped, and to whose care Mr. Windham, of Norfolk, was entrusted at that University, paid me a visit lately; and after we had talked with indignation and contempt of the poisonous productions with which this age is infested, he said there was now an excellent opportunity for Dr. Johnson to step forth. I agreed with him that you might knock Hume's and Smith's heads together, and make vain and ostentatious infidelity exceedingly ridiculous. Would it not be worth your while to crush such noxious weeds in the moral garden?

'You have said nothing to me of Dr. Dodd. I know not how you think on that subject; though the news-papers give us a saying of your's in favour of mercy to him. But I own I am very desirous that the royal prerogative of remission of punishment should be employed to exhibit an illustrious instance of the regard which GOD'S VICEGERENT will ever shew to piety and virtue. If for ten righteous men the ALMIGHTY would have spared Sodom, shall not a thousand acts of goodness done by Dr. Dodd counterbalance one crime? Such an instance would do more to encourage goodness, than his execution would do to deter from vice.[a] I am not afraid of any bad consequence to society; for who will persevere for a long course of years in a distinguished discharge of religious duties, with a view to commit a forgery with impunity?

'Pray make my best compliments acceptable to Mr. and Mrs. Thrale, by assuring them of my hearty joy that the *Master*, as you call him, is alive. I hope I shall often taste his Champagne—*soberly*.

'I have not heard from Langton for a long time. I suppose he is as usual,

"Studious the busy moments to deceive."

* * * * * *

'I remain, my dear Sir,
'Your most affectionate
'And faithful humble servant,
'JAMES BOSWELL'

underlined: *vice* [H]

[a] *It was not to deter Men from* Vice *that Dodd was hanged . . . it was to secure Men's* Money *from* Forgers *. . .* Vicious Fellows *are let 'Scape every day . . . when* Money *is not concerned.* [H]

On the 23d of June, I again wrote to Dr. Johnson, enclosing a ship-master's receipt for a jar of orange-marmalade, and a large packet of Lord Hailes's 'Annals of Scotland.'

'TO JAMES BOSWELL, ESQ.

'DEAR SIR,

'I HAVE just received your packet from Mr. Thrale's, but have not day-light enough to look much into it. I am glad that I have credit enough with Lord Hailes to be trusted with more copy. I hope to take more care of it than of the last. I return Mrs. Boswell my affection-ate thanks for her present, which I value as a token of reconciliation.

'Poor Dodd was put to death yesterday, in opposition to the recommendation of the jury,—the petition of the city of London,—and a subsequent petition signed by three-and-twenty thousand hands. Surely the voice of the publick, when it calls so loudly, and calls only for mercy, ought to be heard.

'The saying that was given me in the papers I never spoke; but I wrote many of his petitions, and some of his letters. He applied to me very often. He was, I am afraid, long flattered with hopes of life; but I had no part in the dreadful delusion; for as soon as the King had signed his sentence, I obtained from Mr. Chamier an account of the disposition of the court towards him, with a declaration that there *was no hope even of a respite*. This letter im-mediately was laid before Dodd; but he believed those whom he wished to be right, as it is thought, till within three days of his end. He died with pious composure and resolution. I have just seen the Ordinary that attended him. His Address to his fellow-convicts offended the Methodists; but he had a Moravian with him much of his time. His moral character is very bad: I hope all is not true that is charged upon him. Of his behaviour in prison an account will be published.

'I give you joy of your country-house, and your pretty garden; and hope some time to see you in your felicity. I was much pleased with your two letters that had been kept so long in store;[1] and rejoice at Miss Rasay's advancement, and wish Sir Allan success.

'I hope to meet you somewhere towards the north, but am loath to come quite to Carlisle. Can we not meet at Manchester? But we will settle it in some other letters.

'Mr. Seward,[2] a great favourite at Streatham,[a] has been, I think, enkindled by our travels, with a curiosity to see the

underlined:
Seward, favourite at Streatham [H]

[a] *The Favour was ill bestow'd: . . . he was very spiteful to the Mistress—when She lost the Master of the House he was so kindly entertain'd at.* [H]

[1] Since they have been so much honoured by Dr. Johnson, I shall here insert them:

'TO MR. SAMUEL JOHNSON

'MY EVER DEAR AND MUCH-RESPECTED SIR,

'You know my solemn enthusiasm of mind. You love me for it, and I respect myself for it, because in so far I resemble Mr. Johnson. You will be agreeably surprized, when you learn the reason of my writing this letter. I am at Wittemberg, in Saxony. I am in the old church where the Reformation was first preached, and where some of the reformers lie interred. I cannot resist the serious pleasure of writing to Mr. Johnson from the tomb of Melancthon. My paper rests upon the grave-stone of that great and good man, who was undoubtedly the worthiest of all the reformers. He wished to reform abuses which had been introduced into the Church; but had no private resentment to gratify. So mild was he, that when his aged mother consulted him with anxiety on the perplexing disputes of the times, he advised her "to keep to the old religion." At this tomb, then, my ever dear and respected friend! I vow to thee an eternal attachment. It shall be my study to do what I can to render your life happy: and if you die before me, I shall endeavour to do honour to your memory; and, elevated by the remembrance of you, persist in noble piety. May GOD, the father of all beings, ever bless you! and may you continue to love,

'Your most affectionate friend, and devoted servant,
'Sunday, Sept. 30, 1764.'   'JAMES BOSWELL'

'TO DR. SAMUEL JOHNSON

'MY DEAR SIR,   'Wilton-house, April 22, 1775
'EVERY scene of my life confirms the truth of what you have told me, "there is no certain happiness in this state of being."—I am here, amidst all that you know is at Lord Pembroke's; and yet I am weary and gloomy. I am just setting out for the house of an old friend in Devonshire, and shall not get back to London for a week yet. You said to me last Good-Friday, with a cordiality that warmed my heart, that if I came to settle in London we should have a day fixed every week, to meet by ourselves and talk freely. To be thought worthy of such a privilege cannot but exalt me. During my present absence from you, while, notwithstanding the gaiety which you allow me to possess, I am darkened by temporary clouds, I beg to have a few lines from you; a few lines merely of kindness, as a *viaticum* till I see you again. In your "Vanity of Human Wishes," and in Parnell's "Contentment," I find the only sure means of enjoying happiness; or, at least, the hopes of happiness. I ever am, with reverence and affection,

'Most faithfully your's,
'JAMES BOSWELL'

[2] William Seward, Esq. F.R.S. editor of 'Anecdotes of some distinguished persons,' &c. in four volumes, 8vo. well known to a numerous and valuable

Highlands. I have given him letters to you and Beattie. He desires that a lodging may be taken for him at Edinburgh, against his arrival. He is just setting out.

'Langton has been exercising the militia. Mrs. Williams is, I fear, declining. Dr. Lawrence says he can do no more. She is gone to summer in the country, with as many conveniences about her as she can expect; but I have no great hope. We must all die: may we all be prepared!

'I suppose Miss Boswell reads her book, and young Alexander takes to his learning. Let me hear about them; for every thing that belongs to you, belongs in a more remote degree, and not, I hope, very remote, to, dear Sir,

'Your's affectionately,
'June 28, 1777.'   'SAM. JOHNSON'

TO THE SAME

'DEAR SIR,

'THIS gentleman is a great favourite at Streatham, and therefore you will easily believe that he has very valuable qualities. Our narrative has kindled him with a desire of visiting the Highlands after having already seen a great part of Europe. You must receive him as a friend, and when you have directed him to the curiosities of Edinburgh, give him instructions and recommendations for the rest of his journey. I am, dear Sir,

'Your most humble servant,
'June 24, 1777.'   'SAM. JOHNSON'

Johnson's benevolence to the unfortunate was, I am confident, as steady and active as that of any of those who have been most eminently distinguished for that virtue. Innumerable proofs of it I have no doubt will be for ever concealed from mortal eyes. We may, however, form some judgement of it, from the many and very various instances which have been discovered. One, which happened in the course of this summer, is remarkable from the name and

acquaintance for his literature, love of the fine arts, and social virtues. I am indebted to him for several communications concerning Johnson.

[This gentleman, who was born in 1747, and was educated at the Charter-House, and at Oxford, died in London, April 24, 1799. MALONE.]

connection of the person who was the object of it. The
circumstance to which I allude is ascertained by two letters,
one to Mr. Langton, and another to the Reverend Dr.
Vyse, rector of Lambeth,[a] son of the respectable clergyman
at Lichfield, who was contemporary with Johnson, and in
whose father's family Johnson had the happiness of being
kindly received in his early years.

underlined:
Dr. Vyse, rector of
Lambeth [H]
[a] whose   Connection
with Sophia Streatfield
was afterwards so much
talked about, & I sup-
pose never understood:
certainly not at all by
H.L.P. [H & I]

'DR. JOHNSON TO BENNET LANGTON, ESQ.

'DEAR SIR,

'I HAVE lately been much disordered by a difficulty
of breathing, but am now better. I hope your house
is well.

'You know we have been talking lately of St. Cross, at
Winchester; I have an old acquaintance whose distress
makes him very desirous of an hospital, and I am afraid
I have not strength enough to get him into the Chartreux.
He is a painter, who never rose higher than to get his
immediate living, and from that, at eighty-three, he is
disabled by a slight stroke of the palsy, such as does not
make him at all helpless on common occasions, though his
hand is not steady enough for his art.

'My request is, that you will try to obtain a promise of
the next vacancy, from the Bishop of Chester. It is not a
great thing to ask, and I hope we shall obtain it. Dr.
Warton has promised to favour him with his notice, and
I hope he may end his days in peace. I am, Sir,

'Your most humble servant,
'June 29, 1777.'   'SAM. JOHNSON'

'TO THE REVEREND DR. VYSE, AT LAMBETH

'SIR,

'I DOUBT not but you will readily forgive me for
taking the liberty of requesting your assistance in recommending an old friend to his Grace the Archbishop as
Governor of the Charter-house.

'His name is De Groot; he was born at Gloucester; I
have known him many years. He has all the common

claims to charity, being old, poor, and infirm to a great
degree. He has likewise another claim, to which no scholar
can refuse attention; he is by several descents the nephew
of Hugo Grotius; of him, from whom perhaps every man
of learning has learnt something. Let it not be said that in
any lettered country a nephew of Grotius asked a charity
and was refused. I am, reverend Sir,

       'Your most humble servant,
'July 9, 1777.'   'SAM. JOHNSON'

['TO THE REVEREND DR. VYSE, AT LAMBETH

 'If any notice should be taken of the recommendation
which I took the liberty of sending you, it will be necessary
to know that Mr. De Groot is to be found at No. 8, in Pye-
street, Westminster. This information, when I wrote, I
could not give you; and being going*a* soon to Lichfield,
think it necessary to be left behind me.

 'More I will not say. You will want no persuasion to
succour the nephew of Grotius.

    'I am, Sir,
      'Your most humble servant,
'July 22, 1777.'   'SAM. JOHNSON']

*a strangely   express'd
being going!* [H]

'THE REVEREND DR. VYSE TO MR. BOSWELL

'SIR,   'Lambeth, June 9, 1787

 'I HAVE searched in vain for the letter which I spoke
of, and which I wished, at your desire, to communicate to
you. It was from Dr. Johnson, to return me thanks for my
application to Archbishop Cornwallis in favour of poor de
Groot. He rejoices at the success it met with, and is lavish
in the praise he bestows upon his favourite, Hugo Grotius.
I am really sorry that I cannot find this letter, as it is
worthy of the writer. That which I send you inclosed,[1] is
at your service. It is very short, and will not perhaps be
thought of any consequence, unless you should judge
proper to consider it as a proof of the very humane part

     [1] The preceding letter.

which Dr. Johnson took in behalf of a distressed and deserving person. I am, Sir,

'Your most obedient humble servant,
'W. VYSE'[1]

'DR. JOHNSON TO MR. EDWARD DILLY

'SIR,

'To the collection of English Poets I have recommended the volume of Dr. Watts to be added; his name has long been held by me in veneration, and I would not willingly be reduced to tell of him only that he was born and died. Yet of his life I know very little, and therefore must pass him in a manner very unworthy of his character, unless some of his friends will favour me with the necessary information; many of them must be known to you; and by your influence perhaps I may obtain some instruction. My plan does not exact much; but I wish to distinguish Watts, a man who never wrote but for a good purpose. Be pleased to do for me what you can. I am, Sir,

'Your humble servant,
'Bolt-court, Fleet-street,   'SAM. JOHNSON'
   July 7, 1777.'

'TO DR. SAMUEL JOHNSON

'MY DEAR SIR,   'Edinburgh, July 15, 1777

'THE fate of poor Dr. Dodd made a dismal impression upon my mind.

*   *   *   *   *   *

'I had sagacity enough to divine that you wrote his speech to the Recorder, before sentence was pronounced. I am glad you have written so much for him; and I hope to be favoured with an exact list of the several pieces, when we meet.

[1] [Dr. Vyse, at my request, was so obliging as once more to endeavour to recover the letter of Johnson, to which he alludes, but without success; for, April 23, 1800, he wrote to me thus: 'I have again searched, but in vain, for one of his letters, in which he speaks in his own nervous style of Hugo Grotius—De Groot was clearly a descendant of the family of Grotius, and Archbishop Cornwallis willingly complied with Dr. Johnson's request.' MALONE.]

underlined:
friend, Mrs. [H]

ª *Enemy* [H]

'I received Mr. Seward as the friend of Mr. and Mrs. Thrale,ª and as a gentleman recommended by Dr. Johnson to my attention. I have introduced him to Lord Kames, Lord Monboddo, and Mr. Nairne. He is gone to the Highlands with Dr. Gregory; when he returns I shall do more for him.

'Sir Allan Maclean has carried that branch of his cause, of which we had good hopes; the President and one other Judge only were against him. I wish the House of Lords may do as well as the Court of Session has done. But Sir Allan has not the lands of *Brolos* quite cleared by this judgement, till a long account is made up of debts and interests on the one side, and rents on the other. I am, however, not much afraid of the balance.

'Macquarry's estates, Staffa and all, were sold yesterday, and bought by a Campbell. I fear he will have little or nothing left out of the purchase money.

'I send you the case against the negro, by Mr. Cullen, son to Dr. Cullen, in opposition to Maclaurin's for liberty, of which you have approved. Pray read this, and tell me what you think as a *Politician*, as well as a *Poet*, upon the subject.

'Be so kind as to let me know how your time is to be distributed next autumn. I will meet you at Manchester, or where you please; but I wish you would complete your tour of the cathedrals, and come to Carlisle, and I will accompany you a part of the way homewards. I am ever,

'Most faithfully yours,

'JAMES BOSWELL'

'TO JAMES BOSWELL, ESQ.

'DEAR SIR,

'YOUR notion of the necessity of an yearly interview is very pleasing to both my vanity and tenderness. I shall perhaps come to Carlisle another year; but my money has not held out so well as it used to do. I shall go to Ashbourne, and I purpose to make Dr. Taylor invite you. If you live awhile with me at his house, we shall have much time to ourselves, and our stay will be no expence to us or him. I shall leave London the 28th; and after some stay at

Oxford and Lichfield, shall probably come to Ashbourne about the end of your Session; but of all this you shall have notice. Be satisfied we will meet somewhere.

'What passed between me and poor Dr. Dodd, you shall know more fully when we meet.

'Of law-suits there is no end; poor Sir Allan must have another trial, for which, however, his antagonist cannot be much blamed, having two Judges on his side. I am more afraid of the debts than of the House of Lords. It is scarcely to be imagined to what debts will swell, that are daily increasing by small additions, and how carelessly in a state of desperation debts are contracted. Poor Macquarry was far from thinking that when he sold his islands he should receive nothing. For what were they sold? and what was their yearly value? The admission of money into the Highlands will soon put an end to the feudal modes of life, by making those men landlords who were not chiefs. I do not know that the people will suffer by the change; but there was in the patriarchal authority something venerable and pleasing. Every eye must look with pain on a *Campbell* turning the *Macquarries* at will out of their *sedes avitæ*, their hereditary island.

'Sir Alexander Dick is the only Scotsman liberal enough not to be angry that I could not find trees, where trees were not. I was much delighted by his kind letter.

'I remember Rasay with too much pleasure not to partake of the happiness of any part of that amiable family. Our ramble in the islands hangs upon my imagination, I can hardly help imagining that we shall go again. Pennant seems to have seen a great deal which we did not see: When we travel again, let us look better about us.

'You have done right in taking your uncle's house. Some change in the form of life, gives from time to time a new epocha of existence. In a new place there is something new to be done, and a different system of thoughts rises in the mind. I wish I could gather currants in your garden. Now fit up a little study, and have your books ready at hand; do not spare a little money, to make your habitation pleasing to yourself.

'I have dined lately with poor dear ———.[a] I do not think he goes on well. His table is rather coarse, and he

index sign:
When we travel etc. [I]

marginal line:
You have . . . a new
[H]

[a] *Langton* [H & I]

has his children too much about him.[1] But he is a very good man.

'Mrs. Williams is in the country, to try if she can improve her health; she is very ill. Matters have come so about, that she is in the country with very good accommodation; but age, and sickness, and pride, have made her so peevish that I was forced to bribe the maid to stay with her, by a secret stipulation of half a crown a week over her wages.

'Our CLUB ended its session about six weeks ago. We now only meet to dine once a fortnight. Mr. Dunning, the great lawyer, is one of our members. The Thrales are well.

'I long to know how the negro's cause will be decided. What is the opinion of Lord Auchinleck, or Lord Hailes, or Lord Monboddo?

> 'I am, dear Sir,
>> 'Your most affectionate, &c.

'July 22, 1777.'   'SAM. JOHNSON'

'DR. JOHNSON TO MRS. BOSWELL

'MADAM,

'THOUGH I am well enough pleased with the taste of sweetmeats, very little of the pleasure which I received at the arrival of your jar of marmalade arose from eating it. I received it as a token of friendship, as a proof of reconciliation, things much sweeter than sweetmeats, and upon this consideration I return you, dear Madam, my sincerest thanks. By having your kindness I think I have a double security for the continuance of Mr. Boswell's, which it is not to be expected that any man can long keep, when the influence of a lady so highly and so justly valued operates against him. Mr. Boswell will tell you that I was always faithful to your interest, and always endeavoured to exalt you in his estimation. You must now do the same for me. We must all help one another, and you must now consider me as, dear Madam,

> 'Your most obliged
>> 'And most humble servant,

'July 22, 1777.'   'SAM. JOHNSON'

[1] This very just remark I hope will be constantly held in remembrance by parents, who are in general too apt to indulge their own fond feelings for

'MR. BOSWELL TO DR. JOHNSON

'MY DEAR SIR,   'Edinburgh, July 28, 1777

'THIS is the day on which you were to leave London, and I have been amusing myself in the intervals of my law-drudgery, with figuring you in the Oxford post-coach. I doubt, however, if you have had so merry a journey as you and I had in that vehicle last year, when you made so much sport with Gwyn, the architect. Incidents upon a journey are recollected with peculiar pleasure; they are preserved in brisk spirits, and come up again in our minds, tinctured with that gaiety, or at least that animation with which we first perceived them.'

*   *   *   *   *   *

[I added, that something had occurred, which I was afraid might prevent me from meeting him; and that my wife had been affected with complaints which threatened a consumption, but was now better.]

'TO JAMES BOSWELL, ESQ.

'DEAR SIR,

'Do not disturb yourself about our interviews: I hope we shall have many; nor think it any thing hard or unusual, that your design of meeting me is interrupted. We have both endured greater evils, and have greater evils to expect.

'Mrs. Boswell's illness makes a more serious distress. Does the blood rise from her lungs or from her stomach? From little vessels broken in the stomach there is no danger. Blood from the lungs is, I believe, always frothy, as mixed with wind. Your physicians know very well what is to be done. The loss of such a lady would, indeed, be very afflictive, and I hope she is in no danger. Take care to keep her mind as easy as possible.

their children at the expence of their friends. The common custom of introducing them after dinner is highly injudicious. It is agreeable enough that they should appear at any other time; but they should not be suffered to poison the moments of festivity by attracting the attention of the company, and in a manner compelling them from politeness to say what they do not think.

queried: *they should not* etc. [H]

'I have left Langton in London. He has been down with the militia, and is again quiet at home, talking to his little people, as I suppose you do sometimes. Make my compliments to Miss Veronica.[1] The rest are too young for ceremony.

'I cannot but hope that you have taken your country-house at a very seasonable time, and that it may conduce to restore or establish Mrs. Boswell's health, as well as provide room and exercise for the young ones. That you and your lady may both be happy, and long enjoy your happiness, is the sincere and earnest wish of, dear Sir,

'Your most, &c.,

'Oxford, Aug. 4, 1777.'   'SAM. JOHNSON'

'MR. BOSWELL TO DR. JOHNSON

[Informing him that my wife had continued to grow better, so that my alarming apprehensions were relieved: and that I hoped to disengage myself from the other embarrassment which had occurred, and therefore request-ing to know particularly when he intended to be at Ashbourne.]

'TO JAMES BOSWELL, ESQ.

'DEAR SIR,

'I AM this day come to Ashbourne, and have only to tell you, that Dr. Taylor says you shall be welcome to him, and you know how welcome you will be to me. Make haste to let me know when you may be expected.

'Make my compliments to Mrs. Boswell, and tell her, I hope we shall be at variance no more. I am, dear Sir, your most humble servant,

'Aug. 30, 1777.'   'SAM. JOHNSON'

'TO JAMES BOSWELL, ESQ.

'DEAR SIR,

'ON Saturday I wrote a very short letter, immediately upon my arrival hither, to shew you that I am not less

marginal line:
time about . . . 1795.
MALONE [H]

[1] [This young lady, the authour's eldest daughter, and at this time about five years old, died in London, of a consumption, four months after her father, Sept. 26, 1795. MALONE.]

desirous of the interview than yourself. Life admits not of delays; when pleasure can be had, it is fit to catch it: every hour takes away part of the things that please us, and perhaps part of our disposition to be pleased. When I came to Lichfield, I found my old friend Harry Jackson dead. It was a loss, and a loss not to be repaired, as he was one of the companions of my childhood. I hope we may long continue to gain friends; but the friends which merit or usefulness can procure us, are not able to supply the place of old acquaintance, with whom the days of youth may be retraced, and those images revived which gave the earliest delight. If you and I live to be much older, we shall take great delight in talking over the Hebridean Journey.

'In the mean time it may not be amiss to contrive some other little adventure, but what it can be I know not; leave it, as Sidney says,

"To virtue, fortune, time, and woman's breast;"[1]

for I believe Mrs. Boswell must have some part in the consultation.

[1] [By an odd mistake, in the first three editions we find a reading in this line, to which Dr. Johnson would by no means have subscribed; *wine* having been substituted for *time*. That errour probably was a mistake in the transcript of Johnson's original letter, his hand-writing being often very difficult to read. The other deviation in the beginning of the line (*virtue* instead of *nature*) must be attributed to his memory having deceived him; and therefore has not been disturbed.

The verse quoted is the concluding line of a sonnet of Sidney's, of which the earliest copy, I believe, is found in Harrington's translation of Ariosto, 1591, in the notes on the eleventh book:—'And therefore,' says he, 'that excellent verse of Sir Philip Sidney in his first ARCADIA, (which I know not by what mishap is left out in the printed booke, [4to. 1590,] is in mine opinion worthie to be praised and followed, to make a good and virtuous wife:

"Who doth desire that chast his wife should bee,
     First be he true, for truth doth truth deserve;
Then be he such, as she his worth may see,
     And, alwaies one, credit with her preserve:
Not toying kynd, nor causelessly unkynd,
     Not stirring thoughts, nor yet denying right,
Not spying faults, nor in plaine errors blind,
     Never hard hand, nor ever rayns [reins] too light;
As far from want, as far from vaine expençe,
     Th' one doth enforce, the t'other doth entice:
Allow good companie, but drive from thence
     All filthie mouths that glorie in their vice:
This done, thou hast no more but leave the rest
     To *nature*, fortune, *time*, and woman's breast." '

Marginal notes:

exclamation point: *but the friends* etc. [H]

exclamation point: *with whom* etc. [H]

two marginal lines: *The verse . . . of Sidney's* [H]

'One thing you will like. The Doctor, so far as I can judge, is likely to leave us enough to ourselves. He was out to-day before I came down, and, I fancy, will stay out to dinner. I have brought the papers about poor Dodd, to show you, but you will soon have dispatched them.

'Before I came away, I sent poor Mrs. Williams into the country, very ill of a pituitous defluxion, which wastes her gradually away, and which her physician declares himself unable to stop. I supplied her as far as could be desired, with all conveniences to make her excursion and abode pleasant and useful. But I am afraid she can only linger a short time in a morbid state of weakness and pain.

'The Thrales, little and great, are all well, and purpose to go to Brighthelmstone at Michaelmas. They will invite me to go with them, and perhaps I may go, but I hardly think I shall like to stay the whole time; but of futurity we know but little.

'Mrs. Porter is well; but Mrs. Aston, one of the ladies at Stowhill, has been struck with a palsy, from which she is not likely ever to recover. How soon may such a stroke fall upon us!

'Write to me, and let us know when we may expect you.
    'I am, dear Sir,
        'Your most humble servant,
'Ashbourne, Sept. 1, 1777.'   'SAM. JOHNSON'

'MR. BOSWELL TO DR. JOHNSON
'Edinburgh, Sept. 9, 1777

[After informing him that I was to set out next day, in order to meet him at Ashbourne;—]

I take this opportunity to add, that in ENGLAND'S PARNASSUS, a collection of poetry printed in 1600, the second couplet of this sonnet is thus corruptly exhibited: 'Then *he be* such as *he* his *words* may see,
        And alwaies one credit *which* her preserve:'
a variation, which I the rather mention, because the readings of that book have been triumphantly quoted, when they happened to coincide with the sophistications of the SECOND Folio edition of Shakspeare's plays in 1632, as adding I know not what degree of authority and authenticity to the latter: as if the corruptions of one book (and that abounding with the grossest falsifications of the authours from whose works its extracts are made) could give any kind of support to another, which in every page is still more adulterated and unfaithful. See Mr. Steevens's Shakspeare, vol. xx. p. 97, 5th edit. 1803. MALONE.]

'I have a present for you from Lord Hailes; the fifth book of "Lactantius," which he has published with Latin notes. He is also to give you a few anecdotes for your "Life of Thomson," who I find was private tutor to the present Earl of Hadington, Lord Hailes's cousin, a circumstance not mentioned by Dr. Murdoch. I have keen expectations of delight from your edition of the English Poets.[1]

'I am sorry for poor Mrs. Williams's situation. You will, however, have the comfort of reflecting on your kindness to her. Mr. Jackson's death, and Mrs. Aston's palsy, are gloomy circumstances. Yet surely we should be habituated to the uncertainty of life and health. When my mind is unclouded by melancholy, I consider the temporary distresses of this state of being as "light afflictions," by stretching my mental view into that glorious after-existence, when they will appear to be as nothing. But present pleasures and present pains must be felt. I lately read "Rasselas" over again with satisfaction.

'Since you are desirous to hear about Macquarry's sale, I shall inform you particularly. The gentleman who purchased Ulva, is Mr. Campbell, of Auchnaba: our friend Macquarry was proprietor of two-thirds of it, of which the rent was 156l. 5s. 1½d. This parcel was set up at 4,069l. 5s. 1d. but it sold for no less than 5,540l. The other third of Ulva, with the island of Staffa, belonged to Macquarry of Ormaig. Its rent, including that of Staffa, 83l. 12s. 2½d.—set up at 2,178l. 16s. 4d.—sold for no less than 3,540l. The Laird of Col wished to purchase Ulva, but he thought the price too high. There may, indeed, be great improvements made there, both in fishing and agriculture; but the interest of the purchase-money exceeds the rent so very much, that I doubt if the bargain will be profitable. There is an island called Little Colonsay, of 10l. yearly rent, which I am informed has belonged to the Macquarrys of Ulva for many ages, but which was lately claimed by the Presbyterian Synod of Argyll, in consequence of a grant made to them by Queen Anne. It is believed that their claim will be dismissed, and that Little Colonsay will also be sold for the advantage of Macquarry's creditors. What think you of purchasing this island, and

two marginal lines:
for the . . . endowing a
[H]

---

[1] [See p. 351, n. MALONE.]

endowing a school or college there, the master to be a clergyman of the Church of England? How venerable would such an institution make the name of DR. SAMUEL JOHNSON, in the Hebrides! I have, like yourself, a wonderful pleasure in recollecting our travels in those islands. The pleasure is, I think, greater than it reasonably should be, considering that we had not much either of beauty or elegance to charm our imaginations, or of rude novelty to astonish. Let us, by all means, have another expedition. I shrink a little from our scheme of going up the Baltick.[1] I am sorry you have already been in Wales; for I wish to see it. Shall we go to Ireland, of which I have seen but little? We shall try to strike out a plan when we are at Ashbourne. I am ever

'Your most faithful humble servant,

'JAMES BOSWELL'

'TO JAMES BOSWELL, ESQ.

'DEAR SIR,

'I WRITE to be left at Carlisle, as you direct me; but you cannot have it. Your letter, dated Sept. 6, was not at this place till this day, Thursday, Sept. 11; and I hope you will be here before this is at Carlisle.[2] However, what you

---

[1] It appears that Johnson, now in his sixty-eighth year, was seriously inclined to realize the project of our going up the Baltick, which I had started when we were in the Isle of Sky; for he thus writes to Mrs. Thrale; Letters, Vol. I. page 366:

'Ashbourne, Sept. 13, 1777

'BOSWELL, I believe, is coming. He talks of being here to-day: I shall be glad to see him: but he shrinks from the Baltick expedition, which, I think, is the best scheme in our power: what we shall substitute, I know not. He wants to see Wales; but, except the woods of *Bachycraigh*, what is there in Wales, that can fill the hunger of ignorance, or quench the thirst of curiosity?[a] We may, perhaps, form some scheme or other; but, in the phrase of *Hockley in the Hole*, it is pity he has not a *better bottom*.'

[a] *This was mere Badinage I believe.* [H]

Such an ardour of mind, and vigour of enterprize, is admirable at any age; but more particularly so at the advanced period at which Johnson was then arrived. I am sorry now that I did not insist on our executing that scheme. Besides the other objects of curiosity and observation, to have seen my illustrious friend received, as he probably would have been, by a prince so eminently distinguished for his variety of talents and acquisitions as the late King of Sweden; and by the Empress of Russia, whose extraordinary abilities, information, and magnanimity, astonish the world, would have afforded a noble subject for contemplation and record. This reflection may possibly be thought too visionary by the more sedate and cold-blooded part of my readers; yet I own, I frequently indulge it with an earnest, unavailing regret.

[2] It so happened. The letter was forwarded to my house at Edinburgh.

have not going, you may have returning; and as I believe I shall not love you less after our interview, it will then be as true as it is now, that I set a very high value upon your friendship, and count your kindness as one of the chief felicities of my life. Do not fancy that an intermission of writing is a decay of kindness. No man is always in a disposition to write; nor has any man at all times something to say.

'That distrust which intrudes so often on your mind is a mode of melancholy, which, if it be the business of a wise man to be happy, it is foolish to indulge; and, if it be a duty to preserve our faculties entire for their proper use, it is criminal. Suspicion is very often an useless pain. From that, and all other pains, I wish you free and safe; for I am, dear Sir,

'Most affectionately yours,

'Ashbourne, Sept. 11, 1777.'   'SAM. JOHNSON'

On Sunday evening, Sept. 14, I arrived at Ashbourne, and drove directly up to Dr. Taylor's door. Dr. Johnson and he appeared before I had got out of the post-chaise, and welcomed me cordially.

I told them that I had travelled all the preceding night, and gone to bed at Leek, in Staffordshire; and that when I rose to go to church in the afternoon, I was informed there had been an earthquake, of which, it seems the shock had been felt in some degree at Ashbourne. JOHNSON. 'Sir, it will be much exaggerated in public talk: for, in the first place, the common people do not accurately adapt their thoughts to the objects; nor, secondly, do they accurately adapt their words to their thoughts: they do not mean to lie; but, taking no pains to be exact, they give you very false accounts. A great part of their language is proverbial. If any thing rocks at all, they say *it rocks like a cradle;* and in this way they go on.'

The subject of grief for the loss of relations and friends being introduced, I observed that it was strange to consider how soon it in general wears away. Dr. Taylor mentioned a gentleman of the neighbourhood as the only instance he had ever known of a person who had endeavoured to *retain* grief. He told Dr. Taylor, that after his

Lady's death, which affected him deeply, he *resolved*ᵃ that the grief, which he cherished with a kind of sacred fondness, should be lasting; but that he found he could not keep it long. JOHNSON. 'All grief for what cannot in the course of nature be helped, soon wears away; in some sooner, indeed, in some later; but it never continues very long, unless where there is madness, such as will make a man have pride so fixed in his mind, as to imagine himself a king; or any other passion in an unreasonable way: for all unnecessary grief is unwise, and therefore will not be long retained by a sound mind. If, indeed, the cause of our grief is occasioned by our own misconduct, if grief is mingled with remorse of conscience, it should be lasting.' BOSWELL. 'But, Sir, we do not approve of a man who very soon forgets the loss of a wife or a friend.' JOHNSON. 'Sir, we disapprove of him, not because he soon forgets his grief; for the sooner it is forgotten the better, but because we suppose, that if he forgets his wife or his friend soon, he has not had much affection for them.'

I was somewhat disappointed in finding that the edition of the English Poets, for which he was to write Prefaces and Lives, was not an undertaking directed by him: but that he was to furnish a Preface and Life to any poet the booksellers pleased. I asked him if he would do this to any dunce's works, if they should ask him. JOHNSON. 'Yes, Sir; and *say* he was a dunce.' My friend seemed now not much to relish talking of this edition.

On Monday, September 15, Dr. Johnson observed, that every body commended such parts of his 'Journey to the Western Islands,' as were in their own way. 'For instance, (said he,) Mr. Jackson (the all-knowing) told me there was more good sense upon trade in it, than he should hear in the House of Commons in a year, except from Burke. Jones commended the part which treats of language; Burke that which describes the inhabitants of mountainous countries.'

After breakfast, Johnson carried me to see the garden belonging to the school of Ashbourne, which is very prettily formed upon a bank, rising gradually behind the house. The Reverend Mr. Langley, the head-master, accompanied us.

While we sat basking in the sun upon a seat here, I
introduced a common subject of complaint, the very small
salaries which many curates have, and I maintained, that
no man should be invested with the character of a clergyman, unless he has a security for such an income as will
enable him to appear respectable; that, therefore, a clergyman should not be allowed to have a curate, unless he
gives him a hundred pounds a year; if he cannot do that,
let him perform the duty himself. JOHNSON. 'To be sure,
Sir, it is wrong that any clergyman should be without a
reasonable income; but as the church revenues were sadly
diminished at the Reformation, the clergy who have
livings, cannot afford, in many instances, to give good
salaries to curates, without leaving themselves too little;
and, if no curate were to be permitted unless he had a
hundred pounds a year, their number would be very
small, which would be a disadvantage, as then there would
not be such choice in the nursery for the church, curates
being candidates for the higher ecclesiastical offices,
according to their merit and good behaviour.' He explained
the system of the English Hierarchy exceedingly well. 'It
is not thought fit (said he) to trust a man with the care of a
parish till he has given proof as a curate that he shall
deserve such a trust.' This is an excellent *theory:* and if the
practice were according to it, the Church of England would
be admirable indeed. However, as I have heard Dr.
Johnson observe as to the Universities, bad practice does
not infer that the *constitution* is bad.

We had with us at dinner several of Dr. Taylor's neighbours, good civil gentlemen, who seemed to understand
Dr. Johnson very well, and not to consider him in the
light that a certain person did, who being struck, or
rather stunned by his voice and manner, when he was
afterwards asked what he thought of him, answered, 'He's
a tremendous companion.'[a]

Johnson told me, that 'Taylor was a very sensible acute
man, and had a strong mind: that he had great activity
in some respects, and yet such a sort of indolence, that if
you should put a pebble upon his chimney-piece, you would
find it there, in the same state, a year afterwards.'

underlined:
certain person [H]

[a] *George told Peter
Garrick so, & Peter
told again.* [H & I]

And here is a proper place to give an account of John-son's humane and zealous interference in behalf of the Reverend Dr. William Dodd, formerly Prebendary of Brecon, and chaplain in ordinary to his Majesty; celebrated as a very popular preacher, an encourager of charitable institutions, and authour of a variety of works, chiefly theological. Having unhappily contracted expensive habits of living, partly occasioned by[a] licentiousness of manners, he in an evil hour, when pressed by want of money, and dreading an exposure of his circumstances, forged a bond, of which he attempted to avail himself to support his credit, flattering himself with hopes that he might be able to repay its amount without being detected. The person, whose name he thus rashly and criminally presumed to falsify, was the Earl of Chesterfield, to whom he had been tutor, and who, he perhaps, in the warmth of his feelings, flattered himself would have generously paid the money in case of an alarm being taken, rather than suffer him to fall a victim to the dreadful conse-quences of violating the law against forgery,[b] the most dangerous crime in a commercial country: but the un-fortunate divine had the mortification to find that he was mistaken. His noble pupil appeared against him, and he was capitally convicted.

Johnson told me that Dr. Dodd was very little acquainted with him, having been but once in his company, many years previous to this period (which was precisely the state of my own acquaintance with Dodd); but in his distress he bethought himself of Johnson's persuasive power of writing, if haply it might avail to obtain for him the Royal Mercy.[c] He did not apply to him directly, but, extra-ordinary as it may seem, through the late Countess of Harrington,[1] who wrote a letter to Johnson, asking him to employ his pen in favour of Dodd. Mr. Allen, the printer, who was Johnson's landlord and next neighbour in Bolt-court, and for whom he had much kindness, was one of Dodd's friends, of whom, to the credit of humanity be it recorded, that he had many who did not desert him, even after his infringement of the law had reduced him to the

a *gross* inserted be-fore *licentiousness* [H]

b *Ld. Kirkwall did do Something of this Sort, I forget how much; to save or screen Charles Wynne of Plasnewydd two or Three Years ago 1819.* [H & I]

c *If the King could have saved any Man —he would have saved Ryland, whom he per-sonally loved; but hav-ing tried his Interest for that Man, now said he If I am ever solicited to pardon forgery, you shall be made to remember these Arguments.* [H]

[1] [Caroline, eldest daughter of Charles Fitzroy, Duke of Grafton, and wife of William, the second Earl of Harrington. MALONE.]

state of a man under sentence of death. Mr. Allen told me
that he carried Lady Harrington's letter to Johnson, that
Johnson read it walking up and down his chamber, and
seemed much agitated, after which he said, 'I will do
what I can;'—and certainly he did make extraordinary
exertions.

He this evening, as he had obligingly promised in one
of his letters, put into my hands the whole series of his
writings upon this melancholy occasion, and I shall present my readers with the abstract which I made from the
collection; in doing which I studied to avoid copying what
had appeared in print, and now make part of the edition
of 'Johnson's Works,' published by the Booksellers of
London, but taking care to mark Johnson's variations in
some of the pieces there exhibited.

Dr. Johnson wrote in the first place, Dr. Dodd's 'Speech
to the Recorder of London,' at the Old Bailey, when
sentence of death was about to be pronounced upon him.

He wrote also 'The Convict's Address to his unhappy
Brethren,' a sermon delivered by Dr. Dodd, in the chapel
of Newgate. According to Johnson's manuscript it began
thus after the text, *What shall I do to be saved?*—'These were
the words with which the keeper, to whose custody Paul
and Silas were committed by their prosecutors, addressed
his prisoners, when he saw them freed from their bonds by
the perceptible agency of divine favour, and was, therefore,
irresistibly convinced that they were not offenders against
the laws, but martyrs to the truth.'

Dr. Johnson was so good as to mark for me with his own
hand, on a copy of this sermon which is now in my possession, such passages as were added by Dr. Dodd. They are
not many: Whoever will take the trouble to look at the
printed copy, and attend to what I mention, will be
satisfied of this.

There is a short introduction by Dr. Dodd, and he also
inserted this sentence, 'You see with what confusion and
dishonour I now stand before you;—no more in the pulpit
of instruction, but on this humble seat with yourselves.'
The *notes* are entirely Dodd's own, and Johnson's writing
ends at the words, 'the thief whom he pardoned on the
cross.' What follows was supplied by Dr. Dodd himself.

The other pieces mentioned by Johnson in the above-mentioned collection, are two letters, one to the Lord Chancellor Bathurst, (not Lord North, as is erroneously supposed,) and one to Lord Mansfield;—A Petition from Dr. Dodd to the King;—A Petition from Mrs. Dodd to the Queen;—Observations of some length inserted in the news-papers, on occasion of Earl Percy's having presented to his Majesty a petition for mercy to Dodd, signed by twenty thousand people, but all in vain. He told me that he had also written a petition for the city of London; 'but (said he, with a significant smile) they *mended* it.'[1]

The last of these articles which Johnson wrote is 'Dr. Dodd's last solemn Declaration,' which he left with the sheriff at the place of execution. Here also my friend marked the variations on a copy of that piece now in my possession. Dodd inserted, 'I never knew or attended to the calls of frugality, or the needful minuteness of painful œconomy;' and in the next sentence he introduced the words which I distinguish by *Italicks;* 'My life for some *few unhappy* years past has been *dreadfully erroneous.*' Johnson's expression was *hypocritical;* but his remark on the margin is 'With this he said he could not charge himself.'[a]

Having thus authentically settled what part of the 'Occasional Papers,' concerning Dr. Dodd's miserable

[a] *The Man was right enough I dare say. Lookers-on when they see Words & Actions so discordant, fancy there must be Hypocrisy . . . but no, a Fellow shall be tempted beyond what he can bear, & act Crimes which he abhors sincerely. George Henry Glasse was a Character of the same Sort . . . but he hanged himself Poor Fellow!* [H]

[1] Having unexpectedly, by the favour of Mr. Stone, of London Field, Hackney, seen the original in Johnson's handwriting, of 'The Petition of the City of London to his Majesty, in favour of Dr. Dodd,' I now present it to my readers, with such passages as were omitted inclosed in crotchets, and the additions or variations marked in Italicks.

'That William Dodd, Doctor of Laws, now lying under sentence of death *in your Majesty's gaol of Newgate,* for the crime of forgery, has for a great part of his life set a useful and laudable example of diligence in his calling, [and as we have reason to believe, has exercised his ministry with great fidelity and efficacy,] *which, in many instances, has produced the most happy effect.*

'That he has been the first institutor, [or] *and* a very earnest and active promoter of several modes of useful charity, and [that] therefore [he] may be considered as having been on many occasions a benefactor to the publick.

'[That when they consider his past life, they are willing to suppose his late crime to have been not the consequence of habitual depravity, but the suggestion of some sudden and violent temptation.]

'[That] *Your Petitioners* therefore considering his case, as in some of its circumstances unprecedented and peculiar, *and encouraged by your Majesty's known clemency,* [they] most humbly recommend the said William Dodd to [his] *your* Majesty's most gracious consideration, in hopes that he will be found not altogether [unfit] *unworthy* to stand an example of Royal Mercy.'

situation, came from the pen of Johnson, I shall proceed
to present my readers with my record of the unpublished
writings relating to that extraordinary and interesting
matter.

I found a letter to Dr. Johnson from Dr. Dodd, May 23,
1777, in which, 'The Convict's Address' seems clearly to
be meant:

'I am so penetrated, my ever dear Sir, with a sense of
your extreme benevolence towards me, that I cannot find
words equal to the sentiments of my heart. * * * *

'You are too conversant in the world to need the slightest hint from me, of what infinite utility the Speech[1] on the
aweful day has been to me. I experience, every hour, some
good effect from it. I am sure that effects still more salutary
and important, must follow from *your kind and intended
favour.* I will labour —GOD being my helper,—to do justice
to it from the pulpit. I am sure, had I your sentiments
constantly to deliver from thence, in all their mighty force
and power, not a soul could be left unconvinced and
unpersuaded.' * * * * * * * *

He added: 'May GOD ALMIGHTY bless and reward,
with his choicest comforts, your philanthropick actions,
and enable me at all times to express what I feel of the
high and uncommon obligations which I owe to the *first
man* in our times.'

On Sunday, June 22, he writes, begging Dr. Johnson's
assistance in framing a supplicatory letter to his Majesty:

'If his Majesty could be moved of his royal clemency to
spare me and my family the horrours and ignominy of a
publick death, which the *publick* itself is solicitous to wave,
and to grant me in some silent distant corner of the globe
to pass the remainder of my days in penitence and prayer,
I would bless his clemency and be humbled.'

This letter was brought to Dr. Johnson when in church.
He stooped down and read it, and wrote, when he went
home, the following letter for Dr. Dodd to the King:

'SIR,

'MAY it not offend your Majesty, that the most
miserable of men applies himself to your clemency, as his

---

[1] His Speech at the Old Bailey, when found guilty.

last hope and his last refuge; that your mercy is most earnestly and humbly implored by a clergyman, whom your Laws and Judges have condemned to the horrour and ignominy of a publick execution.

'I confess the crime, and own the enormity of its consequences, and the danger of its example. Nor have I the confidence to petition for impunity; but humbly hope, that publick security may be established, without the spectacle of a clergyman dragged through the streets, to a death of infamy, amidst the derision of the profligate and profane; and that justice may be satisfied with irrevocable exile, perpetual disgrace, and hopeless penury.

'My life, Sir, has not been useless to mankind. I have benefited many. But my offences against GOD are numberless, and I have had little time for repentance. Preserve me, Sir, by your prerogative of mercy, from the necessity of appearing unprepared at that tribunal, before which Kings and Subjects must stand at last together. Permit me to hide my guilt in some obscure corner of a foreign country, where, if I can ever attain confidence to hope that my prayers will be heard, they shall be poured with all the fervour of gratitude for the life and happiness of your Majesty. I am, Sir,

'Your Majesty's, &c.'

Subjoined to it was written as follows:

'TO DR. DODD

'SIR,

'I MOST seriously enjoin you not to let it be at all known that I have written this letter, and to return the copy to Mr. Allen in a cover to me. I hope I need not tell you, that I wish it success.—But do not indulge hope.— Tell nobody.'

It happened luckily that Mr. Allen was pitched on to assist in this melancholy office, for he was a great friend of Mr. Akerman, the keeper of Newgate. Dr. Johnson never went to see Dr. Dodd. He said to me, 'it would have done *him* more harm, than good to Dodd, who once expressed a desire to see him, but not earnestly.'

Dr. Johnson, on the 20th of June, wrote the following letter:

'TO THE RIGHT HONOURABLE CHARLES JENKINSON

'SIR,

'SINCE the conviction and condemnation of Dr. Dodd, I have had, by the intervention of a friend, some intercourse with him, and I am sure I shall lose nothing in your opinion by tenderness and commiseration. Whatever be the crime, it is not easy to have any knowledge of the delinquent, without a wish that his life may be spared; at least when no life has been taken away by him. I will, therefore, take the liberty of suggesting some reasons for which I wish this unhappy being to escape the utmost rigour of his sentence.

'He is, so far as I can recollect, the first clergyman of our church who has suffered publick execution for immorality; and I know not whether it would not be more for the interests of religion to bury such an offender in the obscurity of perpetual exile, than to expose him in a cart, and on the gallows, to all who for any reason are enemies to the clergy.

'The supreme power has, in all ages, paid some attention to the voice of the people; and that voice does not least deserve to be heard, when it calls out for mercy. There is now a very general desire that Dodd's life should be spared. More is not wished; and, perhaps, this is not too much to be granted.

'If you, Sir, have any opportunity of enforcing these reasons, you may, perhaps, think them worthy of consideration: but whatever you determine, I most respectfully intreat that you will be pleased to pardon for this intrusion, Sir,

'Your most obedient
'And most humble servant,
'SAM. JOHNSON'

It has been confidently circulated, with invidious remarks, that to this letter no attention whatever was paid by Mr. Jenkinson, (afterwards Earl of Liverpool), and that he did not even deign to shew the common civility of owning the receipt of it. I could not but wonder at such conduct in the noble Lord, whose own character and just elevation in life, I thought, must have impressed him with all due regard for great abilities and attainments. As the story had been much talked of, and apparently from good authority, I could not but have animadverted upon it in this work, had it been as was alledged; but from my earnest love of truth, and having found reason to think that there might be a mistake, I presumed to write to his Lordship, requesting an explanation; and it is with the sincerest pleasure that I am enabled to assure the world, that there is no foundation for it, the fact being, that owing to some neglect, or accident, Johnson's letter never came to Lord Hawkesbury's hands. I should have thought it strange indeed, if that noble Lord had undervalued my illustrious friend; but instead of this being the case, his Lordship, in the very polite answer with which he was pleased immediately to honour me, thus expresses himself:—'I have always respected the memory of Dr. Johnson, and admire his writings; and I frequently read many parts of them with pleasure and great improvement.'

All applications for the Royal Mercy having failed, Dr. Dodd prepared himself for death; and, with a warmth of gratitude, wrote to Dr. Johnson as follows:

'June 25, *Midnight*

'ACCEPT, thou *great* and *good* heart, my earnest and fervent thanks and prayers for all thy benevolent and kind efforts in my behalf.—Oh! Dr. Johnson! as I sought your knowledge at an early hour in life, would to heaven I had cultivated the love and acquaintance of so excellent a man!—I pray GOD most sincerely to bless you with the highest transports—the infelt satisfaction of *humane* and benevolent exertions!—And admitted, as I trust I shall be, to the realms of bliss before you, I shall hail *your* arrival there with transports, and rejoice to acknowledge that you was my Comforter, my Advocate, and my *Friend!* GOD *be ever* with *you!*'

exclamation point:
I shall hail etc. [H]

Dr. Johnson lastly wrote to Dr. Dodd this solemn and soothing letter:

'TO THE REVEREND DR. DODD

'DEAR SIR,

'THAT which is appointed to all men is now coming upon you. Outward circumstances, the eyes and the thoughts of men, are below the notice of an immortal being about to stand the trial for eternity, before the Supreme Judge of heaven and earth. Be comforted: your crime, morally or religiously considered, has no very deep dye of turpitude. It corrupted no man's principles; it attacked no man's life. It involved only a temporary and reparable injury. Of this, and of all other sins, you are earnestly to repent; and may GOD, who knoweth our frailty, and desireth not our death, accept your repentance, for the sake of his Son JESUS CHRIST, our Lord.

'In requital of those well intended offices which you are pleased so emphatically to acknowledge, let me beg that you make in your devotions one petition for my eternal welfare. I am, dear Sir,

'Your most affectionate servant,

'June 26, 1777.'   'SAM. JOHNSON'

Under the copy of this letter I found written, in Johnson's own hand, 'Next day, June 27, he was executed.'

To conclude this interesting episode with an useful application, let us now attend to the reflections of Johnson at the end of the 'Occasional Papers,' concerning the unfortunate Dr. Dodd.—'Such were the last thoughts of a man whom we have seen exulting in popularity, and sunk in shame. For his reputation, which no man can give to himself, those who conferred it are to answer. Of his publick ministry the means of judging were sufficiently attainable. He must be allowed to preach well, whose sermons strike his audience with forcible conviction. Of his life, those who thought it consistent with his doctrine, did not originally form false notions. He was at first what he endeavoured to make others; but the world broke down his resolution, and he in time ceased to exemplify his own instructions.

'Let those who are tempted to his faults, tremble at his punishment; and those whom he impressed from the pulpit with religious sentiments, endeavour to confirm them, by considering the regret and self-abhorrence with which he reviewed in prison his deviations from rectitude.'[1a]

a very fine! [H]

Johnson gave us this evening, in his happy discriminative manner, a portrait of the late Mr. Fitzherbert of Derbyshire. 'There was (said he) no sparkle, no brilliancy in Fitzherbert; but I never knew a man who was so generally acceptable. He made every body quite easy, overpowered nobody by the superiority of his talents, made no man think worse of himself by being his rival, seemed always to listen, did not oblige you to hear much from him, and did not oppose what you said. Every body liked him; but he had no friends, as I understand the word, nobody with whom he exchanged intimate thoughts. People were willing to think well of every thing about him. A gentleman was making an affecting rant, as many people do, of great feelings about "his dear son," who was at school near London;[b] how anxious he was lest he might be ill, and what he would give to see him. "Can't you (said Fitzherbert,) take a post-chaise and go to him?" This, to be sure, *finished* the affected man, but there was not much in it.[2] However, this was circulated as wit for a whole winter, and I believe part of a summer too;[c] a proof that he was no very witty man. He was an instance of the truth of the observation, that a man will please more upon the whole by negative qualities than by positive; by never offending, than by giving a great deal of delight. In the first place,

b at Eton [H]

c They said it was so dry a Thing; & so it was. [H]

marginal line:
*observation, that . . .
of delight* [H]

---

[1] [See Dr. Johnson's final opinion concerning Dr. Dodd, in vol. iii. under April 18, 1783. MALONE.]

[2] Dr. Gisborne, Physician to his Majesty's Household, has obligingly communicated to me a fuller account of this story than had reached Dr. Johnson. The affected Gentleman was the late John Gilbert Cooper, Esq. authour of a Life of Socrates, and of some poems in Dodsley's collection. Mr. Fitzherbert found him one morning, apparently, in such violent agitation, on account of the indisposition of his son, as to seem beyond the power of comfort. At length, however, he exclaimed, 'I'll write an Elegy.' Mr. Fitzherbert being satisfied, by this, of the sincerity of his emotions, slyly said, 'Had not you better take a post-chaise and go and see him?' It was the shrewdness of the insinuation which made the story be circulated.

men hate more steadily than they love; and if I have said
something to hurt a man once, I shall not get the better of
this, by saying many things to please him.'

Tuesday, September 16, Dr. Johnson having mentioned
to me the extraordinary size and price of some cattle
reared by Dr. Taylor, I rode out with our host, surveyed
his farm, and was shewn one cow which he had sold for a
hundred and twenty guineas, and another for which he
had been offered a hundred and thirty. Taylor thus described to me his old schoolfellow and friend, Johnson: 'He
is a man of a very clear head, great power of words, and a
very gay imagination; but there is no disputing with him.
He will not hear you, and having a louder voice than you,
must roar you down.'

In the afternoon I tried to get Dr. Johnson to like the
Poems of Mr. Hamilton of Bangour, which I had brought
with me: I had been much pleased with them at a very
early age: the impression still remained on my mind; it was
confirmed by the opinion of my friend the Honourable
Andrew Erskine, himself both a good poet and a good
critick, who thought Hamilton as true a poet as ever wrote,
and that his not having fame was unaccountable. Johnson,
upon repeated occasions, while I was at Ashbourne, talked
slightingly of Hamilton. He said, there was no power of
thinking in his verses, nothing that strikes one, nothing
better than what you generally find in magazines; and
that the highest praise they deserved was, that they were
very well for a gentleman to hand about among his friends.
He said the imitation of *Ne sit ancilla tibi amor, &c.* was too
solemn; he read part of it at the beginning. He read the
beautiful pathetick song, 'Ah the poor shepherd's mourn-
ful fate,' and did not seem to give attention to what I had
been used to think tender elegant strains, but laughed at
the rhyme, in Scotch pronunciation, *wishes* and *blushes*,
reading *wushes*—and there he stopped. He owned that the
epitaph on Lord Newhall was pretty well done. He read
the 'Inscription in a Summer-house,' and a little of the
imitations of Horace's Epistles; but said he found nothing
to make him desire to read on. When I urged that there
were some good poetical passages in the book, 'Where
(said he,) will you find so large a collection without some?'

I thought the description of Winter might obtain his approbation:

> 'See Winter, from the frozen north
> Drives his iron chariot forth!
> His grisly hand in icy chains
> Fair Tweeda's silver flood constrains,' &c.

He asked why an '*iron* chariot'? and said 'icy chains' was an old image. I was struck with the uncertainty of taste, and somewhat sorry that a poet whom I had long read with fondness, was not approved by Dr. Johnson. I comforted myself with thinking that the beauties were too delicate for his robust perceptions. Garrick maintained that he had not a taste for the finest productions of genius: but I was sensible, that when he took the trouble to analyse critically, he generally convinced us that he was right.

underlined:
Reverend, Seward [H]
ᵃ*Father to Miss Seward*
[H]

In the evening the Reverend Mr. Seward,ᵃ of Lichfield, who was passing through Ashbourne in his way home, drank tea with us. Johnson described him thus:—'Sir, his ambition is to be a fine talker; so he goes to Buxton, and such places, where he may find companies to listen to him. And, Sir, he is a valetudinarian, one of those who are always mending themselves. I do not know a more disagreeable character than a valetudinarian, who thinks he may do any thing that is for his ease, and indulges himself in the grossest freedoms: Sir, he brings himself to the state of a hog in a stye.'

Dr. Taylor's nose happening to bleed, he said, it was because he had omitted to have himself blooded four days after a quarter of a year's interval. Dr. Johnson, who was a great dabbler in physick, disapproved much of periodical bleeding. 'For (said he) you accustom yourself to an evacuation which Nature cannot perform of herself, and therefore she cannot help you, should you from forgetfulness or any other cause omit it; so you may be suddenly suffocated. You may accustom yourself to other periodical evacuations, because, should you omit them, Nature can supply the omission; but Nature cannot open a vein to blood you.'[1]—'I do not like to take an emetick, (said

[1] [Nature, however, may supply the evacuation by an hæmorrhage. KEARNEY.]

Taylor,) for fear of breaking some small vessels.'—'Poh! (said Johnson,) if you have so many things that will break, you had better break your neck at once, and there's an end on't. You will break no small vessels:' (blowing with high derision.)

I mentioned to Dr. Johnson, that David Hume's persisting in his infidelity, when he was dying, shocked me much. JOHNSON. 'Why should it shock you, Sir? Hume owned he had never read the New Testament with attention. Here then was a man who had been at no pains to enquire into the truth of religion, and had continually turned his mind the other way. It was not to be expected that the prospect of death would alter his way of thinking, unless GOD should send an angel to set him right.' I said, I had reason to believe that the thought of annihilation gave Hume no pain. JOHNSON. 'It was not so, Sir. He had a vanity in being thought easy. It is more probable that he should assume an appearance of ease, than so very improbable a thing should be, as a man not afraid of going (as, in spite of his delusive theory, he cannot be sure but he may go,) into an unknown state, and not being uneasy at leaving all he knew. And you are to consider, that upon his own principle of annihilation he had no motive to speak the truth.' The horrour of death, which I had always observed in Dr. Johnson, appeared strong to-night. I ventured to tell him, that I had been, for moments in my life, not afraid of death; therefore I could suppose another man in that state of mind for a considerable space of time. He said, 'he never had a moment in which death was not terrible to him.' He added, that it had been observed, that scarce any man dies in publick, but with apparent resolution; from that desire of praise which never quits us. I said, Dr. Dodd seemed to be willing to die, and full of hopes of happiness. 'Sir, (said he,) Dr. Dodd would have given both his hands and both his legs to have lived. The better a man is, the more afraid is he of death, having a clearer view of infinite purity.' He owned, that our being in an unhappy uncertainty as to our salvation, was mysterious; and said, 'Ah! we must wait till we are in another state of being, to have many things explained to us.' Even the powerful mind of Johnson seemed foiled by futurity. But I thought, that the gloom of uncertainty in solemn religious speculation, being mingled with hope, was yet[a] more consolatory than the emptiness of infidelity. A man can live in thick air, but perishes in an exhausted receiver.[b]

[a] *yet* crossed out; *at least* written in [H]

[b] *very well said.* [H]

Dr. Johnson was much pleased with a remark which I told him was made to me by General Paoli:—'That it is impossible not to be afraid of death; and that those who at the time of dying are not afraid, are not thinking of death, but of applause, or something else, which keeps death out of their sight: so that all men are equally afraid of death when they see it; only some have a power of turning their sight away from it better than others.'

On Wednesday, September 17, Dr. Butter, physician at Derby, drank tea with us; and it was settled that Dr. Johnson and I should go on Friday and dine with him. Johnson said, 'I'm glad of this.' He seemed weary of the uniformity of life at Dr. Taylor's.

Talking of biography, I said, in writing a life, a man's peculiarities should be mentioned, because they mark his character. JOHNSON. 'Sir, there is no doubt as to peculiarities: the question is, whether a man's vices should be mentioned; for instance, whether it should be mentioned that Addison and Parnell drank too freely; for people will probably more easily indulge in drinking from knowing this; so that more ill may be done by the example, than good by telling the whole truth.' Here was an instance of his varying from himself in talk; for when Lord Hailes and he sat one morning calmly conversing in my house at Edinburgh, I well remember that Dr. Johnson maintained, that 'If a man is to write *A Panegyrick*, he may keep vices out of sight: but if he professes to write *A Life*, he must represent it really as it was;' and when I objected to the danger of telling that Parnell drank to excess, he said, that 'it would produce an instructive caution to avoid drinking, when it was seen, that even the learning and genius of Parnell could be debased by it.' And in the Hebrides he maintained, as appears from my 'Journal,'[1] that a man's intimate friend should mention his faults, if he writes his life.

two marginal lines: *instance of . . . calmly conversing* [H]

[1] Journal of a Tour to the Hebrides, 3d edit. p. 240.

He had this evening, partly, I suppose, from the spirit
of contradiction to his Whig friend, a violent argument
with Dr. Taylor, as to the inclinations of the people of
England at this time towards the Royal Family of Stuart.
He grew so outrageous as to say, 'that if England were
fairly polled, the present King would be sent away to-
night, and his adherents hanged to-morrow.' Taylor, who
was as violent a Whig as Johnson was a Tory, was roused
by this to a pitch of bellowing. He denied, loudly, what
Johnson said; and maintained, that there was an abhorrence against the Stuart family, though he admitted that
the people were not much attached to the present King.[1a]
JOHNSON. 'Sir, the state of the country is this: the people
knowing it to be agreed on all hands that this King has not
the hereditary right to the crown, and there being no hope
that he who has it can be restored, have grown cold and
indifferent upon the subject of loyalty, and have no warm
attachment to any King. They would not, therefore, risk
any thing to restore the exiled family. They would not
give twenty shillings a piece to bring it about. But if a
mere vote could do it, there would be twenty to one; at
least there would be a very great majority of voices for it.
For, Sir, you are to consider, that all those who think a
King has a right to his crown, as a man has to his estate,
which is the just opinion, would be for restoring the King
who certainly has the hereditary right, could he be trusted
with it; in which there would be no danger now, when
laws and every thing else are so much advanced: and every
King will govern by the laws. And you must also consider,
Sir, that there is nothing on the other side to oppose to
this: for it is not alledged by any one that the present
family has any inherent right: so that the Whigs could not
have a contest between two rights.'

Dr. Taylor admitted, that if the question as to hereditary
right were to be tried by a poll of the people of England,
to be sure the abstract doctrine would be given in favour
of the family of Stuart; but he said, the conduct of that

[a] *The People even
then were beginning
to lose all Attachment
to Royalty: no King
would have pleased
them. 1819.* [H]

[1] Dr. Taylor was very ready to make this admission, because the party
with which he was connected was not in power. There was then some truth
in it, owing to the pertinacity of factious clamour. Had he lived till now, it
would have been impossible for him to deny that his Majesty possesses the
warmest affection of his people.

family, which occasioned their expulsion, was so fresh in the minds of the people, that they would not vote for a restoration. Dr. Johnson, I think, was contented with the admission as to the hereditary right, leaving the original point in dispute, *viz.* what the people upon the whole would do, taking in right and affection; for he said, people were afraid of a change, even though they think it right. Dr. Taylor said something of the slight foundation of the hereditary right of the house of Stuart. 'Sir, (said Johnson,) the house of Stuart succeeded to the full right of both the houses of York and Lancaster, whose common source had the undisputed right. A right to a throne is like a right to any thing else. Possession is sufficient, where no better right can be shown. This was the case with the Royal Family of England, as it is now with the King of France:[a] for as to the first beginning of the right, we are in the dark.'

Thursday, September 18. Last night Dr. Johnson had proposed that the crystal lustre, or chandelier, in Dr. Taylor's large room, should be lighted up some time or other. Taylor said, it should be lighted up next night. 'That will do very well, (said I,) for it is Dr. Johnson's birth-day.' When we were in the Isle of Sky, Johnson had desired me not to mention his birth-day. He did not seem pleased at this time that I mentioned it, and said (somewhat sternly,) 'he would *not* have the lustre lighted the next day.'

Some ladies, who had been present yesterday when I mentioned his birth-day, came to dinner to-day, and plagued him unintentionally, by wishing him joy. I know not why he disliked having his birth-day mentioned, unless it were that it reminded him of his approaching nearer to death, of which he had a constant dread.

I mentioned to him a friend of mine who was formerly gloomy from low spirits, and much distressed by the fear of death, but was now uniformly placid, and contemplated his dissolution without any perturbation. 'Sir, (said Johnson,) this is only a disordered imagination taking a different turn.'

We talked of a collection being made of all the English Poets who had published a volume of poems. Johnson told me, 'that a Mr. Coxeter,[1] whom he knew, had gone the greatest length towards this; having collected, I think, about five hundred volumes of poets whose works were little known; but that upon his death Tom Osborne bought them and they were dispersed, which he thought a pity, as it was curious to see any series complete; and in every volume of poems something good may be found.'

He observed, that a gentleman of eminence in literature[a] had got into a bad style of poetry of late. 'He puts (said he) a very common thing in a strange dress till he does not know it himself, and thinks other people do not know it.' BOSWELL. 'That is owing to his being so much versant in old English poetry.' JOHNSON. 'What is that to the purpose, Sir? If I say a man is drunk, and you tell me it is owing to his taking much drink, the matter is not mended. No, Sir, —— [b] has taken to an odd mode. For example: he'd write thus:

> "Hermit hoar, in solemn cell,
> Wearing out life's evening gray."

Gray evening is common enough; but *evening gray* he'd think fine.—Stay;—we'll make out the stanza:

> "Hermit hoar, in solemn cell,
> Wearing out life's evening gray:
> Smite thy bosom, sage, and tell,
> What is bliss? and which the way?"'

BOSWELL. 'But why smite his bosom, Sir!' JOHNSON. 'Why to shew he was in earnest,' (smiling).—He at an after period added the following stanza:

> 'Thus I spoke; and speaking sigh'd;
> —Scarce repress'd the starting tear;—
> When the smiling sage reply'd—
> —Come, my lad, and drink some beer.'[2]

---

[1] [Thomas Coxeter, Esq. who had also made a large collection of old plays, and from whose manuscript notes the Lives of the English Poets, by Shiels and Cibber, were principally compiled, as should have been mentioned in a former page. See pp. 280, 281 of this volume. Mr. Coxeter was bred at Trinity College, Oxford, and died in London, April 17, 1747, in his fifty-ninth year. A particular account of him may be found in 'The Gentleman's Magazine' for 1781, p. 173. MALONE.]

[2] As some of my readers may be gratified by reading the progress of this little composition, I shall insert it from my notes. 'When Dr. Johnson and I

I cannot help thinking the first stanza very good solemn poetry, as also the first three lines of the second. Its last line is an excellent burlesque surprize on gloomy sentimental enquirers. And, perhaps, the advice is as good as can be given to a low-spirited dissatisfied being:—'Don't trouble your head with sickly thinking: take a cup, and be merry.'

Friday, September 19, after breakfast, Dr. Johnson and I set out in Dr. Taylor's chaise to go to Derby. The day was fine and we resolved to go by Keddlestone, the seat of Lord Scarsdale, that I might see his Lordship's fine house. I was struck with the magnificence of the building; and the extensive park, with the finest verdure, covered with deer, and cattle, and sheep, delighted me. The number of old oaks, of an immense size, filled me with a sort of respectful admiration; for one of them sixty pounds was offered. The excellent smooth gravel roads; the large piece of water formed by his Lordship from some small brooks, with a handsome barge upon it; the venerable Gothic church, now the family chapel, just by the house; in short, the grand group of objects agitated and distended my mind in a most agreeable manner. 'One should think (said I,) that the proprietor of all this *must* be happy.'—'Nay, Sir, (said Johnson), all this excludes but one evil—poverty.'[1a]

were sitting *tête-à-tête* at the Mitre-tavern, May 9, 1778, he said, "Where is bliss," would be better. He then added a ludicrous stanza, but would not repeat it, lest I should take it down. It was somewhat as follows; the last line I am sure I remember:

> "While I thus   cried,
>   seer,
> The hoary   reply'd,
> Come, my lad, and drink some beer."

'In spring, 1779, when in better humour, he made the second stanza, as in the text. There was only one variation afterwards made on my suggestion, which was changing *hoary* in the third line to *smiling*, both to avoid a sameness with the epithet in the first line, and to describe the hermit in his pleasantry. He was then very well pleased that I should preserve it.'

[1] When I mentioned Dr. Johnson's remark to a lady of admirable good sense and quickness of understanding, she observed, 'It is true, all this excludes only one evil; but how much good does it let in?'—To this observation much praise has been justly given. Let me then now do myself the honour to mention that the lady who made it was the late Margaret Montgomerie, my very valuable wife, and the very affectionate mother of my children, who, if they inherit her good qualities, will have no reason to complain of their lot. *Dos magna parentum virtus.*

Our names were sent up, and a well-drest elderly house-keeper, a most distinct articulator, shewed us the house; which I need not describe, as there is an account of it published in 'Adams's Works in Architecture.' Dr. Johnson thought better of it to-day, than when he saw it before; for he had lately attacked it violently, saying, 'It would do excellently for a town-hall. The large room with the pillars (said he) would do for the Judges to sit in at the assizes; the circular room for a jury-chamber; and the room above for prisoners.' Still he thought the large room ill lighted, and of no use but for dancing in; and the bed-chambers but indifferent rooms; and that the immense sum which it cost was injudiciously laid out. Dr. Taylor had put him in mind of his *appearing* pleased with the house. 'But (said he) that was when Lord Scarsdale was present. Politeness obliges us to appear pleased with a man's works when he is present. No man will be so ill bred as to question you. You may therefore pay compliments without saying what is not true. I should say to Lord Scarsdale of his large room, "My Lord, this is the most *costly* room that I ever saw;" which is true.'

Dr. Manningham, physician in London, who was visiting at Lord Scarsdale's, accompanied us through many of the rooms, and soon afterwards my Lord himself, to whom Dr. Johnson was known, appeared, and did the honours of the house. We talked of Mr. Langton. Johnson, with a warm vehemence of affectionate regard, exclaimed, 'The earth does not bear a worthier man than Bennet Langton.' We saw a good many fine pictures, which I think are described in one of 'Young's Tours.' There is a printed catalogue of them, which the housekeeper put into my hand; I should like to view them at leisure. I was much struck with Daniel interpreting Nebuchadnezzar's dream, by Rembrandt.—We were shown a pretty large library. In his Lordship's dressing room lay Johnson's small Dictionary: he shewed it to me, with some eagerness, saying, 'Look ye! *Quæ regio in terris nostri non plena laboris.*' He observed, also, Goldsmith's 'Animated Nature;' and said, 'Here's our friend! The poor Doctor would have been happy to hear of this.'

In our way, Johnson strongly expressed his love of driving fast in a post-chaise. 'If (said he) I had no duties,

marginal line:
an account . . . it to-day
[H]

and no reference to futurity, I would spend my life in driving briskly in a post-chaise with a pretty woman; but she should be one who could understand me, and would ^a add something to the conversation.'^a I observed, that we were this day to stop just where the Highland army did in 1745. JOHNSON. 'It was a noble attempt.' BOSWELL. 'I wish we could have an authentick history of it.' JOHNSON. 'If you were not an idle dog you might write it, by collecting from every body what they can tell, and putting down your authorities.' BOSWELL. 'But I could not have the advantage of it in my life-time.' JOHNSON. 'You might have the satisfaction of its fame, by printing it in Holland; and as to profit, consider how long it was before writing came to be considered in a pecuniary view. Baretti says, he is the first man that ever received copy-money in Italy.' I said that I would endeavour to do what Dr. Johnson suggested; and I thought that I might write so as to venture to publish my 'History of the Civil War in Great Britain in 1745 and 1746,' without being obliged to go to a foreign press.'[1]

When we arrived at Derby, Dr. Butter accompanied us to see the manufactory of china there. I admired the ingenuity and delicate art with which a man fashioned clay into a cup, a saucer, or a teapot, while a boy turned round a wheel to give the mass rotundity. I thought this as excellent in its species of power, as making good verses in its species. Yet I had no respect for this potter. Neither, indeed, has a man of any extent of thinking for a mere verse-maker, in whose numbers, however perfect, there is no poetry, no mind. The china was beautiful, but Dr. Johnson justly observed it was too dear; for that he could have vessels of silver, of the same size, as cheap as what were here made of porcelain.

I felt a pleasure in walking about Derby, such as I always have in walking about any town to which I am not accustomed. There is an immediate sensation of novelty; and one speculates on the way in which life is passed in it,

[1] I am now happy to understand that Mr. John Home, who was himself gallantly in the field for the reigning family, in that interesting warfare, but is generous enough to do justice to the other side, is preparing an account of it for the press.

which, although there is a sameness every where upon the whole, is yet minutely diversified. The minute diversities in every thing are wonderful. Talking of shaving the other night at Dr. Taylor's, Dr. Johnson said, 'Sir, of a thousand shavers, two do not shave so much alike as not to be distinguished.' I thought this not possible, till he specified so many of the varieties in shaving;—holding the razor more or less perpendicular;—drawing long or short strokes;—beginning at the upper part of the face, or the under;—at the right side or the left side. Indeed, when one considers what variety of sounds can be uttered by the windpipe, in the compass of a very small aperture, we may be convinced how many degrees of difference there may be in the application of a razor.

We dined with Dr. Butter,[1] whose lady is daughter of my cousin Sir John Douglas, whose grandson is now presumptive heir of the noble family of Queensberry. Johnson and he had a good deal of medical conversation. Johnson said, he had somewhere or other given an account of Dr. Nichols's discourse '*De Animâ Medicâ.*' He told us 'that whatever a man's distemper was, Dr. Nichols would not attend him as a physician, if his mind was not at ease; for he believed that no medicines would have any influence. He once attended a man in trade, upon whom he found none of the medicines he prescribed had any effect; he asked the man's wife privately whether his affairs were not in a bad way? She said no. He continued his attendance some time, still without success. At length the man's wife told him she had discovered that her husband's affairs *were* in a bad way. When Goldsmith was dying, Dr. Turton said to him, "Your pulse is in greater disorder than it should be, from the degree of fever which you have: is your mind at ease?" Goldsmith answered it was not.'[a]

After dinner, Mrs. Butter went with me to see the silk-mill which Mr. John Lombe had[2] had a patent for, having brought away the contrivance from Italy. I am not very

---

[1] [Dr. Butter was at this time a practising physician at Derby. He afterwards removed to London, where he died in his 79th year, March 22, 1805. He is authour of several medical tracts. MALONE.]

[2] See Hutton's History of Derby, a book which is deservedly esteemed for its information, accuracy, and good narrative. Indeed the age in which we live is eminently distinguished by topographical excellence.

conversant with mechanicks; but the simplicity of this machine, and its multiplied operations, struck me with an agreeable surprize. I had learnt from Dr. Johnson, during this interview, not to think with a dejected indifference of the works of art, and the pleasures of life, because life is uncertain and short; but to consider such indifference as a failure of reason, a morbidness of mind; for happiness should be cultivated as much as we can, and the objects which are instrumental to it should be steadily considered as of importance with a reference not only to ourselves, but to multitudes in successive ages. Though it is proper to value small parts, as

'Sands make the mountain, moments make the year;'[1]

yet we must contemplate, collectively, to have a just estimation of objects. One moment's being uneasy or not, seems of no consequence; yet this may be thought of the next, and the next, and so on, till there is a large portion of misery. In the same way one must think of happiness, of learning, of friendship. We cannot tell the precise moment when friendship is formed. As in filling a vessel drop by drop, there is at last a drop which makes it run over; so in a series of kindnesses there is at last one which makes the heart run over. We must not divide the objects of our attention into minute parts, and think separately of each part. It is by contemplating a large mass of human existence, that a man, while he sets a just value on his own life, does not think of his death as annihilating all that is great and pleasing in the world, as if actually *contained in his mind*, according to Berkeley's reverie. If his imagination be not sickly and feeble, it 'wings its distant way' far beyond himself, and views the world in unceasing activity of every sort. It must be acknowledged, however, that Pope's plaintive reflection, that all things would be as gay as ever, on the day of his death,[a] is natural and common.[b] We are apt to transfer to all around us our own gloom, without considering that at any given point of time there is, perhaps, as much youth and gaiety in the world as at another. Before I came into this life, in which I have had so many pleasant scenes, have not thousands and ten

[a] *I feel glad always to know that it will be so.* [J]

[b] *I don't know how common . . . but not natural in the least to me. I am glad other people go on,—if I am forced to stop.* [H]

[1] Young.

thousands of deaths and funerals happened, and have not families been in grief for their nearest relations? But have those dismal circumstances at all affected *me?* Why then should the gloomy scenes which I experience, or which I know, affect others? Let us guard against imagining that there is an end of felicity upon earth, when we ourselves grow old, or are unhappy.

Dr. Johnson told us at tea, that when some of Dr. Dodd's pious friends were trying to console him by saying that he was going to leave 'a wretched world,' he had honesty enough not to join in the cant;—'No, no (said he,) it has been a very agreeable world to me.' Johnson added, 'I respect Dodd for thus speaking the truth; for, to be sure, he had for several years enjoyed a life of great voluptuousness.'

He told us, that Dodd's city friends stood by him so, that a thousand pounds were ready to be given to the gaoler, if he would let him escape. He added, that he knew a friend of Dodd's, who walked about Newgate for some time on the evening before the day of his execution, with five hundred pounds in his pocket, ready to be paid to any of the turnkeys who could get him out, but it was too late; for he was watched with much circumspection. He said, Dodd's friends had an image of him made of wax, which was to have been left in his place; and he believed it was carried into the prison.

Johnson disapproved of Dr. Dodd's leaving the world persuaded that 'The Convict's Address to his unhappy Brethren' was of his own writing. 'But, Sir, (said I,) you contributed to the deception; for when Mr. Seward expressed a doubt to you that it was not Dodd's own, because it had a great deal more force of mind in it than any thing known to be his, you answered,—"Why should you think so? Depend upon it, Sir, when any man knows he is to be hanged in a fortnight, it concentrates his mind wonderfully."' JOHNSON. 'Sir, as Dodd got it from me to pass as his own, while that could do him any good, that was an *implied promise* that I should not own it. To own it, therefore, would have been telling a lie, with the addition of breach of promise, which was worse than simply telling a lie to make it be believed it was Dodd's. Besides, Sir, I did not *directly* tell a lie: I left the matter uncertain. Perhaps I thought that Seward would not believe it the less to be mine for what I said, but I would not put it in his power to say I had owned it.'

He praised Blair's sermons: 'Yet,' said he, (willing to let us see he was aware that fashionable fame, however deserved, is not always the most lasting,) 'perhaps, they may not be re-printed after seven years; at least not after Blair's death.'

He said, 'Goldsmith was a plant that flowered late. There appeared nothing remarkable about him when he was young; though when he had got high in fame, one of his friends began to recollect something of his being distinguished at College.[1] Goldsmith in the same manner recollected more of that friend's early years, as he grew a greater man.'

I mentioned that Lord Monboddo told me, he awaked every morning at four, and then for his health got up and walked the room naked, with the window open, which he called taking *an air bath;* after which he went to bed again, and slept two hours more. Johnson, who was always ready to beat down any thing that seemed to be exhibited with disproportionate importance, thus observed: 'I suppose, Sir, there is no more in it than this, he wakes at four, and cannot sleep till he chills himself, and makes the warmth of the bed a grateful sensation.'

I talked of the difficulty of rising in the morning. Dr. Johnson told me, 'that the learned Mrs. Carter, at that period when she was eager in study, did not awake so early as she wished, and she therefore had a contrivance, that, at a certain hour, her chamber-light should burn a string to which a heavy weight was suspended, which then fell with a strong sudden noise: this roused her from sleep, and then she had no difficulty in getting up.' But I said *that* was my difficulty; and wished there could be some medicine invented which would make one rise without pain, which I never did, unless after lying in bed a very long time. Perhaps there may be something in the stores of Nature which could do this. I have thought of a pully to raise me

[1] [He *was* distinguished in college, as appears from a circumstance mentioned by Dr. Kearney. See vol. i. p. 292. MALONE.]

gradually; but that would give me pain, as it would counteract my internal inclination. I would have something that can dissipate the *vis inertiæ*, and give elasticity to the muscles. As I imagine that the human body may be put, by the operation of other substances, into any state in which it has ever been; and as I have experienced a state in which rising from bed was not disagreeable, but easy, nay, sometimes agreeable; I suppose that this state may be produced, if we knew by what. We can heat the body, we can cool it; we can give it tension or relaxation; and surely it is possible to bring it into a state in which rising from bed will not be a pain.

Johnson observed, that 'a man should take a sufficient quantity of sleep, which Dr. Mead says is between seven and nine hours.' I told him, that Dr. Cullen said to me, that a man should not take more sleep than he can take at once. JOHNSON. 'This rule, Sir, cannot hold in all cases; for many people have their sleep broken by sickness; and surely, Cullen would not have a man to get up, after having slept but an hour. Such a regimen would soon end in a *long sleep*.'[1] Dr. Taylor remarked, I think very justly, that 'a man who does not feel an inclination to sleep at the ordinary times, instead of being stronger than other people, must not be well; for a man in health has all the natural inclinations to eat, drink, and sleep, in a strong degree.'

Johnson advised me to-night not to *refine* in the education of my children. 'Life, (said he) will not bear refinement: you must do as other people do.'

As we drove back to Ashbourne, Dr. Johnson recommended to me, as he had often done, to drink water only: 'For (said he) you are then sure not to get drunk; whereas,

marginal line:
Johnson observed . . . is between [H]

queried:
For (said he) etc. [H]

[1] This regimen was, however, practised by Bishop Ken, of whom Hawkins (*not Sir John*) in his Life of that venerable Prelate, page 4, tells us, 'And that neither his study might be the aggressor on his hours of instruction, or what he judged his duty, prevent his improvements; or both, his closet addresses to his GOD; he strictly accustomed himself to but one sleep, which often obliged him to rise at one or two of the clock in the morning, and sometimes sooner; and grew so habitual, that it continued with him almost till his last illness. And so lively and chearful was his temper, that he would be very facetious and entertaining to his friends in the evening, even when it was perceived that with difficulty he kept his eyes open; and then seemed to go to rest with no other purpose than the refreshing and enabling him with more vigour and chearfulness to sing his morning hymn, as he then used to do to his lute before he put on his cloaths.

if you drink wine, you are never sure.' I said, drinking
wine was a pleasure which I was unwilling to give up.
'Why, Sir, (said he,) there is no doubt that not to drink
wine is a great deduction from life; but it may be necessary.' He however owned, that in his opinion a free use of
wine did not shorten life; and said, he would not give less
for the life of a certain Scotch Lord (whom he named)[a]
celebrated for hard drinking, than for that of a sober man.
'But stay, (said he, with his usual intelligence, and accuracy of enquiry,) does it take much wine to make him
drunk?' I answered, 'a great deal either of wine or strong
punch.'—'Then (said he) that is the worse.' I presume to
illustrate my friend's observation thus: 'A fortress which
soon surrenders has its walls less shattered, than when a
long and obstinate resistance is made.'

I ventured to mention a person who was as violent a
Scotchman as he was an Englishman; and literally had the
same contempt for an Englishman compared with a
Scotchman, that he had for a Scotchman compared with
an Englishman; and that he would say of Dr. Johnson,
'Damned rascal! to talk as he does of the Scotch.' This
seemed, for a moment, 'to give him pause.' It, perhaps,
presented his extreme prejudice against the Scotch in a
point of view somewhat new to him by the effect of
contrast.

By the time when we returned to Ashbourne, Dr. Taylor
was gone to bed. Johnson and I sat up a long time by
ourselves.

He was much diverted with an article which I shewed
him in the 'Critical Review' of this year, giving an account
of a curious publication, entitled, 'A Spiritual Diary and
Soliloquies, by John Rutty, M.D.' Dr. Rutty was one of
the people called Quakers, a physician of some eminence
in Dublin, and authour of several works. This Diary,
which was kept from 1753 to 1775, the year in which he
died, and was now published in two volumes octavo,
exhibited, in the simplicity of his heart, a minute and
honest register of the state of his mind; which, though frequently laughable enough, was not more so than the
history of many men would be, if recorded with equal
fairness.

two marginal lines:
said he . . . be necessary
[H]

[a] *was it Lord Kelly?*
[H]

The following specimens were extracted by the Reviewers:

'Tenth month, 1753.

'23. Indulgence in bed an hour too long.

'Twelfth month, 17. An hypochrondriack obnubilation from wind and indigestion.

'Ninth month, 28. An over-dose of whisky.

'29. A dull, cross, cholerick day.

'First month, 1757–22. A little swinish at dinner and repast.

'31. Dogged on provocation.

'Second month, 5. Very dogged or snappish.

'14. Snappish on fasting.

'26. Cursed snappishness to those under me, on a bodily indisposition.

'Third month, 11. On a provocation, exercised a dumb resentment for two days, instead of scolding.

'22. Scolded too vehemently.

'29. Dogged again.

'Fourth month, 29. Mechanically and sinfully dogged.'

Johnson laughed heartily at this good Quietist's self condemning minutes; particularly at his mentioning, with such a serious regret, occasional instances of '*swinishness* in eating, and *doggedness of temper*.' He thought the observations of the Critical Reviewers upon the importance of a man to himself so ingenious and so well expressed, that I shall here introduce them.

After observing that 'There are few writers who have gained any reputation by recording their own actions,' they say,

'We may reduce the egotists to four classes. In the *first* we have Julius Cæsar: he relates his own transactions; but he relates them with peculiar grace and dignity, and his narrative is supported by the greatness of his character and achievements. In the *second* class we have Marcus Antoninus: this writer has given us a series of reflections on his own life; but his sentiments are so noble, his morality so sublime, that his meditations are universally admired. In the *third* class we have some others of tolerable credit, who have given importance to their own private history by an intermixture of literary anecdotes, and the occurrences of their own times: the celebrated *Huetius* has published an entertaining volume upon this plan, "*De rebus ad eum pertinentibus.*" In the *fourth* class we have the journalists, temporal and spiritual: Elias Ashmole, William Lilly, George Whitefield, John Wesley, and a thousand other old women and fanatick writers of memoirs and meditations.'

I mentioned to him that Dr. Hugh Blair, in his lectures on Rhetorick and Belles Lettres, which I heard him deliver at Edinburgh, had animadverted on the Johnsonian style as too pompous; and attempted to imitate it, by giving a sentence of Addison in 'The Spectator,' No. 411, in the manner of Johnson. When treating of the utility of the pleasures of imagination in preserving us from vice, it is observed of those 'who know not how to be idle and innocent,' that 'their very first step out of business is into vice or folly;' which Dr. Blair supposed would have been expressed in 'The Rambler,' thus: 'Their very first step out of the regions of business is into the perturbation of vice, or the vacuity of folly.'[1] JOHNSON. 'Sir, these are not the words I should have used. No, Sir; the imitators of my style have not hit it. Miss Aikin has done it the best;[a] for she has imitated the sentiment as well as the diction.'

I intend, before this work is concluded, to exhibit specimens of imitation of my friend's style in various modes; some caricaturing or mimicking it, and some formed upon it, whether intentionally, or with a degree of similarity to it, of which, perhaps, the writers were not conscious.

In Baretti's Review, which he published in Italy, under the title of 'FRUSTA LETTERARIA,' it is observed, that Dr. Robertson the historian had formed his style upon that of '*Il celebre Samuele Johnson.*' My friend himself was of that opinion;[b] for he once said to me, in a pleasant humour,

----

[1] When Dr. Blair published his 'Lectures,' he was invidiously attacked for having omitted his censure on Johnson's style, and, on the contrary, praising it highly. But before that time Johnson's 'Lives of the Poets' had appeared, in which his style was considerably easier, than when he wrote 'The Rambler.' It would, therefore, have been uncandid in Blair, even supposing his criticism to have been just, to have preserved it.

'Sir, if Robertson's style be faulty, he owes it to me; that is, having too many words, and those too big ones.'

I read to him a letter which Lord Monboddo had written to me, containing some critical remarks upon the style of his 'Journey to the Western Islands of Scotland.' His Lordship praised the very fine passage upon landing at Icolm-kill:[1] but his own style being exceedingly dry and hard, he disapproved of the richness of Johnson's language, and of his frequent use of metaphorical expressions. JOHNSON. 'Why, Sir, this criticism would be just, if, in my style, superfluous words, or words too big for the thoughts, could be pointed out; but this I do not believe can be done. For instance; in the passage which Lord Monboddo admires, "We were now treading that illustrious region," the word *illustrious* contributes nothing to the mere narration; for the fact might be told without it: but it is not, therefore, superfluous; for it wakes the mind to peculiar attention, where something of more than usual importance is to be presented. "Illustrious!"—for what? and then the sentence proceeds to expand the circumstances connected with Iona. And, Sir, as to metaphorical expression, that is a great excellence in style, when it is used with propriety, for it gives you two ideas for one;—conveys the meaning more luminously, and generally with a perception of delight.'

He told me, that he had been asked to undertake the new edition of the *Biographia Britannica,* but had declined it; which he afterwards said to me he regretted. In this

[1] 'WE were now treading that illustrious island, which was once the luminary of the Caledonian regions, whence savage clans and roving barbarians derived the benefits of knowledge, and the blessings of religion. To abstract the mind from all local emotion would be impossible, if it were endeavoured, and would be foolish, if it were possible. Whatever withdraws us from the power of our senses, whatever makes the past, the distant, or the future, predominate over the present, advances us in the dignity of thinking beings. Far from me, and from my friends, be such frigid philosophy, as may conduct us, indifferent and unmoved, over any ground which has been dignified by wisdom, bravery, or virtue. The man is little to be envied, whose patriotism would not gain force upon the plain of Marathon, or whose piety would not grow warmer among the ruins of Iona.'

marginal line: senses, whatever . . . frigid philosophy [H]

Had our Tour produced nothing else but this sublime passage, the world must have acknowledged that it was not made in vain. Sir Joseph Banks, the present respectable President of the Royal Society, told me, he was so much struck on reading it, that he clasped his hands together, and remained for some time in an attitude of silent admiration.

marginal line: Sir Joseph . . . silent admiration [H]

regret many will join, because it would have procured us more of Johnson's most delightful species of writing; and although my friend Dr. Kippis[1] has hitherto discharged the task judiciously, distinctly, and with more impartiality than might have been expected from a Separatist, it were to have been wished that the superintendence of this literary Temple of Fame had been assigned to 'a friend to the constitution in Church and State.' We should not then have had it too much crowded with obscure dissenting teachers, doubtless men of merit and worth, but not quite to be numbered amongst 'the most eminent persons who have flourished in Great Britain and Ireland.'[2]

On Saturday, September 20, after breakfast, when Taylor was gone out to his farm, Dr. Johnson and I had a

---

[1] [After having given to the publick the first five volumes of a new edition of BIOGRAPHIA BRITANNICA, between the years 1778 and 1793, Dr. Kippis died, October 8, 1795; and the work is not likely to be soon completed. MALONE.]

[2] In this censure which has been carelessly uttered, I carelessly joined. But in justice to Dr. Kippis, who, with that manly candid good temper which marks his character, set me right, I now with pleasure retract it; and I desire it may be particularly observed, as pointed out by him to me, that, 'The new Lives of dissenting Divines, in the first four volumes of the second edition of the "Biographia Britannica," are those of John Abernethy, Thomas Amory, George Benson, Hugh Broughton the learned Puritan, Simon Browne, Joseph Boyse of Dublin, Thomas Cartwright the learned Puritan, and Samuel Chandler. The only doubt I have ever heard suggested is, whether there should have been an article of Dr. Amory. But I was convinced, and am still convinced, that he was entitled to one, from the reality of his learning, and the excellent and candid nature of his practical writings.

'The new Lives of clergymen of the Church of England, in the same four volumes, are as follows: John Balguy, Edward Bentham, George Berkley Bishop of Cloyne, William Berriman, Thomas Birch, William Borlase, Thomas Bott, James Bradley, Thomas Broughton, John Brown, John Burton, Joseph Butler Bishop of Durham, Thomas Carte, Edmund Castell, Edmund Chishull, Charles Churchill, William Clarke, Robert Clayton Bishop of Clogher, John Conybeare Bishop of Bristol, George Costard, and Samuel Croxall.—"I am not conscious (says Dr. Kippis) of any partiality in conducting the work. I would not willingly insert a Dissenting Minister that does not justly deserve to be noticed, or omit an established clergyman that does. At the same time, I shall not be deterred from introducing Dissenters into the Biographia, when I am satisfied that they are entitled to that distinction, from their writings, learning, and merit."'

Let me add that the expression 'A friend to the Constitution in Church and State,' was not meant by me, as any reflection upon this Reverend Gentleman, as if he were an enemy to the political constitution of his country, as established at the revolution, but, from my steady and avowed predilection for a Tory, was quoted from 'Johnson's Dictionary', where that distinction is so defined.

serious conversation by ourselves on melancholy and madness; which he was, I always thought, erroneously inclined to confound together. Melancholy, like 'great wit,' may be, 'near allied to madness;' but there is, in my opinion, a distinct separation between them. When he talked of madness, he was to be understood as speaking of those who were in any great degree disturbed, or as it is commonly expressed, 'troubled in mind.' Some of the ancient philosophers held, that all deviations from right reason were madness; and whoever wishes to see the opinions both of ancients and moderns upon this subject, collected and illustrated with a variety of curious facts, may read Dr. Arnold's very entertaining work.[1]

Johnson said, 'A madman loves to be with people whom he fears; not as a dog fears the lash: but of whom he stands in awe.' I was struck with the justice of this observation. To be with those of whom a person, whose mind is wavering and dejected, stands in awe, represses and composes an uneasy tumult of spirits,[2] and consoles him with the contemplation of something steady, and at least comparatively great.

marginal line: whom a . . . an uneasy [H]

underlined: something steady [H]

He added, 'Madmen are all sensual in the lower stages of the distemper. They are eager for gratifications to sooth their minds, and divert their attention from the misery which they suffer; but when they grow very ill, pleasure is too weak for them, and they seek for pain.[3a] Employment, Sir, and hardships, prevent melancholy.

a For what does Life inherit
But countless Woes, chequer'd with transient Good!
Hence nobler Souls, tir'd with the tedious and disrelish'd Pleasure
Seek for their Solace in acknowledg'd Ill,
Danger and Toil and Pain.
Graham's Telemachus. [H]

two marginal lines: torment to . . . it relieves [H]

[1] 'Observations on Insanity,' by Thomas Arnold, M.D. London, 1782.

[2] [Cardan composed his mind tending to madness, (or rather actually mad, for such he seems in his writings, learned as they are,) by exciting voluntary pain. V. Card. Op. et Vit. KEARNEY.]

[3] We read in the Gospels, that those unfortunate persons, who were possessed with evil spirits, (which, after all, I think is the most probable cause of madness, as was first suggested to me by my respectable friend Sir John Pringle,) had recourse to pain, tearing themselves and jumping sometimes into the fire, sometimes into the water. Mr. Seward has furnished me with a remarkable anecdote in confirmation of Dr. Johnson's observation. A tradesman who had acquired a large fortune in London, retired from business, and went to live at Worcester. His mind, being without its usual occupation, and having nothing else to supply its place, preyed upon itself, so that existence was a torment to him. At last he was seized with the stone; and a friend who found him in one of its severest fits, having expressed his concern, 'No, no, Sir, (said he) don't pity me; what I now feel is ease, compared with that torture of mind from which it relieves me.'

I suppose in all our army in America, there was not one man who went mad.'

We entered seriously upon a question of much importance to me, which Johnson was pleased to consider with friendly attention. I had long complained to him that I felt myself discontented in Scotland, as too narrow a sphere, and that I wished to make my chief residence in London, the great scene of ambition, instruction, and amusement: a scene, which was to me, comparatively speaking, a heaven upon earth. JOHNSON. 'Why, Sir, I never knew any one who had such a *gust* for London as you have: and I cannot blame you for your wish to live there: yet, Sir, were I in your father's place, I should not consent to your settling there; for I have the old feudal notions, and I should be afraid that Auchinleck would be deserted, as you would soon find it more desirable to have a country-seat in a better climate. I own, however, that to consider it as a *duty* to reside on a family estate is a prejudice; for we must consider, that working-people get employment equally, and the produce of land is sold equally, whether a great family resides at home or not; and if the rents of an estate be carried to London, they return again in the circulation of commerce; nay, Sir, we must perhaps allow, that carrying the rents to a distance is a good, because it contributes to that circulation. We must, however, allow, that a well-regulated great family may improve a neighbourhood in civility and elegance, and give an example of good order, virtue, and piety; and so its residence at home may be of much advantage. But if a great family be disorderly and vicious, its residence at home is very pernicious to a neighbourhood. There is not now the same inducement to live in the country as formerly; the pleasures of social life are much better enjoyed in town; and there is no longer in the country that power and influence in proprietors of land which they had in old times, and which made the country so agreeable to them. The Laird of Auchinleck now is not near so great a man as the Laird of Auchinleck was a hundred years ago.'

I told him, that one of my ancestors never went from home without being attended by thirty men on horseback. Johnson's shrewdness and spirit of enquiry were exerted

marginal line:
social life . . . *old times* [H]

upon every occasion. 'Pray (said he,) how did your ancestor support his thirty men and thirty horses when he went at a distance from home, in an age when there was hardly any money in circulation?' I suggested the same difficulty to a friend who mentioned Douglas's going to the Holy Land with a numerous train of followers. Douglas could, no doubt, maintain followers enough while living upon his own lands, the produce of which supplied them with food; but he could not carry that food to the Holy Land; and as there was no commerce by which he could be supplied with money, how could he maintain them in foreign countries?

I suggested a doubt, that if I were to reside in London, the exquisite zest with which I relished it in occasional visits might go off, and I might grow tired of it. JOHNSON. 'Why, Sir, you find no man, at all intellectual, who is willing to leave London. No, Sir, when a man is tired of London, he is tired of life; for there is in London all that life can afford.'

two marginal lines: *tired of . . . can afford* [H]

To obviate his apprehension, that by settling in London I might desert the seat of my ancestors, I assured him that I had old feudal principles to a degree of enthusiasm; and that I felt all the *dulcedo* of the *natale solum*. I reminded him, that the Laird of Auchinleck had an elegant house, in front of which he could ride ten miles forward upon his own territories, upon which he had upwards of six hundred people attached to him; that the family seat was rich in natural romantick beauties of rock, wood, and water; and that in my 'morn of life' I had appropriated the finest descriptions in the ancient Classicks, to certain scenes there, which were thus associated in my mind. That when all this was considered, I should certainly pass a part of the year at home, and enjoy it the more from variety, and from bringing with me a share of the intellectual stores of the metropolis. He listened to all this, and kindly 'hoped it might be as I now supposed.'

He said, 'A country gentleman should bring his lady to visit London as soon as he can, that they may have agreeable topicks for conversation when they are by themselves.'[a]

[a] *but they would not willingly go home to talk with One another, I fear. The Lady would like London as well as Boswell did.* [H & I]

As I meditated trying my fortune in Westminster Hall, our conversation turned upon the profession of the law in England. JOHNSON. 'You must not indulge too sanguine hopes, should you be called to our bar. I was told, by a very sensible lawyer, that there are a great many chances against any man's success in the profession of the law; the candidates are so numerous, and those who get large practice so few. He said, it was by no means true that a man of good parts and application is sure of having business, though he, indeed, allowed that if such a man could but appear in a few causes, his merit would be known, and he would get forward; but that the great risk was, that a man might pass half a life-time in the Courts, and never have an opportunity of shewing his abilities.'[1]

We talked of employment being absolutely necessary to preserve the mind from wearying and growing fretful, especially in those who have a tendency to melancholy; and I mentioned to him a saying which somebody had related of an American savage, who, when an European was expatiating on all the advantages of money, put this question: 'Will it purchase *occupation?*' JOHNSON. 'Depend upon it, Sir, this saying is too refined for a savage.[a] And, Sir, money *will* purchase occupation; it will purchase all the conveniences of life; it will purchase variety of company; it will purchase all sorts of entertainment.'

I talked to him of Forster's 'Voyage to the South Seas,' which pleased me; but I found he did not like it. 'Sir, (said he,) there is a great affectation of fine writing in it.' BOSWELL. 'But he carries you along with him.' JOHNSON. 'No, Sir, he does not carry *me* along with him; he leaves me behind him: or rather, indeed, he sets me before him; for he makes me turn over many leaves at a time.'

On Sunday, September 21, we went to the church of Ashbourne, which is one of the largest and most luminous

marginal line:
advantages of . . . *Sir this* [H]

[a] *besides yt a Savage does not want Occupation   his Felicity in Life (if he has any) is in Leisure* [I]

queried and underlined:
will [H]

[1] Now, at the distance of fifteen years since this conversation passed, the observation which I have had an opportunity of making in Westminster Hall, has convinced me, that, however true the opinion of Dr. Johnson's legal friend may have been some time ago, the same certainty of success cannot now be promised to the same display of merit. The reasons, however, of the rapid rise of some, and the disappointment of others equally respectable, are such as it might seem invidious to mention, and would require a longer detail than would be proper for this work.

that I have seen in any town of the same size. I felt great satisfaction in considering that I was supported in my fondness for solemn publick worship by the general concurrence and munificence of mankind.

Johnson and Taylor were so different from each other, that I wondered at their preserving an intimacy. Their having been at school and college together, might, in some degree account for this; but Sir Joshua Reynolds has furnished me with a stronger reason; for Johnson mentioned to him, that he had been told by Taylor he was to be his heir.[a] I shall not take upon me to animadvert upon this; but certain it is that Johnson paid great attention to Taylor. He now, however, said to me, 'Sir, I love him; but I do not love him more; my regard for him does not increase. As it is said in the Apocrypha, "his talk is of bullocks."[1] I do not suppose he is very fond of my company. His habits are by no means sufficiently clerical: this he knows that I see; and no man likes to live under the eye of perpetual disapprobation.'

index sign:
a stronger reason etc.
[H]

underlined:
by Taylor . . . his heir
[H]

two exclamation points:
was to be his heir [I]

a His fondness for Reynolds too . . . Ay & for Thrale; had a Small dash of Interest to keep it warm. [H & I]

marginal line:
and no . . . of perpetual
[H]

I have no doubt that a good many sermons were composed for Taylor by Johnson. At this time I found, upon his table, a part of one which he had newly begun to write: and *Concio pro Tayloro* appears in one of his diaries. When to these circumstances we add the internal evidence from the power of thinking and style, in the collection which the Reverend Mr. Hayes had published, with the *significant* title of 'Sermons *left for publication* by the Reverend John Taylor, LL.D.' our conviction will be complete.

I, however, would not have it thought, that Dr. Taylor, though he could not write like Johnson, (as, indeed, who could?) did not sometimes compose sermons as good as those which we generally have from very respectable divines. He shewed me one with notes on the margin in Johnson's hand-writing; and I was present when he read another to Johnson, that he might have his opinion of it, and Johnson said it was 'very well.' These, we may be sure, were not Johnson's; for he was above little arts, or tricks of deception.

two marginal lines:
footnote 1 [H]

[1] Ecclesiasticus, chap. xxxviii. v. 25. The whole chapter may be read as an admirable illustration of the superiority of cultivated minds over the gross and illiterate.

Johnson was by no means of opinion, that every man of a learned profession should consider it as incumbent upon him, or as necessary to his credit, to appear as an authour. When in the ardour of ambition for literary fame, I regretted to him one day that an eminent Judge had nothing of it, and therefore would leave no perpetual monument of himself to posterity; 'Alas, Sir, (said Johnson) what a mass of confusion should we have, if every Bishop, and every Judge, every Lawyer, Physician, and Divine, were to write books.'

I mentioned to Johnson a respectable person of a very strong mind, who had little of that tenderness which is common to human nature; as an instance of which, when I suggested to him that he should invite his son, who had been settled ten years in foreign parts, to come home and pay him a visit, his answer was, 'No, no, let him mind his business.' JOHNSON. 'I do not agree with him, Sir, in this. Getting money is not all a man's business: to cultivate kindness is a valuable part of the business of life.'[a]

In the evening, Johnson being in very good spirits, entertained us with several characteristical portraits; I regret that any of them escaped my retention and diligence. I found from experience, that to collect my friend's conversation so as to exhibit it with any degree of its original flavour, it was necessary to write it down without delay. To record his sayings, after some distance of time, was like preserving or pickling long-kept and faded fruits, or other vegetables, which, when in that state, have little or nothing of their taste when fresh.

I shall present my readers with a series of what I gathered this evening from the Johnsonian garden.

'My friend, the late Earl of Corke, had a great desire to maintain the literary character of his family: he was a genteel man, but did not keep up the dignity of his rank. He was so generally civil, that nobody thanked him for it.'

'Did we not hear so much said of Jack Wilkes, we should think more highly of his conversation. Jack has a great variety of talk, Jack is a scholar, and Jack has the manners of a gentleman. But after hearing his name sounded from pole to pole, as the phœnix of convivial felicity, we are disappointed in his company. He has always been *at me:*

a but he was not sure the Kindness would increase on Acquaintance I suppose—it seldom does. Like Dr. Moore's Man in some Novel who resolutely avoided seeing his Sister, because he was not used to her, he said, & was sure he should not like her. [H]

marginal line: *dignity of . . . civil, that* [H]

but I would do Jack a kindness, rather than not. The contest is now over.'

'Garrick's gaiety of conversation has delicacy and elegance: Foote makes you laugh more; but Foote has the air of a buffoon paid for entertaining the company. He, indeed, well deserves his hire.'

'Colley Cibber once consulted me as to one of his birth-day Odes, a long time before it was wanted. I objected very freely to several passages. Cibber lost patience, and would not read his Ode to an end. When we had done with criticism, we walked over to Richardson's, the authour of "Clarissa," and I wondered to find Richardson displeased that I "did not treat Cibber with more *respect*." Now, Sir, to talk of *respect* for a *player!*" (smiling disdainfully.) BOSWELL. 'There, Sir, you are always heretical: you never will allow merit to a player.' JOHNSON. 'Merit, Sir, what merit? Do you respect a rope-dancer, or a ballad-singer?' BOSWELL. 'No, Sir: but we respect a great player, as a man who can conceive lofty sentiments, and can express them gracefully.' JOHNSON. 'What, Sir, a fellow who claps a hump on his back, and a lump on his leg, and cries, "*I am Richard the Third*"? Nay, Sir, a ballad-singer is a higher man, for he does two things; he repeats and he sings: there is both recitation and musick in his perform-ance; the player only recites.' BOSWELL. 'My dear Sir! you may turn any thing into ridicule. I allow, that a player of farce is not entitled to respect; he does a little thing: but he who can represent exalted characters, and touch the noblest passions, has very respectable powers; and man-kind have agreed in admiring great talents for the stage. We must consider, too, that a great player does what very few are capable to do; his art is a very rare faculty. *Who* can repeat Hamlet's soliloquy, "To be, or not to be," as Garrick does it?' JOHNSON. 'Any body may. Jemmy, there (a boy about eight years old, who was in the room) will do it as well in a week.' BOSWELL. 'No, no, Sir: and as a proof of the merit of great acting, and of the value which mankind set upon it, Garrick has got a hundred thousand pounds.'[a] JOHNSON. 'Is getting a hundred thousand pounds a proof of excellence? That has been done by a scoundrel commissary.'

[a] *No No—scarcely half as much.* [H & I]

This was most fallacious reasoning. I was *sure*, for once, that I had the best side of the argument. I boldly maintained the just distinction between a tragedian and a mere theatrical droll; between those who rouse our terrour and pity, and those who only make us laugh. 'If (said I) Betterton and Foote were to walk into this room, you would respect Betterton much more than Foote.' JOHNSON. 'If Betterton were to walk into this room with Foote, Foote would soon drive him out of it. Foote, Sir, *quatenùs* Foote, has powers superiour to them all.'

On Monday, September 22, when at breakfast, I unguardedly said to Dr. Johnson, 'I wish I saw you and Mrs. Macaulay together.' He grew very angry; and, after a pause, while a cloud gathered on his brow, he burst out, 'No, Sir; you would not see us quarrel, to make you sport. Don't you know that it is very uncivil to *pit* two people against one another?' Then, checking himself, and wishing to be more gentle, he added, 'I do not say you should be hanged or drowned for this; but it *is* very uncivil.' Dr. Taylor thought him in the wrong, and spoke to him privately of it; but I afterwards acknowledged to Johnson that I was to blame, for I candidly owned, that I meant to express a desire to see a contest between Mrs. Macaulay and him; but then I knew how the contest would end; so that I was to see him triumph.' JOHNSON. 'Sir, you cannot be sure how a contest will end; and no man has a right to engage two people in a dispute by which their passions may be inflamed, and they may part with bitter resentment against each other. I would sooner keep company with a man from whom I must guard my pockets, than with a man who contrives to bring me into a dispute with somebody that he may hear it. This is the great fault of ——,[a] (naming one of our friends) endeavouring to introduce a subject upon which he knows two people in the company differ.' BOSWELL. 'But he told me, Sir, he does it for instruction.' JOHNSON. 'Whatever the motive be, Sir, the man who does so, does very wrong. He has no more right to instruct himself at such risk, than he has to make two people fight a duel, that he may learn how to defend himself.'

[a] *Beauclerc, but then he did it slyly.* [H]

He found great fault with a gentleman of our acquaintance for keeping a bad table. 'Sir, (said he,) when a man
is invited to dinner, he is disappointed if he does not get
something good. I advised Mrs. Thrale, who has no card-
parties at her house,[a] to give sweet-meats, and such good
things, in an evening, as are not commonly given, and she
would find company enough come to her;[b] for every body
loves to have things which please the palate put in their
way, without trouble or preparation.' Such was his
attention to the *minutiæ* of life and manners.

underlined:
her house [1]

[a] *in the Borough of
Southwark* [1]

underlined:
*and she would find,
enough come to her* [1]

[b] *there* inserted after
her [1]

He thus characterised the Duke of Devonshire, grandfather of the present representative of that very respectable
family: 'He was not a man of superiour abilities, but he
was a man strictly faithful to his word. If, for instance, he
had promised you an acorn, and none had grown that
year in his woods, he would not have contented himself
with that excuse: he would have sent to Denmark for it. So
unconditional was he in keeping his word; so high as to the
point of honour.' This was a liberal testimony from the
Tory Johnson to the virtue of a great Whig nobleman.

Mr. Burke's 'Letter to the Sheriffs of Bristol, on the
affairs of America,' being mentioned, Johnson censured
the composition much, and he ridiculed the definition of a
free government, *viz.* 'For any practical purpose, it is
what the people think so.'[1]—'I will let the King of France
govern me on those conditions, (said he,) for it is to be
governed just as I please.' And when Dr. Taylor talked of
a girl being sent to a parish workhouse, and asked how
much she could be obliged to work, 'Why, (said Johnson,)
as much as is reasonable: and what is that? as much as *she
thinks* reasonable.'

Dr. Johnson obligingly proposed to carry me to see
Islam, a romantick scene, now belonging to a family of the
name of Port, but formerly the seat of the Congreves. I
suppose it is well described in some of the Tours. Johnson
described it distinctly and vividly, at which I could not
but express to him my wonder; because, though my eyes,
as he observed, were better than his, I could not by any
means equal him in representing visible objects. I said, the
difference between us in this respect was as that between a

exclamation point
and underlined:
Islam, Port [H]

---

[1] Edit. 2, p. 53.

man who has a bad instrument, but plays well on it, and a man who has a good instrument, on which he can play very imperfectly.

I recollect a very fine amphitheatre, surrounded with hills covered with woods, and walks neatly formed along the side of a rocky steep, on the quarter next the house, with recesses under projections of rock, overshadowed with trees; in one of which recesses, we were told, Congreve wrote his 'Old Bachelor.' We viewed a remarkable natural curiosity at Islam; two rivers bursting near each other from the rock, not from immediate springs, but after having run for many miles under ground. Plott, in his 'History of Staffordshire,'[1] gives an account of this curiosity; but Johnson would not believe it, though we had the attestation of the gardener, who said, he had put in corks, where the river *Manyfold* sinks into the ground, and had catched them in a net, placed before one of the openings where the water bursts out. Indeed, such subterraneous courses of water are found in various parts of our globe.[2]

Talking of Dr. Johnson's unwillingness to believe extraordinary things, I ventured to say, 'Sir, you come near Hume's argument against miracles, "That it is more probable witnesses should lie, or be mistaken, than that they should happen."' JOHNSON. 'Why, Sir, Hume, taking the proposition simply, is right. But the Christian revelation is not proved by the miracles alone, but as connected with prophecies, and with the doctrines in confirmation of which the miracles were wrought.'

He repeated his observation, that the differences among Christians are really of no consequence. 'For instance, (said he,) if a Protestant objects to a Papist, "You worship images;" the Papist can answer, "I do not insist on *your* doing it; you may be a very good Papist without it: I do it only as a help to my devotion."' I said, the great article of Christianity is the revelation of immortality. Johnson admitted it was.

In the evening, a gentleman farmer, who was on a visit at Dr. Taylor's, attempted to dispute with Johnson in

[1] Page 89.

[2] See Plott's 'History of Staffordshire,' p. 88, and the authorities referred to by him.

favour of Mungo Campbell, who shot Alexander, Earl of Eglintoune, upon his having fallen, when retreating from his Lordship, who he believed was about to seize his gun, as he had threatened to do. He said he should have done just as Campbell did. JOHNSON. 'Whoever would do as Campbell did, deserves to be hanged; not that I could, as a juryman, have found him legally guilty of murder; but I am glad they found means to convict him.' The gentleman farmer said, 'A poor man has as much honour as a rich man; and Campbell had *that* to defend.' Johnson exclaimed, 'A poor man has no honour.'[a] The English yeoman, not dismayed, proceeded: 'Lord Eglintoune was a damned fool to run on upon Campbell, after being warned that Campbell would shoot him if he did.' Johnson, who could not bear any thing like swearing, angrily replied, 'He was *not* a *damned* fool; he only thought too well of Campbell. He did not believe Campbell would be such a *damned* scoundrel, as to do so *damned* a thing.' His emphasis on *damned*, accompanied with frowning looks, reproved his opponent's want of decorum in *his* presence.

Talking of the danger of being mortified by rejection, when making approaches to the acquaintance of the great, I observed, 'I am, however, generally for trying, "Nothing venture, nothing have."' JOHNSON. 'Very true, Sir; but I have always been more afraid of failing, than hopeful of success.' And, indeed, though he had all just respect for rank, no man ever less courted the favour of the great.

During this interview, at Ashbourne, Johnson seemed to be more uniformly social, cheerful, and alert, than I had almost ever seen him. He was prompt on great occasions and on small. Taylor, who praised every thing of his own to excess, in short, 'whose geese were all swans,' as the proverb says, expatiated on the excellence of his bull-dog, which he told us, was 'perfectly well shaped.' Johnson, after examining the animal attentively, thus expressed the vain-glory of our host:—'No, Sir, he is *not* well shaped; for there is not the quick transition from the thickness of the fore-part, to the *tenuity*—the thin part—behind,—which a bull-dog ought to have.' This *tenuity* was the only *hard word* that I had heard him use during this interview, and it will be observed, he instantly put another expression in its place.

underlined:
poor, no [H]

three exclamation points and underlined:
poor man has no honour
[1]

[a] *Shocking!* [H]

Taylor said, a small bull-dog was as good as a large one.
JOHNSON. 'No, Sir: for, in proportion to his size, he has
strength: and your argument would prove, that a good
bull-dog may be as small as a mouse.' It was amazing how
he entered with perspicuity and keenness upon every thing
that occurred in conversation. Most men, whom I know,
would no more think of discussing a question about a
bull-dog, than of attacking a bull.

I cannot allow any fragment whatever that floats in my
memory concerning the great subject of this work to be
lost. Though a small particular may appear trifling to
some, it will be relished by others; while every little spark
adds something to the general blaze: and to please the true,
candid, warm admirers of Johnson, and in any degree
increase the splendour of his reputation, I bid defiance to
the shafts of ridicule, or even of malignity. Showers of them
have been discharged at my 'Journal of a Tour to the
Hebrides;' yet it still sails unhurt along the stream of time,
and as an attendant upon Johnson,

'Pursues the triumph, and partakes the gale.'

One morning after breakfast, when the sun shone bright,
we walked out together, and 'pored' for some time with
placid indolence upon an artificial water-fall, which Dr.
Taylor had made by building a strong dyke of stone across
the river behind the garden. It was now somewhat obstructed by branches of trees and other rubbish, which had
come down the river, and settled close to it. Johnson,
partly from a desire to see it play more freely, and partly
from that inclination to activity which will animate, at
times, the most inert and sluggish mortal, took a long pole
which was lying on a bank, and pushed down several
parcels of this wreck with painful assiduity, while I stood
quietly by, wondering to behold the sage thus curiously
employed, and smiling with an humorous satisfaction each
time when he carried his point. He worked till he was quite
out of breath; and having found a large dead cat so heavy
that he could not move it after several efforts, 'Come,' said
he, (throwing down the pole,) 'you shall take it now;'
which I accordingly did, and being a fresh man, soon made
the cat tumble over the cascade. This may be laughed at

as too trifling to record; but it is a small characteristic trait in the Flemish picture which I give of my friend, and in which, therefore, I mark the most minute particulars. And let it be remembered, that 'Æsop at play' is one of the instructive apologues of antiquity.

I mentioned an old gentleman of our acquaintance whose memory was beginning to fail. JOHNSON. 'There must be a diseased mind, where there is a failure of memory at seventy. A man's head, Sir, must be morbid, if he fails so soon.' My friend, being himself now sixty-eight, might think thus: but I imagine, that *threescore and ten*, the Psalmist's period of sound human life in later ages, may have a failure, though there be no disease in the constitution.

Talking of Rochester's Poems, he said, he had given them to Mr. Steevens to castrate[1] for the edition of the Poets, to which he was to write Prefaces. Dr. Taylor (the only time I ever heard him say any thing witty)[2] observed, that 'if Rochester had been castrated himself, his exceptionable poems would not have been written.' I asked if Burnet had not given a good Life of Rochester. JOHNSON. 'We have a good *Death:* there is not much *Life.*' I asked whether Prior's Poems were to be printed entire: Johnson said, they were. I mentioned Lord Hailes's censure of Prior in his Preface to a collection of 'Sacred Poems,' by various hands, published by him at Edinburgh a great many years ago, where he mentions, 'those impure tales which will be the eternal opprobrium of their ingenious authour.' JOHNSON. 'Sir, Lord Hailes has forgot. There is nothing in Prior that will excite to lewdness. If Lord Hailes thinks there is, he must be more combustible than other people.' I instanced the tale of 'Paulo Purganti and his Wife.' JOHNSON. 'Sir, there is nothing there, but that his wife wanted to be kissed, when poor Paulo was out of pocket. No, Sir, Prior is a lady's book. No lady is ashamed to have it standing in her library.'

The hypochondriack disorder being mentioned, Dr. Johnson did not think it so common as I supposed.

marginal line:
Prefaces. Dr. . . . . if Rochester [H]

marginal line:
There is . . . tale of [H]

[1] [This was unnecessary, for it had been done in the early part of the present century, by Jacob Tonson. MALONE.]

[2] I am told, that Horace, Earl of Orford, has a collection of *Bon-Mots* by persons who never said but one.

'Dr. Taylor (said he) is the same one day as another. Burke and Reynolds are the same. Beauclerk, except in pain, is the same. I am not so myself; but this I do not mention commonly.'

I complained of a wretched changefulness, so that I could not preserve, for any long continuance, the same views of any thing. It was most comfortable to me to experience in Dr. Johnson's company, a relief from this uneasiness. His steady vigorous mind held firm before me those objects which my own feeble and tremulous imagination frequently presented in such a wavering state, that my reason could not judge well of them.

Dr. Johnson advised me to-day, to have as many books about me as I could; that I might read upon any subject upon which I had a desire for instruction at the time. 'What you read *then*, (said he,) you will remember; but if you have not a book immediately ready, and the subject moulds in your mind, it is a chance if you have again a desire to study it.' He added, 'If a man never has an eager desire for instruction, he should prescribe a task for himself. But it is better when a man reads from immediate inclination.'

He repeated a good many lines of Horace's Odes, while we were in the chaise; I remember particularly the Ode '*Eheu fugaces.*'

He said, the dispute as to the comparative excellence of Homer or Virgil[1] was inaccurate. 'We must consider (said he) whether Homer was not the greatest poet, though Virgil may have produced the finest poem.[2] Virgil was indebted to Homer for the whole invention of the structure of an epick poem, and for many of his beauties.'

He told me, that Bacon was a favourite authour with him; but he had never read his works till he was compiling

[1] I am informed by Mr. Langton, that a great many years ago he was present when this question was agitated between Dr. Johnson and Mr. Burke; and, to use Johnson's phrase, they 'talked their best;' Johnson for Homer, Burke for Virgil. It may well be supposed to have been one of the ablest and most brilliant contests that ever was exhibited. How much must we regret that it has not been preserved.

[2] [But where is the *inaccuracy*, if the admirers of Homer contend, that he was not only prior to Virgil in point of time, but superiour in excellence? J. BOSWELL.]

the English Dictionary, in which, he said, I might see Bacon
very often quoted. Mr. Seward recollects his having mentioned, that a Dictionary of the English Language might
be compiled from Bacon's writings alone, and that he had
once an intention of giving an edition of Bacon, at least of
his English works, and writing the Life of that great man.
Had he executed this intention, there can be no doubt that
he would have done it in a most masterly manner. Mallet's
Life of Bacon has no inconsiderable merit as an acute and
elegant dissertation relative to its subject; but Mallet's
mind was not comprehensive enough to embrace the vast
extent of Lord Verulam's genius and research. Dr. Warburton therefore observed, with witty justness, 'that Mallet
in his Life of Bacon had forgotten that he was a philosopher; and if he should write the Life of the Duke of
Marlborough, which he had undertaken to do, he would
probably forget that he was a General.'

marginal line:
*Warburton therefore
. . . . a General* [H]

Wishing to be satisfied what degree of truth there was in
a story which a friend of Johnson's and mine had told me
to his disadvantage, I mentioned it to him in direct terms;
and it was to this effect: that a gentleman who had lived
in great intimacy with him, shewn him much kindness,
and even relieved him from a spunging-house, having
afterwards fallen into bad circumstances, was one day,
when Johnson was at dinner with him, seized for debt, and
carried to prison; that Johnson sat still undisturbed, and
went on eating and drinking; upon which the gentleman's
sister, who was present, could not suppress her indignation:
'What, Sir, (said she,) are you so unfeeling, as not even to
offer to go to my brother in his distress; you who have been
so much obliged to him?' And that Johnson answered,
'Madam, I owe him no obligation; what he did for me
he would have done for a dog.'

Johnson assured me, that the story was absolutely false:
but like a man conscious of being in the right, and desirous
of completely vindicating himself from such a charge, he
did not arrogantly rest on a mere denial, and on his general
character, but proceeded thus:—'Sir, I was very intimate
with that gentleman, and was once relieved by him from
an arrest; but I never was present when he was arrested,
never knew that he was arrested, and I believe he never

was in difficulties after the time when he relieved me. I
oved him much; yet, in talking of his general character,
I may have said, though I do not remember that I ever
did say so, that as his generosity proceeded from no
principle, but was a part of his profusion, he would do for
a dog what he would do for a friend: but I never applied
this remark to any particular instance, and certainly not
to his kindness to me. If a profuse man, who does not value
his money, and gives a large sum to a whore, gives half as
much, or an equally large sum to relieve a friend, it cannot
be esteemed as virtue. This was all that I could say of that
gentleman; and, if said at all, it must have been said after
his death. Sir, I would have gone to the world's end to
relieve him.[a] The remark about the dog, if made by me,
was such a sally as might escape one when painting a
man highly.'

On Tuesday, September 23, Johnson was remarkably
cordial to me. It being necessary for me to return to Scotland soon, I had fixed on the next day for my setting out,
and I felt a tender concern at the thought of parting with
him. He had, at this time, frankly communicated to me
many particulars, which are inserted in this work in their
proper places; and once, when I happened to mention that
the expence of my jaunt would come to much more than I
had computed, he said, 'Why, Sir, if the expence were to
be an inconvenience, you would have reason to regret it;
but, if you have had the money to spend, I know not that
you could have purchased as much pleasure with it in
any other way.'

During this interview at Ashbourne, Johnson and I
frequently talked with wonderful pleasure of mere trifles
which had occurred in our tour to the Hebrides; for it had
left a most agreeable and lasting impression upon his mind.

He found fault with me for using the phrase to *make*
money. 'Don't you see (said he) the impropriety of it? To
make money is to *coin* it: you should say *get* money.' The
phrase, however, is, I think, pretty current. But Johnson
was at all times jealous of infractions upon the genuine
English language, and prompt to repress colloquial bar-
barisms; such as *pledging myself*, for *undertaking; line*, for
department, or *branch*, as, the *civil line*, the *banking line*. He

---

Marginal notes:

underlined:
generosity, principle [H]
queried, exclama-
tion point, and mar-
ginal line:
profusion, he . . . any
particular [H]

[a] *I wonder who the*
Man was. [H & I]

was particularly indignant against the almost universal use of the word *idea* in the sense of *notion*, or *opinion*, when it is clear that *idea* can only signify something of which an image can be formed in the mind. We may have an *idea* or *image* of a mountain, a tree, a building; but we cannot surely have an *idea* or *image* of an *argument* or *proposition*. Yet we hear the sages of the law 'delivering their *ideas* upon the question under consideration;' and the first speakers in parliament 'entirely coinciding in the *idea* which has been ably stated by an honourable member;'—or 'reprobating an *idea* unconstitutional, and fraught with the most dangerous consequences to a great and free country.'[a] Johnson called this 'modern cant.'[b]

I perceived that he pronounced the word *heard*, as if spelt with a double *e*, *heerd*, instead of sounding it *herd*, as is most usually done.[1] He said, his reason was, that if it were pronounced *herd*, there would be a single exception from the English pronunciation of the syllable *ear*, and he thought it better not to have that exception.

He praised Grainger's 'Ode on Solitude,' in Dodsley's collection, and repeated, with great energy, the exordium:

'O Solitude, romantick maid,
Whether by nodding towers you tread;
Or haunt the desart's trackless gloom,
Or hover o'er the yawning tomb;
Or climb the Andes' clifted side,
Or by the Nile's coy source abide;
Or, starting from your half-year's sleep,
From Hecla view the thawing deep;
Or, at the purple dawn of day,
Tadnor's marble waste survey;'[c]

observing, 'This, Sir, is very noble.'

In the evening our gentleman-farmer, and two others, entertained themselves and the company with a great number of tunes on the fiddle. Johnson desired to have 'Let ambition fire thy mind,' played over again, and appeared to give a patient attention to it; though he owned to me that he was very insensible to the power of musick.

[a] *so they do still; but not so much since a foolish Character in some foolish Drama, is made to say nothing but* —'I've an Idea.' [H]

[b] *he called it very properly* [H & I]

[c] *Or, at etc. partly struck out* [H & I]

Or in yon Roofless Cloyster stray: quote it right [H]

quote it right Or Tadmor's & or in yon roofless Cloyster stray [I]

[d] *I have hard it so pronounced since the reign of Queen Ann, 'Tis a provincial Pronunciation, but I forget the Province* [H]

& is so now by Caernarvonshire Gentlemen & Ladies—I guess not why; but I have hard them do it [I]

marginal line: *to it . . . that it* [H]

[1] [In the age of Queen Elizabeth, this word was frequently written, as doubtless it was pronounced, *hard*.[d] MALONE.]

I told him that it affected me to such a degree, as often to agitate my nerves painfully, producing in my mind alternate sensations of pathetic dejection, so that I was ready to shed tears; and of daring resolution, so that I was inclined to rush into the thickest part of the battle. 'Sir (said he,) I should never hear it, if it made me such a fool.'

Much of the effect of musick, I am satisfied, is owing to the association of ideas. That air, which instantly and irresistibly excites in the Swiss, when in a foreign land, the *maladie du pais*, has, I am told, no intrinsick power of sound. And I know from my own experience, that Scotch reels, though brisk, make me melancholy, because I used to hear them in my early years, at a time when Mr. Pitt called for soldiers 'from the mountains of the north,' and numbers of brave Highlanders were going abroad, never to return. Whereas the airs in 'The Beggar's Opera,' many of which are very soft, never fail to render me gay, because they are associated with the warm sensations and high spirits of London.—This evening, while some of the tunes of ordinary composition were played with no great skill, my frame was agitated, and I was conscious of a generous attachment to Dr. Johnson, as my preceptor and friend, mixed with an affectionate regret that he was an old man, whom I should probably lose in a short time. I thought I could defend him at the point of my sword.[a] My reverence and affection for him were in full glow. I said to him, 'My dear Sir, we must meet every year, if you don't quarrel with me.' JOHNSON. 'Nay, Sir, you are more likely to quarrel with me, than I with you. My regard for you is greater almost than I have words to express; but I do not chuse to be always repeating it; write it down in the first leaf of your pocket-book, and never doubt of it again.'

I talked to him of misery being 'the doom of man,' in this life, as displayed in his 'Vanity of Human Wishes.' Yet I observed that things were done upon the supposition of happiness; grand houses were built, fine gardens were made, splendid places of publick amusement were contrived, and crowded with company. JOHNSON. 'Alas, Sir, these are only struggles for happiness. When I first entered Ranelagh, it gave an expansion and gay sensation to my mind, such as I never experienced any where else. But, as

[a] *very comical* [H]

Xerxes wept when he viewed his immense army, and considered that not one of that great multitude would be alive a hundred years afterwards, so it went to my heart to consider that there was not one in all that brilliant circle, that was not afraid to go home and think; but that the thoughts of each individual there, would be distressing when alone.' This reflection was experimentally just. The feeling of languor,[1] which succeeds the animation of gaiety, is itself a very severe pain; and when the mind is then vacant, a thousand disappointments and vexations rush in and excruciate. Will not many even of my fairest readers allow this to be true?[a]

[a] Too true [I]

I suggested, that being in love, and flattered with hopes of success; or having some favourite scheme in view for the next day, might prevent that wretchedness of which we had been talking. JOHNSON. 'Why, Sir, it may sometimes be so as you suppose; but my conclusion is in general but too true.'

While Johnson and I stood in calm conference by ourselves in Dr. Taylor's garden, at a pretty late hour in a serene autumn night, looking up to the heavens, I directed the discourse to the subject of a future state. My friend was in a placid and most benignant frame of mind. 'Sir, (said he,) I do not imagine that all things will be made clear to us immediately after death, but that the ways of Providence will be explained to us very gradually.' I ventured to ask him whether, although the words of some texts of Scripture seemed strong in support of the dreadful doctrine of an eternity of punishment, we might not hope that the denunciation was figurative, and would not literally be executed. JOHNSON. 'Sir, you are to consider the intention of punishment in a future state. We have no reason to be sure that we shall then be no longer liable to offend against GOD.[b] We do not know that even the angels are quite in a state of security; nay, we know that some of them

[b] yet Melancthon said one Reason which reconciled him to Death was—That he should sin no more. [H]

[1] Pope mentions,
   'Stretch'd on the rack of a too easy chair.'
But I recollect a couplet quite apposite to my subject in 'Virtue, an Ethick Epistle,' a beautiful and instructive poem, by an anonymous writer, in 1758; who, treating of pleasure in excess, says,
   'Till languor, suffering on the rack of bliss,
   Confess that man was never made for this.'

have fallen. It may therefore, perhaps, be necessary, in order to preserve both men and angels in a state of rectitude, that they should have continually before them the punishment of those who have deviated from it; but we may hope that by some other means a fall from rectitude may be prevented. Some of the texts of Scripture upon this subject, are, as you observe, indeed strong; but they may admit of a mitigated interpretation.' He talked to me upon this awful and delicate question in a gentle tone, and as if afraid to be decisive.[a]

[a] *I hope so, Who* can *speak* decisively? [H]

I hope so. [I]

After supper I accompanied him to his apartment, and at my request he dictated to me an argument in favour of the negro who was then claiming his liberty, in an action in the Court of Session in Scotland. He had always been very zealous against slavery in every form, in which I with all deference thought that he discovered 'a zeal without knowledge.' Upon one occasion, when in company with some very grave men at Oxford, his toast was, 'Here's to the next insurrection of the negroes in the West Indies.' His violent prejudice against our West Indian and American settlers appeared whenever there was an opportunity. Towards the conclusion of his 'Taxation no Tyranny,' he says, 'how is it that we hear the loudest *yelps* for liberty among the drivers of negroes?' and in his conversation with Mr. Wilkes[1] he asked, 'Where did Beckford and Trecothick learn English?' That Trecothick could both speak and write good English is well known. I myself was favoured with his correspondence concerning the brave Corsicans. And that Beckford could speak it with a spirit of honest resolution even to his Majesty, as his 'faithful Lord-Mayor of London,' is commemorated by the noble monument erected to him in Guildhall.[b]

[b] *Beckford spoke miserable English — but any Language that insulted any King, was welcome to the City of London* [I]

The argument dictated by Dr. Johnson was as follows:

'It must be agreed that in most ages many countries have had part of their inhabitants in a state of slavery; yet it may be doubted whether slavery can ever be supposed the natural condition of man. It is impossible not to conceive that men in their original state were equal; and very difficult to imagine how one would be subjected to another but by violent compulsion. An individual may,

[1] See page 316 of this volume.

indeed, forfeit his liberty by a crime; but he cannot by that crime forfeit the liberty of his children. What is true of a criminal seems true likewise of a captive. A man may accept life from a conquering enemy on condition of perpetual servitude; but it is very doubtful whether he can entail that servitude on his descendants; for no man can stipulate without commission for another. The condition which he himself accepts, his son or grandson perhaps would have rejected. If we should admit, what perhaps may with more reason be denied, that there are certain relations between man and man which may make slavery necessary and just, yet it can never be proved that he who is now suing for his freedom ever stood in any of those relations. He is certainly subject by no law, but that of violence, to his present master; who pretends no claim to his obedience, but that he bought him from a merchant of slaves, whose right to sell him never was examined. It is said that according to the constitutions of Jamaica he was legally enslaved; these constitutions are merely positive; and apparently injurious to the rights of mankind, because whoever is exposed to sale is condemned to slavery without appeal; by whatever fraud or violence he might have been originally brought into the merchant's power. In our own time Princes have been sold, by wretches to whose care they were entrusted, that they might have an European education; but when once they were brought to a market in the plantations, little would avail either their dignity or their wrongs. The laws of Jamaica afford a Negro no redress. His colour is considered as a sufficient testimony against him. It is to be lamented that moral right should ever give way to political convenience. But if temptations of interest are sometimes too strong for human virtue, let us at least retain a virtue where there is no temptation to quit it. In the present case there is apparent right on one side, and no convenience on the other. Inhabitants of this island can neither gain riches nor power by taking away the liberty of any part of the human species. The sum of the argument is this:—No man is by nature the property of another: The defendant is, therefore, by nature free: The rights of nature must be some way forfeited before they can be justly taken away; That the defendant has by

I have read, conversed, and thought much upon the subject, and would recommend to all who are capable of conviction, an excellent Tract by my learned and ingenious friend John Ranby, Esq. entitled 'Doubts on the Abolition of the Slave Trade.' To Mr. Ranby's 'Doubts,' I will apply Lord Chancellor Hardwicke's expression in praise of a Scotch Law Book, called 'Dirleton's Doubts;' 'HIS *Doubts*, (said his Lordship,) are better than most people's *Certainties*.'

When I said now to Johnson, that I was afraid I kept him too late up, 'No, Sir, (said he,) I don't care though I sit all night with you.' This was an animated speech from a man in his sixty-ninth year.[a]

[a] *not from Johnson, who delighted to sit up all Night, & lie a Bed all Day.* [H]

Had I been as attentive not to displease him as I ought to have been, I know not but this vigil might have been fulfilled; but I unluckily entered upon the controversy concerning the right of Great-Britain to tax America, and attempted to argue in favour of our fellow-subjects on the other side of the Atlantick. I insisted that America might be very well governed, and made to yield sufficient revenue by the means of *influence*, as exemplified in Ireland, while the people might be pleased with the imagination of their participating of the British constitution, by having a body of representatives, without whose consent money could not be exacted from them. Johnson could not bear my thus opposing his avowed opinion, which he had exerted himself with an extreme degree of heat to enforce; and the violent agitation into which he was thrown, while answering, or rather reprimanding me, alarmed me so, that I heartily repented of my having unthinkingly introduced the subject. I myself, however, grew warm, and the change was great, from the calm state of philosophical discussion in which we had a little before been pleasingly employed.

I talked of the corruption of the British Parliament, in which I alledged that any question, however unreasonable or unjust, might be carried by a venal majority; and I spoke with high admiration of the Roman Senate, as if composed of men sincerely desirous to resolve what they should think best for their country. My friend would allow no such character to the Roman Senate; and he maintained that the British Parliament was not corrupt, and

that there was no occasion to corrupt its members; asserting
that there was hardly ever any question of great importance
before Parliament, any question in which a man might
not very well vote either upon one side or the other. He
said there had been none in his time except that respecting
America.

We were fatigued by the contest, which was produced by
my want of caution; and he was not then in the humour to
slide into easy and cheerful talk. It therefore so happened,
that we were after an hour or two very willing to separate
and go to bed.

On Wednesday, September 24, I went into Dr. Johnson's room before he got up, and finding that the storm of
the preceding night was quite laid, I sat down upon his
bed-side, and he talked with as much readiness and good
humour as ever. He recommended to me to plant a considerable part of a large moorish farm which I had purchased, and he made several calculations of the expence
and profit; for he delighted in exercising his mind on the
science of numbers. He pressed upon me the importance
of planting at the first in a very sufficient manner, quoting
the saying '*In bello non licet bis errare:*' and adding, 'this
is equally true in planting.'

I spoke with gratitude of Dr. Taylor's hospitality; and
as evidence that it was not on account of his good table
alone that Johnson visited him often, I mentioned a little
anecdote which had escaped my friend's recollection, and
at hearing which repeated, he smiled. One evening, when
I was sitting with him, Frank delivered this message; 'Sir,
Dr. Taylor sends his compliments to you, and begs you
will dine with him to-morrow. He has got a hare.'—'My
compliments (said Johnson) and I'll dine with him—hare
or rabbit.'

After breakfast I departed, and pursued my journey
northwards. I took my post-chaise from the Green Man,
a very good inn at Ashbourne, the mistress of which, a
mighty civil gentlewoman, courtseying very low, presented
me with an engraving of the sign of her house; to which
she had subjoined, in her own hand-writing, an address in
such singular simplicity of style, that I have preserved it
pasted upon one of the boards of my original Journal at

this time, and shall here insert it for the amusement of my readers:

'*M. KILLINGLEY*'s *duty waits upon Mr.* Boswell, *is exceedingly obliged to him for this favour; whenever he comes this way, hopes for a continuance of the same. Would Mr.* Boswell *name the house to his extensive acquaintance, it would be a singular favour conferr'd on one who has it not in her power to make any other return but her most grateful thanks, and sincerest prayers for his happiness in time, and in a blessed eternity.*

'*Tuesday morn.*'

From this meeting at Ashbourne I derived a considerable accession to my Johnsonian store. I communicated my original Journal to Sir William Forbes, in whom I have always placed deserved confidence; and what he wrote to me concerning it is so much to my credit as the biographer of Johnson, that my readers will, I hope, grant me their indulgence for here inserting it: 'It is not once or twice going over it (says Sir William,) that will satisfy me; for I find in it a high degree of instruction as well as entertainment; and I derive more benefit from Dr. Johnson's admirable discussions than I should be able to draw from his personal conversation; for, I suppose there is not a man in the world to whom he discloses his sentiments so freely as to yourself.'

I cannot omit a curious circumstance which occurred at Edensor-inn, close by Chatsworth, to survey the magnificence of which I had gone a considerable way out of my road to Scotland. The inn was then kept by a very jolly landlord, whose name, I think, was Malton. He happened to mention that 'the celebrated Dr. Johnson had been in his house.'[a] I enquired *who* this Dr. Johnson was, that I might hear my host's notion of him. 'Sir, (said he,) Johnson, the great writer; *Oddity*, as they call him. He's the greatest writer in England; he writes for the ministry; he has a correspondence abroad, and lets them know what's going on.'

My friend, who had a thorough dependance upon the authenticity of my relation without any *embellishment*, as *falsehood* or *fiction* is too gently called, laughed a good deal at this representation of himself.

[a] *Ay marry! he might very well remember it* [1]

'MR. BOSWELL TO DR. JOHNSON

'MY DEAR SIR,   Edinburgh, Sept. 29, 1777

'BY the first post I inform you of my safe arrival at my own house, and that I had the comfort of finding my wife and children all in good health.

'When I look back upon our late interview, it appears to me to have answered expectation better than almost any scheme of happiness that I ever put in execution. My Journal is stored with wisdom and wit; and my memory is filled with the recollection of lively and affectionate feelings, which now, I think, yield me more satisfaction than at the time when they were first excited. I have experienced this upon other occasions. I shall be obliged to you if you will explain it to me; for it seems wonderful that pleasure should be more vivid at a distance than when near. I wish you may find yourself in a humour to do me this favour; but I flatter myself with no strong hope of it; for I have observed, that unless upon very serious occasions, your letters to me are not *answers* to those which I write.

[I then expressed much uneasiness that I had mentioned to him the name of the gentleman[a] who had told me the story so much to his disadvantage, the truth of which he had completely refuted; for that my having done so might be interpreted as a breach of confidence, and offend one whose society I valued:—therefore earnestly requesting that no notice might be taken of it to any body, till I should be in London, and have an opportunity to talk it over with the gentleman.]

[a] *who was he?* [I]

'TO JAMES BOSWELL, ESQ.

'DEAR SIR,

'You will wonder, or you have wondered, why no letter has come from me. What you wrote at your return, had in it such a strain of cowardly caution as gave me no pleasure. I could not well do what you wished; I had no need to vex you with a refusal. I have seen Mr.————,[b] and as to him have set all right, without any inconvenience, so far as I know, to you. Mrs. Thrale had forgot the story.[c] You may now be at ease.

[b] *who?* [I]

[c] *I believe I never heard it— it seems new to me now   1808.* [I]

I forgot it again; & cannot now guess the Man's Name H.L.P. 1817. [H]

'And at ease I certainly wish you, for the kindness that you showed in coming so long a journey to see me. It was pity to keep you so long in pain, but, upon reviewing the matter, I do not see what I could have done better than I did.

'I hope you found at your return my dear enemy and all her little people quite well, and had no reason to repent of your journey. I think on it with great gratitude.

'I was not well when you left me at the Doctor's, and I grew worse; yet I staid on, and at Lichfield was very ill. Travelling, however, did not make me worse; and when I came to London, I complied with a summons to go to Brighthelmstone, where I saw[a] Beauclerk, and staid three days.

'Our CLUB has recommenced last Friday, but I was not there. Langton has another wench.[1] Mrs. Thrale is in hopes of a young brewer. They got by their trade last year a very large sum, and their expences are proportionate.

'Mrs. Williams's health is very bad. And I have had for some time a very difficult and laborious respiration; but I am better by purges, abstinence, and other methods. I am yet, however, much behind-hand in my health and rest.

'Dr. Blair's sermons are now universally commended; but let him think that I had the honour of first finding and first praising his excellencies. I did not stay to add my voice to that of the publick.

'My dear Friend, let me thank you once more for your visit; you did me great honour, and I hope met with nothing that displeased you. I staid long at Ashbourne, not much pleased, yet awkward at departing. I then went to Lichfield, where I found my friend at Stow-hill[2] very dangerously diseased. Such is life. Let us try to pass it well, whatever it be, for there is surely something beyond it.[b]

'Well, now, I hope all is well, write as soon as you can to, dear Sir,

'Your affectionate servant,

'London, Nov. 25, 1777.'   'SAM. JOHNSON'

'TO DR. SAMUEL JOHNSON

'MY DEAR SIR,   'Edinburgh, Nov. 29, 1777

'THIS day's post has at length relieved me from much uneasiness, by bringing me a letter from you. I was, indeed,

---

[a] *with* written in after *was* [printer's error for *saw*] [I]

[b] *Yes   truly — & something better than the best of us can dream of deserving—or wretched will be our Lot. Christ died for us however, & let that be our Hope: one Drop of such Blood would surely have saved us, & He gave it all.* [H]

---

[1] A daughter born to him.   [2] Mrs. Aston.

doubly uneasy;—on my own account and yours. I was very anxious to be secured against any bad consequences from my imprudence in mentioning the gentleman's name who had told me a story to your disadvantage; and as I could hardly suppose it possible, that you would delay so long to make me easy, unless you were ill, I was not a little apprehensive about you. You must not be offended when I venture to tell you that you appear to me to have been too rigid upon this occasion. The "*cowardly caution which gave you no pleasure*," was suggested to me by a friend here, to whom I mentioned the strange story, and the detection of its falsity, as an instance how one may be deceived by what is apparently very good authority. But, as I am still persuaded, that as I might have obtained the truth, without mentioning the gentleman's name, it was wrong in me to do it, I cannot see that you are just in blaming my caution. But if you were ever so just in your disapprobation, might you not have dealt more tenderly with me?

'I went to Auchinleck about the middle of October, and passed some time with my father very comfortably.

* * * * * *

'I am engaged in a criminal prosecution against a country schoolmaster, for indecent behaviour to his female scholars. There is no statute against such abominable conduct; but it is punishable at common law. I shall be obliged to you for your assistance in this extraordinary trial. I ever am, my dear Sir,

'Your faithful humble servant,

'JAMES BOSWELL'

About this time I wrote to Johnson, giving him an account of the decision of the *Negro cause*, by the Court of Session, which by those who hold even the mildest and best regulated slavery in abomination, (of which number I do not hesitate to declare that I am none,) should be remembered with high respect, and to the credit of Scotland; for it went upon a much broader ground than the case of *Somerset*, which was decided in England;[1] being truly the general question, whether a perpetual obligation

[1] See State Trials, Vol. XI. p. 339, and Mr. Hargrave's argument.

of service to one master in any mode should be sanctified by the law of a free country. A negro, then called *Joseph Knight*, a native of Africa, having been brought to Jamaica in the usual course of the slave trade, and purchased by a Scotch gentleman in that island, had attended his master to Scotland, where it was officiously suggested to him that he would be found entitled to his liberty without any limitation. He accordingly brought his action, in the course of which the advocates on both sides did themselves great honour. Mr. Maclaurin has had the praise of Johnson, for his argument[1] in favour of the negro, and Mr. Macconochie distinguished himself on the same side, by his ingenuity and extraordinary research. Mr. Cullen, on the part of the master, discovered good information and sound reasoning; in which he was well supported by Mr. James Ferguson, remarkable for a manly understanding, and a knowledge both of books and of the world. But I cannot too highly praise the speech which Mr. Henry Dundas generously contributed to the cause of the sooty stranger. Mr. Dundas's Scottish accent, which has been so often in vain obtruded as an objection to his powerful abilities in Parliament, was no disadvantage to him in his own country. And I do declare, that upon this memorable question he impressed me, and I believe all his audience, with such feelings as were produced by some of the most eminent orations of antiquity. This testimony I liberally give to the excellence of an old friend, with whom it has been my lot to differ very widely upon many political topicks: yet I persuade myself without malice. A great majority of the Lords of Session decided for the negro. But four of their number, the Lord President, Lord Elliock, Lord Monboddo, and Lord Covington, resolutely maintained the lawfulness of a *status*, which has been acknowledged in all ages and countries, and that when freedom flourished, as in old Greece and Rome.

[1] The motto to it was happily chosen:

'*Quamvis ille niger, quamvis tu candidus esses.*'[a]

I cannot avoid mentioning a circumstance no less strange than true, that a brother Advocate in considerable practice, but of whom it certainly cannot be said, *Ingenuas didicit fideliter artes*, asked Mr. Maclaurin, with a face of flippant assurance, 'Are these words your own?'[b]

[a] *very good* [H]

underlined:
these words your own [I]

[b] *does he mean that the Man could not read Virgil's Bucolics? too bad! too bad!* [I]

'TO JAMES BOSWELL, ESQ.

'DEAR SIR,

'THIS is the time of the year in which all express their good wishes to their friends, and I send mine to you and your family. May your lives be long, happy, and good. I have been much out of order, but, I hope, do not grow worse.

'The crime of the schoolmaster whom you are engaged to prosecute is very great, and may be suspected to be too common. In our law it would be a breach of the peace and a misdemeanour: that is, a kind of indefinite crime, not capital, but punishable at the discretion of the Court. You cannot want matter: all that needs to be said will easily occur.

'Mr. Shaw, the authour of the Gaelick Grammar, desires me to make a request for him to Lord Eglintoune, that he may be appointed Chaplain to one of the new-raised regiments.

'All our friends are as they were; little has happened to them of either good or bad. Mrs. Thrale ran a great black hair-dressing pin into her eye;[a] but by great evacuation she kept it from inflaming, and it is almost well. Miss Reynolds has been out of order, but is better. Mrs. Williams is in a very poor state of health.

'If I should write on, I should, perhaps, write only complaints, and therefore I will content myself with telling you, that I love to think on you, and to hear from you; and that I am, dear Sir,

                                    'Yours faithfully,
'December 27, 1777.'   'SAM JOHNSON'

[a] *So She did.* [H]
so She did Poor silly Soul! [J]

'TO DR. SAMUEL JOHNSON

'DEAR SIR,   'Edinburgh, Jan. 8, 1778

'Your congratulations upon a new year are mixed with complaint: mine must be so too. My wife has for some time been very ill, having been confined to the house these three months by a severe cold, attended with alarming symptoms.

[Here I gave particular account of the distress which the person, upon every account most dear to me, suffered;

and of the dismal state of apprehension in which I now was: adding that I never stood more in need of his consoling philosophy.]

'Did you ever look at a book written by Wilson, a Scotchman, under the Latin name of *Volusenus*, according to the custom of literary men at a certain period? It is entitled "*De Animi Tranquillitate.*" I earnestly desire tranquillity. *Bona res quies;* but I fear I shall never attain it: for, when unoccupied, I grow gloomy, and occupation agitates me to feverishness.

* * ' * * * *

'I am, dear Sir,

'Your most affectionate humble servant,

'JAMES BOSWELL'

'TO JAMES BOSWELL, ESQ.

'DEAR SIR,

'To a letter so interesting as your last, it is proper to return some answer, however little I may be disposed to write.

'Your alarm at your lady's illness was reasonable, and not disproportionate to the appearance of the disorder. I hope your physical friend's conjecture is now verified, and all fear of a consumption at an end: a little care and exercise will then restore her. London is a good air for ladies; and if you bring her hither, I will do for her what she did for me—I will retire from my apartments for her accommodation. Behave kindly to her, and keep her cheerful.

'You always seem to call for tenderness. Know then, that in the first month of the present year I very highly esteem and very cordially love you. I hope to tell you this at the beginning of every year as long as we live; and why should we trouble ourselves to tell or hear it oftener?

'Tell Veronica, Euphemia, and Alexander, that I wish them, as well as their parents, many happy years.

'You have ended the negro's cause much to my mind. Lord Auchinleck and dear Lord Hailes were on the side of liberty. Lord Hailes's name reproaches me; but if he saw my languid neglect of my own affairs, he would rather pity than resent my neglect of his. I hope to mend, *ut et mihi vivam et amicis.* I am, dear Sir,

> 'Yours affectionately,

'Jan. 24, 1778.'   'SAM. JOHNSON'

'My service to my fellow-traveller, Joseph.'

Johnson maintained a long and intimate friendship with Mr. Welch, who succeeded the celebrated Henry Fielding as one of his Majesty's Justices of the Peace for Westminster; kept a regular office for the police of that great district; and discharged his important trust, for many years, faithfully and ably. Johnson, who had an eager and unceasing curiosity to know human life in all its variety, told me, that he attended Mr. Welch in his office for a whole winter, to hear the examinations of the culprits; but that he found an almost uniform terror of misfortune, wretchedness, and profligacy. Mr. Welch's health being impaired, he was advised to try the effect of a warm climate; and Johnson, by his interest with Mr. Chamier, procured him leave of absence to go to Italy, and a promise that the pension or salary of two hundred pounds a year, which Government allowed him, should not be discontinued. Mr. Welch accordingly went abroad, accompanied by his daughter Anne, a young lady of uncommon talents and literature.

marginal line: an almost . . . being impaired [H]

'TO SAUNDERS WELCH, ESQ. AT THE ENGLISH COFFEE-HOUSE, ROME

'DEAR SIR,

'To have suffered one of my best and dearest friends to pass almost two years in foreign countries without a letter, has a very shameful appearance of inattention. But the truth is, that there was no particular time in which I had anything particular to say; and general expressions of good will, I hope, our long friendship is grown too solid to want.

'Of public affairs you have information from the newspapers, wherever you go, for the English keep no secret; and of other things, Mrs. Nollekens informs you. My intelligence could therefore be of no use; and Miss Nancy's letters made it unnecessary to write to you for information: I was likewise for some time out of humour, to find that motion, and nearer approaches to the sun, did not restore your health so fast as I expected. Of your health, the accounts have lately been more pleasing; and I have the gratification of imagining to myself a length of years which I hope you have gained, and of which the enjoyment will be improved by a vast accession of images and observations which your journeys and various residence have enabled you to make and accumulate. You have travelled with this felicity, almost peculiar to yourself, that your companion is not to part from you at your journey's end; but you are to live on together, to help each other's recollections, and to supply each other's omissions. The world has few greater pleasures than that which two friends enjoy, in tracing back, at some distant time, those transactions and events through which they have passed together. One of the old man's miseries is, that he cannot easily find a companion able to partake with him of the past. You and your fellow-traveller have this comfort in store, that your conversation will be not easily exhausted; one will always be glad to say what the other will always be willing to hear.

'That you may enjoy this pleasure long, your health must have your constant attention. I suppose you propose to return this year. There is no need of haste: do not come hither before the height of summer, that you may fall gradually into the inconveniences of your native clime. July seems to be the proper month. August and September will prepare you for the winter. After having travelled so far to find health, you must take care not to lose it at home; and I hope a little care will effectually preserve it.

'Miss Nancy has doubtless kept a constant and copious journal. She must not expect to be welcome when she returns, without a great mass of information. Let her review her journal often, and set down what she finds herself to have omitted, that she may trust to memory as little as possible, for memory is soon confused by a quick succession of things:[a] and she will grow every day less confident of the truth of her own narratives, unless she can recur to some written memorials. If she has satisfied herself

queried:
is soon confused etc. [H]
[a] *how true that is!* [H]

has been in better health these three weeks than for some years past. I believe I have evaded till I could send you a copy of Lord Hailes's opinion on the negro's cause, which he wishes you to read, and correct any errours that there may be in the language; for, (says he,) "we live in a critical though not a learned age; and I seek to screen myself under the shield of Ajax." I communicated to him your apology for keeping the sheets of his "Annals" so long. He says, "I am sorry to see that Dr. Johnson is in a state of languor. Why should a sober Christian, neither an enthusiast nor a fanatick, be very merry or very sad?" I envy his Lordship's comfortable constitution; but well do I know that languor and dejection will afflict the best, however excellent their principles. I am in possession of Lord Hailes's opinion in his own hand-writing, and have had it for some time. My excuse then for procrastination must be, that I wanted to have it copied; and I have now put that off so long, that it will be better to bring it with me than send it, as I shall probably get you to look at it sooner, when I solicit you in person.

'My wife, who is, I thank GOD, a good deal better, is much obliged to you for your very polite and courteous offer of your apartment: but, if she goes to London, it will be best for her to have lodgings in the more airy vicinity of Hyde-Park. I, however, doubt much if I shall be able to prevail with her to accompany me to the metropolis; for she is so different from you and me, that she dislikes travelling; and she is so anxious about her children, that she thinks she should be unhappy if at a distance from them. She therefore wishes rather to go to some country place in Scotland, where she can have them with her.

'I purpose being in London about the 20th of next month, as I think it creditable to appear in the House of Lords as one of Douglas's Counsel, in the great and last competition between Duke Hamilton and him.

* * * * * *

'I am sorry poor Mrs. Williams is so ill: though her temper is unpleasant, she has always been polite and obliging to me. I wish many happy years to good

Mr. Levett, who I suppose holds his usual place at your breakfast-table.[1]

'I ever am, my dear Sir,
'Your affectionate humble servant,
'JAMES BOSWELL'

TO THE SAME

'MY DEAR SIR,   'Edinburgh, Feb. 28, 1778

'YOU are at present busy amongst the English poets, preparing, for the public instruction and entertainment, Prefaces, biographical and critical. It will not, therefore, be out of season to appeal to you for the decision of a controversy which has arisen between a lady and me concerning a passage in Parnell. That poet tells us, that his Hermit quitted his cell

"———— to know the world by sight,
To find if *books* or *swains* report it right;
(For yet by *swains alone* the world he knew,
Whose feet came wand'ring o'er the nightly dew.)"

I maintain, that there is an inconsistency here; for as the Hermit's notions of the world were formed from the reports both of *books* and *swains*, he could not justly be said to know by *swains alone.*[a] Be pleased to judge between us, and let us have your reasons.[2]

[a] *it is* Irish [I]

'What do you say to "*Taxation no Tyranny,*" now, after Lord North's declaration, or confession, or whatever else his conciliatory speech should be called? I never differed from you in Politicks but upon two points,—the Middlesex Election, and the Taxation of the Americans by the British *Houses of Representatives.* There is a *charm* in the word *Parliament,* so I avoid it. As I am a steady and a warm Tory,

[1] Dr. Percy, the Bishop of Dromore, humourously observed, that Levett used to breakfast on the crust of a roll, which Johnson, after tearing out the crumb for himself, threw to his humble friend.[b]

underlined:
threw to [H]

[b] *Johnson would not have liked to hear this of himself—but I feel as if I remembered some thing of the sort. 1819.* [H]

[Perhaps the word *threw* is here too strong. Dr. Johnson never treated Levett with contempt; it is clear indeed from various circumstances, that he had great kindness for him. I have often seen Johnson at breakfast, accompanied, or rather attended, by Levett, who had always the management of the tea-kettle. MALONE.]

[2] [See this subject discussed in a subsequent page, under May 3, 1779. MALONE.]

I regret that the King does not see it to be better for him to receive constitutional supplies from his American subjects by the voice of their own assemblies, where his Royal Person is represented, than through the medium of his British subjects. I am persuaded that the power of the Crown, which I wish to increase, would be greater when in contact with all its dominions, than if "the rays of regal bounty"[1] were to "shine" upon America, through that dense and troubled body, a modern British Parliament. But, enough of this subject; for your angry voice at Ashbourne upon it, still sounds aweful "in my mind's *ears.*"

'I ever am, my dear Sir,
'Your most affectionate humble servant,
'JAMES BOSWELL'

TO THE SAME

'MY DEAR SIR,   'Edinburgh, March 12, 1778

'THE alarm of your late illness distressed me but a few hours; for on the evening of the day that it reached me, I found it contradicted in "The London Chronicle," which I could depend upon as authentick concerning you, Mr. Strahan being the printer of it. I did not see the paper in which "the approaching extinction of a bright luminary" was announced. Sir William Forbes told me of it; and he says he saw me so uneasy, that he did not give me the report in such strong terms as he read it. He afterwards sent me a letter from Mr. Langton to him, which relieved me much. I am, however, not quite easy, as I have not heard from you; and now I shall not have that comfort before I see you, for I set out for London to-morrow before the post comes in. I hope to be with you on Wednesday morning; and I ever am, with the highest veneration,

'My dear Sir, your most obliged,
'Faithful, and affectionate humble servant,
'JAMES BOSWELL'

---

[1] Alluding to a line in his 'Vanity of Human Wishes,' describing Cardinal Wolsey in his state of elevation:
'Through him the rays of regal bounty shine.'

On Wednesday, March 18, I arrived in London, and was informed by good Mr. Francis, that his master was better, and was gone to Mr. Thrale's at Streatham, to which place I wrote to him, begging to know when he would be in town. He was not expected for some time; but next day having called on Dr. Taylor, in Dean's-yard, Westminster, I found him there, and was told he had come to town for a few hours. He met me with his usual kindness, but instantly returned to the writing of something on which he was employed when I came in, and on which he seemed much intent. Finding him thus engaged, I made my visit very short, and had no more of his conversation, except his expressing a serious regret that a friend of ours[a] was living at too much expence, considering how poor an appearance he made: 'If (said he) a man has splendour from his expence, if he spends his money in pride or in pleasure, he[b] has value: but if he lets others spend it for him, which is most commonly the case, he has no advantage from it.'

On Friday, March 20, I found him at his own house, sitting with Mrs. Williams, and was informed that the room formerly allotted to me was now appropriated to a charitable purpose; Mrs. Desmoulins,[1] and I think her daughter, and a Miss Carmichael,[c] being all lodged in it. Such was his humanity, and such his generosity, that Mrs. Desmoulins herself told me, he allowed her half-a-guinea a week. Let it be remembered, that this was above a twelfth part of his pension.

His liberality, indeed, was at all periods of his life very remarkable. Mr. Howard, of Lichfield, at whose father's house Johnson had in his early years been kindly received, told me, that when he was a boy at the Charter-house, his father wrote to him to go and pay a visit to Mr. Samuel Johnson, which he accordingly did, and found him in an upper room, of poor appearance. Johnson received him with much courteousness, and talked a great deal to him, as to a school-boy, of the course of his education, and other particulars. When he afterwards came to know and understand the high character of this great man, he recollected his condescension with wonder. He added, that when he

[a] *meaning Langton* [H]

[b] *was that Langton?* [I]

underlined:
Miss Carmichael [H & I]
[c] *That was Poll.* [H]
Oh—That was Poll: I had forgotten who Poll was. [I]

[1] Daughter of Dr. Swinfen, Johnson's godfather, and widow of Mr. Desmoulins, a writing-master.

was going away, Mr. Johnson presented him with half-a-guinea; and this, said Mr. Howard, was at a time when he probably had not another.

We retired from Mrs. Williams to another room. Tom Davies soon after joined us. He had now unfortunately failed in his circumstances, and was much indebted to Dr. Johnson's kindness for obtaining for him many alleviations of his distress. After he went away, Johnson blamed his folly in quitting the stage, by which he and his wife got five hundred pounds a year. I said, I believed it was owing to Churchill's attack upon him,

'He mouths a sentence, as curs mouth a bone.'

JOHNSON. 'I believe so too, Sir. But what a man is he, who is to be driven from the stage by a line? Another line would have driven him from his shop.'[a]

I told him that I was engaged as Counsel at the bar of the House of Commons to oppose a road-bill in the county of Stirling, and asked him what mode he would advise me to follow in addressing such an audience. JOHNSON. 'Why, Sir, you must provide yourself with a good deal of extraneous matter, which you are to produce occasionally, so as to fill up the time; for you must consider, that they do not listen much. If you begin with the strength of your cause, it may be lost before they begin to listen. When you catch a moment of attention, press the merits of the question upon them.' He said, as to one point of the merits, that he thought 'it would be a wrong thing to deprive the small landholders of the privilege of assessing themselves for making and repairing the high roads; *it was destroying a certain portion of liberty, without a good reason, which was always a bad thing.*' When I mentioned this observation next day to Mr. Wilkes, he pleasantly said, 'What! does *he* talk of liberty? *Liberty* is as ridiculous in *his* mouth as *Religion* in *mine.*' Mr. Wilkes's advice as to the best mode of speaking at the bar of the House of Commons, was not more respectful towards the senate, than that of Dr. Johnson. 'Be as impudent as you can, as merry as you can, and say whatever comes uppermost. Jack Lee is the best heard there of any Counsel; and he is the most impudent dog, and always abusing us.'

[a] *& then he would have had no Bone to mouth.* [H]

In my interview with Dr. Johnson this evening, I was quite easy, quite as his companion; upon which I find in my Journal the following reflection: 'So ready is my mind to suggest matter for dissatisfaction, that I felt a sort of regret that I was so easy. I missed that awful reverence with which I used to contemplate MR. SAMUEL JOHNSON, in the complex magnitude of his literary, moral, and religious character. I have a wonderful superstitious love of *mystery;* when, perhaps, the truth is, that it is owing to the cloudy darkness of my own mind. I should be glad that I am more advanced in my progress of being, so that I can view Dr. Johnson with a steadier and clearer eye. My dissatisfaction to-night was foolish.[a] Would it not be foolish to regret that we shall have less mystery in a future state? That "we now see in a glass darkly," but shall "then see face to face"?'—This reflection, which I thus freely communicate,[b] will be valued by the thinking part of my readers, who may have themselves experienced a similar state of mind.

[a] *very foolish indeed* [H]

[b] I *think tis like Insanity to feel so; & very like Insanity to confess such stuff* [J]

He returned next day to Streatham, to Mr. Thrale's; where, as Mr. Strahan once complained to me, 'he was in a great measure absorbed from the society of his old friends.' I was kept in London by business, and wrote to him on the 27th, that a separation from him for a week, when we were so near, was equal to a separation for a year, when we were at four hundred miles distance. I went to Streatham on Monday, March 30. Before he appeared, Mrs. Thrale made a very characteristical remark:—'I do not know for certain what will please Dr. Johnson: but I know for certain that it will displease him to praise any thing, even what he likes, extravagantly.'

At dinner he laughed at querulous declamations against the age, on account of luxury,—increase of London,—scarcity of provisions,—and other such topicks. 'Houses (said he) will be built till rents fall; and corn is more plentiful now than ever it was.'

I had before dinner repeated a ridiculous story told me by an old man, who had been a passenger with me in the stage-coach to-day. Mrs. Thrale, having taken occasion to allude to it, in talking to me, called it 'The story told you by the old *woman.*'—'Now, Madam, (said I,) give me leave to catch you in the fact: it was not an old *woman*, but an old *man*, whom I mentioned as having told me this.'[a] I presumed to take an opportunity, in presence of Johnson, of shewing this lively lady how ready she was, unintentionally, to deviate from exact authenticity of narration.

Thomas à Kempis (he observed) must be a good book, as the world has opened its arms to receive it. It is said to have been printed, in one language or other, as many times as there have been months since it first came out.[1] I always was struck with this sentence in it: "Be not angry that you cannot make others as you wish them to be, since you cannot make yourself as you wish to be."[2][b]

He said, 'I was angry with Hurd about Cowley, for having published a selection of his works: but, upon better consideration, I think there is no impropriety in a man's publishing as much as he chooses of any authour, if he does not put the rest out of the way. A man, for instance, may print the Odes of Horace alone.' He seemed to be in a more indulgent humour, than when this subject was discussed between him and Mr. Murphy.

When we were at tea and coffee, there came in Lord Trimlestown, in whose family was an ancient Irish peerage, but it suffered by taking the generous side in the troubles of the last century.[3] He was a man of pleasing conversation, and was accompanied by a young gentleman, his son.

I mentioned that I had in my possession the Life of Sir Robert Sibbald, the celebrated Scottish antiquary, and founder of the Royal College of Physicians at Edinburgh, in the original manuscript in his own hand writing; and that it was, I believed, the most natural and candid account of himself that ever was given by any man. As an instance,

[a] *Mrs. Thrale knew there was no such Thing as an old Man: when a Man gets Superannuated they call him an old Woman.* [H]

but there is no such Thing as an old Man: when any Man talks such Twaddling Stuff as This, I call him an old Woman. [I]

[b] *The very best Thing in any Book.* [H & I]

index sign: *a young gentleman* etc. [H]

[c] *Impossible!* [I]

---

[1] [The first edition was in 1492. Between that period and 1792, according to this account, there were three thousand six hundred editions. But this is very improbable.[c] MALONE.]

[2] [The original passage is: Si non potes te talem facere, qualem vis, quomodo poteris alium ad tuum habere beneplacitum? De Imit. Christ. Lib. i. Cap. xvi. J. BOSWELL.]

[3] [Since this was written, the attainder has been reversed; and Nicholas Barnewall is now a peer of Ireland with this title. The person mentioned in the text had studied physick, and prescribed *gratis* to the poor. Hence arose the subsequent conversation. MALONE.]

he tells that the Duke of Perth, then Chancellor of Scotland, pressed him very much to come over to the Roman Catholick faith: that he resisted all his Grace's arguments for a considerable time, till one day he felt himself, as it were, instantaneously convinced, and with tears in his eyes ran into the Duke's arms, and embraced the ancient religion; that he continued very steady in it for some time, and accompanied his Grace to London one winter, and lived in his household; that there he found the rigid fasting prescribed by the church very severe upon him; that this disposed him to reconsider the controversy, and having then seen that he was in the wrong, he returned to Protestantism. I talked of some time or other publishing this curious life. MRS. THRALE. 'I think you had as well let alone that publication. To discover such weakness exposes a man when he is gone.' JOHNSON. 'Nay, it is an honest picture of human nature. How often are the primary motives of our greatest actions as small as Sibbald's, for his re-conversion.' MRS. THRALE. 'But may they not as well be forgotten?' JOHNSON. 'No, Madam, a man loves to review his own mind. That is the use of a diary or journal.' LORD TRIMLESTOWN. 'True, Sir. As the ladies love to see themselves in a glass;[a] so a man likes to see himself in his journal.' BOSWELL. 'A very pretty allusion.' JOHNSON. 'Yes, indeed.' BOSWELL. 'And as a lady adjusts her dress before a mirrour, a man adjusts his character by looking at his journal.' I next year found the very same thought in Atterbury's 'Funeral Sermon on Lady Cutts;' where having mentioned her Diary, he says, 'In this glass she every day dressed her mind.' This is a proof of coincidence, and not of plagiarism; for I had never read that sermon before.

Next morning, while we were at breakfast, Johnson gave a very earnest recommendation of what he himself practised with the utmost conscientiousness: I mean a strict attention to truth, even in the most minute particulars. 'Accustom your children (said he) constantly to this; if a thing happened at one window, and they, when relating it, say that it happened at another, do not let it pass, but instantly check them; you do not know where deviation from truth will end.' BOSWELL. 'It may come to the door:

[margin note:]
[a] *True, but when the Lady grows old & ugly, She says*
Venus, take my Votive Glass,
Since I am not what I was:
What from this day I shall be,
Venus! let me never see.
1817. [H]

two marginal lines:
I mean ... the most [H]

and when once an account is at all varied in one circumstance, it may by degrees be varied so as to be totally
different from what really happened.' Our lively hostess,
whose fancy was impatient of the rein, fidgeted at this, and
ventured to say, 'Nay, this is too much. If Mr. Johnson
should forbid me to drink tea, I would comply, as I should
feel the restraint only twice a day; but little variations in
narrative must happen a thousand times a day, if one is not
perpetually watching.' JOHNSON. 'Well, Madam, and you
ought to be perpetually watching. It is more from carelessness about truth than from intentional lying, that there is
so much falsehood in the world.'

marginal line:
Madam, and . . . the
world [H]

In his review of Dr. Warton's 'Essay on the Writings
and Genius of Pope,' Johnson has given the following
salutary caution upon this subject: 'Nothing but experience could evince the frequency of false information, or
enable any man to conceive that so many groundless
reports should be propagated, as every man of eminence
may hear of himself. Some men relate what they think, as
what they know; some men of confused memories and
habitual inaccuracy, ascribe to one man what belongs to
another; and some talk on without thought or care. A few
men are sufficient to broach falsehoods, which are afterwards innocently diffused by successive relaters.'[1] Had
he lived to read what Sir John Hawkins and Mrs. Piozzi
have related concerning himself, how much would he have
found his observation illustrated. He was indeed so much
impressed with the prevalence of falsehood, voluntary or
unintentional, that I never knew any person who upon
hearing an extraordinary circumstance told, discovered
more of the *incredulus odi*. He would say with a significant
look and decisive tone, 'It is not so. Do not tell this again.'[2a]
He inculcated upon all his friends the importance of perpetual vigilance against the slightest degrees of falsehood;
the effect of which, as Sir Joshua Reynolds observed to me,

a & he said so to a
Man who related El-
liots Defence of Gibral-
tar—he thought Every
Thing false. [H]

[1] Literary Magazine, 1756, p. 37.

[2] The following plausible, but over-prudent counsel on this subject is
given by an Italian writer, quoted by '*Rhedi de generatione insectarum*,' with
the epithet of '*divini poetae*.'

> 'Sempre à quel ver ch' a faccia di menzogna
> Dee l' uom chiudere le labbra quanto ei puote;
> Però chez zenza colpa fa vergogna.'

has been, that all who were of his *school* are distinguished for a love of truth and accuracy, which they would not have possessed in the same degree, if they had not been acquainted with Johnson.

Talking of ghosts, he said, 'It is wonderful that five thousand years have now elapsed since the creation of the world, and still it is undecided whether or not there has ever been an instance of the spirit of any person appearing after death. All argument is against it; but all belief is for it.'

He said, 'John Wesley's conversation is good, but he is never at leisure. He is always obliged to go at a certain hour. This is very disagreeable to a man who loves to fold his legs and have out his talk, as I do.'

On Friday, April 3, I dined with him in London, in a company where were present several eminent men, whom I shall not name, but distinguish their parts in the conversation by different letters.

F. 'I have been looking at this famous antique marble dog of Mr. Jennings, valued at a thousand guineas, said to be Alcibiades's dog.' JOHNSON. 'His tail then must be docked. That was the mark of Alcibiades's dog.' E. 'A thousand guineas! The representation of no animal whatever is worth so much. At this rate a dead dog would indeed be better than a living lion.' JOHNSON. 'Sir, it is not the worth of the thing, but of the skill in forming it which is so highly estimated. Every thing that enlarges the sphere of human powers, that shows man he can do what he thought he could not do, is valuable. The first man who balanced a straw upon his nose; Johnson who rode upon three horses at a time; in short, all such men deserve the applause of mankind, not on account of the use of what they did, but of the dexterity which they exhibited.' BOSWELL. 'Yet a misapplication of time and assiduity is not to be encouraged. Addison, in one of his "Spectators," commends the judgement of a King, who as a suitable reward to a man that by long perseverance had attained to the art of throwing a barley-corn through the eye of a needle, gave him a bushel of barley.' JOHNSON. 'He must have been a King of Scotland, where barley is scarce.' F. 'One of the most remarkable antique figures of an animal

marginal line:
JOHNSON. 'He ...
of Scotland [H]

proposition.' C. 'Holland is very unhealthy, yet it is exceedingly populous.' JOHNSON. 'I know not that Holland is unhealthy. But its populousness is owing to an influx of people from all other countries. Disease cannot be the cause of populousness, for it not only carries off a great proportion of the people; but those who are left are weakened, and unfit for the purposes of increase.'

R. 'Mr. E., I don't mean to flatter, but when posterity reads one of your speeches in parliament, it will be difficult to believe that you took so much pains, knowing with certainty that it could produce no effect, that not one vote would be gained by it.' E. 'Waving your compliment to me, I shall say in general, that it is very well worth while for a man to take pains to speak well in parliament. A man, who has vanity, speaks to display his talents; and if a man speaks well, he gradually establishes a certain reputation and consequence in the general opinion, which sooner or later will have its political reward. Besides, though not one vote is gained, a good speech has its effect. Though an act which has been ably opposed passes into a law, yet in its progress it is modelled, it is softened in such a manner, that we see plainly the Minister has been told, that the members attached to him are so sensible of its injustice or absurdity from what they have heard, that it must be

a was this Erskine? [H] altered.'[a] JOHNSON. 'And, Sir, there is a gratification of pride. Though we cannot out-vote them, we will out-argue them. They shall not do wrong without its being shown both to themselves and to the world.' E. 'The House of Commons is a mixed body. (I except the Minority, which I hold to be pure, [smiling] but I take the whole House.) It is a mass by no means pure; but neither is it wholly corrupt, though there is a large proportion of corruption in it. There are many members who generally go with the minister, who will not go all lengths. There are many honest well-meaning country gentlemen who are in parliament only to keep up the consequence of their families. Upon most of these a good speech will have influence.' JOHNSON. 'We are all more or less governed by interest. But interest will not make us do every thing. In a case which admits of doubt, we try to think on the side which is for our interest, and generally bring ourselves to act accordingly. But the subject must admit of diversity of colouring; it must receive a colour on that side. In the House of Commons there are members enough who will not vote what is grossly unjust or absurd. No, Sir, there must always be right enough, or appearance of right, to keep wrong in countenance.' BOSWELL. 'There is surely always a majority in parliament who have places, or who want to have them, and who therefore will be generally ready to support government without requiring any pretext.' E. 'True, Sir, that majority will always follow

queried: *always a majority* etc. [H]

"*Quo clamor vocat et turba faventium.*"'

BOSWELL. 'Well, now, let us take the common phrase, Place-hunters. I thought they had hunted without regard to any thing, just as their huntsman, the Minister, leads, looking only to the prey.'[1] J. 'But taking your metaphor, you know that in hunting there are few so desperately keen as to follow without reserve. Some do not choose to leap ditches and hedges and risk their necks, or gallop over steeps, or even to dirty themselves in bogs and mire.' BOSWELL. 'I am glad there are some good, quiet, moderate political hunters.' E. 'I believe in any body of men in England I should have been in the Minority; I have always been in the Minority.' P. 'The House of Commons resembles a private company. How seldom is any man convinced by another's argument; passion and pride rise against it.' R. 'What would be the consequence, if a Minister, sure of a majority in the House of Commons, should resolve that there should be no speaking at all upon his side.' E. 'He must soon go out. That has been tried; but it was found it would not do.'———

E. 'The Irish language is not primitive; it is Teutonick, a mixture of the northern tongues; it has much English in it.' JOHNSON. 'It may have been radically Teutonic; but English and High Dutch have no similarity to the eye, though radically the same. Once when looking into Low Dutch, I found, in a whole page, only one word similar to

[1] Lord Bolinbroke, who, however detestable as a metaphysician, must be allowed to have had admirable talents as a political writer, thus describes the House of Commons, in his 'Letter to Sir William Windham;'—'You know the nature of that assembly; they grow, like hounds, fond of the man who shews them game, and by whose halloo they are used to be encouraged.'

two marginal lines: *assembly; they . . . be encouraged* [H]

English; *stroem*, like *stream*, and it signified *tide*.' E. 'I
remember having seen a Dutch Sonnet, in which I found
this word, *roesnopies*. Nobody would at first think that this
could be English; but, when we enquire, we find *roes*, rose,
and *nopie*, knob; so we have *rosebuds*.'

JOHNSON. 'I have been reading Thicknesse's Travels,
which I think are entertaining.' BOSWELL. 'What, Sir, a
good book?' JOHNSON. 'Yes, Sir, to read once; I do not
say you are to make a study of it, and digest it; and I
believe it to be a true book in his intention. All travellers
generally mean to tell truth; though Thicknesse observes,
upon Smollett's account of his alarming a whole town in
France by firing a blunderbuss, and frightening a French
nobleman till he made him tie on his portmanteau, that he
would be loth to say Smollett had told two lies in one page;
but he had found the only town in France where these
things could have happened. Travellers must often be
mistaken. In every thing, except where mensuration can
be applied, they may honestly differ. There has been, of
late, a strange turn in travellers to be displeased.'

E. 'From the experience which I have had,—and I have
had a great deal,—I have learnt to think *better* of mankind.'
JOHNSON. 'From my experience I have found them worse
in commercial dealings, more disposed to cheat, than I had
any notion of; but more disposed to do one another good
than I had conceived.' J. 'Less just and more beneficent.'
JOHNSON. 'And really it is wonderful, considering how
much attention is necessary for men to take care of themselves, and ward off immediate evils which press upon
them, it is wonderful how much they do for others. As it is
said of the greatest liar, that he tells more truth than falsehood; so it may be said of the worst man, that he does more
good than evil.' BOSWELL. 'Perhaps from experience men
may be found *happier* than we suppose.' JOHNSON. 'No,
Sir; the more we enquire we shall find men the less happy.'
P. 'As to thinking better or worse of mankind from experience, some cunning people will not be satisfied unless
they have put men to the test, as they think. There is a
very good story told of Sir Godfrey Kneller, in his character of a justice of the peace. A gentleman brought his
servant before him, upon an accusation of having stolen

some money from him; but it having come out that he had laid it purposely in the servant's way, in order to try his honesty, Sir Godfrey sent the master to prison.'[1] JOHNSON. 'To resist temptation once, is not a sufficient proof of honesty. If a servant, indeed, were to resist the continued temptation of silver lying in a window, as some people let it lye, when he is sure his master does not know how much there is of it, he would give a strong proof of honesty. But this is a proof to which you have no right to put a man. You know, humanly speaking, there is a certain degree of temptation, which will overcome any virtue. Now, in so far as you approach temptation to a man, you do him an injury;[a] and, if he is overcome, you share his guilt.' P. 'And when once overcome, it is easier for him to be got the better of again.' BOSWELL. 'Yes, you are his seducer; you have debauched him. I have known a man resolve to put friendship to the test, by asking a friend to lend him money, merely with that view, when he did not want it.' JOHNSON.'That is very wrong, Sir. Your friend may be a narrow man, and yet have many good qualities: narrowness may be his only fault. Now you are trying his general character as a friend, by one particular singly, in which he happens to be defective, when, in truth, his character is composed of many particulars.'

[a] *you do the Devil's Work for him.* [H & I]

E. 'I understand the hogshead of claret, which this society was favoured with by our friend the Dean, is nearly out; I think he should be written to, to send another of the same kind. Let the request be made with a happy ambiguity of expression, so that we may have the chance of his sending *it* also as a present.' JOHNSON. 'I am willing to offer my services as secretary on this occasion.' P. 'As many as are for Dr. Johnson being secretary hold up your hands.—Carried unanimously.' BOSWELL. 'He will be our Dictator.' JOHNSON. 'No, the company is to dictate to me. I am only to write for wine; and I am quite disinterested, as I drink none; I shall not be suspected of

---

[1] Pope thus introduces this story:

'Faith in such case if you should prosecute,
I think Sir Godfrey should decide the suit,
Who sent the thief who stole the cash away,
And punish'd him that put it in his way.'

Imitations of Horace, Book II. Epist. ii.

having forged the application. I am no more than humble *scribe*.' E. 'Then you shall *pre*scribe.' BOSWELL. 'Very well. The first play of words to-day.' J. 'No, no; the *bulls* in Ireland.' JOHNSON. 'Were I your Dictator, you should have no wine. It would be my business *cavere ne quid detrimenti Respublica caperet*, and wine is dangerous. Rome was ruined by luxury,' (smiling.) E. 'If you allow no wine as Dictator, you shall not have me for your master of horse.'

On Saturday, April 4, I drank tea with Johnson at Dr. Taylor's, where he had dined. He entertained us with an account of a tragedy written by a Dr. Kennedy, (not the Lisbon physician.) 'The catastrophe of it (said he) was, that a King, who was jealous of his Queen with his prime-minister, castrated himself.[1] This tragedy was actually shewn about in manuscript to several people, and, amongst others, to Mr. Fitzherbert, who repeated to me two lines of the Prologue:

> "Our hero's fate we have but gently touch'd;
> The fair might blame us, if it were less couch'd."

It is hardly to be believed what absurd and indecent images men will introduce into their writings, without being sensible of the absurdity and indecency. I remember Lord Orrery told me, that there was a pamphlet written against Sir Robert Walpole,[a] the whole of which was an allegory on the PHALLICK OBSCENITY. The Duchess of Buckingham asked Lord Orrery *who* this person was? He answered he did not know. She said, she would send to Mr. Pulteney, who, she supposed, could inform her. So then, to prevent her from making herself ridiculous, Lord Orrery sent her Grace a note, in which he gave her to understand what was meant.'

He was very silent this evening; and read in a variety of books; suddenly throwing down one, and taking up another.

a *Walpole* deserv'd *it see Page 54:* [p. 298 of this volume] *but I doubt his understanding it better than the Duchess of Buckingham. Which of them all knows the Meaning of the Delphic Oracle?—or of ye Word Adelphi—critically?* [I]

---

[1] The reverse of the story of *Combabus*, on which Mr. David Hume told Lord Macartney, that a friend of his had written a tragedy. It is, however, possible, that I may have been inaccurate in my perception of what Dr. Johnson related, and that he may have been talking of the same ludicrous tragical subject that Mr. Hume had mentioned.

[The story of Combabus, which was originally told by Lucian, may be found in Bayle's Dictionary. MALONE.]

He talked of going to Streatham that night. TAYLOR. 'You'll be robbed, if you do: or you must shoot a high-wayman. Now I would rather be robbed than do that; I would not shoot a highwayman.' JOHNSON. 'But I would rather shoot him in the instant when he is attempting to rob me, than afterwards swear against him at the Old Bailey, to take away his life, after he has robbed me. I am surer I am right in the one case, than in the other. I may be mistaken as to the man when I swear; I cannot be mistaken, if I shoot him in the act. Besides, we feel less reluctance to take away a man's life, when we are heated by the injury, than to do it at a distance of time by an oath, after we have cooled.' BOSWELL. 'So, Sir, you would rather act from the motive of private passion, than that of publick advantage.' JOHNSON. 'Nay, Sir, when I shoot the highwayman, I act from both.' BOSWELL. 'Very well, very well.—There is no catching him.' JOHNSON. 'At the same time, one does not know what to say. For perhaps one may, a year after, hang himself from un-easiness for having shot a highwayman.[1] Few minds are fit to be trusted with so great a thing.' BOSWELL. 'Then, Sir, you would not shoot him?' JOHNSON. 'But I might be vexed afterwards for that too.'

Thrale's carriage not having come for him, as he ex-pected, I accompanied him some part of the way home to his own house. I told him, that I had talked of him to Mr. Dunning a few days before, and had said, that in his company we did not so much interchange conversation, as listen to him; and that Dunning observed, upon this, 'One is always willing to listen to Dr. Johnson;' to which I answered, 'That is a great deal from you, Sir.'—'Yes, Sir, (said Johnson,) a great deal indeed. Here is a man willing

---

[1] The late Duke of Montrose was generally said to have been uneasy on that account; but I can contradict the report from his Grace's own authority. As he used to admit me to very easy conversation with him, I took the liberty to introduce the subject. His Grace told me, that when riding one night near London, he was attacked by two highwaymen on horseback, and that he instantly shot one of them, upon which the other galloped off; that his servant, who was very well mounted, proposed to pursue him and take him,[a] but that his Grace said, 'No, we have had blood enough: I hope the man may live to repent.' His Grace, upon my presuming to put the question,[b] assured me, that his mind was not at all clouded by what he had thus done in self-defence.

[a] & the Servt. pro-posed it, that He might get 40 L. as a scrupu-lous Man he ought to have Made the Fellow amends indeed, but People never are con-sistently scrupulous. [H]

[b] but what a Man was Boswell to put such a Question. [I]

to listen, to whom the world is listening all the rest of the year.' BOSWELL. 'I think, Sir, it is right to tell one man of such a handsome thing, which has been said of him by another. It tends to increase benevolence.' JOHNSON. 'Undoubtedly it is right, Sir.'

On Tuesday, April 7, I breakfasted with him at his house. He said, 'nobody was content.' I mentioned to him a respectable person in Scotland whom he knew; and I asserted, that I really believed he was always content. JOHNSON. 'No, Sir, he is not content with the present; he has always some new scheme, some new plantation, something which is future. You know he was not content as a widower; for he married again.' BOSWELL. 'But he is not restless.' JOHNSON. 'Sir, he is only locally at rest. A chymist is locally at rest; but his mind is hard at work. This gentleman has done with external exertions. It is too late for him to engage in distant projects.' BOSWELL. 'He seems to amuse himself quite well; to have his attention fixed, and his tranquillity preserved by very small matters. I have tried this; but it would not do with me.' JOHNSON. (laughing) 'No, Sir; it must be born with a man to be contented to take up with little things. Women have a great advantage that they may take up with little things, without disgracing themselves: a man cannot, except with fiddling. Had I learnt to fiddle, I should have done nothing else.' BOSWELL. 'Pray, Sir, did you ever play on any musical instrument?' JOHNSON. 'No, Sir. I once bought me a flagelet; but I never made out a tune.' BOSWELL. 'A flagelet, Sir!—so small an instrument?[1] I should have liked to hear you play on the violoncello. *That* should have been *your* instrument.' JOHNSON. 'Sir, I might as well have played on the violoncello as another; but I should have done nothing else. No, Sir; a man would never undertake great things, could he be amused with small. I once tried knotting. Dempster's sister undertook to teach me; but I could not learn it.' BOSWELL. 'So, Sir, it will be related in pompous narrative, "Once for his amusement he tried

[1] When I told this to Miss Seward, she smiled, and repeated, with admirable readiness, from 'Acis and Galatea,'

'Bring me a hundred reeds of ample growth,
To make a pipe for my CAPACIOUS MOUTH.'

knotting; nor did this Hercules disdain the distaff."'
JOHNSON. 'Knitting of stockings is a good amusement.
As a freeman of Aberdeen I should be a knitter of stockings.' He asked me to go down with him and dine at Mr.
Thrale's at Streatham, to which I agreed. I had lent him
'An Account of Scotland, in 1702,' written by a man of
various enquiry, an English chaplain to a regiment
stationed there. JOHNSON. 'It is sad stuff, Sir, miserably
written, as books in general then were. There is now an
elegance of style universally diffused. No man now writes
so ill as Martin's Account of the Hebrides is written. A
man could not write so ill, if he should try. Set a merchant's
clerk now to write, and he'll do better.'

He talked to me with serious concern of a certain female
friend's 'laxity of narration, and inattention to truth.' —
'I am as much vexed (said he) at the ease with which she
hears it mentioned to her, as at the thing itself. I told her,
"Madam, you are contented to hear every day said to you,
what the highest of mankind have died for, rather than
bear."—You know, Sir, the highest of mankind have died
rather than bear to be told they had uttered a falsehood.
Do talk to her of it: I am weary.'

BOSWELL. 'Was not Dr. John Campbell a very inaccurate man in his narrative, Sir? He once told me, that he
drank thirteen bottles of port at a sitting.'[1] JOHNSON.
'Why, Sir, I do not know that Campbell ever lied with pen
and ink; but you could not entirely depend on any thing
he told you in conversation, if there was fact mixed with it.
However, I loved Campbell: he was a solid orthodox man:
he had a reverence for religion. Though defective in

[1] Lord Macartney observes upon this passage, 'I have heard him tell
many things, which, though embellished by their mode of narrative, had
their foundation in truth; but I never remember any thing approaching to
this. If he had written it, I should have supposed some wag had put the
figure of one before the three.'—I am, however, absolutely certain that Dr.
Campbell told me it, and I gave particular attention to it, being myself a
lover of wine, and therefore curious to hear whatever is remarkable concerning drinking. There can be no doubt that some men can drink, without
suffering any injury, such a quantity as to others appears incredible. It is
but fair to add, that Dr. Campbell told me, he took a very long time to this
great potation; and I have heard Dr. Johnson say, 'Sir, if a man drinks very
slowly, and lets one glass evaporate before he takes another, I know not how
long he may drink.' Dr. Campbell mentioned a Colonel of Militia who sat
with him all the time, and drank equally.

practice, he was religious in principle; and he did nothing grossly wrong that I have heard.'[1]

I told him, that I had been present the day before, when Mrs. Montague, the literary lady, sat to Miss Reynolds for her picture; and that she said, 'she had bound up Mr. Gibbon's History without the last two offensive chapters;[a] for that she thought the book so far good, as it gave, in an elegant manner, the substance of the bad writers *medii ævi*, which the late Lord Lyttleton advised her to read.' JOHNSON. 'Sir, she has not read them: she shews none of this impetuosity to me: she does not know Greek, and, I fancy, knows little Latin. She is willing you should think she knows them; but she does not say she does.' BOSWELL. 'Mr. Harris, who was present, agreed with her.' JOHNSON. 'Harris was laughing at her, Sir. Harris is a sound sullen scholar; he does not like interlopers. Harris, however, is a prig, and a bad prig.[2] I looked into his book, and thought he did not understand his own system.' BOSWELL. 'He says plain things in a formal abstract way, to be sure; but his method is good: for to have clear notions upon any subject, we must have recourse to analytick arrangement.' JOHNSON. 'Sir, it is what every body does, whether they will or no. But sometimes things may be made darker by definition. I see a *cow*. I define her, *Animal quadrupes ruminans cornutum*. But a goat ruminates, and a cow may have no horns. *Cow* is plainer.' BOSWELL. 'I think Dr. Franklin's definition of *Man* a good one—"A tool-making animal."' JOHNSON. 'But many a man never made a tool: and suppose a man without arms, he could not make a tool.'

Talking of drinking wine, he said, 'I did not leave off wine because I could not bear it; I have drunk three bottles of port without being the worse for it. University College has witnessed this.' BOSWELL. 'Why then, Sir,

[a] *That was eating the Woodcock without the Grail [Thrail:* 1] *& Toast I suppose.—1817* [H & I]

queried: *Harris, however* etc. [H]

[b] *I wonder he lived so long.* [H]

[c] *but who was the satisfactory Doctor?* [H]
who was the Physician? [I]

[1] [Dr. John Campbell died about two years before this conversation took place; Dec. 10, 1776.[b] MALONE.]

[2] What my friend meant by these words concerning the amiable philosopher of Salisbury, I am at a loss to understand. A friend suggests, that Johnson thought his *manner* as a writer affected, while at the same time the *matter* did not compensate for that fault. In short, that he meant to make a remark quite different from that which a *celebrated gentleman* made on a very eminent physician: 'He is a coxcomb, but a *satisfactory coxcomb*.'

[The *celebrated gentleman*[c] here alluded to, was the late Right Honourable William Gerard Hamilton. MALONE.]

did you leave it off?' JOHNSON. 'Why, Sir, because it is so much better for a man to be sure that he is never to be intoxicated, never to lose the power over himself. I shall not begin to drink wine again till I grow old, and want it.' BOSWELL. 'I think, Sir, you once said to me, that not to drink wine was a great deduction from life.' JOHNSON. 'It is a diminution of pleasure, to be sure; but I do not say a diminution of happiness. There is more happiness in being rational.' BOSWELL. 'But if we could have pleasure always, should not we be happy? The greatest part of men would compound for pleasure.' JOHNSON. 'Supposing we could have pleasure always, an intellectual man would not compound for it. The greatest part of men would compound, because the greatest part of men are gross.' BOSWELL. 'I allow there may be greater pleasure than from wine. I have had more pleasure from your conversation. I have indeed; I assure you I have.' JOHNSON. 'When we talk of pleasure, we mean sensual pleasure. When a man says he had pleasure with a woman, he does not mean conversation, but something of a very different nature. Philosophers tell you, that pleasure is *contrary* to happiness. Gross men prefer animal pleasure. So there are men who have preferred living among savages. Now what a wretch must he be, who is content with such conversation as can be had among savages! You may remember an officer at Fort Augustus, who had served in America, told us of a woman whom they were obliged to *bind*, in order to get her back from savage life.' BOSWELL. 'She must have been an animal, a beast.' JOHNSON. 'Sir, she was a speaking cat.'

I mentioned to him that I had become very weary in a company where I heard not a single intellectual sentence, except that 'a man who had been settled ten years in Minorca was become a much inferiour man to what he was in London, because a man's mind grows narrow in a narrow place.' JOHNSON. 'A man's mind grows narrow in a narrow place, whose mind is enlarged only because he has lived in a large place: but what is got by books and thinking is preserved in a narrow place as well as in a large place. A man cannot know modes of life as well in Minorca as in London; but he may study mathematicks as well in

Minorca.' BOSWELL. 'I don't know, Sir; if you had remained ten years in the Isle of Col, you would not have been the man that you now are.' JOHNSON. 'Yes, Sir, if I had been there from fifteen to twenty-five; but not if from twenty-five to thirty-five.' BOSWELL. 'I own, Sir, the spirits which I have in London make me do every thing with more readiness and vigour. I can talk twice as much in London as any where else.'

Of Goldsmith, he said, 'He was not an agreeable companion, for he talked always for fame. A man who does so, never can be pleasing. The man who talks to unburthen his mind, is the man to delight you. An eminent friend of ours[a] is not so agreeable as the variety of his knowledge would otherwise make him, because he talks partly from ostentation.'

Soon after our arrival at Thrale's, I heard one of the maids calling eagerly on another, to go to Dr. Johnson. I wondered what this could mean. I afterwards learnt, that it was to give her a Bible, which he had brought from London as a present to her.

He was for a considerable time occupied in reading 'Memoires de Fontenelle,'[b] leaning and swinging upon the low gate into the court, without his hat.

I looked into Lord Kames's 'Sketches of the History of Man;' and mentioned to Dr. Johnson his censure of Charles the Fifth, for celebrating his funeral obsequies in his life-time, which, I told him, I had been used to think a solemn and affecting act. JOHNSON. 'Why, Sir, a man may dispose his mind to think so of that act of Charles; but it is so liable to ridicule, that if one man out of ten thousand laughs at it, he'll make the other nine thousand nine hundred and ninety-nine laugh too.'[c] I could not agree with him in this.

Sir John Pringle had expressed a wish that I would ask Dr. Johnson's opinion what were the best English sermons for style. I took an opportunity to-day of mentioning several to him. 'Atterbury?' JOHNSON. 'Yes, Sir, one of the best.' BOSWELL. 'Tillotson?' JOHNSON. 'Why, not now. I should not advise a preacher at this day to imitate Tillotson's style; though I don't know; I should be cautious of objecting to what has been applauded by so many

underlined: *eminent friend* [H]

[a] *Burke I suppose.* [H]
who was that? Burke I suppose. [I]

[b] *I wonder how he liked the Story of the Asparagus.* [H]

[c] *& Miss Edgworth does laugh at it in her Castle Rackrent, where Sir Condy obliges the People to wake him (as the Irish Phrase is) while yet alive* [H]
The Man in Castle Rackrent who would have himself wak'd as the Irish express it before his Death, exemplifies Johnson's Assertion. [I]

suffrages.—*South* is one of the best, if you except his peculiarities, and his violence, and sometimes coarseness of
language.—*Seed* has a very fine style; but he is not very
theological.—*Jortin's* sermons are very elegant.—*Sherlock's*
style too is very elegant, though he has not made it his
principal study.—And you may add *Smallridge*. All the
latter preachers have a good style. Indeed, nobody now
talks much of style: every body composes pretty well.
There are no such inharmonious periods as there were a
hundred years ago. I should recommend Dr. *Clarke's*
sermons, were he orthodox. However, it is very well known
where he is not orthodox, which was upon the doctrine of
the Trinity, as to which he is a condemned heretick; so one
is aware of it.' BOSWELL. 'I like Ogden's Sermons on
Prayer very much, both for neatness of style and subtilty
of reasoning.' JOHNSON. 'I should like to read all that
Ogden has written.' BOSWELL. 'What I wish to know is,
what sermons afford the best specimen of English pulpit
eloquence.' JOHNSON. 'We have no sermons addressed to
the passions, that are good for any thing; if you mean that
kind of eloquence.' A CLERGYMAN: (whose name I do
not recollect.)[a] 'Were not Dodd's sermons addressed to
the passions?' JOHNSON. 'They were nothing, Sir, be they
addressed to what they may.'

At dinner, Mrs. Thrale expressed a wish to go and see
Scotland. JOHNSON. 'Seeing Scotland, Madam, is only
seeing a worse England. It is seeing the flower gradually
fade away to the naked stalk. Seeing the Hebrides, indeed,
is seeing quite a different scene.'

Our poor friend, Mr. Thomas Davies, was soon to have
a benefit at Drury-lane theatre, as some relief to his unfortunate circumstances. We were all warmly interested
for his success, and had contributed to it. However, we
thought there was no harm in having our joke, when he could
not be hurt by it. I proposed that he should be brought on
to speak a Prologue upon the occasion; and I began to
mutter fragments of what it might be: as, that when now
grown *old*, he was obliged to cry, 'Poor Tom's *a-cold;'*—
that he owned he had been driven from the stage by a
Churchill, but that this was no disgrace, for a Churchill
had beat the French;—that he had been satyrised as

marginal lines:
suffrages.—South . . .
and sometimes [H]

[a] *Mr. Embry.* [H]

'mouthing a sentence as curs mouth a bone,' but he was now glad of a bone to pick.—'Nay, (said Johnson,) I would have him to say,

"Mad Tom is come to see the world again."'

He and I returned to town in the evening. Upon the road, I endeavoured to maintain, in argument, that a landed gentleman is not under any obligation to reside upon his estate; and that by living in London he does no injury to his country. JOHNSON. 'Why, Sir, he does no injury to his country in general, because the money which he draws from it gets back again in circulation; but to his particular district, his particular parish, he does an injury. All that he has to give away is not given to those who have the first claim to it. And though I have said that the money circulates back, it is a long time before that happens. Then, Sir, a man of family and estate ought to consider himself as having the charge of a district, over which he is to diffuse civility and happiness.'[1]

Next day I found him at home in the morning. He praised Delany's 'Observations on Swift;' said that his book and Lord Orrery's might both be true, though one viewed Swift more, and the other less, favourably; and that, between both, we might have a complete notion of Swift.

Talking of a man's resolving to deny himself the use of wine, from moral and religious considerations, he said, 'He must not doubt about it. When one doubts as to pleasure, we know what will be the conclusion. I now no more think of drinking wine than a horse does. The wine upon the table is no more for me, than for the dog that is under the table.'

On Thursday, April 9, I dined with him at Sir Joshua Reynolds's, with the Bishop of St. Asaph, (Dr. Shipley,) Mr. Allan Ramsay, Mr. Gibbon, Mr. Cambridge, and Mr. Langton.[a] Mr. Ramsay had lately returned from Italy, and entertained us with his observations upon Horace's villa, which he had examined with great care. I relished this much, as it brought fresh into my mind what I had

[a] *All dead* *1820!* [H]

---

[1] [See, however, pp. 402, 403, where his decision on this subject is more favourable to the absentee. MALONE.]

viewed with great pleasure thirteen years before. The
Bishop, Dr. Johnson, and Mr. Cambridge, joined with
Mr. Ramsay, in recollecting the various lines in Horace
relating to the subject.

Horace's journey to Brundusium being mentioned,
Johnson observed, that the brook which he describes is to
be seen now, exactly as at that time; and that he had often
wondered how it happened, that small brooks, such as
as this, kept the same situation for ages, notwithstanding
earthquakes, by which even mountains have been
changed, and agriculture, which produces such a variation upon the surface of the earth. CAMBRIDGE.
'A Spanish writer has this thought in a poetical conceit.
After observing that most of the solid structures of Rome
are totally perished, while the Tiber remains the same,
he adds,

> " Lo que èra Firme huió solamente,
>   Lo Fugitivo permanece y dura." '

JOHNSON. 'Sir, that is taken from *Janus Vitalis:*

> "_____ _____ _____ immota labescunt;
>   Et quæ perpetuò sunt agitata manent." '

The Bishop said, it appeared from Horace's writings
that he was a cheerful contented man. JOHNSON. 'We
have no reason to believe that, my Lord. Are we to think
Pope was happy, because he says so in his writings? We
see in his writings what he wished the state of his mind to
appear. Dr. Young, who pined for preferment, talks with
contempt of it in his writings, and affects to despise every
thing that he did not despise.' BISHOP OF ST. ASAPH.
'He was like other chaplains, looking for vacancies: but that
is not peculiar to the clergy. I remember, when I was with
the army, after the battle of Lafeldt, the officers seriously
grumbled that no general was killed.'[a] CAMBRIDGE. 'We
may believe Horace more, when he says,

> " Romæ Tibur amem, Ventosus Tibure Romam;"

than when he boasts of his consistency:

> " Me constare mihi scis, et decedere tristem,
>   Quandocunque trahunt invisa negotia Romam." '

[a] and I remember Cor-
bet Parry said he him-
self had called out in the
midst of the Battle at
Fontenoy 'Come, stand
thick Gentlemen, that a
Young Man may rise
among you.' [H]

BOSWELL. 'How hard is it that man can never be at rest.'
RAMSAY. 'It is not in his nature to be at rest. When he
is at rest, he is in the worst state that he can be in; for he
has nothing to agitate him. He is then like the man in the
Irish song,

> "There liv'd a young man in Ballinacrazy,
> Who wanted a wife for to make him un*ai*sy."'

Goldsmith being mentioned, Johnson observed, that it
was long before his merit came to be acknowledged: that
he once complained to him, in ludicrous terms of distress,
'Whenever I write any thing, the publick *make a point* to
know nothing about it:' but that his 'Traveller'[1] brought
him into high reputation. LANGTON. 'There is not one
bad line in that poem; not one of Dryden's careless verses.'
SIR JOSHUA. 'I was glad to hear Charles Fox say, it was
one of the finest poems in the English language.' LANG-
TON. 'Why were you glad? You surely had no doubt of
this before.' JOHNSON. 'No; the merit of "The Traveller"
is so well established, that Mr. Fox's praise cannot augment it, nor his censure diminish it.' SIR JOSHUA. 'But
his friends may suspect they had too great a partiality for
him.' JOHNSON. 'Nay, Sir, the partiality of his friends was
always against him. It was with difficulty we could give
him a hearing. Goldsmith had no settled notions upon any
subject; so he talked always at random. It seemed to be his
intention to blurt out whatever was in his mind, and see
what would become of it. He was angry too, when catched
in an absurdity; but it did not prevent him from falling
into another the next minute. I remember Chamier,[2] after
talking with him some time, said, "Well, I do believe he
wrote this poem himself: and, let me tell you, that is
believing a great deal." Chamier once asked him, what he
meant by *slow*, the last word in the first line of "The
Traveller,"

> "Remote, unfriended, melancholy, slow."

Did he mean tardiness of locomotion? Goldsmith, who
would say something without consideration, answered,

[1] [First published in 1765. MALONE.]

[2] [Anthony Chamier, Esq. a member of the LITERARY CLUB, and
Under-Secretary of State. He died Oct. 12, 1780. MALONE.]

"Yes." I was sitting by, and said, "No, Sir, you do not mean tardiness of locomotion; you mean, that sluggishness of mind which comes upon a man in solitude." Chamier believed then that I had written the line, as much as if he had seen me write it. Goldsmith, however, was a man, who, whatever he wrote, did it better than any other man could do. He deserved a place in Westminster-Abbey; and every year he lived, would have deserved it better. He had, indeed, been at no pains to fill his mind with knowledge. He transplanted it from one place to another; and it did not settle in his mind; so he could not tell what was in his own books.'

We talked of living in the country. JOHNSON. 'No wise man will go to live in the country, unless he has something to do which can be better done in the country. For instance; if he is to shut himself up for a year to study a science, it is better to look out to the fields, than to an opposite wall. Then, if a man walks out in the country, there is nobody to keep him from walking in again; but if a man walks out in London, he is not sure when he shall walk in again. A great city is, to be sure, the school for studying life; and "The proper study of mankind is man," as Pope observes.' BOSWELL. 'I fancy, London is the best place for society, though I have heard that the very first society of Paris is still beyond any thing that we have here.' JOHNSON. 'Sir, I question if in Paris such a company as is sitting round this table could be got together in less than half a year. They talk in France of the felicity of men and women living together: the truth is, that there the men are not higher than the women, they know no more than the women do, and they are not held down in their conversation by the presence of women.' RAMSAY. 'Literature is upon the growth, it is in its spring in France: here it is rather *passée*.' JOHNSON. 'Literature was in France long before we had it. Paris was the second city for the revival of letters: Italy had it first, to be sure. What have we done for literature, equal to what was done by the Stephani and others in France? Our literature came to us through France. Caxton printed only two books, Chaucer and Gower, that were not translations from the French; and Chaucer, we know, took much from the Italians. No, Sir, if literature be in its spring in France, it is a second spring; it is after a winter. We are now before the French in literature; but we had it long after them. In England, any man who wears a sword and a powdered wig, is ashamed to be illiterate.[a] I believe it is not so in France.[b] Yet there is, probably, a great deal of learning in France, because they have such a number of religious establishments; so many men who have nothing else to do but to study. I do not know this; but I take it upon the common principles of chance. Where there are many shooters, some will hit.'

We talked of old age. Johnson (now in his seventieth year,) said, 'It is a man's own fault, it is from want of use, if his mind grows torpid in old age.'[1] The Bishop asked, if an old man does not lose faster than he gets. JOHNSON. 'I think not, my Lord, if he exerts himself.' One of the company rashly observed, that he thought it was happy for an old man that insensibility comes upon him. JOHNSON: (with a noble elevation and disdain,) 'No, Sir, I should never be happy by being less rational.' BISHOP OF ST.

underlined: ashamed to . . . I believe [H]

[a] True. [H]

[b] certainly. Because Birth secures that Respect upon the Continent which England gives only to Money or to Merit. A Continental Nobleman is not ashamed either of Poverty or Ignorance. [H]
marginal line: is from . . . in old [H]

marginal line: JOHNSON: (with . . . less rational [H]

[1] [Hobbes was of the same opinion with Johnson on this subject; and in his answer to D'Avenant's Preface to GONDIBERT, with great spirit explodes the current opinion, that the mind in old age is subject to a necessary and irresistible debility.

'And now while I think on't, (says the philosopher,) give me leave, with a short discord, to sweeten the harmony of the approaching close. I have nothing to object to your poem, but dissent only from something in your preface, sounding to the prejudice of age. It is commonly said, that old age is a return to childhood: which methinks you insist on so long, as if you desired it should be believed. That's the note I mean to shake a little. That saying, meant only of the weakness of body, was wrested to the weakness of mind, by froward children, weary of the controlment of their parents, masters, and other admonitors.

'Secondly, the dotage and childishness they ascribe to age, is never the effect of time, but sometimes of the excesses of youth, and not a returning to, but a continual stay with, childhood. For they that want the curiosity of furnishing their memories with the rarities of nature in their youth, and pass their time in making provision only for their ease, and sensual delight, are children still, at what years soever; as they that coming into a populous city, never going out of their inn, are strangers still, how long soever thay have been there.

'Thirdly, there is no reason for any man to think himself wiser to-day than yesterday, which does not equally convince he shall be wiser to-morrow than to-day.

'Fourthly, you will be forced to change your opinion hereafter, when you are old; and in the mean time you discredit all I have said before in your commendation, because I am old already.—But no more of this.'

Hobbes, when he wrote these pleasing and sensible remarks, was sixty-two years old, and D'Avenant forty-five. MALONE.]

ASAPH. 'Your wish then, Sir, is γηράσκειν διδασκόμενος.' JOHNSON. 'Yes, my Lord.' His Lordship mentioned a charitable establishment in Wales, where people were maintained, and supplied with every thing, upon the condition of their contributing the weekly produce of their labour; and he said, they grew quite torpid for want of property. JOHNSON. 'They have no object for hope. Their condition cannot be better. It is rowing without a port.'

One of the company asked him the meaning of the expression in Juvenal, *unius lacertæ.* JOHNSON. 'I think it clear enough; as much ground as one may have a chance to find a lizard upon.'

Commentators have differed as to the exact meaning of the expression by which the poet intended to enforce the sentiment contained in the passage where these words occur. It is enough that they mean to denote even a very small possession, provided it be a man's own:

> 'Est aliquid, quocunque loco quocunque recessu,
> Unius sese dominum fecisse lacertæ.' [a]

This season there was a whimsical fashion in the news-papers of applying Shakspeare's words to describe living persons well known in the world; which was done under the title of 'Modern Characters from Shakspeare;' many of which were admirably adapted. The fancy took so much, that they were afterwards collected into a pamphlet. Somebody said to Johnson, across the table, that he had not been in these characters. 'Yes (said he) I have. I should have been sorry to be left out.' He then repeated what had been applied to him,

> 'You must borrow me GARGANTUA's mouth.'

Miss Reynolds not perceiving at once the meaning of this, he was obliged to explain it to her, which had something of an awkward and ludicrous effect. 'Why, Madam, it has a reference to me, as using big words, which require the mouth of a giant to pronounce them. Gargantua is the name of a giant in Rabelais.' BOSWELL. 'But, Sir, there is another amongst them for you:

> "He would not flatter Neptune for his trident,
> Or Jove for his power to thunder."'

marginal note:

marginal line: γηράσκειν . . . estab-lishment [H]

[a] *Lizards are so com-mon in Italy, the Thought occur'd natu-rally to Juvenal: an Englishman wd be absurd to talk so.* [I]

JOHNSON. 'There is nothing marked in that. No, Sir, Gargantua is the best.' Notwithstanding this ease and good humour, when I, a little while afterwards, repeated his sarcasm on Kenrick,[1] which was received with applause, he asked, '*Who* said that?' and on my suddenly answering, —*Gargantua*, he looked serious, which was a sufficient indication that he did not wish it to be kept up.[a]

 [a] *to be sure he did.* [H]

When we went to the drawing-room, there was a rich assemblage. Besides the company who had been at dinner, there were Mr. Garrick, Mr. Harris of Salisbury, Dr. Percy, Dr. Burney, the Honourable Mrs. Cholmondeley,[b] Miss Hannah More,[c] &c. &c.

[b] *Poor dear!* [H]

[c] *All dead but the last nam'd in 1820* [H]

After wandering about in a kind of pleasing distraction for some time, I got into a corner, with Johnson, Garrick, and Harris. GARRICK. (to Harris,) 'Pray, Sir, have you read Potter's Æschylus?' HARRIS. 'Yes; and think it pretty.' GARRICK. (to Johnson.) 'And what think you, Sir, of it?' JOHNSON. 'I thought what I read of it *verbiage:* but upon Mr. Harris's recommendation, I will read a play. (To Mr. Harris.) Don't prescribe two.' Mr. Harris suggested one, I do not remember which. JOHNSON. 'We must try its effect as an English poem; that is the way to judge of the merit of a translation. Translations are, in general, for people who cannot read the original.' I mentioned the vulgar saying, that Pope's Homer was not a good representation of the original. JOHNSON. 'Sir, it is the greatest work of the kind that has ever been produced.' BOSWELL. 'The truth is, it is impossible perfectly to translate poetry. In a different language it may be the same tune, but it has not the same tone. Homer plays it on a bassoon; Pope on a flagelet.'[d] HARRIS. 'I think heroick poetry is best in blank verse; yet it appears that rhyme is essential to English poetry, from our deficiency in metrical quantities. In my opinion, the chief excellence of our language is numerous prose.' JOHNSON. 'Sir William Temple was the first writer who gave cadence to English prose.[2] Before his time they were careless of

[d] *Homer play'd it on the Organ; Pope on a Cremona Fiddle.* [H]

---

[1] See vol. i. p. 354.

[2] [The authour in Vol. i. p. 147, says, that Johnson once told him, 'that he had formed his style upon that of Sir William Temple, and upon Chambers's Proposal for his Dictionary. He certainly was mistaken; or, if

arrangement, and did not mind whether a sentence ended with an important word or an insignificant word, or with what part of speech it was concluded.' Mr. Langton, who now had joined us, commended Clarendon. JOHNSON. 'He is objected to for his parentheses, his involved clauses, and his want of harmony. But he is supported by his matter. It is, indeed, owing to a plethory of matter that his style is so faulty: every *substance*, (smiling to Mr. Harris,) has so many *accidents*.—To be distinct we must talk *analytically*. If we analyse language, we must speak of it grammatically; if we analyse argument, we must speak of it logically.' GARRICK. 'Of all the translations that ever were attempted, I think Elphinston's Martial the most extraordinary.[a] He consulted me upon it, who am a little of an epigrammatist myself, you know. I told him freely, "You don't seem to have that turn." I asked him if he was serious; and finding he was, I advised him against publishing. Why, his translation is more difficult to understand than the original. I thought him a man of some talents; but he seems crazy in this.' JOHNSON. 'Sir, you have done what I had not courage to do. But he did not ask my advice, and I did not force it upon him, to make him angry with me.' GARRICK. 'But as a friend, Sir—.' JOHNSON. 'Why, such a friend as I am with him—no.' GARRICK. 'But if you see a friend going to tumble over

[a] *he said true.*
Hast unroll'd to the Horns my dear Friend my dear Book?
And roll'd as perus'd doest resign?
are two Lines of Elphinston's Martial & nobody can wish two more. [I]

---

he imagined at first that he was imitating Temple, he was very unsuccessful for nothing can be more unlike than the simplicity of Temple and the richness of Johnson.'

This observation of our authour, on the first view, seems perfectly just; but, on a closer examination, it will, I think, appear to have been founded on a misapprehension. Mr. Boswell understood Johnson too literally. He did not, I conceive, mean, that he endeavoured to imitate Temple's style in all its parts; but that he formed his style on him and Chambers, (perhaps the paper published in 1737, relative to his second edition, entitled CONSIDERATIONS, &c.) taking from each what was most worthy of imitation. The passage before us, I think shows, that he learned from Temple to modulate his periods, and, *in that respect only*, made him his pattern. In this view of the subject there is no difficulty. He might learn from Chambers, compactness, strength, and precision (in opposition to the laxity of style which had long prevailed); from Sir Thomas Browne, (who was certainly one of his archetypes,) *pondera verborum*, vigour and energy of expression; and from Temple, harmonious arrangement, the due collocation of words, and the other arts and graces of composition here enumerated: and yet, after all, his style might bear no striking resemblance to that of any of these writers, though it had profited by each. MALONE.][b]

[b] *A beautiful Note.* [H]

a precipice?' JOHNSON. 'That is an extravagant case, Sir. You are sure a friend will thank you for hindering him from tumbling over a precipice: but, in the other case, I should hurt his vanity, and do him no good. He would not take my advice. His brother-in-law, Strahan, sent him a subscription of fifty pounds, and said he would send him fifty more, if he would not publish.' GARRICK. 'What! eh! is Strahan a good judge of an Epigram? Is not he rather an *obtuse* man, eh?' JOHNSON. 'Why, Sir, he may not be a judge of an Epigram: but you see he is a judge of what is *not* an Epigram.' BOSWELL. 'It is easy for you, Mr. Garrick, to talk to an authour as you talked to Elphinston; you, who have been so long the manager of a theatre, rejecting the plays of poor authours. You are an old Judge, who have often pronounced sentence of death. You are a practised surgeon, who have often amputated limbs; and though this may have been for the good of your patients, they cannot like you. Those who have undergone a dreadful operation, are not very fond of seeing the operator again.' GARRICK. 'Yes, I know enough of that. There was a reverend gentleman, (Mr. Hawkins,) who wrote a tragedy, the SIEGE of something,[1] which I refused.' HARRIS. 'So, the siege was raised.' JOHNSON. 'Ay, he came to me and complained; and told me, that Garrick said his play was wrong in the *concoction*. Now, what is the concoction of a play!' (Here Garrick started, and twisted himself, and seemed sorely vexed; for Johnson told me, he believed the story was true.) GARRICK. 'I—I—I— said, *first* concoction.'[2] JOHNSON. (smiling.) 'Well, he left out *first*. And Rich, he said, refused him *in false English:* he could shew it under his hand.' GARRICK. 'He wrote to me in violent wrath, for having refused his play: "Sir, this is growing a very serious and terrible affair. I am resolved to publish my play. I will appeal to the world; and how will your judgement appear?" I answered, "Sir, notwithstanding all the seriousness, and all the terrours, I have no

---

[1] It was called 'The Siege of Aleppo.' Mr Hawkins, the Authour of it, was formerly Professor of Poetry at Oxford. It is printed in his 'Miscellanies,' 3 Vols. 8vo.

[2] [Garrick had high authority for this expression. Dryden uses it in his preface to OEDIPUS. MALONE.]

objection to your publishing your play; and as you live at a great distance, (Devonshire, I believe,) if you will send it to me, I will convey it to the press." I never heard more of it, ha! ha! ha!'

On Friday, April 10, I found Johnson at home in the morning. We resumed the conversation of yesterday. He put me in mind of some of it which had escaped my memory, and enabled me to record it more perfectly than I otherwise could have done. He was much pleased with my paying so great attention to his recommendation in 1763, the period when our acquaintance began, that I should keep a journal; and I could perceive he was secretly pleased to find so much of the fruit of his mind preserved; and as he had been used to imagine and say that he always laboured when he said a good thing,—it delighted him, on a review, to find that his conversation teemed with point and imagery.

I said to him, 'You were, yesterday, Sir, in remarkably good humour; but there was nothing to offend you, nothing to produce irritation or violence. There was no bold offender. There was not one capital conviction. It was a maiden assize. You had on your white gloves.'

index sign: *There was* etc. [H]

Hr found fault with our friend Langton for having been too silent. 'Sir, (said I,) you will recollect that he very properly took up Sir Joshua for being glad that Charles Fox had praised Goldsmith's "Traveller," and you joined him.' JOHNSON. 'Yes, Sir, I knocked Fox on the head, without ceremony. Reynolds is too much under Fox and Burke at present. He is under the *Fox star*, and the *Irish constellation*. He is always under some planet.' BOSWELL. 'There is no Fox star.' JOHNSON. 'But there is a dog star.' BOSWELL. 'They say, indeed, a fox and a dog are the same animal.'

I reminded him of a gentleman,[a] who, Mrs. Cholmondeley said, was first talkative from affectation, and then silent from the same cause; that he first thought, 'I shall be celebrated as the liveliest man in every company;' and then, all at once, 'O! it is much more respectable to be grave and look wise.' 'He has reversed the Pythagorean discipline, by being first talkative, and then silent. He reverses the course of Nature too; he was first the gay

[a] *I do not know who this was.* [I]

butterfly, and then the creeping worm.' Johnson laughed
loud and long at this expansion and illustration of what
he himself had told me.

We dined together with Mr. Scott (now Sir William
Scott, his Majesty's Advocate General,)[1] at his chambers
in the Temple, nobody else there. The company being
small, Johnson was not in such spirits as he had been the
preceding day, and for a considerable time little was said.
At last he burst forth: 'Subordination is sadly broken
down in this age. No man, now, has the same authority
which his father had, except a gaoler. No master has it
over his servants: it is diminished in our colleges; nay, in
our grammar-schools.' BOSWELL. 'What is the cause of
this, Sir?' JOHNSON. 'Why, the coming in of the Scotch,'
(laughing sarcastically.) BOSWELL. 'That is to say, things
have been turned topsy-turvy.—But your serious cause.'
JOHNSON. 'Why, Sir, there are many causes, the chief of
which is, I think, the great increase of money. No man
now depends upon the Lord of a Manour, when he can
send to another country, and fetch provisions. The shoe-
black at the entry of my court does not depend on me. I
can deprive him but of a penny a day, which he hopes
somebody else will bring him; and that penny I must carry
to another shoe-black, so the trade suffers nothing. I have
explained, in my "Journey to the Hebrides," how gold
and silver destroy feudal subordination. But, besides,
there is a general relaxation of reverence. No son now
depends upon his father, as in former times. Paternity used
to be considered as of itself a great thing, which had a right
to many claims. That is, in general, reduced to very small
bounds. My hope is, that as anarchy produces tyranny,
this extreme relaxation will produce *freni strictio*.'[a]

Talking of fame, for which there is so great a desire, I
observed, how little there is of it in reality, compared with
the other objects of human attention. 'Let every man
recollect, and he will be sensible how small a part of his
time is employed in talking or thinking of Shakspeare,
Voltaire, or any of the most celebrated men that have ever
lived, or are now supposed to occupy the attention and

[a] *So it did in France. it produc'd* Buonaparte *who held the* Frenum *strictly enough, but not too strictly: They are going to run Riot again, now he is safe in the rocky Cage of St. Helena. 1817.* [H]

& so it has in France Buonapart holds his Reins tight at least. [I]

[1] [Now (1804,) Judge of the Court of Admiralty, and Master of the Faculties. MALONE.]

admiration of the world. Let this be extracted and compressed; into what a narrow space will it go!' I then slily introduced Mr. Garrick's fame, and his assuming the airs of a great man. JOHNSON. 'Sir, it is wonderful how *little* Garrick assumes. No, Sir, Garrick *fortunam reverenter habet.* Consider, Sir; celebrated men, such as you have mentioned, have had their applause at a distance; but Garrick had it dashed in his face, sounded in his ears, and went home every night with the plaudits of a thousand in his *cranium.* Then, Sir, Garrick did not *find,* but *made* his way to the tables, the levees, and almost the bed-chambers of the great. Then, Sir, Garrick had under him a numerous body of people; who, from fear of his power, and hopes of his favour, and admiration of his talents, were constantly submissive to him. And here is a man who has advanced the dignity of his profession. Garrick has made a player a higher character.' SCOTT. 'And he is a very sprightly writer too.' JOHNSON. 'Yes, Sir; and all this supported by great wealth of his own acquisition. If all this had happened to me, I should have had a couple of fellows with long poles walking before me, to knock down every body that stood in the way. Consider, if all this had happened to Cibber or Quin, they'd have jumped over the moon. —Yet Garrick speaks to *us.*' (smiling.) BOSWELL. 'And Garrick is a very good man, a charitable man.' JOHNSON. 'Sir, a liberal man. He has given away more money than any man in England. There may be a little vanity mixed: but he has shewn, that money is not his first object.' BOSWELL. 'Yet Foote used to say of him, that he walked out with an intention to do a generous action; but turning the corner of a street, he met with the ghost of a halfpenny, which frightened him.' JOHNSON. 'Why, Sir, that is very true, too; for I never knew a man of whom it could be said with less certainty to-day, what he will do to-morrow, than Garrick; it depends so much on his humour at the time.' SCOTT. 'I am glad to hear of his liberality. He has been represented as very saving.' JOHNSON. 'With his domestic saving we have nothing to do. I remember drinking tea with him long ago, when Peg Woffington made it, and he grumbled at her for

marginal notes:
marginal line: *wonderful how ... Sir; celebrated* [H]

marginal line: *applause at ... his cranium* [H]

marginal line: *profession. Garrick ... sprightly writer* [H]

marginal line: *man, a ... any man* [H]

making it too strong.[1] He had then begun to feel money in his purse, and did not know when he should have enough of it.'

On the subject of wealth, the proper use of it, and the effects of that art which is called economy, he observed, 'It is wonderful to think how men of very large estates not only spend their yearly incomes, but are often actually in want of money. It is clear they have not value for what they spend. Lord Shelburne told me, that a man of high rank, who looks into his own affairs, may have all that he ought to have, all that can be of any use, or appear with any advantage, for five thousand pounds a year. Therefore a great proportion must go in waste; and indeed, this is the case with most people, whatever their fortune is.' BOSWELL. 'I have no doubt, Sir, of this. But how is it? What is waste?' JOHNSON. 'Why, Sir, breaking bottles, and a thousand other things. Waste cannot be accurately told, though we are sensible how destructive it is. Economy on the one hand, by which a certain income is made to maintain a man genteelly, and waste on the other, by which, on the same income, another man lives shabbily, cannot be defined. It is a very nice thing; as one man wears his coat out much sooner than another, we cannot tell how.'

We talked of war. JOHNSON. 'Every man thinks meanly of himself for not having been a soldier, or not having been at sea.' BOSWELL. 'Lord Mansfield does not.' JOHNSON. 'Sir, if Lord Mansfield were in a company of General Officers and Admirals who have been in service, he would shrink; he'd wish to creep under the table.' BOSWELL. 'No; he'd think he could *try* them all.' JOHNSON. 'Yes, if he could catch them: but they'd try him much sooner. No, Sir; were Socrates and Charles the Twelfth of Sweden both present in any company, and Socrates to say, "Follow me, and hear a lecture in philosophy;" and Charles, laying his hand on his sword, to say, "Follow me, and dethrone the Czar;" a man would be ashamed to follow Socrates.[a] Sir, the impression is universal: yet it is strange. As to the sailor, when you look down from the

marginal line:
with any . . . a year [H]

queried:
he would shrink etc. [H]

[a] *curious!* [H]
[b] *I have heard him tell it another way—how he stole the Tea (before it was made) out of the Cup she put it in by way of measuring— & then lamented its strength & deep colour.* [I]

[1] When Johnson told this little anecdote to Sir Joshua Reynolds, he mentioned a circumstance which he omitted to-day :—'Why (said Garrick) it is as red as blood.'[b]

quarter-deck to the space below, you see the utmost extremity of human misery: such crowding, such filth, such stench!' BOSWELL. 'Yet sailors are happy.' JOHNSON. 'They are happy as brutes are happy, with a piece of fresh meat,—with the grossest sensuality. But, Sir, the profession of soldiers and sailors has the dignity of danger. Mankind reverence those who have got over fear, which is so general a weakness.' SCOTT. 'But is not courage mechanical, and to be acquired?' JOHNSON. 'Why, yes, Sir, in a collective sense. Soldiers consider themselves only as part of a great machine.' SCOTT. 'We find people fond of being sailors.' JOHNSON. 'I cannot account for that, any more than I can account for other strange perversions of imagination.'

marginal line: grossest sensuality ... danger. Mankind [H]

marginal line: sailors' JOHNSON ... strange perversions [H]

His abhorrence of the profession of a sailor was uniformly violent; but in conversation he always exalted the profession of a soldier. And yet I have, in my large and various collection of his writings, a letter to an eminent friend, in which he expresses himself thus: 'My god-son called on me lately. He is weary, and rationally weary, of a military life. If you can place him in some other state, I think you may increase his happiness, and secure his virtue. A soldier's time is passed in distress and danger or in idleness and corruption.' Such was his cool reflection in his study; but whenever he was warmed and animated by the presence of company, he, like other philosophers, whose minds are impregnated with poetical fancy, caught the common enthusiasm for splendid renown.

He talked of Mr. Charles Fox, of whose abilities he thought highly, but observed, that he did not talk much at our CLUB. I have heard Mr. Gibbon remark, 'that Mr. Fox could not be afraid of Dr. Johnson; yet he certainly was very shy of saying any thing in Dr. Johnson's presence.' Mr. Scott now quoted what was said of Alcibiades by a Greek poet, to which Johnson assented.[1]

[1] [Wishing to discover the ancient observation here referred to, I applied to Sir William Scott on the subject, but he had no recollection of it.—My old and very learned friend, Dr. Michael Kearney, formerly senior fellow of Trinity College, Dublin, and now Arch-deacon of Raphoe in Ireland, has, however, most happily elucidated this passage. He remarks to me that 'Mr. Boswell's memory must here have deceived him; and that Mr. Scott's observation must have been, that "Mr. Fox, in the instance mentioned,

He told us, that he had given Mrs. Montague a catalogue of all Daniel Defoe's works of imagination; most, if
not all of which, as well as of his other works, he now
enumerated, allowing a considerable[a] share of merit to a
man, who, bred a tradesman, had written so variously and
so well. Indeed, his 'Robinson Crusoe' is enough of itself
to establish his reputation.

He expressed great indignation at the imposture of the
Cock-lane Ghost, and related, with much satisfaction,
how he had assisted in detecting the cheat, and had
published an account of it in the news-papers. Upon this
subject I incautiously offended him, by pressing him with
too many questions, and he shewed his displeasure. I
apologised, saying that 'I asked questions in order to be
instructed and entertained; I repaired eagerly to the
fountain; but that the moment he gave me a hint, the
moment he put a lock upon the well, I desisted.'—'But,
Sir, (said he,) that is forcing one to do a disagreeable
thing:' and he continued to rate me. 'Nay, Sir, (said I,)
when you have put a lock upon the well, so that I can no
longer drink, do not make the fountain of your wit play
upon me and wet me.'

He sometimes could not bear being teazed with questions. I was once present when a gentleman[b] asked so many,
as, 'What did you do, Sir?' 'What did you say, Sir?' that
he at last grew enraged, and said, 'I will not be put to the
question. Don't you consider, Sir,[c] that these are not the
manners of a gentleman? I will not be baited with what
and why; what is this? what is that? why is a cow's tail
long? why is a fox's tail bushy?'[d] The gentleman, who
was a good deal out of countenance, said, 'Why, Sir, you
are so good, that I venture to trouble you.' JOHNSON.
'Sir, my being so good is no reason why you should be so ill.'

might be considered as the reverse of Phæax, of whom, as Plutarch relates in
the Life of Alcibiades, Eupolis the tragedian said: It is true he can talk, and yet
he is no speaker.'"

If this discovery had been made by a scholiast on an ancient authour, with
what ardour and exuberant praise would Bentley or Taylor have spoken of
it!—Sir William Scott, to whom I communicated Dr. Kearney's remark, is
perfectly satisfied that it is correct. A few other observations have been
communicated by the same gentleman. Every classical reader will lament
that they are not more numerous. MALONE.]

underlined:
considerable [1]

[a] considerable is no
Word for De Foe; in
some Respects his merit
is transcendent—in
his History of the
Plague there are Pas-
sages that freeze one
with Horror. [1]

marginal line:
put a . . . a disagreeable
[H]

[b] himself. [H]

[c] This Gentleman was
his own dear Self—
James Boswell Esq—
[1]

[d] 'I have been put so
to the Question by Bozzy
this Morning—said Dr.
Johnson one day—that
I am now panting for
Breath. What sort of
Questions did he ask I
wonder . . . Why one
Question was Pray Sir
can you tell why an
Apple is round & a
Pear pointed? Would
not such Talk make a
Man hang himself?'
[H]

Talking of the Justitia hulk at Woolwich, in which
criminals were punished, by being confined to labour, he
said, 'I do not see that they are punished by this: they
must have worked equally, had they never been guilty of
stealing. They now only work; so, after all, they have
gained; what they stole is clear gain to them; the confinement is nothing. Every man who works is confined: the
smith to his shop, the tailor to his garret.' BOSWELL.
'And Lord Mansfield to his Court.' JOHNSON. 'Yes, Sir.
You know the notion of confinement may be extended,
as in the song "Every island is a prison." There is, in
Dodsley's Collection, a copy of verses to the authour of
that song.'[1]

Smith's Latin verses on Pococke, the great traveller,[2]
were mentioned. He repeated some of them, and said they
were Smith's best verses.

He talked with an uncommon animation of travelling
into distant countries; that the mind was enlarged by it,
and that an acquisition of dignity of character was derived
from it. He expressed a particular enthusiasm with respect
to visiting the wall of China. I catched it for the moment,
and said I really believed I should go and see the wall of
China had I not children, of whom it was my duty to take
care. 'Sir, (said he,) by doing so, you would do what would
be of importance in raising your children to eminence.
There would be a lustre reflected upon them from your
spirit and curiosity. They would be at all times regarded   index sign:
as the children of a man who had gone to view the wall of   *a man who* etc. [H]
China. I am serious, Sir.'

When we had left Mr. Scott's, he said, 'Will you go home
with me?' 'Sir, (said I,) it is late; but I'll go with you for
three minutes.' JOHNSON. 'Or *four*.' We went to Mrs.

---

[1] [I have in vain examined Dodsley's Collection, for the verses here referred
to; nor has the name of the authour been ascertained. The song alluded to
begins with the words,
   'Welcome, welcome, brother debtor—'
It consists of several stanzas, in one of which it is said, that
   'Every island is a prison.' MALONE.]

[2] [Smith's Verses are on Edward Pococke, the great Oriental linguist; he
travelled it is true; but Dr. Richard Pococke, late Bishop of Ossory, who
published Travels through the East, is usually called *the great traveller*.
KEARNEY.]

Williams's room, where we found Mr. Allen the printer, who was the landlord of his house in Bolt-court, a worthy obliging man, and his very old acquaintance; and what was exceedingly amusing, though he was of a very diminutive size, he used, even in Johnson's presence, to imitate the stately periods and slow and solemn utterance of the great man.—I this evening boasted, that although I did not write what is called stenography, or short-hand, in appropriated characters devised for the purpose, I had a method of my own of writing half words, and leaving out some altogether, so as yet to keep the substance and language of any discourse which I had heard so much in view, that I could give it very completely soon after I had taken it down. He defied me, as he had once defied an actual short-hand writer; and he made the experiment by reading slowly and distinctly a part of Robertson's 'History of America,' while I endeavoured to write it in my way of taking notes. It was found that I had it very imperfectly; the conclusion from which was, that its excellence was principally owing to a studied arrangement of words, which could not be varied or abridged without an essential injury.

underlined:
laying [H]

On Sunday, April 12, I found him at home before dinner; Dr. Dodd's poem, entitled 'Thoughts in Prison,' was laying upon his table. This appearing to me an extraordinary effort by a man who was in Newgate for a capital crime, I was desirous to hear Johnson's opinion of it: to my surprize, he told me he had not read a line of it. I took up the book and read a passage to him. JOHNSON. 'Pretty well, if you are previously disposed to like them.' I read another passage, with which he was better pleased. He then took the book into his own hands, and having looked at the prayer at the end of it, he said, 'What *evidence* is there that this was composed the night before he suffered? *I* do not believe it.' He then read aloud where he prays for the King, &c. and observed, 'Sir, do you think that a man, the night before he is to be hanged, cares for the succession of a royal

marginal line:
composed this . . . a
man [H]

family?—Though, he *may* have composed this prayer then. A man who has been canting all his life, may cant to the last.—And yet, a man who has been refused a pardon after so much petitioning, would hardly be praying thus fervently for the King.'

most dutiful attachment to the noble House of Northumberland, could not sit quietly and hear a man praised, who had spoken disrespectfully of Alnwick Castle and the Duke's pleasure-grounds, especially as he thought meanly of his travels. He therefore opposed Johnson eagerly. JOHNSON. 'Pennant in what he has said of Alnwick, has done what he intended; he has made you very angry.' PERCY. 'He has said the garden is trim, which is representing it, like a citizen's parterre, when the truth is, there is a very large extent of fine turf and gravel walks.' JOHNSON. 'According to your own account, Sir, Pennant is right. It *is* trim. Here is grass cut close, and gravel rolled smooth. Is not that trim? The extent is nothing against that; a mile may be as trim as a square yard. Your extent puts me in mind of the citizen's enlarged dinner, two pieces of roast-beef, and two puddings. There is no variety, no mind exerted in laying out the ground, no trees.' PERCY. 'He pretends to give the natural history of Northumberland, and yet takes no notice of the immense number of trees planted there of late.'[a] JOHNSON. 'That, Sir, has nothing to do with the *natural* history; that is *civil* history. A man who gives the natural history of the oak, is not to tell how many oaks have been planted in this place or that. A man who gives the natural history of the cow, is not to tell how many cows are milked at Islington. The animal is the same, whether milked in the Park or at Islington.' PERCY. 'Pennant does not describe well; a carrier who goes along the side of Lochlomond would describe it better.' JOHNSON. 'I think he describes very well.' PERCY. 'I travelled after him.' JOHNSON. 'And *I* travelled after him.' PERCY. 'But, my good friend, you are short-sighted, and do not see so well as I do.' I wondered at Dr. Percy's venturing thus. Dr. Johnson said nothing at the time: but inflammable particles were collecting for a cloud to burst. In a little while Dr. Percy said something more in disparagement of Pennant. JOHNSON. (pointedly,) 'This is the resentment of a narrow mind, because he did not find every thing in Northumberland.' PERCY. (feeling the stroke,) 'Sir! you may be as rude as you please.' JOHNSON. 'Hold, Sir! Don't talk of rudeness; remember, Sir, you told me, (puffing hard with

queried:
a mile etc. [H]

[a] *The very finest old Beech Trees I ever saw—are at Inverary.* [H]

passion struggling for a vent,) I was short-sighted. We have done with civility. We are to be as rude as we please.' PERCY. 'Upon my honour, Sir, I did not mean to be uncivil.' JOHNSON. 'I cannot say so, Sir; for I *did* mean to be uncivil, thinking *you* had been uncivil.' Dr. Percy rose, ran up to him, and taking him by the hand, assured him affectionately that his meaning had been misunderstood; upon which a reconciliation instantly took place. JOHNSON. 'My dear Sir, I am willing you shall *hang* Pennant.' PERCY. (resuming the former subject,) 'Pennant complains that the helmet is not hung out to invite to the hall of hospitality. Now I never heard that it was a custom to hang out a *helmet*.'[1][a] JOHNSON. 'Hang him up, hang him up.'[b] BOSWELL. (humouring the joke,) 'Hang out his skull instead of a helmet, and you may drink ale out of it in your hall of Odin, as he is your enemy; that will be truly ancient. *There* will be "Northern Antiquities."'[2] JOHNSON. 'He's a *Whig*, Sir; a *sad dog*, (smiling at his own violent expressions, merely for *political* difference of opinion.) But he's the best traveller I ever read; he observes more things than any one else does.'

I could not help thinking that this was too high praise of a writer who traversed a wide extent of country, in such haste, that he could put together only curt frittered fragments of his own, and afterwards procured supplemental intelligence from parochial ministers, and others not the best qualified or most impartial narrators, whose ungenerous prejudice against the house of Stuart glares in misrepresentation; a writer, who at best treats merely of superficial objects, and shews no philosophical investigation of character and manners, such as Johnson has exhibited in his masterly 'Journey,' over part of the same ground; and who it should seem from a desire of ingratiating himself with the Scotch, has flattered the people of North-Britain so inordinately and with so little

marginal line:
say so . . . uncivil,
thinking [H]
underlined:
did [H]

[a] *Yes Yes, that it* was; & *it was in Percy's way to know it—more than in Pennants way.* [H]

[b] *I am unwilling Pennant should be hang'd to pacify Dr. Percy—there* my *nationality comes in.—but how miserably do* all *these Wits and Scholars shew in such a Concave Mirror as this Book is.* [I]

---

[1] [It certainly was a custom, as appears from the following passage in Perceforest, vol. iii. p. 108:—'fasoient mettre au plus hault de leur hostel un *heaulme, en signe* que tous les gentils hommes et gentilles femmes entrassent hardiment en leur hostel comme en leur propre,' &c. KEARNEY.]

[The authour's second son, Mr. James Boswell, had noticed this passage in Perceforest, and suggested to me the same remark. MALONE.]

[2] The title of a book translated by Dr. Percy.

discrimination, that the judicious and candid amongst them must be disgusted, while they value more the plain, just, yet kindly report of Johnson.

Having impartially censured Mr. Pennant, as a Traveller in Scotland, let me allow him, from authorities much better than mine, his deserved praise as an able Zoologist; and let me also from my own understanding and feelings, acknowledge the merit of his 'LONDON,' which, though said to be not quite accurate in some particulars, is one of the most pleasing topographical performances that ever appeared in any language. Mr. Pennant, like his countrymen in general, has the true spirit of a *Gentleman*.[a] As a proof of it, I shall quote from his 'LONDON' the passage, in which he speaks of my illustrious friend. 'I must by no means omit *Bolt-court*, the long residence of Doctor SAMUEL JOHNSON, a man of the strongest natural abilities, great learning, a most retentive memory, of the deepest and most unaffected piety and morality, mingled with those numerous weaknesses and prejudices which his friends have kindly taken care to draw from their dread abode.[1] I brought on myself his transient anger, by observing that in his tour in *Scotland*, he once had "long and woeful experience of oats being the food of men in *Scotland* as they were of horses in *England*." It was a national reflection unworthy of him, and I shot my bolt. In return he gave me a tender hug.[2] *Con amore* he also said of me, " *The dog is a Whig:*"[3] I admired the virtues of Lord *Russel*, and pitied his fall. I should have been a Whig at the Revolution. There have been periods since in which I should have been, what I now am, a moderate Tory, a supporter, as far as my little influence extends, of a well-poised balance between the crown and people: but should the scale preponderate against the *Salus populi*, that moment may it be said, "*The* dog's a *Whig!*"'

index sign and underlined:
spirit [H]

[a] *1817. so he has: I wish He had the Style of a Gentleman; but his perverse Imitation of Counting House Brevity, leaving the Personal Pronoun out so perpetually; teazes a Reader more than one could imagine. his style resembles a Letter in the Spectator, recommending Whittington to the Temple of Fame.* [H]

So he has; and yet he borrows a pityful Commercial Style; Fruit of his Whiggism; leaving out the personal Pronouns as if he were Clerk in a Merchant's Counting house & not a Descendant of Vortigern. [I]

[1] This is the common cant against faithful Biography. Does the worthy gentleman mean that I, who was taught discrimination of character by Johnson, should have omitted his frailties, and, in short, have *bedawbed* him as the worthy gentleman has bedawbed Scotland?

[2] See Dr. JOHNSON's 'Journey to the Western Islands,' p. 296:—see his Dictionary article, *oats:*—and my 'Voyage to the Hebrides,' first edition.—PENNANT.

[3] Mr. Boswell's Journal, p. 386.—PENNANT.

We had a calm after the storm, staid the evening and supped, and were pleasant and gay. But Dr. Percy told me he was very uneasy at what had passed; for there was a gentleman there who was acquainted with the Northumberland family, to whom he hoped to have appeared more respectable, by shewing how intimate he was with Dr. Johnson, and who might now, on the contrary, go away with an opinion to his disadvantage. He begged I would mention this to Dr. Johnson, which I afterwards did. His observation upon it was, 'This comes of *stratagem;* had he told me[a] that he wished to appear to advantage before that gentleman, he should have been at the top of the house all the time.' He spoke of Dr. Percy in the handsomest manner. 'Then, Sir, (said I,) may I be allowed to suggest a mode by which you may effectually counteract any unfavourable report of what passed. I will write a letter to you upon the subject of the unlucky contest of that day, and you will be kind enough to put in writing as an answer to that letter, what you have now said, and as Lord Percy is to dine with us at General Paoli's soon, I will take an opportunity to read the correspondence in his Lordship's presence.' This friendly scheme was accordingly carried into execution without Dr. Percy's knowledge. Johnson's letter placed Dr. Percy's unquestionable merit in the fairest point of view; and I contrived that Lord Percy should hear the correspondence, by introducing it at General Paoli's as an instance of Dr. Johnson's kind disposition towards one in whom his Lordship was interested. Thus every unfavourable impression was obviated that could possibly have been made on those by whom he wished most to be regarded. I breakfasted the day after with him, and informed him of my scheme, and its happy completion, for which he thanked me in the warmest terms, and was highly delighted with Dr. Johnson's letter in his praise, of which I gave him a copy. He said, 'I would rather have this than degrees from all the Universities in Europe. It will be for me, and my children and grand-children.' Dr. Johnson having afterwards asked me if I had given him a copy of it, and being told I had, was offended, and insisted that I should get it back, which I did. As, however, he did not desire me to destroy either the original or the copy, or forbid me to

[a] *but who* does *tell such Things?* [H & I]

let it be seen, I think myself at liberty to apply to it his general declaration to me concerning his own letters, 'That he did not choose they should be published in his life time; but had no objection to their appearing after his death.' I shall therefore insert this kindly correspondence, having faithfully narrated the circumstances accompanying it.

'TO DR. SAMUEL JOHNSON

'MY DEAR SIR,

'I BEG leave to address you in behalf of our friend Dr. Percy, who was much hurt by what you said to him that day we dined at his house;[1] when, in the course of the dispute as to Pennant's merit as a traveller, you told Percy that "he had the resentment of a narrow mind against Pennant, because he did not find every thing in Northumberland." Percy is sensible that you did not mean to injure him; but he is vexed to think that your behaviour to him on that occasion may be interpreted as a proof that he is despised by you, which I know is not the case. I have told him, that the charge of being narrow-minded was only as to the particular point in question; and that he had the merit of being a martyr to his noble family.

'Earl Percy is to dine with General Paoli next Friday; and I should be sincerely glad to have it in my power to satisfy his Lordship how well you think of Dr. Percy, who, I find, apprehends that your good opinion of him may be of very essential consequence;[a] and who assures me, that he has the highest respect and the warmest affection for you.[b]

underlined:
essential consequence [H]
[a] *Proof that his Mind was narrow.* [H]
[b] *a Lye on both Sides.* [H]

'I have only to add, that my suggesting this occasion for the exercise of your candour and generosity, is altogether unknown to Dr. Percy, and proceeds from my good-will towards him, and my persuasion that you will be happy to do him an essential kindness. I am, more and more, my dear Sir,

'Your most faithful

'And affectionate humble servant,

'JAMES BOSWELL'

[1] Sunday, April 12, 1778.

'TO JAMES BOSWELL, ESQ.

'SIR,

'THE debate between Dr. Percy and me is one of those foolish controversies, which begin upon a question of which neither party cares how it is decided, and which is, nevertheless, continued to acrimony, by the vanity with which every man resists confutation. Dr. Percy's warmth proceeded from a cause which, perhaps, does him more honour than he could have derived from juster criticism. His abhorrence of Pennant proceeded from his opinion that Pennant had wantonly and indecently censured his patron. His anger made him resolve, that, for having been once wrong, he never should be right. Pennant has much in his notions that I do not like; but still I think him a very intelligent traveller. If Percy is really offended, I am sorry; for he is a man whom I never knew to offend any one. He is a man very willing to learn, and very able to teach; a man, out of whose company I never go without having learned something. It is sure that he vexes me sometimes, but I am afraid it is by making me feel my own ignorance. So much extension of mind, and so much minute accuracy of enquiry, if you survey your whole circle of acquaintance, you will find so scarce, if you find it at all, that you will value Percy by comparison. Lord Hailes is somewhat like him: but Lord Hailes does not, perhaps, go beyond him in research; and I do not know that he equals him in elegance. Percy's attention to poetry has given grace and splendour to his studies of antiquity. A mere antiquarian is a rugged being.

'Upon the whole, you see that what I might say in sport or petulance to him, is very consistent with full conviction of his merit.   'I am, dear Sir,

'Your most, &c.

'April 23, 1778.'   'SAM. JOHNSON'

'TO THE REVEREND DR. PERCY, NORTHUMBER-
LAND-HOUSE

'DEAR SIR,

'I WROTE to Dr. Johnson on the subject of the *Pennantian* controversy; and have received from him an answer which will delight you. I read it yesterday to Dr. Robertson, at the Exhibition; and at dinner to Lord Percy, General Oglethorpe, &c. who dined with us at General Paoli's; who was also a witness to the high *testimony* to your honour.

'General Paoli desires the favour of your company next Tuesday to dinner, to meet Dr. Johnson. If I can, I will call on you to-day. I am, with sincere regard,

'Your most obedient humble servant,

'South Audley-street, April 25.'   'JAMES BOSWELL'[1]

On Monday, April 13, I dined with Johnson at Mr. Langton's, where were Dr. Porteus, then Bishop of Chester, now of London, and Dr. Stinton. He was at first in a very silent mood. Before dinner he said nothing but 'Pretty baby,' to one of the children.[a] Langton said very well to me afterwards, that he could repeat Johnson's conversation before dinner, as Johnson had said that he could repeat a complete chapter of 'The Natural History of Iceland,' from the Danish of *Horrebow*, the whole of which was exactly thus:

'CHAP. LXXII. *Concerning Snakes*

'There are no snakes to be met with throughout the whole island.'

At dinner we talked of another mode in the news-papers of giving modern characters in sentences from the classicks, and of the passage

> 'Parcus deorum cultor, et infrequens,
> Insanientis dum sapientiæ
> Consultus erro, nunc retrorsùm
> Vela dare, atque iterare cursus
> Cogor relictos:'

being well applied to Soame Jenyns; who, after having wandered in the wilds of infidelity, had returned to the

[a] *Bozzy was like a Man in Mrs. Inchbald's Comedies—I forget his Name—who brings People together for his own Sport, & they Sometimes quarrel; but make it up so often, that he is at length happily perswaded of his own Benevolence. 1817.* [H]

---

[1] Though the Bishop of Dromore kindly answered the letters which I wrote to him, relative to Dr. Johnson's early history; yet, in justice to him, I think it proper to add, that the account of the foregoing conversation, and the subsequent transaction, as well as of some other conversations in which he is mentioned, has been given to the publick without previous communication with his Lordship.

Christian faith. Mr. Langton asked Johnson as to the
propriety of *sapientiæ consultus*. JOHNSON. 'Though *consultus* was primarily an adjective, like *amicus* it came to be
used as a substantive. So we have *Juris consultus*, a consult
in law.'

We talked of the styles of different painters, and how
certainly a connoisseur could distinguish them. I asked, if
there was as clear a difference of styles in language as in
painting, or even as in hand-writing, so that the composition of every individual may be distinguished? JOHNSON.
'Yes. Those who have a style of eminent excellence, such
as Dryden and Milton, can always be distinguished.'[a] I
had no doubt of this; but what I wanted to know was,
whether there was really a peculiar style to every man
whatever, as there is certainly a peculiar hand-writing,
a peculiar countenance, not widely different in many,
yet always enough to be distinctive:

> '————— facies non omnibus una,
> Nec diversa tamen.'——

The Bishop thought not; and said, he supposed that many
pieces in Dodsley's collection of poems, though all very
pretty, had nothing appropriated in their style, and in that
particular could not be at all distinguished. JOHNSON.
'Why, Sir, I think every man whatever has a peculiar style,
which may be discovered by nice examination and comparison with others: but a man must write a great deal to
make his style obviously discernible. As logicians say, this
appropriation of style is infinite *in potestate*, limited *in actu*.'

Mr Topham Beauclerk came in the evening, and he and
Dr. Johnson and I staid to supper. It was mentioned that
Dr. Dodd had once wished to be a member of THE LITER-
ARY CLUB. JOHNSON. 'I should be sorry if any of our
Club were hanged. I will not say but some of them deserve
it.'[1] BEAUCLERK (supposing this to be aimed at persons
for whom he had at that time a wonderful fancy, which,
however, did not last long,) was irritated, and eagerly
said, 'You, Sir, have a friend (naming him)[b] who deserves
to be hanged; for he speaks behind their backs against
those with whom he lives on the best terms, and attacks

[a] *It seems* not. *The
Lines always quoted as
Dryden's, beginning*

> *To die is landing on
> some silent Shore*

*are Garth's Lines after
all. Mr. Mangin
shew'd them to me in
the Dispensary.* 1817.
[H]

marginal line:
should be . . . it.'
BEAUCLERK [H]

underlined:
naming him [H]
[b] Steevens [H]

[1] See *ante*, p. 340.

them in the news-papers. *He* certainly ought to be *kicked.*'
JOHNSON. 'Sir, we all do this in some degree: " *Veniam
petimus damusque vicissim.*" To be sure it may be done so
much, that a man may deserve to be kicked.' BEAUCLERK.

'He is very malignant.' JOHNSON. 'No, Sir; heᵃ is not
malignant. He is mischievous, if you will. He would do no
man an essential injury; he may, indeed, love to make sport
of people by vexing their vanity. I, however, once knew an
old gentleman who was absolutely malignant. He really
wished evil to others, and rejoiced at it.' BOSWELL. 'The

ᵇ *was the Man Mr.
Boswell himself?* [I]
ᶜ *Who could this be?
I think it was Steevens:
oh yes.* [H]

gentleman,ᵇ Mr. Beauclerk, against whom you are so violent, is, I know, a man of good principles.ᶜ BEAUCLERK.
'Then he does not wear them out in practice.'

Dr. Johnson, who, as I have observed before, delighted
in discrimination of character, and having a masterly
knowledge of human nature, was willing to take men as
they are, imperfect, and with a mixture of good and bad
qualities, I suppose thought he had said enough in defence
of his friend, of whose merits, notwithstanding his exceptionable points, he had a just value; and added no more
on the subject.

On Tuesday, April 14, I dined with him at General
Oglethorpe's, with General Paoli and Mr. Langton.
General Oglethorpe declaimed against luxury. JOHNSON.
'Depend upon it, Sir, every state of society is as luxurious
as it can be. Men always take the best they can get.'
OGLETHORPE. 'But the best depends much upon our-
selves; and if we can be as well satisfied with plain things,
we are in the wrong to accustom our palates to what is
high-seasoned and expensive. What says Addison in his
"Cato," speaking of the Numidian?

"Coarse are his meals, the fortune of the chace,
    Amid the running stream he slakes his thirst,
Toils all the day, and at the approach of night,
    On the first friendly bank he throws him down,
Or rests his head upon a rock till morn;
    And if the following day he chance to find
A new repast, or an untasted spring,
    Blesses his stars, and thinks it luxury."

Let us have *that* kind of luxury, Sir, if you will.' JOHNSON.

'But hold, Sir; to be merely satisfied, is not enough. It is in refinement and elegance that the civilized man differs from the savage. A great part of our industry, and all our ingenuity is exercised in procuring pleasure; and, Sir, a hungry man has not the same pleasure in eating a plain dinner, that a hungry man has in eating a luxurious dinner. You see I put the case fairly. A hungry man may have as much, nay, more pleasure in eating a plain dinner, than a man grown fastidious has in eating a luxurious dinner.[a] But I suppose the man who decides between the two dinners, to be equally a hungry man.'

Talking of different governments,—JOHNSON. 'The more contracted power is, the more easily it is destroyed. A country governed by a despot is an inverted cone. Government there cannot be so firm, as when it rests upon a broad basis gradually contracted, as the government of Great Britain, which is founded on the parliament, then is in the privy-council, then in the King.' BOSWELL. 'Power, when contracted into the person of a despot, may be easily destroyed, as the prince may be cut off.[b] So Caligula wished that the people of Rome had but one neck, that he might cut them off at a blow.' OGLETHORPE. 'It was of the Senate he wished that. The Senate by its usurpation controuled both the Emperour and the people. And don't you think that we see too much of that in our own parliament?'

Dr. Johnson endeavoured to trace the etymology of Maccaronick verses, which he thought were of Italian invention from Maccaroni; but on being informed that this would infer that they were the most common and easy verses, maccaroni being the most ordinary and simple food, he was at a loss; for he said, 'He rather should have supposed it to import in its primitive signification, a composition of several things;[1] for Maccaronick verses are

[a] *It is not put fairly yet . . . A Gentleman who is hungry will like the luxurious Dinner best . . . A poor Man will like the plain Dinner, tho' hungry enough to devour the Ragouts with something resembling Pleasure. he would eat Roast Beef longer though, . . . than he would Fricandeau made by the first Cook in France . . . The rich Man not so; He is accustom'd to have as Milton says Taste after Taste upheld with kindliest Change. and would prefer bonne Cuisine. 1817* [H]

[b] *True: therefore France fell, & therefore England stood the Shock of 1794.* [H]

underlined: *pulmentum . . . butyro* [H]

[c] *Bravo Malone! almost always right.* [H]

---

[1] [Dr. Johnson was right in supposing that this kind of poetry derived its name from *maccherone.* 'Ars ista poetica (says Merlin Coccaie, whose true name was Theophilo Folengo,) nuncupatur ARS MACARONICA, a *maca-ronibus* derivata; qui *macarones* sunt quoddam pulmentum, farina, caseo, butyro compaginatum, grossum, rude, et rusticanum. Ideo MACARONICA nil nisi grossedinem, ruditatem, et VOCABULAZZOS debet in se continere.' Warton's Hist. of Eng. Poet. ii. 357. Folengo's assumed name was taken up in consequence of his having been instructed in his youth by Virago Coccaio. —He died in 1544. MALONE.][c]

verses made out of a mixture of different languages, that is, of one language with the termination of another.' I suppose we scarcely know of a language in any country, where there is any learning, in which that motley ludicrous species of composition may not be found. It is particularly droll in Low Dutch. The '*Polemo-middinia*' of Drummond of Hawthornden, in which there is a jumble of many languages moulded, as if it were all in Latin, is well known. Mr. Langton made us laugh heartily at one in the Grecian mould, by Joshua Barnes, in which are to be found such comical *Anglo-hellenisms* as Κλυββοισιν εβανχθεν: they were banged with clubs.

END OF VOLUME II